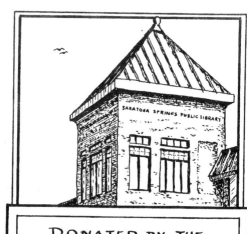

THE
DODGERS

ALSO BY THE AUTHORS

Yankees Century: 100 Years of New York Yankees Baseball
Red Sox Century: 100 Years of Red Sox Baseball
Ted Williams: A Portrait in Words and Pictures
DiMaggio: An Illustrated Life
Jackie Robinson: Between the Baselines

EDITED BY GLENN STOUT

Best American Sports Writing 1991–present (series editor for annual volumes)
Best American Sports Writing of the Century (with David Halberstam)
Chasing Tiger: The Tiger Woods Reader
Impossible Dreams: A Red Sox Collection
Top of the Heap: A Yankees Collection

BY RICHARD A. JOHNSON

A Century of Boston Sports: Photographs and Memories
The Boston Braves
The American Game (co-editor with Lawrence Baldassaro)
Fall Classics: The Best Writing about the World Series' First 100 Years (co-editor with Bill Littlefield)

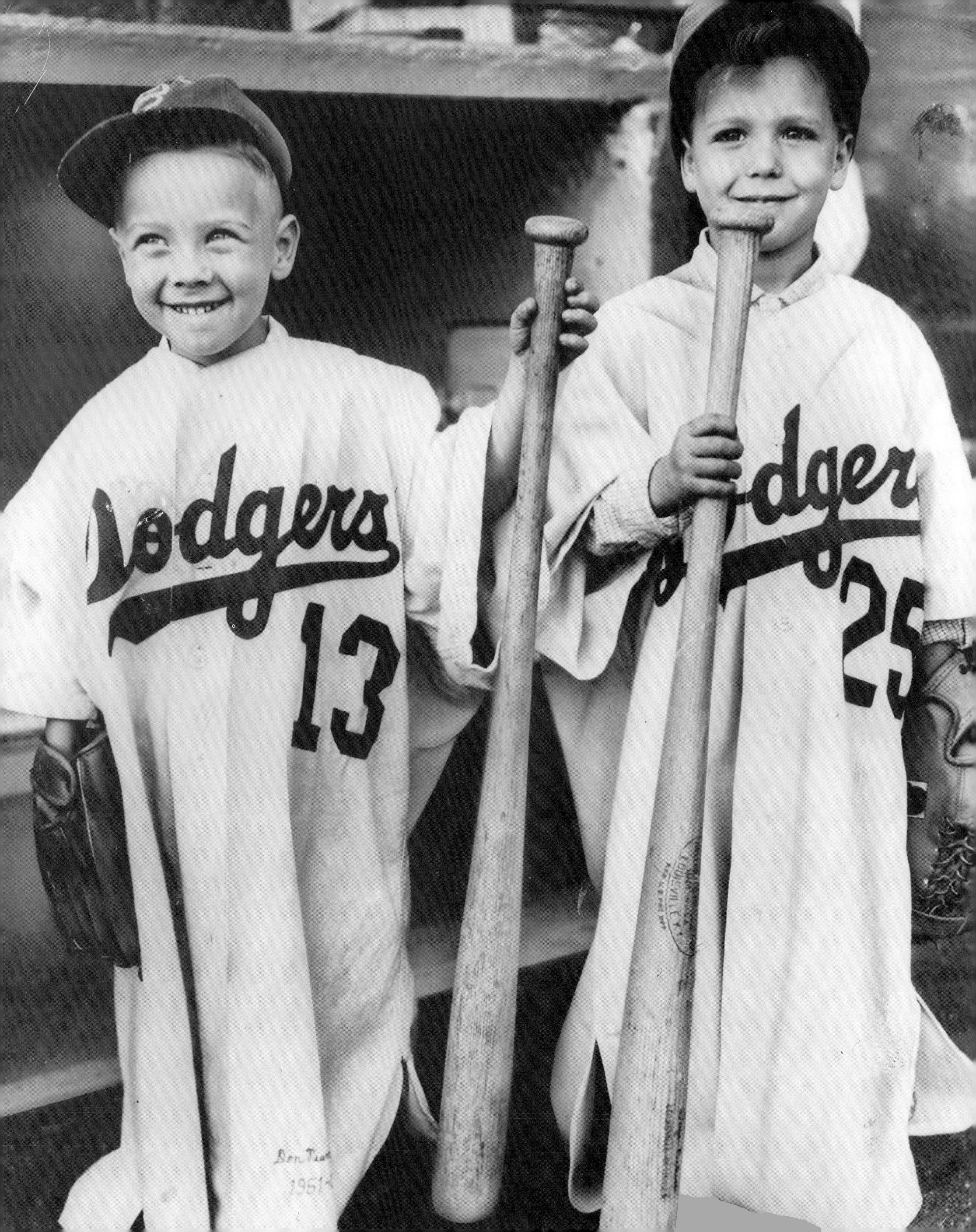
13
25
1951

THE DODGERS

120 YEARS OF DODGERS BASEBALL

TEXT BY **GLENN STOUT**

PHOTOGRAPHS SELECTED AND EDITED BY

RICHARD A. JOHNSON

HOUGHTON MIFFLIN COMPANY

BOSTON   NEW YORK

2004

For information about permission to reproduce selections from
this book, write to Permissions, Houghton Mifflin Company,
215 Park Avenue South, New York, New York 10003.

Visit our Web site: www.houghtonmifflinbooks.com.

Library of Congress Cataloging-in-Publication Data

Stout, Glenn, date.
The Dodgers : 120 years of Dodgers baseball / text by Glenn Stout ;
photographs selected and edited by Richard A. Johnson.
p. cm.
Includes index.
ISBN 0-618-21355-4
1. Los Angeles Dodgers (Baseball team) — History. 2. Brooklyn Dodgers
(Baseball team) — History. I. Title.
GV875.L6S834 2004
796.357'64'0979494 — dc22   2004047545

Book design by Julia Sedykh
Typefaces: Scala and Fairplex

Printed in the United States of America

KPT 10 9 8 7 6 5 4 3 2 1

"Monument to Walter" by Jim Murray. Copyright © 2004 by the Los
Angeles Times. Reprinted with permission. "Obit to the Dodgers" by
Dick Young. Copyright © 1956 by the New York Daily News, L.P., and
first published by the *New York Daily News*. Reprinted by permission.

ENDPAPERS
Front: Ebbets Field, 1956. *Back:* Los Angeles Coliseum, 1959.

CONTENTS

ACKNOWLEDGMENTS

Special thanks go to John Taylor Williams, agent extraordinaire, and Hope Denekamp of Fish & Richardson, and to editor Susan Canavan, Sarah Gabert, Gracie Doyle, Laura Noorda, Larry Cooper, and Julia Sedykh of Houghton Mifflin for taking on another project of this scope. I'm grateful to Pat Kelly, Bill Burdick, and Tim Wiles of the National Baseball Hall of Fame, Susan April, Jay Kaplan, Elizabeth Harvey and the staff of the Brooklyn Public Library, the staff of the Lamont Library at Harvard University, the staff of the Boston Public Library, and the UCLA Sports Information Department. Thanks to Bob Ahrens for his insight, the Zeckendorfs, John Cronin of the *Boston Herald,* Mark Rucker of Transcendental Graphics, Joe Sullivan and Jim Wilson of the *Boston Globe,* Bill Plaschke, Jane Leavy, Dave Anderson, Howard and Veronique Bryant, Denise Bousquet, the late Doc Kountze, Tony Morante, Max Frazee, the Dodger players — particularly Ed Stevens, Howie Schultz, and Gene Hermanski — the Los Angeles Dodgers organization, and the many writers who covered the team for so many years, without whom this book would have been impossible. Finally, thanks to Michele Lee Amundsen for her wisdom and support, Richard and Mary Thaler for support in New York, and the trustees and staff of the Sports Museum for their overall support and goodwill.

INTRODUCTION

When you say you're a Dodger, everybody knows
you're in the major leagues.

— **Tommy Lasorda**

Of all the teams in professional sports, the Dodgers are unique. No other team uses the name, and as onetime manager Tommy Lasorda pointed out, the pronoun refers only to the Dodgers of baseball — nothing else. The name is as distinctive in Tokyo or San Pedro de Macorís as it is in Bensonhurst or Hollywood.

Yet while that name may mean different things to different people, in the end it refers to only one franchise. The Brooklyn Dodgers and the Dodgers of Los Angeles can certainly be seen as separate entities. Virtually every other book ever written about the team splits them in half, focusing on either one or the other, or perhaps on the moment one ended and the other began. There are still fans of the Brooklyn Dodgers who evince a profound disinterest and even dislike for their West Coast progeny, while many L.A. Dodger fans are essentially ignorant about the team's past.

That approach is easy and obvious, but also misleading, for it ignores reality. Where it really matters, on the field where the game is played and not in the front office, they have been just one team — the Dodgers — and from that perspective they are larger and more resilient than when considered only in terms of their tenure in either Brooklyn or Los Angeles. One of the goals of this book is to look at the Dodgers of both places and see how and where and why they remain connected and to find within "the Dodgers" a common spirit that informs us about the teams of both places.

In the course of writing this book, the authors necessarily began in Brooklyn and ended in Los Angeles, but along the way the story of the Dodgers is also the story of one of the signature franchises of the national pastime. Theirs is an inherently American story that follows a familiar path, a story of immigration, assimilation, migration, and change. And as

such an inherently American tale, the history of the Dodgers repeatedly touches on some of the most profound transformations that have taken place in the history of this nation, from segregation to integration, from bigotry to diversity, from urbanization to suburbanization. In the story of the Dodgers these issues are not told remotely through statistics or policy but through flesh-and-blood characters like Jackie Robinson, Sandy Koufax, Walter O'Malley, and Fernando Valenzuela. They are a part of the day-to-day story of a baseball team trying to win championships, turn a profit, and engage their fans.

Yet while these issues are part of the Dodgers' story, they are not the main narrative. In this book, as well as in our two earlier team histories, *Red Sox Century* and *Yankees Century*, at each step we have tried to tell the story of how and why a team wins when it does, how and why a team loses, and, most important, why the final score has come to matter to so many.

While we researched and wrote those other titles, the Dodgers were never very far away. Their battles with the Yankees at Ebbets Field, Dodger Stadium, and Yankee Stadium are legendary, and Dodger history has intersected with that of the Red Sox on a number of occasions, from the 1916 World Series to Robinson's "tryout" with Boston in 1945 to the acquisition of Pee Wee Reese. In the larger saga of baseball, the Dodgers are always elbowing their way in, demanding attention. It became clear that the logic of history required us to tell their story next.

The Dodgers, whether in Los Angeles or Brooklyn, have always occupied an enormous place in the history of the game. If the Red Sox are the most interesting team in baseball history, and the Yankees the most successful, the Dodgers are perhaps the most essential. The modern game of baseball as we know it was created in Brooklyn, and the Dodgers of Brooklyn helped carry the game from the 19th century to the modern era. Beginning in 1945 with the signing of Jackie Robinson, the Dodgers also played a central role in ushering the game into its contemporary form. Even the move to Los Angeles foreshadowed many of the controversies that have challenged professional baseball for much of the past five or six decades. The Dodgers, like no other team, have borne witness to the evolution of baseball from an amateur pastime played by gentlemen to a multibillion-dollar business. They were there at the beginning, and more than 100 years later are one of the few teams to have survived.

But baseball is more than box scores, season records, and stories. In the mind's eye, the game lives on in images, snapshots of players and plays and games and ballparks. While I spent the past few years researching the text of this volume, my colleague Richard Johnson went on a similar quest to ferret out the pictures that illuminate the Dodgers' story. Their visual history is at least equal to that of any team that has ever played the game. Through that imagery we have been informed about not only the players and the places they played but also the position that both hold in the hearts of fans.

The best part about writing a book is the enormous learning process. This one began nearly a decade ago with a project on Jackie Robinson, which sent me to gaze at Dodger Stadium rising from the foothills of Chavez Ravine and to search for the ghostly presence of Ebbets Field on the streets of Brooklyn. I have spent hundreds of hours in libraries, in Brooklyn and elsewhere, reading the collected works of such luminaries as Chadwick, Holmes, Smith, Kahn, Young, Murray, Newhan, Plaschke, and others. I have watched hours of film and video, pored over hundreds of books, and talked to dozens of people for whom the Dodgers were not an abstract notion but a living presence.

In that time I have grown to think of them not as of either Brooklyn or Los Angeles, but as one team, the Dodgers. Although they have changed tremendously since first emerging in Brooklyn more than 100 years ago, that evolution is part of what makes theirs a compelling story. The Dodgers have rarely been predictable or boring for long. Change — sometimes to the consternation of their fans — has been a constant in their story, but change is also what has separated them from other teams and made them essential to professional baseball. By evolving the way they have since their birth so long ago, the Dodgers have only added to their legacy. They remain unique, inimitable, and unmistakable.

In Brooklyn — and in Los Angeles — the Dodgers still matter.

— **GLENN STOUT**
June 2004

Prologue

DODGER WINTER

HE WAS A DODGER.

As he busied himself closing his Harlem liquor store on the evening of January 27, 1958, Roy Campanella was, for the first and only time of his life, just that—a Dodger. That was all and that was enough.

The Dodgers had played for the last time at Ebbets Field the previous September 24. They then walked off the diamond before 6,702 desultory fans as Gladys Goodding played a dirge on her organ. Since then, the appellation "Brooklyn" that had for so long preceded the word "Dodgers" no longer applied, not even as they went on to finish the season with three final games in Philadelphia, where a still-obscure bonus baby named Sandy Koufax mopped up their final game, a 2–1 loss. By spring the city of Los Angeles would take possession of the Dodger name. But for now it was still impossible to imagine the Dodgers in the sunshine of an endless summer, playing in the sterile, supersized Los Angeles Coliseum in front of fans who had to check the scorecard to match the player's name with his number and face. In Brooklyn fans knew the players not just by their number but by the cars they drove and by their nicknames, just like any other guy in the neighborhood.

The heart and soul of the Brooklyn Dodger franchise were their loyal and often colorful fans. For decades these fans embraced the team's offbeat underdog image and rejoiced with their dynasty of the 1950s.

Pee Wee. Duke. Oisk. Newk. Campy. Even Sal Maglie, after coming over in a 1956 trade with the rival Giants, had been embraced by Brooklyn. As a Giant, he had earned his nickname "the Barber" for both his grizzled look and his ability to give hitters a close shave, throwing under their chin and backing them off the plate, a tactic he had used most successfully against Brooklyn. Then, Brooklyn fans had spat out his nickname like an epithet. But as a Dodger, Maglie's moniker suddenly became a term of endearment. His trade to the hated Yankees near the end of the 1957 season, as the Dodgers fell out of the race and their last season in Brooklyn wound down, was somehow symbolic. They were throwing in the towel.

But now those days were gone. Campanella and his teammates knew that, and accepted it, even if they all weren't exactly thrilled with the notion of pulling up stakes and making the trek all the way across the country to California for the 1958 season.

They had had a long time to grow accustomed to the idea, but it had still been something of a shock when the official announcement was made on October 8 by way of a simple press release that read, "The stockholders and directors of the Brooklyn Baseball Club have today met and unanimously agreed that necessary steps be taken to draft the Los Angeles territory." Walter O'Malley had been threatening to move the team for several years as he and a host of New York politicians hemmed and hawed over the building of a new ballpark. O'Malley wanted more than the politicians were willing to give, and the politicians grated over what they perceived as O'Malley's greed. As they waltzed the team into infinity, Brooklyn fans signed petitions and wrote letters and formed committees and wore pins that made good copy for the newspaper columnists, but no one who really mattered paid their empty protests any attention.

In the off-season Campy usually worked days and left the store to his trusted staff at night. This evening he was at his store — Roy Campanella's Choice Wines and Liquors at the corner of Seventh and 134th Street — only because later that night he was supposed to do a television interview to help raise funds for the Harlem YMCA. He had arrived at the store at 11:00 A.M. and kept himself busy the rest of the day, killing time until the scheduled 10:00 P.M. interview. But at 9:00 P.M., broadcaster Harry Wismer called and asked if he could put the interview off for a week so he could better promote Campanella's appearance and raise additional money. That was fine with Campy. He was a catcher, a baseball laborer,

and he thrived on work of any kind. He helped a clerk close the store at midnight and then rearrange stock before sending the man home. A few minutes later, at 1:30 A.M., Campanella prepared to leave.

Despite his lucrative liquor business and his success in Brooklyn, Campanella was beginning to look forward to the move. The store could run without him, and although he regretted having to give up his oceanside home and small yacht, he had already rented a house for his family in the Lincoln Park section of Redondo Beach. He had been to Los Angeles twice already in the off-season, appearing at a luncheon welcoming the Dodgers in November, and again just a few weeks earlier, representing the Dodgers in a television tribute to Ethel Barrymore.

His teammates had been split on the move. Some, like first baseman Gil Hodges, had settled in Brooklyn and felt at home there. Others, like native Californian Duke Snider, regretted leaving but also looked forward to playing closer to home. Campanella didn't really want to leave either, but at the age of 36 and bothered by nerve damage to his hands, he was coming off two subpar seasons in which he hit .219 and .242 with only 33 home runs. He was at a stage in his career where the aches and pains he had accumulated over more than 20 years of pro baseball no longer disappeared overnight. The sun and heat would feel good. He promised club owner Walter O'Malley that he wouldn't retire until after the Dodgers' proposed new ballpark was finished.

But it was the new place that really intrigued him, that made him begin to look more favorably at the move to Los Angeles. Since World War II, Los Angeles had become self-aware and was beginning to burst with civic pride. The sleepy city suddenly realized that it belonged in the same conversation with other great American metropolises like Chicago, Philadelphia, and New York. Now L.A. had the evidence that it was truly a major league city, that the metaphor was reinforced by reality. The city was absolutely giddy over the prospect of major league baseball.

Originally, O'Malley had thought the Dodgers could play in L.A.'s Wrigley Field, where his triple-A franchise had played before crowds of as much as 20,000, while waiting for a new park to be built. But now it was clear that the ballpark wasn't nearly large enough to accommodate the Dodgers and their new fans. That sent O'Malley looking elsewhere, first to the Rose Bowl and then the Los Angeles Coliseum, which had been built for the 1932 Olympic Games and patterned

Roy Campanella makes his emotional return to baseball at the Los Angeles Coliseum on May 7, 1959, as fans light matches in the darkness in tribute to the paralyzed Dodger hero.

after its Roman ancestor. The Coliseum wasn't a ballpark, but there was really no other option. In fact, turning the stadium into a ballpark was, at best, a bad fit, and an obviously temporary solution. The footprint of a baseball diamond didn't fit neatly into the oval-shaped field of the Coliseum — the shoe simply wasn't wide enough and couldn't enclose an outfield with anything close to the normal dimensions. After taking into consideration the sun and the arrangement of the seats, and at the cost of some $200,000, they had finally decided to wedge the field into the corner of the closed end of the stadium. It was an unsatisfactory solution, but the only one that was really feasible.

Yet the end result made Campanella smile. While it would be some 440 feet to the temporary fences in the right-center power alley, and 420 feet to the fence in center field, left field would be confined by the immovable concrete stands of the Coliseum. At the left-field foul line it would be only 251 feet from home plate, barely 320 feet at the power alley, softball dimensions.

Two hundred and fifty-one feet. For Campanella, still a pull hitter, a fence only 251 feet away was as tempting as the notion of walking into his back yard and being able to pick an orange from his own tree. Never mind that it would be protected by a 40-foot chicken-wire screen stretching some 140 feet toward left-center field. He knew he could still turn on the fastball, knew he could still get the ball in the air, knew he

could hit the ball 251 feet almost by accident. In 1953 he had hit a career-best 41 home runs and earned MVP honors in the National League. In the Coliseum, taking aim at that extraordinarily short porch, Campanella was convinced his power would return and he could hold off prospect John Roseboro, already touted as the Dodgers' catcher of the future. Even at his age, he might be able to crack 40-plus home runs again, maybe more, maybe enough to win the home run title or even, if his legs held up, collect another MVP Award. Yes, the California sun and those 251 feet could make him young again.

Since Jackie Robinson had retired after the end of the 1956 season, Campanella, perhaps more than any of his teammates, had been the quintessential Dodger. The son of an Italian father and African American mother raised in a mixed neighborhood in Philadelphia, Campanella epitomized the melting pot ideal that was the Dodgers, the first team to integrate and still the most racially mixed team in baseball. And in the years right after the war, after Robinson broke the color line in 1947, Brooklyn had been the perfect place for Campanella to play. After nine long years in the Negro Leagues, he had followed Robinson to Brooklyn in 1948, and he had thrived. Brooklyn had always been a place where people of various races and ethnicities lived — there had been a significant black presence in Brooklyn for more than 100 years. For the first time in their star-crossed history, the Dodgers were the right team in the right place at the right time.

In the years immediately after World War II, after Robinson broke in, Brooklyn and the Dodgers had seemed to epitomize a new America, a place where race and ethnicity didn't matter as much anymore. Younger Brooklyn, the kids, worshiped Robinson from the start, and they had mixed easily on the streets and in the stands. But Campanella, even more than Jackie, was the perfect player for the time, and symbolic of this changing attitude. More than Robinson, both blacks *and* ethnic whites identified with him and counted him as their own, for Campanella did not push racial issues as vigorously as Robinson. Campanella looked like Brooklyn, and Brooklyn looked like the multiracial society some envisioned for America. The throngs who swarmed Ebbets Field to see the Dodgers contained that promise, and when the Dodgers won, that promise seemed confirmed.

Reality, however, had not lived up to the dream. While the children of Brooklyn may have looked at the borough and at the Dodgers with idealism and wide-eyed optimism, some adults saw things differently. By 1950 white flight to Long Island was the order of the day as Brooklyn turned blacker and browner and age-old suspicions and fear took hold. To some, cozy old Ebbets Field now seemed more cramped and seedy. Yes, the Dodgers were still symbolic of Brooklyn, but that symbolism wasn't all positive anymore. The Dodgers had led the NL in attendance in 1946, 1947, and 1949, but crowds had slipped thereafter, down some 700,000 fans in 1957 from a record 1.8 million in 1947.

Maybe things would be different in California. In contrast to Brooklyn, which was a place long-time residents were leaving, drawn to the new schools and tract housing on Long Island, California was a place people were moving *to*. But in one respect Los Angeles was not dissimilar from Brooklyn, or at least from the way Brooklyn had been until very recently.

Race was not as important in Los Angeles as it was in so many other places in America. Oh, it still mattered, but the divisions in society weren't quite so pronounced, and the bigotry was less obvious. Mexican influence was everywhere in California, and over the last 30 years thousands of African Americans had migrated there and often found somewhat less prejudice than farther east or in the South. It was a place where Campanella, surrounded by his teammates and with

the notoriety of being a major leaguer, could be comfortable, where blacks and whites and Mexicans mixed, if not always easily, without the overt, aggressive segregation still in place in so much of America. Already, in his two short visits to California, he hadn't encountered any racial problems, not even when he looked for a place to live. He would be one of the mainstays of the bridge that would carry the team from Brooklyn to Los Angeles, a player who could bring to the new place an important element of the place they had left behind, a player who could eventually help Los Angeles residents embrace these Dodgers, as Brooklyn fans once had. Just as his bat could turn the Coliseum into a ballpark, in his own understated way Campanella the man could help turn the sprawling city of Los Angeles into a neighborhood.

If Campanella was not thinking these things that night as he straightened the shelves, took inventory, counted the cash register, and closed his store, such thoughts were not far away. For now, in the dark of early morning, he was more concerned about the weather. On that night in Harlem the weather was the sort that made one dream of California. It was cold — below freezing — with a brisk wind, a spit of snow, and a mix of slush and ice along the curb.

After locking up the store he made his way to a nearly new 1957 Chevy sedan. He climbed in and paused for a moment before turning the key in the ignition. His own car, a station wagon big enough to transport his family, his wife Ruthe and three children, was being fixed. He had rented a replacement so he could drive to Manhattan for the now-canceled interview.

He was careful as he pulled onto the Harlem streets and headed downtown. The new car felt different in his hands. As his headlights cut through the darkness and he made his way out of the city and across the Triborough Bridge toward his home on Long Island's North Shore, he remembered that unlike his own vehicle, the rental car didn't have snow tires. He was a cautious driver anyway, but was even more so now.

He crawled home cautiously, turning the usual 45-minute drive into a trip of more than an hour. The roads were better than he expected, for the combination of traffic and salt had melted the snow. As he drove through Glen Cove, only five miles from his home in Morgan's Island, he began to relax.

There was less traffic farther out on the island, and it was turning colder. The road still looked wet in places, but the surface was growing icy. As Campanella hugged the speed limit and negotiated a turn, he spied the glare of his headlights illuminating a frozen patch of highway. He turned the wheel, but the car didn't respond as the tires spun and turned but failed to grip the road. The car, not unlike a hanging curveball, went straight instead of turning. The result was no less violent.

He knew it before it happened, but there was nothing he could do. The road turned from beneath the car as the car continued forward. It smashed into a telephone pole and then started to flip over. Campanella's massive body was suddenly loose in the car — seat belts were common only in racing cars at the time. He flew forward against the steel steering wheel and windshield as the car ground to a stop, then whiplashed back as the automobile lurched over on its side, tumbling from the seat to the floor, becoming wedged beneath the dashboard on the passenger's side as the car grotesquely folded in around him. Then it was quiet, the only sound the engine running and the spinning wheels, going nowhere.

Campanella was in shock. Pain radiated from his head. He knew he had wrecked the car. He thought of a ruptured gasoline line, of the ghastly pictures in the newspaper of automobiles that had caught fire and burned.

He thought first to turn off the car, to stop the gasoline from coursing through the engine. He reached for the ignition.

He reached up to where he believed the ignition to be, but his hand did not move. He reached again and still the hand did not move. Then he tried to move himself, to hoist himself free from the wreckage, but again, he did not move. *I'm paralyzed*, he thought, and then the thought formed words he heard himself speak aloud.

"O Lord, have mercy on me."

A neighbor had heard the unmistakable sound of the crash. A physician, he instinctively grabbed his doctor's bag and ran out of his house to where he saw the headlights shin-

---

Roy Campanella at his Harlem liquor store in December 1955 displaying the rewards of his day job following the announcement that he won a third National League MVP Award to join the two he is holding.

ing askew through the bare trees. He called out as he neared the car and heard a garbled moan. The neighbor also thought of the gasoline and turned off the car. Inside he found a man wedged between twisted metal moaning over and over again. He reached in his bag, then found the man's arm and stabbed it with a needle, shooting him with morphine to stop the pain. The doctor noticed that the man didn't flinch, and soon the moaning stopped.

The police arrived a few minutes later and tried to free the man from the car but could not extract the large man through the twisted metal. A half-hour later a tow truck roughly pulled the car upright as an officer crawled on top of the man and tried to hold him rigid as the car flopped and rocked. Only then, with crowbars, could they pry back the metal, force open a door, pull him free, and place him on a stretcher. Only then did they become certain the man who could not move was a Dodger. It was Roy Campanella.

Was a Dodger. Roy Campanella's neck was broken, a fracture and dislocation of the fifth and sixth vertebrae, something nearly five hours of surgery could not fix. He was paralyzed below the shoulders, with only his arms capable of movement, and then just barely, a halting motion that seemed to mock the athlete he had been.

Campanella's injury was another blow to Brooklyn fans, the worst possible news piled on top of what they had thought was already the worst possible news. Campy had been one of them, and in an instant, he was changed, his long, storied career over as suddenly as a car crash. Although they knew their experience was not the same, they believed that in a small way they knew how he felt. When the Dodgers left Brooklyn, they too had been cut down, their passion made inert, and their lives irrevocably split in half, into before and after. They had been cut off from their team just as suddenly as Campanella had been cut off from his body, leaving a hole that was both invisible and undeniable. Not even word a week later that Walter O'Malley, whose name was now usually preceded by a string of epithets on the Brooklyn streets, had tripped and broken his ankle had soothed the Brooklynites. Why couldn't Campanella have tripped and fallen? they asked. Why couldn't O'Malley have been behind the wheel?

Los Angeles felt for Campanella too, but from afar. There he was a sidebar, a wire report, a stranger on the side of the road. Oh, they slowed as they passed on the freeway and shook

The accident scene in Glen Cove, N.Y., where Roy Campanella's car skidded into a light pole in the early hours of January 28, 1958.

their heads in a combination of pity and genuine sympathy, but they did not stop, for they did not yet really know him. The Dodgers weren't theirs — not yet.

But excitement for the coming season was building. Players were already making appearances, sorting through endorsement opportunities, meeting stars, and laughing over their newfound celebrity. They would all gather soon in Los Angeles to hold a clinic for youngsters at Wrigley Field, and the club was already scheduling tryouts to participate in its "Dodger Rookies" program, a team-sponsored league for the best high school prospects in the area. Local Little Leagues were being swamped with applicants. The 1958 schedule had just been released, and more than 500,000 tickets had already been sold, including more than 30,000 for the opener against the Giants. Team officials beamed and announced they hoped to draw more than 80,000 fans for the first game in the 100,000-plus capacity of the Coliseum. The club had already taken in nearly $2 million in advance orders. Plans for luncheons, parades, banquets, and other celebrations were in full swing. L.A. was going big league. April was right around the corner.

Welcome, Dodgers.

In our sun-down perambulations, of late, through the outer parts of Brooklyn, we have enjoyed several parties of youngsters playing "base," a game of ball. We wish such sights were more common among us. In the practice of athletic and manly sports, the young men of nearly all our American cities are very deficient. . . . Clerks are shut up from early morning till nine or ten o'clock at night—apprentices, after their day's works, either go to bed, or lounge about in places where they benefit neither body or mind—and all classes seem to act as though there were no commendable objects of pursuit in the world except making money, and tenaciously sticking to one's trade or occupation. . . . Let us go forth awhile, and get better air in our lungs. Let us leave our close rooms, and the dust and corruption of stagnant places, and taste some of the good things. . . . The game of ball is glorious.

—**Walt Whitman**, *Brooklyn Daily Eagle*, July 23, 1846

THE GLORIOUS GAME

THE DODGERS ARE BROOKLYN'S PRODIGAL SON.

Baseball wasn't born in Brooklyn, but it might as well have been. Baseball and Brooklyn grew up simultaneously as both were shaped and changed by the same forces. Although baseball evolved from a boys' game into the national pastime in countless places, in Brooklyn that growth coincided with the evolution of the community. Baseball and Brooklyn, its fans and its players, would eventually become synonymous. Few other places have exerted such an influence on the game.

In its infancy, baseball was first played in Brooklyn on unnamed fields, nurtured on the roughly manicured greens of the Union and Capitoline Grounds in Williamsburg, then raised in hardship and shaped by struggle in Washington Park in Park Slope and Eastern Park on Jamaica Bay, before reaching adulthood in Flatbush, at Ebbets Field. There thousands stood as proud parents and uncles and cousins as the boy became a man and the man made the Dodgers name a symbol of pride. Brooklyn was home to the first professional player, the first paid admission, the first ballpark, the first curveball, the first African American in the major leagues, even the first box score and baseball writer. The vocabulary of the game is pure Brooklynese.

The Brooklyn Atlantics claimed five national champions in the decade from 1860 to 1870. Among their stars were left fielder John "Death to Flying Things" Chapman, Joe "Old Reliable" Start, and shortstop Dicky Pearce, who was credited with developing the bunt.

And then, just as the Brooklyn boy reached maturity, the Dodgers left home. But unlike the progeny in biblical parable, major league baseball has never returned to Brooklyn. This son set forth and never looked back after landing in Los Angeles, a place that was not so much a city as a state of mind, in some ways as different from Brooklyn as the surface of the moon. Yet the two places were also oddly similar, for each was a place that looked to the rest of America with disdain, as if no other place really mattered. It was in Los Angeles—not Brooklyn—that the Dodgers finally fulfilled the promise of their long history. In a city of stars the Dodgers emerged as a star in their own right, becoming one of baseball's wealthiest and most dominant franchises and quickly achieving what Brooklyn fans had only dreamt of.

Nearly 50 years after the Brooklyn Dodgers took the field for the last time, the city of neighborhoods that became a borough of New York still stands apart when emblazoned with the Dodgers name. And after nearly 50 years in the harsh sun and bright lights of Los Angeles, the Dodgers name is not yet emblazoned across that anthologized city. They are of Los Angeles, but the city is still best defined by other institutions—Hollywood, the highways, and, in sports, the basketball Lakers.

The Dodgers are now both apart from and a part of both places. Although their history is still steeped in its Brooklyn beginnings, their more recent past and their future are not yet essential to a full portrait of Los Angeles. The Dodgers are still settling in.

The irony, of course, is that even in Brooklyn it took decades for the team that became the Dodgers to develop and grow inseparable from its home. In the early days there was Brooklyn, and there was baseball, but there were no Dodgers. It would in fact take nearly half a century for the Dodgers and Brooklyn to become synonymous.

Before baseball, Brooklyn was a separate city—of New York but not a part of it. Wedged hard between the shores of Upper New York Bay, the East River, Newtown Creek, and Jamaica Bay on the western edge of Long Island, Brooklyn, from the beginning, served as the more pastoral adjunct to Manhattan, which by 1800 was already a thriving city of nearly 40,000. Brooklyn was little more than a seaside village of a couple of thousand souls surrounded by farmland and the even smaller towns of Bushwick, Flatbush, Williamsburg, and other wide spots in the roads that served as conduits for the commerce of the rest of Long Island.

The precursors of baseball, a wide variety of English bat and ball games played by children, were being played in the streets of New York as far back as the 18th century. But "base ball," a codified, organized game played by adults, did not really take hold until the 1840s, when young men looking for a thrill adapted it to their own purposes. And even then, a relatively flat expanse of grass large enough to play on, roughly four acres square, was hard to come by in Manhattan, where land was cleared and then built upon in a matter of weeks. The first New York team, the Knickerbockers, was formed in 1842, and it was no accident that by 1846 they were already looking elsewhere, to New Jersey's Elysian Fields, for a place to play. Indeed, it was the search for space that first brought the game to Brooklyn.

Brooklyn boomed as baseball did, becoming one of the first commuter suburbs as the businessmen of Manhattan fled the already crowded streets and returned to Brooklyn each night by ferry. The city grew quickly as a growing number of immigrants from Ireland, England, and Germany found work on the docks, in the Navy Yard, and with the numerous manufacturers that hugged the shore of the East River. The population of Brooklyn tripled every decade from 1800 to 1860. By 1854 baseball too had jumped the East River to Brooklyn, where the relative availability of open land and the popularity of the new, more organized game spawned a number of clubs that sought to imitate the Knickerbockers. At first, these Brooklyn-based clubs, the Excelsiors, the Eckfords, the Atlantics, and others, played wherever they could—in South Brooklyn, at the foot of Court Street, in Greenpoint, and in other places lost to history. By 1857 Brooklyn sported no fewer than four well-organized, formal baseball clubs. One year later they were invited to join an association of clubs in Manhattan to create what can be considered the first baseball league, the National Association of Base Ball Players. For the next 100 seasons, at least one and sometimes several teams in the most elite baseball leagues in the country would call Brooklyn home.

In Brooklyn the game quickly shed its genteel reputation as a game for gentlemen as workers and tradesmen became the game's most numerous and enthusiastic participants. As the population of Brooklyn exploded from fewer than 100,000 in 1850 to nearly 300,000 in 1860, nearly half of them foreign-born, the number of clubs playing baseball also increased.

The young immigrants were drawn to the game because it gave them a sense of community lacking in the workplace

The Atlantic baseball club of Brooklyn was a workingman's team comprising dock workers and day laborers. Many of their games matched them against gentlemen's clubs such as the Excelsiors of Brooklyn and the Eckfords of Manhattan.

and, significantly, an outlet for the tradition of gambling many of them had carried across the Atlantic from Ireland and England. They brought baseball to the streets.

This point was dramatically driven home in 1858, when all-star teams from New York and Brooklyn—called "picked nines"—agreed to meet in a best-of-three series played at roughly one-month intervals beginning on July 20. The two clubs agreed to meet on neutral ground, the Fashion Race Course on Long Island, where a rough diamond was laid out before the sturdy stone grandstand. That cost money, so for the first time spectators were charged admission to watch, paying 50¢ each to offset the cost of preparing the grounds. Baseball would never be the same again, for this was the point at which the pastime began to be viewed as a business. There was money to be made.

The participants were shocked when thousands of fans traveled by every available mode of transportation—by carriage, buggy, train, horseback, and even on foot—to witness the contests. While touts worked the stands taking bets (with Brooklyn installed as the 20–15 favorite), the grounds surrounding the racecourse took on the character of a carnival as vendors hawked wares and opportunists relieved the naive of their hard-earned cash through every manner of games of chance. The crowd also included what the papers delicately referred to as "beauty in female form," demonstrating the growing popularity of the sport. The game would barely be recognized as baseball today. The ball was thrown underhanded

from a distance of only 45 feet. The batsman could call for a pitch of his liking, and balls caught on the first bounce were counted as outs. But the end result pleased many in the crowd, for New York won the series in three hard-fought games, capturing the first game 22–18, losing to Brooklyn in game two 29–8, then knocking Brooklyn back in the finale 29–18. It would not be the last time a Brooklyn nine fell beneath the shadow of their counterparts from New York.

But New York's dominance would initially be short-lived. Over the next decade the best baseball in the world was played in Brooklyn as the Excelsiors, Eckfords, and Atlantics traded championships back and forth and the play on the field was spiced by increasingly bitter and bare-knuckled displays in the stands. From the start, Brooklyn fans saw themselves as an extension of their team.

In one notable contest at the end of the 1860 season, passions ran unchecked. Atlantic fans, upset that their team was losing to the more established Excelsiors and fearful that they would soon lose the bets they had placed on their favorites, rioted in the sixth inning. The fight spilled over onto the field, forcing the Excelsiors to withdraw and players from both teams to call the aborted match a draw. No longer in its infancy, baseball had entered an extended and unruly adolescence, with Brooklyn at its center. As the *Brooklyn Eagle* bragged, "Nowhere has the National game of Base Ball taken firmer hold than in Brooklyn. . . . If we are ahead of the big city [New York] in nothing else, we can beat her in baseball." Not to mention in the stands, for Brooklyn's feisty partisans soon earned a reputation as the most rabid and unruly in the country. Fans from New York began to travel to Brooklyn with trepidation.

With so much interest in baseball, it was not long before Brooklyn also spawned the baseball press. Brooklynite Harry Chadwick, although born in England and a fan of cricket, fell hard for baseball. He began covering contests for several newspapers, inventing the box score and unintentionally giving baseball-crazed fans fodder both literary and statistical for discussion long after the game ended. Now its nuances could be debated with some authority, even by those who hadn't attended the game in the first place. The baseball season became endless. Each game could be replayed and debated in detail.

And it was no accident that the birth of baseball writing roughly coincided with the emergence of baseball's first star player, Excelsior pitcher James Creighton, for now the exploits of individual players and games could be compared to those who had come before. Now baseball had a history.

The modern game of baseball evolved through a periodic bending of the rules, and the 19-year-old Creighton bent his arm to give the game an important evolutionary nudge. At the time the pitcher was required to throw the ball underhanded with a stiff arm. Apart from the location of the pitch and — barely — its speed, the hurler was unable to affect the ball in any other way. His job was simply to put the ball in play — the game didn't really start until the batsman swung.

But the crafty Creighton bent his arm slightly while keeping it nominally stiff. This small adjustment allowed him to make an almost undetectable snap while bringing his arm forward at great speed, dramatically increasing the velocity of the pitch. He further discovered that if he also snapped his wrist upon releasing the ball, the effect was increased. Now he could not only pitch the ball faster than his peers but put spin on the ball, which made it more difficult for the batter to hit the ball squarely. And once speed became part of the equation, its sudden absence could be just as disruptive to the batter. We can credit Creighton for inventing both the fastball and its counterpart, the change of pace.

JAMES CREIGHTON,

Pitcher James Creighton of the Excelsiors became baseball's first martyr when he died in 1862. It is thought that he ruptured his bladder, or perhaps his spleen, while swinging his bat. Creighton was the first pitcher to deliver a fastball with the snap of his wrist.

The style was as controversial as it was successful. Both opponents and the press debated Creighton's revolutionary adaptation before finally arriving at the conclusion that while it may have bent the rules, it did not break them. Besides, fans were awed by Creighton's magical delivery, which caused one Brooklyn reporter to wonder, "Now that we have seen it [the pitch] attentively, our wonder is that such experienced batsmen . . . could ever be mastered by it the way they were."

Creighton rapidly became the first dominant pitcher in the game and elevated the pitcher to the most important player on the field, just as the forward pass in football changed the nature of the position of quarterback. As a result, when Creighton pitched, the Excelsiors became baseball's best team.

Batters were unaccustomed to hitting against a pitcher who had the ability to make them swing and miss. Creighton was nearly unbeatable, for he flung his arm forward with such speed that the wrist snap was virtually undetectable. That made Creighton a valuable commodity, and he was soon approached by other clubs eager for his services. To retain him, and thus remain baseball's preeminent team, the Excelsiors began to pay Creighton a small salary to keep him on their squad, even though that violated the spirit of what was still an "amateur" game. Such payments, however, were nearly impossible to prove. Meanwhile, as other pitchers tried their best to emulate Creighton, he continued to dominate. The Excelsiors toured the known baseball world in 1860, playing all comers in such distant outposts as Buffalo and Rochester before turning south and sweeping through Pennsylvania, Maryland, and Delaware. Outside Brooklyn, Creighton and the Excelsiors went undefeated.

But that meant little, for everyone knew that Brooklyn baseball was a cut above the game played elsewhere, and the local Atlantics already believed they were the better club, a matter that could be settled definitively only on the field. Over the course of three afternoons in July and August, the Excelsiors and Atlantics met to determine the championship of Brooklyn, which was at the time the equivalent of the championship of the known world.

In the first contest on July 19, Creighton's vaunted speed befuddled his opponents, and the Excelsiors thumped their counterparts 28–4 on their home ground before nearly 10,000 spectators. Two weeks later, before nearly 15,000 on the Atlantics' grounds in Bedford, it was a different story. By the middle of the game the Atlantic hitters had become accustomed to Creighton's speed and were beginning to adjust. They suddenly solved the pitcher and hung on to win 15–14 after Excelsior catcher Joseph Legget, representing the tying run, unwisely tried to stretch a single into a double. He was thrown out, and the Atlantics were mobbed by the giddy crowd as they left the field.

That set up the rubber match at the Putnam Grounds on August 23. Baseball cranks from throughout the East descended on the grounds in numbers never seen before: nearly 20,000 crowded around the field. If the first game belonged to the Excelsiors and the second to the Atlantics, this contest belonged to the fans.

With the Excelsiors leading 8–6 in the fifth inning, the mob came unglued over an umpire's decision that went against the Atlantics. When the Excelsiors took the field in the sixth, they found themselves the targets of fruit and assorted garbage. Captain Legget pulled his team from the field and spirited them away. Thus, each club could declare victory.

The Excelsiors sat out the 1861 season but resumed play in 1862. By then both the Atlantics and Eckfords laid claim to being the best team in Brooklyn. With Creighton on the mound, the Excelsiors were confident that they would soon resume their rightful place atop the baseball world.

But it was as if Creighton's early success extracted a price, and when retribution came, it was swift and irrefutable. In October he was reportedly either bothered by a sore arm or had made the decision to jump to the Atlantics and was refusing to pitch. On October 14, 1862, in the Excelsiors' final game of the season, Creighton played second base.

In midgame Creighton, a dangerous hitter, drove the ball over the heads of the opposing outfielders. He raced from the plate only to collapse as he rounded first, then rose again and struggled to reach home, whereupon he bent over in tremendous pain. Concerned teammates and spectators helped him from the field to his father's Brooklyn home.

The *Eagle* reported that he had "sustained an internal injury occasioned by the strain while batting," but other reports indicated that he entered the game already injured from his participation in a cricket match. Regardless, for the next four days he remained bedridden, delirious with pain, before dying of what was reported to be internal bleeding caused by a ruptured bladder. Thus, Creighton, the game's first great pitcher, also became its first martyr.

The Civil War, which threw much of New York into an uproar as draft riots spread and young men joined the military, nearly caused a temporary halt to the growth of the game in Brooklyn as a number of teams were forced to fold. But the game survived the Civil War. Soldiers from Brooklyn and New York brought their game with them and spread the gospel to the South and West, where soldiers and civilians alike fell in love with the game. Like Creighton's slightly bent arm, the war allowed baseball to take an evolutionary leap that otherwise might have taken decades or might never have taken place at all. Wherever soldiers gathered in great numbers, in large encampments, on training grounds, and even in prisoner-of-war camps, they played baseball. The regional pastime turned into a game with national appeal.

It was perfectly attuned to the times. The only equipment needed was a ball of some kind, a stout stick, and an open field. The organization of men into teams reinforced the soldierly camaraderie of military service while giving players an escape from the rigors of the war. The game demanded little of participants physically but required a certain degree of mental focus for both players and spectators. And during that time, across the innings of an afternoon, the war momentarily faded.

Meanwhile, the game was too well rooted in Brooklyn to disappear from there entirely, even during the war. In 1862 an ice rink operator named William Cammeyer, taking note of the increasingly large crowds he saw at baseball games, opened the first "ballpark" adjacent to his rink in Williamsburg. He enclosed the field with a six-foot fence, installed benches seating perhaps 1,500 spectators, and opened the gates. To offset the cost of construction, he charged fans 10¢ admission, sold concessions, and in the winter flooded the field for ice skating. Soon afterward another entrepreneur opened a second such park, the Capitoline Grounds.

Another pitching genius soon emerged from the streets of Brooklyn. In 1866 Arthur Cummings, an amateur on one of Brooklyn's many junior teams, took note of the way a clamshell curves when thrown through the air, and after a period of experimentation discovered he could get a thrown baseball to curve by violently snapping his wrist. Thus was born the "curved ball." Although Cummings's method was mechanically unsound and eventually resulted in a dislocated wrist, his discovery paved the way for later practitioners who discovered less damaging ways of imparting the same effect. The diminutive pitcher moved up to pitch for the Brooklyn Stars in 1867 and enjoyed a decade of success, earning the nickname "Candy" for his sweet tosses.

But the game was changing rapidly, and Brooklyn soon lost its preeminent place in the baseball world. While Brooklyn remained a hotbed of the game, the success of the Cincinnati-based professional Red Stockings in 1869 sent the game headlong down the path to professionalism. They went undefeated until June 14, 1870, when Brooklyn's Atlantics defeated them 8–7 in ten innings at the Capitoline Grounds after man-

In 1884 Brooklyn joined the American Association and the team was soon known as the "Trolley Dodgers" as the result of the difficulties that players experienced getting to their home at Washington Park in the Red Hook section of Brooklyn. The 1889 team won the pennant with a record of 93–44. They are (front row) Mike Hughes; (middle row, left to right) George Pinkney, Bob Caruthers, Hub Collins, manager Bill McGunnigle, Oyster Burns, Bob Clark, and Tommy Lovett; (back row) Germany Smith, Pop Corkhill, Adonis Terry, Dave Foutz, Darby O'Brien, Doc Bushong, and Joe Visner.

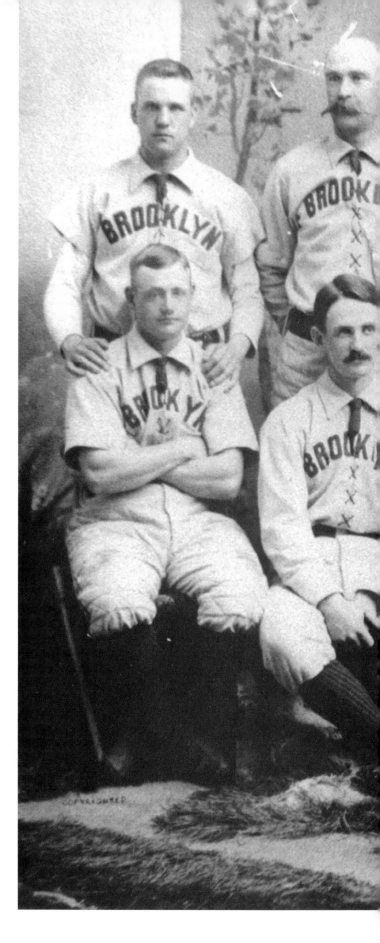

ager Harry Wright eschewed an offered draw. But the victory was, in a sense, the last game of baseball's infancy, for over the next decade baseball transformed from a game into a business. There was no going back.

Although the Eckfords, Mutuals, and Atlantics continued to represent baseball in Brooklyn, initially the city was left out when the National League was formed in 1876. But the success of the National League inspired the birth of a second major league, the American Association, in the winter of 1881. The Association initially planned to include the Brooklyn Atlantics in their fold, but Atlantic owner Billie Barnie was underfinanced. After he failed either to sign players or to secure a place to play, Brooklyn was dropped in favor of Baltimore.

Barnie's personal failure was not representative, however, of Brooklyn's enduring interest in baseball. There were still more places that wanted teams than there were leagues to play in, and Brooklyn was one of those places. The team that would become the Dodgers would soon be born.

If the game on the field evolved from a periodic bending of the rules, the game as a business grew when the desire for profit intersected with the public appetite for the game. In the winter of 1882–83 three men recognized both the financial potential of the game and Brooklyn's long-standing interest in the sport. The city had recently been swept by an industrial boom and sported a population of more than 500,000 souls, most of them working and with few places to spend any extra cash. The three were determined to take advantage of both.

George Taylor, the night editor of the *New York Herald,* noticed that his readers had a seemingly unending appetite for baseball news. Charles Byrne, a former journalist, was a real estate investor who owned a piece of a gambling house in Manhattan with his brother-in-law, Joseph Doyle.

The three men came together and decided that Brooklyn was ripe for exploitation. A new professional league, the Interstate Association, was being formed, and Brooklyn was a natural site for a franchise. They recruited a fourth investor, Frederick Abell, who owned a lucrative and opulent casino and gambling parlor in Narragansett Beach, Rhode Island, and made a successful application for a franchise in the new league.

Their timing was perfect. Brooklyn was the third most populous city in the country and the largest without a professional team. The Brooklyn Bridge, after nearly 15 years of

work, was nearing completion and would open in May. From Brooklyn's perspective, the bridge would serve not to link Brooklyn to Manhattan, but the other way around. Town boosters boasted that Brooklyn would soon usurp its island neighbor as an economic power. The city was bursting with pride and activity as the bridge inspired a torrent of other transportation plans to replace the obsolete horse-drawn streetcars that snaked down most major thoroughfares. Although the elevated steam-powered railways, so popular on Manhattan, had yet to make their way to Brooklyn, plans were already under way to add elevated cars and thereby link the bridge to the rest of Brooklyn. Brooklyn was prepared to boom.

The four men were perfectly equipped to take full advantage of this anticipated boom. Taylor knew baseball and knew how to promote the game. Byrne's real estate background made him the obvious choice to find a place to play, while Doyle and Abell knew full well that the real money in baseball was made off the field, through gambling, concessions, and the saloons that usually popped up around ballparks to serve the crowd. Brooklyn was wide open.

Byrne got busy and soon located a place for an enclosed ballpark in a swale near the Gowanus Canal in Red Hook, between Fourth and Fifth Avenues and Third and Fifth Streets, just west of Prospect Park. An old stone house on the property known as Gowanus House had been George Washington's headquarters during the Battle of Long Island. At the cost of $30,000, the park featured a wooden grandstand seating 2,500 that looked down on the field, which was placed in the swale below the surrounding landscape, and a so-called free stand that held another 2,000 patrons. The partners decided to honor Washington by calling the proposed park Washington Park. Then they decided to save some money and turn the old headquarters into a ladies' room.

While work on the park was under way, Taylor advertised far and wide for ballplayers, seeking what the *New York Clipper* called "men of intelligence, and not street corner roughs who may happen to possess some skill." Eventually some 40 players were secured, and the club was formally accepted into the Interstate League. This ballclub was the genealogical forebear of the Dodgers.

But far more important than any player acquired by Taylor and Byrne was a certain 24-year-old young man of various talents hired to produce the scorecards and fill in wherever else he was needed in the organization, which included everything from keeping the books and selling the tickets to sweeping the floors. Charles Hercules Ebbets, who despite his young age had already served as a draftsman, publisher, printer, and assemblyman in the New York legislature, joined the club at the lowest rung of the organization as a valuable jack-of-all-trades. He would eventually have as great an impact on the team as any other man in franchise history.

Under the direction of Byrne, who served as field manager, the club went almost unnoticed for the first few weeks of its existence. Although the "Grays" began their season on May 1, the new ballpark was not yet complete. The club opened its inaugural season with a 9–6 loss to the Quickstep club in Wilmington, New Jersey, then was forced to play its first home game in Newark and its second in Prospect Park, where 1,000 fans turned out and left happy, for not only did the team win 7–1, but since the game was played in a public park, no admission fee was charged.

By the time Washington Park was ready on May 12, the Grays were not yet headline material in the Brooklyn papers. The much-anticipated opening of the Brooklyn Bridge was only a few weeks off, and it dominated the news. Brooklyn was falling all over itself with predictions of future grandeur. The *Daily Eagle* even went so far as to deride a recent article in a New York newspaper that advocated combining New York and Brooklyn into one municipality. Brooklynites saw no need for such a subservient relationship. Such stories and other breaking news — such as the tale of a scandalous marriage of a "white girl" and a "very black Negro" who moved to Brooklyn to avoid tar-and-feathering in Greenpoint, bumped the baseball news to the back pages. Nevertheless, Brooklyn was a baseball town, and some 6,000 fans paid their money to witness the first game in the new park, including a few old-timers who had played for the Excelsiors and Atlantics.

They saw a sloppy ballgame in which the visiting club from Trenton made 12 errors and handed Brooklyn a 13–6 win. But the victory was no harbinger of success. The crowd would prove to be the largest of the season, and by midyear the Grays, with a record of 15–17, were far behind the 27–8 first-place Merritt Club.

Fortunately for Brooklyn, however, the Merritts ran out of money and folded. As the owners of the best-financed team in the fledgling league, Mr. Byrne and company proceeded to sign the pick of the disbanded club, turning the also-ran Grays into world beaters. They closed the season with a rush, sweeping first-place Harrisburg four in a row late in the sea-

NL BATTING CHAMPIONS

1892	Dan Brouthers	.335
1913	Jake Daubert	.350
1914	Jake Daubert	.329
1918	Zack Wheat	.335
1932	Lefty O'Doul	.368
1941	Pete Reiser	.343
1944	Dixie Walker	.357
1949	Jackie Robinson	.342
1953	Carl Furillo	.344
1962	Tommy Davis	.346
1963	Tommy Davis	.326

son to take a half-game lead into the final day. With another win over Harrisburg on September 29, they could capture the Interstate pennant.

On the mound for the Grays was pitcher William "Adonis" Terry, who had joined the team in midseason just before the infusion of talent from the Merritts and who was one of the few veteran players on the team not released after arrival — by season's end the Grays' starting lineup included only two players from Opening Day. Terry's chiseled profile and handsome mustache made ladies swoon and gave him his nickname, which rescued an otherwise obscure player from anonymity. Against Harrisburg, he pitched just well enough to win, 11–6, helped out by the sun, which conveniently set before the ninth inning could be played, and by Harrisburg's cleanup hitter, John Shetzline, who struck out three times and made a baserunning gaff so bad he was fined $50 by his manager. Nevertheless, the victory made Brooklyn champions.

Byrne, who had become the dominant partner among the owners, celebrated by pulling his team from the league, which soon passed into oblivion. Brooklyn joined the three-year-old American Association, which was vying with the National League to be baseball's preeminent professional league. The eight-team circuit included teams from cities ignored by the NL, such as St. Louis, Louisville, Cincinnati, Baltimore, Pittsburgh, and Philadelphia, and went head to head with the National League only in New York. Competition in the AA was unquestionably better than that of the Interstate League, and so was the profit potential.

And that was the only solace the Brooklyns had over their first few seasons in the AA, for they were only nominally competitive, beating up on the league also-rans and in turn being beat up by the first division, particularly the power-

house St. Louis Browns. The only thing distinctive about the club was their propensity to provide the occasional memorable moment. Even the *Daily Eagle* recognized that this team was different: the paper commented about the "glorious uncertainty" of the national game that was best expressed by the Brooklyn team. The variation in the quality of their performance from one day to the next could be maddening.

Pitcher Sam Kimber provided the first such moment, an exclamation point on an otherwise forgettable first season in the AA. As the Grays played out the string in the waning days of the 1884 season, Kimber took the mound on October 4 for ninth-place Brooklyn against eighth-place Toledo and pitcher Tony Mullane before a Saturday crowd of 1,200 at Washington Park.

Both pitchers were at the top of their game, perhaps helped by the fact that on the cool fall day, with little at stake, hitters on both clubs were anxious to end the game as quickly as possible. Brooklyn was held in check by Mullane, and on the rare occasion when they did get a hit, the Grays almost immediately ran into outs.

Kimber was even more effective as inning after inning Toledo went down without a base hit. Finally, after ten innings, umpire John Dykler was forced to call the scoreless game because of darkness. Kimber had a no-hitter, but not a victory.

In the off-season before the 1885 season, the Cleveland franchise of the National League disbanded. Just as they had pursued the orphans of the Merritts, Byrne and company

---

Washington Park was located between Third and Fifth Streets and bordered by Fourth and Fifth Avenues in Red Hook. This photograph depicts a Decoration Day crowd watching the Dodgers play the St. Louis Browns. Note the overflow crowd, dressed to the nines, watching the game from both the rooftops and the outfield perimeter.

swept in and signed six players for an aggregate cost of some $9,000 — no small figure — plus Cleveland manager Charlie Hackett. The infusion of talent was supposed to make the ballclub a contender.

But there was bad blood between the players from Cleveland and the Brooklyn holdovers from 1884. Manager Hackett, thought the holdovers, favored his own players, while Hackett's charges apparently believed their Brooklyn teammates got preference from the manager. Both were united in their distaste for their manager. The result was a team that worked against itself.

As a young pitcher named John "Phenomenal" Smith made his debut on June 17, players from both cliques were peeved: each side believed one of its men was even more phenomenal and deserving of the start than Smith. Each faction then welcomed the rookie to the big leagues by trying to outdo each other with poor play. Former Cleveland shortstop Germany Smith and Brooklyn veteran catcher Jackie Hayes played "top this" all game long — each man committed 7 errors, helping the team to the astounding total of 28 errors as the Grays lost to the Browns, 18–5.

Byrne went ballistic after the game, firing Hackett, meting out fines to everyone involved, and taking over as manager himself. While the club played nominally better ball for the remainder of the year, they still finished in fifth place, 26 games behind the Browns.

Although their play improved in 1886 and garnered them a third-place finish, the Grays were still no match for the Browns, who won the pennant some 16 games ahead of the Brooklyn team. The highlights of the season were two more meaningless midseason games a few weeks apart. The first, which took place on June 24 at Washington Park, is still the most one-sided victory in club history.

Visiting Baltimore sent their young phenom Matt Kilroy to the mound opposite Adonis Terry. Known for his fastball, young Kilroy entered the game with a record of 15–8 — not bad for a team whose cumulative record was a dismal 19–27.

But Kilroy threw *too* hard. Catchers of the day were not equipped with oversized mitts and other protective equipment of the modern age, and Baltimore catcher Chris Fullmer's thin gloves provided little protection. He started the game with hands so sore that from the start he had a hard time holding on to Kilroy's offerings.

This put the pitcher into a quandary. When he threw fastballs, Fullmer let the balls pass and Brooklyn runners raced around the bases. When he took something off the ball, Brooklyn's hitters belted it all over the lot.

Neither solution was satisfactory, since each resulted in a wave of Brooklyn players crossing the plate. By the time Kilroy and Fullmer were pulled with no outs in the third, Brooklyn led 11–1. Their replacements proved little better and the game ended at 25–1 in Brooklyn's favor. Every player in the lineup scored at least one run and collected at least one hit, and all but one knocked in a run.

One month later, on July 24, the Grays indulged in another memorable contest, as Terry no-hit St. Louis 1–0 before a crowd of 7,000 at Washington Park. But the Grays, despite the third-place finish in 1886, slumped back again in 1887 to finish sixth as the Browns won their third pennant in a row with no end in sight.

Part of Brooklyn's problem on the field was Charles Byrne. While his knowledge of baseball had been sufficient to manage the team in the Interstate League, he was ill prepared for the higher class of play in the AA, and even less prepared to adapt to the constant evolution of the game, which required an intimate and creative knowledge of the sport that he lacked. Although the American Association and the National League wouldn't agree to a common set of rules until 1886, in 1885 the AA had followed the NL's lead and begun to allow overhand pitching. That changed *everything*, and baseball began to look much more like the game that is played today. Of course, there were still changes to be made, particularly in ball and strike counts and the pitching distance, but after overhand pitching was allowed, even the most casual of modern fans would recognize the game as baseball.

Fortunately, Byrne would soon recognize the folly of being both owner and manager, for at the same time that baseball the game was evolving and growing on the field, so too was baseball the business. Byrne would prove far better as a businessman than a field general.

In the waning days of the 1887 season, the St. Louis Browns and the NL champion Detroit Wolverines both smelled a potential windfall in the offing. For the past several seasons the AA and NL champions had met in a lucrative yet unofficial postseason "world's series." This time Detroit owner Freddie Stearns had an even better idea.

He proposed not a short best-of-seven or -nine "home and home" series, but a fifteen-game barnstorming extravaganza played in no fewer than ten different cities, including Brooklyn.

Not only was pitcher "Adonis" Terry a notorious ladies' man, but he also was a superb competitor, winning 20 or more games three times for the club. His best season came in 1890, when Brooklyn joined the National League and Terry won 26 games while helping lead the Dodgers to the pennant.

The series promised to provide a windfall for the two owners, particularly Chris Von der Ahe of the Browns, who, in addition to the $12,500 players' share to be divided among the members of his club, offered his players only $100 more for winning the series. Disgruntled, the Browns quickly lost their enthusiasm for playing and were drubbed by Detroit ten games to five.

In the wake of the defeat, Von der Ahe and player-manager Charles Comiskey broke the team up, shedding those players they felt were over the hill or had not given their best effort against Detroit. Byrne, true to form, picked up the pieces, buying star hurler "Parisian" Bob Caruthers for $8,500 and pitcher Dave Foutz for $6,000, with catcher Doc Bushong thrown in for good measure. Simultaneously, Byrne purchased the New York Metropolitans, originally thinking he could move the team elsewhere. When that plan fell through, Byrne retained the heart of the club and sold off the spare parts.

Almost overnight the Grays went from a pretender to a contender. Byrne chose to return to the front office and hired Bill McGunnigle to manage the club. McGunnigle had enjoyed a fine career as a catcher and occasional pitcher. But his reputation as an innovator and manager far outweighed his worth as a player. To this day he remains the most successful manager in club history.

In 1875 McGunnigle was credited with being the first player to wear a glove, and he later pioneered the use of removable baseball spikes. But in a managerial career that began in the Massachusetts League in 1874 and continued in the New England League, International League, Northwestern League, and National League, McGunnigle proved himself to be perhaps the best manager in the game. From 1874 to 1887 he won seven pennants and never finished lower than fourth. McGunnigle usually managed while wearing a suit, hat, and spats, directing his players over the diamond with a wave of a baseball bat. Byrne could not have made a better choice. Acquiring McGunnigle would prove to be as important as the addition of Caruthers and Foutz.

But not in 1888. Although Brooklyn was much improved, the gap between the Grays and the Browns was still substantial. Foutz's arm was going dead, and he would soon become more of a first baseman than a pitcher. Although Brooklyn led the league in midseason following a four-game sweep of the Browns, the club immediately collapsed. The Browns rolled to another pennant while Brooklyn, with a meaningless late-season surge, finished in second place.

Yet for the first time they began to be something close to beloved by Brooklyn fans. In the off-season several players had married, causing the press to refer to the team as the "Bridegrooms." By the spring of 1889 the nickname had taken hold.

As they entered the 1889 season, expectations for the former bachelors were high. Byrne's club had been supplemented by even more high-priced talent with the purchase of Thomas "Oyster" Burns and several other players, giving the Grooms one of the better players in the league at virtually every position. Adonis Terry was the only player left on the roster from the old Grays.

They did not disappoint. From the start of the season the Grooms and the Browns marched through the league in lockstep, giving Brooklyn fans their first pennant race of note.

Although the franchise subsequently became known for the passion and drama of its championship pursuits, this first race was nearly the equal of much more recent pennant chases.

The two teams entered September with identical 71–36 records. When St. Louis fell to Columbus on September 1, the Bridegrooms nudged ahead. "The tumble has come at last," opined the *Daily Eagle*. Most fans believed the pennant would be decided when the Browns traveled to Brooklyn a week later for three games.

There was already bad blood between the two teams, some stemming from the sale of Caruthers and Foutz two years earlier, but much of it arising from the fast and loose umpiring that made every game in the league contentious beyond belief. It seemed as if every close decision was open to both argument and appeal. League officials were constantly putting out fires, ruling on forfeits, then changing their minds. With only one umpire on the field and both of his eyes facing the same direction, it was impossible for him to see everything. It was more or less accepted practice for players to get away with anything they could, whether that meant cutting the corners while running the bases, interfering with runners, or blocking the view of fielders. An earlier series between the two clubs in St. Louis had been marred by such shenanigans. But the events of September 7 set a new standard for controversy.

With over 15,000 rabid fans in attendance, Caruthers faced Elton Chamberlain in what was, to that point, the most important game in franchise history for Brooklyn. The Bridegrooms chose to bat first and got off to a quick start. Darby O'Brien topped a ball to shortstop and was safe on an error. He went to second on a passed ball before Hub Collins doubled him home. Foutz's line drive single scored Collins, and Brooklyn led 2–0.

But neither Caruthers nor his counterpart was particularly sharp, and only some sharp fielding by each team stopped the fourth inning from turning into a Waterloo as each club had two men thrown out at home. In the fifth St. Louis broke through when Charlie Duffee singled, then allowed himself to be hit by the throw, making second and causing the game to be halted for some time as Brooklyn argued that he had done so intentionally. Which of course he had, but umpire Fred Goldsmith was in no mood to make such a judgment. Duffee scored on a hit to make the score 2–1 Brooklyn.

In the sixth, however, St. Louis forged ahead, sandwiching three hits around a sacrifice to take a 3–2 lead. Then, as the afternoon light began to dim, things turned strange. The Browns were eager to have the game finished and escape with a win.

The seventh inning began, noted one newspaper, at 5:40 P.M. "with a cloudy atmosphere but the sun still well up in the west." When Caruthers was hit by a pitch, Browns catcher

Bill McGunnigle was both a baseball pioneer, having been credited with being the first player to use a glove and wear removable baseball spikes, and a superb manager, having won pennants in five leagues, including the National League. In his second season as Brooklyn manager, McGunnigle led the team to the American Association championship.

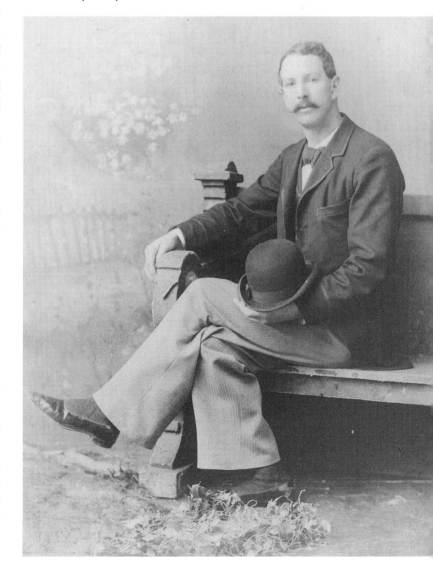

Right-handed pitcher Dave "Scissors" Foutz was reported to have won $245 while betting on his team during the 1889 season. Prior to the Dodgers' 1889 postseason series with the New York Giants, he told fellow pitcher Bob Caruthers he'd pay him $50 if he won and expected to be paid the $50 if he lost.

Milligan argued at length, keeping an eye on the dwindling light. When the next man was also hit by a pitch and Milligan resumed his complaint, Goldsmith caved in and ruled that the hitter had not gotten out of the way, which caused Brooklyn to argue. The half-inning took a full ten minutes, and all the while the sun continued to set.

St. Louis scored again in the bottom of the seventh to lead 4–2. But before play began in the eighth, the Browns absconded with the ball and dunked it in a bucket of water. This caused another brief delay before umpire Goldsmith discovered the ruse and ordered that a new ball be put in play.

The eighth inning was a joke. The visiting Browns argued nearly every pitch, then sauntered back into position after each play. Owner Chris Von der Ahe earned Goldsmith's wrath by placing lit candles in front of the Browns' bench, leading the partisan crowd to hurl beer mugs at the bench, toppling the candles and causing a small fire to break out along the edge of the stands. By the time the fire was put out, order restored, and the scoreless inning completed, a full half-hour had passed.

By now it really was too dark to play, but Goldsmith was determined to see the game to its conclusion, and Brooklyn came to bat to lead off the ninth. Shortstop Germany Smith struck out, but Browns catcher Jocko Milligan lost the ball in the dwindling light. It rolled past, allowing Smith to make first.

This was too much for the Browns. Charles Comiskey pulled his team from the field, according to the *Daily Eagle*, "to the disgust of every impartial spectator." Goldsmith ordered them back out, but Comiskey refused, and fans pelted his club with bottles while the umpire stood at home plate consulting his watch for a moment. He then called the game a forfeit and gave the Bridegrooms a 9–0 victory, at which point the crowd rioted, breaking the windows of the clubhouse that housed the Browns, where they huddled in fear before being rescued by a complement of police.

That was hardly the end of it. On the following day, Sunday, the two teams were supposed to play the second game of the series in Ridgewood to skirt local blue laws. Brooklyn showed, as did some 17,000 of their fans, but the Browns wanted the Saturday game replayed in its entirety. Brooklyn refused, and the Browns refused to play, resulting in yet another forfeit in Brooklyn's favor. To calm the crowd, the Bridegrooms played a five-inning exhibition. To the relief of almost everyone, the final game of the series was rained out before yet another forfeit could be declared.

For much of the next month charges and countercharges were lobbed back and forth between the two clubs, and the AA eventually reached something of a compromise that pleased neither team, ruling that St. Louis had in fact won the September 7 game 4–2 while upholding the forfeit the following day and fining the Browns $1,500. Brooklyn hung on to win the pennant by two games, leading one local poet to wax in a poem entitled "The Brooklyn Champions": "Terry, so genial so suave and so neat, / Here's to Caruthers, who cannot be beat, Ever and always they'll find honors meet . . . / Now of brave Byrne we'll raise a great noise, / Shout for McGunnigle who shares in our joys."

Over in the National League, the Giants had swept to the pennant. Giants owner Jim Mutrie and Byrne quickly reached an agreement to play the first all–New York world's series, a best-of-11 affair scheduled to begin on October 18 in Manhattan at the Polo Grounds. A subway series it was not, however, for just as Brooklyn and Manhattan were not yet linked politically, neither was there a subway between the two cities. Travelers back and forth were still forced to use carriages or aboveground trains.

And while fans were excited about the series, it was hardly the honored spectacle the World Series is today. The games were viewed for what they were — an exhibition. Similar meetings between the NL and AA champions since 1884 had hardly been memorable. Not only had the games been marred by rumors of fixes or other arrangements that undercut the drama of the series, but the arguing, rough play, and trickery that besmirched so many regular season games increased exponentially in the postseason. Moreover, clubs that fell behind in the series lost interest and pooh-poohed the significance of the contests, while the owners pushed to play the full complement of games even after victory in the series had been decided. It was as much a sideshow as a series of real import, but it made for great theater.

It is impossible to overstate the effect of gambling on these contests, for wagers were made not only by the fans but by the players themselves. On the precipice of the series, the *New York World* reported that Dave Foutz had earned $245 gambling on the regular season. He collected his bets and immediately put $100 on the first game of the series. But he did not wager on Brooklyn's fortunes. Instead, he wagered with Bob Caruthers, promising to pay the pitcher $50 if he won, while Caruthers would have to pay Foutz $50 if he lost. "This, if true, ought to be stopped by Mr. Byrne," sniffed the *Eagle*. "It makes players too anxious about winning their bets to play coolly in a match."

The series opened on October 18 in Manhattan at the Polo Grounds. In contrast to the mighty Giants, Brooklyn fans looked upon their club as the underdog that the local betting line made them out to be. They were "the village nine from Long Island" compared to Manhattan's behemoths, the Giants. It had already become clear that Brooklyn, as a city, was rapidly falling beneath New York's shadow. The Brooklyn Bridge had not brought New York to Brooklyn but Brooklyn to New

As a ballplayer, attorney, manager, and executive, there wasn't much that John Montgomery Ward didn't achieve in the national pastime. In 1891, following the demise of the Players' League, Ward was hired to manage the Dodgers, where he lasted just two seasons.

York. Increasingly, Brooklyn was becoming a place that people either passed through on their way to the big city or returned to at the end of the day.

Similarly, the American Association played Brooklyn to the more powerful National League's Manhattan. The Bridegrooms, as AA champions, were seen as something lesser than the NL pennant winner. That perception would linger even after the team joined the NL, and for the remainder of the club's tenure in Brooklyn. No matter how many games they won or how successful they were, Brooklyn's team would always play the role of the underdog, the lovable loser, a status the club and its fans eventually came to cherish and even to cultivate. Although that underdog status would at times prove to be both profitable and artistically successful, it would also lay the groundwork for the perception that the Brooklyn club was somehow less significant to the game than other teams, particularly other New York teams. Brook-

NL WINNING PERCENTAGE LEADERS

Year	Player	Pct.	Year	Player	Pct.
			1953	Carl Erskine	.769
			1955	Don Newcombe	.800
			1956	Don Newcombe	.794
			1961	Johnny Podres	.783
1890	Tom Lovett	.744	1963	Ron Perranoski	.842
1899	Jim Hughes	.824	1964	Sandy Koufax	.792
1900	Joe McGinnity	.763	1965	Sandy Koufax	.765
1920	Burleigh Grimes	.676	1973	Tommy John	.696
1940	Freddie Fitzsimmons	.889	1974	Andy Messersmith	.769
1942	Larry French	.789	1976	Rick Rhoden	.800
1949	Preacher Roe	.714	1985	Orel Hershiser	.864
1951	Preacher Roe	.880			

lyn would operate on the margins of the national pastime, an insular club that meant everything to its hometown but one that elsewhere didn't matter much at all. This perception of the club, which first appeared during the 1889 world's series, would eventually lead to the removal of the team from Brooklyn some 69 seasons later. Ironically, that would take place at the precise moment when, owing to their groundbreaking role as the first team to embrace integration, they were finally beginning to forge a new identity and take on a significance that reached far beyond their borough. This helps to explain the enduring appeal of that team today, for in a sense there is a greater level of interest in the Brooklyn Dodgers now than there was for most of their years spent in Brooklyn. Just as the city of Brooklyn would become a victim of pure geography, so too would the team that would become the Dodgers.

They cemented their identity in game one of the series. After Brooklyn took a 5–0 lead in the first inning, a wild seventh determined the game. Trailing 6–5, the Giants stormed back to score five runs and take a 10–6 lead, only to see Brooklyn fight back with two runs of their own. It was 5:00, and the Giants wanted the game called, but the day was clear and the sun would not set for another 15 minutes. The umpires ordered that the game continue. The Giants went down scoreless in the eighth, and as the sun hung on the horizon, Brooklyn responded with four runs to take a 12–10 lead. That was enough for the arbiters, who called the game at 5:15, just one minute before the sun blinked closed. The *Eagle* summed it up by noting that "the unexpected did happen, and Brooklyn's David knocked out New York's great Goliath and took initiatory steps for becoming giant killers."

That view, however, was purely parochial. The Giants groused that Brooklyn unfairly stalled in order to have the game called. Manhattan newspapers echoed the charge.

The Giants won game two before a crowd of more than 16,000 in Brooklyn, but when Brooklyn took games three and four, their eventual victory seemed all but assured. The Giants, however, took another view, for both their 8–7 loss in game three and their 10–7 defeat in game four were marred by delaying tactics by Brooklyn that caused both games to be called prematurely on account of darkness. In the first contest, umpire John Gaffney called the game with the Giants at the plate and the bases loaded in the last of the ninth. In the second game, with the game tied at 7–7 in the sixth, Brooklyn won when Oyster Burns lofted a fly ball into the twilight with two men on. The ball fell untouched, and three runs scored. As soon as they did, Gaffney called the game.

Interest in the series should have been at a fever pitch. Instead, the opposite was true. The shenanigans of games three and four led to widespread charges in some quarters of "Hippodroming"—arranging games in order to guarantee the extension of the series so that each club could make as much money as possible. The St. Louis–based *Sporting News,* still smarting over the regular season defeat of its beloved Browns, took another view. Its headline screamed:

MURDER!
That is The Cry of the New Yorks
Brooklyn Succeeds by Treachery

Such taunts, combined with the deteriorating October weather, kept crowds down to only a few thousand hardy souls. The Giants were able to enforce an earlier starting time for the remainder of the series, making called games a thing of the past. When forced to play a full nine innings, Brooklyn proved no match for its NL counterpart. The Giants won the next five games to take the series six games to three. "Hosanna," wrote an anonymous correspondent for *The Sporting News,* "which means Glory to God in the highest. The New York Giants have wiped out the robbery of the Browns by the Brooklyns. They have beaten the Bogus Champions without half trying." Within only a few weeks, however, the series would pass from memory.

Since 1885 the Brotherhood of Professional Ball Players, led by attorney and star player John Montgomery Ward, had sought to protect player rights while baseball's professional

leagues virtually ignored them. Days after the end of the series, the Brotherhood announced the formation of the Players' League and released a manifesto that opined: "Players have been bought sold and exchanged as though they were sheep instead of American citizens." Organizers of the circuit announced plans to place a team in Brooklyn and build a ballpark along an elevated line in East New York known as Eastern Park. They began trying to entice players to jump their contracts in the AL and NL and join the fledgling organization, which promised to share profits with its members.

Charles Byrne looked into the future and did not like what he saw. Two major leagues were plenty; three would be way too much. Ten days after the Players' League went public, Byrne pulled his team from the AA and joined the National League, a crippling blow to the American Association, which rapidly lost several more clubs. Partner Frederick Abell took

---

Charles Hercules Ebbets rose from ticket-taker to baseball magnate on sheer will and effort. After he was rewarded with shares of team stock for his work as club secretary, Ebbets was elected team president in January 1898 and soon moved the club back to South Brooklyn, where he built a new version of Washington Park.

a more pragmatic approach—he hedged his bet and invested in the Players' League New York franchise. Although another Brooklyn franchise in the AA was quickly cobbled together, the "Gladiators" would not last the season. The future of Brooklyn baseball appeared to lie with either Byrne's Bridegrooms in the NL or John Montgomery Ward's "Wonders" of the Players' League.

The Players' League was a grand idea light-years ahead of its time. Had it succeeded, professional baseball would probably be a radically different organization without the rancor between players and management that characterizes the game today. But although the Players' League succeeded in swiping much of the best talent from both the AA and the NL, increased competition made it virtually impossible for any team to earn a profit. Most National League owners could take the hit, but the fledgling PL could not. The 1890 campaign would be both its first and last.

Meanwhile, the Bridegrooms began the 1890 season virtually unscathed, since most of its players had resisted offers from the PL. Pitcher Tom Lovett emerged as the equal of Terry and Caruthers, giving the Bridegrooms a three-man pitching rotation that was the best in baseball. The club was a juggernaut and swept through the season to another pennant and yet another postseason appearance in the world's series, this time representing the National League against AA champion Louisville.

Yet no one really cared. Although the Players' League was staggered by the end of the season and would soon fall, most fans correctly believed that the best players in the game were in the PL. Attendance for the Bridegrooms dropped from over 350,000 in 1889 to a pathetic 37,000 in 1890—Brooklyn's entry in the Players' League drew twice as many fans. A meeting between the NL and AA champs held little meaning or interest, a point underscored when, with the series tied at three games apiece with one tie and attendance dwindling to only a couple of hundred fans, both clubs decided to cave to the cold weather and call the whole thing off.

As soon as the season ended, more changes came to Brooklyn. The Players' League folded and the Brotherhood collapsed. This left George Chauncey, who had financed the Brooklyn entry in the Players' League, with a ballpark but no team. Although he'd lost money in 1890, his interest in the game was purely financial, and the National League was now poised to take advantage of the collapse of the Brotherhood—player salaries would drop almost in half, and begin-

ning in 1891 the NL would have little competition. Meanwhile, Byrne and company were still stinging from their financial losses. When Chauncey offered to invest in the NL club, Byrne readily agreed.

But Chauncey had no intention of being a silent partner. He wanted to make a few changes. Foremost, he wanted the new team to play at Eastern Park, which he owned, along with much of the surrounding real estate. And he also wanted John Montgomery Ward, the deposed Brotherhood boss, former pitcher, and infielder-manager of the Wonders, installed as manager of the Bridegrooms. Byrne, desperate for Chauncey's cash, agreed, and McGunnigle, despite two pennants and a second-place finish in three seasons, was dismissed and passed into anonymity. To this day, no subsequent Dodger manager has matched his record.

And the Dodgers they soon would be. Trolley lines crisscrossed Brooklyn with little plan or forethought. Eastern Park was several miles removed from downtown Brooklyn, almost inaccessible except by rail. An elevated train line dumped fans near the park, but to reach the stands they were forced to cross several sets of railroad tracks that sent electric trolley cars from Greenpoint to Coney Island.

The newfangled contraptions proved a challenge for both drivers and pedestrians, neither of whom seemed to realize that the added weight of the mechanized cars made them much more difficult to stop than the horse-drawn variety. The result was carnage. Accidents became daily occurrences. Barely a week went by without one or more Brooklyn residents meeting his or her demise by trolley, and countless more were maimed. As such, surviving Brooklynites began to be known as "trolley dodgers" for their skill at cheating death. Over the next few years the briefer moniker "Dodgers" would become attached to the players of the baseball team, although they would prove most adept at dodging first place.

For the Dodgers' first few seasons in the National League are among the least memorable in club history. The club made money, but the National League was now a virtual monopoly, and many league clubs became less concerned with winning. Most club owners played it fast and loose, and by the end of the decade it was not uncommon for the owner of one club to own a piece of another in what became referred to as "syndicate" baseball.

In this environment, the Dodgers floundered. Monte Ward lasted only a few seasons as manager before giving way to Dave Foutz in 1893. But Foutz was no improvement, and he too was let go after the Dodgers finished the 1896 season in ninth place. He died a short time later.

The most significant event during this period took place in the front office. When Chauncey bought in, he quickly noticed that although Byrne, Doyle, and Abell were the titular leaders of the franchise, young Charlie Ebbets seemed to be doing all the work. Chauncey sold Ebbets some stock, and the young ticket-taker's career as a baseball magnate was under way.

Ebbets's rise coincided with a series of fortuitous events that would send the team into the 20th century in an entirely new form. First, within a few short years the triumvirate of Byrne, Doyle, and Abell would quietly pass from the scene. Doyle died after the 1896 season, and Ebbets took over his position as club secretary, and in 1897 Byrne became too ill to run the franchise. The club desperately needed a new leader.

Abell, who was now the majority stockholder, wasn't interested. He'd always been an absentee owner and did not want a larger role. Neither was Chauncey. That left Ebbets.

His long apprenticeship was about to pay a hefty dividend. He was Brooklyn to his bones and already had some strong ideas in regard to the future of the franchise. Foremost was its return to Brooklyn proper from the relative obscurity of East New York, a move that served several purposes. Over the last decade the club's identity as a Brooklyn institution had become increasingly murky. At the same time, so had Brooklyn's civic identity. The rapid growth of the city had strained its financial resources to the breaking point, and in 1897 the New York legislature offered a way out of the fiscal crisis. On January 1, 1898, the city of Brooklyn was subsumed into a new municipality made up of the boroughs of Manhattan, the Bronx, Staten Island, Brooklyn, and Queens. It was humiliating. Later that evening Ebbets was elected president of the Dodgers. Byrne died a few days later, and one of Ebbets's first acts was to move the club back to South Brooklyn, returning to the borough one of its most visible institutions just as the city itself was losing its hegemony. Brooklynites never forgot — Ebbets was one of them. Their city may have been taken away, but their ballclub had returned.

In less than four months Ebbets built a ballpark on leased land between First and Third Streets and Second and Third Avenues and even called it Washington Park to hark back to the club's original home. Unfortunately, that was the only change he was able to make before the start of the 1898 season.

The ballclub was terrible. Pitcher Brickyard Kennedy and first baseman Candy LaChance were the only veterans of ability, while youthful outfielders Jimmy Sheckard and Fielder Jones were just beginning to make their mark. The Dodgers finished tenth in the twelve-team league. Ebbets fired manager Billie Barnie in midseason, and when his replacement, player-manager Mike Griffin, quit after three games, Ebbets himself went to the bench, an experience that taught him that his talents were best utilized behind a desk.

The season had been a disaster, not just for Ebbets and the Dodgers but for most of the league. The Spanish-American War had distracted fans, and attendance was down everywhere. Moreover, syndicate baseball had caused fans to question the integrity of league play, further sapping interest in the game. And New York Giants owner Andrew Freedman had announced his intention to fight the Dodgers at every turn. Even though his club played in the upper reaches of Manhattan, he didn't want to share greater New York with *anyone*. A politically well-connected member of Tammany Hall, the political machine that ran New York, Freedman used his influence to block a proposed subway stop that would service Washington Park.

Ebbets, rightfully, was more concerned with the Dodgers than the rest of the league. He supported syndicate play, and it was in Brooklyn that syndicate baseball would demonstrate its full creative power, for when two or more teams were owned by the same group of men, players could be transferred wholesale from one team to another. A tail-ender could turn into a contender overnight, and that was precisely the strategy Ebbets hoped to use.

He even dreamed of forcing the Giants from New York. The Dodgers were better positioned than just about any team in the game to take advantage of the benefits of syndicate ball. Even though Brooklyn was technically just a borough of New York, that borough was still larger than every other city in the league save Chicago and Philadelphia. In a sense, Brooklyn fans were the largest untapped market in baseball.

All they needed was a winning team to get them into the ballpark.

THE SUPERBAS

BEGINNING IN 1859 AND FOR THE REST OF THE CENTURY, SIX ENGLISH-born brothers of Irish ancestry known as the Hanlons wowed crowds across Europe and America with their inimitable form of theatrical acrobatics. Far from being crude vaudeville performers, the Hanlon Brothers created complicated and dazzling comic-dramatic musical spectacles built around pantomime and flamboyant gymnastics. The shows featured the most dangerous stuntwork of the time, including trapeze work, somersaults performed atop ladders, and tumbling. Their act was roughly akin to a small-scale version of today's popular Cirque du Soleil, with a touch of the Marx Brothers. George Hanlon once described the brothers' productions as "work in which fantasy, agility, and true realism play an equal role." In the late 1890s their final production, "Superba," played to packed houses all across the country.

In Baltimore another Hanlon produced a similarly successful series of shows that also mixed "fantasy, agility, and true realism." Oriole manager Ned Hanlon was the director of baseball's most innovative show, the Orioles. Beginning in 1899, he would bring his magic to Brooklyn.

Frederick Abell had been fishing for a partner to bail out the Dodgers for several seasons, and for several seasons he had looked longingly at Harry Von der Horst's Baltimore Orioles,

"Iron Man" Joe McGinnity pitched just one season for Brooklyn in 1900 and made the most of it while leading the National League with 29 victories from 45 starts and 347 innings pitched.

National League pennant winners under Ned Hanlon in 1895 and 1896. But Von der Horst hadn't needed Abell then. The championship club was making money.

By 1899 that had all changed. Boston had taken over as NL champ, and the Orioles, despite remaining one of the best clubs in the league, began to suffer at the box office. Baltimore was a great baseball town, but it just wasn't big enough to produce a profit during a less-than-championship campaign; as infielder John McGraw later observed: "Baltimore was never a town to support a loser." Ned Hanlon's talents were going to waste.

Hanlon had had a so-so career as a player before being named manager of the Baltimore Orioles in 1892. Although not related to his theatrical namesakes, Hanlon proved no less adept at drawing crowds to witness a form of baseball in which fantasy, agility, and true realism played equal roles. Baseball had never seen anything like it. Hanlon became the game's first great manager, and he would lead the Brooklyn Dodgers into the next century.

In the 1890s the evolution of the game of baseball finally slowed as the game approached the delicate balance between pitching, hitting, and defense that gives it much of its contemporary appeal. Substantive changes were relatively few compared to the more dynamic 1880s, and skill levels increased as the NL became the only major league. Thus, for the first time it became possible to stand back from the game, analyze its structure, and exploit its nuances. No one was better at this than Ned Hanlon.

His Baltimore Orioles were the game's original master craftsmen, the first technicians of what became known as "inside," or "scientific," baseball, what is sometimes referred to today as "little ball." By way of the bunt, the steal, the hit-and-run, the sacrifice, place hitting, daring, and guile, Hanlon's Orioles displayed all the dexterity of a production by the Hanlon Brothers.

Hanlon and his Orioles either invented or refined a host of strategies, ranging from the hit-and-run play to the "Baltimore chop" and the now-standard practice of having fielders back one another up. They played with an aggressive style that kept pressure on the opposition and took advantage of every opportunity, including those that violated the spirit, if not the letter, of the rules.

While Hanlon's Orioles were bunting and stealing their way around the bases, they also realized that the single umpire usually used in league games had only one set of eyes and could look at only one place at a time. So when the umpire's head was turned, Oriole runners were not above cutting the corners around the bases or grabbing, tripping, or otherwise interfering with opposition runners. They hid extra balls in the outfield grass, flashed mirrors in the eyes of hitters and fielders, faked being hit by pitches, doctored the baselines, and buried concrete in front of home plate to accommodate the Baltimore chop. Hanlon even hired a full-time groundskeeper to manicure the field to the Orioles' advantage—tilting the grade of the baselines, cutting the grass to the length favored by the Orioles, and wetting the base paths according to Hanlon's whim. He was widely acknowledged as the savviest leader in the game. Fans took to wearing buttons that read simply "Ask Hanlon." Even Von der Horst wore one.

The Orioles were also not without talent. Their roster included some of the best players of the era: outfielders Joe Kelley and Wee Willie Keeler—made famous by his admonition to "Keep the eye clear and hit 'em where they ain't"—infielder John McGraw, shortstop Hughie Jennings, and catcher Wilbert Robinson. They probably would have won anyway, but their intimidating tactics beat many opponents before the first pitch was thrown. They fought and argued and complained constantly, badgering the umpire and the opposition into submission. Baltimore fans loved them, while crowds turned out in force elsewhere in the league to jeer the swaggering champs. They were one of the most loved and hated teams in baseball history.

Soon after the 1898 season, Von der Horst and Abell came together, for each had what the other wanted and envisioned an arrangement that would put Baltimore's players in Brooklyn's larger and more lucrative market. Each man purchased a portion of the other's ballclub and would eventually own 40 percent of each. Charles Ebbets was offered the opportunity to buy as well, and he would eventually own 10 percent of each club, as would manager Ned Hanlon.

Now there was nothing to prevent the creation of a superteam. Hanlon would take over as manager of the Dodgers and bring all his better players with him, apart from McGraw and Robinson, who balked at the move and were allowed to stay in Baltimore. Some lesser lights and a few promising youngsters, such as outfielder Jimmy Sheckard, were sent to Baltimore to prevent the utter collapse of that club, although Sheckard would eventually return to Brooklyn.

The rest of the league howled. *The Sporting News* referred to Messrs. Von der Horst, Abell, and their brethren as a "mal-

THE FATHER OF ALL MANAGERS

Manager Ned Hanlon fathered many sons. Nearly 100 years after he last managed a major league baseball team, his progeny still direct their charges from the major league dugout.

As manager of both the Orioles and the Dodgers, Hanlon headed up clubs that were noteworthy not just for their success (most prominently in Baltimore) but for their aggressive and innovative style of play. These clubs pursued victory by any means necessary, which sometimes included the intimidation of both the umpires and the opponent as well as the bending and even breaking of the rules.

Hanlon set the standard for this approach, and over the century his influence on his offspring has resulted in an extraordinary number of winning ballclubs, pennants, and world championships. As manager of the Orioles, Hanlon tutored no less than four men who went on to successful and significant careers managing in the major leagues. Hughie Jennings manned Detroit from 1907 through 1920, winning pennants his first three years at the helm. Joe Kelley managed Cincinnati for four years and Boston for one. Then of course there was Wil Robinson, who, after managing Baltimore in 1902, managed the Robins from 1914 through 1931, winning two pennants.

But the legacy that runs from Hanlon through John McGraw is perhaps the strongest and longest-lasting, for not only did McGraw seem to take more from Hanlon and to pass that knowledge on to his charges, but the lineage that runs through McGraw is the most successful in the game.

Like Hanlon, John McGraw was the dominant manager of his time. He led the Giants from 1902 through 1932,

winning ten pennants and three world championships, in 1905, 1921, and 1922. Although a number of former Giants later became big league managers — such as Bill Terry and Frankie Frisch, who between them won four of five National League pennants between 1933 and 1937 — it was Casey Stengel who best passed on McGraw's legacy.

Stengel, of course, won nothing in his three seasons as manager of the Dodgers and six at the helm of the Braves, but once he became manager of the Yankees, he put together a record equal to that of any manager in the history of the game, winning ten pennants and seven world championships in twelve seasons. While Stengel and his teams were not as combative as those of Hanlon and McGraw, his creative and innovative use of the platoon system — which McGraw had successfully employed in his use of Stengel himself in 1922 and 1923, when Stengel hit .368 and .339 — was a huge factor in his success.

In Stengel's wake came manager Yogi Berra and, most notably, Billy Martin, whom Stengel loved like a son. Martin was a throwback, a combination of Hanlon and McGraw incarnate, someone who employed not only Hanlon's creativity but McGraw's belligerence and drive. While Martin's personal problems were legion, he also won with every team he managed — for a while — capturing division titles or pennants with Minnesota, Detroit, the Yankees, and Oakland, leading the Texas Rangers to a second-place finish, winning a world championship with the Yankees in 1977.

Like Hanlon, McGraw, and Stengel, Martin also influenced another generation of managers, most notably Mike Hargrove and Lou Piniella, who in recent years have captured a series of division titles and

Manager Ned Hanlon was the first master of the "little game" within baseball. His scrappy Baltimore Oriole teams perfected the use of the bunt, steal, hit-and-run, double steal, and sacrifice. Many of his former players, such as John McGraw, Hugh Jennings, and Wilbert Robinson, also enjoyed storied and successful managerial careers.

pennants. Piniella steered the Reds to a world championship in 1990 and the Seattle Mariners to a record number of wins in 2001.

Today the managerial DNA that can be traced back all the way to Hanlon seems strongest in Piniella, who is now with Tampa Bay. In an era when most baseball managers seem cut from the same increasingly corporate cloth, Piniella still does things the old-fashioned way. Whenever the feisty manager leaps from the dugout to cover home plate with dirt and go head to head with an umpire, one can almost imagine the smiles on the ancestral visages of Hanlon, McGraw, Stengel, and Martin.

Attaboy, son.

Right-hander William "Brickyard" Kennedy won 174 games for the Dodgers and completed a franchise record 279 starts during the decade he pitched for the team. Not only did the durable Kennedy win 20 or more games for the Dodgers four times, but he also lost 20 or more for an equal number of seasons.

From the first game of the season it became clear that Brooklyn and defending champion Boston were the class of the league. On Opening Day, before 22,000 at Washington Park, the Bostons outlasted Brooklyn 1–0 in 11 long innings. But Brooklyn took the next two games to announce that their time had come.

The influx of talent created a powerhouse. Before long, the press had taken note of the nature of the team and begun to refer to them as the "Superbas," a play on the popular Hanlon Brothers production of the same name.

Superb they were. Jennings, Keeler, and Kelley all hit over .300 in 1899, while expatriate Oriole pitchers Jay Hughes and Doc McJames combined to win nearly 50 games. Holdovers Jack Dunn and Brickyard Kennedy were nearly as good. For a time the "Dodger" name faded from use.

The Superbas took over first place on May 22 in the midst of a 22-game home winning streak. They then assumed command in the race in June and held on from there, although both Boston and Philadelphia tried to keep pace. The new Dodgers outlasted both and won their first NL pennant with a record of 101–47, eight games ahead of Boston.

But there was no postseason series to look forward to in 1899, and the pennant was an accomplishment that spawned only a muted celebration among Brooklyn fans. The Temple Cup, which had matched the two NL clubs with the best records since 1894, had been abandoned after the 1897 season when it became clear that neither players nor fans took the contests very seriously. Although the National League was loath to admit it, without a second league to challenge it for superiority, the baseball season was something of an empty exercise for most clubs. Interest flagged as team after team fell out of the race and lost interest in the outcome of the season.

The fallout was tangible. The combined effects of syndicate baseball—which gave almost every game an unsavory tinge—and the lack of drama in the pennant race stifled attendance, particularly for the league's tail-enders. In January the more powerful magnates elected to be done with the have-nots. The league paid Baltimore, Washington, Louisville, and Cleveland to go away quietly.

It was the best thing that could ever have happened, although for none of the reasons the NL magnates had in mind. They hoped that dropping the league's weaker sisters would increase attendance everywhere, not to mention save on travel costs. It would do both in 1900, but the real impact

odorous gang," but in short order most clubs soon realized that it was better and better business to join in the syndicate shenanigans themselves rather than watch the Dodgers run away from the field. St. Louis and Cleveland entered into a similar arrangement, and Cincinnati and New York would become entwined as well.

was another year off. The Western League, a minor league circuit based in the Midwest, was looking to expand under ambitious young president Ban Johnson, a former sportswriter. Cleveland was an attractive and suddenly wide-open market. Johnson recruited a wealthy shipping baron, Charles Somers, to back expansion and placed teams in Cleveland and Chicago. Although the league was still considered a minor league, Johnson's excursion into both a former and a current major league market should have given the NL a hint of what was soon to come — a challenge from Johnson to their status as the dominant league in the land. But the National League was so arrogant and so consumed with its own increasingly penny-ante political pissing matches that it dismissed Johnson out of hand. The 1900 National League season proceeded absolutely oblivious to the fact that it would be professional baseball's last season under the anachronistic 19th-century model. The game would soon be forcibly thrust into the next millennium.

Players from the four eradicated clubs were not equally dispersed throughout the remainder of the league or cut loose. Rather, their rights were purchased as each defunct club was paid off to disappear. As a result, Hanlon's Superbas, with their convoluted ownership, were able to remain the league's dominant team. They added Baltimore outfielder Jimmy Sheckard and, more important, pitcher Joe McGinnity. McGinnity had led the league with 28 wins in 1899, and his addition to the Brooklyn roster was a coup. Dubbed "Iron Man" owing to his background as a steelworker, the nickname would soon prove to be an accurate assessment of his skills, for later in the 1900 season he would pitch and win on six consecutive days.

Other players who were either spare parts or, like John McGraw and Wil Robinson, had balked at going to Brooklyn were simply sold off. McGraw and Robinson were sent to the relative Siberia of St. Louis, where their skills would do little to help that club. But Brooklyn wasn't the only club to take advantage of the contraction of the league.

Barney Dreyfuss owned both Pittsburgh and Louisville, and the demise of the Louisville club allowed him to create one roster from two squads. In 1899 both teams had finished in the middle of the pack, within a few games of .500. Now the cream of both squads was suddenly concentrated in Pittsburgh. Pitcher Deacon Phillippe and Rube Waddell joined established stars Jack Chesbro, Jess Tannehill, and Sam Leever to form the deepest staff in the league, and a trio of youngsters — Tommy Leach, Claude Ritchey, and Honus Wagner — plus manager-outfielder Fred Clarke, bolstered the everyday lineup. Although the youthful club had yet to come into full flower, Hanlon's club suddenly had some competition.

The two teams were evenly matched from the beginning of the season and provided an intriguing contrast. The Superbas followed the model of Hanlon's old Baltimore team, which had averaged well over .300 as a team during his tenure and would be among the last teams to do so until the late 1920s. They were a tough, aggressive, high-scoring club with a decidedly 19th-century character, a team that slugged and sacrificed and stole its way around the bases with abandon.

But the game was changing. Rule modifications were beginning to tip the balance of the game in favor of pitching and defense at the expense of hitting, and in 1901 the foul strike rule — which made all foul balls strikes save those made with the count at two strikes — would add to that trend. At the same time hurlers were becoming more adept and

Hall of Fame first baseman Hughie Jennings came to Brooklyn via the Orioles in 1899 and batted just .279 in 188 games spread over three seasons for the team.

more talented as a new generation who grew up with the 60-foot, 6-inch distance began to reach the majors and discovered ever more inventive ways to doctor the baseball. Ballparks were increasing in size, and in some places fences were more than 500 feet from the field.

The result would soon be termed the Dead Ball Era, a time when the ball was soft and hard to see, runs were difficult to come by, and scientific baseball ruled. It was as if the game had settled down from its stormy beginnings on the field to a calmer and less tempestuous form more concerned with craft and artistry than brute force. Baseball's best teams would be those built around pitching, pitching, and more pitching, and that was something that Pittsburgh — dubbed the "Pirates" for their crass kidnapping of Louisville's stars — seemed to anticipate. They represented the future of the game, while the Superbas would soon become standard-bearers for a bygone age. The 1900 season was the fulcrum between the two eras, and the ensuing pennant race would be a contrast between the two styles as Brooklyn's brainy brawn and bravado went up against Pittsburgh's stingy and almost revolutionary dependence on pitching. Over the course of that season and the subsequent world's series — the last of its kind — the game turned a page and entered the modern era.

Brooklyn did not waltz to the pennant unchallenged. Philadelphia was the early leader as the Superbas struggled through April and May to play .500 baseball. But a favorable schedule in June led to a nine-game victory streak, and the Superbas dashed through the month with only five losses. By the end of June the surge had propelled them into first place as the Athletics collapsed, and by the start of September they led by a comfortable eight games. But then the Pirates got going.

The principal reason was one man — Honus Wagner. Although still primarily an outfielder, in 1900 Wagner had his first truly magnificent season, batting .381 — more than 100 points above the league average — and leading the league in average, doubles, triples, slugging, and steals (38). Outwardly awkward, the bowlegged star possessed incredible speed and sure hands that made him invaluable for the new era just coming into focus.

But it was too late for the Pirates in 1900. As September turned to October, it became apparent that the Superbas would outlast the youthful chargers from the Steel City — they carried a three-game lead into the final two weeks of the season. But while the season had been successful on the field, off the field it had not.

Despite their fine play, the Superbas failed to draw crowds in sufficient numbers to Brooklyn — average attendance was barely 2,000 fans per game. Ebbets, who despite his minimal stake in the club operated the team on a day-to-day basis, blamed the low attendance on a lack of support from the New York press. He believed they were jealous of his team's accomplishments and had failed to underscore their superiority to fans. "Since a year ago last May the Brooklyns have shown their superiority over the other teams," he opined. "Take any other sport where the contestants are unevenly matched and the public will desert it." That was precisely the kind of self-delusion that would soon bring the National League to its knees. Ebbets, like the rest of his fellow owners, was incapable of seeing that they were the reason for their own demise.

Although the team had proved to be a fine draw on the road, that hadn't been enough to offset the losses at home, and Ebbets and Von der Horst were in the red for the season. One big reason was Ebbets's insistence on charging 50¢ for general admission, then the league standard. That was a dear price at the time, but as a monopoly the National League felt it had the right to extort the public. Ebbets even had to deflect rumors that he would move the team for the 1901 season. The rumors cut attendance even further. Although he had no intention of moving, he admitted that, "if we can get a fair price, we would sell, and the purchaser would be at liberty to take the club where he pleases," but, he cautioned, "there will be no reduction in prices." The result left Ebbets eager to make any additional dollars that he could.

The Pirates had been the only team in the league to make any real money, earning Barney Dreyfuss $30,000 as 250,000 fans flocked to see the dashing young team, in particular Honus Wagner. He was the near-perfect player for the Dead Ball Era, one whose bat control and speed combined to make him an awesome offensive tool in an era when offense would be hard to come by.

Pittsburgh fans couldn't get enough of their club, and a quirk in the scheduling had kept the Superbas and Pirates apart except for three games over the last two months of the season, including the final five weeks. Meanwhile, some disputed games in Cincinnati left the Pirates and their fans feeling cheated out of a chance to win the championship. After the Superbas clinched the pennant on October 3 to give Hanlon his fifth pennant in seven tries as manager, the *Pittsburgh Chronicle Telegraph* stepped into the breach and offered to sponsor a postseason world's series between the two clubs.

Charlie Ebbets had been thinking along the same lines. In fact, over the final month of the season he had added Pittsburgh's scores to the right-field scoreboard to drum up interest in the rivalry. Brooklyn fans had cheered and booed at every change of the score, giving Ebbets some hope that a postseason series just might get him into the black for the season.

But no Brooklyn sponsor emerged, and Ebbets wasn't about to risk his own money. The newspaper's proposed series was a Pittsburgh proposition all the way, and the paper wanted every game of the best-of-five series to be played in Pittsburgh. Ebbets didn't like it, but he was hardly in a position to complain. In fact, in some ways it was a better proposition all around, for he would incur few expenses. While his return would be less than if the games had been played in Brooklyn, any additional take was a windfall he couldn't ignore. He agreed.

Both clubs were confident of victory. Pittsburgh clearly had been the better team over the final months of the season and had won 11 of the 19 meetings between the two clubs in the regular season. They blamed their losses on what one Pittsburgh paper referred to as Hanlon's "questionable tricks to keep his team from being crushed," the usual combination of tripping runners, cutting corners, and stalling. They also intimated that some of the clubs at the bottom of the league, most notably Cincinnati, had laid down for Brooklyn while battling the Pirates to the death. Similarly, Brooklyn sniffed that many of their losses to Pittsburgh had come early in the season before their vaunted offense got untracked. Statistically, they argued, they were clearly the better team.

Yet no amount of hyperbole could change the fact that the series would be starting in mid-October at a time when the leaves were being stripped from the trees and Pittsburgh was taking on the dull gray tinge of the approaching winter. The raw weather made the fans' decision to go to Exposition Park a difficult one, and despite the newspaper's incessant hyping of the series, or perhaps because of it, Pirate fans viewed the series as an exhibition and little more. They knew that they'd lost the pennant and that this set of games wasn't going to change that.

Even some of the players were less than enthusiastic. Brooklyn infielder Lave Cross had never won a championship

In five seasons with the Dodgers, Hall of Fame outfielder Willie Keeler continued to "hit 'em where they ain't" while batting .358. His batting mark stands as the highest career average in Dodger franchise history.

in his long career and was looking forward to the series to provide an exclamation point. Yet he found the Pittsburgh fans singularly unenthralled with the proceedings and wholly lacking in enthusiasm. He moaned to a reporter at the start of the series, "I have been in baseball a great many years and have always had a desire to feel how it is to be with a championship team. Now that I have had my desire, it isn't such a great thing after all. Although I don't drink I expected to be wined and dined, figuratively speaking, and to see the team made much of. But it's an off year I guess."

NL STOLEN BASE LEADERS

1892	Monte Ward	94
1903	Jimmy Sheckard	67
1942	Pete Reiser	20
1943	Arky Vaughan	20
1946	Pete Reiser	34
1947	Jackie Robinson	29
1949	Jackie Robinson	37
1952	Pee Wee Reese	30
1960	Maury Wills	50
1961	Maury Wills	35
1962	Maury Wills	104
1963	Maury Wills	40
1964	Maury Wills	53
1965	Maury Wills	94
1975	Davey Lopes	77
1976	Davey Lopes	63

A fair crowd of some 4,000 fans turned out for the first game of the series on Monday, October 15, a bit more than the average but far less than the capacity of the park. Hanlon chose to pitch his hot hand, the well-rested McGinnity, while Fred Clarke countered with Pittsburgh's eccentric hurler Rube Waddell. Although Waddell probably had the best "stuff" in the game, he was a handful, prone to drinking and jumping the club at a moment's notice.

In fact, the morning before the first game Exposition Park was the site of football practice for the Duquesne University football team. When Waddell arrived for the game, he decided to join the practice and dashed across the field for a full two hours before the park was cleared for the baseball game.

When the game began, it was made clear that Waddell had left the better part of his game on the gridiron. In the third he was battered for six hits as the Superbas took a 3–0 lead, and the margin was five runs when Pittsburgh came to bat in the eighth. Then Waddell, the football player, made another appearance. In the eighth inning McGinnity was caught in a rundown between third base and home. With Waddell holding the ball and giving chase, the Iron Man zigged as Waddell zagged, and the two collided, Waddell's knee hitting McGinnity's head.

McGinnity fell to the ground like a tackling dummy and stayed there. As his teammates gathered around, he finally stirred and after a few minutes stood, a visible lump rising from his scalp.

Today such a collision would probably send a player to the hospital for observation. But McGinnity didn't even leave the game — he came out to pitch the next inning. But it was not entirely because of his innate toughness. McGinnity, like other players of the era, was keenly aware that if he got hurt, he didn't get paid. The players enjoyed few rights of any kind. The standard reserve clause in every contract that bound a player to a team for life was enforced entirely at the discretion of the team. Injured players were often released and not paid, a possibility that every player was aware of. They didn't like it, but as yet they had no choice. That would soon change, but for the time being, if a player could still walk, he played, and McGinnity could still walk.

He could barely pitch, though, and staggered through the ninth, giving up two runs. Nevertheless, the Superbas emerged with a 5–2 win.

Deteriorating weather the next day cut the crowd by more than half, and it became clear that the only real interest in the series came from the gamblers, many of whom had traveled from Brooklyn hoping to catch Pittsburgh fans betting with their hearts over their heads. But after the first game the wise guys made Brooklyn the favorite, and their backers could find few takers.

The bottom dropped out after game two. Brooklyn's Frank Kitson completely outpitched Sam Leever as the Pirates made six errors that delivered four runs to Brooklyn. The 4–2 win put them only a game away from victory.

As the series continued, interest in the games continued to wane. When Pittsburgh bounced back with a 10–0 win in game three as Leever beat Harry Howell, the *Brooklyn Daily Eagle* devoted only a few paragraphs to the game. When Brooklyn swept to victory the following day behind Joe McGinnity, who scattered eight hits in the 6–1 win, the paper was somewhat more enthusiastic, touting the victory as evidence of a Brooklyn "World's Championship." The paper decreed that Brooklyn's victory was the result of their superior "scientific" batting—their ability to wear out Pittsburgh's hurlers by fouling off pitch after pitch and then placing the ball precisely where they wanted it.

For their victory the Superbas won a silver cup, which they received the next evening during a ceremony at Pittsburgh's Alvin Theater between acts of the play *Papa's Wife*. Captain Joe Kelley accepted the trophy but had to apologize for the fact that half the team was missing—including McGinnity, who was already on his way back to the foundry he operated in McAlester, Oklahoma. His teammates had planned to give the trophy to the pitcher, but most members of the team were apparently less than happy with the fruits of victory, which had earned them only $30 or so per game, supplemented by some cuff links donated by Charles Ebbets. Most players looked on them with disdain, for Pittsburgh owner Barney Dreyfuss had magnanimously given the Pirates some $2,500 to be divided among his players—losing had paid off. As soon as the ceremony ended, most of the Brooklyn players bolted from the theater before the start of act two. They left so quickly that they even forgot to take the trophy; it was boxed and shipped to Brooklyn a few days later.

It was, perhaps, the least exciting and least remembered world championship in the annals of baseball, over so quickly and so devoid of drama that in the ensuing decades in most quarters it was rarely mentioned and was considered less of an achievement than even the most tainted Temple Cup championship. Yet in Brooklyn, improbably, it would grow in importance over time and take on a meaning none could imagine, not unlike the way the Red Sox 1918 world championship looms so large over that franchise today. For although no one knew it, the 1900 season would be the last time the phrase "world's championship" would be paired with the name of a baseball team from Brooklyn for more than five decades. That would be no accident of fate but the result of front office failures, myopia, and bad managing.

In the wake of their victory, Charles Ebbets, instead of looking to repeat as champion, seemed eager to undermine his own ballclub. As the *Eagle* reported, "It is evident that the Brooklyns are too strong for the rest of the league so far as winning the pennants is concerned," and the paper prophesied that Ebbets would soon sell both Joe Kelley and Hughie Jennings "for the purpose of reducing expenses and making the race of 1901 closer." Ebbets was already on record as saying he believed that would lead to an increase in attendance.

His timing and logic could not have been worse. Ban Johnson and his American League were just about ready to turn baseball on its head. Just two days before the start of the postseason series with the Pirates, Johnson moved his American League into Baltimore and Washington and announced that the league was minor no more. He was ready to join the big leagues.

The National League laughed it off. At the league meeting a month later, Johnson petitioned for an audience with his National League elders. He wanted the NL to accept him as an equal partner and was ready to accept the same playing rules and respect the reserve clause, content to build his league with younger players, minor leaguers, and players whose NL contracts had expired. He was confident that his league would be competitive and that within a few short years the level of play between the two circuits would be indistinguishable.

But the National League was in no mood to share and was so convinced of its superiority that it saw no reason to. The NL patted Johnson on the head, showed him the door, and then told him to get lost.

Johnson was aptly described by one colleague as a man who "always remembers a friend but never forgets an enemy." The war was on. If the National League didn't want to share major league baseball, Johnson was determined to take it by force. In a matter of days Johnson told his American League investors that his league would no longer respect the reserve clause and go after only players whose contracts had expired.

The American League was ready and eager to outbid the National League for talent, and the players were equally eager to have another market competing for their services. There was already real dissent between the players and the National League. They weren't naive and had long recognized that they were chattel with few rights—the Players' League had provided proof of that. The previous summer they had made a move to organize—Brooklyn's Hughie Jennings had been one of the leaders. The existence of the American League suddenly gave players a real alternative and some leverage.

The National League badly underestimated Johnson, whose primary financial backer, Charles Somers, had enough cash to make good on Johnson's threat. And while it took the NL forever to make a decision, as the owners and their convoluted syndicate system made every issue a nightmare of tangled motives and mutual distrust, Johnson *was* the American League. He could move quickly and decisively.

As a result, Johnson outflanked the National League at every turn. He recognized that Pittsburgh, not Brooklyn, was the team of the future. When the American League began pursuing those National League players not yet under contract for 1901 but who had been turned down by Honus Wagner, the Pirates became off-limits.

Johnson's reason to let the Pirates be was twofold. One, he hoped to convince owner Barney Dreyfuss to jump leagues and take his team with him. That would force the National League to make peace, if not bring it down entirely, leaving Johnson's American League as the reigning monopoly. But if Pittsburgh remained in the NL, Johnson wanted the Pirates to become an unchallenged dynasty. If they romped to a pennant in 1901, there would be no pennant race in the NL and league attendance would surely suffer, giving fans reason to look toward the American League.

Brooklyn, by default, paid the price. They became a special target of the new league, not only because they were a threat to Pittsburgh's supremacy, but because of their location in greater New York. While Johnson was not yet prepared to mount an invasion to go head to head against the National League in New York, he had his sights on what was already baseball's largest market. His eventual invasion of New York would be made easier if he could weaken Brooklyn.

Neither Ebbets, Von der Horst, nor any other NL owner saw any of this coming, and by the time they realized it was happening it was too late. Like every other NL owner, Ebbets fiddled and balked and pounded his fist and whined as the American League offered players double their usual salary to jump leagues. The National League pleaded with the players to show loyalty, but most players weren't fools—that concept was a two-way street.

Over the next few seasons the Superbas would suffer the slow death of a thousand cuts, bleeding more than their share of red ink as the NL tried to stave off Johnson's challenge. Their championship club would quickly devolve into a downtrodden, second-rate franchise.

Before the winter snows had given way to the spring of 1901, third baseman Lave Cross, still yearning for a championship, had signed with the American League Philadelphia Athletics. Outfielder Fielder Jones signed up with the Chicago White Sox. Aging malcontent Hughie Jennings was sold to the Phillies for $3,000. Even more significantly, both Joe McGinnity and Harry Howell returned to Baltimore. That extracted 34 victories from the pitching staff and more than 200 runs from the offense. Meanwhile, the Pirates began the 1901 season a year older and demonstrably better.

The Dodgers struggled all year to fill the gaps in their lineup, and it didn't help when Brickyard Kennedy came down with a sore arm. Without the best players, and in a changing game, Hanlon wasn't much of a genius anymore. The Pirates took command in June and, as expected, romped to a pennant, seven and a half games ahead of Philadelphia. Brooklyn finished third, another two games back. Although the National League retained the bulk of baseball talent, fans took to American League baseball in droves, in part because it charged only 25¢ for general admission as opposed to the NL standard of 50¢. The new league outdrew the NL by nearly two to one. Although attendance actually increased slightly in Brooklyn, in cities where the two leagues went head to head, such as Boston, Philadelphia, and Chicago, the National League trailed badly, and that hurt visiting Brooklyn's bottom line.

Ebbets, however, would eventually benefit personally from Brooklyn's deteriorating financial situation. He had made the decision to stay in the game for the long haul. Over the next few years, as Von der Horst and Abell lost interest, Ebbets would pick up the pieces. While his determination would save the franchise for his beloved borough, it would also keep the club chronically underfunded and very much at the bottom of New York's baseball ladder. Like the team he commanded, Ebbets himself would eventually come to be seen as a beloved if ragtag figure.

The 1902 season brought more misery to Hanlon's team. Another round of contracts expired as many of Brooklyn's most talented players wisely made themselves available in a bidding war between the two leagues. Once again, Brooklyn couldn't compete. Joe Kelley and rookie sensation Jimmy Sheckard, who hit .354 in 1901 and led the league in slugging, jumped to Baltimore, while second baseman Tom Daly went to Chicago.

But perhaps it didn't matter anyway. The Pirates moved into first place on May 4 and never looked back. Brooklyn wasn't bad against other clubs, but against the Pirates they were horrible, winning only six of fourteen games. They finished second, but it was the worst second-place finish in the history of the game. Put it this way — they finished closer to last place than first, 26½ games ahead of the last-place Giants but 27½ games behind Pittsburgh. Remarkably, attendance held in Brooklyn, but it tumbled elsewhere, and 1902 was yet another season of losses for the National League.

Ban Johnson went in for the kill. After Dreyfuss turned down another entreaty to switch leagues, Johnson went after the Pirates, sneaking into Pittsburgh, checking into a hotel under an assumed name, and meeting with players. When he left Pittsburgh, he had almost every player of value, save for Honus Wagner, on an American League contract.

The brazen act decimated the National League, and over the next few weeks more and more players jumped to the AL. Now the National League, not Johnson, wanted to talk peace. In mid-December, they started talking.

Johnson was still agreeable, for although his league was winning at the gate and with recent defections was the near-equal of the NL on the field, it was still costly to compete with the NL. He wasn't necessarily against either monopolies or syndicate baseball — the AL was, in effect, one big syndicate controlled by Johnson, and as far as he was concerned, a monopoly that included the American League was just swell.

On January 9, 1903, the National League met in Cincinnati, Johnson's old hometown. This time he was invited to attend — in fact, he was the honored guest. Over the next ten days Johnson and the NL owners hashed out a host of issues, ranging from territorial claims to the rights of players recently signed by the NL, as well as more mundane matters like scheduling and rules.

In the end Johnson got most of what he wanted, but not without screaming and whining from certain NL quarters. Brooklyn was one of the more vocal opponents of the truce.

Together with the Giants, the Dodgers strongly opposed the peace agreement between the two circuits. Both objected to article five of the agreement, which gave the American League the right to put a team in Manhattan, effectively cutting the New York market into thirds. Ebbets was doubly upset because none of the key players he had lost to the American League were returned to Brooklyn. That was the price he paid for a lack of foresight. What had been one of the game's great teams only a few years earlier was now almost entirely emasculated.

The two New York clubs were outvoted and outflanked. Peace between the leagues was declared on January 19, 1903, ushering in baseball's modern age. As soon as the agreement was signed, Johnson began to make good on his promise to bring a team to New York. No subsequent act would have more of an impact on the future of major league baseball in Brooklyn, for in the end, of the three original New York teams, only one would survive.

It is impossible to overstate how Ebbets, who was the man on the ground, and Von der Horst, who still controlled the purse, failed to protect their interests at what would prove to be the critical moment for the future of the franchise. Their failures from 1901 to 1903 would position Brooklyn as New York's least powerful and most marginalized team. By allowing the American League to field a New York franchise, Brooklyn gave up their claim to all but their own borough, beginning the dynamic that would eventually cause Walter O'Malley to move the team to Los Angeles five decades later. But at the same time, they were little worse than their fellow magnates in the National League, none of whom, save perhaps Barney Dreyfuss, seemed to grasp their precarious position, for teams in Chicago, Philadelphia, and Boston ended up sharing their city with other teams as well.

It is unclear whether Brooklyn believed that a third team in New York, since it had to be placed in Manhattan, would somehow help them by weakening the Giants — after all, the Giants, under owner Andrew Freedman, had worked against Brooklyn by blocking a subway line. Circumstance, however, suggests that Brooklyn probably didn't factor this effect into the equation, for they had sided with the Giants in opposing the peace, and as the American League grappled with Tammany Hall to find a place to play, Brooklyn remained out of the fray.

Nevertheless, for Brooklyn the only drama over the next few seasons would not often take place on the field at Wash-

"Bad Bill" Dahlen played to near–Hall of Fame caliber during a career in which his superb fielding skills at short were more than matched by his ability to hit to all fields with power. In 1903 the Dodgers made one of their worst trades of all time by sending Dahlen to the rival Giants for infielder Charlie Babb and pitcher John Cronin.

ington Park. The real drama was behind the scenes as Ebbets tried to wrest full control of the ballclub. And during the 1903 season Brooklyn's position as an afterthought in New York's baseball universe was underscored.

The big reason was John McGraw. In 1902 McGraw, who had played for Hanlon at Baltimore, almost engineered a coup that could have brought down the American League and preserved NL dominance. Working behind the scenes, he helped facilitate a purchase of the AL Baltimore franchise by NL interests. Those interests then transferred the best Baltimore talent—including Joe McGinnity and McGraw himself—to the National League, leaving Baltimore seriously outclassed by the rest of the league. Ban Johnson, however, leapt in and took control of the team, restocking it with players, preserving the integrity of his league as a major league circuit, and making the decision to move Baltimore to New York in 1903. Meanwhile, the addition of McGraw, who

became manager, and McGinnity to the Giants would help turn them from an also-ran into a powerhouse.

McGraw, his playing career nearly over owing to a bad knee, put his considerable energy and fire into his role as manager. He took the lessons he learned from Hanlon, went after players who could put those ideas into effect on the field, and adapted them to the new game. Of course, it helped that in McGinnity and youthful Christy Mathewson he had the two best pitchers in the league. In 1903 they combined for 800 innings pitched, starting 100 of New York's 139 games and winning 61, one of the best one-two pitching combinations ever. McGraw's Giants emerged as the biggest challengers to Pittsburgh's dominance.

Although a midseason slump that saw them lose 11 of 13 cost them a chance at a pennant, the Giants nevertheless finished only 6½ games out, in second place, while drawing almost 600,000 fans, by far the best in baseball. Fans were drawn to the combative McGraw as they would be in a later generation to the fiery Billy Martin, and as they had once been drawn to Hanlon.

And what of Hanlon's Superbas? That ballclub was becoming just about as relevant as the aging acrobats. No one asked Ned anymore, although home attendance held firm as Brooklyn fans still turned to baseball out of habit. But the Superbas operated in McGraw's shadow for most of the season. They were an afterthought everywhere but in their own borough. The Giants and the new American League team, officially unnamed but already occasionally being referred to as the Yankees owing to the location of their ballpark just north of the Giants' Polo Grounds, sucked up all the press coverage in Manhattan and most of the fans from the hinterlands. For much of that time Brooklyn's history would be told not so much through their own accomplishments but by way of comparison with New York's other teams. Locally, that pennant race often mattered more than either the AL or NL as the three New York teams competed with each other first and then with teams from elsewhere. In almost every way, and in almost every season, Brooklyn would finish third and last in that three-team private league.

They weren't a bad team in 1903, starting out playing .500 baseball and sticking to it, but they were emblematic of the kind of team they would be for too many seasons over the ensuing decades. Only a few players—shortstop Bill Dahlen and slugging Jimmy Sheckard, who had returned—were the kind of stars fans turned out to see. The Giants had McGinnity, Mathewson, and McGraw himself, while the Yankees had Willie Keeler. Brooklyn's pitching staff, while nominally effective, was only a collection of names — Henry Schmidt, Oscar Jones, and Ned Garvin. Only Garvin was possessed of what sportswriters referred to as "color" or personality, and his came from a bottle of rye. That would drive him first from Brooklyn and then from the national pastime in only a few more seasons.

The Superbas were made even more irrelevant when the Pirates faced the Boston Americans in a best-of-nine "world's series," the first between the two leagues. While in some ways this matchup shared much with such tainted championships as the Temple Cup and the 1900 Brooklyn-Pittsburgh debacle, for it too was marred by periods of suspicious play, fans didn't seem to care. Gallons of ink had been spilled detailing the war between the two leagues, creating a rivalry that had never existed between the old American Association and the National League, and there was genuine interest in the question of who was better.

Brooklyn was ill equipped to adjust to the changes happening all around it. Hanlon was increasingly out of touch with the game, and the franchise was losing money. The club made a few deals, but there was no direction to any of them as Ebbets bought out Von der Horst, he and Hanlon disagreed on almost everything, and the team remained unable to take on much salary.

No deal made any difference except to weaken the club, and none more so than the trade of Bill Dahlen to the Giants. Since the day he had joined the league in 1891, Dahlen had been one of the best-fielding shortstops in baseball, a tough, valuable player who could steal a base when required, hit with surprising power, and do all the little things that helped a team, the kind of things that were becoming even more important in the Dead Ball Era. He had joined Brooklyn in 1899 and over the next few seasons had been as responsible as any other player on the team for their success, a Hall of Fame–caliber player. He was 33 years old, ancient for the era, but as yet had shown few signs of slowing down.

But no one in baseball was better at sensing weakness than John McGraw, and it was common knowledge that the Brooklyn front office was a mess. Von der Horst was sick and looking to sell, and Ebbets and Hanlon were both grappling to be in position to buy him out. Ebbets was committed to staying in Brooklyn, but Hanlon wanted to move the team back to Baltimore, where he felt more comfortable.

Charles Ebbets borrowed heavily to gain control of the Dodgers at a time when his New York rivals, the Giants and Highlanders, had reached the top of their respective leagues. It took Ebbets nearly a decade to imitate their success.

In December 1903 John McGraw contacted Hanlon with a proposal, offering infielder Charlie Babb and pitcher John Cronin for Dahlen. Both were over 30 and had done absolutely nothing to distinguish themselves. On a wins-and-losses basis, there was absolutely no reason to make the deal. But wins and losses weren't driving the Superbas anymore.

It was a terrible deal, for it not only weakened Brooklyn but strengthened the Giants. And that may have been the idea all along.

Hanlon, in his eagerness to buy a controlling interest in the team, may well have been eager to undermine Ebbets, and the best way to do that was at the box office. For Ebbets, unlike Hanlon, didn't have a great deal of money that wasn't already wrapped up in the ballclub. A few down seasons would leave him in no position to add to his share of the team's stock, giving Hanlon the opportunity to take over.

The abrasive Dahlen was thrilled when he heard about the deal—he knew a sinking ship and had made his dissatisfaction known. He left the Superbas with this observation to chew on: "It has always been my ambition to play in New York City. Brooklyn is all right, but if you're not with the Giants you might as well be in Albany."

Bill Dahlen was the perfect addition to the Giants, while his loss was devastating to the not-so Superbas. Dahlen led the league in RBIs in 1904 for the Giants, while Charlie Babb faded to gray and Jack Cronin lost 23 games. The Giants won 22 more games than they had in 1903, finishing in first place with a record of 106–47. McGraw credited Dahlen. Albany—er, Brooklyn—lost 31 more to finish seventh, 56–97, 50 full games in arrears.

Over in the American League the Yankees fought Boston down to the final day before losing the pennant. Some 1.2 million fans turned out to watch baseball in New York in 1904, but barely 200,000 of those were in Brooklyn. In four short years Brooklyn had been rendered irrelevant.

The Superbas reached their nadir in 1905, finishing last, 48–104, a bad club in every way. Even worse, the Giants treated them with haughty disdain. In one celebrated incident in midseason, the Giants came to Brooklyn, and while they were beating the bejesus out of the Superbas, a row broke out on the field. While McGraw was arguing his case with an umpire, Ebbets, sitting in a nearby box, tried to inject himself into the conversation. McGraw told him where to get off, at which point Ebbets took umbrage, asking McGraw if he had just called him what he thought he had.

McGraw, never one to back down, reportedly told Ebbets, "No. I called you a ———," an even nastier epithet. A flushed and flustered Ebbets babbled that he'd bring the matter up before the league, a threat McGraw found quite amusing, and he laughed in his face. The manager knew he was more valuable to the league than Ebbets and knew they'd do absolutely nothing. Ebbets was completely humiliated.

After the season came to a welcome end, it became obvious that Hanlon and Ebbets could no longer coexist. Ebbets finally fired the once-great manager, only to have Hanlon, who owned a small portion of stock in the team, try to fight his

A game at Washington Park between Brooklyn and Chicago in 1912. At the time the Dodgers still attracted over 300,000 fans to watch a second-division team. Construction on Ebbets Field was well under way; the new park would open the following April.

ouster in court, a ploy that failed. Hanlon moved on to Cincinnati, where over the next two seasons he demonstrated that he was managing a game with which he was no longer familiar. Then he returned to his beloved Baltimore and went into the real estate business. Over time the Superba moniker — no longer appropriate — would also pass. Over the next several seasons the club would more often be known somewhat awkwardly as only "Brooklyn."

Ebbets was the last man standing. In his zeal to take full financial control of the franchise, he borrowed heavily, taking in a more or less silent partner, a furniture dealer named Henry Medicus, to provide some capital. It may have been a good deal for Ebbets, but it was a lousy deal for Brooklyn. Even though Ebbets generally turned a profit, for Washington Park was cheap to run and he kept salaries down, that didn't mean the ballclub was rolling in the clover. The franchise remained in a state of benign poverty, its status at the bottom of New York's baseball universe all but set in stone even as the Yankees floundered on the northern shore of Manhattan for the next decade.

Incredibly, hardly anyone noticed, for the ballclub's status perfectly matched the borough's own deteriorating self-image in regard to Manhattan. Over the ensuing decades, it would not be Brooklyn's fault that the Dodgers became what they became. The blame should have been placed on Ebbets and Ebbets alone, yet Brooklyn fans and a boosterish press gave him a total pass because, well, he was from Brooklyn, and increasingly Brooklyn blamed its problems on anything and everything else. So did Ebbets. In recent years he'd become obsessed with the local ban on Sunday baseball, blaming it for the club's failure to draw larger crowds. He'd shown some creativity trying to get around it, even going so far in 1904 as to play an admission-free game. He did, however, make scorecards not only a mandatory purchase but color-coded them according to seating section and made them identical in price to the cost of a ticket. Alas, local officials were not amused, and the next time he tried the ploy his pitcher and catcher were placed under arrest.

Over the ensuing years of Ebbets's reign, almost every time he was faced with any decision that, in retrospect, could be viewed as wrong for the franchise, he made that choice. Already, almost inexorably, the skids were being greased to send the ballclub elsewhere. Ebbets, although neither he nor anyone else realized it, was laying the track for Brooklyn's departure.

He made two such poor decisions in the off-season between 1905 and 1906. The first of these wrong moves was hiring former Boston outfielder Patsy Donovan as manager. Donovan had been a star when Hanlon was a genius, then became a thoroughly undistinguished manager in Pittsburgh, St. Louis, and Washington, finishing as high as fourth place only once. Like Hanlon, the new game seemed to befuddle Donovan. That made him perfect for Brooklyn, for whom the game of baseball was, increasingly, a mystery.

Ebbets's next decision was perhaps even more egregious, for it did for the Cubs what the trade of Dahlen had done for the Giants the previous year. Outfielder Jimmy Sheckard was about the only player of value left on the squad, and at age 27, he was still young enough to be attractive to other teams. The Cubs offered Ebbets four players for Sheckard — starting third baseman Doc Casey, starting outfielder Billy Maloney, backup outfielder Jack McCarthy, and pitcher Buttons Briggs.

Brooklyn did improve in 1906 with the four new players, although Briggs never pitched an inning and Maloney and Casey were disappointments. They finished fifth. Unfortunately, with Sheckard, the Cubs finished first, an extraordinary 116–38, 50 games ahead of Brooklyn.

And there, more or less, Brooklyn would stay for the next six seasons, never finishing higher than fifth, never finishing closer to first place than a dreadful 33½ games, and never, ever being in the race for a pennant after the first week of the season.

Beyond the hyperbole of the local sports pages, Ebbets didn't really seem to care, for he did little to change things. Amazingly enough, the crowds at Washington Park held firm at around 300,000 per season, no matter how the team performed. Brooklyn fans seemed satisfied with a club whose roster included only two or three players worth watching.

The first such player of the era was pitcher George Rucker, who in 1904 joined the Augusta, Georgia, team in the Sally League, where his teammates included pitcher Ed Cicotte, later made infamous in the Black Sox scandal, and Ty Cobb. Sportswriter Grantland Rice, not yet a legend, saw Rucker pitch and dubbed the left-hander "Napoleon," after the emperor, a nickname that was quickly shortened to just plain "Nap." Rucker, who had a marvelous curveball that took him several seasons to learn to control, was drafted by Brooklyn in 1907 and immediately became the best pitcher on a bad team. On September 5, 1908, he even threw a no-hitter, beating Boston 8–0, striking out 14. The *Eagle* termed the accomplishment "harder than the score would indicate," for in the ninth inning Boston sent three right-handed hitters to bat in place of the three lefties scheduled. But Rucker "bowled them down all the same." Unfortunately, such spectacular performances were not enough to overcome the club's generally mediocre performance. Although Rucker was widely considered one of the best pitchers in baseball, he was rarely more than a .500 hurler for Brooklyn.

More proof of the club's aptitude for average performance can be seen in the addition of two other players of merit, neither of whom made much of a difference in his first few seasons. In the waning days of the 1909 season, the club added outfielder Zack Wheat, who over time would prove to be the best Brooklyn player before World War II, a title that, if not for Wheat, would have been held by first baseman Jake Daubert, who made his debut in 1910. Yet it would be several more seasons before their combined talents lifted the club from its malaise.

Ebbets's energies were focused elsewhere. He was looking to move.

By 1908 it was apparent that Washington Park was becoming obsolete. Ebbets had maxed out the park, adding seats to within 15 feet of home plate. And Brooklyn was changing as the area around the park became more industrial. The *Eagle* complained about the "congested, smoke laden atmosphere" and the stench that wafted over the park from the nearby Gowanus Canal. It was hardly an idyllic location to watch a baseball game.

Then too, the era of the wooden ballpark was just about over. Because of the risk of fire, insurance costs for wooden parks such as Washington Park were rising rapidly, cutting into profits. It was time to build a new ballpark, but that would prove no easier than building a winning team.

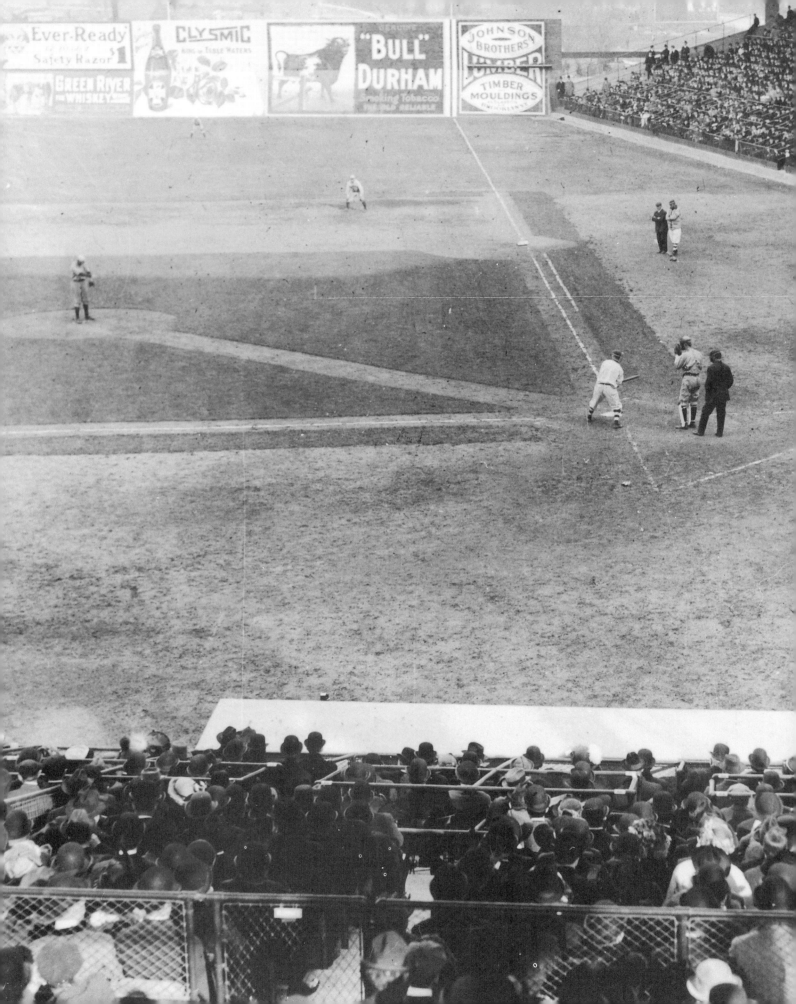

THE ROBINS OF
EBBETS FIELD

EBBETS FIELD.

Those two words are perhaps the most important and evocative in Brooklyn Dodger history.

Ebbets Field was the parlor room where Dodger fans and their heroes first met, the front stoop where they told stories, and the barroom where they celebrated and sometimes commiserated on long, warm summer nights. In cozy old Ebbets Field the line between the field and the stands was blurred, the differences between the players and the fans less pronounced than elsewhere. They could hear each other talking, and they could talk with each other.

Without Ebbets Field, it is entirely possible that the Dodgers would have become just another ballclub. Yet without Ebbets Field, it is also entirely possible that a team named the Dodgers might still call Brooklyn home. Ebbets Field was simultaneously the best ballpark in the world and the worst ballpark for the long-term future of major league baseball in Brooklyn.

When Charles Ebbets first fantasized over a new ballpark for Brooklyn, he did not dream of a park filled with people for

The first game at Ebbets Field was an exhibition game between the Yankees and Dodgers. Right-hander Ray Caldwell pitched for the Yankees in a losing effort as the Dodgers, helped by Casey Stengel's inside-the-park home run — the first home run ever at Ebbets Field — won 3–2.

decades to come, but of a palace decked out in bunting for its first Opening Day, a place that would reflect his own improbable rise to club president and owner. Although by necessity it would be built of concrete and steel, he had no intention of building a utilitarian structure. Ebbets's ballpark would provide proof that after a long campaign he had finally conquered the franchise and made it his own.

Yet from the very beginning Ebbets's grandiose vision would be colored by his precarious financial situation, which caused him to scale back his plans even before the first shovel of earth was moved. The unintentional result would be a ballpark that in many ways reflected the era much more than any other park built at the time, including Boston's vaunted Fenway Park. Unlike so many other new concrete-and-steel structures, Ebbets Field would be almost impossible to renovate or otherwise adapt to the evolving needs of the ballclub. Ebbets simply couldn't afford to look forward or to plan for the future, and even though he once pronounced that "baseball is in its infancy," his ballpark would be a crib that was quickly outgrown. Within only a few years its limitations would be made obvious, and in the long run Ebbets Field would prove to be an impediment to the team's continuing financial health. The destiny of Ebbets Field would be the team's abandonment of Brooklyn and all the resulting nostalgia.

From the start, Ebbets's plans for the new park were driven by his wallet. Land costs and public transportation concerns determined the new park's location. He was offered the Washington Park site for $350,000, but that was too pricey. At each step construction costs and political considerations determined the park's design and construction timetable. At no time did Ebbets pause, ask, What does the franchise require? and then take steps to build a park that responded to that question. Instead, he built a park that forced all other elements of the franchise — from the players to the fans to the front office — to adapt.

Ebbets's search for affordable land that was accessible to public transportation led him to an underdeveloped area of Flatbush east of Prospect Park known variously as "Pigtown," "Goatville," "Tin-Can Alley," and "Crow Hill." Although the *Eagle* would later describe the area as blessed with "the pure air of the suburbs," it was in fact a squalid, mostly Italian neighborhood of a few ramshackle homes and weed-infested lots where one could in fact find pigs, goats, crows, and tin cans in abundance. But better neighborhoods were pressing in on either side, and within a couple of blocks there was

access, by transfer, to a multitude of rail and subway lines. Ebbets was particularly impressed by the fact that the site was only 20 minutes by subway from lower Manhattan and Wall Street. Naively, he believed that one day his ballclub would draw substantial numbers of fans from Manhattan, a wish that would never be fulfilled. He was so enamored with the notion that he ignored protests from Brooklynites, who complained that the site was in the middle of nowhere. It would be Ebbets's good fortune that Brooklyn would grow around the site and leave it, in fact, in the middle, more or less centrally located within the borough. One of the ballpark's great strengths was purely accidental.

Ebbets knew he had to watch costs. Wanting to retain complete control over a franchise to which he had devoted his life, he planned to build the park himself. He quickly realized that if landowners or speculators got wind of his plans, they'd jack up the prices. So in 1908 he formed a dummy corporation named Pylon Construction and hired a straw man named Edward Brown to surreptitiously buy somewhere between 20 and 40 separate but contiguous parcels needed for the new park. Pylon made its first purchase in September, and over the next few years the plan worked like a charm as piece after piece was quietly purchased from oblivious residents eager for a little cash. Then the plan ground to a halt. One owner of a tiny but essential portion of the property reportedly couldn't be located. And without that sliver of land, Ebbets's other acquisitions were rendered worthless.

In a story that sounds apocryphal, agents were reportedly dispatched far and wide to ferret out the property owner. The search cost thousands and brought them to Europe and California before the title-holder was finally located in New Jersey. The landowner then sensed that the parcel was somewhat more important to Pylon than it was letting on. He demanded what was variously reported as a sum between $500 and $2,000 for the parcel, which was valued at only $100. Ebbets gladly paid — he'd have paid ten times as much if he had to.

By December 1911, after three years and at the cost of approximately $200,000, Ebbets had finally acquired four and a half contiguous acres in a shape known as a trapezium — a four-sided figure in which no two sides were parallel. He knew this awkward shape would be large enough for his park, for as the *Eagle* later reported, the "total area [is] about the same as the second Washington Park," consisting of 475 feet of frontage on Bedford Avenue, 478 feet on Sullivan Street, 637 feet on Cedar Street, and 450 feet on Montgomery Street.

Once Ebbets acquired those four and a half acres, he stopped buying land and made plans to start construction on architect Charles Randall Van Burick's plans for the ballpark, which he estimated would cost another $400,000 or so. Were he to spend more on land, he'd either have to pare back some features of the original design or make the structure more utilitarian.

But there was another reason to rush into construction. In 1911 the Giants had been displaced from the Polo Grounds by a fire. While they rebuilt, they played at the Yankees' ramshackle wooden park, the Hilltop Grounds, before moving back into a renovated concrete-and-steel Polo Grounds in 1912. Now the Yankees' ballpark seemed even more tawdry, not to mention dangerous and even more expensive to insure.

They too needed a new park. Co-owners Frank Farrell and William Devery, two notorious gamblers and corrupt members of Tammany Hall, had already squandered hundreds of thousands of dollars on harebrained schemes to build a ballpark on filled land or floating in the East River, plans that had cost them much of their ill-gotten fortunes. Everyone knew they were almost out of time and just about out of money.

Ebbets thought he had a solution. As the *Eagle* reported, Ebbets believed that it would be impossible for the Yankees to find a place to play in Manhattan. "There will be no space to devote to baseball playgrounds," opined the newspaper, which then paraphrased Ebbets by stating that the team would have little choice but to "cross the river and share with

Brooklyn the handsomest home of a ballclub in the country." Ebbets believed he could rent it for top dollar. That erroneous belief would prove to be another serious miscalculation.

On January 2, 1912, Ebbets unveiled his plans to the public. When asked what he would call his park, he first responded, "Washington Park." Then the press cajoled him into naming it after himself, although in truth Ebbets needed little convincing.

Ebbets Field, at least on the surface, would be a palace. Although built of concrete and steel, it would appear far more substantial, for most surfaces were faced with either brick or cement plaster, disguising the basic framework. The grandstand would be supported by a series of Roman columns and arches extending from the building's dominant feature, a central rotunda, 80 feet across and 27 feet high. The grand space would be faced with marble and glazed brick and contain 12 grand gilt ticket booths and entryways. The space was to be lit by a grand brass chandelier with 12 arms made to look like bats and the bulbs designed in imitation of baseballs. The floor would be decorated with a mosaic of a huge baseball, replete with stitches.

For most Dodger fans, Ebbets Field was home. Its memory is embraced by expatriates who still long for Ebinger's Blackout cakes and Sunday doubleheaders. This photograph depicts Ebbets Field as it looked in its inaugural season of 1913.

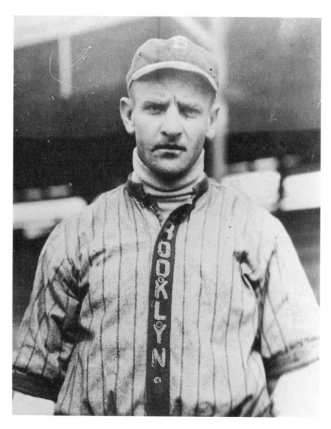

Outfielder Casey Stengel arrived in Brooklyn in 1912 and played his first full major league season at newly opened Ebbets Field. In six seasons with the Dodgers, Stengel batted for the same .272 average he reached in his rookie season. In the 1916 World Series, Stengel led all Dodger regulars with a .364 batting average.

The press and public oohed and aahed at the plans. No one, including Ebbets, yet realized that the combination of the grandiose design on an inadequate plot of land with an insufficient infrastructure for concessions and fan amenities — like bathrooms — had sealed the fate of the franchise and set into motion a dynamic that would help push the team from Brooklyn within five decades.

The pinched four-and-a-half-acre plot was too small, requiring the park to occupy every available inch of space — sidewalks bordering the park would be only nominally wider than those on surrounding streets. The second deck of the grandstand sat directly atop the first deck and, owing to its concrete-and-steel construction, was virtually impossible to renovate or expand. In comparison to other concrete-and-steel parks built at the time, even the original dimensions of the field were undersized. Other parks, whose outfield fences were sometimes as far as 500 feet from home plate, could eventually add thousands of outfield seats and still leave plenty of room to play. But the field dimensions of Ebbets Field left no extra room in right field and very little in left and center. In only a few years even Ebbets would recognize that the park was too small, and within 20 years it would effectively be "built out."

And that was just inside the park. Outside the walls the situation was no better, for the club was confined by the surrounding streets. Despite providing a small parking lot opposite the main entrance at the time the park was built, over the years the club would fail to anticipate fans' increasing dependence on the automobile — it would never provide more than 700 spaces. By the time it became apparent there was a need for substantially more parking, most nearby lots were all in private hands, costing the team an important revenue stream, while parked cars on surrounding streets sometimes angered local merchants. While similar situations plagued most other clubs that built parks during the era, the density of Brooklyn coupled with the need to drive through the heart of the borough on surface streets made the problem more pronounced. In short, from the moment ground was first broken, Ebbets Field was an anachronism, one that in each ensuing season would prove to be less and less adequate.

That is not to say it was not a wonderful place to watch a baseball game — it was that and more, a glorious Globe Theater of a place where the mob felt like part of the game, for its cozy dimensions and double-decked grandstand put fans almost on the field. The quirks of its construction and shape made for exciting baseball in which both speed and power had a place. But tastes would change over the years, and by the time the Dodgers left Brooklyn some of their constituents found the park more claustrophobic than cozy.

All these elements would eventually combine to make Ebbets Field obsolete before its time. Most parks of the era lasted into the 1970s, while Fenway Park, Wrigley Field, and Tiger Stadium all made it into the new millennium, and Fenway and Wrigley seem likely to celebrate their centennials. In contrast, Ebbets Field died before age 50.

The irony was that at the time the park was built it easily could have been made larger. There was plenty of land available elsewhere in Brooklyn as well as adjacent to Ebbets Field, for early pictures of the park show the park surrounded by mostly empty lots, and Ebbets had the political connections necessary to reroute a street or two. Had he had either the money or the will, the park could have been larger and less cramped. But Ebbets simply didn't have the means to acquire more land, much less finance the building of the actual park.

Groundbreaking took place on March 4 with the usual complement of local politicians on hand for the photo op, including borough president Alfred Steers, Ebbets, team treasurer Henry Medicus, and Ebbets's son, Charlie Jr., the club secretary. The attitude of the assembled multitudes reflected the sentiment expressed by the *Eagle,* which lauded the day in a story that began: "Rejoice and be glad, all ye fans. Doff your lids and bow obeisance to Charles H. Ebbets, boss of the Brooklyn Baseball Club and eminent magnate of the national game." But when Ebbets drove the silver spade into the ground to turn over the first spadeful of earth, one witty bystander quipped, "Dig up a couple of new players, Charlie." There were laughs all around, but everyone knew the sentiment was no laughing matter.

Over the past few seasons the Dodgers had ceased to be a competitive team as Ebbets had run players and managers in and out to no effect. Player-manager Harry Lumley had replaced Patsy Donovan at the helm in 1909. He was replaced, in turn, by Bill Dahlen, who accepted an offer to return to his own personal Albany in 1910. But none of these moves made any difference in the standings — Dahlen's tenure was marked by mediocrity on the field and his still out-of-control temper, which culminated in an on-field fistfight in 1912 with umpire Cy Rigler.

And in 1912 the construction of Ebbets Field gave the Dodgers — the old name had slowly worked its way back into use, although the *Eagle* still used "Superbas" — a pass for at least one more season. The Giants ran away with the pennant while the Dodgers struggled mightily to stay atop an even more pathetic Boston in last place.

All the while construction continued on the ballpark. Originally, Ebbets hoped that it would be finished before the end of the season, but as building commenced he learned the same lesson American League owner and founder Ban Johnson had learned when he moved the Yankees into New York in 1903.

In New York the construction of a new ballpark always caused baseball to intersect awkwardly with politics. In 1903 Johnson had learned that unless he put some cash in the right pockets and eventually sold the team to some Sons of Tammany Hall, building a ballpark in New York was about as

Left-hander George "Nap" Rucker spent his entire ten-year career with the Dodgers and just barely hung on to enjoy the 1916 National League championship. His 2.42 ERA and 134 career victories indicate both his skill and the dismal position of the team during most of his tenure. His best season was 1911, when he went 22–18 for a seventh-place club.

(Left to right) Dodger president Charles Ebbets, manager Wilbert Robinson, with Dodger co-owners Ed and Steve McKeever. For a large share of the team, the McKeevers completed the contracting job on Ebbets Field in 1913.

realistic as filling New York Harbor. Similarly, Ebbets overestimated his political influence and as a result, during the early days of construction, he ran into a series of delays and cost overruns. By July he was running out of money. Most work on the park had been confined to moving piles of dirt around.

Ebbets appealed to his fellow club owners for some financial help, but they weren't disposed to bail out a fellow owner—they had their own problems. He had to look elsewhere.

Just as Frank Farrell and William Devery had swept in and offered Ban Johnson a way out in 1903, the McKeever brothers, Stephen and Edward, two wealthy construction magnates who already had a piece of the Ebbets Field contract, now offered Ebbets an escape from his troubles.

The method of their success should have provided a warning to Ebbets, but he never saw it coming until too late. Early in the brothers' careers they had been thwarted in their attempts to land lucrative contracts on such massive civic projects as the Brooklyn Bridge. Instead, they settled for grim tasks like hauling away dead animals that died and were left in the street.

What particularly galled the brothers was that they were often the lowest bidders on such projects. They even appealed to the courts for help, only to learn that no matter what the law said, in practice civic contracts were awarded only to those with the right connections. And that meant membership in Tammany Hall, New York's political machine, for membership in Tammany carried with it the implicit approval to indulge in what Boss Tweed had once referred to as "honest graft." That Tammany tradition allowed Tammany-connected businessmen and contractors to receive lucrative government contracts as one hand washed the other.

Now the McKeevers went to work. Steve McKeever joined Tammany Hall and rapidly rose in the organization. He eventually served four years on the board of aldermen and was even asked to run for state office several times. In the interim, a string of lucrative contracts came his way, and lo and behold Edward McKeever's construction firm suddenly began landing contracts as well, including one to provide all the stone for the New York Central Railroad tracks from New York City to Buffalo. That was a lot of rock, and contracts like that weren't easy to get.

Each brother eventually cashed out and sold his company, earning millions. They then kept busy going into business with each other in Brooklyn, investing in real estate and building houses in Greenpoint in a neighborhood that became known as "McKeeversville." The two served on various corporate and charitable boards and invested in racehorses. They were among the most well connected—and hence well respected—businessmen in Brooklyn. Stephen McKeever was even referred to as "Judge."

When Ebbets's troubles became pronounced, the Mc-Keevers moved in and made an offer Ebbets couldn't refuse. Ebbets needed money, which they had in buckets, and connections, which they also had in abundance. In return, the McKeevers looked at the books, saw the team had earned a $50,000 profit in 1911, and welcomed Ebbets as a partner. For half the team, they'd finish building his ballpark.

But the deal was a bit more complicated than it first appeared, for the end result was two corporations: the team, controlled by Ebbets, and the ballpark and property, controlled by the McKeevers. It was an awkward arrangement that would eventually cause trouble. But for now, although it wasn't what Ebbets wanted, he had little other choice and was able to retain his club presidency. Besides, if he didn't take the deal, he would have to sell. He accepted the brothers' offer and mirabile dictu, construction suddenly proceeded much more smoothly than before, but at a total cost of three-quarters of a million dollars. While neither the cheapest nor the most expensive ballpark of the concrete-and-steel era, in which parks were built for between $200,000 and $1.5 million, on a square footage basis Ebbets Field was near the top of the scale.

In the off-season Ebbets's grand plan to bring the Yankees to Brooklyn as a tenant fell through. The Giants scooped him. It wouldn't be the last time.

The Yankees and Giants had been bitter enemies when the Yankees first invaded Manhattan, but the two clubs had recently forged a mutually beneficial relationship. The Giants seemed to realize that the Dodgers and their new ballpark, not the Yankees, were their foremost rivals — finishing behind a league rival was unacceptable. The thaw between the Yanks and Giants began when the two played a mutually lucrative end-of-the-season exhibition series in 1910. Then the Yankees allowed the Giants to play in Hilltop Park while the Polo Grounds was rebuilt after the fire. Now the Yankees' lease at Hilltop Park was due to expire, and the Giants magnanimously offered them use of the Polo Grounds for $30,000 a year. The Yankees accepted.

Brooklyn was left in the lurch. Ebbets didn't even have the opportunity to make a serious pitch to the Yankees. It was the first time, but not the last, that the two clubs would, if not conspire, at least cooperate to keep the Dodgers in their place.

There was great excitement as the Dodgers barnstormed their way back north in the spring of 1913 for the much-anticipated opening of Ebbets Field. Yet they were shocked to pick up the *Eagle* on the morning of April 1 and learn that manager Bill Dahlen and Jake Daubert had come to blows in a hotel in Richmond, Virginia, and it took "a half dozen husky porters to separate them."

"The upshot of the melee," reported a correspondent, "is that Daubert quit the team and went home while Dahlen wired his resignation to Boss Ebbets." Those who read no

Crowds gather on the street outside Ebbets Field prior to the first game at the Flatbush landmark. Over 25,000 jammed into the park for the exhibition game with the Yankees.

further may well have thrown the paper to the ground in disgust at another temper tantrum by Dahlen. Those who did not were alerted to the fact that it was April Fools' Day. It had in fact been a quiet spring, the main drama being the battle for center field between veteran Herb Moran and brash young rookie Charley Stengel. Stengel, who had debuted the previous September by making four hits in his first game, and seven in his first eleven at bats, had pushed Moran to the side with his play and captured the attention of the press with his personality. Good thing, because for the Dodgers the faux story detailing the fight between Daubert and Dahlen would serve as the highlight of the season.

Ebbets and company exploited the new ballpark to the fullest extent possible during the 1913 season. The park was unofficially inaugurated on April 5, when the Yankees and Dodgers played an exhibition.

"All roads in Greater New York led to Brooklyn's new ballpark this fine day and joy reigned supreme in the heart of every blessed fan," wrote the *Eagle,* at least until the fans arrived at the park, where someone failed to provide a key to open up the 25¢ and 50¢ sections of the park. The crowd spilled over into the street and blocked traffic. Fortunately, the key was located in time for most of the throng to make their way inside and witness the first sign of trouble between Messrs. Ebbets and McKeever. Mrs. Edward McKeever was given the honor of raising the flag, while the privilege of throwing out the first pitch went to Ebbets's winsome daughter Genevieve. Such awkward balancing of rights and privileges between the two families would take an inordinate amount of time and effort over the ensuing seasons.

More than 25,000 fans pushed their way into the park, wondering at the splendor of the rotunda and basking in the extra-wide seats, made so because they shared an armrest with the adjacent chair, rather than each having two of its own, an innovation since repeated in virtually every ballpark and stadium in the world. But more than 10,000 were turned away, several thousand of whom figured out they could still watch the game from the hilltop on Bedford Avenue or from a spot on Montgomery Street referred to as "McKeever's Bluff," where one enterprising neighborhood resident built 300 bleacher seats and charged 50¢ a head. Ebbets, however, may well have been dismayed to discover "a tremendous out-

Mrs. Ed McKeever hoists the Stars and Stripes over Ebbets Field on April 5, 1913, prior to the ballpark's first game against the New York Yankees.

pouring of rabid Manhattanite cranks" — Yankee fans who had taken the long trip downtown and would spend their money the rest of the season in the Polo Grounds.

The start was delayed briefly when Mrs. McKeever discovered there was no flag to raise on the flagpole, but it was quickly located and unfurled. Nap Rucker was honored with the start, and he retired the Yankees in order in the first. When George Cutshaw singled with one out in the second for the Dodgers' first hit, the park seemed christened.

Stengel scored the first run and hit the first home run in the fifth, although Zack Wheat had wowed the crowd during batting practice by dropping a pitch over the right-field fence. Stengel's drive to left-center fell short of the wall and eluded Yankee center fielder Harry Wolter, who then kicked the ball as he chased it down, turning a double into an inside-the-park home run. Brooklyn then weathered a New York rally in the ninth and won the game 3–2 in the final half when Wheat scored from third as third baseman Red Smith singled up the middle.

Ebbets Field was not much like the park that would be mourned and eulogized 40-some years later. The grandstand down each line stopped abruptly far short of the fences, and an uncovered set of stands stretched out from there to the left-field fence, some 413 feet from home. But while it was 450 feet to the fence in dead center, it was only a cozy 301 feet in right. The outfield in left and center was enclosed by a spare wood fence that was higher inside the park than on the street, for the field was below grade. In right field there was a concrete barrier 19 feet tall, the bottom half of which was cantilevered inward, a structural feature placed inside the park because there was no room outside. In center field was an immense flagpole and equally immense flag. The park could hold only 22,000 fans comfortably, although several thousand more could be squeezed in.

After this "Grand Opening," Brooklyn opened the stadium under more pomp and similar circumstances four days later in the "Special Opening" for the season debut against Philadelphia. Before the season was up they would test young Genevieve Ebbets's arm by also celebrating a "Regular Opener," "Ebbets Day," "Cornerstone Day," "Dedication Day," and, just to keep things even, "McKeever Day."

Each subsequent celebration lost a little luster. A second exhibition with the Yankees drew another good crowd, but the "Grand Opening," the first official game at the park, was anticlimactic. As Thomas Rice wrote in the *Eagle*, "A gazook with a wise and throbbing head has remarked that it is no time for mirth or laughter in the cold, gray dawn of the morning after. . . . One Game does not make a season, and an opening day is 153 games from closing day, the president of the Don't Worry Club reminds us, in a champagne tinted note, but, doggone it, we wanted to win that first game!" That game was lost in the first as Benny Mayer dropped a fly ball that gave Philadelphia the only run they would need and Tom Seaton beat Nap Rucker 1–0.

The most memorable moment in the contest took place not on the field but in the stands. Poor weather left fans less than eager to take their seats. Most tried to cram into the rotunda, a situation that quickly went from the comical to the dangerous before park security got control of the situation and prevented fans from being crushed in the stampede.

Still, perhaps spurred on by the new park, the Dodgers got off to a surprisingly quick start as the Giants unexpectedly stumbled. As late as mid-May the Dodgers were challenging for first place, and with the weather ready to warm, Ebbets and company looked forward to a season both successful and lucrative.

They got half their wish. A ten-game losing streak in early July sent the team plummeting, although fans kept coming out to Ebbets Field, setting a franchise record with home attendance of nearly 350,000, some 70,000 more than in any previous season. Jake Daubert led the league with a .350 batting average, but the Giants won another pennant and the Dodgers finished seventh again. Apart from cosmetics, nothing had changed.

The status quo wasn't enough anymore. In a little over a year the team had changed both the ballpark and the ownership. That left only the players and the manager, and everyone in baseball knows it is far easier to fire a manager than an entire team of players.

Fans had grown impatient, and in the off-season the *Eagle* reported that the McKeever brothers had also made their dissatisfaction known: "[They] have long been known to be favorable to a change." Ebbets tried to argue against the move, and for more than a month Dahlen's fate was left hanging as the ballclub played an extended exhibition series in Cuba under the direction of Jake Daubert. But on November 17 Dahlen was finally let go.

There was rampant speculation that Daubert would stay on as player-manager, or that ex-Dodger Fielder Jones, who was "sorry he had ever quit Brooklyn," would return, or that

Hughie Jennings could be enticed away from Detroit. Jake Stahl, who had led the Red Sox to a pennant in 1912, was also available.

Then another option became available, someone who served a purpose even larger than improving the team.

For the past several seasons, former Dodger catcher Wilbert Robinson had served on the staff of Giants manager John McGraw. McGraw had put Robinson in charge of the club's young pitchers, and he'd also coached third base.

The contrast in styles worked. Robinson was as quick with a smile as McGraw was with an insult. He played the good cop to McGraw's more brash and volatile bad cop. Robinson had nursed along a series of younger pitchers, beginning with Rube Marquard in 1910, followed by Jeff Tesreau in 1912 and Al Demaree in 1913, building them back up after McGraw's sharp tongue shredded their confidence. Over time the press began to recognize the key role Robinson played in the Giants' success. No other coach of the era was considered more valuable.

But McGraw wasn't comfortable with that. The more praise was lavished on Robinson, the less McGraw liked having him around, and the relationship between the two cooled. At a drunken bash after the 1913 World Series, in which the Giants fell to the Athletics in five games, McGraw criticized Robinson for some of his coaching decisions at third, leading Robinson to tell McGraw he hadn't managed very well either. With that, McGraw fired his old teammate.

Although Robinson had pondered returning home to Baltimore and taking care of his business interests there, Ebbets met with him and made a persuasive pitch. In Brooklyn, Robinson would have a chance to move out from under McGraw's shadow and demonstrate that he had in fact had something to do with the Giants' success. Ebbets announced Robinson's appointment as Brooklyn manager on November 17.

It was one of the wisest decisions he ever made. Since the demise of Hanlon's Superbas, Ebbets himself had been the public face of the franchise, a role he had come to share, awkwardly, with the McKeevers. Now that job fell to Robinson.

He was perfectly equipped for the job. The newspaper guys who followed the club all knew him and were fond of the portly man Damon Runyon called "Uncle Wilbert," although his competitors favored "Uncle Robbie." Publicly, Robinson was something of a Tommy Lasorda, a garrulous and enthusiastic man whose occasional crudity was kept hidden by the

Dodger manager Wilbert Robinson poses with Yankee manager Bill Donovan prior to an exhibition game between the Yankees and Dodgers at Ebbets Field in 1916. Robinson served as coach and chief lieutenant to Giants manager John McGraw before being hired by the Dodgers.

press of that era. Robinson knew more than a little baseball and excelled at getting the most out of his players. And as a protégé of both Hanlon and McGraw—two of baseball's most successful managers—Robinson had the credibility that Lumley and Dahlen had lacked.

On his first day on the job, he wowed the press at a drink-filled press conference and reception at which Ed McKeever quipped, in an obvious dig at Ebbets, "By Gad [sic], we've got a *real* manager now." And to hear Robinson talk, the Dodgers had the pennant in their back pocket. Rucker was "the best left-hander in the league. [Pat] Ragan too is a first class righthander, while I never saw Reulbach pitch better ball than he did against the Giants last season. . . . If Frank Allen can master control of the ball he'll be a big help to us. . . . Control is the whole thing in pitching." For the record, Ragan had

Wilbert Robinson made a habit of picking up star players in the twilight of their careers, and such was the case with left-handed pitcher Rube Marquard. In six seasons with the Dodgers, Marquard contributed to two National League championships in 1916 and 1920 while compiling an overall won-lost record of 56–48.

gone 15–18 in 1913, Rucker was 14–15, Ed Reulbach 7–6, and Frank Allen 4–18.

But Uncle Robbie's task would soon be made even more difficult. Another team was coming to Brooklyn.

The six-team Federal League, following the rough model of Ban Johnson's American League, chose the 1914 season to mount a challenge to the two established leagues. The circuit added two teams, moved east, went head to head against AL and NL teams in Chicago, St. Louis, Pittsburgh, and Brooklyn, and began raiding players from established teams by offering outrageous contracts.

The Dodgers, née Superbas and rapidly becoming known as the "Robins" after the dear uncle, suddenly had some competition. Robert Ward, owner of the Brooklyn-based Ward Bakery Company, announced his intention to rebuild Washington Park and place his club, dubbed the "Tip Tops" after his best-selling brand of bread, in Brooklyn.

The announcement could have been a disaster for the Robins. But the addition of Uncle Robbie made the McKeevers feel vested in the fortunes of the club. At a time when many of their brethren in the AL and NL chose to retrench, the Robins went on a rare spending spree.

Robinson wanted a shortstop, so Ebbets and the McKeevers got him one — veteran Joe Tinker, who had played a key role in the Cubs' legendary infield of the Franklin Adams poem "Tinker to Evers to Chance." Tinker was now wasted on Cincinnati, and the Reds were worried he'd jump to the Federal League. Before he could, they sold him to Brooklyn for $25,000.

Ebbets also knew that Tinker would be a target of the Feds, so he arranged for $10,000 of the purchase price to go directly to the player. He thought that figure, coupled with a contract offer of $7,000 in annual salary, would be plenty to entice Tinker to Brooklyn. But the offer barely made an impression on the shortstop. The ex-Cub wanted to return to Chicago and signed on as player-manager of the Federal League Chicago Whales.

At length, Ebbets got his money back from the Reds, but the Fed threat caused the Robins to make a critical decision. Good young players and established veterans alike were receiving contract offers from the new circuit that were three and four times what the established leagues were offering. Brooklyn's roster, with Stengel, Daubert, and Wheat all in their twenties, was particularly attractive to the new league.

NL teams had two options — either stand pat, let players walk away, and go on austerity measures and hope to outlast the new league, or try to outspend and eventually bankrupt the new circuit. Each strategy carried considerable risks.

In Brooklyn they decided to pay and fight — Ebbets had to put fans in his brand-new ballpark. Over the winter Ebbets locked up his most valuable players with lucrative, multiyear contracts. Jake Daubert was the big winner, getting a five-year deal worth $9,000 a year. Ebbets locked up Wheat and Stengel as well. The few players he did lose were expendable anyway.

And everyone else's loss was Brooklyn's gain as the Fed raids weakened almost every other club in the NL. Over the next few seasons Robinson would prove adept at enticing lesser lights overlooked by both the Feds and the other established teams to come and play for him, for after paying Daubert and the others, there was precious little money left to fill out the roster. Robinson's personal popularity would make the difference.

But in 1914 the major difference Robinson made was in the press. The sportswriters loved him. He kept them entertained and was always good for a story.

Good thing, because for most of Robinson's first seasons the Robins were terrible. They were a good hitting club with no pitching, even though Jeff Pfeffer emerged as an ace and in 1914 Daubert took aim at his second straight batting title. In a strange season marked by the "Miracle" Boston Braves comeback from last place on July 18 to a pennant, the Dodgers made a similar surge to end the season on an up note. In late August they were mired in last place, but in September they won 18 of their final 26 to pull into fifth place with a 75–79 record.

In any other season, that would have been cause for optimism. But competition from the Tip Tops, who charged half of the admission at Ebbets Field, killed the gate. On most days only about a thousand fans milled around brand-spanking-new Ebbets Field. For the season they drew only 122,000 fans, one-third as many as in 1913.

But there was no turning back. No one but the Feds was buying players now, so there was no way to dump salary or otherwise cut costs. The Robins chose to keep up their aggressive pursuit of talent and hope a rise in the standings would lead to an increase at the box office.

The way to go was clear. The team had no trouble scoring but needed more pitching, and Robinson had always been adept at managing a pitching staff. The 1915 season was marked by a yearlong pursuit of pitching talent. It was a good time to be looking. In an effort to save money, most teams in baseball were cutting loose marginal talent. The existing two major leagues had already cut rosters to a bare-bones 21 players in an effort to save some dough. There was pitching to be had if one knew where to look.

Robinson not only knew where to look but knew how to turn marginal talent into winning pitchers. A life in baseball—and a generally affable one at that—had given him many connections. Robinson had pioneered the notion of inviting pitchers and catchers to spring training a couple of weeks before other players, and his reputation as an innovative pitching guru followed him to Brooklyn.

One of the first pitchers he pursued was former A's star Jack Coombs. The former 20-game winner had been injured and then had fallen out of favor with Connie Mack, who had decided to break up his once-championship club and rebuild. Coombs was only 31, and Robinson thought he had some value. Where others discarded sore arms, Robinson nursed them back to health, for the extended spring training period was a primitive form of rehab. He then added Sherry Smith

and Wheezer Dell, two husky rookies somewhat long in the tooth but with long track records of success in the minor leagues.

That should have been the story of the season—Robinson's aggressive pursuit of pitching—but it was all overshadowed one drizzly day at the start of spring training in the first of several incidents that would forever color the perception of Robinson; long seen as an affable and innovative baseball man, he would come to be viewed as something of a clown.

The airplane was still a novelty, and barnstorming pilots took to dropping baseballs from their planes to announce their arrival in town, all the better to entice spectators to pay for the privilege of taking a joyride. After seeing such a display, a lightbulb went off in Ebbets's head. He wanted to inaugurate the beginning of camp by taking just such a ride and dropping

First baseman Jake Daubert was a classic singles and average hitter for the Dodgers. The nimble-footed Daubert won back-to-back National League batting titles in 1913 and 1914 with averages of .350 and .329, respectively.

a baseball himself in an attempt to set a new record for the baseball drop, currently at 504 feet, representing the height of a few balls caught when dropped off the Washington Monument.

But doctors warned the increasingly frail Ebbets against the stunt. So aviatrix Ruth Law volunteered to perform the task herself. The only question that remained was who would volunteer to catch the sphere.

No one on the team stepped up, so Robinson decided to make a point with his charges and do the deed himself.

At the appointed time, Law took off and began circling skyward over the field as Robinson, given wide berth by a coterie of fans and players, stood wearing a chest protector, glove in hand. He was not taking unnecessary precautions, for a baseball dropped from a height of more than 500 feet reaches maximum velocity. If he missed it and the ball hit his head, he could be killed.

When Law was certain she had reached a sufficient height and was flying directly over Robinson, at a speed of 45 miles per hour, she dropped the orb from the biplane. It hurtled to earth, a small speck growing larger by the instant.

But it was not a baseball; Law had inadvertently left that in her hotel. Not wanting to cause a delay, she had grabbed a grapefruit.

Robinson stared skyward and circled underneath the dropping object, then deftly raised his glove to catch it.

The grapefruit hurtled into the heel of his glove and then to his upper chest, bursting on impact, knocking Robinson flat, and showering him with juice.

The stunned manager, feeling the warm liquid streaming over his face and arms, feared the worst. "Jesus, I'm hit! Help me, lads," he called out. "I'm covered with my own blood." At which point his players fell to the ground laughing and Robinson, opening his eyes, found the eviscerated grapefruit on the ground. Over the years a number of players, including Casey Stengel, took false credit for the substitution of the grapefruit as the story became a legend and the defining anecdote of Robinson's illustrious career.

Once the juice dried and the season began, Brooklyn was in its first pennant race in years. The NL was more balanced than at any other time in its history, and the difference between first place and last place was paper-thin and shifted almost daily.

The Dodgers were absolutely schizophrenic. A poor start seemed to relegate them to the second division, and as late as June 30 they shared last place with Cincinnati. But Robinson never gave up.

In mid-June he had rolled the dice and talked Ebbets into buying Reds pitcher Phil Douglas, a measure of the faith the club had in its manager. Douglas had some of the best stuff in baseball when he was sober, but that wasn't very often. Nevertheless, Robbie thought he could turn Douglas around.

Helped in part by their new pitcher, Brooklyn surged in July, and the club pulled into second place, just a handful of games behind the Phillies.

Adding even more pitching depth with the valuable arms of the Giants' Rube Marquard and the Cubs' Larry Cheney, the Robins spent the next two months stalking Philadelphia, but runs had been hard to come by all year long, and over the final weeks the club's hitting collapsed and they slumped to third. Even Robinson had been powerless to turn Douglas around for long; he didn't last the season and was sold to the Cubs in September.

But there was some good news for the franchise. The Federal League had sued for peace under antitrust laws and folded when it reached a settlement with Organized Baseball, a cause of great joy for both the AL and NL, albeit at the cost of some $600,000. But it was a small price to pay for the end result: the two-part monopoly they enjoyed as the major leagues was restored, and with the Feds out of the way, player salaries would soon drop, in theory making it possible for Ebbets and the McKeevers to make some money. There were smiles all around.

The collapse of the Federal League suddenly made nearly 200 players available to major league clubs. While the level of play in the Federal League had been distinctly subpar, in theory the unleashing upon the majors of the best of the Federal Leaguers should have resulted in a rapid reshuffling of the deck, enabling the more aggressive clubs to rebuild overnight.

But that didn't happen. There were relatively few Federal Leaguers who could make much of a difference, and there were no George Steinbrenners among the owners of the era; the marketplace spread the players throughout both leagues.

The Robins' roster, for example, barely took notice of the Fed collapse: the club added only third baseman Mike Mowery and former Giants catcher Chief Meyers. But now Brooklyn had Cheney and Marquard for a full season, not to mention a spring under the tutelage of Robinson and the experienced gaze of Myers. Robinson recognized the strength of his ballclub and the relative weakness of the competition, for neither the Phillies nor the Braves had taken bold action in the off-season. Robbie confidently announced, "Give me three fellows who can pitch the ball and four who can hit it and I'll win the pennant." As it turned out, he ended up with more of both than were required.

It was still the Dead Ball Era, and from the start of the season Robbie had his club scratching for runs in the best fashion of the old Orioles. On May 1, Tommy Rice observed that "the Superbas have received as much instruction in inside baseball as any team in the big leagues," noting that of their first five victories, "two were gained by the use of the squeeze play, one was clinched by the squeeze play and one was virtually earned by the hit and run applied at a psychological moment."

And that's exactly how they won, scratching out runs while the league's deepest pitching staff held the opposition at bay. Zack Wheat emerged as a full-fledged star of the first order. The quiet outfielder, allegedly half-Cherokee, named after Zachary Taylor and Jefferson Davis, was a native son of the middle border of southwest Missouri. His left-handed swing was perfect for Ebbets Field, and he was a rare commodity at the time, a player who could hit with what passed for power when few others did. Batting cleanup behind Daubert and Stengel, Wheat drove the ball to the gaps with doubles and triples and knocked them home. When he was due to hit, the club tended to play more conservatively, while the bottom of the order played inside ball to perfection.

Stengel too emerged as a local star and fan favorite. Now dubbed "Casey" after his hometown of Kansas City, he bounced back from a subpar 1915, when he was reportedly sick with venereal disease, to bring the considerable energy of his personality onto the field. For thus far in his career Stengel had been a disappointment and had failed to fulfill the promise

As the Dodger left fielder for 18 seasons, Zack Wheat established franchise records for games played (2,322), at bats (8,859), doubles (464), triples (171), and hits (2,804) while helping lead the Dodgers to pennants in 1916 and 1920.

he showed as a rookie and in his first few seasons. Healthy again and playing regularly as part of a four-man contingent that Robinson used in the outfield, Stengel now made his personality part of his game. Part clown, part pest, and a 100 percent pure ballplayer, with the emphasis on *play*, Stengel lit a fire under the club. Chief Meyers even credited Stengel with being the difference on the 1916 pennant winner, telling Lawrence Ritter, "It was Casey who kept us on our toes."

He also kept fans on the edge of their seats, with both his flamboyant, daring, and occasionally inexplicable play and stunts on the base paths and his never-ending banter and constant interaction with fans, both on the field and off. Stengel was everywhere in Brooklyn — showing up at Coney Island, popping into parties, swaggering down the street, often with a girl on his arm and a beer in his hand. He was the player who made the Robins part of the neighborhood. In

Left-hander Sherry Smith pitched one of the great losing games in World Series history when he was defeated by Babe Ruth and the Red Sox in game two of the 1916 Series at Braves Field by a score of 2–1. After surrendering a run in the first, Smith shut out the Red Sox for 12⅓ innings before the Boston team scratched out a run in the 14th for the win.

that sense Stengel was perhaps the first true Dodger, for he created the cartoonish, lovable, slightly off-kilter persona of the team that would characterize it for the next three decades. With players like Stengel around, a good day at Ebbets Field did not necessarily require victory. Wins were nice, but Stengel and his progeny made losses not only livable but laughable and even lovable.

In 1916 there would be both glee and victory in Brooklyn. On May 2 the Dodgers beat the Giants 5–3 in the Polo Grounds on a freak home run by — who else? — Stengel. In years past, balls hit off the facade facing the upper tier of seats in right field had — unfairly — remained in play, but for the 1916 season it had been decided that those drives were home runs. Stengel's hit, described as a "profound wallop," knocked in three and gave the Dodgers a lead they never surrendered in the 8–5 win. The victory sent them into first place and caused Tommy Rice to ask of the Brooklyn faithful, "Where are you going this afternoon?"

For the next week the Dodgers and Phillies traded first place back and forth like a hot potato, leading Tommy Rice to wax eloquent: "Life is considerably worth living hereabouts, is it not, when the Superbas are back in first place. . . . Yea, right smart joy is to be found in Flatbush."

That joy was due in no small part to the disappearance of the Giants as a threat. Over the past several seasons, age had reduced the great Christy Mathewson to mortality and the Giants had tumbled into last place in 1915. Although they were already on the rebound, they were not yet a bona-fide contender, and their absence had left a void atop the National League.

Early on everything seemed to be breaking Brooklyn's way, particularly in their early season battles with Philadelphia for the top spot. On May 5, pitcher Wheezer Dell, just a few days after the birth of his son, who weighed in at an impressive 12 pounds, shut out the Phillies 2–0 to pull Brooklyn into first. The next game ended with perhaps the most unlikely home run in franchise history.

Jeff Pfeffer and Erskine Mayer of the Phillies battled each other to a standoff into the 11th. Then Brooklyn infielder George Cutshaw stepped to the plate.

As Tommy Rice described it, "Cutshaw's whack took the form of a vicious line drive near the right field foul line. It should have gone to the concrete wall and been good for anywhere between one and three bases, according to its carom. It did no such thing. It landed on a hard spot near the foul line a foot or two from the concrete. It bounded up, and up, following the wall, and literally climbed over, pausing a moment to laugh at [Philadelphia outfielder] Homer Cravath. How the climb was made and what peculiarity of 'English' was imparted to the hit when it first landed on the ground will never be explained by a finite mind." Cutshaw tore around the bases for the winning run on a ball that today would be scored a ground-rule double. No one in the park could recall ever seeing a ball take a similar route out, not even in practice.

The Dodgers took advantage and opened a small lead in the standings over Philadelphia as Boston fell back. But as they did, all eyes turned to the Giants, who somehow managed to steal the headlines in Manhattan for most of the summer. While on an extended road trip, the also-ran Giants strung together an incredible 17 consecutive wins, which would prove to be only a footnote to a later surge. Yet in Brooklyn the Giants' streak meant little, for it never brought New York closer than a few games to Brooklyn. When it was over, the club went into an extended slide, but the streak illustrated just how tough it was for the Dodgers to make any inroads into the baseball consciousness of Manhattan. Every time it seemed that something was about to happen in Flatbush, the Giants—and later the Yankees—remained capable of casting Brooklyn in shadow.

Robinson's charges opened up and held the lead like a racehorse turning from the quarter-pole then tearing down the backstretch. In a season bereft of much offense, Brooklyn had the best pitching and the best hitting in the league.

They would need both. In early September the Phillies and the Braves momentarily pulled into a tie with Brooklyn. Although Boston soon fell off and the Robins nudged ahead, they could not shake the Phillies.

The Giants, after a fashion, came to their rescue. After the early season surge, McGraw's club had stumbled badly, falling below .500 for the season. McGraw retooled, and beginning on September 8, the team jelled. They won their next 26 consecutive games, still the all-time record.

It was Brooklyn's good fortune that, once again, they all but avoided the Giants during their historic run. Although the streak started with a win over Brooklyn, the Robins had just taken two of three from the New Yorkers and then didn't play them again until the streak was over. In contrast, both Boston and Philadelphia fell under the Giants' onslaught.

On the last day of September the Robins and Phillies met

NL SLUGGING PERCENTAGE LEADERS

1901	Jimmy Sheckard	.534
1906	Harry Lumley	.477
1916	Zack Wheat	.461
1919	Hy Myers	.436
1941	Pete Reiser	.558
1953	Duke Snider	.627
1956	Duke Snider	.598
1985	Pedro Guerrero	.577

in Brooklyn with the season on the line in an odd, split-admission morning and afternoon doubleheader at Ebbets Field, for the game the day before had been rained out. Attendance had rebounded dramatically in 1916, but Ebbets wasn't shy about raking in as much extra cash as he could—when the Robins were out of town, Ebbets Field was available for rent. He naively believed he could fill Ebbets Field twice for the two games.

But in those pre-radio days it was difficult to spread the word. Only 7,000 fans made use of their rain checks for the morning contest, and many were less than thrilled to learn that they'd witness only one game, not two as was customary after a rain-out. And when the Phillies raked Pfeffer for a 7–2 win, they were doubly disappointed, for the win vaulted the Phillies into first by percentage points.

More than 16,000 turned out for game two, including thousands who thought their rain checks from the day before qualified them for admission. But for the third time that season, the Robins regained first place within hours of losing it to the Phillies. And they did it the hard way, beating ace Grover Cleveland Alexander 6–1. On that same day the Giants' streak ended at 26 games when they lost to Boston.

The win gave Brooklyn the edge entering the final days of the season. After beating the Giants 2–0 on October 1, a Robins win over New York on October 2 coupled with a doubleheader sweep by the Braves over Philadelphia delivered the pennant to Brooklyn.

Or was it more than that? For the pennant-clinching game against the Giants raised more questions than it answered.

To open the game, three of the first four Giants bunted—hardly a strategy designed to beat the Robins into submission—but Brooklyn played nervous baseball, and after Art Fletcher homered, the Giants led 3–0. After that odd start, New York played the rest of the game without enthusiasm, apart from their aversion to fielding the ball on defense and their aversion to scoring while at bat. Routine ground balls rolled through for hits, players ran into outs, and starting pitcher Pol Perritt even pitched from the full windup with men on base.

The tip-off that something wasn't quite on the square came in the sixth. With the Dodgers leading 6–5, McGraw stormed off and left the team under the control of second baseman Buck Herzog, and he failed to manage any more games that season. The Dodgers rolled to a 9–6 win to clinch the pennant.

After the game, McGraw intimated to a reporter that his team had given the game to Brooklyn and "almost turned the game into a farce," missing signs and making other egregious errors. Writers speculated that fondness for Robinson and some of the ex-Giants now playing for Brooklyn might have explained New York's lack of motivation, while others reported that McGraw had made a huge bet that the Giants

In 11 seasons with the Dodgers, outfielder Hy Myers batted a solid .282 and legged out 97 triples. He is shown here stroking a first-inning inside-the-park home run off Red Sox left-hander Babe Ruth in the second game of the 1916 World Series in Boston. It was the last earned run surrendered by Ruth in World Series play until the fourth game of the 1918 Series, a stretch of 29²/₃ consecutive scoreless innings.

Shortstop Ivy Olson had a nightmare of a World Series in 1916 as he made four of the thirteen errors charged to the Dodgers in the five-game contest. Red Sox players openly exhorted teammates within earshot of the mortified Olson to "hit it to Ivy."

would finish third. When their loss on October 1 made that impossible, he had reamed out the team, which in turn had laid down as a show of nonsupport.

It cast a cloud over the pennant, and for the third time that season the Giants pushed the Dodgers into a subordinate role despite the Brooklyn team's lofty record, for the Dodgers had beaten the Giants 15 times over the course of the season on the way to a 94–60 record. Robinson was incensed. He thought McGraw had cast aspersions on the game out of pure spite and to diminish Robinson's achievement, and afterward he fumed that McGraw had "pissed on my pennant." In another era baseball might well have investigated the many charges being thrown around, but in 1916 the game was none too eager to air its dirty laundry. Gambling was baseball's dirty little secret, as common around major league baseball as street urchins sneaking over the fence, and just as easily tolerated. The incident faded from view.

Nevertheless, Brooklyn celebrated its first pennant of the 20th century. When Zack Wheat caught the final out, he tossed the ball into the stands, and the players snake-danced around the clubhouse. They knew this would probably be their last chance in 1916 to rejoice, for although they were going to the World Series, few gave them a chance of beating the defending world champion Boston Red Sox. In a poll of national baseball scribes, Boston was the heavy favorite, collecting 13 of 17 votes. Oddsmakers whose opinions really mattered similarly gave Brooklyn little chance.

Under manager Bill Carrigan, the defending world champions were known as the most fundamentally sound team in baseball. They had gone 91–63 and beat out seven contenders to win the pennant as the top seven teams in the AL had all finished within fifteen games of the top and had all been in the race into September. All this was accomplished despite the loss of outfielder Tris Speaker, arguably one of the best players in baseball, who had inexplicably been sold to Cleveland before the start of the season. And to this point in their history, every time the Red Sox had played in the World Series, they had won.

Although the two teams were not dissimilar, for each depended on the depth of its pitching staff, Boston edged the Dodgers in experience. This would be Boston's third appearance in the fall classic since 1912.

Both team owners salivated at the prospect of making as much extra money as possible. Boston owner Joe Lannin worked out a deal with the Braves to play home games at

Braves Field, which held more fans than Fenway Park. And Charlie Ebbets jacked up ticket prices to an unheard-of $5 per ticket.

The Dodgers left for Boston on October 6 after a parade that began before a throng of thousands at Ebbets Field, traveled slowly down Bedford Avenue to the Bedford YMCA, went on to Borough Hall, then to the offices of the *Brooklyn Eagle*, and finally arrived at Grand Central Station for the one o'clock train to Boston. For much of the way in Brooklyn the streets were lined by fans, and thousands had gathered at Borough Hall. For a group that had never celebrated a pennant before, it wasn't a bad show.

Thousands more turned out the next day at Braves Field, including the usual Boston suspects, such as the famous fan group the "Royal Rooters," and the normal embarrassment of Massachusetts politicians. In Brooklyn, as was the custom during the series, a huge crowd gathered opposite the *Brooklyn Daily Eagle* office to watch a replay on a manned scoreboard, while another 10,000 did the same on Newspaper Row in Manhattan.

But the series did not unfold as most expected. Both managers made curious choices to start game one.

Boston's ace in 1916 had been the 21-year-old left-hander Babe Ruth, who had led the team with 23 wins and a league-best 1.75 ERA. Nearly as good were both Dutch Leonard and Carl Mays, each of whom had won 18 games and pitched nearly as well as Ruth. At the bottom of Boston's rotation, whose five members had won 89 of their 91 victories that season, were Ernie Shore and Rube Foster. While neither was a slouch, winning 17 and 13 games, respectively, they hadn't approached the dominance of the top three. Yet Boston manager Bill Carrigan, wary of Ruth's youthful enthusiasm, chose to pass him over in game one. Instead, he chose Shore.

Robinson trumped him. He took a look at the Boston lineup, which often sported four left-handers, and made the decision to go almost entirely with left-handed pitching. This meant passing over his two best pitchers in 1916, 25-game winner Jeff Pfeffer and 18-game winner Larry Cheney. To start game one, he too picked his number-four starter, lefty Rube Marquard.

It was a case of overmanaging at its worst. Of all the Boston left-handed batters, none, either singly or in combination, merited such respect. Harry Hooper and Larry Gardner were good but not fearsome hitters. Relegating Pfeffer and Cheney to the bullpen was akin to sitting Zack Wheat so he would be available to pinch-hit. Brooklyn would quickly pay for their manager's departure from common sense.

Marquard and Shore both started off strong as Boston's rooters serenaded everyone with their usual cacophony of song, but as Tommy Rice noted with some dismay afterward, "Rube was not a howling success. He had the knack of getting into a hole when there was no occasion for letting the batter have the edge." In the seventh inning, with the score 2–1 in favor of Boston, he stumbled off the precipice, albeit with a little help. After Hal Janvrin doubled, first shortstop Ivy Olson then second baseman George Cutshaw botched routine chances to plate one. Duffy Lewis of Boston sacrificed, then Larry Gardner had the good sense to ground another ball to Cutshaw, who threw home both late and wide, then Everett Scott knocked in the third run of the inning with a sacrifice fly. A disinterested Pfeffer came on in the eighth to mop up and gave Boston another run on two walks and a hit to make the score 6–1.

Many in the crowd began to leave, but as they started to stream toward the exits in the ninth, Shore ran out of steam. For the first time all game, the few Brooklyn rooters held sway, and one fan played a counterpoint to the Royal Rooters by beating a tin pie pan for all it was worth. Thus inspired, the Robins used a series of walks, hit batsmen, and nub hits to push across three runs, chase Shore, then score another when reliever Carl Mays was greeted with an infield hit.

Jake Daubert stepped up to the plate living out every little boy's dream: two out, last of the ninth, bases loaded, and trailing by a run. The tenth Brooklyn batter of the inning, he'd started the comeback with a walk, and no one yet had hit the ball out of the infield in the air; only Stengel's slow roller through the right side had made it there at all. Boston fans were stunned and silent while Brooklyn partisans were apoplectic.

Submarine pitcher Carl Mays was successful because his style of pitching induced ground balls, most of which were hit at fielders—the *Eagle* described his style as "a messenger boy delivering in the most important message of the hour—it sneaks over." Daubert, who hit second in the Brooklyn batting order, was successful because he would slap a ground ball the other way and three times out of ten the ball found a hole.

Both men did their job, but the odds favored Mays and held true. Daubert smacked a chopper to the hole, but Everett Scott of Boston was one of the best glove men in the league. He fielded the ball cleanly and threw across the diamond to Dick Hoblitzell at first.

Daubert ran well but not well enough—as he saw Hoblitzell stretch out to receive the throw, he slid headlong into the bag. Umpire Hank O'Day's clear eye called both Daubert, and Brooklyn, out. Boston won 6–5. "If my legs had been made of rubber," moaned Daubert after the contest, "we'd have brought home that old ballgame." That may have been true, but when he chose to dive for the bag, he rendered his legs insignificant.

Brooklyn entered game two—after an off-day owing to Boston's blue laws, which, like Brooklyn's, still banned Sunday baseball—desperate for a win. Yet Robinson again passed over both Pfeffer—now in the doghouse after his game-one performance—and Cheney, choosing Sherry Smith to start the game opposite Boston left-hander Babe Ruth, who was enjoying his first truly great season on the mound.

Hy Myers led off and drew blood, knocking the ball to center field, where it bounced over Tilly Walker's head and then into the no-man's-land of deep center field. He raced around the bases, and Brooklyn led, 1–0, before an out had been made.

Ruth had been anxious to pitch, for Carrigan had passed him over completely in the 1915 World Series, and he was determined to make good. He did. Myers's drive would end the scoring for Brooklyn that day.

But Sherry Smith was nearly his equal. After giving up a single run in the third when Ruth's ground ball scored Scott, for the next ten innings the two pitchers were near-perfect, neither giving up a run. The game entered the 14th inning under dwindling light that announced the end was near, still tied 1–1.

By this time both club owners and a fair number of players were squinting over at the umpiring crew hoping they'd call the game, for if it had to be replayed, there would be a $100,000 windfall in receipts. But the 14th inning had already started, and the umpires were determined that it would finish.

Smith finally broke down, walking Hoblitzell to start the inning. He was sacrificed to second, and then Del Gainer pinch-hit for Larry Gardner, who'd looked awful against Smith.

Gainer ripped the ball to left. An inning or two earlier Wheat, a fine fielder, would have caught the ball. But in the twilight he got a late start, and the ball dropped in. Boston scored to take the game, and Gainer's single became known in baseball lore as the "$100,000 Hit."

Brooklyn fans sagged. As the two teams left immediately for South Station to catch a train to New York for game three, the Robins' prospects looked dim.

Although Ebbets Field looked festive on the morning of October 10 for its first-ever World Series game, it was anything but. Put off by Ebbets's price gouging, the club's performance, and a cold spell, a crowd of somewhat less than the announced total of 21,087 turned out for the game. Early arrivals even made bonfires on the sidewalk before entering the park. By game time vast portions of the stands—in some places as many as ten rows in an entire section—were empty. Nevertheless, there were still some enterprising boys who cared enough to climb the upper reaches of a tree on Bedford Avenue to watch for free, and nearby housetops were reportedly packed five and six rows deep with freeloaders.

The less intrepid missed the best game Brooklyn played, although Robinson stubbornly stuck to his strategy of throwing the wrong pitcher, this time plucking Jack Coombs from the pile while Pfeffer and Cheney burned. Staked to a 4–0 lead, Coombs then faltered, but Pfeffer stepped in and handily retired the last eight to give Brooklyn the win, sending a few hundred fans into a spontaneous postgame celebration on the field.

Yet while the players were trying to figure out how to score off Boston's pitching, Ebbets and the McKeevers were trying to figure how to make a score with their accountant. Both were interested in cashing in. Interest in the franchise had never been more intense—nearly 500,000 fans had filled Ebbets Field that summer—and fears that the United States might be drawn into the European war made it unlikely that the condition of the franchise would continue to improve.

Coney Island restaurateur Charles Feltman was keenly interested in buying the team, as was Tammany Hall's Jim Gaffney. There was some speculation, quickly denied, that Gaffney, the former owner of the Boston Braves, was simply acting as a front man for John McGraw. Despite the ongoing World Series, Brooklyn's owners weren't shy about discussing a potential sale. Steve McKeever announced that his asking price was $2 million—$500,000 for the team, $950,000 for the ballpark, and the rest a healthy profit.

Such talk didn't help the Robins on the field or in the stands. Although the crowd for game four was somewhat larger and more enthusiastic, Boston's Dutch Leonard was near-perfect while Marquard was not, and Boston won handily 6–2 to take command of the series.

The clubs returned to Boston for game five, but the eventual outcome was not in doubt. Pfeffer finally got a chance to start, but Boston scored three early runs and Ernie Shore scattered only three hits as Boston won the game 3–1, and the series four games to one.

Each Brooklyn player received $2,645, since the Boston crowds had made up for the disappointing ones in Brooklyn. Criticism of Robinson, while common in Brooklyn, was voiced sotto voce, for the manager's personal popularity left him above much public criticism. Although many believed that Robinson had cost the team any chance it had to win by bypassing Pfeffer and Cheney, in Brooklyn such criticisms were left unspoken. For many, the pennant had been enough. Most fans followed the lead of Tommy Rice, who chose to boost the manager, writing, "We do not believe that any other manager extant other than you Uncle Wilbert Robinson could have won a pennant with the Superbas."

The World Series was a different matter. Teams win championships with pitching and defense, and Brooklyn hadn't displayed either. The team had collected thirteen errors in only five games, including four by shortstop Ivy Olson, whom the Red Sox taunted throughout the Series, admonishing each other within earshot of the infielder to "hit it to Ivy."

Outsiders were not so kind. The ink wasn't dry on the scorebook for the final game and already the Robins were being knocked off the top of the barrel. Beyond the borough, many came to the conclusion that in reality the Giants had truly been the best team in the NL. Brooklyn's uninspired performance in the Series seemed to prove that they had been, at best, accidental pennant winners before the Giants' furious onslaught, while the empty seats in the stands during the Series demonstrated that not even their own fans had believed in them.

No one was surprised at either outcome. That was Brooklyn for you. No one ever stayed at the top for very long.

1917–1937

FLOCKING TO THE BUMS

A DYNASTY WAS NOT DESTINED TO GROW IN BROOKLYN—NOT YET. THEIR achievement in 1916 was the result of a good but not great team peaking in a season in which no National League club was much better than average. And the Robins were old. Every key player was either over 30 or rapidly approaching that benchmark. The next few seasons would not be kind to the franchise, its players, or their manager. Of course, compared with what was happening in the rest of the world, things were not so bad.

The United States, after months of posturing and debate, entered the Great War in the fall of 1917, and by that time Brooklyn's 1916 pennant was as much a part of the past as Serbian Archduke Ferdinand, whose assassination had sparked the conflict. Any chance that Ebbets or the McKeevers would sell out went up in smoke over the battlefields of Europe as a nervous uncertainty took hold in America. The Giants took command of the National League race in June and swept to the pennant. Brooklyn, meanwhile, slumped across the board, not helped by injuries to Wheat and Daubert.

Yet for Uncle Wilbert things were even worse. Prior to the World Series, he had been considered something of a managerial wunderkind, for as a coach for the Giants and as manager

The 1917 Dodgers at spring training at the resort spa of Hot Springs, Arkansas. Following their 1916 pennant, the team was already developing a reputation as not only a skilled but a colorful cast of characters. (Bottom row, left to right) Hy Myers, Chief Meyers, and Ivy Olson; (second row) Jim Hickman and Zack Wheat; (at the top) outfielder Jim Johnston.

of Brooklyn, he had left his imprint on four pennants in six seasons.

But the World Series loss, particularly the way he lost it—keeping his best pitchers off the mound until it was too late—damaged his reputation. It was clear too that by the spring of 1917 Brooklyn's time was up. They shared Hot Springs during spring training with the Red Sox and were beaten so soundly that it was obvious they weren't in the Boston club's class, no matter who pitched. Their desultory play in 1917 seemed to confirm that the 50-year-old manager was out of touch. No team had ever fallen further, faster, than the seventh-place Robins, and meanwhile attendance dropped by half.

Nevertheless, throughout much of the 1917 season there had been open speculation that Robinson would be named manager of the Yankees at the end of the season, for Yankee

Who better to lead the team that columnist Westbrook Pegler called the "Daffiness Boys" than former Dodger outfielder Casey Stengel? In three seasons as Brooklyn manager, Stengel led the team to finishes of sixth, fifth, and seventh place.

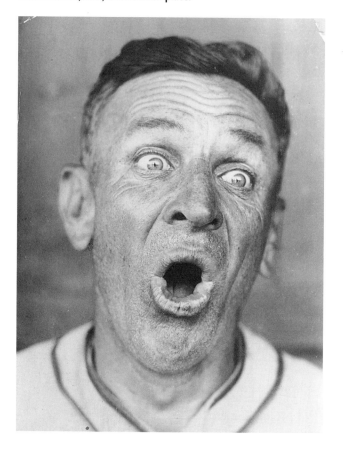

co-owner Tillinghast l'Hommedieu Huston was a close friend. Both men were part of a baseball salon of sorts that formed at the Dover Hall Club in Brunswick, Georgia, where they hunted, drank, and told stories over the Hot Stove League. Huston openly lobbied his partner, Jacob Ruppert, to hire Robinson. But after the Series, Robinson lost his luster. Huston was overseas using his engineering acumen as part of the American expeditionary force when Ruppert hired Miller Huggins instead.

Robinson's mood matched his club's performance. His son, who had been chronically ill, died in the off-season, and grief sent the usually affable manager into darkness. Then the war heated up and turned baseball upside down. Draft-eligible players either had to sign up or go to work in the war industries.

Ebbets and Robinson tried to retool, dumping George Cutshaw and Casey Stengel to the Pirates for pitchers Burleigh Grimes and Al Mamaux. Ebbets had grown tired of Stengel's antics, and the outfielder wrote his own ticket out of town when he returned his contract for 1917, which cut his pay by $1,400, by writing Ebbets a not-so-tongue-in-cheek "Dear Charlie" letter. Telling the owner he must have had Stengel confused with team handyman Red Hanrahan, Casey then bitched to the press that "it seems reasonable that if he [Ebbets] charges such high prices to see his players perform, he should meet the fans halfway by giving them the opportunity to watch high-priced players." Ebbets disagreed and dumped the man who was arguably the team's most popular, albeit overpaid, player, for no one had taken better advantage of the overtures from the Feds to negotiate a high salary.

By spring there was no way of telling who would be available for the upcoming season as the war played havoc with rosters throughout baseball. Over the course of the season the Dodgers would eventually lose such stalwarts as Pfeffer and Sherry Smith. They got off to a poor start and then got worse as the Cubs outdistanced the Giants in the abbreviated season, which ended in early September. Brooklyn finished a quiet seventh again and was never a factor. Without Stengel around, there was little excitement.

Stengel relished his periodic returns to Brooklyn. In Pittsburgh he was just another player, but in Brooklyn he remained a celebrity, and fans treated him as if he had never left. Over the next few seasons Stengel would reward them with a series of unforgettable antics staged for their benefit. In May 1919 he outdid himself.

After misplaying a ball in the outfield and taking a razzing from the Brooklyn crowd, Stengel paid a visit to the Dodger bullpen on his way back to the dugout between innings. Pitcher Leon Cadore had captured a sparrow and was amusing his teammates with the bird.

Stengel had an idea and asked Cadore for the bird. He placed it under his cap and proceeded to the visitors' dugout.

Later that inning Stengel stepped up to the plate. The Brooklyn crowd again hooted him good-naturedly for his earlier error. Stengel paused grandly until the crowd quieted, then, when he was certain that all eyes were on him, he turned toward the stands, solemnly bowed, then doffed his cap. As the *New York Times* recounted, "From out of the darkness of the headpiece flew an irate but much relieved sparrow."

After the war ended on November 11, 1918, baseball rushed to return to normal, although after an almost two-year hiatus, no one was quite sure what normal was anymore. In the spring of 1919 Robinson felt flush with players, but so did everyone else as veterans returned to battle the upstarts who had made a name for themselves during the war.

One other old face was missing: Jake Daubert. Like Stengel, Daubert also had contract issues when Ebbets, like every other club owner, rolled back salaries after the inflationary days of the Federal League. Even though the 1918 season had ended early, Daubert's contract ran through October 14. He wanted his money—over $2,000. Daubert eventually filed suit and the Dodgers settled, but in the interim they dumped the old star to the Cincinnati Reds for outfielder Tommy Griffith.

When the dust finally settled in 1919, the Dodgers discovered that they didn't have much, and what little they had wasn't in the lineup for long as injuries decimated the team. A quick start went for naught, and the Dodgers puttered around .500, finishing fifth with a record of 69–71, with no sign that things were about to improve. Meanwhile, Daubert helped lead the Reds to a pennant and a World Series win over the White Sox.

For Brooklyn, 1920 would be a lot like 1916—another season in which Robinson's strength, the ability to put together a pitching staff whose depth made up for its lack of singular brilliance, would be enough to set the Dodgers apart from a rather undistinguished crowd. The only new face in the lineup was second baseman Pete Kilduff. But just like 1916, hardly anyone outside of Brooklyn would notice.

Baseball was changing, or at least one player was changing baseball. Changes in the game, including the generous use of new baseballs throughout each game and the banning of trick pitches such as the spitter, tilted the game toward the offense, and Babe Ruth showed just how to take advantage of those changes. Ruth, eschewing the pitcher's mound for the batter's box, had been sold to the Yankees in 1920. And in 1920 he dramatically underscored the new era, cracking a record 54 home runs. As the *Spalding Guide* stated, "All home run records in Base Ball, no matter in what league, were broken in 1920 by George Herman Ruth," changing baseball forevermore. In only two short seasons Ruth had lifted the modern single-season home run record from 24, set by Gavvy Cravath in Philadelphia's cozy Baker Bowl, to more than double that mark. From 1920 onward the game of baseball would revolve around the home run.

Except in Brooklyn. For the time being, the Dead Ball Era still lived on at Ebbets Field. In a sense, Brooklyn's upcoming pennant would be the last won by a team still rooted in the style of the 1890s.

There were signs in the spring that Brooklyn, healthy again, was a different ballclub. With Ruth, the Yankees were expected to be much improved, yet the Robins dumped the Yankees in five straight spring games. Afterward, Robinson held court before the press and lectured them on the difference a year made. "Let's look at last year," he said. "We started the season crippled, became crippleder in mid-season and ended up the cripplingest outfit in the land, yet we finished fifth. . . . Look at us [now]. Not a cripple in the lot."

The early season tested the Robins, for seven of their first 21 games went into extra innings, but Robinson's pitching staff was up to the task. That was never more obvious than on May 1, 1920, in Boston.

Spring had yet to arrive in Boston, and Braves Field, hard by the Charles River, was buffeted by a cold, raw wind blowing in from the outfield. Fewer than 3,000 stalwart fans turned out for what has to be considered one of the most remarkable games in baseball history.

The Robins' Leon Cadore faced off against Boston's Joe Oeschger in a matchup of right-handed pitchers known for nothing more than their ability to hold down a spot in the starting rotation without particular distinction—each would struggle throughout his career, without lasting success, to become more than a .500 pitcher. But on this day each man may well have pitched one of the two best games ever thrown in the major leagues.

For the first nine innings the game unfolded without distinction. Oeschger was sharp from the outset, but in the fifth Brooklyn catcher Ernie Krueger worked him for a walk. Cadore then smashed a hot one-hopper that Oeschger knocked down. Cadore was out but Krueger advanced, and Ivy Olson knocked him in with a hard single.

Cadore, on the other hand, was in and out of trouble as the Braves hit him early and often for 11 hits in regulation, only to strand runners all over the lot. In the fifth, Walton Cruise hit a long fly over center fielder Wally Hood's head. On any other day the drive would have been a certain home run in cavernous Braves Field, but on this day it was slowed by the soggy grounds, and Hood was forced to pull up with a triple.

It was at this point, as Tommy Rice wrote, that "Zach Wheat entered the hall of fame"—almost. Walter Holke lofted a short fly over third. Wheat tore in as third baseman Jimmy Johnston and Olson both went back for the ball and Cruise, thinking the ball would drop in, started for home.

Wheat made a catch at his shoetops, and spying Cruise halfway to home, kept running for third. Cruise then recovered and tore back to the base as Wheat tried to beat him to the bag for a rare unassisted double play.

Cruise dove in ahead of Wheat, who nevertheless earned the applause of the crowd for his heads-up play. Cruise then scored on Tony Boeckel's third hit of the day to tie the score, 1–1.

Boeckel nearly scored on Rabbit Maranville's hit, but the relay from Hood to Cadore to home put him out and the score remained tied.

And there it would stay as the game entered an extended period of suspended animation and tested the truism that baseball games are played without regard to the passage of time. Inning after inning Oeschger and Cadore trudged to the mound, and inning after inning neither team could score as each managed to turn in double plays with the bases loaded, stopping the only semblance of rallies. Cadore, after his early struggles, settled in as the game went into extra innings—no Boston runner even made it to third, and only two got as far as second. Meanwhile, Oeschger was almost perfect, giving up only a single hit in the 16th and two more the following inning.

But that was it. Innings 17, 18, 19, and 20 all passed quietly, as did 21, 22, and 23. The record for the longest major league game was 24 innings, set by the Red Sox and A's in 1906 when Jack Coombs and Joe Harris each twirled com-

plete games before Harris weakened and the A's won 4–1. When Cadore and Oeschger both pitched shutout ball in the 24th, the game entered rarefied air.

Fans sat stunned, as did the members of the press. Neither manager moved to replace his hurler, for each was superb, and starting pitchers were expected to finish what they started. The concept of "pitch counts" was as unknown as the rotator cuff injury.

By inning 26 the game, which had started at 3:00 P.M., was nearly four hours old, and behind the low clouds the sun was beginning to lose its influence. Each team went down quietly, and the umpires conferred in the twilight.

The Robins' Ivy Olson begged that the umpire let the game continue for at least another inning, for he saw the poetry in playing *one* game that lasted the equivalent of *three* full contests. But Olson was alone in that desire, and the arbiters chose to call the contest.

The exhausted combatants staggered off the field. Only then was it possible to stand back and look at their accomplishments. Each pitcher faced 85 batters, walked 7, and struck out 4, Cadore scattering 15 hits and Oeschger only 11. More remarkable, though, was that each man got stronger as the game went on. Over the final 13 innings, Cadore gave up only two scratch hits while Oeschger threw a rare midgame no-hitter, giving up no hits over the final nine—in fact, he missed a "perfect game" of sorts by walking Hood in inning 22.

How many pitches did each man throw? No one kept an accurate count, but even then the average batter saw between three and four pitches per at bat. It seems reasonable that each man broke the 300 barrier, and by midgame neither was bothering to make warm-up tosses before each inning. Even more remarkably, each man would pitch again within the week and finish the season without apparent arm trouble, although Uncle Robbie would later complain that Cadore was nothing more than a "six-inning pitcher," and later both men would admit to never being quite the same.

Yet once again, the achievement fell into shadow elsewhere, for on that same day Babe Ruth hit his first home run as a Yankee, knocking the Robins-Braves game from the headlines in Manhattan. It would not be the first time in 1920 that Brooklyn's accomplishments would be swamped by other events.

Even more remarkably, the Robins went on to play 13 innings the very next day back in Brooklyn in a 4–3 loss to Philadelphia in which Burleigh Grimes, one of 17 pitchers who had been allowed to continue to use the spitball after its ban, went the distance opposite George Smith. The Robins then returned to Boston the next day, and Sherry Smith and Dana Fillingim both went 19 innings as Brooklyn fell 2–1. Thus, in only three days the Robins played a remarkable 58 innings using only three pitchers, the equivalent of six and a half full games.

While Brooklyn gained nothing in the standings, the performance announced to the rest of the league that Brooklyn's pitching was superb, as was the team's desire and pluck. Moreover, the club won over the Brooklyn fans. For the first time since the 1890s, Brooklyn fandom began to develop a reputation as one of the more vocal and colorful groups in the country.

The war had been kind to Brooklyn, at least for those who hadn't been called into the service or afflicted with the postwar Spanish influenza. The Brooklyn Navy Yard, already over 100 years old, had emerged as the Navy's major shipbuilding and supply depot and employed as many as 18,000 in 1918. Postwar industry had flocked to Brooklyn to take advantage of its disciplined and battle-tested workforce, and the borough flourished as the 1920s roared.

The old ethnic divisions that had bifurcated the borough were beginning to break down under the heading phrase "I'm from Brooklyn," and identification with its neighborhoods, and even individual streets, began to be more important than where one's parents or grandparents were born. Brooklyn's role in the war had instilled residents with pride, and for perhaps the first time since the opening of the Brooklyn Bridge the burg began to thump its chest and shake its fist toward Manhattan, sloughing off the inferiority complex it had suffered under for more than three decades.

Attendance at Ebbets Field boomed as fans with extra money regularly made their way to the park, for the team was playing winning ball and the ballpark was a fortress in the center of Brooklyn. By midsummer, with the club managing to stay in the pennant race, Brooklyn had suddenly become a place that opposing teams were beginning to dread.

"Brooklyn fans," opined *Baseball Magazine,* "particularly on a weekday, gather at Ebbets Field with two fell purposes in view. One is to ride the members of the opposing team . . . the other is to ring execration and vituperation on the hapless head of Ivan Olson." The thin-skinned shortstop, who wasn't much of a fielder although he had led the league in hits in 1919, had become their favorite whipping boy since his per-

Wilbert Robinson conveyed an image that was equal parts cherished uncle and doting schoolmaster. In 18 seasons with the Dodgers, he captured two pennants and led the team to a winning record with a career .506 winning percentage. He was elected to the Hall of Fame in 1945.

Pitcher Leon Cadore shared a feat that will never be duplicated as he and Boston Braves pitcher Joe Oeschger both pitched a complete 26 innings in a 1–1 tie at Braves Field in Boston. Both pitchers easily broke the 300-pitch barrier. Cadore slept for 36 hours after the game. Both men pitched again within a week of their marathon.

But wherever Brooklyn trod, the Giants were rarely far away. After a horrible start while second baseman Frankie Frisch suffered from appendicitis, the Giants began a familiar surge when he returned in July. As August turned into September the Robins struggled through a western road trip, the Reds began to collapse, and the Giants suddenly looked like the safest bet to win the pennant. With Ruth hitting home runs for the Yankees like no man before him, the Robins, despite their stellar record, were below the fold again.

And it was getting worse by the day. Charges that something hadn't been right in the 1919 World Series, in which the heavily favored White Sox had fallen to the Reds, were coming to a head as the "Black Sox" scandal was unveiled in all its unsavory glory before a Cook County, Illinois, grand jury. Brooklyn? Who cared?

Well, the Robins did. The Reds faded under their proximity to the stench, while the Giants, with a pennant seemingly in their grasp, were knocked off track when John McGraw brawled with Broadway actor William Boyd at a New York speakeasy in mid-August, then had to leave the team to nurse his wounds and defend himself in court. When he returned, the Giants lost momentum. On September 10 and 11 the Robins won back-to-back doubleheaders over the Cardinals at Ebbets Field to open up a four-and-a-half-game lead over the Giants.

Yet even that accomplishment attracted little notice. For as the crowds migrated toward Ebbets Field on September 11 for the doubleheader, packing the trolleys to the gills, the reason the club had once earned the name "Dodgers" was made apparent again. As the *Eagle* described it, at 2:10 P.M., "a runaway Flatbush Ave. car operated by a strikebreaking motorman, jammed to the running boards with people, crashed into a standing car at Malbone St. and Flatbush Avenue." The corner, "thick with fans on their way to Ebbets Field . . . resembled a battlefield." One man was killed and 87 injured.

But the Robins seemed oblivious. They won the pennant going away, beating the Giants on September 27 despite finding an illegal flattened bat allegedly used by New York against them a few days before. When the Giants lost to the Braves the following day, the pennant was Brooklyn's.

And on that day headlines everywhere but in Brooklyn told not of their victory but of the $100,000 promised to the White Sox to lose the 1919 World Series. The Cook County grand jury handed down its indictments the next day.

formance in the 1916 Series. Unable to ignore the crowd, Olson inadvertently egged them on by letting it be known that he heard every word, even wearing cotton in his ears. Old-time fans were put off by the behavior, as one spectator of some 36 years complained in the *Eagle* of the "leather-lunged auctioneers and peddlers who have made life miserable for both the players and the fair-minded patrons . . . pessimism and home boys . . . [that] do not know the first thing about any branch of the sport." But such protesters were in the minority, and a relatively silent one at that.

Led by Grimes, who had gained command of his spitter at the precise time it was made even more effective because most others were forced to abandon the pitch, the Robins edged into first place in late June, lost their grip, then pulled ahead again in early July—"steady as Old Dobbin," according to *Spalding,* as the race turned into a two-team contest in July and August between the Reds and Brooklyn.

There was some speculation that the 1920 World Series, scheduled to be a best-of-nine affair, would be canceled, and Brooklyn players were even questioned by the local district attorney as to whether they had been approached by gamblers. When they stated they had not, plans for the Series, scheduled to begin on October 5, were made in earnest.

To the great surprise of most, the Cleveland Indians headed off Ruth and the Yankees to capture the American League pennant, a victory made even more poignant by the death of Cleveland shortstop Ray Chapman on August 16 when he was struck by a pitched ball from the hand of New York pitcher Carl Mays. The Indians seemed to rally after his death and entered the Series the sentimental favorite of fans all over the country, at least among those dwindling numbers who still cared in the wake of the unfolding scandal of 1919. The resulting Series would have been one of the more anonymous in memory had it not been made memorable by a single spectacular play.

Uncle Wilbert had plenty of time to set his rotation for the Series. Unlike 1916, one member of his starting staff stood far above the crowd — Burleigh Grimes. The spitballer, with his ever-present stubble that made him look middle-aged and a frame that echoed his first name, was unquestionably the staff ace, leading the club with 304 innings, 33 starts, and 23 wins to go with his stellar 2.22 ERA.

But Robinson, once again, eschewed conventional wisdom. Marquard was his favorite and protégé. In the 1912 World Series he had beaten Boston twice and outpitched both Mathewson and Smoky Joe Wood. In subsequent Series appearances, however, in 1913 and 1916, he'd stumbled badly. He'd been a valuable member of the Robins' six-man starting staff in 1920, but his 10 wins and 3.22 ERA were the worst of the six. The Indians, like the 1916 Red Sox, tended toward the left side and had hit .303 as a team, led by Tris Speaker's .388. But Speaker, rare among managers of the era, liked to platoon, which rendered such a strategy moot. Robinson, nevertheless, again decided to pass over his best pitcher. Marquard got the start in game one.

Speaker made the wiser choices. Not only did he insert right-handed-hitting Joe Wood and Joe Evans into his lineup to offset Robinson's selection, but he passed over 31-game winner Jim Bagby for 24-game winner Stan Coveleski. That move made sense too, for Coveleski, despite his record, had actually pitched slightly better than Bagby. Like Grimes, he too was still allowed to use the spitball.

NL ERA LEADERS

1924	Dazzy Vance	2.16
1928	Dazzy Vance	2.09
1930	Dazzy Vance	2.61
1957	Johnny Podres	2.66
1962	Sandy Koufax	2.54
1963	Sandy Koufax	1.88
1964	Sandy Koufax	1.74
1965	Sandy Koufax	2.04
1966	Sandy Koufax	1.73
1980	Don Sutton	2.21
1984	Alejandro Pena	2.48
2000	Kevin Brown	2.58

But perhaps the smartest decision had been made a week earlier by Cleveland president Jim Dunn. The awkward, best-of-nine series was supposed to open in the American League city for the first three games, then move to Brooklyn for games four through seven before returning to Cleveland. But Dunn complained that he needed time to prepare his grounds.

1917

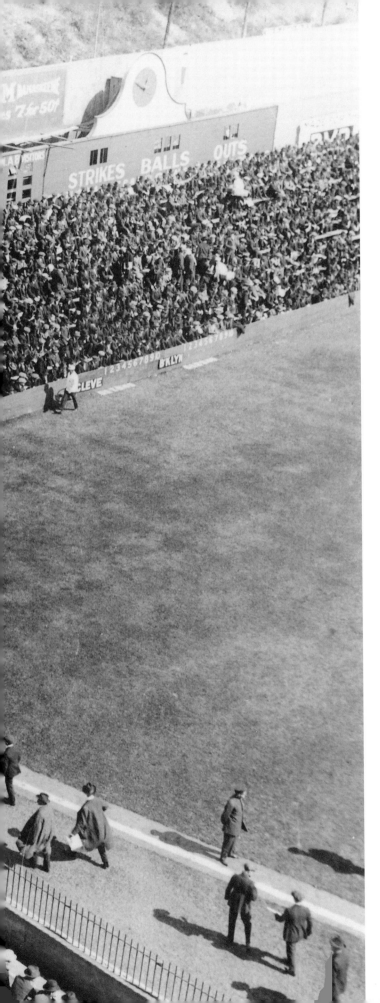

He asked for—and received—a reversal of venue, a move that would pay great dividends.

The oddsmakers favored the Indians 6–5, although reading the papers in the wake of the Black Sox scandal, one would scarcely have known that gambling still existed in baseball in 1920. Up to that time baseball and gambling were, for many fans, a dual pursuit, and it was commonplace for newspapers to print the wagers of bettors great and small. But in 1920 the game suddenly acted as if gambling had as much to do with baseball as mah-jongg. It didn't. It just went underground.

Game one was oddly without drama, played with all the passion of a spring training meeting, albeit one played in conditions more familiar in winter. The game took place in a gale that, in the words of the *Eagle*, left all observers "shivering at the diamondside" and the crowd, a "daily crop of dead grandmothers," stiff and silent.

And the weather told the story. Indian first baseman George Burns opened the second inning with a high fly that was first called for by shortstop Ivy Olson, then by Pete Kilduff at second, and finally by first baseman Ed Konetchy before the gust subsided and sent the ball toward Kilduff again, who watched it drop untouched.

By then Burns was running flat out for second, which Olson had left uncovered as he watched the curious path of the ball. Konetchy picked up the ball and threw toward the bag anyway. The ball found its way to Wheat in deep left while Burns circled the bases to score the game's first run. The play so perplexed the game's official scorers that the scoring was put to a vote, which gave Burns a single and three-base error on Konetchy's throw. The Indians made it 2–0 when Wood walked, went to third on Joe Sewell's single, and scored when Steve O'Neill ripped a double down the line.

Those two runs were all Cleveland needed, although they added a third. The Robins scored only once off Coveleski, when Wheat doubled and came around on two infield hits. Marquard didn't last the game—Robinson pinch-hit for him in the sixth and turned the game over to Cadore.

Afterward, the aging pitcher even admitted he might not have been the best pick that day, making note of the cold weather and saying, "You know, I'm not a young man any-

Fans enter temporary bleachers placed along Ebbets Field's left-field wall on October 5, 1920, prior to the first game of the 1920 World Series.

more, seeing as I have had 13 years' service in the National League, and I think if it had been a good hot day there would have been another story to tell."

In game two Robinson — finally — turned to Grimes, and Speaker responded by sending Bagby to the mound. The spit-baller answered the call, scattering only seven hits and helping his own cause by scoring Brooklyn's second run in the 3–1 win, going the distance despite a badly turned ankle suffered on the bases after his base hit.

All Brooklyn was in flower for game three. The sun burned hot and bright, and Brooklyn fans responded in kind, doffing their hats and coats and, for the first time all series, giving the Indians a taste of the behavior that had made Ebbets Field such a difficult place for visiting teams to play all year long. They rooted long and loud all game, helped out, as the *Eagle* noted, by "John Barleycorn . . . spouting wit from nickel-plated lips." Wheat keyed a first-inning rally after an error by shortstop Joe Sewell that chased Cleveland starter Ray Cald-well, and Sherry Smith held Cleveland to only three hits as the Robins won 2–1.

The team traveled to Cleveland in high spirits. But the Indians were going home to play a series-record four straight home games and were confident. George Currie of the *Eagle* captured the club's mood when he wrote: "As the Tribe left Ebbets Field the sound of grindstone shrieking against sharpening tomahawk was plainly audible. Bowstrings were tested, arrowheads repointed, quivers refilled and war clubs banished."

Of course, as everyone knows, good pitching beats good hitting, and if Robinson had followed that adage, the Robins might well have left the Indians scattered upon the ground and beaten after game four. A 3–1 advantage, even in a best-of-nine series, would have been nearly insurmountable.

But in regard to pitching, Robinson had other ideas, and before game four his hand was forced. Most expected him to turn to old favorite Rube Marquard to start the game.

Marquard, however, was thinking of other things. In Cleveland's Winton Hotel the night before the game, the local press heard Marquard bragging that he had a field box for the game for which he had paid $260 and was looking to sell for $400 or more. There was intense interest in the Series in Cleveland, and tickets with a face value of $3.30 were going for upward of $20, while $4.40 reserved seats were getting $35.

Hmm. The local press apparently saw an angle in Marquard's greed, for when he tried to sell the tickets, the buyer was an undercover Cleveland detective. The morning before game four, Marquard was arrested.

He became, in a sense, the first victim of the fallout from the Black Sox scandal, for almost overnight baseball began holding its players to a previously unknown moral standard of public purity. He was released on personal recognizance and scheduled for arraignment the next day. When he got to the park, he did not find the ball in his glove. That honor belonged to Leon Cadore.

As Rice commented, "Every camp follower of the Super-bas was astonished . . . the critics did not think he had done anything to warrant his selection," except, perhaps, hold on to his tickets.

Cadore was wild from the start, and when he wasn't, he was hittable. After giving up two runs in the first, in the second inning he was pulled some 24 innings shy of his limit as Robinson turned to Al Mamaux to stem the tide. He was only nominally successful and was relieved in turn by the disgraced Marquard in the third. But by the time the inning ended, Brooklyn trailed by five and was a beaten team. Coveleski went the distance, giving up only five hits, as Brooklyn fell 5–1 and Cleveland evened the series.

Momentum had swung their way. And in game five they demonstrated the precise degree to which that was true.

Robinson turned back to Grimes, and Speaker chose Bagby in a game that matched the two winningest pitchers. But from the outset the Indians hit Grimes as if they knew what was coming.

And they did. As shortstop Joe Sewell revealed years later, the Indians had noticed that every time the Brooklyn catcher signaled for Grimes to throw the spitball, second basemen Pete Kilduff reached down for a small handful of dirt to dry his fingers in the event the wet ball was hit his way.

Armed with such information, the Indians laid off the pitch and waited for Grimes's fastball. After Charlie Jamieson and Bill Wambsganss led off with singles, Tris Speaker dropped a bunt.

Grimes had a play, but when he reached for the ball, he lost his footing and fell. The bases were loaded and no one was out.

Slugging Cleveland outfielder Elmer Smith stepped to the plate, and Grimes got ahead, first throwing a ball, then cutting the plate with two beautiful spitballs that Smith let pass.

The veteran pitcher decided to waste a pitch, to see if Smith would chase after a high fastball. On second base, Kilduff telegraphed the pitch — he did not reach down for a handful of dirt.

And although Grimes threw the ball high, it was not high enough, and Smith knew what was coming. He pulled the ball deep over the right-field wall for a grand-slam home run, the first in Series history, and Cleveland led 4–0.

In the fourth inning Cleveland erupted for a second time. In order to pitch to Bagby, Grimes intentionally walked Cleveland catcher Steve O'Neill to put runners on first and second. But the Cleveland pitcher followed Smith's lead and drove the ball over the center-field fence to make the score 7–0.

But Brooklyn wasn't finished — yet. They had been hitting Bagby but had failed to score owing to a third-inning double play. In the fifth Kilduff singled to left, and then Miller singled to center. There were two on and no out as pitcher Clarence Mitchell, who had relieved Grimes in the fourth, stepped in.

Mitchell was no slouch. He'd played 15 games in the field in 1920 to go along with his 19 pitching appearances, and the left-hander matched up well against Bagby. Besides, trailing 7–0, there was no reason to pinch-hit unless Brooklyn drew closer. The count was 2-and-1 when Bagby threw his fourth

pitch, Kilduff dancing off second and Miller on first, and Cleveland second baseman Bill Wambsganss playing Mitchell to pull, stationed a few steps onto the outfield grass.

Then, as Rice wrote, "Mitchell, a wicked batter . . . leaned on a shoot from Bagby's right-handed delivery, what he declared later was one of the hardest swings he had made this season. The ball shot like a bullet toward right field, three steps to the right of Wambsganss and four feet over his head.

"Wambsganss took the three steps toward second on the run, leaped as high as he could, and caught the ball squarely in his gloved hand. Kilduff and Miller had started with the crack of the bat, and justly so, for the blow had all the earmarks of a double or triple.

"It was not a hit and run play. Remember that . . . Wambsganss was thrown off his balance when three feet or more off the ground and his body off perpendicular to the right when his gloved hand received impact of the ball. As he came down

Indians player-manager Tris Speaker receives a commemorative horseshoe-shaped floral arrangement from Cleveland fans before game four of the 1920 World Series.

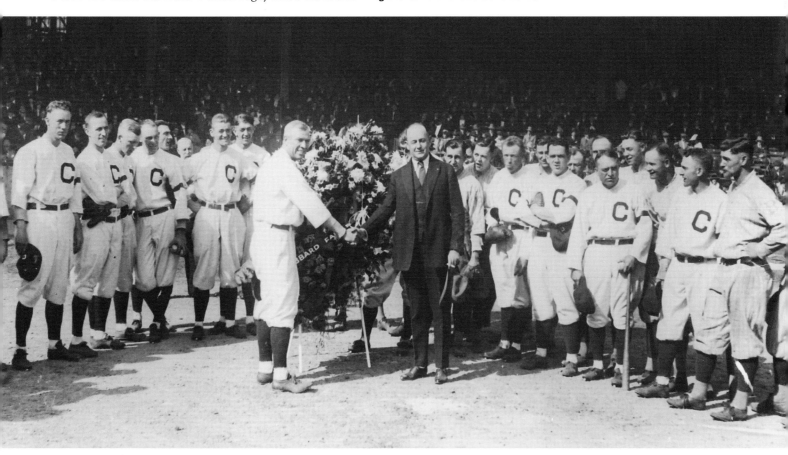

Just prior to the fourth game of the 1920 World Series, Rube Marquard (right) was arrested by the Cleveland police for scalping tickets for a field box to the game in which he was scheduled to pitch. After his release from custody, Marquard discovered that manager Wilbert Robinson (left) had passed him over for Leon Cadore in the series rotation.

For a moment, everyone on the field and off stood dumbfounded before slowly realizing what had occurred. Wambsganss himself later said, "I was dazed beyond description," and was still unsure of precisely what had happened until umpire Tommy Connolly informed him that he had in fact made three outs. Then stunned amazement found expression in the throats and hands of the crowd, and a great roar grew as the Indians sprinted from the field and the Robins looked befuddled.

Only once before, in 1909, had a similar unassisted play been made, by Cleveland shortstop Neal Ball. In the Cleveland stands in 1920 was Cy Young, who as a Boston pitcher had seen the first play and now was the only man on earth to see it twice.

The play broke Brooklyn thoroughly, even though Rice reminded everyone later that it was "absolutely unmarred by stupidity of the base runners." It didn't matter. Cleveland rolled to an 8–1 win and took command of the Series.

Brooklyn was falling apart. At his hotel later that evening Robinson exploded and hurled a glass of bourbon and ice at a reporter. Then the next day Marquard went to court. While he was fined only one dollar for his transgression, baseball looked upon him as a pariah. Ebbets and the McKeevers were beside themselves, for the stunt had embarrassed them in front of their peers. NL president John Heydler issued what proved to be an empty threat to ban the pitcher then and there. "Baseball doesn't want men of his caliber," he sniffed, "and I don't think he'll be back in the league next season."

Insult was added to injury in game six. Duster Mails, a flamboyant failure in Brooklyn a few years before, pitched the best game of the Series against his old teammates. Mails, whose inflated opinion of his skills had led him to precede his surname with the adjective "the Great," was all that and more that day. After telling his teammates, after the first inning, "You boys get me one run and we'll win," they did just that as the Great One lived up to his name, giving up only three hits. By this time the *Spalding Guide* noted, "the Brooklyns were a team with their backs to the wall fighting mechanically."

The Series was all but over. Brooklyn went down quietly in game seven, playing, again according to *Spalding,* "like the fisherman who is looking for the second bite of 'the one that got away,'" knowing the futility of that pursuit. Coveleski beat the Robins for the third time, this time shutting them out, 3–0.

he staggered, but recovered in an instant and dashed for second with the sole idea of doubling Kilduff, unassisted. Kilduff had barely time to halt in his stride for third, for which he had covered two-thirds the distance, when Wamby reached second and doubled him off. . . . Wamby, thoroughly satisfied with retiring two men in one fell swoop, turned to his left and found Otto Miller within ten feet of him, pulling up in his stride.

"A great light broke on Wambsganss. He saw a third runner, one who could be retired by tagging. . . . Then it was that Wamby understood that he had the opportunity of three lifetimes of a ballplayer, to make a triple play unassisted. He darted at Miller, touched him on the body with the ball, and history had been made."

Robinson tried to blame the Brooklyn hitters, saying, "The real cause of our defeat was due to a batting slump," and it was true to a point, for the Robins were outscored 21 to 8, but they were also outpitched, outrun, and outfielded by similar margins. And it was also true that for the second time in a World Series Robinson's own mismanagement of the pitching staff had kept his best pitchers off the mound at critical moments.

The rest of baseball did not look favorably upon Brooklyn's effort. Once again they were seen as a team whose regular season performance had been something of a mirage.

Devastating losses often lead to devastating consequences, and so it would be for Brooklyn. The next few seasons would lay the groundwork for a pennant drought that lasted two decades.

The humiliated Marquard was dealt away in December, as the club gratefully accepted Cincinnati pitcher Dutch Ruether in trade, for Rube was about finished anyway and Ruether was five years younger. And that was Brooklyn's biggest problem—age, not only in the field but in the front office. The entire starting lineup, apart from Kilduff, was on the wrong side of 30, and Robinson, Ebbets, and the McKeevers were all prone to looking backward more than to the future.

Ebbets in particular was starting to fade. At age 61, he had a bad heart and was already in his fifth decade with the organization. He was growing increasingly cranky, particularly at contract time, although the Dodgers had never been more profitable, and in recent years that had kept the McKeever brothers happy to sit in their box in the stands without interfering too much in the day-to-day operation of the club. The team had made a fortune in 1920, drawing over 800,000 fans.

But among such clover there was real trouble. Not since 1915, when they outdrew the Yankees, had Brooklyn been as high as second in attendance among New York's three teams. And now the Yankees, with Ruth, and a rebounding Giants club were far more popular than Brooklyn's favorites. The Giants and Yankees—particularly the Yankees—had appeal not only throughout the city but outside New York. All Brooklyn had was Brooklyn and the occasional Long Island or

DODGERS BY ANY OTHER NAME

If not for Dazzy (Vance), there never would have been the "Daffiness Boys." Ditto for Rube (Bressler) and Chick (Fewster), Babe (Herman) and Jigger (Statz), Watty (Clark) and Sloppy (Thurston), and Jumbo Jim (Elliott), Lefty (O'Doul), Pea Ridge (Day), Ownie (Carroll), and Boom Boom (Beck). Part of the appeal the Brooklyn Dodgers had among their fans during the era of the so-called Daffiness Boys was the assortment of monikers, nicknames, and handles among the players. Never has a roster of players been so artfully named.

The names still roll off the tongue like an orchestra falling down the steps. Curly Onis. Whitey Ock. Frenchy Bordagaray. The Dodgers collected nicknames like other teams collected talent. In the 1920s and 1930s it seemed that if a player didn't have a name that brought a smile every time it was uttered, the Dodgers of Uncle Robbie (Wilbert Robinson), Max Carey (Maximillian Carinus), and Casey (Charles Stengel) weren't interested. Finishing sixth or seventh was somehow made more palatable by the knowledge that either Sloppy Thurston or Boom Boom Beck was pitching, Buzz Boyle and Jigger Statz were in the outfield, Chick Fewster and Rabbit Maranville were turning the double play, and Snooks Dowd was waiting on the bench.

How could fans not have loved a team whose play—and players—seemed as if they were plucked off some sandlot? After all, if Sloppy pitched sloppy or Boom Boom was belted, expectations were met, making a tidy game by Sloppy or a whitewash by Boom Boom appear all the more spectacular. And the nicknames gave the players another dimension, making them appear instantly familiar and likable. For Sloppy was actually Hollis and

Boom Boom was really Walter, as was Rabbit. Curly was Manuel, Buzz was Ralph, Watty was William, Rube was Raymond, Lefty was Francis, Whitey was Harold, Chick was Wilson, Pea Ridge was Clyde, Frenchy was Stanley, Ownie was Owen, and Jigger was Arnold. Even Dazzy was only really Clarence.

What baseball fan of sound mind and body would ever choose to root for Hollis and Clyde and Clarence when offered the option of cheering for Sloppy and Pea Ridge and Dazzy?

Besides, on the Dodgers even the players who used their real names were colorful enough. Consider, for instance, that pitcher Van Lingle Mungo was always known by his given name.

Perhaps he should have been nicknamed Bill.

Queens expatriate. In Manhattan, the Bronx, Westchester, and New Jersey, the Robins scarcely registered on the meter, and there was no way they could even begin to spend as much as their nearest rivals.

Moreover, in the years after their performance in the 1920 World Series Brooklyn fans began to experience a pronounced fatalism concerning their club. As the Yankees and Giants took turns winning championships, Brooklyn's fans would soon learn not to expect to win anymore—or, to some degree, not to care. For fans, the attraction became Ebbets Field—or rather, the atmosphere in and around Ebbets Field, where, as much as any player, the fans became the stars and the game simply a foil for their amusement.

The Robins peaked early in 1921. In late April they went on a winning streak that eventually stretched to eleven games, coming from behind no less than eight times. The streak culminated in a ninth-inning win over the Giants on May 2, when they scored two in the ninth to beat Carl Hubbell, 4–3. But there was already trouble.

They were not a good hitting team in an age when, increasingly, hitting was about all that mattered. Their margin was paper-thin, and when the Giants ended Brooklyn's streak on May 3 with a come-from-behind 3–2 win of their own and Al Mamaux and Jeff Pfeffer went down with injuries, Brooklyn was exposed. Pitching depth—and the slugging of Zack Wheat—had been their only strength.

Ebbets and Robinson tried to shake things up with a few trades, but Brooklyn didn't have much to offer, and most deals were relatively even swaps or for players on the margin of the big leagues, such as their cash purchase of Cubs pitcher Abraham Lincoln "Sweetbreads" Bailey. He was terrible and appeared in only seven games for Brooklyn, his last in the major leagues, but he had a great name. Over the next decade or so, it would often appear as if Brooklyn acquired players solely because of their offbeat monikers—no team, ever, would have a lineup of names as colorful as those of Brooklyn in the 1920s and 1930s.

All the elements for a long decline were in place—aging players, an unresponsive front office, a manager who appeared stuck in an earlier era, and a fan base that seemed content with the status quo. And then there was the press.

The *Brooklyn Eagle,* the largest daily paper in Brooklyn, was the de facto voice of the ballclub. Beat man Tommy Rice wrote in an entertaining, florid, and overtly urbane style—he often led readers through an extended and verbose preamble before letting them know who had won the game. Rice's in-game descriptions, by the time he got around to them, were precise. But he did not view the club critically. To this point the newspaper was a booster: in love with Uncle Robbie, ever-respectful of Ebbets—whom it referred to as the "Squire of Flatbush"—and submissive before the powerful McKeevers. As the club deteriorated over the next few decades, the *Eagle,* as much as any other factor, would share responsibility for its decline, for the paper shaped public opinion in regard to the team. Wins and losses simply would never be as important in Brooklyn because everyone already knew, in their hearts, that Brooklyn had fallen behind the rest of New York. It was still a fabulous place, and much beloved by residents, but Brooklyn's aspirations as a place were as well defined as its borders. Just as the traffic on the bridge flowed in only one direction, so too did expectations for the ballclub. To criticize them or hold them to the higher standard set by the Giants and Yankees was, in a sense, to admit to Brooklyn's shortcomings. To ignore the final score and exalt in the character of the team and its personality was to celebrate the same about Brooklyn.

What success the club had over the next few seasons would be almost accidental. In fact, most of that success was due almost entirely to their purely accidental acquisition of the greatest pitcher in franchise history before Sandy Koufax—Clarence Arthur "Dazzy" Vance.

Vance, a native of Orient, Iowa, acquired his nickname from a neighbor who referred to all things great and grand—like his shotgun—as a "dazzy." Vance, a red-haired, florid-faced right-hander with a potent fastball and a devastating curve, got a late start in professional baseball, making his first appearance with Red Cloud in the Nebraska State League at age 21 in 1912. For the next ten years he bounced around the minor leagues, enthralling teams with his potential but constantly battling arm woes. In three major league trials—with Pittsburgh and the Yankees—he was horrible.

Then luck came to the fun-loving Vance. While playing poker, he banged his elbow on a table and injured it. A doctor then performed modest surgery that miraculously cured his arm. Then, while pitching for New Orleans in the Southern League at age 31 in 1921, Vance pitched every *fifth* day as opposed the then-standard four.

The combined result improved his control, gave new life to his fastball, and allowed him to pitch without breaking down. He won 21 games and for the first time became known as something of a strikeout artist.

Spitball artist Burleigh Grimes won 20 or more games for the Dodgers four times, including the 1920 pennant-winning season, when he won 23 games and led the league in winning percentage at .676.

Reluctantly, after scout Larry Sutton gave his recommendation, Ebbets bought the cow. Vance was invited to Clearwater for spring training as a 31-year-old rookie—albeit one whose right arm, following surgery, felt 21.

From the start, he was equal to or better than any pitcher on the team, and his flamboyant style quickly made him a fan favorite. Vance used an exaggerated wind-up, with a high leg kick, and shredded the fabric of his right sleeve to distract the hitters. Although that move was eventually outlawed, in combination Vance looked nothing like a major league pitcher until the ball exploded from his hand. He had always known how to pitch, surviving for years on guile, but now he had the pitches to put his methods into practice and would throw any pitch at any time.

Still, the result in 1922 was a rather typical Robinson club that featured good pitching—Vance led the league in strikeouts and won 18 games, while Grimes added 17 and Dutch Ruether 21—Zack Wheat, and little else. The club finished fifth behind the world champion Giants—who beat the Yankees in the World Series—then slid to sixth in 1923 as the Yankees defeated New York for their first title. The Robins' attack was even weaker than usual, for Wheat missed several months with an injury that not even the addition of first baseman Jack Fournier, who hit 22 home runs and batted .351, could offset.

The club was quickly becoming the laughingstock of the league, for Robinson, growing older and taking on more responsibility as Ebbets's health failed, was overwhelmed. Columnist Westbrook Pegler dubbed the club "the Daffiness Boys," and increasingly Robinson led the parade of daffiness. Baseball historian Harold Seymour, who served as the club's batboy for a time in the mid-1920s, later recalled that in the middle of a game it was not uncommon for Robbie to argue strategy with fans. The manager created a sort of kangaroo court known as "the Bonehead Club," in which players had to pay fines for making stupid plays, and then became its first member when he turned in an incorrect lineup card. His growing reputation for ineptitude wasn't helped in the spring of 1923 when the club traveled from Clearwater to Lakeland for a spring contest with the Indians, only to find the ballpark empty and the Indians relaxing at their hotel. Robinson and his chagrined team were a day early.

All of which made the club's performance in 1924 all the more surprising. For much of the year the club dog-paddled along a few games above .500. The Giants took command in

But it didn't matter. At his age, Vance was still viewed as just another big league failure, a career minor league pitcher like hundreds of others talented enough to eke out a living on the margins, the kind of guy who was the reason *The Sporting News* still ran classified ads from minor league teams seeking players. Vance was a dime-a-dozen guy who was absolutely interchangeable with dozens of veteran hurlers. He often bragged that there wasn't a team in baseball that didn't include at least three players he already knew from his earlier travels. He would always have a job but had done nothing to set himself apart.

Not even Brooklyn wanted him, although they were interested in his catcher, Hank DeBerry. When they approached New Orleans and asked about DeBerry, New Orleans balked at selling the catcher unless Brooklyn took Vance as well. There was nothing odd about the request. Minor league teams made money selling players, and they did so by any means available. Sometimes you did have to buy the whole cow just to get the cream.

Clarence Arthur "Dazzy" Vance pitched his first full major league season at the advanced age of 31 in 1922. Two seasons later he enjoyed perhaps the greatest season of any Dodger pitcher in the 20th century when he led the league in wins (28–6), ERA (2.16), complete games (30), and strikeouts (262).

June, and as late as August 9 the fourth-place club trailed New York by 13½ games and seemed headed to their accustomed finish in the second division.

But at this precise moment a fortuitous schedule quirk allowed destiny and the right arm of Dazzy Vance to take over. The club won three straight and then had two off-days. Vance pitched out of turn, squeezed in an extra start, and won, running the streak to four games before Burleigh Grimes lost to the Reds. That was followed by a six-game streak as spitballer Bill Doak, a former 20-game winner picked up from St. Louis in June, suddenly started pitching well, as did journeyman Rube Erhardt, giving the club a more than two-man staff for the first time all year. Suddenly it was 1920—and 1916—all over again.

The run coincided with the Giants' worst stretch of baseball since May, and in only ten days the Robins had pulled into third and cut the Giants' lead to seven and a half. That margin held when the Giants came to Ebbets Field for a three-game set on August 29 looking to bury the Dodgers.

But once again the schedule favored Brooklyn. After their road trip they enjoyed two days off, allowing Vance to open the series with an extra day of rest under his belt.

He was pitching better than at any time in his life. Already 22–4 and the winner of 10 in a row, Vance was coming off a 15-strikeout performance that had led Tommy Rice to ask whether he was faster than the great Walter Johnson of the Senators. While Rice opined that both Johnson and Cy Young threw harder, Hank DeBerry, who had hit against Johnson, claimed that Dazzy was his equal. Still, no one, not even the eternally optimistic Rice, expected the Robins to top the Giants. "They can hardly hope to pass the Giants at this stage," he wrote, for New York had beaten Brooklyn in 8 of 12 tries already.

All hope seemed to leave Brooklyn in the first when Frankie Frisch smashed a ball off Vance's hand. With his pitcher doubled over in pain, Robinson told Dutch Ruether to warm up. But Vance demanded to stay in the game and struck out eight in beating the Giants 3–1. Doak and then Grimes followed with wins, and suddenly the lead was down to four and a half games, with a month left to play.

Then came perhaps the most remarkable four days in franchise history. Because of bad weather earlier in the year, three consecutive doubleheaders against the seventh-place Phillies had been scheduled in Philadelphia beginning on September 1, followed by another in Boston. Robinson went for broke and pitched Vance twice during the string. Brooklyn won all 8 games as Vance ran his personal streak to 12 and the club won its 13th contest in a row.

Bill Doak beat Boston 1–0 on September 6 for Brooklyn's 15th straight victory, and Tommy Rice later wrote, "At 4:00 P.M., Saturday September 6, 1924, those Brooklyn Superbas led the National League. At 7 P.M. those said Superbas were third in the National League. 'Twas better to have led then lost than never led at all." In game two pitcher Art Decatur threw the game away with a tenth-inning error, and Brooklyn dropped behind both the Giants and Pittsburgh. Shakespeare, after all, is the master tragedian.

And in the Globe Theater that was Ebbets Field, the mob was living and dying. The Giants came in on September 7 with the season at stake. In a raucous contest, Brooklyn heavily oversold the ballpark, distributing at least 30,000 tickets. As ticket-holders tried to press into the park in which there was no more room, they were joined by some 6,000 gate-crashers, who used a telephone pole to pry the iron gates from their hinges and then pushed into the park, trampling the unfortunate in their path, injuring dozens, and sending at least one young boy to the hospital with a fractured skull.

It was madness on and off the field as the throng heaved back and forth in the stands and spilled into the outfield as hardly a single spectator watched the game from the seat he was supposed to be in. Umpire Bill Klem and his crew were stuck outside and needed a police escort to reach the field. And then, once the game started, pitchers Burleigh Grimes and Jake Beckley of the Giants were battered inside the ropes like heavyweights as 11 ground-rule doubles were called on balls lost in the crowd and Grimes, as best he could, scattered an incredible 17 hits. He could have won too, but when Brooklyn shortstop Johnny Mitchell made a critical error in the seventh that led to five New York runs, the opportunity was lost.

Although Brooklyn would come back to beat the Giants in the next two games as Vance won his 13th in a row on the way to 15 straight, in the end the pennant was lost on September 7, when the McKeevers blamed the police for the mess that happened that day and the police blamed the McKeevers. Still, the club held on until the next-to-last day of the season, only to finish second, 92–62, one and a half games behind — as always — the Giants.

Somehow that day served to turn a page in the history of the franchise: just as it marked the turning point of the 1924 season, so too would the 1924 season serve as a similar ful-

Contractor and part owner Ed McKeever passed away only eleven days after the death of Charles Ebbets on April 18, 1925.

crum for the fortunes of the team. Perhaps, for all his faults, it had been Ebbets who had held the team together, the stubborn force of his will taking what was essentially a 19th-century franchise fully one-quarter of the way into the next century and making it seem possible that one day they might win it all. At least when he was alive it was clear that Robinson managed the team, Ebbets paid the bills, and the McKeevers took care of the ballpark. But when Ebbets died, so did the clarity of those roles, and with it the possibility that in spite of everything the team might just win anyway.

Ebbets had been hampered by heart problems for years; over the last few years the McKeevers had been trying to get him to retire, but Ebbets wouldn't have it. In the fall of 1924, as a rumor circulated that he was about to step down, Ebbets told the press, "I am in baseball till I die." Then, as usual, he fought his players hard over contracts for the upcoming season. Bill Doak wanted to be rewarded for his performance in

1924, but he and Ebbets were $1,000 apart. Neither man budged, and Doak ended up sitting out the season and selling real estate in Florida.

Which is exactly what Ebbets was buying. When he arrived in Clearwater for spring training in the spring of 1925, he thought nothing of dropping a quarter of a million dollars on a land deal to build a hotel, then fell ill. Eschewing his Brooklyn home, he returned to his hotel suite at Manhattan's Waldorf Astoria, where he was too weak to leave his bed.

Brooklyn opened the season, and no one thought they had a chance at the pennant. Doak's replacement, a rookie named Jess Rush who was described as sporting "an elongated India rubber neck" and "the stately grace peculiar to a giraffe," lasted all of two starts.

Ebbets didn't make it through the first week of the season. He died on April 18 of heart disease.

The funeral on April 22 at Brooklyn's Church of the Holy Trinity was huge. Brooklyn fans crowded the sidewalks outside the service and stood on ledges to glimpse his casket as it left the church. The National League wanted to cancel all games that day but was dissuaded by the Ebbets family. Instead, the flags at NL ballparks were lowered to half-staff for a month, and the Robins wore mourning bands on their sleeves. Ebbets was buried in Brooklyn, at Greenwood Cemetery, also the final resting place of Henry Chadwick.

Sixty-six-year-old Ed McKeever took over as club president, but he wasn't well either. Almost immediately he contracted the flu, and only 11 days after Ebbets's death he too passed away. Brother Steve became president, pending a meeting of team shareholders in May.

Steve McKeever wanted to stay on, but the club's convoluted ownership structure, which after the deaths of Ebbets and Ed McKeever spread the shares between a number of heirs, was suddenly both unwieldy and unpredictable. The Ebbets faction feared that the McKeever backers would dump Robinson, while the McKeever faction feared that the manager — whom they were beginning to loathe and who, in Ebbets's absence, they would blame for the team's on-field problems and rapid tumble at the gate in 1925 — would receive a virtual lifetime contract. And then there were elements of each group that simply wanted to cash in and sell the team.

The proceedings took on the air of a bloodless coup d'état. When the shareholders met in May, McKeever was certain he would be named club president, and equally certain he would soon replace Robinson with his own man. But he didn't control enough votes, and the Ebbets faction remained loyal to the past. They handed the presidency to Uncle Robbie, who they were convinced would run the club in a business-as-usual fashion, which included staying on as manager, sort of.

McKeever was livid. After all, it was his money that had bailed out the team, built Ebbets Field, and enabled Ebbets to stay afloat, largesse that eventually made Ebbets a millionaire and proved to be lucrative for all parties. And now he was being passed over in favor of a bumbling manager who'd blown two World Series and hadn't even shown he could get his team to the park on time. Yet there was little McKeever could do — for now.

Robinson was thrilled with his promotion, owing in no small part to the way it made him look. Hell, not even John McGraw was a team president. Damn few managers were.

That was because damn few managers could be, or even cared to be, for the two jobs were antithetical. Even Connie Mack, who owned and managed the A's from their inception in 1901, didn't take over the club presidency until 1937. And even as Robinson attempted to fill both posts, Cardinals manager Branch Rickey, who also served as the club's business manager, had realized he couldn't serve two masters and resigned his bench post.

The contradiction in the two positions was obvious. How could Robinson, as club president, negotiate a contract with a player one day, arguing his salary down, and then expect the player to do his best the next? There was a reason club leadership had evolved into two posts, just as there is a reason today it has evolved into at least three, with the addition of a general manager.

At first Robinson seemed to sense that the job was too big for him. He named Zack Wheat "assistant manager" and traded in his jersey and seat on the bench for a suit and a seat in the stands. But he never told Wheat precisely what, as assistant manager, he was supposed to do.

Almost from the first day Robinson kept dictating what was happening on the field, first by making suggestions in regard to the lineup, then by offering in-game strategic suggestions, and finally by moving down from the stands and back to the bench, where he put the uniform back on and resumed his old role. As he did, all baseball began to laugh — first at Robinson and then, increasingly, at his players as they began to run roughshod over their beleaguered leader and under his watch the club accumulated an increasingly bizarre cast of characters.

The Robins could hit in 1925, but apart from Vance, who won 22, no one could pitch, not even Grimes, whose ERA ballooned to over 5.00 as he lost command of the spitter and the club fell to sixth, a horrific 68–85. Vance provided the high point as the club played out the string, no-hitting Philadelphia on September 13.

But even that achievement was not without an element of the bizarre, for in his previous start, also against Philadelphia, Vance had spun a one-hitter, giving up only a second-inning single to the one and only Nelson "Chicken" Hawks. On this day Vance managed to hold Hawks hitless too but lost his shutout when the batter lofted a fly to left that Jimmy Johnston misplayed, allowing Hawks to make third and score on a fly ball as Brooklyn won 10–1.

The decay that began in 1925 ossified in 1926 as the Robinson-McKeever rift deepened. Robinson tried to rebuild in the off-season but ended up adding mostly hard-drinking,

---

Dodger executive Steve McKeever also became an adversary of Wilbert Robinson. After a verbal feud in 1926, the two men refused to speak to one another.

all-but-washed-up veterans like Rabbit Maranville. He joined the fun-loving Brooklyn crew, which, headed by the untouchable Vance, called itself the "Four-for-Oh" club — a convoluted reference to the 0-for-4 a hitter was bound to collect after a night on the town with the crew, when they could often be heard pledging to one another, "All for one and four-for-oh." The only player of value Robinson added to the mix was minor league slugger Babe Herman, whose prowess at the plate was matched only by his ineptitude in the field. His reputation — and by extension that of Robinson and the entire team — was made on August 15, 1926, as the Dodgers, who had nominally been in the pennant race, faded.

They were the "Dodgers" again — and more or less forevermore — even as the *Eagle* clung to the "Superbas" or "Robins" for a few more seasons. Earlier in the year Uncle Wilbert had taken offense at a caption in a *New York Sun* cartoon that he believed questioned his business acumen. The president-manager complained to the *Sun*, and editor Joe Vila responded by dropping coverage of Brooklyn road games and banning the mention of Robinson's name or even the nickname "Robins" in the *Sun*. Vila chose to use instead the old "Dodger" nickname, a moniker that in fact had been occasionally used along with "the Robins" and "the Superbas" for years. In time other papers would follow suit.

The incident was also the last straw between Steve McKeever and Robinson. When McKeever complained that Robinson's snit had cost the team valuable coverage by the *Sun*, the manager reportedly told him to "mind your own business," to which McKeever replied that the ballclub was in fact "*his* business." The two stopped talking, a situation that did nothing to improve the fortunes of the club.

And after the events of August 15, it was clear that they needed help. What began innocently enough as a rare Dodger rally became instead a lasting emblem of the futility of their chances.

Babe Herman came to bat against Boston with one out and the bases loaded — Hank DeBerry on third, Dazzy Vance on second, and Chick Fewster on first — and drove a line drive to right.

The ball looked as if it might be caught, and the runners hesitated until it rattled off the wall. Herman steamed into second and slid in safe just before the throw, then heard the second baseman yelling for the shortstop to throw home. Herman assumed that Fewster was ahead of him and that both DeBerry and Vance had already scored.

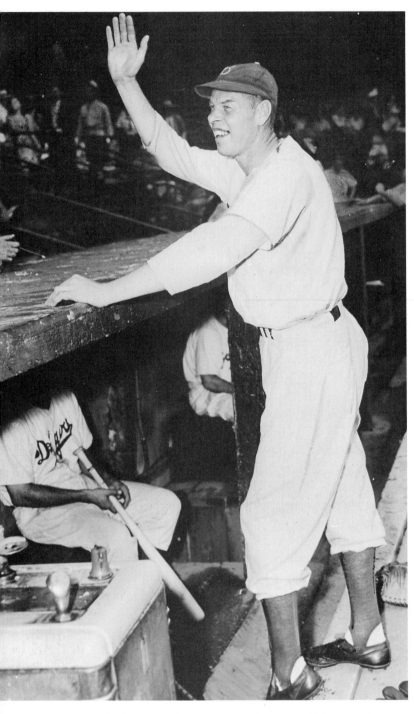

Floyd Caves "Babe" Herman was the greatest hitting talent in Dodger history. His poor fielding is the subject of countless anecdotes, yet he achieved back-to-back single-season batting averages of .381 and .393 in 1929 and 1930. He never won a National League batting crown, however, despite his .339 career batting average in seven years with Brooklyn.

The throw went home, and as it did, Herman lit out for third. Only it wasn't Fewster dashing between third and home — it was Vance, who had gotten such a late start that now he was afraid he'd be put out and was headed back to third.

But that was where Chick Fewster was. He saw Vance coming and started to backtrack to second, whereupon Herman, oblivious and, in a sense, blameless — for by all rights Vance should have scored — slid past him.

That put three players — Vance, Herman, and Fewster — more or less at the same place at the same time, in contradiction of not only the laws of physics but the laws of baseball. The Daffiness Boys were not confined by rules of any kind, however, including those both immutable and universal.

Confusion reigned. With some hesitation, the umpire correctly called Herman out for passing Fewster as Vance arrived back at third and piped in, "I'm safe!" He was, for the base was rightfully his. Meanwhile, a befuddled Fewster assumed that he was out and the inning was over. He wasn't, but he needed to be on some base, and although second base was available, he wasn't about to go back. As he wandered away, Boston shortstop Doc Gatreau was the only player on the field who clearly knew what was happening. He grabbed the ball from the third baseman and tagged Fewster. *Now* he was out, and the umpire told him so.

Deadpanned Fewster, "I thought I was out five minutes ago."

Somewhat inexplicably, Herman was blamed for the gaffe, which sportswriters incorrectly referred to as "tripling into a double play," even though the hit was scored a double. If fault could be assigned to anyone, it properly belonged to Vance. And for the record, Herman's hit caused no lasting damage — except to his reputation — for it knocked in the winning run of the game.

Over the next few years the Dodgers led the league — in fact all baseball — in virtually no significant statistical category but the anecdote, playing the not always unwilling straight man to just about any misadventure or antic the game of baseball could offer. They were not unlike the New York Mets of a later era, minus the excuse of expansion and the utter futility on the field.

For three seasons running they finished sixth even as Herman established himself as one of the league's best hitters (as opposed to best players, which he was not), Vance continued to dazzle every fifth day, and, too late, the club adopted the power game best seen on display in Yankee Stadium as players like outfielder Johnny Frederick and Del Bissonette added the occasional home run to the Dodger arsenal.

Not that anyone noticed much outside of Brooklyn, for in the Bronx the Yankees of Ruth and Gehrig reigned supreme, while the Giants, with stars like Bill Terry, Mel Ott, and Carl Hubbell, kept the Dodgers soundly in third. Attendance lingered several hundred thousand fans behind the throngs at Yankee Stadium and the Polo Grounds as Robinson, overmatched in his role, stocked the club with a revolving door of aging veterans. Wheat, his legs gone, was released in 1926, and Grimes was traded to the Phillies, who promptly shipped him over to the hated Giants.

The off-field battle between Robinson and McKeever was usually more compelling than the pennant race anyway. Steve McKeever wanted Robinson replaced, but the club president had both the title and the votes and refused to step down. The Dodger hierarchy at the time included four voting directors — Robinson and Joe Gilleaudeau, the husband of Ebbets's daughter Genevieve, on one side, and McKeever and club legal eagle Ed York on the other. All votes ended in ties and, as was baseball custom, all ties went to the runner, which meant Robinson stayed. In retribution, McKeever tried to starve him out, refusing to spend money on players. By 1928 the Dodger scouting "staff" was a party of two.

In Brooklyn fans watched the conflict with more bemusement than anger, but organized baseball took another view: the open trench warfare, which gave the team little chance to win, was embarrassing and undercut the integrity of the league.

In February 1930, baseball commissioner Judge Kenesaw Mountain Landis decided to step in: he brokered a deal that rewarded Robinson with another two-year contract as manager if he agreed to give up the club presidency. The presidency went to York, a not very dynamic personality described as a "soft wind blowing through the office." McKeever remained treasurer, and Landis installed a fifth director, Dutch Carter, a politically connected Brooklyn resident, to ensure the end of the voting deadlock in the front office.

Freed of his desk responsibilities, Robinson went back to what he did best in 1930, and to the surprise of everyone, the Dodgers once again contended for the pennant, riding a big winning streak in May and June into first place. Herman was the key: after hitting .381 in 1929, he was even better in 1930, lifting his average to .393.

But Herman alone was not enough, and despite spending a total of 75 days in first place, the Dodgers lacked depth. In September it cost them.

The Giants, Cubs, Cardinals, and Dodgers all entered September in the thick of the race. But as the Dodgers shut out Chicago 6–0 on September 11, outfielder Rube Bressler broke his finger making a diving catch of a drive by Hack Wilson. Two days later Johnny Frederick made what Tommy Holmes of the *Eagle* called "the most spectacular catch this reporter

Former Red Sox pitcher turned outfielder Frank "Lefty" O'Doul led the National League in batting average twice in his 11-year career, with his second title coming with Brooklyn in 1932 when he hit .368.

1917

has ever witnessed," going parallel to stab a line drive by the Reds' Leo Durocher, but as he made his leap he tore a thigh muscle.

The club held it together for a few more days, teasing the Flatbush fans by moving into first place with a win over the Reds, their 11th straight. Brooklyn was beside itself as club attendance breached the one million mark for the first time and applications for World Series tickets topped 50,000, a pleasant quandary for a club that was allowed to sell only 28,000 tickets per game. Even Holmes admitted that Ebbets Field was "woefully inadequate" and blamed the "doughty old baron of Maple Street," McKeever, for not adding seats to the park. The treasurer responded by making plans to add 500 temporary bleachers in center field for the Series.

But the effort to get to first seemed to exhaust the club. The Cardinals were the hot team down the stretch, despite the temporary loss of hard-drinking pitcher Flint Rhem. Scheduled to pitch against Brooklyn on September 17, he claimed that on the previous day he had been abducted by "Brooklyn gangsters" from in front of the Alamac Hotel. The kidnappers then told him, "We're going to get you drunk so you won't be able to pitch against our Robins." He claimed he was taken to a "log cabin" where his keepers forced liquor down his throat.

The "kidnappers," of course, proved to be Rhem's own thirst, and the log cabin a Manhattan gin joint. By the time he sobered up, the Cardinals had swept into first place anyway. The Dodgers faded to fourth, six games out.

Instead of heralding a new age for the team, 1931 proved to be a tease, although McKeever did break ground on a small expansion of Ebbets Field: he tore down the left-field bleachers and began a two-year project to wrap the grandstand around the corner. But the glow of 1930 didn't last. In the off-season the club made a series of trades without Robinson's okay, undercutting his authority, and on Opening Day of 1931 Robinson lost track of the batting order. The club then dropped its first five on its way to a quiet fourth-place finish. That season too the Depression took hold in Brooklyn, cutting attendance by nearly 300,000 and leaving the new seats unneeded and unfilled. While the expansion was long over-

His lyrical name inspired one of the great sports-related jazz ballads, and in 11 years with the Dodgers right-hander Van Lingle Mungo won 109 games with 1,031 strikeouts. His best season was 1934, when he went 18–16 and led the league with 38 starts.

due, it took place at the wrong time, for it left the club cash-starved at the worst possible moment. After years of profitability, if not profligacy, the club wouldn't turn another profit for almost a decade.

It was a foregone conclusion that, at age 67, Robinson would be let go at the end of the 1931 season, and on October 31 he was replaced by former infielder and coach Max Carey. Robbie went quietly after 18 years, his legacy a team that was beloved not for their play but for the way they played. Still, in the long run even this long-overdue move was not a step forward but only a shift to the side, for Robinson's removal had been plan A on McKeever's agenda for so long that he had completely ignored what came next. There was no plan B.

Over the next few seasons the Dodgers simply faded to gray; as the Daffiness Boys grew old, they were not very good and not even very colorful. On January 23, 1932, the Brooklyn chapter of the Base Ball Writers' Association of America provided definitive evidence of the end of an era when it met to select, officially, the team nickname. A week earlier McKeever and company had let the writers know that since the unofficial "Robins" was no longer appropriate, they would agree to any name the writers came up with.

"Dodgers" was the obvious choice, since it had been in widespread use for years. But it was not the only name under consideration. According to the *Eagle*'s Tommy Holmes, some writers favored a brand-new name altogether — the "Kings," a reference to Kings County, whose borders were identical with Brooklyn's. In the end, however, "Dodgers" won in a landslide. As the *Eagle*'s Ed Hughes accurately noted a short time later, "It is the only nickname in the National League that is in some way attached to the native character and traits . . . it is authentic, drawn from life." So too were the Dodgers, warts and all.

The team was changing fast. Pitcher Dolf Luque and outfielder Rube Bressler were released in 1932, and Babe Herman — arguably the best Dodger hitter to that time — was dealt to Cincinnati. Many Brooklyn fans never forgave Carey for trading the club's most popular player, and a year later he may have sealed his fate when 42-year-old Dazzy Vance, hampered by sciatica, was traded to St. Louis. Although he would return as a reliever a year later, it wasn't the same as before.

Carey lasted two disappointing seasons and had little impact apart from squandering some thousands on questionable trades, such as his 1932 purchase of fading slugger Hack Wilson from the Cubs for $45,000. Although Wilson had been a great hitter and held the RBI record of 190 for a

season, what the press referred to as his "sorrow drowning antics" — alcohol — cut his career short, and he would leave little mark in Brooklyn.

By 1934 the Dodgers were an afterthought. In a famous incident in the winter of 1934, *New York Times* baseball writer Ross McGowan asked Giants manager Bill Terry, who had led the Giants to a world championship in his first season after taking over for John McGraw, what he thought about the Dodgers.

"Brooklyn?" quipped Terry. "Is Brooklyn still in the league?"

The words stung. The Dodgers had just hired a general manager, Bob Quinn, who in the 1920s had run the Red Sox into the ground. He wanted the league to take action against Terry, which only reinforced the notion that the Giants manager was right and gave his comment greater play. Quinn then decided to shake things up and fired Carey. His choice as manager was Casey Stengel, who had served the past two seasons as a Dodgers coach.

While Stengel was still nearly 20 years shy of becoming a genius, he had his personality down pat. And the press loved him. He knew what he wanted to do, for he had been taught baseball by McGraw and Robinson, but he simply didn't have the players. As he said shortly after arriving, "The pitching staff isn't as bad as it appears; it only seems that way." He could have said the same about the team, but they still weren't very good.

The highlight of his reign came early, at the end of the 1934 season. The Giants, in a pitched battle with the surging Cardinals for the pennant, needed only two wins over the Dodgers in the final two games of the season to clinch the crown. They were already thinking of the World Series. After all, they'd gone a stellar 14–6 against Brooklyn.

But Terry's comments earlier in the year incited Dodger partisans to make a raucous trek to the Polo Grounds, leading one paper to note that "most of the fans seemed pro-Brooklyn." And if there was anything Stengel knew how to do, it was play to the crowds.

The Dodgers won the first game 5–1 as Van Lingle Mungo outpitched Roy Parmelee to dump the Giants into a tie for first. Both teams then pulled out all the stops in the finale.

As the Giants watched the scoreboard and saw that the Cardinals had moved ahead of Cincinnati, the Dodgers turned bold. They scratched back from a 4–0 first-inning deficit to tie the score off Freddie Fitzsimmons in the eighth.

When they did, three Brooklyn fans raced through the stands, one ringing a cowbell, one tooting an automobile horn, and a third holding up a placard that read: YEP, BROOKLYN IS STILL IN THE LEAGUE.

The game entered the tenth, and the desperate Terry called on both staff aces, Hal Schumacher and then Carl Hubbell, to try to stop the Dodger tide. Neither could, and Brooklyn swept to an 8–5 victory while the Giants ran off the field in second place. Said Stengel afterward, "The Giants thought we gave 'em a beating Saturday and yesterday. Well, they were right. But I'm still sorry for them when I think of the beating they still have to take. Wait until those wives realize they're not going to get those new fur coats. I've been through it and I know." As a side benefit, the win sent Dazzy Vance, now a member of the Cardinals, to his first and only World Series.

But no collection of quips could save the Dodgers over the next few seasons. The Depression, inside and out of Ebbets Field, was killing the team. The front office, content to preserve its own fortune, watched with apparent disinterest as the club lost both at the gate and in the field. Although radio broadcasts were all the rage in baseball, expanding major league markets dramatically, the Dodgers foolishly entered into a five-year agreement with the Giants and Yankees *not* to broadcast their games, ensuring their market would remain moribund.

Such was the state of their decay that aging Steve McKeever had withdrawn from the board of directors and put his son-in-law, Joe Mulvay, in his place, leaving the club in the hands of Mulvay, Ebbets's son-in-law Joe Gilleaudeau, and a local banker, Harry DeMott, brought on board to watch over the bad investments of his bank.

Each member was preoccupied with his own affairs, and none was particularly eager to do much more than tinker with the edges of the Dodgers and hope they'd lose money at a slower rate. Attendance lingered below 500,000, and the team's indebtedness — all acquired since 1930 — approached one million Depression-era dollars. Business manager Joe Gorman was widely viewed as the man actually running the club. Although he had no authority to do so, he even made trades without Stengel's approval, usually to save money.

The rest of the National League was growing impatient. Brooklyn's indifference hurt everyone, for the Dodgers were an even worse draw on the road than in Brooklyn. After Stengel finished seventh in 1936, he was canned, a move widely seen, as one paper reported it, as "a sacrificial goat to the baseball wolves." Rough-and-tough Burleigh Grimes was named his successor.

Grimes could do no more with what he had than Stengel, apart from doing so with fewer laughs and distractions. In 1937 the Dodgers finished sixth again.

A cartoon in the *Eagle* summed up the state of the team. It shows "Doc Rooter" hovering over a prostrate, uniformed player identified as "Old Play-Boy Dodger."

"He's got enough front office slugs in him to kill an army," notes the Doc. And that was more than enough to kill off the fans too, even in Brooklyn.

But another cartoon would have a more lasting resonance. One afternoon after another Dodger loss in the desultory season of 1937, Willard Mullin, the Manhattan-based sports cartoonist for the *World-Telegram*, hailed a cab outside Ebbets Field. The cabby looked at him through the rearview mirror and asked, "Well, what'd dem bums do today?"

Dem bums. A picture formed in Mullin's mind and made its appearance in the paper the following day. Not of a Dodger player, the presumed bum of the question, but of a Brooklyn *fan*, a grizzled, cigar-chewing, potbellied bum in a tattered hat. Although often overlooked, Mullin's rendering turns the table on the question completely, for it focuses on the futility not on the field but off it, on the Depression-afflicted few who still bothered to turn out at Ebbets Field.

The adoption of the figure as a Dodger term of endearment and even a sign of pride over the next few seasons would prove to be a measure of progress.

THE LIGHT OF DAY

BY THE END OF THE 1937 SEASON, THE DODGERS WERE AS MESSY AS THE character of Mullin's cartoon, a moribund franchise with little reason to exist apart from the momentum of its own offbeat history. But in less than a decade they would undergo one of the most remarkable transformations in baseball history, from a team still rooted in its 19th-century beginnings to the most forward-looking team in the game. The initial agent of change would be Larry MacPhail, a brash, bold, blowsy, abrasive, and mercurial front man unfettered by Dodger history — and even more important, unconcerned with it.

MacPhail was rare for the era — at that time most teams were owned and operated either by so-called gentlemen-sportsmen, well-heeled scions like Boston's Tom Yawkey who bought into baseball for the opportunity it gave them to consort with their heroes, or by long-time baseball families, like the Griffiths of Washington. The men they hired to run their little pastime were almost without exception stolid, solid "baseball men" who did things the way they had always been done. Change occurred at a glacial pace.

MacPhail was another animal, an ultraconfident business-man who was in baseball first and foremost for the money. While the rest of baseball had cowered before the Depression, MacPhail had thrived, giving him immediate credibility.

Batboys Sullivan (left) and Jackie Bodner get into the spirit of things prior to the start of the first-ever World Series game between the Yankees and Dodgers at Yankee Stadium on October 1, 1941.

The Michigan native had studied journalism and law before going into business with a Chicago retailer. He enlisted in the Army the day the United States entered World War I, became a captain, and in the first few confusing days after the Armistice hatched a plan with several other officers to kidnap Kaiser Wilhelm, who was hiding out in Holland, and bring him to justice. MacPhail almost pulled it off, reaching the library at Doorn before being discovered, then escaping with the kaiser's ashtray.

He returned to the Midwest, dabbled in baking and real estate, then went into the automobile business in the 1920s and made a fortune. When the Columbus Red Birds, the Cincinnati Reds' American Association farm club, almost went bust in the first years of the Depression, MacPhail bought the team, sold it to the Cardinals at a profit, then stayed on to run the club for Cardinal president Branch Rickey. In the midst of the Depression MacPhail turned a profit with the Red Birds and set an

Cartoonists have a way of creating national icons. Such was the case with the Republican elephant and the Democratic donkey, which sprang from the pen of the political cartoonist Thomas Nast. And so it was with the Brooklyn Bum, as drawn by famed *New York World-Telegram* sports cartoonist Willard Mullin. In time the franchise embraced the image of the unkempt underdog.

attendance record while others were going broke. In 1934 he was hired by Cincinnati to do the same thing for the Reds.

Given free rein, and plenty of cash after convincing Powell Crosby to buy the team from Sam Weil, MacPhail turned the franchise upside down, building a huge radio network through flagship station WLW, bringing night baseball to the major leagues, pioneering promotions, and goosing interest in the Reds. They were on their way, but Crosby thought MacPhail took too much credit and didn't show enough deference to the owner. MacPhail didn't, and while drunk — for "alcoholic" was another adjective usually attached to his name — he sent Crosby a haymaker. MacPhail had to "resign" in November 1936, but that only enhanced his reputation, for baseball has always had a place for productive drunks.

National League president Ford Frick was worried about Brooklyn, particularly because Steve McKeever and the others who ran the team seemed perfectly content to watch their drab little team muddle along. In early 1937 Frick first tried to talk them into hiring MacPhail, and after the disaster of that season, Joe Gorman, who had been elevated to the GM's job after Bob Quinn resigned, also quit. Frick and Brooklyn's debtors then more or less told the Dodgers they had to hire MacPhail. MacPhail hit the ground running, screaming, and scheming, giving orders before he had even signed a contract and intimidating the banks, to which the Dodgers already owed about a million dollars, into giving him even more credit, for his plan was to start from scratch and spend spend spend — on the ballpark, on the players, and on the front office and organization. He told friends, "I'm going to turn Brooklyn inside out, upside down, and win pennants every year." He signed a three-year contract as "executive vice president" on January 18, 1938, but from that instant no other titled Dodger employee had more influence than the batboy. Tommy Holmes called him "the first real boss the Brooklyn ballclub has had since that wet and chilly day in April of 1925 when Charles S. Ebbets was laid to rest in Greenwood Cemetery." Over the next few years MacPhail would cause Ebbets to roll over in that grave time and time again.

As MacPhail dispensed with the old and brought in the new, 1938 would prove to be a shakeout season. He dumped $200,000 into Ebbets Field, giving the park a much-needed makeover, for most maintenance had been put off for years; changed the Dodger colors from green to blue; hired new ushers and put them in spiffy uniforms; and to the relief of all, installed modern plumbing in the public bathrooms.

On the field change came just as fast. Of all the teams in baseball, the Dodgers were the team most stuck in an earlier era. Despite an inviting fence in right field, over the past two seasons they had hit a combined total of 70 home runs, baseball's worst. Meanwhile, the Yankees had hit 366. So on March 6, for almost $50,000 and a warm body, he bought Phillies first baseman Dolph Camilli, a left-handed dead pull hitter who over that same time period had hit 55 home runs all by himself. Steve McKeever died the next day and was eulogized by Ed Holmes as "the grand old man of Brooklyn baseball," for whom baseball had been a "hobby . . . to preserve a kindly lovable old man." MacPhail left such romance in the dust of activity.

By Opening Day the Dodger lineup was almost completely made over. The tone was set by shortstop Leo Durocher, a firebrand who'd been picked up in October in Gorman's last, and best, trade. Durocher wasn't much of a player, but at least he acted like he cared, using his mouth, which earned him the nickname "the Lip," and on occasion his fists.

The Dodgers were only nominally better, but they didn't have to be much more than that to get fans interested, for MacPhail kept everyone distracted by the constant bustle at the ballpark. You needed a scorecard to keep track.

After first saying he had no plans to add lights to Ebbets Field, he borrowed another $100,000-plus and installed lights, choosing to unveil the new feature on June 15.

The Dodgers were already assured of a good crowd that night, for Cincinnati pitcher Johnny Vander Meer was fresh off throwing a no-hitter. But no promotion was good enough for MacPhail, and he pulled out all the stops.

More than 38,000 fans crowded into Ebbets Field as more than 28,000 seats were sold after 5:00 P.M. Before the game, Olympic track star Jesse Owens gave a long-jump demonstration and then ran races against the Dodger players, losing to outfielder Ernie Koy, and Babe Ruth waved from the stands. And then, at 8:37, as the field began to dim in the twilight and the final strains of "The Star-Spangled Banner" echoed over Brooklyn, a firework was sent into the sky and 615 floodlights blazed. Vander Meer underscored the evening by throwing a second consecutive no-hitter, the first and only major league pitcher to do so. For the first time in years, the Dodgers were at baseball's center stage.

Only three days later MacPhail trumped himself. He hired Babe Ruth as a Dodger coach for the balance of the season for $15,000.

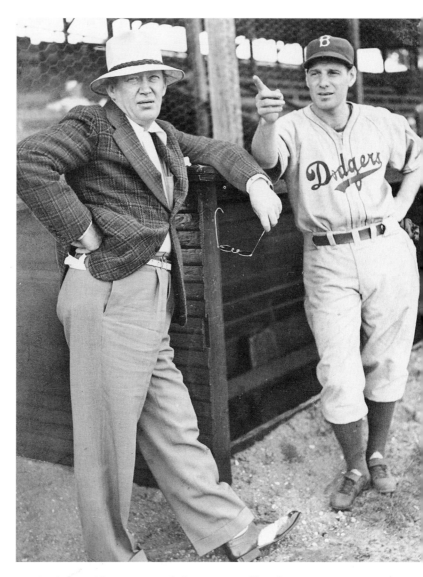

New Dodger president Larry MacPhail came to Brooklyn after an eclectic career as a soldier, auto dealer, and self-made baseball magnate with the Cincinnati Reds. He is shown here meeting with manager Leo Durocher at spring training in 1939.

The Bambino, into his fourth year of retirement, lusted after a managerial post, and there was some speculation that he was being brought in to eventually replace Grimes. Grimes didn't want Ruth around and hadn't even been asked his opinion. But Ruth's reputation for fun left no one willing to take a chance to see if baseball's greatest hitter could be even adequate as a manager. Although MacPhail bluntly told Ruth that his role would be to hit home runs in batting practice, Ruth clung to the false hope that he would take over.

First baseman Dolph Camilli (left) and second baseman Johnny Hudson at spring training in 1939. Before the club broke camp for Brooklyn, Camilli's facial hair was a distant memory.

As usual, MacPhail was right. Ruth boosted attendance, and after a semidisastrous trial as third base coach (he couldn't remember the signs), for the rest of the year he served primarily as a cheerleader from the dugout and a distraction from the Dodgers' place in the standings, which fluttered back and forth between their accustomed sixth and seventh place.

Nevertheless, despite finishing 69–80 and tied for sixth, with Camilli hitting 24 of Brooklyn's 61 home runs, attendance jumped by nearly 200,000 as MacPhail proved you didn't need a winning team to draw a crowd. That still left open the question of just how well a MacPhail team would draw if they did win, which neither the Reds nor the Dodgers had done under his watch. That was his next task.

Step number one was to fire Grimes. The pitching had been terrible in 1938, and while that was hardly Grimes's fault, it was another excuse among many, including his resistance to the hiring of Ruth as coach and an embarrassing charge that the manager had punched a 16-year-old kid in the stomach at Ebbets Field after he asked for an autograph. Besides, MacPhail already had the guy he wanted on board.

His name wasn't Babe Ruth. It was Leo Durocher, the fast-talking, fast-fielding infielder, resident tough guy, and darling of the press. Durocher hadn't been in MacPhail's plans at first, but when several others suggested he was right for the

job—including Grimes—MacPhail warmed to the idea of the fiery shortstop as manager.

After breaking in with the Yankees without particular distinction, Durocher had finally made his mark with the Cardinals in 1934 as the captain of the fun-loving and pennant-winning Gas House Gang. Slick-fielding, feisty holler guys like Durocher often become big league managers, for they leave the impression that guile, desire, and baseball acumen compensate for their lack of skill, a combination of qualities they are presumed capable of instilling in others; Billy Martin is perhaps the most pronounced example of the type. While few such managers have actually been able to endow their players with these qualities, Durocher could. And he could also match MacPhail's enthusiasm and energy, a not insignificant feat.

Not that the two necessarily got along, for both were strong-willed, stubborn, combative, prone to drinking too much, and even more prone to saying too much when they did. And Durocher never really trusted MacPhail, later saying of him, "There is that thin line between genius and insanity, and in

Larry's case it was sometimes so thin you could see it drifting back and forth." Durocher became adept at keeping his balance while toeing that constantly moving line.

MacPhail's second big move took place off the field. In Cincinnati radio broadcasts had been a huge part of the Reds' success, owing in no small part to broadcaster Red Barber, whose understated, homespun approach made baseball the perfect background music on languid summer afternoons. A fair amount of common baseball vernacular — "rhubarb" as a description of an argument, for example — was popularized from the lips of Barber.

Big league baseball on the radio had become a part of the American scene everywhere but in New York. There the Yankees and Giants had bullied the Dodgers into believing that radio would adversely affect attendance, and in 1933 the Dodgers had signed a five-year agreement to stay silent. That agreement expired at the end of the 1938 season, and the two other New York clubs naively expected MacPhail to sign an extension. MacPhail let them believe that was so, but in reality he was pulling out the rug.

Without radio, the Dodger market was in a geographic jail fixed by the borders of Brooklyn itself, for despite ready access by public transportation, few fans ever made their way down there from Manhattan. MacPhail knew that radio, by way of the neighborly Barber, could bring the Dodgers to the street and pull in the casual fan who couldn't always make it to the ballpark. The agreement had served the Yankees and Giants well, but it did nothing for the Dodgers. He got the foot in the door first, hiring Barber and convincing WOR to pay $77,000 to broadcast both home and away games (through re-creation). The result was a windfall of cash and publicity.

For the first time ever, the Dodgers began to chip away at the monolithic economic grip that the Yankees and Giants held over the city. Barber delivered the game in a new form, painting a romantic picture of quirky old Brooklyn and Ebbets Field, celebrating the poetry of neighborhoods like Flatbush, and giving voice to what was special about the Brooklyn team — its intimacy and emotional *sturm und drang*, spiced by players as colorful as the ballpark. His verbal vision worked its way into the American consciousness. Brooklyn wasn't a city, or even a borough, whatever that was. It was a place of people, of characters, and Ebbets Field was where the rest of the world saw them for the first time through Barber. He provided the words, and the mind's eye the picture. Although the Yankees and Giants would soon cave in and begin broadcasting games too, Barber — and MacPhail — had New York's ear.

Now all MacPhail needed was players. He'd seen the success that Rickey enjoyed in St. Louis by way of his far-reaching farm system, and MacPhail set out to do the same, even hiring Rickey's son, Branch Jr., to set things up. In the interim he combed the scrap heap.

The result in 1939 was a scrappy lineup anchored by Camilli and Durocher but filled out by role players like third baseman Cookie Lavagetto and outfielders Ernie Koy and Dixie Walker. While not immensely talented, these Dodgers were not unskilled; unlike the previous generation, they could run and catch. And the pitching staff was made up of a hodgepodge of veterans — Whit Wyatt, Hugh Casey, and Luke Hamlin, many of them receiving their first clear shot in the majors.

The Dodgers turned a corner in 1939, finishing with a rush to take third place — six games in front of the Giants — drawing nearly a million fans, making a profit of more than $100,000, delighting the banks, and giving MacPhail carte blanche to keep going. But MacPhail's greatest acquisition came to him purely by accident.

Harold "Pete" Reiser should be in the Hall of Fame, a member of the small pantheon of genuine "five-tool" players that begins with DiMaggio and includes only a few others, such as Willie Mays. Perhaps no player ever, not even Mickey Mantle, was ever possessed of such prodigious, precocious talent.

And the Cardinals knew it, for the tentacles of their farm system missed nothing, particularly in their own back yard, St. Louis. They'd been watching Reiser since *grade school*. When he showed up at a tryout camp at age 15, they became afraid some other team would spot him, so they moved fast.

Branch Rickey had built an enormously productive and profitable farm system for the Cardinals, stocking the club with talent, selling off his surplus for profit, and bending the rules to his advantage. While he was unquestionably a baseball genius and visionary, much of his success was due to his chutzpah, for he had created the Cardinal farm system by flouting the discreet gentlemen's agreements that were supposed to prevent him from building such an organization. Throughout his career he acted first and worried about the legality of those actions later. His own moral code was the only one that mattered.

He hired 15-year-old Reiser as a driver for scout Charley Barnett. Every time they visited a Cardinal farm club, Reiser worked out, and every time he did the local manager would

beg Barnett to let him stay. Hardly more than a boy, Reiser was already a better player than any of the hundreds of denizens of the lower reaches of the Cardinal system.

In 1937, still underage, Reiser played D-level baseball for several Cardinal farm clubs. Then baseball commissioner Judge Landis, in one of his last acts, stepped in.

He thought the Cardinals' talent monopoly was bad for baseball. Rickey's fast and loose methods finally caught up with him. Landis declared nearly one hundred Cardinal minor leaguers free agents. One of them was Reiser.

Rickey, however, always had a backup plan. Of those one hundred players, one was marked for greatness, and he knew that was Reiser. Rickey and MacPhail were still close, so the Cardinal pooh-bah asked MacPhail to sign Reiser, hide him in the low minors for a few years, and then sell him back to the Cards. MacPhail agreed—it was free money. Durocher, however, apparently knew nothing about the arrangement.

Reiser's talent glittered no matter where he played. After one impressive season playing for the Dodgers' Superior, Wisconsin, franchise in the Northern League, he received an invitation to spring training in 1939 to soak up big league atmosphere before he went back to the bushes.

Durocher couldn't help but notice him, and when the player-manager was knocked out of the lineup with a chest cold, he inserted Reiser into the lineup. Over a three-game stretch against the Cardinals, Reiser did everything but sell popcorn, reaching base 12 times in a row while cracking three home runs and drawing the attention of the press, who dubbed him "Pistol Pete," in reference to the sound the ball made coming off his bat. He was the talk of camp, obscure no more.

Then MacPhail got wind of the performance. Playing Reiser in front of reporters was hardly "hiding" him. He ordered Durocher to stop playing him, first by wire and then in person, leading to the first of several violent exchanges between the two men over the issue. But Reiser kept playing and in weeks became baseball's most sought-after prospect. The Yankees offered MacPhail a small fortune for him—$100,000 and five players.

At the end of camp MacPhail and Durocher got into another of their interminable rows when MacPhail insisted

---

The first night game at Ebbets Field on June 15, 1938, provided a dramatic setting for the second consecutive no-hitter tossed by Cincinnati Reds ace Johnny Vander Meer. The Reds won by a score of 6–0.

1891	Mike Griffin	36
1892	Dan Brouthers	33
1901	Tom Daly	38
1913	Red Smith	40
1929	Johnny Frederick	52
1941	Pete Reiser	39
1970	Wes Parker	47

tell them the Red Sox were accepting offers. But Boston's sudden rejection scared them all away.

By midsummer Reese had played his way back to top-prospect status, and now the offers poured in. Evans begged Cronin to take another look. He refused, and Evans pleaded with Yawkey to keep him, but by now Cronin felt threatened and he still had Yawkey's ear. The Dodgers bought Reese for $75,000 and five players. Durocher, unlike Cronin, knew his days as a starting shortstop were just about over.

MacPhail was his usual whirlwind in the off-season and the first few months of 1940, trading and buying players at a dizzying rate. He bolstered the outfield by adding Joe Vosmik from the Red Sox and, in a huge deal, acquired Durocher's old Cardinal teammate, 1937 Triple Crown winner Ducky Medwick, from the Cardinals for $125,000 and five players on June 12.

He overpaid for Medwick, but that was because of Reiser. The deal both placated Rickey and hid the payoff for the prospect.

The Dodgers were getting closer. With Reiser in the wings, Reese at short, and now Medwick to go along with Camilli and the others, the Dodgers and Reds shared first place into mid-June.

But Brooklyn had no margin for error. Only five days after Medwick was acquired, as the Dodgers played host to the Cardinals, St. Louis pitcher Bob Bowman beaned Medwick, knocking him out cold, sparking a fight on the field, and even sending an enraged MacPhail into the Dodger dugout looking for blood.

To Durocher, the bean ball was part of the game, an essential and effective strategy at that. Although in this case the Dodgers were the victim, Durocher's tenure as a big league manager was marked by bean-ball wars wherever he hung his hat. They helped his teams win a lot of games, but they also cost some guys their careers.

Medwick was never the same, going from great to simply very good. Later that year both Lavagetto and Reese also went down with injuries. Reiser, hitting .378 in Elmira, was brought up, but even he was too little too late. The Dodgers faded to second, and the Reds won the pennant by 12 games.

Both MacPhail and Durocher knew what they needed—more pitching, more depth, and better luck. For 1941 they got all three.

They first added pitcher Kirby Higbe, wasted in Philadelphia, then bought young catcher Mickey Owen from St.

that Reiser be sent back to Elmira. As far as Leo was concerned, Reiser had made the team. So Durocher quit. And MacPhail fired him. Or maybe it was the other way around. But in the end Durocher stayed, and although Reiser was sent down to Elmira again, MacPhail decided the Dodgers were keeping Reiser and he would take care of Rickey some other time.

At the same time another uber-prospect came the Dodgers' way. Several years before, Red Sox farm director Billy Evans, a former umpire, spotted a truly short shortstop, Harold "Pee Wee" Reese, playing under contract to Louisville of the American Association. Despite Reese's size, Evans thought he could eventually supplant Boston player-manager Joe Cronin, who had the yips in the field, as Red Sox shortstop. In order to get him, Boston owner Tom Yawkey bankrolled a deal to buy the whole franchise.

But in the spring of 1939 Cronin got his first look at Reese during an exhibition game. Pee Wee was sick and played poorly. Cronin told Yawkey to get rid of him. The owner complied and ordered Evans to wire every team in baseball and

Dodger manager Burleigh Grimes (left) is joined on the bench at Ebbets Field by fellow Hall of Famers Babe Ruth (center) and Leo Durocher (right) in this 1938 photo. All three were brought to the Dodgers by Larry MacPhail.

Louis, and only a few weeks into the season second baseman Billy Herman was brought in from Chicago. All three deals were essentially purchases, with a few lesser lights thrown in, for an aggregate $230,000. But the Dodgers were rolling in dough, for not only was Ebbets Field full for Dodger games, but MacPhail kept the turnstiles running when the club was out of town too, booking all other sporting events into the park, from car racing to wrestling. The Dodgers were out-drawing the Giants (causing some to ask now if *they* were still in the league) and drawing even with the Yankees. Brooklyn was coming out of the Depression fast as the war industries started to heat up, for Europe was already in turmoil over Nazi aggression. There was money again.

In another key move, Reiser was moved to center field in the spring and proved a natural, for his great speed gave him tremendous range. The Dodgers and Cardinals locked arms in the first week of the season and waltzed away from the league.

The crowds at Ebbets Field were in a state of extended frenzy all season long—Brooklyn never led by more than four games, and the Cardinals never by more than three, as the two clubs exchanged the lead ten times and were tied on eight other occasions. The great characters of the place, such as Hildy Chester, the cowbell-ringing, middle-aged matron of the center-field bleachers, began to take the stage as the rau-cous crowds finally had a team worth rooting for. Durocher's Dodgers and the crowd fed off each other, whipping each

other into a fever pitch as each shook off the Depression. When Leo put his Lip to use and argued with the umpires, which was often, he was backed by 30,000 or more seconds ready to take up his cause. Ebbets Field was easily the most intimidating park in the major leagues.

The Dodgers edged ahead on September 4 and nursed a one-game lead as they traveled to St. Louis on September 11 for a three-game series with the season on the line, for the two clubs would not meet each other again.

At the *Eagle,* journalistic objectivity was increasingly a for-eign concept. When Whit Wyatt blanked the Cards 1–0 in the opener for his 20th win and the Dodgers moved up by two games, Tommy Holmes effused: "Our Brooklyn Dodgers pranced through the fading sunshine toward their locker room at Sportsman's Park with all the high-spirited confi-dence of champions," all made better by the fact that the immensely popular outfielder Dixie Walker—dubbed, in Brooklyn parlance, "the People's Cherce"—doubled in the eighth and scored the winning run on Herman's two-bagger. "Durocher's Flatbush band feels that it will have downhill going from now on," wrote Holmes afterward.

He was right, although the Cardinals stayed nearby and

nearly pushed them to the limit before Brooklyn clinched their first pennant in 21 seasons on September 25. Then the party started.

Brooklyn celebrated like it never had before, as if the whole borough awoke and suddenly found itself the center of the universe. On September 28, a crowd of 60,000, including the Dodgers, paraded from the Grand Army Plaza through Brooklyn. It wasn't supposed to be a parade of 60,000 — that many just joined in. Another million fans lined the street. To be a "Bum" was to be a part of something larger.

The word on the street and the chant of the day was "Murder the Yanks," for their opponent in the upcoming World Series would be the mighty Yankees, pennant winners by 17 games, the team of DiMaggio and his freshly minted 56-game streak, the Bronx Bombers. But Brooklyn, paced by Reiser's league-best .343 batting average and .558 slugging percentage, Camilli's 34 home runs, and a combined 44 wins from Higbe and Wyatt, was hardly impotent.

After more than four decades, it would be the Dodgers' first-ever appearance in a subway series, an event that meant almost as much elsewhere as it did in Brooklyn. The Dodgers were, wrote Martin Kane in the *Eagle*, "a fad with New York's swank international set which hangs out at *Fefe's Monte Carlo* and the *Colony*." Everyone from Mayor LaGuardia to Kate Smith pledged their public allegiance to the Dodgers. They were suddenly baseball's "It" team, the sentimental favorite everywhere but the Bronx. The Yankees had won four of the last five Series, the Giants were down, and the stodgy old

Dodgers were suddenly the newest thing in baseball, a symbol of resilience and pluck spiced by the flamboyance of MacPhail and Durocher.

The smart money, though, still went to the Yankees. They had the home-field advantage and the experience. Nine out of ten scribes in town to cover the Series picked New York, and the wise guys made the Yankees 2–1 favorites.

Sportswriting legend Ring Lardner had a saying that Tommy Holmes took issue with before the Series started. Years earlier Lardner had written, "I am not superstitious, but I do think it is bad luck to bet against the Yankees." In the next week Holmes and the rest of Brooklyn would learn that whenever luck had a role in winning and losing, it usually landed on the Yankees' side. So did skill.

The largest crowd in Series history — nearly 70,000 — filled Yankee Stadium for game one on October 1 and matched Red Ruffing against . . . number-four starter Curt Davis. Like Robinson in both 1916 and 1920, Durocher tried to get cute, writing later that the logic behind starting Davis instead of Wyatt was that if the Dodgers hit in game one, "that would leave us in great shape . . . then we would sur-

---

Prior to the Dodgers' exhibition game against the Yankees at Ebbets Field in April 1940, pitchers Luke Hamlin, Tot Pressnell, and Tex Carleton shiver beneath their standard-issue wool mackinaws. The following year the Yankees returned to Brooklyn for the first of the seven World Series played between the franchises between 1941 and 1956.

prise them with Fitzsimmons instead of Higbe in the third game. And so on." That left 22-game winner Higbe, who hadn't pitched since September 24, cooling his heels for a week and a half. Durocher had Davis, Wyatt, and Larry French all warm up before the game, but that was a ruse the Yankees had seen before, and ignored.

Joe Gordon put the Yankees up with a home run in the second, and entering the seventh the Yankees were ahead 3–1. Then the Dodgers seemed ready to break the game open as an error and two hits scored one and left runners on first and second. But Jimmy Wasdell missed the bunt sign and popped up to third. Pee Wee Reese, who should have taken third on DiMaggio's throw to the plate a moment before, now decided to make amends and tag up.

As Reese said later, "I thought Rolfe was going to fall into the dugout after catching the ball and I thought that third might not be covered." But these were the Yankees. Rolfe didn't fall, Rizzuto covered third, and Reese was out by six feet on a dumb play. "All in a breath," wrote Rud Rennie in the *Herald Tribune*, "the Dodgers were practically out."

Whitlow Wyatt had had the year of his life in 1941, and his mastery continued in game two. He tottered early, only to have the Yankees keep running into outs on the base paths.

Then, in the sixth, the Yankees made another miscue. This time Joe Gordon's throw to first pulled Johnny Sturm off the base and Dixie Walker made first on a routine grounder. When Billy Herman and Dolph Camilli followed with hits, Walker scored, and over the final innings the Yankees squandered several chances. The Dodgers evened the series with a 3–2 win. Thus far the margin between the two clubs was almost indiscernible.

Brooklyn was beside itself for game three, the first Series game in Brooklyn since 1920. While the vast majority of tickets had been sold weeks before, over 40 hours before the gates opened fans began lining up outside Ebbets Field for a chance to buy one of a few thousand bleacher seats scheduled to be sold for game three. Thousands more lined up outside the Dodger offices on Montague Street for the chance to buy a few thousand pricier seats. But their wait for a world championship would prove to be in vain.

For the first seven innings of game three, Yankee pitcher Marius Russo, a Brooklyn native, and forty-year-old "Fat" Freddie Fitzsimmons, the oldest pitcher at the time to ever start a Series game, matched zeroes. But in the seventh Russo bailed out and "cowtailed" a pitch back at Fitzsimmons. It hit

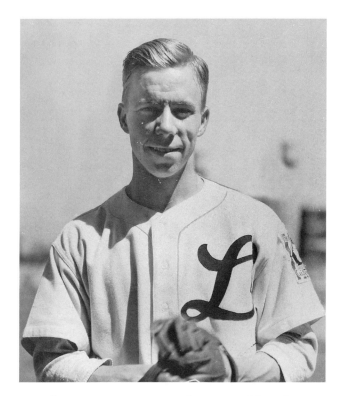

Louisville native Pee Wee Reese was the property of the Red Sox in 1939 and heir apparent to fellow Hall of Fame shortstop Joe Cronin. When Boston owner Tom Yawkey fired Red Sox farm director Billy Evans, Reese was inexplicably deemed expendable and was soon on his way to Brooklyn.

his knee and bounced 60 feet in the air before landing in Reese's glove for the final out. But Fitzsimmons was done and went to the hospital with a chipped kneecap. Hugh Casey replaced him in the eighth with the game still scoreless.

It wasn't for long. With one out, Red Rolfe singled. Then Tommy Henrich hit a ground ball to Camilli at first. But Casey froze, and failed to cover the bag. Then, as DiMaggio hit and Rolfe wandered off second, Casey missed an obvious pickoff play. DiMaggio and Charlie Keller followed with singles, and the Yankees had the only two runs they needed. New York won, 2–0, and led the Series two games to one.

MacPhail was a vicious drunk, and Casey felt his wrath after the game as he berated the pitcher for not warming up properly. It was hardly the way to instill confidence in your ballclub, but then again, neither was having Higbe sitting on his hands for ten days.

Brooklyn absolutely had to win game four, for falling behind the Yankees three games to one was a near-impossible deficit

By the time outfielder Joe Medwick arrived in Brooklyn in 1940, he'd already forged his Hall of Fame credentials with the St. Louis Cardinals. In five seasons with the Dodgers, Medwick batted .303 and helped lead Brooklyn to its first World Series in 21 years.

to surmount. Higbe, at last, took the mound for Brooklyn opposite Atley Donald.

There was rust all over him. He gave up a run in the first and was saved in the third by a catch by Walker. In the fourth he came undone, giving up two more runs and being pulled by Durocher in favor of Larry French. The Yankees led 3–1.

But Brooklyn, at last, started to hit. With two outs in the fourth, Donald walked Mickey Owen and Pete Coscarart. Jim Wasdell pinch-hit for French and doubled, scoring both. And in the fifth, Walker doubled and Reiser hit a home run to center to give the Dodgers the lead. They were four innings away from tying the Series.

And then they were one out away, for Hugh Casey came on in the fifth and cruised into and almost out of the ninth as he easily retired first Johnny Sturm and then Red Rolfe. Brooklyn was at the cusp of a tied Series when Tommy Henrich stepped to the plate. Henrich worked the count full, and then came the pitch that, with the exception of one thrown by Ralph Branca in 1951, is the most infamous in franchise history.

With a contingent of police poised in the Brooklyn dugout to sprint onto the field after the final out, Casey wound up and threw a ball that dropped off the table. Henrich, batting from the left side, swung, saying later, "It was a bad pitch — I mean a ball — but it had me fooled completely." He took a weak half-swing, missing it by a foot and trying, too late, to check his swing. Strike three.

Except the ball also fooled Owen. As Henrich looked back to see umpire Bill McGowan call him out, he also saw the ball skidding crazily toward the Dodger dugout, and the police rushing onto the field thinking the game was over. Owen, instead of dropping to his knees and blocking the low pitch, had simply stabbed at it, and it had glanced off his glove.

Now Henrich tore toward first, and Owen, as described in the *Herald Tribune,* took off, "in a vivid imitation of a man changing a tire, grabbing for monkey wrenches, screwdrivers, inner tubes and a jack and he couldn't find any of them."

By the time he threaded his way through the police and grabbed the ball, Henrich was on first and the Yankees were still alive. And then, as Tommy Holmes wrote none too creatively, "the roof fell in."

With two strikes, DiMaggio singled. And with two strikes, Keller doubled off the right-field screen to put the Yankees ahead, 5–4.

Further details were too excruciating to recount. As Holmes wrote: "The Dodger defense was thoroughly demoralized and the Yanks scored two more runs and there should have been a footnote to the boxscore: 'Three out when the winning runs were scored.'" The Dodgers went quietly in their half, and the Yankees won 7–4 to effectively win the Series, for the next day Brooklyn went down to a quiet little defeat as Tiny Bonham scattered four hits and the Yankees got just enough off Wyatt to win 3–1 and take the Series. "I lost a lot of ballgames in some funny ways," drawled Casey after, "but this is the first time I ever lost by striking out a man." The *Herald Tribune*'s Red Smith came to a similar conclusion. "It could happen only in Brooklyn," he wrote. "Nowhere else in this broad untidy universe, not in Bedlam or in Babel nor in the remotest psychopathic ward nor the sleaziest padded cell . . . could a man win a World Series game by striking out."

In subsequent seasons, much debate has taken place over the question of whether Casey threw a spitball, but Owen said it was a curve and he still made a fundamental mistake by not dropping to his knees and blocking the ball, something he should have been prepared for on a low pitch. After the pitch, Casey had a dozen more chances to throw the last pitch of the game, but couldn't. "When you give the Yankees a reprieve," moaned one Brooklyn rooter, "they leap right out of the chair and electrocute the warden."

Yet Brooklyn didn't mourn, not too much, for the pennant run and the Series were so unexpected after so long a drought that it was easy to assign the miscue to a quirk of fate. Over the next 15 years, however, as the Dodgers made excruciating defeats a matter of course, the 1941 Series defeat would loom ever larger.

In only a few months the Dodgers became something of a backstory, even in Brooklyn. On December 7, the Japanese bombed Pearl Harbor and the United States entered World War II. Franklin Roosevelt ruled that baseball would continue and the 1942 baseball season would unfold in normal fashion as the American war effort took some months to gear up. In fact, few teams were much affected in that first war year. Still, there was also a sense over the course of the season that 1942 might be the last normal season. In Brooklyn there was a frantic pace that suggested a "win now" philosophy, for among Brooklyn's key players, only Reese, Owen, Reiser, Higbe, and Casey were under the age of 30. And by the end of the war no one was sure if even they would return.

The Dodgers were little changed in 1942 apart from the addition of third baseman Arky Vaughan, acquired from the Pirates, a move that looked prescient when Cookie Lavagetto entered the service, the only Dodger regular lost to the team in 1942. Another war victim was night baseball in Brooklyn, for the Navy determined that the wash of light from Ebbets Field backlit ships in the harbor. As a result, 14 scheduled night games began instead at twilight. The Dodgers could use lights in the later innings but were under strict orders to have lights turned off one hour after sunset.

For the first half of 1942 the Dodgers were the best team in baseball and one of the best ever. Only the Cardinals remained even nominally in the race as the Dodgers bolted

Following his release from the Detroit Tigers, Fred "Dixie" Walker, shown here with his imposing 35" bat, reestablished himself with the Dodgers. In eight seasons in Brooklyn, Walker batted .311 and led the league in RBIs in 1945 with 124.

ahead—way ahead. Hitting on all cylinders, the team was paced by Pete Reiser, who seemed determined to follow his extraordinary 1941 season with an even better one. But the season, Reiser's career, and the course of Dodger history turned in July.

Already there was something of a star-crossed character to Reiser, for he had already suffered more serious injuries than many 20-year veterans. In addition to the broken arm he suffered in the minors in 1941, he had suffered two serious beanings that sent him to the hospital and one rude collision with an outfield fence.

So far, though, 1942 had been his year. In one four-game set against Cincinnati he collected an incredible 19 hits in 21 at bats. As the Dodgers went into St. Louis at the beginning of July, he was, without question, the best player in the game and perhaps the best ever, hitting .380 and apparently getting better every day. Durocher would later call him the only player he ever saw who was "better than Willie Mays."

In the 12th inning of a scoreless game, St. Louis outfielder Enos Slaughter hit a drive to deep center, 420-odd feet from home.

No other center fielder in the league, except perhaps the Cardinals' own Terry Moore, could have gotten to the ball. But Reiser, running full out, did, stretching his arm out to grab the ball three feet from the fence.

His next step sent him face first into the unpadded wall. He bounced back like a crash test dummy, and the ball fell loose. He picked it up, and threw to Reese, who just missed nailing Slaughter at home as his inside-the-park home run won the game. But Reiser took only one more step before he collapsed. Durocher had to help him off the field, and he went straight to the hospital.

He'd fractured his skull and suffered his third or fourth concussion in less than a year. St. Louis team physician Robert Hyland advised him to take the rest of the year off, a diagnosis he repeated to the Dodgers.

Yet after two days Reiser talked his way out of the hospital and instead of returning to Brooklyn, as he had promised, followed the Dodgers to Pittsburgh. He sat watching from the stands before Durocher spotted him and told him to put on a uniform, believing the Pirates might pitch differently if they thought Reiser was available to pinch-hit.

He wasn't supposed to be available, and Durocher knew it, but as the game entered extra innings, Durocher couldn't resist the temptation. He asked Reiser if he wanted to hit, and the 23-year-old, with a young man's feeling of invincibility and responsibility, did just that, driving in two runs with a line drive.

Pitcher Curt Davis with Elsie and calf.

Pitchers Whitlow Wyatt (left) and Hugh Casey accounted for four of the five decisions in the 1941 World Series. Wyatt was 1–1 and Casey 0–2 in relief.

Then he collapsed. Hospitalized again, Reiser and the Dodgers were again told that he shouldn't play for the rest of the season.

But to Durocher, Reiser's talent was a drug he couldn't stop using, and when asked to play, the player didn't have the maturity to say no. He played the rest of the year, on and off, but he played badly: half the time he couldn't see the ball, either in the outfield or at the plate. As Durocher wrote later, "We kept expecting him to snap out of it," but you don't just "snap out" of a skull fracture and the attendant debilitating and even life-threatening bleeding and bruising any more than you "snap out" of a broken leg. You have to heal, but Reiser never got the chance.

For all his talent, to MacPhail, Durocher, and the Dodgers Reiser was still a piece of meat, expendable. And Reiser, like every other player at the time, had no rights and no union protection, and he knew full well that if he couldn't play anymore, or if he refused, his career was done and he'd be back in St. Louis, scuffling to make a living like everybody else.

But sending him back out to play was a sin. It was certainly immoral, and in a later era it would have been a crime. It would not be the last time the Dodgers treated an injured player of extraordinary promise in such a myopic and cavalier fashion. Reiser hit only .220 over the final two months of the

1942 season and later admitted, "I cost us the pennant that year"—and probably a few more after that. For a healthy Reiser on the postwar Dodgers could have been the difference in a half-dozen pennant races, playoffs, and World Series. The Dodgers, and not the Yankees, could have been the dominant team of the era. But Reiser was never the same player and would be washed up by age 30. The Dodgers would pay the price.

As Reiser staggered around the outfield over the final two months, the Dodgers staggered to the end as St. Louis surged, winning 43 of their final 51 games. They caught the Dodgers on September 12, and even though Brooklyn won a team-record 104 games, the Cardinals won 106 to win the pennant.

As soon as the season ended, players began to be called into the service or signed up before being drafted. Even Durocher tried to enlist, but he was rejected because of a perforated eardrum. Reiser, after being designated 4-F, was sworn in owing to his youth and notoriety. He'd spend the next three years like most other major leaguers, playing baseball to entertain Uncle Sam, keeping up "morale" by providing bragging rights to service commanders in competition with one another. For while some major leaguers, like the Indians' Bob Feller and Cecil Travis of the Senators, saw combat and served with distinction, most big league ballplayers fought the war in spikes, playing on service teams. Only two major leaguers would lose their lives in combat.

The war stirred something in Larry MacPhail, who still looked back on his World War I service with warmth. Besides, he'd done all he could with the Dodgers. Everyone could tell that most teams would play the next few seasons with 4-Fs, has-beens, and never-would-bes. There wasn't much sport in that. His military experience still had some value, and he wrangled a commission in the Army, leaving a hole atop the Dodger organization.

Only four years before, that job had been seen as the worst in baseball. Now it was a plum. In St. Louis 60-year-old Branch Rickey was similarly restless. A lousy player, he had found his life's work in baseball's backrooms and bush leagues, building an organization out of a team, a franchise out of a ballclub. Yet despite their recent success, he felt he'd accomplished all he could in St. Louis and was beginning to clash with owner Sam Breadon. His son was in Brooklyn, and he wanted to test himself, to see if he could build another farm system as productive as the one he'd built for St. Louis, to see if he could even trump his success there. Besides, there were things he could do in Brooklyn that were impossible in St. Louis. Important things. Significant things. Lucrative things.

Branch Rickey's signing of Jackie Robinson is arguably the most noteworthy moment in baseball history. The basic details — how Rickey scouted Negro League players in secret, called Robinson to his office on August 28, 1945, warned him of the upcoming trials, and, when Robinson asked, "Do you want a ballplayer who's afraid to fight back?" admonished him by saying, "I want a ballplayer with guts enough not to fight back" — are well known and an oft-told part of baseball lore, the worthy subject of a number of books of this length by itself.

Yet that is only part of the story, and one that, perhaps too simplistically, anoints Rickey as baseball's Abraham Lincoln. Just as Lincoln's support of the Emancipation Proclamation

Center fielder Pete Reiser was thought by many to be as talented as Willie Mays. His career was curtailed by numerous injuries, including those suffered when he ran into outfield walls chasing impossible catches. In his Dodger career Reiser batted .306.

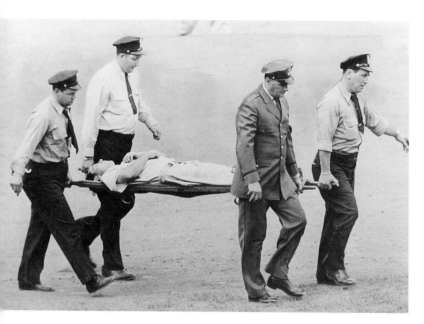

Pete Reiser is carried off the field after he crashed into the concrete wall in left field while chasing a hard-hit fly ball in the fifth inning of the Cardinal-Dodger game of August 1, 1946, at Ebbets Field.

referred to him as "a player, manager, executive, lawyer, preacher, horse-trader, spellbinder, innovator, husband and father and grandfather, farmer, politician, logician, obscurantist, reformer, financier, sociologist, crusader, sharper, father-confessor, checker shark, friend [and] fighter." Rickey was a contradiction of all these terms, for he was both vain and pious, both moral and materialistic, both a genuine trendsetter and someone who took credit where it rightfully belonged to others, a person who could earn the nicknames "the Mahatma" and "El Cheapo" and live up to both simultaneously. Underlying all these behaviors, however, was a not insignificant desire for financial independence and wealth and the attendant freedom that would allow him to do things that were otherwise undoable.

With the Cardinals, where each player sale had put 20 percent of the price directly into his own pocket, he had achieved some of that, but he had still been an employee. In Brooklyn his sights were set higher. He wanted to be atop the echelon, an owner, and a man who set the agenda, not someone who had to find a way to work under someone else's rules. It is important to keep in mind that his desire to break baseball's color line served both parts of his nature, the material *and* the moral, and it also fulfilled both his ego and his obsession with the bottom line. He did what he did to secure his place in history *and* to make money. The two cannot be separated and could not have taken place apart from the unique circumstances of the events about to unfold and the equally unique dynamics of both the Brooklyn baseball franchise and the place itself. There would be a confluence of history and opportunity that had never before taken place in baseball. Rickey would be both an agent of that convergence and a subject of forces larger than himself. No one, not even Rickey, knew what was going to happen next at any step of the process. He is the best example of his own aphorism, "Luck is the residue of design," for he would be the lucky beneficiary even though the larger design was not entirely of his own making.

He took over the Dodgers on October 30, 1942, looked around, and found something of a mess. The Brooklyn farm system, which had grown from five clubs in 1936 to 18 by 1940, was already being scaled back, as it was throughout baseball, by the loss of players to the war. From a high of 310 minor league teams in 1940, there would be only 66 by 1943. The same erosion was affecting the majors, and the Dodgers were already old.

was far more complicated than simply signing the document, so too was Rickey's discovery of Robinson and his decision to break the color line in the first place.

What has often gone less examined in most retellings of the Robinson story is how such a bold and even revolutionary move came to take place and how Robinson, of all Negro Leaguers, came to be chosen. Branch Rickey did not act alone. His signing of Robinson was the logical end result of a much larger process. While Rickey was the catalyst and integral to the event, he was not the first or only voice calling for change. Neither was he the saint that many later biographers tend to make him into, as some accounts of events of the next few years simplistically cast Rickey in the paternalistic and subtly racist role of the great white hero and agent of change, while diminishing or ignoring the contributions of others.

Such a view is incomplete. Robinson's signing was not an event but a process, and the bottom line is that Rickey, first and foremost, was trying to win games for the Dodgers and make money for himself. Social change and moral right, while certainly not insignificant, were not Rickey's only motivation.

Branch Rickey was many things to many people and one of baseball's most complex and complicated characters. If MacPhail is a mess of adjectives, Rickey is an even greater grammatical challenge. The columnist Red Smith once

In the spring of 1943, Rickey told Durocher that "the elevator is already going down" and the Dodgers would not be contenders. Then, for the duration of the war, Rickey essentially ignored the major league team apart from making cursory efforts to keep the bottom from falling out altogether. Most veterans of any value, like Joe Medwick and Dolph Camilli, were simply sold. Instead, he focused his energy on a plan to start rebuilding *now*, to prepare for the end of the war before anyone even knew names like Omaha Beach and Corregidor. During the war the Dodgers would do their part — training at Bear Mountain, helping to sell war bonds and the like — and, while waiting, finished third, seventh, and third and drew reasonable crowds to Ebbets Field; workers at the Navy Yard and elsewhere propped up attendance in Brooklyn more so than in most other major league cities.

Rickey knew that the best young ballplayers were now either already in the service or about to enter it, so what had worked when he was in St. Louis would not work in Brooklyn. He was forced to improvise and find ballplayers not employed overseas. That meant looking at kids in high school too young for the draft — and the Negro Leagues. Not that American blacks were overlooked by the American military, but there was still Negro League baseball during the war, even in New York, where both the Yankees and Giants rented their parks to the black clubs, earning each team a windfall of nearly $100,000 each year. The Dodgers had not done so since 1937, when the Brooklyn Eagles moved to Newark. Rickey was determined to end that advantage.

Although Rickey had done absolutely nothing while with St. Louis to foreshadow his signing of Robinson, he later claimed that he had believed for years that the color line was destined to fall, and he liked to tell the story that spawned his sense of racial awareness. At age 21, while he was the coach of the baseball team at Ohio Wesleyan University, Rickey's catcher, a black man named Charles Thomas, was refused admittance to a hotel. After a humiliating scene in the lobby, Rickey talked the clerk into letting the young man sleep unregistered on a cot in his room, preserving the hotel's lily-white reputation. Rickey later found Thomas rubbing his hands and pulling at his skin, as if to remove the color that had subjugated him.

At least that was what Rickey remembered. Thomas, while acknowledging the incident at the hotel, later claimed to have no recollection of the scene that made such an impression on Rickey.

Before the war, in segregated St. Louis, and while baseball was under the reign of Judge Landis — who believed in the gentleman's agreement that kept big league baseball white — the notion of breaking the color line wasn't tenable. Landis wouldn't allow it, and it was far too risky to attempt in St. Louis. Rickey made no moves to do so, and neither did anyone else in other big league cities. The war would change all that, however, and the agent of change would not be anyone in baseball but primarily the members of the black and leftist press.

The notion of racial equality was just becoming part of the mainstream political discussion. For much of the first third of the 20th century, it resided outside the political mainstream, in socialist and leftist political groups and, significantly, in the black press. Beginning in the 1930s, some dedicated members of the Negro sporting press, a group that would eventually include such figures as Wendell Smith of the *Pittsburgh Courier* and Joe Bostic of the *New York Age*, began a concerted campaign to make the black ballplayer impossible to ignore.

Their goal was nothing less than the integration of American society through sports. Mabrey "Doc" Kountze of the *Boston Guardian* even formed a loose organization called the National Negro Newspaper All-American Association of Sports Editors, the NNNAASE, to coordinate those efforts, which included, in his words, "feeding black sports data into the white daily press to drum up support." They selected black all-American teams and all-conference squads and distributed them nationally through the Associated Negro Press. Members of the group also directly agitated for integration, meeting directly with club officials, calling for tryouts, spreading the word, and planting the seed. It became increasingly impossible for anyone involved in baseball in any way to believe that there were no black ballplayers of major league caliber or that they were content to play in a league of their own.

Even before the war, the African American press had chosen the man they believed could successfully break the color barrier, and it was Jackie Robinson. There were plenty of players with enough talent to succeed in the majors, but Robinson was different. In Robinson, a collegiate football, basketball, track, and baseball star at UCLA, they saw a man who possessed the intangibles necessary to succeed in the majors. Even though baseball had been Robinson's *worst* sport at UCLA (see chapter 6 sidebar), he was easily the best athlete of any color in the entire country. Moreover, he was educated, well-spoken, good-looking, and morally upright — apart from his skin color, his supporters wanted to make sure there was no reason for baseball to reject him. Before Rickey even knew who Robinson was, they were holding him aloft and saying definitively, "This is the man."

As evidence of this, on March 22, 1942, long before Rickey joined the Dodgers, political pressure from the African American press and the Communist *Daily Worker* forced the Chicago White Sox to give Robinson and another player a tryout in Robinson's hometown of Pasadena, where the White Sox held training camp. Robinson's presence was no accident — not only did the black press know that he could be "the one," but they also had on record that White Sox manager Jimmy Dykes had seen Robinson play sandlot ball and already commented favorably upon him. Although no one had any illusions that he'd be signed after the tryout, Dykes told the *Worker*, "I would welcome Negro players on the Sox," and said he thought Robinson was worth $50,000. It was a step.

World War II was giving their efforts traction and pushing the process forward. With each day of combat there was an obvious and unavoidable contradiction between the growing presence of black soldiers in the military and the "whites only" policy of the major leagues. Fair employment legislation spawned by the war was making it increasingly difficult for baseball to cling to its past.

Robinson received his draft notice the day after the Pasadena tryout, giving his candidacy even more legitimacy.

Robinson didn't serve overseas, but as an officer in a segregated cavalry unit, he became something of a cause célèbre and a household name in black America in 1944 when he refused to move to the back of the bus on base, then successfully avoided a court-martial over his private insurrection. Each day the war lasted and each day Robinson spent in uniform provided the undeniable logic that would eventually bring down the color barrier in the major leagues and elsewhere: how could men serve America in the war and then be denied the right to work in their chosen field, particularly when that field was a game?

This climate was taking hold when Rickey came to Brooklyn. What had not been possible a few years before, and certainly not in St. Louis, was suddenly much closer to reality in Brooklyn. The political momentum calling for integration was increasing, and the war provided the convincing moral argument. The Dodgers' need to restock and reload gave Rickey a compelling reason to consider black players for the health of the franchise. And Brooklyn was not St. Louis.

From its very beginning, Brooklyn always had a small but substantial and cohesive middle-class black community. In

Dodger shortstop Pee Wee Reese (second from right) sits among fellow sports stars watching a service ballgame in Guam in the waning days of World War II: (left to right) Heisman Trophy winner Angelo Bertelli, track star Hal Williams, White Sox pitcher John Rigney, Reese, and Hal White of the Detroit Tigers.

1800 the burb was fully one-quarter black and by 1900 was still home to nearly 20,000. In the 1920s the Fulton Street subway connected Brooklyn's blacks to Harlem, and during a housing boom in which more than 100,000 homes were constructed and the borough was essentially built out, blacks began to flock to Brooklyn from Manhattan and elsewhere in increasing numbers, filling the apartments abandoned by homeowners. During that decade the black population of Brooklyn more than doubled, from some 30,000 in 1920 to nearly 70,000 by 1930, and certain sections of Brooklyn, most prominently Bedford-Stuyvesant, began to be known as black neighborhoods.

Predictably, integration was not an easy process. Opposition neighborhood associations sprang up sporadically, some churches tried to segregate, the Ku Klux Klan made the occasional frightening appearance, and there was the widely accepted and expected discrimination when it came to employment, but compared to many other places in the United States, tolerance was not a foreign concept in Brooklyn. Virtually everyone there was only a generation or two removed from immigrant status and to a degree sensitive to the effects of discrimination. In some neighborhoods, such as Brownsville, there was true integration as blacks and Jews lived together on a more or less equal footing.

While Brooklyn was hardly a racial utopia, it wasn't as rigidly and violently segregated as St. Louis. Moreover, in New York, unlike in St. Louis, Brooklyn's blacks had considerable political influence that expanded with the population. And the population did expand. In the 1930s another 50,000 blacks found reason to call Brooklyn home. That was still only about 4 percent of the borough's population, but blacks would soon be the fastest-growing demographic.

Moreover, Brooklyn's blacks were enormous baseball fans. During the 1930s games between white semipro teams and barnstorming black clubs drew huge crowds at Dexter Park, just over the Queens line. They hadn't turned out in force to see the Brooklyn Eagles at Ebbets Field, for the team wasn't very good and the cost was prohibitive. Still, a smattering of black fans had always been visible at Ebbets Field at Dodgers games. As the Depression eased, more and more black faces began to appear in the crowd. In Brooklyn their money was green too.

Very quietly, as part of what would be his larger search for players to stock the Dodger system after the war, Rickey began in 1943 to accumulate information on black players under

Dodger general manager Branch Rickey shakes hands with manager Leo Durocher upon the signing of Durocher's contract for the 1943 season. In 1947 Durocher was suspended for the season by baseball commissioner Albert "Happy" Chandler for consorting with gamblers and exhibiting conduct detrimental to baseball.

the cover of creating a Negro League franchise, the Brooklyn Brown Dodgers, and backing the formation of an entirely new black league, the United States Baseball League. At the same time he cast his net for white players as wide as possible, sending letters inquiring about prospects to some 20,000 high school baseball coaches all across the country. Even Rickey would later admit that he wasn't considering an integrated team just to make a moral statement, saying, "I'm trying to win ballgames." He wanted to make the Dodgers better and more profitable. And in the same way that sending 20,000 letters gave him an edge that helped him eventually sign 400 of the best schoolboy prospects in the country and gave the Dodgers an edge after the war, so too could identifying the best black prospects.

Despite all this, there remained one enormous obstacle for any baseball club interested in lifting the color line: Judge Landis and the other major league owners. In 1943 William Benswanger, owner of the Pittsburgh Pirates, reportedly had wanted to sign the great catcher Josh Gibson, and in 1944 Bill Veeck had wanted to buy the Philadelphia Phillies and stock them with black talent. Landis had blocked both men, know-

Branch Rickey and Jackie Robinson made baseball history in the autumn of 1945 when the former UCLA football star was signed by the Dodgers. Following a successful season in 1946 in which Robinson helped lead the Montreal Royals to a Little World Series title, he was soon on his way to Ebbets Field and everlasting fame as the first African American major leaguer of the 20th century.

ing that he had the support of the other owners. But Rickey was working on that front as well.

While he couldn't topple Landis, he could make his mark among the other baseball magnates. By 1943 the Dodgers' convoluted ownership structure was beginning to come unglued, and Ebbets's heirs, having made their money, were selling out. Rickey, who had purchased a small portion of Dodger stock when he first arrived, was able to increase his holdings as both John Smith, the president of Pfizer Chemical, and Walter O'Malley, the club's attorney, bought in and gave him their support. For the first time since Ebbets had died, the effective control of the team now lay in the hands of one man, Branch Rickey. He could now attend league meetings with the full authority as team owner and president, equal in status with influential zillionaires like Tom Yawkey.

And on November 25, 1944, Judge Landis, whose contract had already been extended through 1953, died of coronary thrombosis. It would take baseball more than six months to name a successor, and when they did it was Happy Chandler, the lame-duck senator from Kentucky. Although Rickey had favored NL president Ford Frick, Chandler's selection would prove to be fortuitous.

So too would the date of November 28, 1944. For on that date Jackie Robinson was given an honorable discharge from the United States Army. At the same time he inquired about a tryout for the Kansas City Monarchs of the Negro National League. Despite not having played baseball for the better part of three seasons, his notoriety, overall athletic ability, and the fact that Negro League rosters were depleted by the war earned him an invitation to a tryout the following April in Houston. While waiting, he took a coaching job at Sam Houston College.

Yet before he played a game in the Negro Leagues, he was again made visible by the black press. In the spring of 1945 baseball was under increasing pressure to integrate. On April 6, Joe Bostic of the *Age* unceremoniously showed up at the Dodgers' Bear Mountain training camp with two Negro Leaguers—Terrence McDuffie and Dave Thomas—and demanded that they be given a tryout. A furious Rickey reluctantly agreed and gave the two players a cursory 45-minute workout. He had already plotted his path and was livid that Bostic, who knew nothing of his plans, presumed to put pressure on him.

Ten days later another tryout was held, this time in Boston. Izzy Muchnick, a Boston city councilman, had been pressuring the Red Sox to integrate and was threatening to block the council's waiver that allowed Sunday baseball if they didn't. He was not acting, as has often been erroneously reported, from political expediency because his district was becoming black. Muchnick was simply a principled man far ahead of his time.

After Red Sox general manager Eddie Collins tried to wiggle out of the situation by sniffing, "No Negro has ever asked to try out," Wendell Smith of the *Courier* worked with Muchnick and brought three Negro Leaguers to Boston. He and Muchnick made it clear—and known to the mainstream press—that *here* were three men who wanted to try out. Unlike the incident at Bear Mountain, which attracted little notice, virtually every black paper in the country—and even most mainstream papers in Boston—followed the confrontation between Muchnick and the Red Sox.

The first two players, 23-year-old outfielder Sam Jethroe and 22-year-old infielder Marvin Williams, were, statistically, among the best players in the Negro Leagues. Jethroe had led the Negro American League in hitting in 1944, and Williams hit .338 in the Negro National League.

The third player was Robinson, who at age 26 had had no baseball experience of note since his desultory season at UCLA. Yet of all the hundreds of players in the Negro Leagues, he was one of three brought to Boston.

That was no accident: he was the man Smith and the other black writers knew had the intangibles that would be needed to be the first—or one of the first—players to integrate major league baseball. He was educated, a veteran who had grown up in an integrated society, already familiar to many whites from his days as a college football star, well spoken, and clearly socially adept. Moreover, Smith and his compatriots in the black press already knew that Robinson could play. They often acted as de facto scouts for Negro League teams, and they alone had seen Robinson playing softball and the odd sandlot game in the years after he left UCLA.

The tryout, which has since become one of the more notorious events in Red Sox history, led to the result everyone expected. The three players, while being praised by Boston coach Hugh Duffy, were not signed, and all three went back to the Negro Leagues.

Just as major league baseball was suffering from a lack of talent owing to the war, so were the Negro Leagues. This gave Robinson a chance to shake the rust off his game. By midyear the shortstop was a star.

At the same time, now that Landis was dead and the war was ending, sending players back in droves, Rickey began to move forward. He directed his scouts to start looking in earnest, telling them to find a player with speed, power, and a strong arm. He already knew that in the end he himself would be the only scout of the character of that player, the "right" man.

That was what made his final selection of Robinson so surprising and lends credence to the notion that once Robinson, elevated by the black press, came into view, Rickey real-ized he had his man and looked no further. For Robinson didn't meet Rickey's criteria at all. Although he was fast, he had little power and a poor throwing arm. At age 26, he was no longer a youngster, and as his experience in the Army demonstrated, he was hardly the kind of man to turn the other cheek.

No matter. Robinson was the one. Facing subpar competition in the Negro Leagues during the 1945 season, Robinson hit .387 in 47 games, a vast improvement over his pathetic .097 mark at UCLA. While Rickey continued to search for other black players, his scouts would follow Robinson closely. He would be the first.

In August Rickey sent superscout Clyde Sukeforth to give Robinson a final look. But he was out of the lineup with a sore shoulder. Nevertheless, on August 28, 1945, Sukeforth delivered Robinson to Rickey at the Dodger offices under the ruse that Rickey wanted to sign Robinson for his black club. Then, in a legendary meeting, the Mahatma unveiled his plans.

In a charged exchange, Rickey graphically described to Robinson how he would be received, role-playing the race-baiting players and fans. Puzzled, Robinson asked, "Mr. Rickey, do you want a player who is afraid to fight back?"

Rickey's response was pointed. "I want a player with guts enough not to fight back," he said. Another role-playing scene ensued, and after Rickey described a player striking Robinson in the face, he boomed, "What do you do now, Jackie? What do you do now?"

"I get it, Mr. Rickey," responded Robinson. "I've got another cheek."

With that, Rickey signed Robinson for a $3,500 bonus and a contract worth $600 a month. There was no turning back.

Although word of the signing slowly leaked out in the Negro press, for most of America the formal announcement on October 23, 1945, struck like a thunderbolt. The war was over, baseball was about to turn the page, and the Dodgers were preparing to take an exponential leap past their competitors.

"LEAVE US GIVE THE YANKEES THE BUMS RUSH!"

IT WASN'T IN THE CARDS!

FIRST

IN BROOKLYN LIFE HAD NEVER BEEN BETTER.

The economic engine that ran the war pulled Brooklyn out of the last vestiges of the Depression as everyone who wasn't fighting went to work. During the war the Navy Yard alone employed as many as 70,000 people in shifts that went around the clock. Millions of soldiers had passed through Brooklyn during the war, and thousands had managed to catch a game or two at Ebbets Field and warmed to its charms. Betty Smith's bittersweet but ultimately inspiring novel *A Tree Grows in Brooklyn* was a national bestseller in 1943. Almost every Hollywood war movie featured a "typical" Brooklyn character, a bare-armed, wisecracking, quasi-tough guy named "Smitty" or "Frankie" who spoke in the invented vernacular of Brooklynese and loved "Dem Bums." Brooklyn had arrived.

By 1946 it seemed as if everyone was coming back with a GI loan in his pocket and a girl around the corner, looking for a piece of the American dream. Many found it in Brooklyn, and the borough boomed. All of a sudden there were kids *every-where*. In a few years the *Brooklyn Eagle* would look at what was

Dodger fans greet shortstop Pee Wee Reese at New York's Pennsylvania Station upon the Dodgers' return from the road on September 19, 1947. Three days later the Dodgers clinched the pennant and yet another World Series matchup with the Yankees.

happening in the gigantic neighborhood and publish a multi-part series that would celebrate the great "mingling of races" on Brooklyn streets, calling it "the civilized world in microcosm" and proclaiming without irony, "Brooklyn *is* America."

That same series would find that nowhere was this truer than "in the great co-mingled shout from 30,000 Brooklyn throats at Ebbets Field." Over the next few seasons a great experiment would take place.

Coming out of the war, few teams in baseball were better positioned than Brooklyn. While others had all but abandoned their scouting networks during combat, Branch Rickey had quietly signed the best young players in baseball. Now, as other teams scrambled to fill rosters, it was a seller's market as Rickey kept the best and sold the rest. After all, his agreement with the Dodgers still delivered 20 percent of the profit from each player sale to his own pocket. And that didn't even include the inroad that Rickey had forged to the Negro Leagues through his signing of Robinson. He was ahead of every curve the game could throw.

The Dodgers had been lucky. Key players like Reese, Reiser, Casey, and Higbe were all still relatively young, although Reiser had contracted pneumonia during the war and run into several more walls while playing ball before finally being discharged. And during the war the Dodgers had found a few gems, such as scrappy second baseman Eddie Stanky, picked up from the Cubs. Already some of the youngsters signed by Rickey, like pitcher Ralph Branca, were ready to contribute, and a dozen more, like Duke Snider and Gil Hodges, were waiting in the wings.

Rickey's only problem was that he had done his job too well. For the organization he had built in St. Louis still hummed along at top efficiency. The Cardinals were similarly flush with talent and over the next few seasons would prove to be Brooklyn's greatest competition for National League supremacy.

But when spring training opened in 1946, the big story was still Jackie Robinson. While the Dodgers trained in Daytona, Robinson was in camp with the Montreal Royals some 30 miles away in Sanford, with about 150 Dodger minor leaguers and officials, all of whom were put on notice that Rickey would not put up with any trouble. And that included trouble from Montreal manager Clay Hopper, a native Mississippian who despite a college education was known to ask others if they really believed that blacks were even human.

Robinson was not the only black player in camp either.

Rickey had also signed pitcher Johnny Wright, a marginal prospect. He was acquired to keep Robinson company as much as anything else, but the college-educated Californian shared nothing with the southern-born pitcher apart from the color of his skin.

There was no overt trouble from the players in camp, but after only a few days the bigoted residents of Sanford kicked the Royals out of town, and they were forced to relocate to Kelly Field in the black district of Daytona. Robinson clearly felt the pressure, however. He struggled early, looking awkward at second base and having trouble hitting curveballs, then came down with a sore arm. Those who wished the major leagues to remain white shared knowing glances.

But in the Royals' final exhibition game, against Rickey's Dodgers, the real Robinson stepped out. The Royals beat the Dodgers 6–1 as Robinson banged out two hits, scored a run, stole a base, and handled five chances in the field. He opened the season as Montreal's starting second baseman.

Meanwhile, Durocher sorted through the dozens of youngsters, vets, and returnees vying for a spot on the Dodger roster. He finally settled on a lineup in which only four players—Reese, Reiser, Stanky, Billy Herman, and Dixie Walker—were truly "regulars," and Herman would soon be dealt away, leaving third base to committee. Elsewhere Durocher platooned according to the situation, such as pairing two youngsters, Ed Stevens and 6'7" Howie Schultz, at first. His players weren't always comfortable—many disliked his methods, which kept them constantly on edge and insecure—but that was the way Durocher liked it, and even the players who hated him grudgingly admitted that once the game started he was one of the smartest managers in the game. The pitching staff, anchored by Higbe, would have made Wil Robinson proud, for it made up for what it lacked in star power with depth. Although the oddsmakers picked the Dodgers to finish fourth, when the Dodgers players were asked by a radio announcer in the spring where they expected to finish the year, to a man they said they expected to finish on top. Except for Pete Reiser. He answered the question more forthrightly—and, as it turned out, accurately—when he quipped that he expected to finish the season in Peck Memorial Hospital, where the ambulances ran from Ebbets Field. He missed by only two days.

Beginning the 1946 season as if the war had never taken place, the Cardinals and Dodgers each vaulted to the lead. For the first half of the season, while the Cardinals looked better on paper, the Dodgers had the edge.

Then St. Louis was hurt by defections to the fledgling Mexican League. Bankrolled by millionaire Jorge Pasqual, the Mexican League waved money at a number of players hoping to entice them away—the Dodgers had already lost Mickey Owen in the spring. But when the Cardinals lost two lesser players and pitcher Max Lanier, 6–0 and playing the best baseball of his career, the balance seemed to tip toward Brooklyn. They led by as many as seven and a half games in early July despite the periodic loss of Reiser, whose preseason prophecy proved to be correct as he kept bouncing in and out of the lineup and Peck Memorial, dislocating a shoulder, tearing a hamstring, and knocking himself out trying to make diving catches.

But little went as expected. Instead of collapsing after losing Lanier, the Cardinals finally surged, sweeping the Dodgers in a four-game series to pull into first on July 18. Then the

HIS WORST SPORT

It is a measure of Jackie Robinson, both as an athlete and as a man, that not only did he succeed in the major leagues, but over the course of his first five seasons he was perhaps the greatest player of his time. Over the course of his brief career he was, without question, one of the greatest players of all time.

And baseball wasn't even his best sport. It was, in fact, the one sport he *couldn't* play initially.

Even if Jackie Robinson had not gained notoriety as the first African American in the major leagues, he would still be considered one of the greatest athletes in American history. Like Olympian Jim Thorpe, who also played professional baseball and football, Robinson was a multisport star who succeeded at virtually every sport he tried. At UCLA, which Robinson attended for a year and a half after spending two years at Pasadena Junior College, he became the first four-letter winner in the history of the university, earning letters in football, track, basketball, and baseball. On the gridiron he was a national figure, averaging nearly 13 yards per carry in 1938. On the basketball court he was a potent scorer during a time when basketball was still played deliberately. As a long jumper, he was world-class, and Robinson was reportedly more than proficient at a host of other sports, such as Ping-Pong and tennis.

But in his only season of baseball at UCLA, Robinson was awful. After starring as a shortstop in junior college, he was overmatched when he moved up to UCLA.

For all intents and purposes, Robinson's baseball career at UCLA consisted of one game, his first. In his first appearance in a Bruins uniform against Los Angeles City College, he banged out four hits and stole home. But once the Bruins began regular season play in 1939 in the California Intercollegiate Athletic Association, Robinson, in nearly 60 at bats over the remainder of the season, collected only *two hits*, ending the season with a batting average of .097, and made ten errors at shortstop.

Those who have written that had he been white Robinson would have been signed by a major league team out of college are dreaming, for it is hard to imagine a more unlikely candidate for the major leagues. All Robinson had was his speed—and he had yet to learn how to use that on the baseball field. Moreover, the CIAA was not one of the better collegiate baseball leagues in the country—college baseball was still dominated by teams from the East Coast. Robinson wasn't just struggling, he was struggling against subpar competition.

For the first time in his life, Jackie Robinson had found a sport he just couldn't play, one that resisted his fabulous athleticism. The following spring he left UCLA, still shy of his degree, just as baseball season was approaching. And in his own autobiography, as if ashamed of it, Robinson completely ignores his baseball career at UCLA.

Yet that embarrassing record may provide some insight into his later success. Robinson played relatively little basketball or football after leaving UCLA, but as if trying to prove to himself that he could conquer baseball, he kept returning to the game. After leaving UCLA, he played in sandlot baseball games and fast-pitch softball at Pasadena's Brookfield Park, and while serving in the military he organized a battalion baseball team and pitched on the officers' fast-pitch softball team. By the time he left the Army, Robinson's skills had matured. He was a ballplayer, good enough for the Negro Leagues and, by extension, the major leagues.

After signing with the Dodgers, Robinson was clearly motivated by the opportunity to break baseball's color line. But that wasn't all. For while he was proving to America that African Americans deserved to play in the major leagues, he was at the same time proving to himself that he could play baseball. To be sure, he was playing for all Americans, but he was also playing for himself, for his own immense pride.

That was a combination that made him unstoppable.

Dodgers pulled ahead again, only to have the Cardinals draw even on August 22. The two teams spent the next five weeks in one of the tightest pennant races in National League history—and one of the most overlooked. For it only served as a grand setup for the first playoff in National League history, a classic World Series, and, in 1947, the falling of the color line. Had that taken place during the heat of the race, a 1946 world championship banner might well have flown above Ebbets Field, for as the Dodgers were battling for the National League pennant, Jackie Robinson was proving to be a revelation.

The excitement in St. Louis and Brooklyn in 1946 was trumped only by that which surrounded the Montreal Royals. For Jackie Robinson of the Royals was clearly the best player in all minor league baseball. Any other player performing at his level would have been called up to Brooklyn, and if he had been, he certainly would have proven to be the difference in the pennant race.

From the moment Robinson made his debut in organized baseball for the Royals versus the Jersey City Giants on April 17, 1946, in Jersey City, there had been little question about either his physical ability or his ability to win over the majority of fans. Before a standing-room-only crowd of 25,000, Robinson grounded out in his first at bat but his second time up cracked a home run. Greeted at home plate with a round of handshakes from the other Royals, Robinson breathed a sigh of relief, saying later, "I wasn't sure if my teammates would shake my hand."

There was no stopping him. His next time up he beat out a bunt, stole second, and scored when he distracted the pitcher into a balk. Then in his fourth appearance he singled and stole two more bases before beating out another bunt in his last at bat and scoring again when he faked the pitcher into a balk. Montreal won 14–1. In *The Sporting News* wrap-up of International League news for the week, Robinson wasn't mentioned until the third paragraph of the story, although the headline writer got it right, titling the story, "Robinson Steals Int. Show." Not a bad debut, one that Wendell Smith referred to as another "Emancipation Day for the Negro Race."

The response of the Jersey City crowd was telling—by the end of the game they were on his side. Robinson drew a crowd everywhere he went, and the same pattern usually followed. Fans first came out of curiosity, or perhaps to root against him, but soon to see his skills and cheer him on. Fully one-third of the total attendance for the International League that season was for games that involved Montreal, and Robinson was mobbed by fans off the field—particularly children—to whom he became a hero. While Robinson hardly had an easy time of it—he was the regular target of racial epithets and shabby treatment by some opponents and off the field almost everywhere but in Montreal—he was a box-office success, and that spoke louder to most opposing teams than anything else. There was little organized resistance to him from other IL teams, and when there was, Robinson stoically stuck to his promise to Branch Rickey to turn the other cheek.

He had an amazing capacity to compartmentalize what was happening, to suppress any frustration he felt and use it to motivate himself on the field. The playing field, in the best way possible, was the only place where Robinson could be himself. Elsewhere, he was cautious and restrained, taking measure of every word and act, revealing little about his inner turmoil, not even in his two rather wooden ghostwritten autobiographies or in innumerable interviews. But on the field, in the context of the game, he could be himself. Actions, not words, would be his legacy.

And on the field he brought a style of play not often seen since the Dead Ball Era anywhere but in the Negro Leagues. Since the emergence of Ruth, the running game had all but faded from view in the major leagues. Robinson brought back the daring, aggressive, and flamboyant style that had first been put into practice by Ned Hanlon in Baltimore and had been best expressed in the play of Ty Cobb. Instead of waiting for something to happen, Robinson made it happen himself by dropping a bunt, stealing a base, or testing an outfielder's arm as he stretched a single into a double. Robinson played as if he had a gear other players lacked. He finished the season hitting a league-best .349—answering any questions regarding whether or not he could "take it"—and leading the Royals to a 100–54 record, 18½ games ahead of second-place Syracuse. The Royals then swept past both Newark and Syracuse in the playoffs to earn the right to play the American Association champion Louisville Colonels in the Little World Series. In that segregated southern city, Robinson not only broke the baseball color line but also led the Royals to the minor league championship.

A similar performance by any other minor leaguer would have resulted in a midseason call-up to the majors, but even if Robinson had hit .500 in 1946, there was no chance that Rickey would call him up during midseason. He was moving deliberately, not so much according to any great plan but because that was simply the way he did things. In fact, he had no great plan that plotted out Robinson's path to the major leagues. Circumstances — and Robinson's own performance — would determine that.

All Rickey knew at the start of the 1946 season was that if Robinson proved he could play, he would spend the entire season in race-tolerant Montreal. Only then, after Robinson had demonstrated not only the ability to play in the majors but the necessary character, would Rickey address the issue of bringing him up to the major leagues. But as of yet, Rickey had no idea precisely how he would accomplish that. He knew there would be resistance — the day Robinson had signed, Dodger outfielder Dixie Walker said ominously, "As long as he isn't with the Dodgers, I'm not worried" — and in 1946 no other baseball owner had rushed to follow Rickey's lead.

But in 1946 Robinson's performance took Rickey by surprise in the same way it did International League pitchers as he danced off third. By June 1946 it was obvious that Robinson was ready for the big leagues *now*, but Rickey was unprepared and unwilling to press the issue of breaking the color line in the major leagues in midseason, no matter what Robinson did. Rickey's caution may have cost the Dodgers a pennant, for Brooklyn and St. Louis would end the scheduled season in a tie with identical 96–58 records.

After the Herman trade, third base had been a trouble spot for the Dodgers. Over half a dozen players, most notably Cookie Lavagetto, shared the position neither with distinction nor with a decent batting average. Although Robinson played second base for Montreal and Brooklyn's Eddie Stanky was well established at that position as well, Stanky had some experience at third, and if Robinson had been white, Stanky undoubtedly would have moved over to make way for the rookie. After Pete Reiser went down in September, first with a hamstring pull and then, with only two days left in the season, a broken ankle, the services of a player with Robinson's skills were even more desperately needed. Even if he had been employed only as an occasional pinch runner, this was a season in which one run could have made the difference in the race, for as Bob Broeg of the *St. Louis Post-Dispatch* commented after the regular season, "As everyone knows from Rangoon to Reykjavík, the Cardinals and Dodgers finished closer together than two postage stamps."

Yet realistically, could Rickey have brought Robinson up at any time in 1946? Not unless he had considered that possibility ahead of time, and he clearly had not, for all the behind-the-scenes machinations that needed to take place for that to

NL TRIPLE LEADERS

1892	Dan Brouthers	20
1901	Jimmy Sheckard	19
1904	Harry Lumley	18
1907	Whitey Alperman	16
1918	Jake Daubert	15
1919	Hy Myers	14
1920	Hy Myers	22
1941	Pete Reiser	17
1945	Luis Olmo	13
1953	Jim Gilliam	17
1959	Wally Moon	11
	Charlie Neal	11
1962	Willie Davis	10
	Maury Wills	10
1970	Willie Davis	16

happen had yet to take place. While the Dodgers fought for the pennant, the one player who could have put them over the top was stuck in Montreal. At this time a Dodger pennant simply wasn't Rickey's number-one priority. Had it been, he

Teammates hoist Harry "Cookie" Lavagetto to their shoulders in a clubhouse celebration after the Dodgers won the fourth game of the 1947 World Series by a score of 3–2. Lavagetto, pinch-hitting for Eddie Stanky, lined a double to right field with two out in the ninth inning to both win the game and break up Yankee pitcher Bill Bevens's bid for the first no-hitter in Series history.

might have tried to find a way to bring Robinson up. And had Rickey done so, it would have been a move as bold and audacious as any Robinson himself made on the base paths, and it would have forced baseball to decide the issue instantaneously and out in the open. But Rickey chose to remain patient, unwilling to test baseball's resolve to remain white in midseason.

Meanwhile, the Dodgers and Cardinals were on a collision course. Ralph Branca had clashed with Rickey over his contract before the 1946 season and spent much of the season in the doghouse before emerging down the stretch as Brooklyn's best pitcher, even starting the first playoff game against St. Louis. Yet he hardly pitched until September and later told author Peter Golenbock that the Dodgers "blew the pennant because Rickey was ticked off at me."

Both teams, as Broeg noted, went "rubber-legged" to the finish, falling to exhaustion as each lost on September 29, the final day of the season. Boston's Mort Cooper first shut out Brooklyn, and the Cardinals took a two-run lead over Chicago. But as the *Eagle* noted: "What started out as a mournful procession for the 32,000 and the countless thousands radioside turned into the gayest party held in our town in five years." The Cubs stormed back to win, 8–3.

That set up the first playoff in National League history, a best-of-three affair beginning, according to a coin toss, with the first game in St. Louis and the remainder in Brooklyn. The Dodgers left immediately for St. Louis as Branch Rickey's past and present were poised to clash. Meanwhile, his future, Robinson, ran rings around Louisville. On his way to St. Louis, Rickey stopped there to watch Robinson in game three of the Little World Series.

He'd have done well to follow the Royals back to Montreal after their 15–6 triumph, for in St. Louis the Dodgers fell to the Cardinals 4–2 as Branca was nicked to death and Howie Pollet worked out of trouble. Then, back in Brooklyn for game two, the Cardinals won the pennant, beating the Dodgers for the 14th time in 22 tries in 1946, 8–4. "The wrong team won," whined Harold Burr in the *Eagle,* and the Dodgers got ready to return nearly $1 million in tickets for the final playoff game and World Series. They had drawn nearly 1.8 million fans, a franchise record, as they continued to tweak Ebbets Field, stuffing extra seats into every possible nook and cranny, a process that had cut the distance to center field by more than 50 feet, to just under 400, and knocked left field from an original 419 to 357. Attendance pressures had transformed the park into a facility increasingly oriented toward offense. Already there were plans for another round of tweaking in 1947.

But even as those plans were being drawn up, the 1947 season was one of the most anticipated in franchise history. Speculation over what Rickey would do with Robinson already held the attention of everyone, including baseball's power brokers, the owners.

Robinson's performance in Montreal in 1946 made it clear to baseball's other owners that Branch Rickey was on the verge of making Robinson a major leaguer. Had Robinson been white, they knew that he would already be in the major leagues. There was no way that a player of Robinson's skills would spend another season in the minors unless they stopped him from making it to the majors. So before Rickey even pressed the issue, they tried to throw up a roadblock.

In early January they convened a secret meeting in New York to consider what was referred to euphemistically in public, when they dared to refer to it at all, as "the race question," a meeting the owners would never even acknowledge took place and the details of which remain sketchy to this day. They were accustomed to taking care of business in the backroom, and for this historic gathering they kept no minutes. Only Commissioner Happy Chandler, who moderated the event, ever spoke on the record about it, as even Rickey remained silent. And even Chandler waited until 1972 before doing so and provided precious few details. "You wouldn't believe what some of those owners said at the meeting," he told the *Washington Star and News*, never indicating precisely who said what. "One of them flat out said that if we let Robinson play they'd burn down the Polo Grounds the first time the Dodgers came in for a series." The goal of the summit was to stop Rickey before he even got started.

According to Chandler, at the start of the meeting Rickey got right to the point and told the other owners that he planned to promote Robinson. He was greeted first with a hostile wall of silence. Then the owners of all 15 other franchises, from Tom Yawkey of the Red Sox to Sam Breadon of the Cardinals and the Phillies' Robert Carpenter Jr., stood and announced their opposition. Any notion that they were simply stewards of the game was exposed as myth. It was a private club — their private club.

But Rickey wasn't finished. He clung to the hope that some club owners, in the privacy of their own thoughts, actually felt differently, that they were just cowards, not bigots. He then introduced a resolution that required a secret ballot, hoping the result might be changed. Again the vote was 15–1. When it was time for cigars and scotch, Rickey stormed away and the other owners congratulated one another for what they thought was a clever and successful dodge. Naively, they believed that Rickey wouldn't dare press the issue again. They'd arrived at their public logic for their position earlier, producing a white paper in 1946 that argued that admitting

blacks into organized baseball would cause irreparable harm to the Negro Leagues. That was true, but in reality they cared not a whit for the Negro Leagues beyond what they received in ballpark rent.

For Rickey and Robinson, however, not all hope was lost. Despite all their anonymous bluster, the men who owned the major leagues were cowards. They had never codified the color line — none of them had ever been willing to put the bigoted policy on a piece of paper for everyone to see — preferring to hide behind the increasingly ludicrous logic of statements such as, "No Negro has ever asked to try out," or the equally ludicrous notion, expressed by a Yankee scout in 1947, that

Following his perilous encounter with Ebbets Field's left-field wall in August 1946, Pete Reiser recovered to help lead the Dodgers to a flatfooted tie with the St. Louis Cardinals and a three-game playoff. Reiser is shown nursing his injured left leg following his game-winning slide against the Cardinals on September 13, 1946.

there were no Negro League players who could "hold down a regular job" in the majors. This even after baseball during the war had somehow found a place for teenagers and obviously handicapped players, including one man — Pete Gray — who had only one arm.

Several days after the secret meeting, Rickey, alone, asked to visit Chandler at his genteel Kentucky home. The commissioner had remained curiously silent during the deliberations, and Rickey wanted to know where he stood on the issue.

Rickey never acknowledged such a meeting, but according to Chandler the Dodger president used his full powers of persuasion to convince Chandler that it was time to break the color line. He even became so desperate that he cautioned there would certainly be race riots if Robinson's promotion was blocked.

Rickey didn't know it, but Chandler had already made his decision. The former Kentucky senator still had political aspirations and, master politician that he was, had found the perfect solution to a situation that had the potential to cost him both his current position and any in his future. He told Rickey, "I'm going to have to meet my Maker some day, and if he asks me why I didn't let this boy play and I say it's because he's black, that might not be a satisfactory answer. So bring him in."

Chandler may have been sincere in that belief, but he was also politically astute — it wasn't his job to make the call on Robinson. He knew there was no formal ban of the black player in the major leagues apart from the owners' craven conspiracy, so there were no grounds to stop Chandler from approving Robinson's contract when it was sent to his office, just as he did hundreds of others. Unless there was some kind of contractual anomaly, he had no authority to act otherwise, for his role in regard to contracts was purely administrative. To change that, the owners would have had to lower their veil of silence and do so publicly. Chandler had rightly concluded that they were unlikely to have the courage of their convictions to do so, for that would certainly entail political and legal problems with emerging fair employment regulations that could reflect badly on both baseball and their other businesses, which blacks and civil rights activists would be certain to boycott. Considering the issue as purely an administrative issue allowed Chandler to have his cake and eat it too: Robinson's contract would simply pass through his office and he would not be required to take a public stand on the issue and alienate his political base.

Brooklyn fans gather on the Ebbets Field turf following the Dodgers' loss to the Boston Braves on the final day of the 1946 season. They are following the progress of the Cardinals' game with the Cubs on the scoreboard in order to learn whether their Dodgers would meet St. Louis in a three-game playoff to decide the pennant. Minutes after this picture was snapped, fans left the park to celebrate the Cardinals' loss and wait in line to purchase playoff tickets.

The door to the future was now wide open—Rickey knew that Chandler would approve Robinson's contract. If Robinson could play, there would be a place for him on the Brooklyn roster. Now all he had to do was make the team.

What ensued was one of the most confusing and maddening spring training camps any organization has ever held, one that has often been lauded since for paving the way for Robinson's promotion, which it did, but not because anything Branch Rickey did that spring worked out the way that he had planned, for virtually none of it did. It was by and large a disaster, later aptly described by Red Smith as Rickey's "weird Chautauqua tour," one that remains shrouded in mystery to this day. Virtually everyone involved with the club that spring—Durocher, Rickey, Robinson, and any number of players and Dodger officials—tells stories about that spring that contradict each other every step of the way. In the end, it was Robinson, by will alone, who made it work, for a lesser man would have fallen apart.

The Dodgers began training in late February, and camp eventually took place in three countries, on two continents, and in two hemispheres: the Dodgers and Royals held spring training in Havana, Cuba, the rest of the system trained in Pensacola, Florida, and both the Dodgers and Royals were scheduled to make extended visits to such distant way stations as Panama and Venezuela.

The decision to train in Cuba has long been assumed to have been for Robinson's benefit, for there he would not face the racism he had experienced in Florida in 1946, and in Cuba Rickey hoped the other Dodgers would become more accustomed to the prevalence of black faces. But as with so many incidents during Robinson's first few seasons, reality was a little different than the revisionist interpretations that followed. The bottom line was that Rickey thought he could make money in Cuba.

Robinson was now one of four African Americans on the Royals roster, which also included pitcher Roy Partlow and the newly signed Roy Campanella and Don Newcombe. Incredibly, although the Hotel Nacional, which housed the Dodgers, was integrated, and the Royals stayed in the clean but spartan barracks of the National Military Academy, a private school, the four black players were given an old car and sent *by Rickey* to a fleabag hotel 15 miles distant. There, segregated from their teammates, they were left to survive on their own without knowing a word of Spanish. Rickey told the men that the slightest racial incident would cause trouble

and he felt it was best to isolate them to make sure no such incident occurred. Yet as a result, Robinson was forced to live in conditions far worse than those of spring training in 1946. He was appalled but turned the other cheek—this time in the face of an act by Rickey.

Rickey was simultaneously trying to exploit the situation for financial gain. Although he spent nearly $25,000 on spring training that year, he thought he could turn a healthy profit by drawing black fans to the ballparks in Cuba, Venezuela, and Panama. In effect, it was yet another Rickey innovation, turning the entire, financially draining spring training experience into one long, lucrative barnstorming tour. Tommy Holmes of the *Eagle* later wrote that the arrangements were primarily made not for Robinson but "to collect a few shekels that would defray the cost of spring training." Instead of ensuring Robinson's success, the approach actually put immediate pressure on him to perform. It was Rickey's naive hope that Robinson would play so well that the Dodger players themselves would ask that he be promoted. That wish would not be fulfilled.

The one "benefit" to the arrangement was unexpected. The press, while interested in Robinson, was kept at bay. Only a few New York papers bothered to send reporters to Cuba. Robinson was left alone—none of the usual Dodger beat writers even bothered to cover the Royals that spring.

Most reports out of camp asked the question, where would Robinson play in 1947 if he made the Dodgers? Second base was apparently out of the question—Stanky had the job and was a Durocher favorite. Rickey encouraged speculation that Robinson would play third, even though Arky Vaughan was returning after two years in the service and a brief retirement. But Durocher apparently had other ideas. On March 2 in Havana he told Ross McGowan of the *Times* that while Robinson was a "damn good ballplayer," Vaughan was his third baseman.

But elsewhere, Rickey was floating another notion. He had told Wendell Smith that "the weakest spot on the Brooklyn roster was first base" and intimated that Robinson would play there, even though Durocher later expressed complete surprise at the move and claimed to be entirely unaware that Robinson had even played first base until spring training was almost over.

Rickey had earlier expressed satisfaction with the tandem of Ed Stevens and Howie Schultz, who were both young and had combined for 87 RBIs and 48 extra-base hits in 1946—

and Schultz had come up big in the playoffs, even hitting a home run. Unbeknownst to Durocher, however, Rickey had changed his mind and was already preparing to make Robinson Brooklyn's first baseman in 1947.

According to Schultz—who, because he also played pro basketball, had permission to arrive late to spring training—when he got on the plane to Havana, Clyde Sukeforth, Dodger scout turned coach, "gave me an indication of what was going to happen." When Schultz got to Cuba, the Dodgers were playing the Yankees in Venezuela. Schultz, known as a fine fielder, was sent to the Royals camp, and "Sukeforth asked me if I would mind working out with Robinson at first."

Schultz immediately realized what was happening. He was being replaced, but to his credit he reacted magnanimously to the situation. He was already thinking that his future might be in basketball, and the Minnesota native recalls that he "didn't have the same feeling toward Robinson as some of the other players." Sadly, it was becoming clear that some of the Dodgers weren't interested in having Robinson as a teammate.

In mid-March, while Schultz was schooling Robinson, a contingent of Dodger players, led by Dixie Walker, decided to take matters into their own hands and stave off Robinson's promotion before it ever happened. They tried to circulate a petition among the players protesting Robinson's presence.

Just who signed on to the plan is still the subject of debate, for everyone but Walker has since tried to distance himself from the event. Bobby Bragan signed, but explained he did so only because he felt he'd be crucified back home in Texas if he did not. Kirby Higbe, from South Carolina, also signed, but later claimed that he had second thoughts and tipped off the Dodgers to the plot. According to Higbe in his autobiography, Pee Wee Reese signed, as did Carl Furillo, something both players later denied. All except for Furillo, a native of Pennsylvania, were from the South.

When Rickey got wind of the move, he had Clyde Sukeforth tell Durocher to intervene. One night the manager roused all the players from bed and had them meet him in the kitchen of the Hotel Nacional. Dressed in his bathrobe, Durocher admonished the team, according to a number of Dodger players, and told them, "If the old man [Rickey] wants

Fans wait in the rain on Montague Street in Brooklyn to purchase tickets to the second game of the 1946 National League playoffs at Ebbets Field.

Dodger manager Leo Durocher mugs with his pal, movie star George Raft, as the pair depart New York for Hollywood several weeks after the Dodgers' defeat in the pennant playoffs. Raft was one of Durocher's unsavory friends whom baseball commissioner Happy Chandler had in mind when he suspended Durocher for the 1947 season.

want to play with Robinson, he'd accommodate them with a trade. As it turned out, Higbe, despite winning 17 games in 1946, would be dealt away with several others in early May in a deal that delivered Pittsburgh outfielder Al Gionfriddo.

As if things were not confusing enough already, another story line was taking shape and dominating the headlines. Since the beginning of camp, Durocher and Larry MacPhail, now the president of the Yankees, had been sparring in the press. Baseball commissioner Happy Chandler was already on Durocher's case for allowing gambling in the clubhouse — Durocher ran a big money card game and regularly fleeced his own players. Then MacPhail was seen sitting with some gamblers during an exhibition series between the Dodgers and Yankees in Havana, and Durocher, through his *Eagle* column ghostwritten by Dodger traveling secretary Harold Parrot and presumably approved by Rickey, made mention of MacPhail's "guests" and added, "If I even said 'hello' to one of those guys, I'd be called before Commissioner Chandler and probably be barred."

MacPhail went off and on March 15 filed a formal charge with Chandler that Durocher was indulging in "conduct detrimental to baseball." At the same time the ex-husband of Durocher's wife, actress Larraine Day, charged Durocher with alienation of affection, dragging Durocher into court and leading the 125,000-member Catholic Youth Organization of Brooklyn to end its affiliation with the team's Knothole Club.

So at the precise time that Rickey was hoping to showcase Robinson before the Dodgers in Panama, Durocher had to leave to defend himself at a California court hearing in regard to the legality of Day's divorce, and the Dodgers shipped half the club, including the anti-Robinson petitioners, back to Havana, leaving Robinson showcased before nobody who mattered. Although Robinson, playing first base, did well in the three-game series versus the major league club that started on March 17, there were no calls from the Dodger players to bring him up. And when the two clubs met up again just over a week later in Havana, Robinson, left to forage for himself, had come down with dysentery and played poorly. Durocher couldn't have been impressed, and he wasn't. He told a reporter he hoped the team could work out a trade for first baseman Johnny Mize.

Even Rickey suddenly seemed unsure. On March 31 Robinson returned to the Royals' lineup as a second baseman, and Rickey claimed he was working on a deal with another NL team that was "the largest offer ever made in baseball," per-

him to play, he's going to play," not revealing his own feelings, although in some subsequent accounts, including his own, his words were more heroic. The next day Rickey met with the players individually and told them that if they didn't

haps to dump the anti-Robinson faction and open up second base for Robinson. But two days later Robinson was back at first base.

Bob Cooke of the *Herald Tribune* summed up the mood precisely, writing: "Log of the good ship Dodger. Men grumbling. Complain about manager leaving early. . . . Hope to make states in another week. . . . Still have enough food to keep squad alive and Rickey talking." Then on April 4 Robinson hurt his back in a collision at first base. As the Dodgers went on a brief barnstorming trip through the South, Robinson and Campanella were sent ahead to Brooklyn for a scheduled two-game set between the Royals and Dodgers at Ebbets Field on April 9.

Then Chandler put a gaping hole in the hull of the already leaky good ship. On April 9 he ruled on MacPhail's charges and stunned everyone by suspending Durocher for the season. Robinson suddenly became an "in other news" kind of story.

Given the Robinson situation, the timing was bizarre, for no one could ever figure out just why Durocher was suspended, including Durocher. A suspension? Over a ghost-written column? Wendell Smith may well have hit the nail on the head when he wrote that the suspension "was not an ordinary brawl" between MacPhail and Durocher, but one fueled by MacPhail's opposition to the Rickey-Robinson plan; MacPhail, Smith wrote, "can't stomach the thought of the lily-white color line being broken." Durocher's suspension may well have been an act of appeasement on Chandler's part. He knew he was going to allow Robinson to be called up, but suspending Durocher at the same time also smacked down Rickey and the Dodgers. Rickey would get Robinson, but MacPhail would have the satisfaction of knowing the move cost the Dodgers their manager.

Another possibility, circumstantial but not without merit, is that Durocher may not have been the staunch supporter of Robinson he later claimed to be. A close examination of the events of that spring reveals that he hardly saw Robinson play. Indications that Rickey was beginning to think of Robinson as a second baseman may well have grated on Durocher—Stanky was his kind of player. The suspension may have been a convenient way to remove Durocher, his input, and, later, his mouth from the entire situation so that Robinson's promotion wouldn't face resistance from within the organization. For once Durocher was out of the picture, there would be no resistance to Rickey's plans. The fact that the press

didn't even speculate that there might have been a connection between the two events lends credence to the notion that there probably was. Increasingly, the New York press had shown its willingness to do Rickey's bidding in regard to Robinson.

Good soldier Clyde Sukeforth was named interim manager, and before the final meeting between the Dodgers and Royals on April 10 Rickey told Robinson it would be his last game as a Royal. After bunting into a double play in the sixth, Robinson was puzzled when his Montreal teammates greeted him with a standing ovation. Then he learned why. Rickey had issued a simple press statement that contained perhaps the most important words in baseball history. "The Brooklyn Dodgers today purchased the contract of Jack Roosevelt Robinson from the Montreal Royals. He will report immediately."

He made his unofficial debut the following day in the first game of a three-game exhibition against the Yankees. The day before, Ed Stevens and Howie Schultz had played first. Now the job was Robinson's. Although he went hitless, a nervous Yankee infield made two errors on two ground balls hit by Robinson, enabling him to reach first. The next day he drove in Brooklyn's only run in a 6–1 loss with a single off Allie Reynolds and finished his soft opening with another hit and two RBIs in the finale.

Although the jury was still out in regard to his reception around the league, Brooklyn fans gave him their vote. Crowds for the first two games hovered around 25,000, a near-packed house of 30,000 showed up for the finale, and in each game there were more black faces than ever seen at Ebbets Field before. Robinson was cheered widely by Brooklyn fans, and Dixie Walker, "the People's Cherce" and widely believed to be the club's most popular player, was booed, owing to his opposition to Robinson.

The Dodgers opened the 1947 season on April 15 against the Boston Braves. Although Robinson and Reese were on the club, the Dodgers were not yet the "Boys of Summer" later rhapsodized by writer Roger Kahn. They were exhausted after spring training, off-balance from the loss of Durocher, and uncertain about Robinson—in regard to both their own feelings about him and the reception they knew awaited them in other cities throughout the league.

Both the pitching rotation and the lineup were unsettled. Half the staff were rookies. No one had staked a claim to third base, and only Reiser and Walker seemed to have secured an outfield spot, although Walker was on the trading block along with Higbe and the other anti-Robinson conspirators. Robinson was apparently the first baseman, but both Schultz and Stevens remained on the roster. Moreover, most of their spring competition had been against semipro and minor league clubs, and the Dodgers hadn't been very impressive. Compared to the Cardinals, who were little changed from 1946, the Dodgers had questions on and off the field.

On Opening Day a large but strangely subdued crowd of 26,643 turned out as vendors hawked "I'm for Jackie" buttons on the street. Joe Hatten started for Brooklyn against Johnny Sain, and the Dodgers won 5–3 in rather workmanlike fashion as Pete Reiser, temporarily healthy, figured in every rally. Robinson had a quiet game and went hitless before being replaced by Schultz in the ninth. He got a nice ovation, but unlike a week earlier, the biggest applause was reserved for Dixie Walker. The *Eagle* termed the size of the crowd "disappointing," perhaps owing to Durocher's absence, but also noted that there was a smallpox scare sweeping Brooklyn.

Robinson got his first hit in game two, a bunt in a 12–6 win. After the game Rickey named 62-year-old Burt Shotton "managerial consultant," in Durocher's stead. With a trustworthy loyalist like Shotton on board—he had played center field for Rickey some 30 years before—Rickey was assured of a quiet and compliant temporary field leader.

Robinson started to perk up at the Polo Grounds against the Giants, but then the Phillies came to Brooklyn. Manager Ben Chapman was from the old school and the Old South, an unapologetic racist and anti-Semite, and under his direction the Phillies gave Robinson a trial by fire.

For three full games they called Robinson everything they could think of in an unceasing barrage. Yet Robinson took it. Howie Schultz remembered that "it was as bad as anything you can imagine. If they said those things today it would cause a civil war." Even some of the Dodgers who were not happy with Robinson's presence—such as Eddie Stanky, who had bluntly told Robinson he did not like playing with him— had their fill of the garbage that spewed forth from the Philadelphia dugout. Stanky even challenged the Phillies to "pick on somebody who can answer back."

Incredibly, even as Robinson was being targeted on the field, Rickey again demonstrated his unique ability to separate baseball the business from all other issues. According to Bob Cooke of the *Herald Tribune,* on April 23 Rickey met with Chapman and general manager Herb Pennock and made a

bizarre pitch for the Phillies franchise to move its entire remaining home schedule to Ebbets Field. That effectively would have put the fox into the hen house, simultaneously making Ebbets Field the home of both the only integrated team in the majors and baseball's most racist franchise, and presumably drawing fans both for and against Robinson, making money off both sides of the "race question." If Cooke's report was accurate, and there is no reason to think it was not, it offers unique insight into the degree to which money figured into Rickey's "great experiment." In this instance morality clearly took a back seat to profit. The Phillies turned him down.

Robinson and the Dodgers, however, were clearly bothered by the experience in Philadelphia. Robinson slumped, and even Brooklyn fans began to pepper Robinson with racial epithets. Their comments were loud enough to be picked up by broadcast microphones and caused the Dodgers to turn them off. Then the club went into Chicago, where the Cubs allegedly voted to go on strike, only to have NL president Ford Frick tell them bluntly they would be banned for life if they did. Robinson was slumping and went hitless in 20 at bats to drop his batting average to .227, a level that rendered his greatest asset, speed, almost irrelevant. Only the fact that the Dodgers started 9–3 saved his place in the lineup, for Schultz and Stevens remained on board.

Racial trouble continued to stalk the team. When the Cardinals came into Brooklyn on May 6, the Cardinals reportedly became the second team to threaten to strike over Robinson, and this time the incident got more play. *Herald Tribune* sports editor Stanley Woodward wrote a famous column about the event in which he quoted Frick telling the players, "If you do this, you'll be suspended from the league. . . . I don't care if it wrecks the National League for five years." Although the Cardinal players later denied the incident ever took place, Woodward's story, which received nationwide play, nevertheless sent out the intended message—baseball would back Robinson, no matter what.

Robinson, true to form and true to his promise to Rickey, remained silent, stoically taking everything being sent his way. He took his promise seriously, for in subsequent interviews and in his biographies he barely addressed the trouble he faced and tended to put the best light on the situation, rarely identifying his tormentors, apart from Chapman, and being circumspect about his own teammates. From the start, Robinson was keenly aware of the historical significance of his promotion and resisted personalizing it. Already, he was taking a much longer view.

The club then went on the road, first to Philadelphia and then to Cincinnati, where the reaction to Robinson turned more ominous. There were death threats, and the Phillies aimed their bats at Robinson as if they were rifles, an act that finally led Frick to tell Chapman to back off. In Cincinnati the FBI even searched nearby rooftops for snipers. At a team meeting, when Burt Shotton informed the team of what was going on, outfielder Gene Hermanski broke the tension when he quipped, "Why don't we all wear the same number — forty-two?" Although Robinson was not yet being welcomed by his teammates, to a man they were developing respect for him. Yet the club was clearly distracted and slumped below .500 for the season.

But while all this was taking place, and despite Robinson's recent slump, the Dodgers sent a message that he was in Brooklyn to stay. On May 9, Schultz was sold to Philadelphia. A few days later Rickey took another tack with Ed Stevens.

According to Stevens, "Mr. Rickey talked to me and told me, 'The job is yours, you've made the club. But could you do me a favor for the ballclub? Let me play Jackie Robinson at first base, you stay in Montreal, and I promise you with a handshake that [in 1948] I'll get rid of Eddie Stanky, put Jackie back on second, and you've got a job for 10 or 15 years.'" The conversation is particularly telling for revealing that Rickey already knew that while Robinson was his first baseman now, his future was at second. Stevens, who had no choice, was sent down, and after the season Rickey conveniently forgot his handshake and sold him to Pittsburgh.

The removal of Schultz and Stevens seemed to give Robinson confidence, for he immediately began playing better. The Dodgers, however, continued to muddle along, playing .500 ball. Their cause was not helped June 4 when Reiser, playing center field, raced back after a fly ball hit by the Pirates' Culley Rikard.

Reiser had a bead on the ball and told himself it would be an easy catch. But the manipulations of the outfield over the past two seasons to accommodate extra seats at Ebbets Field had shortened the distance in center. In the heat of the moment Reiser's instinct took over, and he raced off, oblivious to his rapid approach to the wall.

He learned once again that as tough as he was, concrete was tougher. Just as he caught the ball, he hit the barrier at full speed. The back of his head, turned to make the catch,

On April 15, 1947, Jackie Robinson made history when he became the first African American in the 20th century to play major league baseball. What made Robinson's feat all the more remarkable was that the 28-year-old rookie soon established Hall of Fame credentials in his fourth-best sport. In college Robinson had excelled in both football and basketball and captured a national title in the broad jump.

took the brunt of the collision. He bounced back and fell to the ground like a rag doll, then did not move.

Rikard raced around the bases as the Dodgers rushed to Reiser's aid. As he lay there, umpire Butch Henline looked in his glove, found the ball, and waved Rikard out. The crowd roared, then watched silently as Reiser, after his fourth collision with a wall in five seasons as a Dodger, was carried unconscious off the field on a stretcher for the third time.

He awoke in the Swedish Hospital, where doctors were relieved to discover no fracture. But for Reiser, this would be the final, crushing blow to his career. Although he would return to the lineup a month later and even hit .310 for the balance of the season, the great instinct that allowed him to track down fly balls was gone. At times he was still a dangerous hitter and baserunner, but his days as an everyday player were over, as was any remaining chance he had to make good on his limitless potential. Although no one yet knew it, Reiser's decline took with it the best chance the Dodgers ever had to supplant the Yankee dynasty.

The Dodgers were reeling on all fronts except the box office. Owing primarily to curiosity about Robinson, they were a huge draw on the road, even in segregated St. Louis, where thousands of black fans turned out to see him. Dodger road attendance for the season would be 1,863,542, an NL record at the time, and 55,000 more than the Dodgers drew at home, where attendance kept pace with their record attendance of the previous season.

Nevertheless, these figures reveal a subtle change that went little noticed at the time. The Dodgers were a better draw on the road than at home. And despite Robinson's notoriety and appeal, and in a season in which NL attendance rose by nearly 17 percent, attendance in Brooklyn rose by only 10,000 fans, for the addition of black faces in the crowd was offset by a corresponding subtraction of white ones. Similarly, the crowd at Ebbets Field was younger and contained more children and teenagers than before, a sign of both demographic change and the appeal that Robinson had to kids and young adults whose racial feelings were still malleable. They learned from Robinson, and they were responsible for much of the idealistic, gooey nostalgia that so many still invest in the era. But many parents felt differently.

It wasn't the same. Some older fans — many of them even supportive of Robinson — were nevertheless uncomfortable with the change that suddenly put a black face in the next seat. They were accustomed to a different Ebbets Field and a different team, the lovable, working-class bums who looked like they did and played to a soundtrack of Gladys Goodding's organ and the off-key meanderings of the band of clownish musicians who performed in the stands as the Brooklyn "Sym-Phony." Over the next few seasons these fans would travel to Ebbets Field less and less often. While remaining boosters of the club, many followed the team primarily by radio, and later television. Ebbets Field, which for so long had served as something of an adult clubhouse for many Brooklynites, would become a less popular destination.

Even Rickey had been worried about that. Before the start of the season he met with three dozen black leaders at the Brooklyn YMCA and gave a rousing speech in which he admonished them that "the biggest threat to his success and the one enemy most likely to ruin his success . . . is the Negro people themselves. . . . We don't want parades at the ballpark every night [or] Negroes to strut, and wear badges. . . . We don't want Negroes in the stands gambling, drunk, fighting, being arrested." He asked them to spread the word that Robinson's black fans would be under the same scrutiny as Robinson. The fact that Rickey felt the need for such a meeting is telling, for despite his commitment to bringing down the color line, he was clearly operating under some of the same disquieting racial presumptions as many of the other whites, both in the stands and among baseball's owners. He was afraid black fans lacked the sophistication to mingle with white fans. "Don't ruin it for Jackie" was the phrase of the day in the black community.

The Dodgers were reeling. On June 15, after being crushed by St. Louis, their record was a desultory 27–25.

But Robinson was heating up. After struggling for his first month and surviving his second, he was now beginning to thrive and help make up for the loss of Reiser, thus fulfilling the true role of a teammate — picking up for others. He had weathered the worst, gone through a western road trip, and started to learn the pitchers. While it would be incorrect to say that he had begun to "relax," he had learned to adapt to the pressures he faced and, just as he had done in Montreal, was beginning to channel the anger he often felt at his treatment by fans and players into his game. And even though a number of his Dodger teammates remained distant, either ignoring him off the field or treating him with cursory civility, he had proven to them that by his skills he belonged. And a few, led by captain Pee Wee Reese, began to forge real friendships with Robinson.

When one watches film of Robinson during this initial season, he seems supercharged, as if his energy can barely be contained within his body. Blessed with a football player's build, Robinson fairly seethes with strength and determination, using his legs like others wield a bat. He is always

Dodger manager Burt Shotton gives his team a pep talk on April 18, 1947, at the Polo Grounds following his appointment as Leo Durocher's replacement. Shotton, who managed in street clothes, led the team to the pennant despite the turmoil surrounding Jackie Robinson's historic major league debut.

focused, always on his toes, always pressing forward. One can almost feel his kinetic power and see his eyes burning with a white-hot inner fire. Off the field, he may have just been trying to fit in. But on the field he was trying to take over, a revolution of one, changing the game and changing hearts and minds at the same time, making the case over and over again that he, Jackie Robinson, a black man, is here, visible and undeniable, and that he belongs.

Once it was clear that Robinson wasn't going away and that he was in fact one of the best players on the team, if not in the game, he and his teammates reached a working accommodation. Although history has tended to romanticize the way he was eventually accepted by his teammates, there were true acts of courage and public support. Reese, in particular, made it a point to include Robinson in activities off the field. And on the long train rides between the NL cities, barriers inevitably fell as the team was forced to get to know one another and suspicion fell away.

Over the next week, as the Dodgers won five out of six, Robinson was in the middle of things, doing what was necessary to help the club win. At the same time the questions of spring training were beginning to be answered as Spider Jorgensen captured the third base job, Carl Furillo nailed down right field and filled in for Reiser in center, Ralph Branca

emerged as the staff ace, and Hugh Casey became the best fireman in the league.

The rest of the National League was finally starting to see the player who had terrorized the International League so effectively the previous year. In Pittsburgh on June 24, with the score tied 2–2 and Robinson on third, he faked a dash to home. Pirate hurler Fritz Ostermueller looked at him with disdain and yelled something presumably unprintable. Robinson took off again, only this time he wasn't faking it — he slid into home ahead of the pitch for what proved to be the winning margin. Two days later the Dodgers snuck into first place.

The Braves hung with them for the next ten days as Robinson stayed hot, running a hitting streak he started on June 14 to 20 games before it was finally snapped on the Fourth of July. By then the Dodgers were in first place, 41–30, 14–6 over Robinson's hitting streak, and threatening to pull away. The Braves had Spahn and Sain but still wished for rain when anyone else was on the mound, while the Cardinals, although starting to surge, had gotten off to a horrible start because Stan Musial, who had hit .365 in 1946, came down with appendicitis and was hitting nearly 150 points less. St. Louis manager Eddie Dyer still selected Musial to appear in the All-Star Game to back up Giants slugger Johnny Mize. Although Robinson was clearly having a better year, he was ignored.

And as of July 3, Robinson wasn't the only story anymore. Cleveland owner Bill Veeck, who had purchased the team before the start of the season, signed Larry Doby from the roster of the Newark Eagles and brought him to Cleveland. Now Robinson had tangible evidence that his struggles were not singular but had indeed served a larger purpose, paving the way for others.

At the All-Star break Robinson was hitting .310 and the Dodgers led the Braves by a game. Taking a cue from Robinson, who maintained his torrid pace after the break, the Dodgers took off. They won their final 13 games in July to take command in the pennant race, helped by the return of Pete Reiser, who in between misplaying fly balls was still an occasionally dangerous hitter. When he hit third behind Robinson, the two sometimes created a devastating combination.

In the second half the Dodgers pulled away. As they did, the most egregious acts of bigotry from the stands and the opposition began to fade. But on the field it was a different story, for in the context of the game Robinson remained a target.

Nowhere was that more true than in St. Louis. On August 16, Robinson was spiked by Joe Medwick. And in a celebrated incident two days later, outfielder Enos Slaughter, running to first, viciously spiked Robinson on the leg.

But now he had the support of his teammates, who knew that while Robinson couldn't retaliate, they could. Even Eddie Stanky hoped for the opportunity to give Slaughter some of his own medicine were he to slide into second. And Brooklyn pitchers, tired of seeing Robinson thrown at, let it be known that there would be retribution every time it happened.

On August 26, the second black Dodger, pitcher Dan Bankhead, arrived. But unlike the signing of Johnny Wright, his promotion had nothing to do with providing Robinson

---

Dodger players and their wives and girlfriends celebrate the 1947 pennant at pitcher Hugh Casey's restaurant on Flatbush Avenue. From left are Hank Behrman, Harry Taylor, Pete Reiser, Johnny Jorgensen, Bobby Bragan, and Vic Lombardi.

with a companion. He could pitch, and the Dodgers needed depth going into September.

They ran away from the field as St. Louis lost six straight to fall out of the race. On September 12 Robinson was named the *Sporting News* Rookie of the Year. The club clinched the pennant on September 22, and the next day Robinson was honored with his own "day" at Ebbets Field. Entertainer Bill "Bojangles" Robinson helped with the ceremony and captured the mood when he said, "I'm 69 years old and never thought I'd live to see the day when I'd stand face to face with Ty Cobb in Technicolor."

All Brooklyn celebrated the pennant on September 26 with an enormous parade. The Dodgers finished first with a record of 94–60 as Robinson hit .297, scored 125 runs, and led the league with 29 stolen bases. The team began to make preparations to play the Yankees in the World Series. In a sense the Series was the second true "subway series," for when the Yankees and Giants had met earlier, Series games were played either entirely at the Polo Grounds or, after the building of Yankee Stadium, in parks that were little more than a short walk from each other, as they were on opposite sides of the Harlem River.

The Yankees, like the Dodgers, had been a surprise. This was not the star-laden dynasty that had dominated baseball before the war. DiMaggio was older and less of a force, but the Yankees had made up for their loss of star power by creating a flexible team built around role players and pitching depth, solid pros who knew their jobs. Still, compared to the Dodgers, the Yankees seemed strong and had won the pennant by 12 games.

After the trials and tribulations of the 1947 season in regard to Robinson, it seemed unlikely that the World Series could match the drama of the regular season. Yet it did all that and more.

Beginning in 1947, the Yankees, not the Giants—at least temporarily—became Brooklyn's main rivals. That was a measure of just how far along the club had come, for suddenly a mere pennant wasn't enough. For years the Yankees and Giants had dominated, but now Brooklyn had passed the Giants both on the field and in attendance and were closing in on the Yankees. The addition of Robinson had given the club real appeal among younger New Yorkers—even in Manhattan and the Bronx—and among those who were put off by the Yankees' smug attitude. In a season of firsts, a Brooklyn victory could begin to make the case that the center of

The 1947 World Series between the Dodgers and the Yankees marked the second time the clubs had met in the fall classic in six years. For years the two had met in preseason exhibition games.

New York's baseball universe was not "the House That Ruth Built" but the one built by Charlie Ebbets, and that the Dodgers sat atop the New York baseball throne.

And there was still more at stake in the Series than just settling the question of who was the better team. In addition to Robinson's presence, which represented a personal affront to Larry MacPhail, there was still genuine animosity between the two teams stemming from the MacPhail-Durocher feud, made even worse by the fact that Yankee coach Charlie Dressen, who'd also been suspended for a month after being caught in the crossfire, had formerly served the Dodgers and was viewed as a traitor.

The Series actually started quietly and, for the first two games anyway, unfolded as many expected.

As had happened so many times before during the regular season, Robinson got the Dodgers going. In the first game, with one out in the top of the first at Yankee Stadium, he drew a walk. Before the Series, the Yankees' rookie catcher, Larry (not yet Yogi) Berra had bragged that Robinson hadn't successfully stolen a base against him in 1946 while he was catching for Newark. But Robinson's life was about doing things people said he couldn't do.

He stole second and later said if he ran against Berra every day he'd steal 60 bases. When Reiser tapped back to Spec Shea, Robinson broke for third and got into a rundown, which for anyone else would have been a big mistake. And it was. But only Robinson could stay alive long enough to allow Reiser to make it to second. He scored on Dixie Walker's single to give the Dodgers a 1–0 lead.

Ralph Branca was perfect through four innings, but in the fifth the Yankees blew him out of the game with a five-run

Pete Reiser crosses home plate with the first run of the 1947 World Series at Yankee Stadium after being driven home by Dixie Walker.

and aggressive baserunning to score six runs without a homer—Robinson and Reese had actually tied for the team lead with 12 each during the regular season. The Dodgers then managed to hold on for a 9–8 win.

Game four, as it so often is, was critical, for a Brooklyn loss would force the Dodgers to win the final three games, a near-insurmountable task. Neither team was particularly adept with starting pitching. Journeyman Bill Bevens pitched for New York opposite the Dodgers' Harry Taylor. At best, both men were no better than the number-four starters on their own team.

Which is precisely what made game four so remarkable, one of the most talked about in World Series history, one that Dick Young of the *Daily News* accurately called "the greatest baseball ever played. . . . They'll talk about it forever, those 33,443 fans who saw it. They'll say, 'I was there.'" In a strange way, both men pitched to their expected standard, but Taylor didn't make it out of the first while Bevens nearly made it to the Hall of Fame.

Taylor didn't retire a man in the first inning. After he walked DiMaggio to force in the first run of the game, Shotton pulled him and in desperation brought in Hal Gregg, whose regular season ERA was 5.88.

Gregg managed to work out of trouble and settled in, giving up only a single run in the fourth inning. But for the Yankees, Bevens was on the tightrope, pitching bad but getting results.

He was effectively wild, just wild enough to keep the Dodgers off-balance, and pitched what the *Herald Tribune's* Rud Rennie later called a "most strangely beautiful performance." Nearly every inning he walked one man—or two— and went to a full count on another batter or two only to have the Yankee defense bail him out. The Dodgers finally broke through in the fifth when Bevens walked both Spider Jorgensen and Gregg. An Eddie Stanky bunt and a ground ball by Reese plated a run.

It was then that the odd sight of a "1" under the run column paired with a "0" in the hit column alerted most fans that Bevens, despite his struggles, hadn't given up a hit. On any other day Yankee manager Bucky Harris would have called on reliever Joe Page or someone else, but the Yankees had used five pitchers the day before and the pen was gassed.

At the end of eight, the score was still 2–1 and Bevens was three outs away from pitching a no-hitter, the first in World Series history. Then the already strange game got stranger.

outburst, then held on to win, 5–2. The Yankees won game two in a rout, 10–3. The *Eagle's* Harold Burr moaned, "The Dodgers look like a team that has gone stale . . . it has a listless air about it." As the teams traveled to Brooklyn, the Yankees started preparing to raise another banner over the Stadium.

But at Ebbets Field, in front of the home crowd, the Dodgers were another team. They exploded in the second inning in typical Dodger fashion, using a series of hits, walks,

Burt Shotton, whose understated style caused New York sportswriters to automatically insert the phrase "kindly old" before his name, suddenly awoke and responded with a series of moves as inexplicable today as they were then. Yet they all worked.

For no known reason, he pulled Gregg in favor of reliever Hank Behrman, who immediately loaded the bases. But Hugh Casey came in and got a double-play ball to end the inning and keep the game close.

Bill Bevens went to the mound in the ninth after throwing 120 pitches determined to throw three more and secure his place in baseball history. Catcher Bruce Edwards led off the inning with a long drive to left, but the Yankees' Johnny Lindell drifted back to make the catch short of the fence. Bevens was two outs away.

But he still had trouble throwing strikes. He walked Furillo, and then Spider Jorgensen let him off the hook by popping out, leaving Bevens one out shy of immortality.

Now Shotton awoke and decided to pinch-run for Furillo, inserting Al Gionfriddo into the game as a pinch runner. Gionfriddo was not only faster than Furillo but a better baserunner. On several occasions earlier in the year Furillo had been called out for missing second base while running to third.

Pitcher Hugh Casey was due up next, and Shotton called on Pete Reiser to pinch-hit. Reiser shouldn't have even been on the bench but in his more accustomed place in the hospital. He had broken his ankle in game three but refused to have it put in a cast, insisting that he could still play with the leg heavily taped.

He limped to the plate and worked the count to 2–1. Shotton decided to send Gionfriddo to second, trying to get him into scoring position.

Bevens, at 6'3", took a while to uncoil. Gionfriddo got a good jump but slipped on his first step and Berra made a near-perfect throw as Gionfriddo slid into Phil Rizzuto's tag.

Umpire Bill McGowan hesitated, then called Gionfriddo safe as Rizzuto spun away, certain he was out. The pitch was called a ball, making the count 3–1.

Now Yankee manager Bucky Harris made a move. As Red Smith noted later, he violated "all ten commandments of the

Cookie Lavagetto is mobbed by teammates, fans, policemen, and Ebbets Field ushers following his dramatic game-winning hit that broke up Bill Bevens's no-hitter with two outs in the ninth inning of game four of the 1947 World Series. Lavagetto's pinch-hit double scored teammates Al Gionfriddo and Eddie Miksis and was the last hit of his ten-year major league career.

With the Dodgers holding an 8–5 lead in the sixth inning of game six of the 1947 World Series, Brooklyn left fielder Al Gionfriddo, who'd just entered the game as a defensive replacement for Eddie Miksis, made one of the great catches in Series history when he robbed Joe DiMaggio of a game-tying home run with two outs and the world championship on the line for New York.

dugout" and ordered Bevens to walk Reiser, putting the winning run — and a healthy baserunner — on first.

Shotton countered by calling Reiser back to the dugout — he could barely walk — and sending in Eddie Miksis to pinch-run. Eddie Stanky was due up next. Bat in hand, he started to stroll from the dugout.

Then Shotton called him back. Stanky couldn't believe it. He hadn't been pinch-hit for all season long and had handled Bevens as well as any other Brooklyn batter that day, walking twice, bunting for a sacrifice, and popping up. Moreover, he rarely struck out and was second in the league in walks, 103 to Pee Wee Reese's 104.

Even more surprising was Shotton's choice to hit in his stead — Cookie Lavagetto, another right-handed hitter.

Before the war, Lavagetto had been a valuable part of the Dodgers, but after he returned from the service, Branch Rickey bluntly told him he'd lost it and had tried to convince Lavagetto to take a job as a manager in the low minors. But

Lavagetto stubbornly held on. He had hardly played in 1947, coming to bat only 69 times, and he was hitless in the Series. His big moment had come on September 11 when his pinch-hit had beat the Cardinals, but it was hardly a trend. If Arky Vaughan hadn't already been called on, Shotton never would have put in Lavagetto.

Even Lavagetto was shocked. When Shotton called on him, he admitted later, he "thought [Shotton] wanted to bring me in as a pinch-runner. He had to tell me twice that he wanted me to go up and hit."

Stanky slammed his bat to the ground as Lavagetto took his place and stepped in against Bevens. The pitcher threw an inside fastball, and Lavagetto swung through it, putting Bevens up 0–1.

Now the pitcher wanted to work him and keep Lavagetto from pulling the ball. He threw a pitch away, trying to get Lavagetto to chase, to pull the ball on the ground.

The ball was right where Bevens wanted it. But Lavagetto wasn't trying to pull — he was just trying to make contact. He swung, a little late, and hit the ball flush. The drive sliced to right.

Gionfriddo and Miksis took off. In right field Yankee outfielder Tommy Henrich, playing Lavagetto to pull in front of the scoreboard, raced back and to his left, the ball sailing over his head.

He had two choices — play it safe and catch the ball as it caromed off the wall and try to nail Miksis at home or go for the catch. He tried to save the no-hitter.

He leaped up, still some eight or ten feet from the wall, and still short of the drive. The no-hitter was gone. It hit squarely in the middle of the Gem Blade sign, then bounced back, off Henrich's chest and then past him as he tried to stop and gather in the ball.

It was too late. Gionfriddo scored easily, and Miksis was crossing the plate as his relay throw came in to George McQuinn. The Dodgers, with but a single hit, had won 3–2 and evened the Series. Brooklyn blew its top. Lavagetto pulled in at second and then was swamped by his delirious teammates. Red Barber told the country, "Friends, they're killing Lavagetto . . . his own teammates . . . they're tearing him to pieces." And as they did, Bill Bevens walked off the mound alone. In the rough truth of Dick Young, "Now he was just another loser."

Brooklyn was beside itself. Wrote Young: "The Faithful hugged each other in the stands . . . others ran out to the center of the diamond and buried Lavagetto in their caresses." Tommy Holmes noted: "Forty-five minutes after the game was over there were still several thousand fans wandering around the ballpark in a bubble-headed daze. They didn't want to go home. They didn't want to go anywhere . . . this may have been the greatest World Series game, this 3–2 decision the Dodgers plucked out of the fire at the 59th minute of the 11th hour."

He may well have been right, and Dodger fans certainly would have been happy if the day had never come to an end, for they still had to win two of the next three, and the Yankees were still the Yankees and the Dodgers the Dodgers.

Shotton proved that in game five the next day. His hunches the day before gave him the false confidence of a poker player who once had drawn to an inside straight and thought he could do it again.

Shotton didn't like revealing his choice of pitcher until the day of the game. When he walked into the Dodger clubhouse for game five — late, for he'd spent much of the night meeting with Rickey — he walked past Vic Lombardi and Branca, both of whom were hoping to pitch, and over to 22-year-old Rex Barney, 5–2 with a 4.75 ERA, and told him he was pitching. Like Wil Robinson so many years before, in the middle of the World Series a Dodger manager was playing 52-pickup with his pitching staff.

Branca and Lombardi were both stunned. When Shotton saw the looks on their faces, he hastily blubbered, "I suppose both of you boys are disappointed, but I can only use one of you at a time." All year long the Dodgers had shaken their heads at Shotton's moves, but this was something else. Thirty-eight wins sat on the bench in the biggest game of the year.

Barney pitched well, but the Yankees' Spec Shea was better. He took a 2–1 lead into the ninth. Once again the game came down to the last batter, Lavagetto, pinch-hitting for Hugh Casey, with the tying run on second. But this time Casey's replacement struck out, and the Yankees were going home with a 3–2 Series lead.

Lombardi got the start in game six, but after the Dodgers took an early 4–0 lead, he was shelled. Now Branca came on — he would hold the Yankees off until the Dodgers regained the lead and provided their fans with one more memorable moment. Leading 8–5 in the sixth, there were two on

when Al Gionfriddo tracked down Joe DiMaggio's deep drive to left, making a spectacular one-handed catch at the "415" sign and causing DiMaggio to make a rare emotional display as he kicked the dirt in disappointment after the catch. Brooklyn held on, and the Series was tied. Tommy Holmes quipped afterward, in reference to the trade of Kirby Higbe that had delivered Gionfriddo, "The longer you live around these Dodgers of ours the more likely you are to concede that Branch Rickey is an authentic, licensed genius after all."

But the Dodgers were spent, and genius could not help them now. Shotton's top three starters, Lombardi, Branca, and Hatten, had all pitched in game six, and thus far in the Series the Dodgers had used 22 pitchers because not a single starter had made it past the fifth. And Hugh Casey, who'd appeared in five games already, had bruised his ribs in a collision. All Shotton had left now was Hal Gregg.

The game all but ended in the first inning. Thus far Brooklyn had run wild on Yogi Berra. In game seven Bucky Harris started Aaron Robinson, and in this game it was Aaron, not Jackie, who was the difference. In the first inning both Robinson and Reese reached first base. And each was thrown out trying to steal second by the Yankee catcher.

Brooklyn battled back to take a 2–0 lead in the second, but Bill Bevens came on in relief of a struggling Spec Shea, and he and Joe Page slammed the door the rest of the way. Meanwhile, the Yankees chipped away and took advantage of a misplay by Eddie Miksis in left that turned Snuffy Stirnweiss's pop fly into a two-run triple. New York won, 5–2, to take the Series.

With the end of the Series, it was as if a great group hallucination loosened its grip on Brooklyn. After all that had happened — the weird spring training, Durocher's suspension, and Robinson breaking the color line — a world championship to top it off was too much to ask. As Holmes wrote, "Everyone should have known that the 1947 Dodgers are still in the formative stage. . . . It seems incredible, nevertheless it is true, that if the Dodgers could have got a competent nine-inning pitching performance anywhere in the World Series, they could have been world champions."

"There will come a day."

The Dodgers' first world championship was still somewhere in the distance.

THE LORDS OF FLATBUSH

TOMMY HOLMES WAS RIGHT IN A SENSE. THE DODGERS WERE IN A FORMA-tive stage. But no one as yet had any idea of the extent to which that was true.

After the 1947 season, despite winning a pennant, the Dodgers were unfinished. While they were the darlings of their fans and the Lords of Flatbush, the future was uncertain. And before moving forward, Branch Rickey was determined to make some changes.

Durocher was a big part of those changes. Presumably, now that the 1947 season was over, he was eligible to return and his reinstatement was a mere formality. In fact, one day after the World Series the *Eagle* reported that Durocher received a statement from Chandler indicating that he was eligible to return. But the key word was *eligible*. He still needed a con-tract with Rickey.

Rickey, however, wasn't too eager to give him one. He had never been fully enamored of the manager. While Rickey respected Durocher as a game tactician, he also felt threatened by him — Durocher was both a better player and a better tactician than Rickey had ever been, and by sheer force of Durocher's personality, Rickey was con-fronted by those facts regularly. Also, Rickey had never been com-fortable with Durocher's morals — the man gambled, which offended Rickey, who wouldn't even attend a ballgame on Sun-

Dodger fans line up for Opening Day tickets in 1949. Among the throng are (front row, left to right) Sylvia Jacobs, Mrs. Carrie Koschnick, and Gregory Musco in this photograph from Brook-lyn's paper of record, the *Eagle*.

day. Had Rickey not felt forced into supporting Durocher against MacPhail the year before, he'd probably have fired the manager by now anyway. Durocher simply wasn't Rickey's guy.

Despite the fact that Durocher had been a guest of the club during the Series and had been paid his full contract for 1947—albeit after pressing the issue—when the *Eagle*'s Harold Burr called Rickey to ask when Durocher would be offered a contract, Rickey cryptically told him, "Why don't you go fishing?" A few days later he answered the same question hyperbolically, saying, "Last spring I didn't decide on my manager until the National League season was three or four days old." While he added that he had no intention of waiting that long this time, he did note, "We have several months left to make that decision." Naming a manager—particularly Durocher—wasn't a priority.

Increasingly, Rickey's only priority was his own plans. In the wake of the Series, the *Eagle* reported that after game one Rickey had moaned that in Robinson he had "the best second baseman in the game . . . but I've got to play him at first. The Dodgers are going to have a good club eventually, but it's still in the making." Apparently, and despite 94 wins and a pennant, he still held to that notion.

He let Durocher dangle into December before reluctantly signing him to a contract for 1948, but not before inserting a clause that allowed it to be canceled at any time. Rickey then reminded Durocher just whose team it was by finally trading Dixie Walker, along with Vic Lombardi and Hal Gregg, to Pittsburgh for shortstop Billy Cox, journeyman pitcher Preacher Roe, and infielder Gene Mauch. Rickey then announced that Cox would play third for the Dodgers, which was something of a surprise to Durocher. Then in short order Rickey damned Eddie Stanky with faint praise. While calling him "the most valuable player on the club" and noting that "you win pennants with ballplayers like Stanky," he also said, "He can't run, he can't throw and can't field . . . If I could find a better first baseman," he added, "I'd shift Jackie Robinson to second."

Durocher was being set up, something that was made clear to the manager a short while later when he was called to Brooklyn to weigh in on a contract dispute with Stanky, who wanted $2,500 more than Rickey wanted to pay him. When Durocher backed the player and told Rickey to pay up, he gave Rickey the excuse he needed eventually to get rid of both men, which is what the Mahatma probably wanted to do all

along—because circumstances reveal that Rickey had no intention or desire to win the pennant in 1948. Bringing Durocher back in 1948 was a way for Rickey to pacify Brooklyn fans before the trade of the popular Walker, then set up Durocher to be the fall guy for the failure that Rickey was about to bring about as he remade his club. Rickey would then be left free to do what he wanted without taking the blame. And that's just what happened.

In the spring Robinson showed up at camp at Ciudad Trujillo in the Dominican Republic two days late and some 25 pounds overweight. He had spent the winter cashing in on his notoriety. He touted everything from bread to cigarettes in print ads in black newspapers, made a vaudeville-style speaking tour at $2,500 an appearance, inked a book deal with ghostwriter Wendell Smith, signed to appear in a movie version of his life, and traveled the country to appear at a variety of banquets and testimonials. All told, he'd made about $100,000, more than any player in the game at the time.

Durocher was both jealous and angry at Robinson's poor physical condition, which Durocher felt showed him up. He immediately got on Robinson's back, making him run outfield sprints, shag flies, and field grounders for hours to melt off the fat. But this wasn't 1947. Among the Dodgers, Robinson no longer felt as restrained as before, and he resisted the manager. There was bad blood from the start, and the two rarely spoke, their distaste for one another apparent to everyone.

And then, despite Durocher's best efforts to convince Rickey otherwise, Eddie Stanky was traded to the Boston Braves. But *traded* might be the wrong word.

Stanky was given away without any pretense to one of the teams most likely to challenge the Dodgers in 1948, the rapidly improving Boston Braves. All the Dodgers received in return were outfielder Bama Rowell, light-hitting first baseman Ray Sanders, and $40,000. Neither Sanders nor Rowell would ever play in a game for Brooklyn.

The deal was telling. It left the way open for Robinson at second base yet sent Rickey's self-described team MVP to a club certain to fight Brooklyn for the pennant in 1948, for the Braves had finished only eight games behind the Dodgers in 1947. Significantly, it would be the only deal of substance Rickey made during his Dodger tenure with another contender, and it made the Braves much stronger while doing absolutely nothing for Brooklyn—apart from alienating Durocher. And after the last two seasons the Dodgers were already rolling in dough and didn't need another $40,000. Had Rickey really wanted to win in 1948, he would have either kept Stanky or traded him to a noncontender, probably for pitching.

Stanky's racial views probably weren't a factor in the deal. Although he had initially been resistant to Robinson, the way Robinson played had won him over. Durocher said that when he showed up at training camp, Stanky was Robinson's "greatest booster." The whole episode was made even more curious when in the space of the next six weeks the Dodgers dumped Rowell on waivers and sold Sanders back to the Braves for $60,000, making the Stanky deal purely a cash transaction worth $100,000.

What followed was another weird training camp that seemed designed to do everything *but* prepare the club for the start of the season. Durocher went into a snit after the Stanky trade and asked publicly of Rickey, "What was he doing?" Durocher took his anger out on Robinson, playing Eddie Miksis at second base and leaving Robinson on the bench. He got his first good look at Roy Campanella, thought he was already the best catcher in the league, and wanted to hand him the Dodger job, but Rickey wouldn't allow it. The Dodger president wanted credit for breaking the color line in the American Association and had already determined that Campy would play for St. Paul. But that was a vain and empty desire, for Robinson effectively had already done that when he'd played against the circuit's lone southern franchise, Louisville, in the 1946 Little World Series. Durocher also wanted to turn the young backup catcher Gil Hodges into a first baseman only to have Rickey veto that move—he had concluded that it was too dangerous for Reiser in the outfield and wanted him to play first base.

Once again, the Dodgers spent most of the spring playing minor league competition, proving only that they were a pretty fair triple-A team. When they finally left the Dominican Republic, they barnstormed through the South, playing before lucrative capacity crowds and breaking the color barrier in a host of cities as Rickey simultaneously satisfied both his moral and venal desires. But the tour didn't prepare the Dodgers for Opening Day.

Robinson opened the season at second, but he was still overweight, and the Dodgers got off to a slow start. In mid-May they were in fifth place and dropping fast. Reiser was finished. Durocher still preferred Hodges at first and Campanella behind the plate, but when rosters had to be cut down

Jackie Robinson helped lead the Dodgers to six National League pennants and one world championship in his ten-year career with Brooklyn. He is shown here making a leaping catch of a line drive by Danny O'Connell of the Pirates at Ebbets Field on September 22, 1953.

Edwin "Duke" Snider was to Brooklyn what Mays and Mantle were to the Giants and Yankees, a five-tool ballplayer. Snider clouted 40 or more homers for five straight seasons, from 1953 through the Dodgers' final season in Brooklyn in 1957.

on May 15, Campy was sent to St. Paul. It might have been good social policy, but it wasn't a good way to run a baseball team. Durocher retaliated by moving Robinson back to first base.

By the end of May the Dodgers were in sixth place and threatening to drop even further. Durocher was incensed—because of player injuries, he began a road trip with only six

healthy pitchers, and Rickey seemed determined to leave him understaffed. While the organization was bursting with young pitching talent, Rickey seemed loath to bring up more than one man a year, and in 1948 it was Rex Barney, who got the call while Carl Erskine and Don Newcombe languished in the minors, dominating the competition. Robinson, although hitting with more power, was not the same player who had terrorized organized baseball with his speed in 1946 and 1947 — that had almost disappeared from his game.

Then, in a stunning move, the Dodgers asked for waivers on Robinson. For a nominal fee, any other team in the league could have claimed him, and if the Dodgers chose to let him go, he would go for virtually nothing. All seven teams passed.

While the administrative maneuver doesn't necessarily mean a team wants to rid itself of a player, its use in regard to Robinson was curious — Robinson wasn't just any player. Rickey later offered the weak excuse that he was simply using the ploy to "fire up" Robinson. This was a patent lie, for when the move became public, the Dodgers were so embarrassed that they first denied it even happened, an odd response if they were trying to use it for motivational purposes.

Although many subsequent biographers have claimed the move spurred a turnaround for Robinson after a dismal start, that is incorrect, for despite his poor condition he was already hitting over .300 and was among the league leaders in RBIs. What the move did accomplish was to return Robinson back to second base as Rickey asserted his will over Durocher.

At the end of June, after hitting .325 and cracking 13 home runs in 35 games with St. Paul, Campanella was brought back up. The move paid immediate dividends. Durocher put Hodges at first, and the club won 16 of its next 19 to pull back into the pennant race.

But it didn't last. Just before the All-Star break the club dropped six in a row, and during the break Rickey asked Durocher to quit. He refused. Then Giants owner Horace Stoneham asked permission to talk to Shotton, who was now serving as head of the Dodger farm system, about replacing Mel Ott as their manager. Rickey agreed and then offered Stoneham the option of talking to Durocher. Stoneham was thrilled, and when Rickey told Durocher he was free to go to the Giants, the manager, knowing his time was up, quickly "resigned." He joined the Giants and looked forward with relish to the many opportunities he believed he would have to show up Rickey. Rickey brought back kindly old compliant Burt Shotton to do as he was told as Dodger manager.

Shotton didn't resist Rickey's interference. After telling the press he planned to put Robinson back on first and move Hodges back behind the plate, he did no such thing. Now that Durocher was gone, a few of Durocher's ideas—like making Hodges a first baseman and making Campanella the full-time catcher—were now Rickey's ideas and suddenly seemed brilliant. Young Duke Snider became the center fielder as Furillo moved to right. Billy Cox started getting the bulk of playing time at third. Carl Erskine was called up from the minors and gave the pitching staff a jolt.

For six weeks the Dodgers were the best team in the National League, and at the end of August they were pressing the Braves. The team that author Roger Kahn would later dub "the Boys of Summer" was beginning to take shape.

But too many games had been squandered in April and May, and now Stanky and Durocher came back to haunt the Dodgers. After providing the Braves with a spark early in the season, Stanky had broken his hand. Now he returned and put them over the top. Despite the fact that Robinson, his weight finally down below 200 pounds, was beginning to run the bases with abandon again, it was too late for Brooklyn. Durocher's Giants knocked the Dodgers out of the race in early September. The club finished third, seven and a half games out of first. But Rickey got his wishes. He was rid of Durocher, had remade his ballclub, and had broken the color line in the American Association, receiving full credit for the successes and none of the blame for a season he had tossed away. Now he was looking over the horizon, toward the future, where his scouting efforts during the war were about to pay off.

Although two years had passed since Robinson became a Dodger, the color line was still in place everywhere but Brooklyn and Cleveland. In addition to Larry Doby, the Indians had also signed Satchel Paige. But no other team had a black player on the major league roster. The Dodgers could have—and should have—been poised to skim the cream from the Negro Leagues, since they were wildly popular in the black community and would have been the first choice of just about every available player.

But that didn't happen. Not even Rickey was comfortable with the notion of too many black players. He steadfastly stuck to his schedule of one player a year. In 1948 Don Newcombe was unquestionably ready for the majors, but he spent the entire year pitching for Montreal. And Rickey still wanted to make sure that his players had what he paternalistically believed were the right qualities, that they were all "good"

NL HITS LEADERS

1900	Willie Keeler	208
1919	Ivy Olson	164
1950	Duke Snider	199
1962	Tommy Davis	230
1978	Steve Garvey	202
1980	Steve Garvey	200

Negroes who wouldn't rock the boat or threaten white sensibilities. Newcombe was impatient and volatile and pushed Rickey as far as he was willing to go. But older, established black players—save the legendary Paige—were ignored by Rickey and everyone else. The final generation of established Negro League stars found the door to the major leagues still shut tight, even by the Dodgers.

Although the Dodgers would generally remain ahead of the curve in regard to signing black players, they could have started a dynasty that would have left the rest of baseball playing catch-up for decades. Had they aggressively pursued black talent after signing Robinson, no team in baseball could have kept pace, and their lead would have forced others to follow suit or fall even further behind. But instead of moving forward, the Dodgers stood pat. Their farm system was full of talent—primarily white—and that, apparently, was enough.

It was enough because there were continuing signs in the stands at Ebbets Field that Rickey's great experiment was not an unqualified success. In a season when big league attendance surged for the first time to more than 20 million and in which six teams set all-time attendance marks, attendance

With the arrival of Roy Campanella, Gil Hodges was converted from catcher to first baseman, with great success. Always a fan favorite in Brooklyn, Hodges hit 40 or more home runs in 1951 and 1954 and led all regulars with a .364 batting average in the 1953 World Series.

in the middle of the pack in regard to attendance. Only one year after the breaking of the color line, the Dodgers were again only the third-best draw in New York. That said something.

In the Dodger front office, it began to spell change. There was growing trouble between Rickey and the other Dodger owners. Attorney Walter O'Malley, who'd made his fortune on foreclosures during the Depression and now had his fingers in a host of other lucrative businesses, was rapidly accumulating more power and influence. After being appointed club attorney in 1941, by 1945 he owned 25 percent of the club, the same share as Rickey and John Smith. Although Rickey enjoyed their backing and a five-year contract as club president, O'Malley was already looking forward to the end of Rickey's tenure. He simply didn't see the financial return he expected, and he thought Rickey was spending way too much, particularly on the farm system. O'Malley himself wanted to replace Rickey atop the Dodger organization.

That was not all. As early as 1946 O'Malley was already talking about the need for a new ballpark. Not only was Ebbets Field small and increasingly difficult for fans to reach by car, which was rapidly becoming the preferred mode of transportation, but it simply wasn't aging gracefully. MacPhail's improvements were Band-Aids that were already starting to come loose. When the park was full, the baseball was still wonderful but the comfort level wasn't. Postwar fans were increasingly impatient with long lines, smelly bathrooms, and obstructed views.

And from the West Coast there was talk that, with the arrival of commercial air travel, both Los Angeles and San Francisco were beginning to politic for major league teams. Earlier that year, in a column entitled "Baseball and the West Coast Puzzle," Tommy Holmes had written innocently: "There has been another mild movement in the major leagues to expand to ten-club circuits with Los Angeles and San Francisco operating franchises in the National and American Leagues. Commissioner Chandler is supposed to look with favor on this re-organization of baseball geography." Little did he know that within a decade those words would find resonance in Brooklyn.

The big news in the off-season came from Florida. After eschewing the state since bringing up Robinson, the Dodgers purchased a former military camp in Vero Beach and turned it into an enormous training complex for the entire organization. The first complex of its kind, Vero Beach would be a place where players at every level were instructed in playing

at Ebbets Field in 1948 dropped by more than 400,000, *three times* more than that of any other club in baseball. Such a fall couldn't be entirely explained by the Dodgers' drop to third place — other teams fell further that season with little or no drop-off.

The trend was disturbing. In 1947 Dodger attendance had been second only to the Yankees. In 1948 they were eighth, outdrawn even by the Giants, who had finished fifth. And for the rest of their tenure in Brooklyn, the Dodgers would remain

baseball the "Dodger way," making the same plays the same way throughout the system—assembly-line baseball. In Vero Beach most players wouldn't have to worry about who could eat or sleep where—most players, except for the major league roster, were housed in Quonset huts. For the first time in three years, the Dodgers actually had the semblance of a normal spring training camp: morning workouts, afternoon exhibitions, and all the players together under one roof being indoctrinated in the same methods, enabling Dodger brass to evaluate players on a more or less equal footing rather than on their performance in a foreign land against semipro or minor league competition.

The result was that after another barnstorming trip through the South, where Robinson again played before huge crowds and faced the now-familiar concoction of adulation on the field and bigotry off it, the Dodgers opened the season with something resembling a set lineup and pitching rotation.

Gil Hodges settled in at first base, giving the club its first power threat at the position since Dolph Camilli. Robinson and Reese were set in the middle—at age 30, they were the two oldest players in the lineup. Billy Cox adapted his strong arm to third, platooning with Spider Jorgensen. Twenty-two-year-old Duke Snider roamed center field and pulled balls down the right-field line, his swing tailor-made for Ebbets Field. Gap-hitting Carl Furillo and his rocket arm patrolled right, and Campanella was the best catcher in the league. Snider, Hodges, and Campanella had all adapted to the major leagues in 1948 and now were ready to produce, while Furillo, Reese, and Robinson were entering their prime. The only position left unsettled was left field. Had it not been for concrete fences, Pete Reiser would have been knocking on the doors of the Hall of Fame instead of sitting on the bench in Boston, where he had been traded in the off-season. But with Gene Hermanski, Mike McCormick, and a handful of others, Shotton had enough to fill the breach.

Almost overnight the club had almost everything. And they would keep it for nearly a decade and stake a claim as perhaps the best Dodger team ever. Certainly they became the most beloved and remembered. Reese and Robinson could run, and the defense was probably the best in club history, while Hodges, Snider, and Campanella gave the club the home run bats they'd been looking for since before the war.

The pitching staff too suddenly seemed set. Since coming to Brooklyn, Preacher Roe had refined a spitball, which he paired with a slow curve to give hitters fits. Steady Joe Hatten

still won more than he lost, while Ralph Branca, Rex Barney, Erv Palica, and Erskine were among the best young pitchers in baseball. Only Roe and Hatten were in their thirties; the others were babies in their early twenties. And there was more pitching knocking on the door as the fruits of Rickey's wartime scouting all ripened at once. Jack Banta and Newcombe had been big winners the year before in triple A, where the two Dodger farm clubs, St. Paul and Montreal, faced each other in the Little World Series.

But it was still spring for the Boys of Summer. Robinson, after an off-season spent working at the Harlem YMCA, was in great shape. After two seasons, Rickey lifted his admonition to Robinson to turn the other cheek, and the ballplayer seemed to relish the opportunity, telling a reporter before the

Dodger right fielder Carl Furillo was as great a fielder as he was a hitter. Furillo, known as the "Reading Rifle" for both his throwing ability and his Pennsylvania hometown, hit .299 in fifteen seasons with the Dodgers.

start of the season, "They better be rough on me this year because I'm going to be rough on them."

The Dodgers opened the season by dumping the Giants 10–3 before a record crowd of 34,530 at Ebbets Field. They seemed to announce that this was a different Dodger team as Furillo, Campanella, and Robinson—hitting cleanup for Shotton—all cracked home runs. Then Robinson inexplicably slumped.

So too did the Dodgers, who found it hard to score. Although Robinson was his old self, running wild on the bases, he simply wasn't getting on very often. Entering May,

In seven seasons with the Dodgers, left-handed pitcher Elwin "Preacher" Roe won over 70 percent of his decisions with an overall won-lost record of 93–37. He also won two of three World Series decisions.

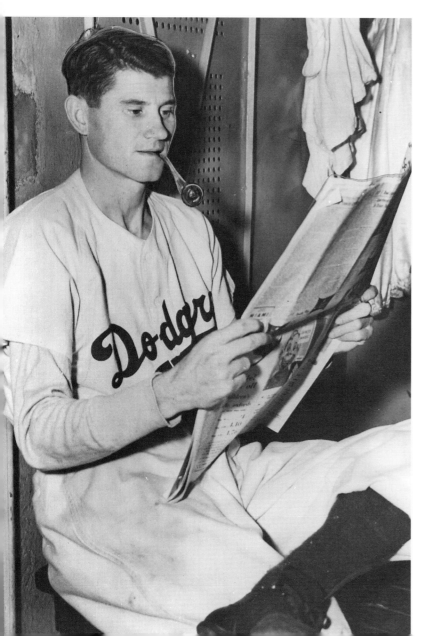

the Dodgers were a pedestrian 7–6 and Robinson was hitting only .200.

Then he got hot and the Dodgers took off. In the middle of the lineup Robinson was the catalyst and gave the Dodgers a unique advantage. While he protected Snider and knocked in the men ahead of him, if the Dodgers went down in order in the first inning Robinson led off the second. Then his role changed: his job was to get on base while worrying pitchers to distraction and ensuring that Campanella, Hodges, and Furillo received a steady diet of fastballs. In May he hit .400 to lift his average to above .360 while leading the league in RBIs. As he did, every other Dodger regular, save for Furillo, got hot too. The Dodgers pulled into first place, and by the middle of June it was a two-team race between Brooklyn and St. Louis as Robinson carried the load.

One other factor figured in the surge—Don Newcombe. The fourth black Dodger in history after Robinson, Dan Bankhead (who after a brief trial in 1947 was back in the minors), and Campanella, Newcombe was called up in the middle of the month and was soon taking a regular turn in the rotation. A power pitcher, Newcombe was a perfect addition to the staff, an intimidating presence who allowed the Dodger rotation to present a confounding set of contrasts to the opposition: the fastballs of Barney and Newcombe interspersed with the comparatively softer tosses of Hatten, Branca, and—excruciatingly so—Preacher Roe.

Now the Dodgers had all the pieces they thought they needed to win a world championship, and they entered what was essentially one gigantic, six-year-long pennant race—a stretch of time during which the National League pennant race was so close that *every* single game the Dodgers played mattered, every player was important, every win critical, and every loss devastating. From 1949 through 1954 the Dodgers finished either in first place by no more than five games or in second by one or two, taking their fans on an extended emotional roller coaster as thrilling as the Cyclone at Coney Island, with lofty highs followed quickly by breathtaking lows and twists and turns that threatened to rip fans out of their seats. Every time they appeared out of the race, teetering like a milk bottle in the game on the midway, they would improbably right themselves. And every time they threatened to run away from the field, they would just as improbably begin to wobble and stagger as if they were addicted to uncertainty. Every inning was played as though it was the bottom of the ninth and the entire season was on the line with *everything* at

NL SHUTOUTS LEADERS

Year	Player	Shutouts
1912	Nap Rucker	6
1921	Clarence Mitchell	3
1922	Dazzy Vance	5
1925	Dazzy Vance	4
1928	Doug McWeeny	4
	Dazzy Vance	4
1930	Dazzy Vance	4
1935	Van Lingle Mungo	4
1940	Whitlow Wyatt	5
1941	Whitlow Wyatt	7
1949	Don Newcombe	5
1957	Johnny Podres	6
1959	Roger Craig	4
	Don Drysdale	4
1963	Sandy Koufax	11
1964	Sandy Koufax	7
1966	Sandy Koufax	5
1971	Al Downing	5
1972	Don Sutton	9
1975	Andy Messersmith	7
1980	Jerry Reuss	6
1981	Fernando Valenzuela	8
1984	Orel Hershiser	4
	Alejandro Pena	4
1987	Bob Welch	4
1988	Orel Hershiser	8
1989	Tim Belcher	8
1990	Mike Morgan	4
1994	Ramon Martinez	3
1995	Hideo Nomo	3

stake. And on the other side, almost always, were the Yankees, smug and secure, lying in wait at the finish line, ready to knock off the exhausted winner.

For most of the summer and into the fall, however, the Dodgers were concerned not with the Yankees but with the Cardinals. Like the Dodgers, they too were in the midst of a run in which every game counted—beginning in 1941 and running through 1949, they finished either first or second in the NL, never more than a handful of games from the top spot. But unlike the Dodgers, the Cardinals had a pitching staff that was getting old, and 1949 would be their last shot at the postseason for more than a decade.

The two clubs met with everything at stake on September 22 in St. Louis in a split doubleheader. Newcombe faced Max

Rookie pitcher Don Newcombe admires himself in the mirror of Buddy Lee's men's store in Brooklyn. After winning 17 games, Newcombe joined Lee's sales staff in the off-season.

Lanier in the first game, and Roe pitched opposite Harry Brecheen in the second.

Robinson, playing the best baseball of his career, entered the game leading the NL in batting, RBIs, and stolen bases. The day before, in a 5–0 win over Chicago, Robinson had stolen home for the fifth time that season, ending what the *Eagle* called Brooklyn's "crucifixion" of the Cubs, their 17th win in 22 tries over Chicago. But the Cardinals weren't the Cubs.

Game one against the Cardinals was as close as the pennant race as Lanier and Newcombe matched each other into the eighth. Then the Cardinals' Enos Slaughter, with the count 0–2, took a pitch for a ball that started the Dodgers—particularly Robinson—barking. Slaughter dumped a double down the line, and then a walk and a bunt loaded the bases.

Shotton sent coach Clyde Sukeforth out to calm Newcombe, and as the Dodger infield gathered around the pitcher, Robinson—no wallflower anymore—started in on home plate ump Bill Stewart, talking to his teammates but making sure Stewart could hear every word. Then, as Harold Burr described it, "Jackie made the magnificent gesture, holding his windpipe to indicate that Stewart had choked up in a game vital to the Dodgers." Stewart tossed him from the game, and Robinson had to be restrained. Joe Garagiola then hit a ground ball to Eddie Miksis, who had moved from third to second after Robinson's ejection. The ball skipped over his glove, and the Cardinals won 1–0 to move two and a half ahead with only eight left to play. Brooklyn's bottle was tottering.

Then, as Harold Rosenthal of the *Tribune* noted: "Roe stepped in [and] placed his bony frame between the Dodgers and disaster. . . . He looks like someone out of the Legend of Sleepy Hollow . . . [but] tonight he looked like Mr. America." He tossed a shutout, facing only 29 batters, and the Dodgers stayed on their feet.

The Cardinals, who had been in first place since August 20, started to waver. Brooklyn won the next day, 19–6, and the Dodgers drew close, then improbably pulled ahead on September 29 as the Cardinals lost four in a row. With two games left Brooklyn had a chance to clinch, but Branca, who had been battling arm trouble in the second half of the season, lost to the Phillies. On the final day of the season, October 2, Brooklyn led by one game, and they had a train waiting to take them to St. Louis for another best-of-three playoff.

Both Newcombe and the Phillies' Russ Meyer went into the game looking for win number 18, but as one reporter noted, "Both had plenty of time to adjust their ties properly long before the contest ended." Each was gone by the end of the fourth inning. After Newcombe blew a five-run lead, Barney failed too. Then sidearming Jack Banta came on for Brooklyn.

A pitcher Rosenthal described as a "young gawky kid with a ticklish fastball" then held Philadelphia at bay into the tenth. Meanwhile, Stan Musial was stepping up for the Cardinals, smacking two home runs as the Cards crushed the Cubs 13–5.

Then Reese singled, Miksis sacrificed him to second, and two singles, by Snider and Luis Olmo around an intentional walk to Robinson, plated two runs. Banta held on, and the Dodgers were in the World Series again.

No place ever celebrated a pennant better than Brooklyn, and the Dodgers were at the peak of their popularity. Twenty-five thousand fans met their train at Penn Station, and the *Eagle* put out an open call for "twenty-five open autos" to carry the Dodgers in a parade the next day. When one of the Dodger wives told a reporter she might not be able to attend the first game of the Series because she didn't have a baby-sitter, volunteers swamped the *Eagle* with offers to watch the Dodger little ones.

Amid all that glee, it was easy to forget that the Dodgers still had to beat the Yankees, who had staged a late season comeback of their own to knock out the Boston Red Sox over the final two days and steal a pennant, their first under former Brooklyn outfielder and manager Casey Stengel. While still an object of amusement in Brooklyn, and fondly recalled, Stengel was beginning to change that impression with his skillful manipulation of the Yankee roster in 1949. Managing a team eviscerated by injuries — every Yankee regular had missed significant portions of the season, except Phil Rizzuto, who was one of only two Yankees to play in more than 116 games — Stengel had platooned New York into the World Series. And now they were as healthy as they'd been at anytime during the season, which was to say that only Berra, who had a broken thumb, and Henrich, with a bad back, were diminished. In addition, New York was far more rested than Brooklyn and enjoyed the home-field advantage.

Yankee Stadium and Ebbets Field presented a significant difference between the two teams in the postseason — in the long run, it may have been the difference that made one team a dynasty. The Dodger offense was much better at home than in Yankee Stadium, where hits that would have been home runs or wall-rattling doubles at Ebbets Field fell harmlessly into the hands of the Yankee outfield. On the other hand, the Yankees had little trouble adapting to Ebbets Field — their power traveled better than Brooklyn's. In six World Series meetings between 1947 and 1956, the Yankees would out-homer the Dodgers 45 to 31 — 26 to 22 at Ebbets Field and a whopping 19 to 9 at Yankee Stadium.

And in the first two games at Yankee Stadium, Brooklyn's power didn't have subway fare. In game one both the Yankees' Allie Reynolds and Don Newcombe were dominant. But in the eighth Tommy Henrich dropped his bat head on a down-and-in curveball and hooked it into the seats. The Yankees won, 1–0.

Brooklyn battled back the next day as the Yankees, unaccustomed to the spitter Roe euphemistically referred to as his "forkball," did nothing against him despite the fact that after being struck by a line drive he pitched half the game with a hole drilled in the nail of a finger on his nonpitching hand. This time the Dodgers won 1–0, not on a home run, but

---

Dodger manager Burt Shotton (left) congratulates Yankee manager Casey Stengel following the Yankees' 10–6 win in the fifth and decisive game of the 1949 World Series at Ebbets Field.

New York developer William Zeckendorf attempted to purchase Branch Rickey's shares in the Dodgers before Walter O'Malley made his successful counteroffer. One can only speculate as to whether a successful Zeckendorf bid would have helped keep the franchise in Brooklyn.

because Robinson opportunistically went from second to third on a foul out to Yankee second baseman Jerry Coleman, putting him in position to score the winning run.

Then it was on to Brooklyn, where the Series turned in the ninth inning of game three. With the score tied at 1–1 and one out, Brooklyn starting pitcher Ralph Branca walked Yogi Berra. After DiMaggio popped up, Bobby Brown singled and Gene Woodling walked to load the bases. With Cliff Mapes due up, Stengel called on left-handed slugger Johnny Mize, a late season addition acquired for just such situations, to pinch-hit.

Shotton had options. He hadn't used a relief pitcher yet in the Series, and Branca, after a magnificent performance, was clearly tiring. But at the same time, if the Dodgers had a glar-

ing weakness, it was left-handed relief pitching. All Shotton had at his disposal were Joe Hatten and Paul Minner. Hatten was primarily a starter, while Minner had rarely been used in critical situations and was very much the last option.

He stayed with Branca, and Mize jumped on a pitch, pulling it on a line 330 feet to right field, where it rattled off the screen, scoring two. In Yankee Stadium it might have been caught. In Brooklyn it meant the ballgame. Now Shotton turned to Jack Banta, who gave up a single to Jerry Coleman, and all of a sudden the score was 4–1.

Stengel operated differently. When starter Tommy Byrne had gotten in trouble in the fourth, he had turned to his relief ace, Joe Page, who had given up only one hit until the final inning. And although he wavered, giving up solo home runs to both Luis Olmo and Roy Campanella in the ninth, he struck out Bruce Edwards to end the game.

It also effectively ended the Series. In game four Shotton panicked and called on Newcombe with two days' rest, but he didn't have it. The Yankees knocked him out in the fourth and won 6–4. Game five was even worse. New York jumped out to a 5–0 lead and cruised to a 10–6 victory. The Yankees were champions again.

This time Brooklyn was not so understanding. In a column that Tommy Holmes bitterly described as "what you might call a mop up piece," he was blunt, calling Shotton "the goat." What was the highlight of the Series? "To a Dodger fan, there wasn't anything high about any of it," he wrote. Brooklyn fans weren't just happy to be in the Series, as they had been in 1941 and 1947, or close, as in 1946. In 1949 they'd responded, and attendance bounced back to 1.6 million, a rise of nearly 250,000, and a positive sign in a season in which overall attendance at major league games began an inexorable slide that over the next five years would amount to a decrease of some 30 percent. But in subsequent seasons Brooklyn fans increasingly refused to be fooled. Apart from the postseason, weekends, and late season contests against such rivals as the soon-to-be-rejuvenated Giants, the number of empty seats at Ebbets Field would grow at an alarming rate. For weekday games and contests against also-rans that didn't matter, fans stayed home.

The tenor of Ebbets Field was evolving. The generation of fans who as kids and young adults had embraced the Bums and given the club its reputation were now leaving Brooklyn. In their place was a new breed—fans who were more concerned with wins and losses and, significantly, increasing numbers of black fans whose allegiance was to Robinson, not to the team he represented.

Brooklyn, like the rest of postwar America, was starting to change. The great sprint toward the suburbs had begun as the potato fields of Long Island, now fertilized by black-topped highways, sprouted row upon row of identical homes with back yards and brand-new schools. "We're moving for the children" was the excuse heard over and over in Brooklyn. Over the next decade nearly 150,000 people, nearly all of them white, would flee Brooklyn, and more than 160,000 blacks and Puerto Ricans would take their place.

At the same time baseball was changing from a game people played on the sandlots and saw in person to one played in organized youth leagues, listened to on the radio, and, increasingly, watched on television. Of the 39 million home radios in America in 1949, 26 million had tuned in to the World Series. NBC also broadcast the Series on television. While relatively few consumers had television sets, taverns all over New York tuned in and then sold places at the bar like box seats. With all due respect to those who have referred to a later Dodger year as "the last good season," the last good season was in fact 1949. That was the last year when Brooklyn baseball was all that later nostalgia would make it out to be. The next eight seasons would be marked by declining crowds, frustrating play, and, in 1950 in particular, front office disarray.

Branch Rickey had only one year left on his contract, and Walter O'Malley was marking off the days. He'd disagreed with Rickey's expenditures at Vero Beach and on the pro football Dodgers, which Rickey bought in 1948 and then sold after one season after taking a bath when no one came out to watch them. Even the farm system, which Rickey had built back up to 26 teams, the most of any team in baseball, was under attack. Minor league attendance was acutely affected by the availability of major league broadcasts, and the Dodgers would soon start to fall in line with other clubs, operating fewer teams and signing fewer players. As the date approached when Rickey's contract would expire, so too did his influence.

Rickey, who knew that O'Malley wanted to take over, had no interest in staying on as a silent partner. Now Rickey's greater concern became protecting his investment so that when he sold out he'd receive top dollar. For the first time in his tenure with the Dodgers, he virtually stopped selling off players. Not only was the market suddenly smaller with the collapse of the minor leagues, but all that Dodger talent was suddenly worth more to him sitting in the farm system, making the franchise look as strong as possible, than sold for his ten cents on the dollar.

The only good news for the Dodgers came when Jackie Robinson was named National League MVP, receiving more votes than Stan Musial. Sportswriter Tom Meany accurately described him at the time as the man who "can beat you more ways than any other player in baseball." Indeed. Robinson had led the league with a .342 batting average and 37 stolen bases while knocking in 124 runs (second only to Ralph Kiner), cracking 203 hits (second to Musial), and scoring 122 runs (behind only the Cardinal outfielder and Pee Wee Reese). He had done everything, all year long, until the World Series, where he hit only .188 and played a role in only two of the Dodgers' fourteen runs.

For all their achievements in 1949, the Series against the Yankees had exposed a few holes remaining on the ballclub—namely, left-handed relief pitching and depth. Yet Rickey and the Dodgers did nothing of consequence in the off-season. They stood pat and it cost them.

The Dodgers opened the 1950 season with a team almost indistinguishable from the one that ended 1949. The starting lineup, essentially unchanged, was still one of the most powerful in the game. Robinson, despite suffering from a badly sprained ankle that limited his ability to run, hit better than at any other time in his career. On July 1 he was leading the league with a .371 batting average and 53 RBIs, the odds-on favorite to win another MVP Award. Snider, Hodges, and Campanella continued to improve.

Had they had any relief pitching, they'd have clinched the pennant in August. As it was, although Newcombe and Roe were dependable, the rest of the rotation was a tossup as ten other men were eventually tried in the rotation. The bullpen was even worse. Time after time the Dodger offense seemed to put a game on ice only to see the bullpen give it up. Instead of fighting for first place, the Dodgers entered July having lost five of six. They were desperately trying to stay in the race—and above .500.

And in a disturbing development, another Dodger trait began to emerge. Perhaps no team in baseball history ever produced as much young pitching talent as the Dodgers from the late 1940s through the 1960s. Almost every season a youngster or two would emerge who seemed destined to become an ace. A few years before it had been Ralph Branca, then Erskine and Barney, and in 1949 it was Jack Banta. Later it would be Karl Spooner, Sandy Koufax, and other now-forgotten phenoms.

But as an organization, no team was ever worse at protecting young pitchers than Brooklyn. Both Erskine and Banta were forced by Shotton to pitch while hurt and never fulfilled their promise. Others, like Barney and Branca, would collapse under the weight of expectations as their early failures were too often chalked up to a lack of guts. After promising starts, pitcher after pitcher in the Dodger organization would essentially be washed up by age 30, if they even made it that far.

There were also other distractions. Dodger co-owner John L. Smith died in mid-July. Although he had once been a Rickey backer, over the last few seasons he had slowly shifted allegiance to O'Malley. Now that he was gone, the attorney was able to wrest control of the club away from the long-standing club president.

Robinson was one of the Dodgers who sensed the writing on the wall. O'Malley didn't care for Robinson personally, particularly after his two-year injunction in regard to fighting back expired. The new, less-deferential Robinson grated on him. O'Malley referred to Robinson as "Rickey's prima donna," and in mid-August Robinson made his feelings known. When asked his position in regard to the behind-the-scenes battle over the Dodgers, Robinson bluntly offered, "It wouldn't surprise me if I were traded," and intimated that a trade wouldn't exactly break his heart either. Rickey denied that Robinson was on the block but seemed resigned to his loss of influence as even he admitted, "Of course I don't mean that Robinson can't be had for any price."

While the Dodgers stumbled, the Philadelphia Phillies, paced by starter Robin Roberts and screwball-throwing reliever Jim Konstanty, had the pitching the Dodgers lacked. Their energetic, opportunistic offense and solid defense suddenly made the "Whiz Kids" a formidable opponent, and they entered September with a double-digit lead over third-place Brooklyn.

The Dodgers still trailed by nine games on September 19. Despite having five games left with the Phillies, the Dodgers

Dodger fans do a premature victory dance on the Ebbets Field dugout on October 1, 1950, as they cheer Pee Wee Reese's sixth-inning, game-tying home run against the Phillies on the final day of the 1950 season. Their hopes were soon dashed as Dick Sisler of the Phillies socked a three-run home run off Don Newcombe in the ninth to send the pennant to Philadelphia.

had only 16 games remaining in the ensuing 12 days of the season, and the lead looked insurmountable.

But the Phillies were starting to fray. Seventeen-game winner Curt Simmons, a member of the National Guard, had been called into the service on September 10. Rookie Bob Miller, who had won his first eight games, hurt his arm. Swingman Bubba Church was hit in the face by a line drive and missed more than a week, while hard-hitting outfielder Andy Seminick was limping around on a separated ankle. All of a sudden the Phillies were in trouble.

They slumped and the Dodgers surged, taking two from the Phillies on September 23 and 24 to draw to within five games. Then a bomb dropped.

The Rickey-O'Malley feud bubbled over. Knowing Rickey had no interest in remaining after his term as president expired, for Rickey knew he would not be reappointed, O'Malley had offered Rickey the same $350,000 he had initially paid for his one-quarter stake in the team. Rickey found the offer insulting. But now word leaked out that Rickey had another buyer. Real estate developer William Zeckendorf offered Rickey a cool $1.05 million for his original $350,000 investment. As a member of the firm Webb and Knapp, one of the largest real estate development companies in the country, Zeckendorf's big local score to date had been quietly piecing together a vast portion of midtown à la Charlie Ebbets for about $6 million, then packaging it into a single parcel and selling it — with Robert Moses's blessing — to the United Nations for $8.5 million of Rockefeller charity funds. Fully half the club was on the block — Rickey's quarter of the club plus a similar portion held by Smith's heirs, who reportedly wanted $1.5 million for their quarter stake. O'Malley enjoyed the right of first refusal, and there were obvious signs that Rickey, after selling out, planned to take his money and join the Pirates. At the most critical juncture of the season, Rickey was preparing to jump ship, and Shotton, a Rickey favorite, was widely perceived to be a lame duck.

The Dodger players had every reason to pack it in, for over the next five days they were scheduled to play four doubleheaders while the Phillies played three of their own, a grueling schedule at any time but particularly so now. Jackie Robinson set the tone for the team. Instead of bemoaning Rickey's departure, whose impending loss he certainly felt, or holding it up as an excuse, Robinson was stoic. He said Rickey's decision "means nothing to me. I just play ball."

And over the next five days the Dodgers did just that. They suddenly had the edge in pitching depth and weathered the week in better shape than the Phillies, winning six games while Philadelphia, which now seemed to be turning to starter Robin Roberts every other game, won only twice. On September 29, behind a sparse Ebbets Field crowd of just over 5,000, including Philadelphia pitcher Russ Meyer, who took a swing at a Brooklyn photographer, the Dodgers came from behind to sweep the Braves. The wins drew them to within two games of the Phillies.

That set up a showdown with Philadelphia in the final two games of the season. With a sweep, the Dodgers could force another best-of-three playoff where their pitching depth — and home-field advantage — would give them an edge.

For the Dodgers the playoffs, in effect, were already under way. To win the pennant they would have to take four of five, while the Phillies needed to win only one of their remaining two regular season contests. As noted Chicago sportswriter Warren Brown commented, "There hasn't been a finish like this since sporting British officials carried Dorando over the finish line in the 1908 Olympic marathon." The Phillies were out on their feet and the Dodgers were closing fast.

With the season on the line, the Dodgers made it a sprint to the finish. In the next-to-last game of the regular season, Erv Palica outpitched Miller and went the distance as Snider hit a two-run homer in the fifth and Campy cracked a three-run clout in the eighth to give Brooklyn a 7–3 win.

The matchup for the finale favored Brooklyn, with Don Newcombe going up against Philadelphia stalwart Robin Roberts. Each man was in search of his 20th win — but for Roberts this was his third start in five days, and in five previous attempts to win number 20, he'd come up empty.

On this day such things meant nothing. Both pitchers were immense, and the game was scoreless into the sixth, when, with two out, light-hitting Dick Sisler rolled a ground ball quietly through the right side. Del Ennis followed with a short fly ball to center field.

Jackie Robinson ranged back as Snider charged in and seemed to have a bead on the ball, but at the last second Robinson shied away and the ball fell in for a hit. Sisler went to third and scored a moment later when Willie Jones knocked a clean hit to give the Phillies a 1–0 lead.

In the bottom of the inning Pee Wee Reese lofted a towering fly ball to right field. Years later a similar fly ball hit by another shortstop — the Yankees' Bucky Dent in Fenway Park — would remind some of Reese's pop.

Like Dent's fly ball, Reese's hit just cleared the wall and struck the screen. At Ebbets Field such balls inevitably bounced back onto the field. Reese saw it hit and kept running—hard.

But the screen at Ebbets Field was not the soft netting of Fenway Park but wire mesh. Reese's blast struck it gently, then, as Tommy Holmes wrote, the ball "rebounded and stuck on the six-inch ledge for a home run. In all the years that screen has been here, this has happened just once before." The umpires paused, then waved Reese around the bases for a home run. As one Philadelphia writer noted later, "For the remainder of the game fans could see that silly little ball stuck in the screen."

The events of the ninth inning would relegate both Ennis's pop-up and Reese's fly ball to the dimmer recesses of memory. For in the ninth the Dodgers should have won, but did not.

Working on fumes, Roberts walked outfielder Cal Abrams. Reese followed with a single and moved him to second. Then Duke Snider roped a pitch into center field. As the ball began to drop in front of Richie Ashburn, 33,000 fans on hand started celebrating and a great roar enveloped Ebbets Field. They knew the Philadelphia center fielder had an average arm at best and that Abrams was as fast as anyone on the field save Robinson.

Yet as Roberts threw home, both Philadelphia shortstop Granny Hamner and center fielder Ashburn had been breaking toward second. Roberts was supposed to try a pickoff play—Hamner was moving over to take the throw and Ashburn was backing up the play.

Roberts had missed the sign. Yet Hamner's move caused Abrams to hesitate before breaking to third, and Ashburn was racing toward second, as one writer described it, "like a third baseman fielding a bunt."

In the stands fans were already in full embrace and beginning to climb onto the field. The ball took one bounce straight to Ashburn, who came up throwing. Meanwhile, Brooklyn third base coach Milt Stock, oblivious, waved Abrams around third toward home.

Ashburn's perfect throw beat him by 15 feet. Abrams tried to knock the ball loose from catcher Stan Lopata, but he held on and Abrams was out. Brooklyn gasped, and in a heartbeat the stands fell silent and then turned angry. *Whadda ya mean? How could he be out?*

Most fans blamed Abrams for taking a wide turn around third. Those who didn't blamed Stock for sending him home.

While the play has long been derided in Dodger lore as a failure almost on par with another only one year in the offing, it still left men on second and third with one out. Had Robinson caught that short fly in the sixth, it would have mattered not at all. Now he was due up—arguably the best player in baseball over the last two seasons had a chance for redemption.

But the Phillies weren't taking chances. Roberts walked Robinson intentionally, and then Furillo popped on the first pitch. Gil Hodges stepped in with a chance to win the game.

He drove the ball deep to left. Once more, 33,000 stood and screamed and then saw the ball die just shy of the wall and fall into Dick Sisler's glove. Extra innings, 1–1.

Jim Russell (left) and Gil Hodges contemplate their heartbreaking loss to the Phillies on the final day of the 1950 season at Ebbets Field.

And then, in a matter of minutes, the season ended. This game belonged to Robin Roberts, who opened the tenth with a single off Newcombe. Eddie Waitkus, after failing to get down a bunt, then dropped a single into center. After Richie Ashburn hit back to Newcombe for a force-out, the immortal Dick Sisler stepped in. The son of the great George Sisler, former batting star of the St. Louis Browns and currently serving as the Dodgers' chief scout, he shared little on the ballfield with his father but the notoriety of his last name. George Sisler later admitted that as a child Dick had been the worst player of his three sons and that he'd been shocked when the boy made it into pro ball, much less the majors. For Dick Sisler lacked any of the requisite baseball skills in abundance. He was a slap hitter without speed.

But on this day he was the equivalent of his Hall of Fame father. With three hits already to his credit, the son of a legend sliced a ball in the air down the left-field line, and at Ebbets Field such hits by slap hitters sometimes found the seats. Sisler's did, and when the Dodgers went out in the bottom of the inning against a rejuvenated Roberts, the Phillies had won, 4–1, to take the pennant.

"Stock played it right," sighed Shotton after the game, but his lack of enthusiasm in defense of his coach mirrored his ballclub's exhaustion. Robinson's earlier gaffe was never mentioned. Against all odds and with no bullpen, the front office in uproar, and a lame-duck manager, they had nevertheless come within a single game of a pennant.

And now it was over. As soon as the Yankees finished

WHO WAS WILLIAM ZECKENDORF?

At one point in time it looked as if we would take over the Brooklyn Dodgers. John Galbreath, the real estate builder and investor and an owner of the Pittsburgh Pirates, brought his friend Branch Rickey into my office with an offer to sell Rickey's twenty-five percent share in the club. The instant that word of these negotiations got out, our switchboard was jammed with calls from friends angling for box seats, but I never had to test their love by refusal. . . . Rickey's partners had the right to match my offer. They did so and I lost my chance at a lifetime supply of player autographed baseballs.

— The Autobiography of William Zeckendorf (1970)

In most accounts of Dodger history, William Zeckendorf's offer in 1950 to buy Branch Rickey's share of the Dodgers for $1 million has been presented as a ploy, a favor extended to his old friend John Galbreath to help Branch Rickey extract many extra thousands of dollars from Walter O'Malley and the other Dodger partners. In this version, Zeckendorf is described simply as a "real estate developer" — an anonymous, penny-ante builder.

But Bill Zeckendorf was a giant. In the annals of New York's real estate history, he is one of half a dozen of the most important developers in the history of the city, on par with developers who are far better known, such as Harry Helmsley and Donald Trump. One observer described Zeckendorf aptly as someone who "engaged in a real-life game of Monopoly involving some of the most prestigious properties in the United States." He was no one's toady, and his attempt to buy the Dodgers was genuine.

Zeckendorf was born in Illinois in 1905 but moved with his parents to Cedarhurst, Long Island, in 1908. The family then relocated to Manhattan, where Zeckendorf graduated from high school at age 16 and attended New York University before starting to work for an uncle who was a real estate agent. In the midst of the Depression, Zeckendorf made his mark by brokering the sale of a $3 million property, and in 1938 he joined the national real estate and development firm Webb and Knapp as vice president. Now his career really took off.

He persuaded Vincent Astor to allow the company to manage his vast holdings and keyed a massive expansion of the firm. Zeckendorf became a public figure when he was able to parlay his purchase of the Swift meatpacking company and other properties on the East River north of 42nd Street into a site for the United Nations, solving a problem for power broker Robert Moses, earning a huge profit for Webb and Knapp, and leading to his promotion to company president.

He was bold, ambitious, and creative. In 1949 Zeckendorf hired architect I. M. Pei, and under his leadership over the next two decades Webb and Knapp would build $3 billion worth of commercial property and manage the holdings of such high-end clients as Gimbel's, Time Inc., and Macy's and signature New York buildings such as the Chrysler Building. During his tenure the firm played a key role in high-end developments that included the Chase Manhattan Plaza, Century City in Los Angeles, and L'Enfant Plaza in Washington. Zeckendorf is even credited with playing a key role in the development of the World Trade Center.

sweeping the exhausted Phillies in the World Series, attention turned toward Branch Rickey one last time.

To retain control of the Dodgers, O'Malley had to come up with a million dollars to match Zeckendorf's offer. What looked to be a costly endeavor to begin with was now becoming even costlier, and increasingly risky.

Despite their late charge, the Dodgers had taken a bath in 1950. Attendance had dropped to 1.2 million, the lowest figure since the war years. Although some of that drop-off could be blamed on the Dodgers' performance throughout most of 1950, there were signs that something more was at work — even as the Dodgers closed with a rush, until the final two games crowds had been slim. That late September double-header against Boston had been played before an almost empty house, and in the second-to-last game of the season against the Phillies there had been 5,000 empty seats at Ebbets Field. Attendance was down everywhere, but nowhere was it as pronounced as in Brooklyn. This didn't appear to be the right time to spend big on a baseball team, but to sell. Yet O'Malley was diving in. Why?

Part of it was ego, for he lusted for the kind of recognition that had come to the "genius" Branch Rickey, but there was more to it than that. O'Malley was a big guy — in Brooklyn. Owning the Dodgers made him bigger. And he had plans too. Rickey wasn't the only guy with ideas.

But unlike Rickey, who held baseball and his own bank account in more or less equal esteem, O'Malley was first and foremost a businessman, and a confident one at that. He was

By the time the Dodgers came up for sale, Zeckendorf was living on a huge estate in Greenwich, Connecticut, with a 20,000-bottle wine cellar, dabbling in Broadway, and serving on the board of trustees at Long Island University. He was major league. By comparison, Walter O'Malley, who had likewise made his considerably smaller fortune in real estate, was still in the low minors.

According to Zeckendorf's family, his interest in the Dodgers was genuine, and they recall many meetings with Branch Rickey over the issue. Zeckendorf was aware from the start that O'Malley and the other partners had an option on Rickey's shares and hoped his $1 million offer would be enough to dissuade them from exercising that bid. But as Zeckendorf wrote in his autobiography, he had no desire to serve as a "straw man" for Rickey. Just in case O'Malley matched his offer, wrote Zeckendorf, "I had made my offer conditional on a $50,000 agent's fee if my bid were matched." As Zeckendorf wrote later, "In effect, I got a five percent commission for getting Rickey a sale."

Zeckendorf's activities over the next decade or so offer some insight into what might have happened had he been able to purchase the Dodgers, for he had all the connections that O'Malley lacked, and those connections enabled him to proceed with the most ambitious plans of his career. As he once told a reporter, "To do less than the ultimate is to do nothing."

In 1950, just as the Dodger deal was falling apart, Webb and Knapp purchased Roosevelt Field on Long Island. In exchange for donating 48 acres of land for the Meadowbrook Parkway — a Robert Moses project — Webb and Knapp received a cloverleaf of entrances and exits that gave ready access to the 300-acre property. They took advantage of it and at a cost of $35 million built the Roosevelt Field Shopping Center, the largest in the nation. Designed by Pei, the center featured parking for more than 11,000 automobiles as well as art galleries, hotels, bowling alleys, theaters, and a skating rink.

Might this have been the new home of the Dodgers as well? Perhaps, but it seems more likely that Zeckendorf, with a massive firm behind him and a working relationship with Moses, might have been able to parlay those connections into a Brooklyn ballpark, for the bulk of his projects both before and after took place in urban, not suburban, environments.

And in fact, it was Zeckendorf's suburban-based projects that led to his down-

fall. The shopping center slumped in the early 1960s as covered malls drew business away; Zeckendorf was simultaneously pouring his energy and money into an ambitious but misplaced and ill-timed amusement park in the Bronx, Frontierland. Built on the site of what is now Co-op City in Pelham Bay, Frontierland was an American history–based theme park covering 205 acres and built in the shape of the United States. Visitors could stroll through "Old New York" and Chicago — which burned every 20 minutes in a reenactment of the Great Fire — or gaze upon replicas of the Great Lakes that contained 20 million gallons of water.

But alas, access was a problem from the beginning. The park wasn't convenient to public transportation, and the Bronx was difficult for vacationers to reach by automobile. The World's Fair, which opened in 1964, doomed Zeckendorf's dream. In 1965 Webb and Knapp went bankrupt, and Zeckendorf followed suit a few years later.

Nevertheless, his offer to buy the Dodgers may have represented the last great chance the team had to stay in Brooklyn.

someone who believed that a man of his business sense, among the rubes who ran baseball, could make a killing.

William Zeckendorf's interest in the team had intrigued O'Malley even as it angered him. Zeckendorf was no minor figure, but one of the most prominent real estate men in the country. He was a big wheel who ran in big circles in what was fast becoming the biggest game of all in and around New York — real estate. O'Malley was rich, and a big deal in Brooklyn, but not on par with someone like Zeckendorf. But if a guy like Zeckendorf was interested in the Dodgers, well, that said something. And to O'Malley it may have said the magic words — real estate.

Zeckendorf's role in the transaction between O'Malley and Rickey has been all but overlooked in most accounts of Dodger history. But it may have been larger and far more significant than anyone realized at the time. Most have dismissed his offer as merely a favor to Pirate owner and onetime fraternity brother John Galbreath, a ploy to force O'Malley to overpay to get rid of Rickey and free him to join the Pirates. But it is with Zeckendorf that the name of Robert Moses, the man who shaped modern New York and has shared the blame with O'Malley for forcing the Dodgers to California, first appears in the Dodger story. Zeckendorf was not a Moses toady, for most of his projects were privately financed. Yet he knew where the power lay in New York. His quick turnaround on the United Nations property demonstrated his acumen. He knew that Moses, with an insatiable lust for land for his unending stream of civic projects, needed sites for those proj-

Branch Rickey departs the Dodgers on October 26, 1950, as newly elected Dodger president Walter O'Malley (second from left) shakes Rickey's hand. Also on hand were (from left) George A. Barnwell of Manufacturers Trust Company, Judge Henry Ughetta, Bud Holeman of Eastern Airlines, and Hector Racine, president of the Montreal Royals.

ects. For the UN, Zeckendorf had found one, taken a gamble, and bought it, then turned it around and made a tidy profit.

Zeckendorf's comments in September 1950 indicate that he was fully prepared to follow through on his initial offer to buy Rickey's shares and perhaps those of the Smith estate as well, a transaction that could place the Dodgers — and Ebbets Field — in his hands, leaving O'Malley on the fringes. He looked at the deal as "an investment." And since Zeckendorf's primary concern was always real estate — he had no prior or subsequent interest in major league sports — for him Ebbets Field was the prize, a valuable piece of property in the heart of the borough. With his established connection to Moses — and real estate holdings throughout greater New York that were valuable chips in a time of rampant development — he might have eventually been able to accomplish what O'Malley could not: get a new ballpark for the Dodgers.

O'Malley may have sensed that was what Zeckendorf was up to. When he matched Zeckendorf's offer, O'Malley may well have disrupted larger plans of which he was not aware. Although the transaction delivered Ebbets Field into the

O'Malley portfolio, O'Malley didn't have Zeckendorf's bargaining power, with his vast holdings and powerful connections. Had Ebbets Field fallen into Zeckendorf's hands, with his connections, it might have had value beyond its borders. But in the O'Malley portfolio its value was severely limited.

One other factor may have influenced O'Malley's decision—religion. Zeckendorf was Jewish, and at the time there were no other Jewish owners in major league baseball, a situation that the men who ran baseball may not have been eager to see end. Zeckendorf would have had to seek their approval to buy in, but they preferred not to publicize their anti-Semitism. It was better policy to keep Zeckendorf from buying in the first place rather than force him out of the neighborhood after he had already staked a claim.

The end of the Rickey era came, officially, on October 26, 1950. The press was called to Brooklyn's Hotel Bossert, where O'Malley kept a large room to entertain. O'Malley let Rickey have his day as the aging Mahatma made a graceful exit and the two men—who were barely speaking—honored each other with platitudes that fooled no one.

Rickey had led the Dodgers to the most successful and profitable era in their history, to a time that changed the face of baseball forever. Of this there is no doubt. He had ended the era of "Dem Bums" and replaced it with one in which the Dodgers were clearly the most potent franchise in the National League and the most progressive in baseball, one that was pushing to supplant the Yankee dynasty.

Yet at the same time, while at the helm of the Dodgers Rickey had missed several grand opportunities to take the Dodgers even further, to make next year *this* year. Instead, that chimerical season remained a tease, just out of reach, always one trade, one game, one pitch away. It was almost too much to take.

And Dodger fans hadn't seen anything yet.

WAIT TILL NEXT YEAR

IMMEDIATELY FOLLOWING THE PRESS CONFERENCE AT THE HOTEL BOSSERT, there were rapid changes at the Dodger offices on Montague Street. By April 1951 Branch Rickey — his methods, his ideals, and even his name — would cease to be recognized by the Dodger organization.

O'Malley had been waiting for this for a long time, and he didn't mess around. Rickey immediately became an "unperson," and the mere mention of his name engendered a $1 fine in the Dodger offices.

But O'Malley didn't stop with cosmetic changes. Shotton, despite two pennants in three and a half seasons as manager, saw the writing on the wall. He wouldn't even meet with O'Malley, concluding there was no reason to do so just to be fired. He was let go anyway, as was disgraced third base coach Milt Stock. Long-time Dodger employees Buzzie Bavasi and Fresco Thompson — both Rickey protégés who had now changed stripes and were pledging allegiance to O'Malley — were promoted. They split Rickey's front office duties — Bavasi, in effect, became the general manager, running the Dodgers and Montreal, while Thompson took care of the rest of the farm system.

The concept of "profit" took on a new significance within the organization. But it would not be the kind of profit that came

Catcher Roy Campanella (left) is shown in Vero Beach, Fla., at spring training in 1952 with rookie sensation Joe Black. More than one newspaper heralded the 28-year-old rookie as the "New Newk."

from internal investment and the careful harvesting of assets, as under Rickey, but from making cutbacks, cutting corners, and downsizing. Ebbets Field would continue its slow deterioration, and the Dodger farm system, which at 22 teams in 1950 was the largest in baseball, would begin to be slowly trimmed until its scope and size would be on par with those of other clubs, as would its production. Trades, which had already become an increasingly insignificant part of the Dodger philosophy under Rickey because the opposition feared dealing with him, would be few and far between. In little more than a decade the Dodgers would squander their organizational edge.

Even though Rickey was gone, O'Malley still sought to cash in on the reservoir of goodwill the Dodgers had built with their fan base. He embraced the notion—and the image—of the lovable Bums, and variations of the Mullin cartoon began to appear on Dodger publications. The subtle change was telling, for it was a discreet admission that the club was no longer basing its value on success on the field but hewing to another standard—the willingness of its fans to support a team that broke their heart on an annual basis. Over the next few seasons—and never more so than in 1951—the resiliency of Brooklyn fans would be tested again and again.

There was one place, however, where O'Malley could not erase the Rickey name and where he was wise enough not to try—on the field. There, Rickey would live on. The Dodgers would embark on no vast rebuilding program and make no trades involving Jackie Robinson or any other Dodger stalwart. Instead, O'Malley proceeded just as the Cardinals had done: in their post-Rickey era, St. Louis had remained competitive for a number of seasons as the talent already in the majors continued to produce. So too would the Dodgers.

But O'Malley would not add to what Rickey had left behind, and a slow erosion would, in time, take place. Over the next few seasons, as the club came excruciatingly close time and time again to a world championship, the difference between the disappointment of *next year* and the promised glory of *this year* was so thin that it was virtually invisible, yet so enormous it was overwhelming. There were dozens upon dozens of times when one pitch or, more significantly, one player could have tipped the balance and forever changed not only the O'Malley legacy but also the future of the franchise. But that anonymous player never made it to Brooklyn. For want of a penny a fortune was lost, at least for Brooklyn fans, and

the accumulated disappointments continued to chip away at the unique bond the team enjoyed with its supporters. In the end, whether it was true or not, it seemed as if that had been O'Malley's plan all along.

This was never more true than in 1951. The story of that season is generally told within the simplistic framework of a Dodger "collapse" and a Giant "miracle," condensed into a single pitch thrown by Ralph Branca to Bobby Thomson. Yet in reality the 1951 season contained hundreds of moments, junctures, and events just as critical and telling. The 1951 season came down to the final pitch primarily because of what the organization did—or did not do—both before and during the season. That pitch mattered only because the Dodger organization put the ballclub in a position where it could matter. Those failures would resonate through the next few seasons far more than Branca's unfortunate pitch.

At first, none of O'Malley's semantic changes made much of a difference on the field. In Robinson, and in black players throughout baseball, Rickey's legacy would survive in spite of the efforts of O'Malley to erase him from memory. The team that would eventually be mourned by Brooklyn fans was not O'Malley's team, but the Dodgers created by Branch Rickey. From today's perspective, over the next few seasons there were so few changes on the field that it almost seems as if O'Malley was determined to watch Rickey's Dodgers wither on the vine. The fact that they did not is a testimony to their skill in the same way that the club's failure to win multiple world championships is a testimony to O'Malley's failed leadership.

In his first substantive move, O'Malley replaced Shotton, a Rickey guy who reminded O'Malley of Rickey in temperament and bearing as a man of the past. He hired former coach Charlie Dressen, who had served under Durocher in Brooklyn before going over to the Yankees.

When O'Malley hired Dressen, he hired a man like himself, a man who wanted the credit, who felt his achievements had not been properly recognized. Like O'Malley, Dressen was eager to prove himself and had fostered the notion that while serving on Durocher's coaching staff he had been a larger part of Brooklyn's success than the manager. And so far, without Dressen, Durocher had been something of a bust for the Giants. In his words, after taking over in 1948 he'd "backed up the truck," and in 1949 and 1950 the depleted Giants had finished fifth and third. Not bad, but not what they had expected of a Durocher team. In 1951 the Giants manager had a lot to prove too.

In recent years the once-proud Dodger-Giant rivalry had become a thing of the past, for it had become entirely one-sided in Brooklyn's favor. Since winning their last pennant in 1937, the Giants had been consistently mediocre—their third-place finish in 1950 was their best showing since 1942. Attendance at the Polo Grounds was deteriorating at an even greater pace than at Ebbets Field. Having the Yankees across the river didn't help. Increasingly, they drew big crowds only when they played Brooklyn and thousands of Dodger fans turned out hoping to gloat. But by 1951, owing primarily to an influx of African American talent best represented by Monte Irvin and Willie Mays, the Giants were on the precipice of a return to their former glory. They were the pick of contrarians to win the 1951 NL pennant over the more heavily favored Dodgers. Coupled with the venom that flowed between Dressen and Durocher, the rivalry would soon resume.

The Dodgers entered the 1951 season not as a team that had finished second but with the confidence of a defending world champion. The organization treated Philadelphia's pennant as a fluke and blamed Shotton for ruining a sure thing. They acted as if they were destined to win under Dressen in 1951, that it was unthinkable for a team with such obvious talent to lose. Dressen agreed, for such an attitude fed his own ego. Dodger players would quickly tire of the manager's inflated opinion of his role, as he would admonish the team to simply "hold them and I'll think of something."

As a result, the obvious weakness of the 1950 Dodgers—left-handed relief pitching and depth—went unacknowledged and unaddressed. They should have taken a lesson from Stengel's Yankees, who always seemed to have the right pitcher available to match up in the late innings, or the Phillies. In the final month of the 1950 season Jim Konstanty had proven invaluable to the Phillies and kept the team from collapsing despite the loss of players like Curt Simmons, Bob Miller, and Bubba Church. But his impact was dismissed as an anomaly.

Hubris was a trait shared by both Dressen and O'Malley—Dressen was still miffed about being passed over in favor of Stengel as Yankee manager in 1949 and was loath to admit that anything Stengel did showed intelligence. Brooklyn's failure to add or develop a left-handed relief pitcher in 1951 would, in the end, have horrendous consequences.

So too would their lack of depth. The starting lineup was the best in baseball. But beyond that the Dodgers really didn't have a dependable player. Like the Red Sox of the late 1940s,

they were made for the regular season, for crushing the opposition over the long haul, but not to win the close game when they had to.

It took the Dodgers only a few weeks of regular season play to work out the kinks after the off-season. In a prescient Opening Day column, Tommy Holmes warned that "fans must suffer," and although Robin Roberts dumped the Dodgers in the season opener in a reprise of the final game of the previous year, he added that "Roberts beat the Dodgers last opening day and in the final game of the season with the pennant at stake. This year he starts with a victory over Brooklyn on opening day. . . . It begins to look like a system." But the Dodgers were looking neither back nor ahead—yet. In the first week of the season they made a statement to the Giants, the first of a half-dozen occasions when Brooklyn fans thought the Giants were done.

Dodger diehard Dominic Barbuto hangs his head as his Dodgers lose their fifth straight World Series to the Yankees in 1953.

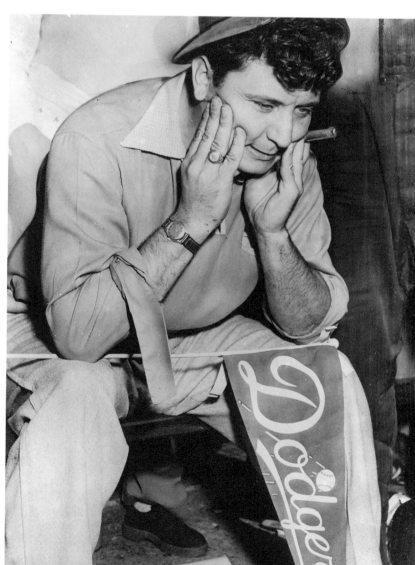

In their first meeting at the Polo Grounds, the Dodgers took three in a row. Moreover, when Durocher ordered his pitchers to try to intimidate the Dodgers with some chin music and both Campanella and Robinson were nicked, their teammates responded by emptying the bench.

At the end of the three-game set, the Giants were 2–5, losers of four in a row. The sweep sent them reeling, and they went on to lose a total of eleven straight, including two more against Brooklyn, before finally winning their third game of the season with an 8–5 win at Ebbets Field on April 30. That was the first of many games that season that would come back to haunt the Dodgers. An overconfident Dressen did everything but throw the game. His starting pitcher Chris Van Cuyk, an end-of-the-roster rookie, lasted exactly eleven pitches and then was relieved by another rookie, Earl Mosser, in his major league debut. Mosser walked the first three men he faced. Giants pitcher Sal Maglie rubbed it in when he threw at Robinson again, and this time Robinson responded by bunting down the first-base line and running over the pitcher when he covered the bag. As the two came up swinging and Durocher took on the umpires, it made great theater for fans, but the escalating violence forced acting baseball commissioner Ford Frick to step in and threaten to fine everyone. In a telling moment, he admonished Robinson in particular and warned him to stop "popping off." O'Malley's

support had been crucial to Frick's appointment, and by slapping down Robinson, who in this instance had been the victim, Frick showed his willingness to do O'Malley's bidding, something he would do again and again over his tenure — ultimately to the great consternation of Brooklyn fans.

On May 13 the Dodgers put away the pesky Boston Braves, coming back from a 6–0 deficit to win 12–6 and move into first place by percentage points. For the next four months they never looked back.

Never before had a Dodger team looked so invincible. Everybody — at least everybody who played regularly — was having one of the best seasons of his career. Hodges, Snider, and Campanella supplied the power, Reese and Robinson ran with abandon, and Furillo and Cox locked down the defense. Preacher Roe was almost unbeatable, Don Newcombe was on his way to winning 20 games for the first time, and Carl Erskine thrived in the rotation and teamed with Ralph Branca as the best third and fourth starters in the league. They hardly needed a fifth. They just started winning and never looked back. Although Cal Abrams entered June hitting almost .500, as soon as he slumped Bavasi made his first

Dodger President Walter O'Malley lets out a laugh as he helps newly hired manager Charlie Dressen with his new uniform at the announcement of Dressen's hiring in November 1950.

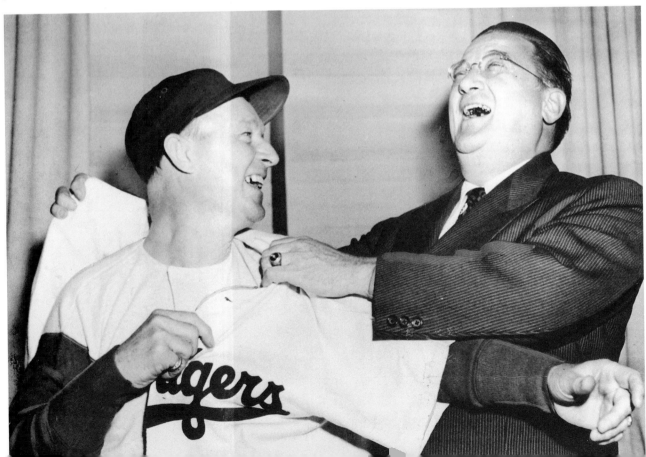

big trade, sending Bruce Edwards, Joe Hatten, Eddie Miksis, and Gene Hermanski—none of whom were playing, but all of whom were proven major leaguers—to the Cubs for veteran outfielder Andy Pafko, catcher Rube Walker, infielder Wayne Terwilliger, and pitcher Johnny Schmitz. The trade bolstered the starting lineup but stripped the team of what little depth it had. The Dodgers also called up Clem Labine from the minors to support Clyde King and Bud Podbielan in the bullpen.

On July 4 the Dodgers dumped the Giants in a doubleheader and Dressen began to gloat. "They're through," he announced of the Giants, rubbing it in Durocher's face. "They'll never bother us again."

But the Giants, despite the losses, were not the same team that had lost 11 games in a row in April. Unlike Dressen, Durocher wasn't so convinced of his own genius that he wouldn't admit to mistakes. Nor was he locked into a set starting lineup. He was, by his own admission, already "desperate." He started tinkering until he found something that worked.

The first something was 20-year-old Willie Mays, a phenom acquired a few years before after the Red Sox and Yankees both passed on him. Mays was hitting almost .500 for triple-A Minneapolis when Durocher brought him up in mid-May and installed him in center field in place of Bobby Thomson. But Mays went 1-for-24 his first week and begged to be sent back to Minneapolis. He had a girl there and told Durocher, "I can't hit up here."

If the Giants had been in the race, Durocher might well have sent Mays back. The Giants organization, while convinced he was the greatest prospect in baseball, also thought he needed more time in the minors and was worried that he'd be drafted—the Korean War was beginning to take a toll on major league rosters. They were prepared to leave Mays in the minors until his service commitment was over.

But Durocher had nothing to lose—the Giants were doing enough of that even before Mays joined them. Durocher told Mays he would be the Giant center fielder "tomorrow, next week, next month." Mays started to hit, and for most of the next 20 years he was arguably the greatest player in the game.

That still didn't solve all of Durocher's problems. Thomson, a solid hitter with occasional power, was in a slump. Hitting just over .200, he suddenly had no regular place to play. Along with Don Mueller and Whitey Lockman, he was one of three quality outfielders fighting for two spots. Over the next two months Durocher figured it out. He first flipped Monte

The Duke of Flatbush, aka Edwin Snider, poses for the *Brooklyn Eagle* in front of his Ebbets Field locker in 1951.

Irvin, uncomfortable at first base, and Lockman. Then, in mid-July, he gambled and moved Thomson, who had come to the majors as a third baseman, back to his old spot, sending Hank Thompson, who wasn't hitting at all, back to the minors. Again, had the Giants been in the race, Durocher probably never would have made either move. But with nothing to lose, all three thrived in their new positions and the Giants gained more offense and, surprisingly, better defense, for the addition of Mays compensated for the occasional struggle of the others. He saved more runs than they could hope to give away, and Giants pitching, led by Sal Maglie and Larry Jansen, was solid.

Meanwhile, the Dodgers ran away like the hare in Aesop's fable. But unlike the hare, they never bothered to take a rest. Maybe they should have.

On August 7 they rolled over the Giants again, taking a day-night doubleheader by winning 7–2 in game one and 7–6 in the second as Sal Maglie went headhunting, Jackie Robinson ran wild in response, and the Dodger fans at Ebbets Field showered Durocher and crew with all manner of garbage and other debris. The Giants had lost their last six games against Brooklyn, and the Dodger lead expanded to eleven and a half games, the greatest margin in franchise history. Dressen gave New York last rites, pronouncing, "The Giants is dead," and Brooklyn fans concurred.

Durocher was livid afterward and took issue with a report that had him conceding the pennant to the Dodgers. He told the *Herald Tribune*'s Harold Rosenthal: "They've [the Dodgers] got to win every one of them. I don't give them a thing until it says up there"—pointing to the Dodgers' scoreboard—"Dodgers win." But the next day the Dodgers won again, 6–5, upping their 1951 record versus New York to 12–3. Rosenthal wrote, "If the Dodgers quit right now and decide to mail the Polo Grounders the remaining seven games on the schedule they'll still finish in front." The lead was 12½ games, and not

even the presence of General Douglas MacArthur in the crowd caused anyone to think the Giants would replicate his return.

On August 11 the Dodgers again appeared to check the body for the last time. After beating the Braves in the first game of a doubleheader, they led the Giants by 13½ games. The game was quietly momentous for another reason—it was the first major league game ever to be televised in color. That led Red Smith of the *Herald Tribune* to warn of "horrors to come." He was referring to the peculiarly resplendent outfit that broadcaster Red Barber wore that day, but he could have been describing the rest of Brooklyn's season. For after losing the second game, the Dodgers lead was down to 13—remember that number.

From then on, with the Dodgers' record a gaudy 70–36 and the Giants' a middling 59–51, Brooklyn's lead began to shrink. The Giants would win and win and win again, losing only *seven* games for the rest of the year. Meanwhile, the

OF SIGNS AND CERTAINTY

The stealing of signs is as old as the game. Since baseball was first played and signs were first used to relay strategic information back and forth between players, opponents have endeavored to steal those signs. This practice can be divided into so-called legitimate sign stealing—such as a base coach relaying a catcher's sign to a hitter, or a player on the bench decoding a base coach's signs for a hitter or runner—and more questionable practices. Illegitimate methods of stealing signs range from batters glancing back to steal the catcher's sign to players or other spotters being stationed far away from home armed with a telescope, video monitor, or other device to steal the catcher's sign and then relay the information to the batter.

There is ample evidence dating from the 19th century that many ballclubs and many players had no qualms about stealing signs by any means possible, including the use of spotters with telescopes. The practice was tolerated with a nod and a wink and considered such a part of the

game that even though within the game it had long been considered morally questionable—like the grounds crew watering down the base paths to slow opposing runners—the practice wasn't even officially banned until 1961.

In 2001 reporter Josh Prager of the *Wall Street Journal* exposed the practice to a wide audience in his story "Giants 1951 Comeback Wasn't All It Seemed." Prager's exhaustively researched report revealed that beginning on July 19 the Giants employed an elaborate sign-stealing system that involved a spotter in the distant recesses of the Giants' clubhouse at the Polo Grounds. With a clear but distant view of home plate, the spotter used a telescope to steal the catcher's signs and relay them electronically to sound a buzzer in both the New York bullpen and the dugout. After experimenting by having players in the dugout yell out code words for various pitches, the Giants finally decided to utilize visual signals relayed from the bullpen.

The title of Prager's story suggests that in light of this practice the Giants' comeback in 1951 must be viewed in an entirely new light—as a spurious, even unsavory achievement. For after the Giants began stealing signs they went on a remarkable 52–18 streak that propelled them into a playoff against the Dodgers. Then, in the final game, Bobby Thomson, armed with the knowledge that Ralph Branca would throw a fastball, hit the home run that broke Brooklyn's heart and delivered a pennant to the Giants. To the casual fan, the story was a shocking revelation, even though it had been referred to, in far less detail, in several previous books.

Yet there was much more to the story. Baseball researcher Dave Smith soon crunched the numbers and discovered that after the Giants began stealing signs, they actually hit *worse* than before in the Polo Grounds, where they were presumed to have an advantage. His research revealed that the real difference in the second half of New York's season

Dodgers began a pattern that would last the rest of the season, winning and losing in more or less equal measure, keeping the Giants' faint hope alive.

On August 14, 15, and 16, the Giants broke Brooklyn's stranglehold with a tough three-game sweep, all close games the Dodgers could have won but did not. They lost the first 4–2 and the second 3–1 when Willie Mays, after catching a drive to right-center off the bat of Duke Snider, turned a full 180 degrees and threw home while falling over. Billy Cox, who perhaps waited a split second too long before leaving third and then failed to run flat out, was thrown out at the plate. Afterward Dressen sniffed, "I'd like to see him do it again." Mays would do just that, over and over, much to the chagrin of hitters throughout baseball. But for the Dodgers, once was enough. The Giants won the third game, 2–1, on a Newcombe wild pitch. Had Snider's drive dropped or Newcombe's pitch been closer to the plate, had Brooklyn won

even one of the three games, they'd have still led by 11½. But now their lead was less than ten games, an important psychological barrier to both clubs. Rosenthal cautioned: "The Dodger lead is even less than it was in 1942 at this time . . . it could be they are getting ready to blow another one on the final day of the season." His was the lone voice uttering such a warning, but the Giants were making a move.

They were also stealing signs in the Polo Grounds. It was hardly the first or the last time such a strategy has been tried in baseball. As revealed by writer Josh Prager in 2001, the club electrician installed a bell and buzzer system, and from mid-July on Giants hitters had the option of knowing precisely what pitch was coming. Yet the question of just how much impact this had on the pennant race is one that has yet to be definitively answered.

Brooklyn did not collapse—not yet. They kept winning, just not as often. They began to bleed from a thousand small

was their pitching staff—after July 19 the staff ERA dropped by more than a run a game. Although that doesn't mean the sign stealing had no effect on the Giants' season, it is certainly reason to pause before casting a cloud over the entire season.

But what of Thomson's at bat? Even if the sign stealing had no demonstrable impact on games during the regular season, might its impact on that particular at bat have been enough to change the season? Thomson denied taking the sign that told him that both pitches he saw would be fastballs. Yet according to Prager, backup catcher Sal Yvars was the player relaying the information from the bullpen. There was a sign for a breaking ball, but if the pitch was a fastball, Yvars was to do nothing, and on the two pitches to Thomson, he did nothing.

That raises more questions than it answers. For one, did Thomson have enough time to check with Yvars? And how certain could Thomson have been about the pitch when, presumably, Yvars also would have done nothing when he did not receive a signal? Remember, Thomson let the first fastball pass. And

Whitey Lockman claimed he was giving the sign from second base—a still legitimate method of gaining an edge. Who was Thomson looking at? Both? Neither?

Would knowledge of the pitch that was coming really make a difference anyway? Even in batting practice, players can't get base hits at will, much less home runs—not every time, not even against pitches thrown at batting practice speed. Furthermore, the Giants' system did not indicate *where* a pitch was going to be thrown, and most players believe that is far more valuable to know than whether a pitch is a fastball or curve. And many players—including many of the 1951 Giants—eschewed the practice entirely, not because they thought it was unfair, but because they found foreknowledge of the pitch distracting. And for the record, in 1951 Bobby Thomson hit thirteen home runs at the Polo Grounds—but only *three* of them after the Giants started stealing signs.

History is a cumulative process that tries to seize the truth from the irretrievable past. Each nugget of new information may bring the truth closer, but rarely does it do so definitively. Such is the case with

the stolen signs of 1951. It is an interesting and compelling story that adds to the richness of one of the most remarkable seasons and games in baseball history. But that is all.

It is neither the only story nor the definitive story, and we can never be certain that it was any more germane to the outcome of the season than a thousand other events of that year, ranging from rain-outs to pop-ups to spitballs. Consider this—perhaps if the Giants had *not* been stealing signs, they might *not* have slumped so dramatically at the plate after July 19. They might in fact have scored an extra run or two and somewhere along the line won one more game and won the pennant during the regular season. Or what if the Dodgers had won the 1951 pennant? Then, would not the sign-stealing story have been seen in the context of the failed strategy it was that led to New York's batting slump and subsequent narrow loss of the pennant? Wouldn't their sign stealing have been framed as the reason the Giants *lost* the pennant?

This much is certain—no one in Brooklyn would have complained about that.

Former teammates Eddie Stanky (left) and Pee Wee Reese pose at Ebbets Field prior to the first of the three playoff games that decided the 1951 National League pennant.

cuts and struggled as exhaustion set in. Roe had a sore shoulder and had to be pushed back. Snider's back was giving him trouble. Almost every Dodger went into a slump both subtle and more pronounced. Meanwhile, the Giants just kept winning—not because they knew what pitch was coming, but because of their pitching. Maglie in particular was immense, and Jim Hearn emerged to give the club a solid third starter.

At the beginning of September, when the Dodgers came to the Polo Grounds for two more games, they led by seven. After they absorbed two lopsided losses, the *Eagle* admitted, "They're still having trouble with those pesky Giants." But the next day Campanella's two home runs keyed a doubleheader sweep of Boston and seemed to stem the Giants' charge.

No one was worried. Or at least no one would admit it. Tommy Holmes reminded readers that in 1916 the Giants had won 17 in a row in May and another 26 straight beginning in mid-August, yet they had finished in fourth place. He concluded that the Giants' 11-game losing streak in April had doomed them to a similar finish. Yet Harold Burr warned that the Dodgers were beginning to wear out: "Jackie Robinson, Duke Snider and Pee Wee Reese all look like tired hitters. But Dressen hasn't got what Rickey called a strong bench, so he doesn't dare give too many of his tarnished stars a rest."

Even Dressen concurred, admitting, "Our bench is weak." But he still thought the Dodgers had the pennant wrapped up and was already looking past the 1951 season. "I'm not going to be caught next year with my hat down over my eyes," he said. "I want another outfielder, a left-handed relief pitcher like [right-hander] Clyde King and a spare first baseman." There was some help in the farm system, namely Junior Gilliam. In his first year in the organization after being signed off the roster of the Baltimore Elite Giants, Gilliam, a switch hitter, was causing some to compare him to Jackie Robinson. In Montreal he was leading the International League in runs scored, running wild on the bases, hitting nearly .300, and displaying uncommon grace and skill at second, at third, and in the outfield. A player of his versatility could have helped the Dodgers in a dozen ways and allowed the starters to receive some periodic rest, but the Royals were in the playoffs. "It would be unfair," said Dressen, to raid the minor league team. It was more unfair to leave the Dodgers undermanned.

There may have been yet another, unspoken reason to leave Gilliam in Montreal. His promotion would open up the prospect of the Dodgers having four black players on the field at the same time when Newcombe pitched. That hadn't been done yet.

On September 8, for what seemed to be about the 10th or 11th time, the Dodgers thought they'd knocked the Giants off for good when Newcombe shut them out on two hits, 9–0, ruining what Burr called the Giants' "evil designs" on a pennant. Although the loss was only New York's fourth in their last 27 games, with 17 games remaining the Dodgers still led by 6½. Then, in what was supposed to be their final meeting of the season the next day, the Dodgers gave Maglie his 20th win of the season, losing 2–1 in another game they could have won. The key play came in the eighth. After Robinson tripled to knock in a run, he made a rare baserunning gaffe. On a ground ball to Bobby Thomson at third, Robinson was caught off base to start a double play.

For Maglie, it was his fifth straight complete-game win over Brooklyn. On the flip side, it was the first time Ralph Branca had lost to the Giants at Ebbets Field since August 1945. The Dodgers—particularly Robinson—hated Maglie for his headhunting, yet it had served its purpose and gotten under their skin. They tried too hard against him, and that was ideal for a pitcher whose success depended on guile more than on speed.

But denial still ran unchecked in Brooklyn. Afterward Holmes gave the Giants their due, calling the game the season's "artistic high peak," but he concluded that after the previous day's win, "the Dodgers feel they have the world by the tail and downhill pull. They're probably right."

Three days later Newcombe left in the first inning of a 6–3 loss to the Phillies with a sore elbow, which Holmes and others questioned as a case of what Holmes called "Imaginitis." Nothing Newcombe did was ever quite enough for Dodger watchers, who expected him to win every game he pitched. He seemed particularly lacking when compared to Maglie, who didn't have half Newcombe's stuff but always seemed to win the big game. Newcombe, on the other hand, was prone to spectacular performances that still resulted in loss. Still, on September 15 an *Eagle* headline crowed, "Flock Concedes NL Pennant to Themselves," and the team started selling World Series tickets. Then they lost to the lowly Pirates 11–2, and their lead was down to five games.

Yet after every Dodger victory—and the rare Giant loss—the *Eagle* and other New York papers confidently declared the race was over. Durocher was still looking at the scoreboard, however, and it still did not say, "Dodgers win."

Brooklyn relished those words like a signature blackout cake from Brooklyn's Ebinger's bakery chain. They could taste the pennant and couldn't *wait* to celebrate. Before playing the Phillies on September 22—Charlie Dressen's birthday—

Members of the Pee Wee Reese Fan Club present their idol with a birthday cake at Ebbets Field on July 23, 1951. With Reese are (left to right) Connie Guida, Barbara Casale, Jerry Reilly, and Loretta Matteo.

they gave him a car, $5,000, and, incredibly, an oil painting that referred to his team as "National League Champions 1951." But the Dodgers ruined his day and lost to the Phillies. With a week left, their lead was down to three games.

Preacher Roe won the next day to push his record to 22–2, and then the Dodgers went into Boston for a doubleheader against the Braves. It was a disaster.

In the first game Branca didn't retire a hitter, giving up three hits and a walk before being pulled as the Braves scored the only six runs they'd need for a 6–3 win. And in game two Erskine was little better. He was knocked out in the second, and the Braves rolled to a 14–2 victory, crushing the Dodgers and their confidence. Meanwhile, the Giants beat Robin Roberts, and now the lead was down to one. And for the first time all season, despite being down a game, the Giants appeared to have the edge.

With five days remaining in the regular season, the Dodgers, 93–56, had five games left to play, two in Boston and three in Philadelphia. The Giants were 93–58. But after playing Philadelphia on September 26, they would enjoy two off-days before ending the season with two in Boston. The Dodgers would have to push to the finish knowing the Giants were watching — and resting. While the Dodgers still controlled their own destiny, if the pennant was still in doubt after the two off-days, the Giants would be in far better shape. For the last two games of the season they would have Maglie,

who'd made only one relief appearance since September 23, and Jansen, with three days' rest, available to pitch.

Both clubs won big on September 26. On the 27th, Durocher and the Giant staff gathered in their offices on 42nd Street to follow Red Barber's account of Brooklyn's game in Boston.

For seven and a half innings, Durocher shadow-managed the Braves and bit his nails as the game entered the last of the seventh tied, 3–3. Then, in a season in which every play loomed larger than the next, perhaps the biggest one to date came along.

With Sam Jethroe on first, Bob Addis on third, and one out, Earl Torgeson stepped in against Roe. Dressen chose to play the infield in and cut off the run at the plate.

Torgeson cooperated and chopped a roller right at Robinson. He threw home, where Campanella was blocking the plate.

Addis came in hard, driving his spikes into Campanella's shins, aiming for the plate blocked behind him. He upended Campanella, who collapsed on top of the runner, but Campy

---

In August 1951, Dodger fans, shown here in full musical celebration at Ebbets Field, felt assured that their team would coast to the pennant. Within weeks their team found themselves in a pennant race with the hated New York Giants led by former Dodger manager Leo Durocher.

held the ball firm. Umpire Frank Dascoli didn't hesitate — he called Addis safe.

Campanella bounced off the ground and started howling, tossing both his mask and mitt to the ground. Dressen and coach Cookie Lavagetto bolted from the dugout to join him in his argument.

One by one, Dascoli started picking them off like ducks on the midway, first tossing Campanella from the game, then Lavagetto, then going down the Dodger bench and tossing one player after the other until the only uniformed personnel left were Rube Walker — who had to replace Campanella — infielder Wayne Terwilliger, the first-base coach, the batboy, and — how could he have missed him? — Dressen himself.

Brooklyn had a chance to tie it in the ninth when Reese hit a double, but instead of Campanella and his 100-plus RBIs due to come to bat, it was Rube Walker and his nine. So Dressen pinch-hit Terwilliger, with his four. Terwilliger grounded out, and when Pafko struck out to end the game, Brooklyn's lead was down to half a game.

Now the Dodgers were coming unglued. Campanella was waiting for the umpires when they entered their dressing room next to the visitors' clubhouse. A guard was called. Jackie Robinson reportedly split the door in half with a mule kick. Dressen called Dascoli incompetent. Dascoli and his crew needed an escort to protect them from the Dodgers as they left the ballpark.

The next day the Dodgers fell to the Phillies as Durocher played manager by radio once more, this time in Boston's Kenmore Hotel. After taking a 3–0 lead, Erskine tired late and Dressen was afraid to go to the pen. The Phillies won 4–3. With two games left, the Dodgers and Giants were tied, and it looked as though they were passing like two elevators, Brooklyn down and New York up.

For six weeks, as the Giants surged, the Dodgers had held them at bay, playing good, almost great, baseball. The word *collapse* hadn't fit the way they played from August 11 through September 14, a time during which they'd gone 21–15 — a .583 win percentage was enough to win the pennant in most seasons. Yet since September 14, they'd won only four of thirteen, including only one of their last five games. The word *collapse* now fit the Dodgers as accurately as the word *miracle* fit the Giants.

Now another factor tilted in New York's favor. While the Dodgers were in Philadelphia, the league held a coin toss to determine home-field advantage in the playoffs. Dodger ticket

NL TOTAL BASES LEADERS

1916	Zack Wheat	262
1919	Hy Myers	223
1941	Pete Reiser	299
1950	Duke Snider	343
1953	Duke Snider	370
1954	Duke Snider	378

manager Jack Collins was the highest-ranking club official still in Brooklyn. He was left to make the call on an outcome no one in the organization had ever imagined would take place.

The Dodgers won the toss. He thought he was doing the right thing and chose to give up home-field advantage in the best-of-three playoff, electing to play the first game at Ebbets Field and giving New York the last two in the Polo Grounds. The Giants couldn't believe their good fortune.

There was a twisted, if mistaken, logic in Collins's thinking. He recalled that back in 1946 the Dodgers had also won the toss and had also erred. They'd won the toss then too and took the home-field advantage by electing to play the first game in St. Louis. But that had forced them to take a 26-hour train trip back and forth across the country twice in a matter of days, something the Dodgers later regretted and blamed for their loss. Recalling that now, he made the opposite decision and chose to have the club play the first game at Ebbets Field.

He had forgotten that it wasn't a 26-hour trip between Brooklyn and the Polo Grounds but a 40-minute subway ride. Common sense and the odds said the Dodgers should have chosen to play the final two games in Brooklyn. So for the second time—but for very different reasons—the Dodgers won the toss but blew the call.

Brooklyn looked finished. As Holmes had intimated at the start of the season, the end was near. Robin Roberts again stood between Brooklyn and first place.

But this time he faltered. Newcombe pitched a shutout opposite Roberts, and Maglie tossed a shutout for the Giants. The season entered the final day. If the Dodgers lost and the Giants won, New York would win the pennant, holding first place for only one day all season—the only day that mattered.

Dressen chose Preacher Roe to start the game on only two days' rest. His other options were Ralph Branca, who after starting the season 12–5 had struggled with a sore arm, and Clem Labine. But Dressen had lost faith in Branca, and he had buried Labine over the final ten days after the pitcher angered his manager by pitching from the stretch against Philadelphia on September 21 and giving up a grand-slam

---

World War I veteran Samuel Maxwell maintained a vigil outside the bleacher entrance of Ebbets Field waiting for World Series tickets he'd hoped might be distributed to veterans and shut-ins. His wait was in vain: the Dodgers dropped a historic three-game playoff to the Giants.

home run. For Roe it was his third straight start with less than the usual four days off, and for the third consecutive start his performance deteriorated. The Phillies got to him early, and he was knocked out in the second as the Dodgers fell behind, 4–0.

By the end of the third inning they trailed 6–1. Walter O'Malley later admitted, "In my mind, I was going over the phrasing for the wire of congratulations." They still trailed 6–5 when word reached Ebbets Field that the Giants, behind Larry Jansen, had beaten Boston 3–2. Now, for the first time all year, what the Dodgers needed to do was clear, elemental, and irrefutable—win or the season was over.

It is a measure of the season that the rest of the game against Philadelphia is barely remembered anywhere beyond the borders of Brooklyn. For over the next few innings Jackie Robinson put on a clutch performance equal to that of any player in the history of the game, far better than Yaz in '67 or Bucky Dent in '78.

Brooklyn forged a tie in the eighth on Rube Walker's two-run double and Carl Furillo's single, and the game entered extra innings. In the tenth the Giants were boarding their train back to New York and announcer Russ Hodges gave the team a play-by-play account over a rail phone as the team chugged through Connecticut. Then, in the twelfth, Newcombe, who in a gutsy performance had come on in the sixth after pitching the previous day and shut the Phillies down, finally faltered, loading the bases. With two out, he faced Eddie Waitkus.

The Philadelphia first baseman hit a rocket by Newcombe's ear. Robinson reacted, leaping sideways to his right. He was, wrote Red Smith, "stretched at full length in the insubstantial twilight, the unconquerable doing the impossible," laid out parallel to the ground, his glove reaching out to try to save the season.

He did. The ball smacked into Robinson's glove and he landed heavily, like a football wide receiver catching the ball in the corner of the end zone. As he landed, his elbow was driven into his side and Robinson rolled and then lay still. After a few minutes he rose weakly and made his way to the dugout as the Philadelphia crowd, which had once been so disdainful of him, cheered the play wildly.

Tommy Holmes had been right on Opening Day, for in the eighth inning Robin Roberts had come on in relief and still stood between Brooklyn and a pennant. But in the fourteenth, with one out and the count one ball and one strike,

Jackie Robinson drove the ball into the left-field stands to give the Dodgers a 9–8 lead. Bud Podbielan held the Phillies scoreless in the bottom of the inning, and now the Dodgers knew how the Giants had felt for six weeks—they were still alive.

But they were also hurting in perhaps the worst way possible. In a few months Roy Campanella would win his first MVP Award in recognition of his 33 home runs, 108 RBIs, and .325 batting average, as well as his stewardship behind the plate. But over the final weeks Campanella had started to come apart. He'd taken a pitch to the head that caused him to bleed from the ears, yet he had kept playing, and playing well. His hands were a swollen mess, the result of a lifetime spent behind the plate. And in the game against Philadelphia, as he legged out a triple, he pulled a hamstring yet kept playing. Now he could barely walk.

There was no time to think about that, however, and hardly any time to breathe, for the playoffs would start the next day at Ebbets Field.

In a sense, game one was the key to the series, for the winner would enter game two with the knowledge that for the first time in weeks the upcoming game would not determine the outcome of the season, that no matter what happened they would live for another day.

Neither club enjoyed the luxury of entering the playoff with a 20-game winner available for game one—Newcombe, Roe, Maglie, and Jansen were all gassed.

But the Giants were in far better shape for the longer haul. Both Erskine and Preacher Roe were nursing sore arms, and neither would pitch in the playoffs. Ralph Branca got the ball for the Dodgers opposite the Giants' Jim Hearn.

It was a quiet contest, as if neither team had the energy to play a game equal to the drama of the previous week. The Dodgers took a 1–0 lead on Pafko's second-inning home run, but in the fourth, after Branca hit Monte Irvin, Bobby Thomson homered—his first off Branca that year but his seventh off Dodger pitching—and the Dodgers trailed 2–1.

In the bottom of the inning they made their last threat, but Roy Campanella, playing with his leg numbed by an anesthetic, bounced into a double play after Snider and Jackie Robinson singled. Had he been able to run, he probably would have beaten the throw and Snider would have scored to tie the game. But the tying run never crossed the plate, and in the eighth Irvin hit a home run off Branca and the Giants emerged with a 3–1 win. After the game the *Eagle* noted that

Jubilant after their 14th-inning 9–8 victory over the Phillies, members of the Dodgers descend on winning pitcher Bud Podbielan. The Dodger victory on the final day of the season combined with the Giants' win over the Boston Braves set up the Dodgers' second National League playoff in six seasons.

the home runs by Thomson and Irvin "lifted the Branca home run total [in 1951] to seventeen and ten of them have been pumped into the stands by Giant batsmen, five of the ten by Irvin." Clearly, this was not the pitcher to have on the mound against the Giants when a home run could mean the ballgame.

Both managers were in a quandary before game two at the Polo Grounds, but for different reasons. Durocher pondered whether to start Maglie on two days' rest or save him for game three, while Dressen found himself with no choice but

Tom McDonough, a bartender at Eisen's Bar in Brooklyn, expresses the feelings of countless Dodger fans as he stands by a miniature coffin, a symbol representing the New York Giants after their 10–0 loss to Brooklyn in the second of three playoff games to decide the 1951 National League pennant.

to turn to the exiled Clem Labine. After winning game one, Durocher could afford to gamble, and so he did. He decided to save Maglie, who was exhausted anyway, for game three and gave the ball to journeyman Sheldon Jones instead. Besides, if the Giants won, Maglie would be able to start the World Series against the Yankees.

The game ended quickly. The Dodgers pounded Jones, hitting five home runs, including one by Rube Walker, playing because Campanella couldn't, and Labine pitched a shutout, winning 10–0. The question went unanswered as to what might have happened over the previous week had Dressen allowed him to pitch. They might have won the pennant or, at the very least, saved Preacher Roe's arm for the playoffs.

Despite the win, things weren't looking good for Brooklyn. Roy Campanella couldn't play. His season was over, and the Dodgers would enter the final game with neither Roe nor the NL MVP-to-be, a devastating loss.

The final game of the playoff is one of the most closely dissected games in the history of baseball, alone the subject of several books. And while the finish was without question one of the most memorable moments in baseball, few accounts

of the playoffs bother to consider the impact of the loss of Roe and Campanella on the Dodgers, but their absence amounted to removing the last two bricks that caused the house to tremble before it fell.

Campanella's loss was particularly devastating, and particularly in the final game. For most of the season he had hit fifth, behind Robinson. That position in the lineup not only forced pitchers to pitch to Robinson but brought Campanella a steady diet of fastballs when Robinson got on base. In this game the fifth spot was taken by Pafko, a good hitter but hardly the intimidating presence of Campanella. Furthermore, Campanella had been a workhorse behind the plate in 1951. Before the final game Campanella wanted to play but was forced to admit that he might have trouble moving behind the plate. So Dressen, impressed by Walker's three hits and home run the day before, decided to ride the hot hand. The rookie had little experience, however, and was facing the awesome responsibility of calling the biggest game of the season.

Both teams went with the best they had. That meant Newcombe, 20–8 for the Dodgers, and Maglie, 22–6 for the Giants, even though both pitchers were spent and began the game with much less than their best stuff.

Brooklyn threatened early. Maglie, who always looked like he needed another night's sleep anyway, pitched that way this time, working deliberately. Furillo led off the game by striking out, but then Reese and Snider both walked on a combined nine pitches.

Jackie Robinson didn't wait around. He ripped the next pitch to left, driving in Reese and sending Snider to second. Maglie was on the brink. But now, instead of Campanella coming to bat, it was Pafko. He hit into a force play, and Hodges popped up. The Dodgers led 1–0, but they'd let Maglie off the hook. He'd retire 13 of the next 14 batters—including two strikeouts by Rube Walker.

Newcombe, meanwhile, was nearly as good. After a quick first, he got lucky in the second. Whitey Lockman singled, and then Bobby Thomson—who had owned the Dodgers in 1951—followed with a line drive between third base and Bobby Cox. It appeared as if the Giants would rally.

Thomson had been in the middle of everything for the Giants all year—displaced by Mays, moved to third base, and then in August moved ahead of Mays in the Giants lineup. And each time, after a bad start, he had made the moves work.

That pattern would be repeated in this game. As he

rounded first Thomson was thinking double. Lockman, however, was making sure that as the tying run he wouldn't be thrown out at third, and he stopped at second. Thomson was more than halfway to a double when he saw Lockman at second, then tried to scramble back to first. Reese's relay to Hodges put him out and Giants fans groaned.

Neither team really threatened again until the seventh. The game was tense, but the crowd was relatively quiet—it was cool and so gloomy that in the third inning the lights were turned on.

In the bottom of the seventh the Giants finally rallied. Monte Irvin led off with a double and Whitey Lockman followed with a bunt in front of home plate.

Attempting a play that a healthy Campanella might have made, Walker jumped out from behind the plate and threw to third to catch Irvin, but he was too late. Then Thomson hit a simple fly ball to left. Irvin tagged up to tie the game before Mays hit into a double play to end the inning.

Newcombe came back into the dugout and told Dressen he was gassed. Before the manager could respond, Robinson jumped in the pitcher's face, challenging him to stay in the game, trying to make him angry. It worked. Newcombe was steamed, but he didn't ask out again.

In the top of the eighth it was Maglie who suddenly seemed to run out of gas. With one out, Reese and Snider singled, putting runners on the corners. Then Maglie threw a wild pitch, and Reese scored the go-ahead run. Maglie walked Robinson intentionally to set up a force-out at second, but Pafko smashed the ball off Thomson's glove at third. Snider scored to make the score Brooklyn 3, Giants 1.

Gil Hodges followed with a pop-up, but Billy Cox cracked another single through Thomson to score Robinson, and now the Dodgers led 4–1. Neither play was ruled an error, but a true third baseman like Cox would have made the play. Thomson was in the lineup because of his bat, not his glove, but now he was wearing goat horns. Rube Walker ended the rally with a groundout. Maglie walked off the field to applause, even a few rounds from suddenly confident and sympathetic Dodger fans. He was due to hit second and was certain to be pulled for a pinch-hitter.

Newcombe cruised through the bottom of the inning on adrenaline, and Larry Jansen, in relief of Maglie, set the Dodgers down in order in the top of the ninth. Pitching in his fourth game in eight days, Newcombe then walked to the mound in the ninth needing only three more outs to put

Jackie Robinson watches to make sure that Bobby Thomson touches all the bases following his pennant-winning ninth-inning home run at the Polo Grounds. As the Giant bench empties to greet Thomson, Dodger relief pitcher Ralph Branca can't bear to watch.

Brooklyn in the World Series. As he warmed up Durocher tried to pump up his club, but the Giants knew the outlook was grim.

Alvin Dark came up first, and Newcombe got ahead of him, 0–2. He didn't have the energy to waste a pitch and threw another strike. Dark hit it off the end of the bat between first and second.

Hodges moved to his right and tried to backhand the ball, but it tipped off his glove toward Robinson, who tried to change direction and stop it, but the ball rolled free for a single.

Dressen froze. With Dark on first, he failed to change the infield defense. Dark's run didn't matter, but Hodges held

Dodger reliever Clem Labine cleans out his Ebbets Field following Brooklyn's playoff defeat in 1951. Labine enjoyed a superb 5–1 season in 1951, topped by his 10–0 shutout victory over the Giants in the second of the three playoff games against the Giants.

him close to the bag, leaving a huge hole on the right side. Dressen should have moved Hodges off the bag so as to close the hole and be in position to turn a double play if the ball was hit hard right at him. Left-handed Don Mueller noticed and pulled the ball to the hole, a simple ground ball, but again between Robinson and Hodges. Dark raced to third.

There was some uneasy stirring in the stands as the enthusiasm and confidence began to shift from Dodger fans to Giant supporters. Monte Irvin stepped in.

Dressen went out to the mound. For several innings Ralph Branca and Clem Labine had been warming up. Coach Clyde Sukeforth had told him that both were ready. But Dressen didn't want to bring in either against Irvin. He stuck with Newcombe.

Irvin, who led the Giants in home runs, RBIs, and batting average, tried to prove his worth. But Newcombe, although tired, was smart. He knew that it was only 279 feet down the line to the stands in left, and he didn't want to give Irvin a chance to pull the ball. He threw a fastball up and away, emptying the tank.

Irvin was thinking home run and tried to pull the ball. But the pitch beat him. He popped the ball up to Hodges for an out.

That brought up lefty Whitey Lockman, a contact hitter with little power, but a hard man to strike out. Had the Dodger bullpen included a left-hander, this would have been the spot to bring him in, to try to get a ground ball and a double play. But there was no one who fit that description available in the pen.

Newcombe was still throwing hard, but not hard enough. He stayed away again, but Lockman went with the pitch and slapped the ball over Cox's head down the left-field line into the corner. Dark scored easily, and Mueller tore for third.

He made it, but paid a price. As he hit the bag he rolled over his ankle, spraining it badly. The game was delayed for several minutes while Mueller was helped off the field and replaced by Clint Hartung. Lockman made second, the tying run, the score 4–2, one out. Bobby Thomson was on deck.

Dressen came out to the mound again. Newcombe was finished. Dressen had called to the bullpen one last time and asked Sukeforth who looked better, Branca or Labine. Sukeforth told him to go with Branca. The coach later remembered that it was the first time all season that Dressen had asked who he thought should pitch rather than just making the decision himself.

That was one reason to bring in Branca.

But there were several reasons more not to. Branca had thrown a full game two days before and had given up a home run to Thomson. The Giants had had his number all year. He hadn't pitched well in the second half. He hadn't thrown much to Rube Walker.

But there was, perhaps, another big reason to pitch Branca. In 17 days he would marry into the Dodger hierarchy when he wed the daughter of Dearie Mulvey, who still owned a block of stock passed down from the McKeevers.

Both Bud Podbielan and Clyde King, the two stalwarts of the Dodger bullpen, were well rested, and Podbielan had been the winning pitcher in the critical game against Philadelphia. But neither was even asked to warm up. Dressen waved Branca in.

It was a long walk. The Polo Grounds buzzed.

Branca took the ball from Dressen. The manager, a former infielder, didn't tell him what to throw and didn't tell the rookie catcher what pitch to call. All Dressen said was, "Get him out." The Dodgers had done their job so far and held the game close, but now Dressen thought of nothing. Nothing.

Durocher was thinking, though. As Thomson started toward the batter's box, Durocher put his arm around him. The manager claimed he told Thomson to look for a fastball, because his home run off Branca two days before had come on a slider. Thomson doesn't remember that. He remembers Durocher telling him, "If you ever hit one, hit one now."

Branca and Walker talked as Dressen walked back to the dugout. Walker wanted the pitcher to get ahead with a fastball, and if he did, come back with another one, up and in. Thomson, like most pull hitters, liked to get his arms out and could be jammed on a pitch up and in.

Branca nodded his head and agreed.

He should have stopped to think. So should have Walker. So should have Dressen. Think.

A home run would beat the Dodgers. The Polo Grounds was huge—except down the lines. It was almost 500 feet to center, and nearly 450 feet to the power alleys. But it was only 260 feet down the right-field line, and 279 in left, where a hitter could even be jammed and still hit the ball out. In his first three times at bat Thomson had hit the ball to left field each time. Think.

A fly ball to the big part of the park would score a run but wouldn't beat the Dodgers—that's why Newcombe had stayed away from both Irvin and Mueller. A ground ball any-

Following his superb 20–9 season in 1951, the Dodgers lost Don Newcombe to military service for two full seasons. Newcombe is shown being fitted for his uniform in February 1952 by Lt. William A. Johnson at Camp Kilmer, N.J.

where wouldn't beat them either. Even a base hit would do nothing more than tie the game. You couldn't walk Thomson intentionally—Mays was too fast to count on a double play. But if Thomson pulled a ball down the line, into the stands, well, that would be the season.

Common Sense said, "Don't throw a pitch that can be pulled in the air," and Experience added, "Keep the ball away,

Television personality Happy Felton served as leader of the Knothole Gang for a generation of young Dodger fans. Felton is shown at Ebbets Field in 1951.

or down, and if you do come inside, make sure it's a ball. Be careful, and remember, there's a rookie on deck, Mays. He's a good one, but he's only 20 years old. Even if Thomson gets on base, he'll be nervous."

Think. Try to get ahead, but keep the ball away. Then change speeds. Throw a breaking ball. See if Thomson's anxious. Make him chase a pitch. Don't let him pull the ball. Think.

But no one thought.

Thomson stepped in and Branca threw. A fastball, right down the middle. Thomson's bat never moved. Strike one.

Did he know it was a fastball? Had he gotten the sign? Was there enough time for Walker to signal for the pitch, the sign to be decoded, the buzzer to be pushed, the sign to be relayed, and Thomson to glance away and process the information? How long does that take? Three seconds, four? Five? Branca was a fast worker, and back then all pitchers worked fast. Did Walker even flash Branca a sign? He'd already called the pitch

on the mound. Anyway, wouldn't he change signals with a new pitcher and a runner on second?

And there it was, a fastball. So why didn't Thomson swing? Isn't that what every hitter looks for anyway, a fastball? Expect the fastball and adjust to everything else — that's the rule. Thomson had just watched a fat one pass. He'd be anxious now. Think. Keep the ball away, maybe waste one. Think.

Branca knew what to do next. So did Walker. It was done, already decided. Another fastball, up and in.

Whitey Lockman saw it from second base. Baserunners are supposed to steal signs, supposed to let the hitter know what's coming whenever they can. That's not cheating; that's heads-up baseball. He later told author Ray Robinson, "I watched Walker cup his hand for the next pitch and motion up and to his left."

What?

"I watched Walker *cup his hand* for the next pitch and motion up and to his left."

So there was no sign? But Lockman also told Josh Prager there was a sign but "I couldn't read the sequence." He held his belt buckle to let Thomson know he didn't know what the pitch was, for with a runner on second the catcher eschews simple signs for more complex patterns.

Was there a sign? The pitch had been called when Branca went to the mound. All Walker did was signal location, remind Branca where to throw the pitch. And there was no sign for location anyway, no way to communicate that from a telescope through a wire to the bullpen. And if Thomson was watching for a signal from the bullpen, why was Lockman giving him a sign? Did he have time to look at Lockman too?

Does it matter? Branca threw the pitch Walker had called for a moment before on the mound. Thomson was looking for a fastball anyway. The ball was up and in. But not too far up, and not too far in. Borderline. And Thomson was ready, anxious — he'd just let a fat one pass.

He swung. The ball hit the bat and sailed, not down the line, where it would curve foul, but some 40 feet fair. A fly ball that went high and then, as everyone remembered later, started to die, to sink down. On the radio Ernie Harwell calmly said, "It's gone," then worried that it wasn't, that he'd just made the biggest mistake of his broadcasting career.

It was a fly ball, but not to where the fence was 279 feet from home, but where a sign said "315," where Andy Pafko took a few steps back and now stood watching, where no other park in major league baseball had a fence, where even at Ebbets Field such fly balls are routine outs, where even though the ball was sinking it had enough. A fly ball not hit on a line but in an arc, then dropping, high enough, just high enough, to breach the wall 16 feet high. Long enough and high enough for the Giants to win the pennant, for Russ Hodges on his television broadcast to scream to the nation, "There's a long drive . . . it's gonna be — I believe — THE GIANTS WIN THE PENNANT! THE GIANTS WIN THE PENNANT! THE GIANTS WIN THE PENNANT! THE GIANTS WIN THE PENNANT!" Long enough and high enough and far enough for time to stop, for the Dodgers to turn and walk out across the field toward the clubhouse, Giants fans streaming past them, Thomson leaping and pinwheeling his arms through the air as he ran the bases. Long enough for Red Smith to note later that as Branca walked off the field, "the number on his back looked huge. Thirteen." Long enough and high enough to end the Dodger season, to squash the dream of a dynasty *again,* long enough to make the moment still hurt some 50 years later.

Long enough to be talked about, envisioned, heard, and seen again, over and over and over. Memorable enough for Red Smith to start his column the next day, "Now it's done. Now the story ends. And there is no way to tell it. The art of fiction is dead." Close enough to still seem like it happened yesterday.

5–4. The Giants' 99–59 to the Dodgers' 98–54. The 157th game of a 154-game season. THE GIANTS WIN THE PENNANT!

Dodger fans were stunned. This was worse than '41, worse than '46, worse than 1950. They had won the pennant, they were sure, when the Giants lost 11 in a row in April, and in July when Dressen said, "The Giants is dead," and in August when the lead was 13½, and in September when Dressen got his painting that said, "National League Champions 1951," and when Newcombe shut out Philadelphia, and when Robinson snagged the line drive and hit the home run. And they were certain they had won when they had scored in the eighth, and when Irvin had popped up, and when Branca threw a first-pitch strike, and when he wound up to throw the next pitch and the ball was headed toward the plate.

And now they had lost. For ten years they were certain that Brooklyn would win, that victory was not just deserved but destined, that Brooklyn could beat its chest again and shake its fist at Manhattan and the rest of the country, that the Bum would be a bum no more. But now, that's what they were, not the team, but the fans. Bums. Bums to believe the Dodgers would win. Suckers.

They tried to forget about it, the fans, but it was hard, and it hurt.

Rookie right-handed pitcher Joe Black filled the void in the Brooklyn staff left by Don Newcombe's departure to military service. Not only did Black win 15 games, but he also dazzled in the opening game of the 1952 World Series at Ebbets Field. In this sequence Black is shown in the ninth inning of that game. He scattered six hits and struck out six Yankees in the 4–2 victory.

In seven seasons with the Dodgers, outfielder Sandy Amoros played a stellar left field. His chief contribution to Dodger glory was his remarkable game-saving catch of Yogi Berra's sinking liner in the seventh game of the 1955 World Series.

Dressen survived it. No one really blamed him, at least not in public and not in print. Nor did they blame O'Malley or mention the hundred reasons why the Giants played in the World Series that year, losing to the Yankees, while the Dodgers did not. It was as if the moment was so painful that no one, anywhere, could bear to look back and see what had gone wrong. They fired Clyde Sukeforth, but to most it came

down to Branca, the man who touched the ball when the Dodgers were still ahead and when the Dodgers were winning the pennant and that one pitch — and not anything else, not really — had been the difference in the season.

Not a lesson was learned from the loss. Over the next two seasons the graph of the Dodgers season would unfold in rough proximity to the way it had in 1951 — they would start fast, open a lead, and coast to the finish. But neither the 1952 nor the 1953 Dodgers would have a team like the 1951 Giants rise up to press them.

Yes, the Dodgers had lost because of Bobby Thomson's home run off Branca, but for a hundred different reasons it never should have come down to that. To blame Branca for the loss is to assign blame to the last man standing in a long row of failure. In the largest sense, the Dodgers lost because of O'Malley's and Dressen's inflated, personal overconfidence that led them to leave the obvious holes in the Dodger lineup after the 1950 season unaddressed — that's what cost Dodgers the 1951 pennant. In particular, the utter lack of left-handed relief pitching and lack of depth left the Dodgers ill equipped to face the final weeks of the season. That's what had made an apparently insurmountable lead surmountable, and that's what sent the Dodgers into the playoffs ill prepared.

More specifically, like their fans, until the very end neither Dressen nor the Dodgers seemed to realize it was even possible for them to lose. Over the final six weeks Dressen's own mistakes, coupled with those of his players and a series of small though unfortunate injuries, left the Dodgers exposed. And in the final days Dressen's exile of Labine and his resulting overdependence on Roe, coupled with Campanella's bad leg, left the team limping into the playoffs undermanned. Branca's pitch was just the period on a long sentence already written, for it never, ever should have come down to that pitch. All he did was throw the ball — everybody else helped place the ball in his hand in a situation with no margin for error. The miracle wasn't that the Giants won the playoff, but that the Dodgers came within one out of winning, for by October the Giants were by far the better team on the field.

That loss looms over all Dodger history like no other game the franchise played before or after. Indeed, in all baseball perhaps only the Red Sox loss to the Mets in game six of the 1986 World Series or their game-seven loss to the Yankees in the 2003 ALCS has caused similar pain among partisan fans. And the shadow it casts has caused observers to overlook the fact that no matter how the 1951 season came out, the

Dodgers should have won one or more world championships in the seasons just prior to 1951 and soon after, but those championships were lost without the drama of 1951. That year's loss was neither an anomaly nor a singular instance of bad luck, but the result of the combined failures of the franchise intersecting all at once.

Yet the organization — O'Malley and Dressen — sloughed off the loss as easily as they had fired Clyde Sukeforth. By the following April, October was not just forgotten — it was as if it had never happened. They had considered 1950 a fluke, and now they put 1951 in the same column. They hadn't changed anything after the 1950 season, and they would change nothing after 1951. Long before it was recognized as a psychological state, the Dodger organization had denial down pat.

The Dodgers still had the best lineup in baseball and were still convinced that would be enough. The pitching staff, however, was beginning to look like a train wreck.

Don Newcombe was gone, drafted into the service. Preacher Roe's 36-year-old arm was almost shot — he needed plenty of rest after every appearance. Ralph Branca fell off a chair in spring training, landed on a Coke bottle, and hurt his back, twisting his pelvis. In 1951 the Dodgers had gotten 85 wins from Newcombe, Roe, Erskine, Branca, and Clyde King. In 1952 they would get only 31 from those same five pitchers.

A few years before, when under Rickey the Dodger farm system was pumping out prospects, they might have packaged a few overrated youngsters and pried away a veteran or two, as they'd done with Roe, to fill the breach. But by now Brooklyn's farm system was shrinking, down to five teams in only two seasons, and they had emptied their reservoir of veterans in 1951 to get Andy Pafko.

But they still had the players Rickey had signed, including former Negro Leaguer Joe Black and a young rookie from Long Island named Billy Loes. Loes stepped into the rotation, while Black, like Newcombe, gave the club an intimidating, dominating presence. The Dodgers finally learned a lesson and installed Black in the bullpen, where for the first time since Hugh Casey they had a pitcher who could come in late and shut the other team down. He was a true fireman.

What helped the Dodgers the most in 1952, however, was not what they added but what the Giants lost. Monte Irvin and Larry Jansen were both injured for much of the year, while Willie Mays, after a poor start, was drafted into the Army. Their lineup just couldn't match up with Brooklyn's anymore. The Dodgers were in their prime. Duke Snider, at

25, was the youngest man in the starting lineup, while Robinson and Reese, both 33, were the oldest.

In 1952 the Dodgers pulled away in June from everyone but New York, and from then on it was a two-team race. On July 22 their record was a stellar 60–22.

Then the Dodgers began to coast. For the rest of the season they played little better than .500 baseball. In late August the Dodgers still led by nearly ten games, but the Giants started surging again. It was beginning to look like 1951 all over again, only this time Dodger observers were alert to New York's footsteps.

On September 6 the Giants swept a doubleheader to draw to within four games. The headline above the box score in the *Eagle* told the story: "Oh, Foul Infamy! Oh, Cursed Day! Oh, Darn Giants!"

The load on the Brooklyn bandwagon grew considerably lighter. Tommy Holmes quoted Durocher as saying, "If we can pull this one out, there'll be 100,000 suicides in Brooklyn," and he was being kind. "The Dodgers," added Holmes, "began to look like Sugar Ray Robinson in the 13th round against Joey Maxim," a bout in which the once-great champion was battered and it became clear his better days were behind him. "What happened to Ray Robinson drew almost universal sympathy," he went on. ". . . The Dodgers . . . can expect nothing but abuse and ridicule." He noted the overall weakness of the pitching staff, save for Black, and noted that even if the Dodgers made it to the pennant, "no staff like this has ever pitched a ball club into the World Series." But the Dodgers took the next two against the Giants; this time New York simply didn't have it. They made one final push to get within three and a half games, but from there the Dodgers pulled away and won the pennant by four and a half and the right to play the Yankees in the World Series.

Dodger supporters, however, were comparatively unimpressed, even blasé. Despite the race, in 1952 crowds at Ebbets Field slumped to their lowest level since the war — barely one million tickets were sold.

Brooklyn was changing faster than anyone cared to admit. Crime was on the rise there as it was elsewhere in urban America after the war, and the *Eagle*, facing an erosion of its readership, had discovered that sensationalized crime coverage sold papers. The paper cut off its nose to spite its face: day after day the latest vicious crime highlighted on the front page sold papers for a day but drove more and more longtime residents — and *Eagle* subscribers — to browse the

DAY BY DAY
IN THE GREAT RACE

SATURDAY, AUGUST 11

Brooklyn Dodgers 8, Boston Braves 1, at Ebbets Field
This victory gives the Dodgers their greatest lead of the season.
  +13½
Brooklyn Dodgers 4, Boston Braves 8, at Ebbets Field
  +13

SUNDAY, AUGUST 12

Brooklyn Dodgers 7, Boston Braves 2, at Ebbets Field
New York Giants 3, Philadelphia Phillies 2, at Polo Grounds
New York Giants 2, Philadelphia Phillies 1, at Polo Grounds
The Giants (59–51) begin the day 13 games behind first-place Brooklyn (70–36). Their sweep over the Phillies starts a 16-game win streak: the Giants will win 39 of their next 47 games.
  +12½

MONDAY, AUGUST 13

Brooklyn Dodgers 7, Boston Braves 6, at Ebbets Field
New York Giants 5, Philadelphia Phillies 2, at Polo Grounds
  +12½

TUESDAY, AUGUST 14

New York Giants 4, Brooklyn Dodgers 2, at Polo Grounds
  +11½

WEDNESDAY, AUGUST 15

New York Giants 3, Brooklyn Dodgers 1, at Polo Grounds
  +10½

THURSDAY, AUGUST 16

New York Giants 2, Brooklyn Dodgers 1, at Polo Grounds
  +9½

FRIDAY, AUGUST 17

Brooklyn Dodgers 3, Boston Braves 1, at Braves Field
Boston Braves 4, Brooklyn Dodgers 3, at Braves Field
New York Giants 8, Philadelphia Phillies 5, at Shibe Park
  +9

SATURDAY, AUGUST 18

Brooklyn Dodgers 5, Boston Braves 3, at Braves Field
New York Giants 2, Philadelphia Phillies 0, at Shibe Park
  +9

SUNDAY, AUGUST 19

Boston Braves 13, Brooklyn Dodgers 4, at Braves Field
New York Giants 5, Philadelphia Phillies 4, at Shibe Park
  +8

MONDAY, AUGUST 20

Both teams off

TUESDAY, AUGUST 21

New York Giants 7, Cincinnati Reds 4, at Polo Grounds
Brooklyn rained out
  +7½

WEDNESDAY, AUGUST 22

Brooklyn Dodgers 4, St. Louis Cardinals 3, at Ebbets Field
Brooklyn Dodgers 8, St. Louis Cardinals 7, at Ebbets Field
New York Giants 4, Cincinnati Reds 3, at Polo Grounds
  +8

THURSDAY, AUGUST 23

St. Louis Cardinals 4, Brooklyn Dodgers 2, at Ebbets Field
  +7½

FRIDAY, AUGUST 24

Brooklyn Dodgers 1, Chicago Cubs 0, at Ebbets Field
New York Giants 6, St. Louis Cardinals 5, at Polo Grounds
  +7½

SATURDAY, AUGUST 25

Chicago Cubs 5, Brooklyn Dodgers 1, at Ebbets Field
New York Giants game against St. Louis Cardinals rained out with New York trailing 3–1
  +7

SUNDAY, AUGUST 26

Pittsburgh Pirates 12, Brooklyn Dodgers 11, at Ebbets Field
Brooklyn Dodgers 4, Pittsburgh Pirates 3, at Ebbets Field
New York Giants 5, Chicago Cubs 4, at Polo Grounds
New York Giants 5, Chicago Cubs 1, at Polo Grounds
+6

MONDAY, AUGUST 27

Brooklyn Dodgers 5, Pittsburgh Pirates 0, at Ebbets Field
Pittsburgh Pirates 5, Brooklyn Dodgers 2, at Ebbets Field
New York Giants 5, Chicago Cubs 4, at Polo Grounds
New York Giants 6, Chicago Cubs 3, at Polo Grounds
+5

TUESDAY, AUGUST 28

Brooklyn Dodgers 3, Cincinnati Reds 1, at Ebbets Field
Pittsburgh Pirates 2, New York Giants 0, at Polo Grounds
+6

WEDNESDAY, AUGUST 29

Brooklyn Dodgers 13, Cincinnati Reds 1, at Ebbets Field
New York Giants 3, Pittsburgh Pirates 1, at Polo Grounds
+6

THURSDAY, AUGUST 30

Brooklyn Dodgers 3, Cincinnati Reds 1, at Ebbets Field
Pittsburgh Pirates 10, New York Giants 9, at Polo Grounds
+7

FRIDAY, AUGUST 31

Both teams off

SATURDAY, SEPTEMBER 1

New York Giants 8, Brooklyn Dodgers 1, at Polo Grounds
+6

SUNDAY, SEPTEMBER 2

New York Giants 11, Brooklyn Dodgers 2, at Polo Grounds
+5

MONDAY, SEPTEMBER 3

Brooklyn Dodgers 7, Boston Braves 2, at Ebbets Field
Brooklyn Dodgers 7, Boston Braves 2, at Ebbets Field
New York Giants 3, Philadelphia Phillies 1, at Polo Grounds
+6

TUESDAY, SEPTEMBER 4

Both teams off. The Dodgers (84–47) have a six-game lead over the Giants (79–54).

WEDNESDAY, SEPTEMBER 5

New York Giants 3, Boston Braves 2, at Braves Field
New York Giants 9, Boston Braves 1, at Braves Field
Brooklyn Dodgers 5, Philadelphia Phillies 2, at Ebbets Field
+5½

THURSDAY, SEPTEMBER 6

Both teams off

FRIDAY, SEPTEMBER 7

New York Giants 7, Boston Braves 3, at Braves Field
Brooklyn Dodgers 11, Philadelphia Phillies 6, at Ebbets Field
+5½

SATURDAY, SEPTEMBER 8

Brooklyn Dodgers 9, New York Giants 0, at Ebbets Field
+6½

SUNDAY, SEPTEMBER 9

New York Giants 2, Brooklyn Dodgers 1, at Ebbets Field
+5½

MONDAY, SEPTEMBER 10

Both teams off

TUESDAY, SEPTEMBER 11

Brooklyn Dodgers 7, Cincinnati Reds 0, at Crosley Field
New York Giants 10, St. Louis Cardinals 5, at Sportsman's Park
+6

WEDNESDAY, SEPTEMBER 12

Cincinnati Reds 6, Brooklyn Dodgers 3, at Crosley Field
New York Giants game against St. Louis Cardinals rained out
+5½

THURSDAY, SEPTEMBER 13

St. Louis Cardinals 6, New York Giants 4, at Sportsman's Park
+6

FRIDAY, SEPTEMBER 14

New York Giants 7, Chicago Cubs 2, at Wrigley Field
Brooklyn Dodgers 3, Pittsburgh Pirates 1, at Forbes Field
  +6

SATURDAY, SEPTEMBER 15

New York Giants 5, Chicago Cubs 2, at Wrigley Field
Pittsburgh Pirates 11, Brooklyn Dodgers 4, at Forbes Field
  +5

SUNDAY, SEPTEMBER 16

Brooklyn Dodgers 6, Chicago Cubs 1, at Wrigley Field
New York Giants 7, Pittsburgh Pirates 1, at Forbes Field
New York Giants 6, Pittsburgh Pirates 4, at Forbes Field
  +4½

MONDAY, SEPTEMBER 17

Chicago Cubs 5, Brooklyn Dodgers 3, at Wrigley Field
  +4

TUESDAY, SEPTEMBER 18

New York Giants 6, Cincinnati Reds 5, at Crosley Field
St. Louis Cardinals 7, Brooklyn Dodgers 1, at Sportsman's Park
  +3

WEDNESDAY, SEPTEMBER 19

Brooklyn Dodgers 3, St. Louis Cardinals 0, at Sportsman's Park
Giants off
  +3½

THURSDAY, SEPTEMBER 20

Cincinnati Reds 3, New York Giants 1, at Crosley Field
Brooklyn Dodgers 4, St. Louis Cardinals 3, at Sportsman's Park
  +4½

FRIDAY, SEPTEMBER 21

Philadelphia Phillies 9, Brooklyn Dodgers 6, at Ebbets Field
Giants off
  +4

SATURDAY, SEPTEMBER 22

Philadelphia Phillies 7, Brooklyn Dodgers 3, at Ebbets Field
New York Giants 4, Boston Braves 1, at Polo Grounds
  +3

SUNDAY, SEPTEMBER 23

Brooklyn Dodgers 6, Philadelphia Phillies 2, at Ebbets Field
New York Giants 4, Boston Braves 1, at Polo Grounds
  +3

MONDAY, SEPTEMBER 24

New York Giants 4, Boston Braves 3, at Polo Grounds
  +2½

TUESDAY, SEPTEMBER 25

Boston Braves 6, Brooklyn Dodgers 3, at Braves Field
Boston Braves 14, Brooklyn Dodgers 2, at Braves Field
  +1

WEDNESDAY, SEPTEMBER 26

Brooklyn Dodgers 15, Boston Braves 5, at Braves Field
New York Giants 10, Philadelphia Phillies 1, at Shibe Park
  +1

THURSDAY, SEPTEMBER 27

Boston Braves 4, Brooklyn Dodgers 3, at Braves Field
New York Giants 10, Philadelphia Phillies 1, at Shibe Park
  +½

FRIDAY, SEPTEMBER 28

Philadelphia Phillies 4, Brooklyn Dodgers 3, at Shibe Park
  Tied

SATURDAY, SEPTEMBER 29

New York Giants 3, Boston Braves 0, at Braves Field
Brooklyn Dodgers 5, Philadelphia Phillies 0, at Shibe Park
  Tied

SUNDAY, SEPTEMBER 30

New York Giants 3, Boston Braves 2, at Braves Field
Brooklyn Dodgers 9, Philadelphia Phillies 8, at Shibe Park
*The Dodgers overcome a 6–1 deficit to win and set the stage for a
playoff with the Giants.*

paper's growing real estate section and then head out to Long Island. Low interest rates and government-backed mortgages for veterans did everything but load the truck.

Yes, crime was getting worse as neighborhoods changed and broke up and the familiar faces were replaced by those of strangers, but it wasn't nearly as bad as the paper made it out to be. Nevertheless, headlines about a crime in Highland Park or Cypress Hills drove people out of not only those neighborhoods but others as well.

The *Eagle* was cautious about assigning blame, at least in words. But it still managed to choose a target. In one particularly repugnant editorial cartoon that appeared in September 1952, crows—black crows—labeled "Thug," "Rapist," "Hoodlum," etc., assail a scarecrow labeled "Sad Lack of Adequate Police Protection." The significance of the crows did not pass readers by. Old Brooklyn—the parents and grandparents of kids just entering school and adolescence—were leaving every day, replaced by blacks and Latinos. The appropriate symbol of Brooklyn was no longer a trolley but a car going on a weekend drive or a moving van. While Ebbets Field was still usually packed to the rafters for a big game on a weekend or holiday, the rest of the time it was almost empty.

And more and more often even at big games there were smatterings of empty seats.

Before the World Series, there was a sense of fatalism among the Brooklyn faithful. The Yankees were 8–5 favorites, and the *Eagle* even called upon the organization to break up the team regardless of the outcome. "The rebuilding can't be postponed much longer," wrote Harold Burr. "The squad could fall apart from senility. It's ancient in vital parts . . . [and] the Flatbushers haven't too much material on their farms." The consensus entering the Series was that this just might be Brooklyn's final chance to win with the group put together by Branch Rickey.

The key move came before the first pitch was even thrown. Dressen, acknowledging that the Dodgers didn't have the pitching to match up with the Yankees, put Joe Black

---

Dodger right fielder Carl Furillo is shown at Yankee Stadium prior to the 1953 World Series pointing to an outfield sign that corresponds exactly to the .344 batting average he attained to lead the National League that season. Following his baseball career, Furillo worked in construction and remained in New York, where he helped build the World Trade Center.

into the starting rotation and selected him to pitch the first game, setting him up for three Series starts, a tacit admission that unless Black came through big, even Dressen thought the Dodgers were done.

The players, however, retained the confidence of a champion. They'd won with Rickey and without him, with Durocher and Shotton and now Dressen, and they weren't easily intimidated. Robinson said that "the younger fellows have beaten the Yankees in the chains" and that "the Yanks don't mean anything" to Joe Black.

The Series was far closer than anybody expected it to be, for the Yankees weren't quite as strong as usual and the Dodgers, if nothing else, were resilient. But every time it seemed as if the Dodgers were about to take control of the Series, the Yankees knocked them down.

Black won game one at Ebbets Field, 4–2, but when Erskine was pounded in game two, there was no Joe Black available in relief to stem the tide, as there had been all year long, and the Yankees won 7–1. Preacher Roe mesmerized New York in game three, 5–3, but when the Yankees beat Black 2–0 in game four, there was a sense that the outcome was decided. Although the Dodgers won game five in extra innings behind Erskine, back in Brooklyn for the final two games New York followed what had thus far proven to be a winning strategy — get into the bullpen. The Dodgers weren't hitting at all — Gil Hodges would go 0-for-21 in the Series and cause Brooklyn priests to offer prayers for him.

When Joe Black was finally knocked out in the sixth inning of game seven, the Yankees chipped away, took the lead, and won 4–2 to take the Series. "Every year," mused Roger Kahn in the *Herald Tribune*, "is next year for the New York Yankees." And increasingly it was beginning to look like next year would never arrive in Brooklyn.

Which is precisely what made 1953 such a shock. The Dodgers did not take the *Eagle*'s advice and rebuild. In fact, they did little beyond prying pitcher Russ Meyer away from the Phillies and promoting two rookies, pitcher Johnny Podres and, finally, infielder Junior Gilliam.

After hitting a career-high 19 home runs in 1952, Robinson showed up at spring training overweight and out of shape, which gave Dressen a reason to take a good look at Gilliam. He liked what he saw. His speed and ability to switch-hit and get on base made him invaluable, and it made Jackie Robinson look slow for the first time in his life.

So Gilliam became the Dodger second baseman, which freed Robinson to give the Dodgers something they'd rarely had in recent years — depth. Left field was still a problem — Andy Pafko had disappointed in 1952 and been sold to Milwaukee — so Robinson became the Dodgers' everyman, splitting his time between the outfield and third base, where Cox, facing some competition, had his best year at the plate.

The result was the most potent Dodger lineup to date — Snider and Campanella both crushed more than 40 home runs, and Campanella won another MVP Award. The Dodgers led both leagues in runs, home runs, batting average, slugging, and just about every other imaginable offensive statistic. They battered the opposition early, and although the Braves kept pace through June, this time the Dodgers surged late, winning 46 of 57 from the All-Star break to Labor Day, on their way to a team record 105 wins. They finished 13 games ahead of the Braves, who after nearly a century in Boston had moved to Milwaukee in 1953.

Throughout most of baseball that was the big story of the season. All the thunder of the Dodger bats was drowned out by the cheers of crowds in Milwaukee. There, county officials had built a ballpark on spec with plenty of parking and courted a major league team, finally convincing the Boston Braves to relocate, the first franchise shift since the Baltimore Orioles had morphed into the New York Yankees in 1903.

They drew 1.8 million fans, by far the best gate in baseball. Every owner in the game took notice, and so did every big city without a baseball team. A new dynamic was suddenly in play — ballclubs were fluid entities that could move, and the government could play a role in the construction of a ballpark.

In Brooklyn they didn't notice, except in the front office, where the Dodgers drew some 600,000 fewer fans than the Braves and made nothing on parking and concessions, which the Braves demonstrated could be significant new sources of income. Milwaukee's success sent shock waves throughout baseball, for it gave the Braves an apparent competitive advantage that no team in baseball — save the Yankees, who still drew well at the Stadium — could touch. Although Milwaukee's fascination with the Braves would last only a decade, in the short term it seemed as if the Braves would be able to outspend everyone. Fueled by huge crowds at County Stadium, over the next few seasons they would be one of the few teams in baseball to expand its farm system.

As the Series approached, Dodger fans were in love again, convinced that this, finally, was the invincible Dodger club

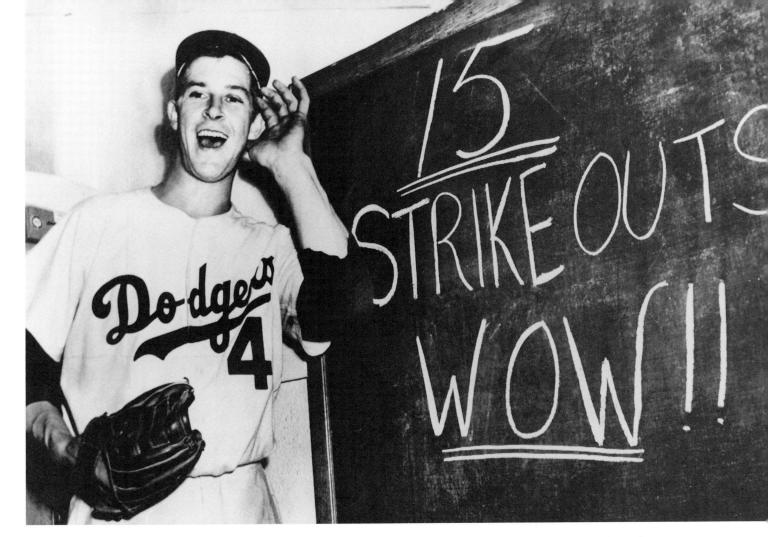

On September 22, 1954, Dodger rookie left-handed pitcher Karl Spooner made his first major league start against the National League champion New York Giants and struck out 15 while shutting them out by a score of 3–0. Over the next year, however, he won only nine more games before arm trouble ended his big league career.

that could not just take down the Yankees but rip them to shreds.

Yet the Dodger offense had covered more than a few flaws. The pitching staff was little better than mediocre. Everybody won — Erskine went 20–6 — but no one was dominant. Black was a mess. After going 15–4 with a 2.15 ERA in 1952, his 1953 ERA ballooned to more than 5.00 after Dressen insisted — disastrously — that he add a slider. On the other hand, the Yankees had the best staff in baseball.

In a sense, the Dodgers lost the Series in game one. Erskine, whom Dressen was counting on for three starts, was shelled early, and Campanella was hit on the hand by Yankee pitcher Allie Reynolds. He'd collect only one extra-base hit the entire Series.

Still, after Erskine rebounded to strike out 14 Yankees and win game four, the Series was tied at two games each. Before game five, however, Dressen seemed to come down with the Dodgers' age-old October managerial malady: he decided to tinker with the pitching staff. Next to Erskine, Russ Meyer had been the Dodgers' most consistent and most prolific

starter all year, going 15–5. Yet Dressen chose 20-year-old rookie Johnny Podres to start game five. By the time he turned to Meyer, the Yankees were well on their way to an 11–7 win.

The Dodgers made it close in game six, but close doesn't count in the World Series either. Dressen skipped over Roe and brought back Erskine on two days' rest, but he didn't have it. With the game tied at 3–3 in the ninth, the Yankees efficiently packaged a walk and two hits into the winning run to take the Series.

The Dodgers had been upset before, but after this loss they were disconsolate, convinced that they were the better team. "We lost," said Reese, "because the Yanks played their

usual game in the Series and we didn't." He was getting tired of saying things like that.

Dressen was more precise. He knew why they lost. He blamed Black, for having an off-year, and the Dodger defense, leaving his own contributions unspoken and unrecognized.

That was the real problem. When the Dodgers won, Dressen crowed and took all the credit, and when they lost, he didn't have a problem pointing fingers. But 1953 was the third season in a row when he'd been outmanaged at the end, once by Durocher and twice by Stengel, and the third season in a row when he'd failed adequately to address the obvious trouble with his team. The Dodger players had done their job, but Dressen still hadn't thought of anything that had worked.

The organization was awfully smug for a team that couldn't seem to win the big one. When the Dodger brass met after the season, Buzzie Bavasi offered, "We'll be content to go with the same team. . . . Who'll beat us?" Uh—the Yankees?

Dressen echoed O'Malley as "Wait Till Next Year" ossified into an organizational trait. For this, he thought he deserved some security and asked for a two-year deal. O'Malley refused. His standard policy was to offer only a one-year contract, and Dressen was getting to be expensive.

Dressen thought O'Malley was bluffing, but he wasn't. He'd grown tired of the way Dressen tried to take credit for everything. That was something O'Malley wanted for himself, and now he had an excuse to get it. Dressen was let go and replaced by taciturn Montreal manager Walter Alston. At

On December 23, 1954, the Dodgers signed 18-year-old Brooklyn native Sanford Koufax as a bonus baby. Joining the former Lafayette High School and University of Cincinnati star at the signing announcement are scout Al Campanis (left) and Dodger vice president Fresco Thompson.

age 42, the former player with one career major league at bat—and an average of .000—was barely older than his players. If he seemed an odd choice to take on a veteran club, it was also true that he was much cheaper than Dressen, or any other option with major league experience, and that for the last six years he had managed Dodger triple-A teams, first in St. Paul and then in Montreal.

In a sense, Alston's appointment split the club. While fully 17 current Dodgers had played for him in the minors, this didn't include anyone in the starting lineup except Gilliam and Snider. In the minors Alston's gruff touch had worked with his young charges, but in the big leagues it wasn't quite as effective.

One more familiar face was ready to go: Red Barber. He too had gotten too big and was making too much money for O'Malley's taste—$60,000. His contract was up, and O'Malley never made an offer. Barber jumped to the Yankees, and O'Malley hired Vin Scully to take his place for a reported $18,000.

For the first half of 1954 the Dodgers won on their reputation. But the Giants, with Mays back from the Army, went

24–4 in June, sweeping Brooklyn at the end of the month, and took command. Roy Campanella had a bad hand and was little more than a part-time player. Alston had trouble commanding respect. Robinson was visibly slowed down and bothered by nagging injuries, and Alston stubbornly insisted that Don Hoak play third base, tossing Cox aside almost completely and forcing Robinson into the outfield. Don Newcombe struggled in his return from the service. Joe Black's comet turned to ash, and as the season unfolded it became clear that the Dodgers simply didn't have enough pitching, enough hitting, or, even more important, the will to make a charge, for in the minor leagues — once again — was a player who could have put the Dodgers over the top.

Down in Fort Worth, the Dodgers' double-A affiliate, young left-hander Karl Spooner was on his way to winning 21 games and striking out nearly 300 hitters, clearly the best prospect in baseball. But like so many others before him, he was left down all season and not brought to Brooklyn until the final week of the season. All he did was shut out the Giants and the Pirates, striking out 27. Had he been brought up at midseason, the Dodgers might have won another pennant.

By the end of the summer Dodger fans seemed to sense that this team was done, that perhaps their time had finally passed, and attendance took another tumble, barely topping one million for the season. In August the *Eagle* even wondered, "Where is everybody? . . . Somehow or other, there's always a reason — or an excuse, depending on your viewpoint — for the small crowds."

There was. The Dodgers, in a sense, were hanging by a thread; the bond between the ballclub and Brooklyn was starting to fray. There was a difference in the crowds now, and it had nothing to do with color or class. The Dodgers weren't loved any less, but the fans had other suitors. The Dodgers weren't the first option for fun anymore. Their story was getting old. There were suddenly a thousand reasons not to go to Ebbets Field — television, the traffic, the parking, the neighborhood, the crime, the rickety seats, the smelly bathrooms, simply the sense that it wasn't at the center of Brooklyn anymore, that Brooklyn, as a place, didn't even have a center anymore.

The drop-off in interest had been happening for years but was masked by the general slide in baseball attendance everywhere. Now, however, it was obvious — all anyone had to do was look at Milwaukee and the more than two million they drew for a third-place team. Once upon a time it had been that way in Brooklyn. But over the past few seasons fans had really only come out to Ebbets Field when the team was winning, or when it looked like they might. Now even that wasn't a given.

Fans didn't believe in the team as they once had. There were moments when it just didn't seem like anyone even cared anymore, when the carrot stick of "next year" seemed as stale and out of fashion as the Brooklyn Bum.

Although the second-place Dodgers made it look good in 1954, never falling too far back, they also never made a believable challenge in the second half, finishing 92–62, five games behind the Giants.

The story of the season was told on September 17. Trailing New York by only three games with nine games left, including three against the Giants, the Dodgers played a makeup game with Cincinnati while New York and Pittsburgh played a doubleheader. If the Giants lost both and Brooklyn won, the lead would be down to a game and a half. It was a big game, a *big* game, and the kind that not so many years before had made Ebbets Field seem like the best place in the world to be.

Only 522 fans paid their way into Ebbets Field.

The Dodgers weren't dead, but they were headed that way.

NEXT YEAR

BROOKLYN FANS REMEMBER 1955 AS THE SEASON WHEN "NEXT YEAR"—
finally and gloriously—became "this year," when the dream of a Dodger world championship was improbably and wonderfully fulfilled. Yet "next year" was also, in a sense, the last year, for it was during the 1955 season that the organization, as so many of its fans had already done, began to scan the real estate ads in earnest and dream of a new and larger home with a yard and some trees and a place to park the car.

Change was coming, almost so slowly that it was hard to see, but it was taking place all around the Dodgers. The ties that bound the team irrevocably to Brooklyn were slowly being severed.

The old Dodgers were starting to go. In December Bavasi sold Preacher Roe and Billy Cox to the Baltimore Orioles for $50,000 and a couple of warm bodies. Roe knew he was through and retired, so eventually Erv Palica was also sent to Baltimore to take his place. Then in January 1955, the entire climate changed.

For 114 years the *Eagle* had been Brooklyn's paper of record, as much a part of what it meant to be a Dodger fan as the Brooklyn Sym-Phony or Red Barber. In the off-season the paper ran at

Twenty-three-year-old Dodger left-hander Johnny Podres relaxes in the visitors' clubhouse at Yankee Stadium following his complete-game 2–0 shutout of the Yankees in the seventh game of the 1955 World Series. Not only did the Dodgers capture their first world championship, but they finally defeated the Yankees in their sixth Series attempt.

least one Dodger story every day, allowing fans to keep in touch, firing up the Hot Stove League, keeping the Dodgers in the conversation from November to March, building anticipation for the upcoming season. There was no sports talk radio, no ESPN, no other way for fans to sate their appetite for all things Dodger. Although the Dodgers were covered during the regular season by no less than nine other daily papers, ranging from the *Times,* the *Daily News,* and the *Post* to the *Long Island Press,* Dodger fans gathered in the pages of the *Eagle,* reading Tommy Holmes and, more recently, young Dave Anderson.

Although the paper had been losing readers for years, it was still profitable, but in the winter the Newspaper Guild called a strike of reporters, which lingered for months. Then, abruptly, on January 28, 1955, just as fans began to look for the first signs of spring, publisher Frank Schroth folded the paper and put it out of business, writing on the last day that "again Brooklyn falls victim to the Manhattan pattern," swallowed up by the city. He mourned the loss of "the last voice that is purely Brooklyn" and cautioned, "The borough seems to be doomed to be cast in Manhattan's shadow." With the loss of the *Eagle,* it was.

The Dodgers and their fans never recovered from the loss. Although other papers covered the Dodgers, none did so with the easy familiarity of the *Eagle.* For years the newspaper had created and maintained a particularly Brooklyn perspective from which most fans viewed the team. While the *Eagle* can certainly be criticized for often serving as a "house organ" and rarely taking a critical view of the club, it was indispensable to the Dodger organization. And even more significantly, had it chosen to, the *Eagle* could have made Jackie Robinson's rookie season much more difficult and problematic, but its understated approach helped pave the way for his acceptance. In the pages of the *Eagle,* Brooklyn fans saw Robinson as a player, not a symbol.

No other newspaper filled the void created when the *Eagle* folded, either individually or cumulatively. Oh, they covered the Dodgers, and in some cases, such as the *Daily News* with Dick Young, Roger Kahn of the *Herald Tribune,* and the *Post's* Milton Gross, covered them extremely well, but it wasn't the same, for in those papers the Dodgers were one of three teams, and in some ways less of New York than the Giants and Yankees. In the *Eagle,* the Dodgers always came first, even when the standings didn't say so. And for Dodger fans, that made the club seem a little more remote, a little more

distanced, and a little less essential to the rhythm of their daily lives. Out on Long Island, where many Brooklyn expatriates had continued to follow their former home through the *Eagle,* picking it up on their commute, the demise of the paper completely severed their ability to do so.

The big news in Dodgertown that spring had to do with Karl Spooner's left shoulder and Jackie Robinson's pride. After his performance at the end of the 1954 season, the Dodgers had penciled Spooner into the starting rotation — he seemed a lock to become a big winner, and a big draw at the gate. But in his first spring training appearance, he hurt his shoulder — from Spooner's later description of the injury, it seems likely it was a rotator cuff tear. But neither medical science nor the Dodgers knew much about that, and true to form, the Dodgers barely acknowledged the injury. Spooner wasn't right, but he kept pitching, even though he opened the season in the bullpen, as Alston chose to go with a rotation of Erskine, Newcombe — who was looking great again — Loes, Russ Meyer, and Johnny Podres.

Robinson and Alston, who hadn't seen eye to eye in 1954, continued to detest one another while standing toe to toe. On April 4, as the Dodgers barnstormed through the South, Alston told the *Herald Tribune's* Roger Kahn that he wasn't sure if Robinson had made the starting lineup — a slap in the face to a player not only of Robinson's notoriety but whose .311 batting average had been second on the team in 1954, his .505 slugging percentage third.

This was news to Robinson, and he exploded. "He ought to talk to me before he talks to the damn press," he said, referring to himself bitterly as an "irregular." And then Alston talked to Robinson in the press again, saying he had a sore arm — that set Robinson off again. "He should have come to me and asked," Robinson said, indicating his arm was fine. "That's the way a ballclub runs; the manager asks. But he didn't ask me and he didn't ask the doc. You get the feeling that he doesn't care, that nothing you do makes any difference to him." At a salary of $40,000 annually, tops on the club, Robinson knew that if he didn't play, under O'Malley he wouldn't remain a Dodger for long.

Robinson wasn't the only player less than enamored with Alston, who almost seemed to be afraid to confront his own players directly and to resent the club's veteran makeup. During the spring he'd toyed with the idea of replacing Reese with Don Zimmer and making Gil Hodges an outfielder. Also, the club now included five black players, and the consensus was that Alston had a problem with that, unless they behaved with cheerful deference, like Campanella usually did.

Such problems between players and management can go one of two ways. Often they break a team apart, and the trouble shows up on the field. But sometimes such problems bring a team together and make them determined to win "in spite of" the manager and management.

The 1955 Dodgers, who were expected to fight it out for second place behind the favored Braves, had the latter response. Robinson and Alston finally had it out and narrowly avoided coming to blows. They agreed to disagree, and the club settled into an uneasy truce. And on April 13 at Ebbets Field, Opening Day, Jackie Robinson was in the starting lineup, as were Reese at shortstop and Hodges at first base. Apart from the addition of Sandy Amoros in the club's perennial problem spot, left field, the lineup was essentially unchanged, although Alston had tinkered with the batting order. Campanella, with his bad hand, began the season in the eighth slot, and Robinson slid down to sixth.

The game had been pushed back a day because of bad weather, but the Pirates were awful to begin with and the Dodgers made them look worse. Erskine scattered seven hits, the Dodgers erupted for five runs in the seventh keyed by Robinson's bunt hit, and the Dodgers won, 6–1.

They were in first place. They never left it. But on Opening Day they drew fewer than 5,000 fans; the Dodgers announced a crowd of "around 4,999," but it seemed considerably smaller to anyone who looked around.

The Dodgers opened the season with ten straight wins, going on the road after Opening Day to beat the Giants twice in the Polo Grounds, the Pirates three times in Pittsburgh, and the Phillies twice in Philadelphia before smacking the Phils down twice more in Brooklyn. The Dodgers were 10–0.

Pitching made the difference early: only twice did the Dodgers staff give up more than four runs, and a favorable schedule also helped. The Giants broke the streak with a 5–4 win on April 22 and took two of three, but the Dodgers then went out and won 11 in a row to up their record to 22–2.

The pennant race was virtually over—everybody else in the league was struggling to play .500 baseball. The only blip came from Don Newcombe, who refused to pitch batting practice until Alston threatened him with suspension. A pissed-off Newcombe complied, and a pissed-off Newcombe was suddenly the best pitcher in the league again. His one-hitter against the Cubs had notched that 11th victory in a row.

Dodger batboy Charlie DiGiovanna greets Dodger slugger Gil Hodges following his fourth-inning home run that put the Dodgers ahead by a score of 4–3 in the fourth game of the 1955 World Series.

NL RBI LEADERS

1919	Hy Myers	73
1941	Dolph Camilli	120
1945	Dixie Walker	124
1953	Roy Campanella	142
1955	Duke Snider	136
1962	Tommy Davis	153

Any lingering questions about the pennant race were answered in early June when the Dodgers went on another tear, winning 16 of 19, pushing the team some 30 games over .500. Of course, they couldn't maintain such a pace, and they didn't, but it didn't matter. School was barely out and already fans were looking ahead to the World Series.

Clearly, however, fans were not looking ahead to the rest of the regular season. Attendance at Ebbets Field was dismal, and the club even started to hold promotions and contests to drum up attendance, something that hadn't been tried very often since the days of MacPhail.

"Eddie Fisher Day," honoring the singing star, fell flat, but a celebration of Pee Wee Reese's birthday in mid-July drew a packed house.

But fans refused to turn out on a regular basis. In 1954 the St. Louis Browns moved to Baltimore, and in 1955 the Athletics transferred to Kansas City, and suddenly two teams that nobody had cared about in years were drawing crowds equal to, or better than, Brooklyn's. The Dodgers were still profitable, but only because television and radio were an increas-

ing part of the club budget. Attendance couldn't begin to pay the bills anymore.

Walter O'Malley started dropping not so small hints that the Dodgers were looking for a new park. Whenever another city or municipality started making noise about building a ballpark to lure a major league team, O'Malley was certain to make mention of it to the press.

He'd already determined that he wanted nothing to do with any kind of refurbished or expanded Ebbets Field. He felt that a renovation was not only problematic from a construction perspective but didn't really solve the larger problem, for it wouldn't provide the club with the parking revenue it wanted.

Although often overlooked, the issue of parking revenue was behind most ballpark plans from the 1950s through the 1970s, just as "luxury boxes" dominate the debate today. Like the luxury box, parking fees represented a new source of revenue unavailable in existing parks. Twenty thousand or 30,000 or 40,000 fans were great, but even better was the income from 10,000 or 15,000 cars at 50¢ or $1 each, a surcharge fans didn't blink at paying. And that was just the beginning. Fans who went to games by public transportation, as had been the norm, tended to arrive just before the game or, if they arrived early, to patronize taverns and restaurants in the surrounding area ahead of time before bolting out to the park to catch the first pitch. In that scenario the only income a club took in was the price of a ticket, a 10¢ scorecard, and maybe a beer and a hot dog. Peanuts.

But fans who drove to the games were different. They not only were generally more affluent but also often arrived early to get a good spot and beat the traffic. And once in the parking lot, they usually had no choice but to go directly inside the park. Instead of buying a beer or a soda outside before the game, fans who arrived by car had to do so inside. They were in the park longer and spent more — a lot more. So although the Dodgers were still drawing nominally well (in 1955 their total attendance of 1.03 million was still the eighth-best in all baseball), they were missing out on the windfall that came from a big parking lot.

The lesson had been learned in Milwaukee. One can say with some assurance that until the 1950s, the business of baseball was primarily baseball, the selling of the game. But since that time baseball has in many ways simply served as a loss leader to extract income from other sources. Baseball has become a front for a parking lot and a restaurant that charges for a seat at the table and could recoup the cost of a dozen frankfurters from the sale of only one.

And then there was the land. That made Brooklyn different from other cities, such as Boston and Philadelphia, which had both recently lost their franchises. The cost of real estate in New York was skyrocketing, and William Zeckendorf's interest in the Dodgers a few years before had alerted O'Malley to the vast potential for profit contained in the few acres on which Ebbets Field sat. If Zeckendorf was interested, logic told O'Malley that Ebbets Field was worth something, and the price was only going up. Not that he would necessarily sell the property and use the proceeds to buy another and build a new park — that model was outdated. The plan was to leverage interest from another city to make New York do something akin to what had been done in Milwaukee: to get civic government to pony up some of the cost by providing the land, the parking lot, the infrastructure, or some combination of all these.

There was no lack of suitors. As Tommy Holmes had written more than a decade before, cities with franchises in the Pacific Coast League, particularly Los Angeles, were starting to make noises about getting major league baseball. The recent franchise moves had only heightened the interest, and late that spring O'Malley alerted the press to the fact that a bond issue to build a stadium was coming to a vote in Los Angeles. Most filed it away as an item in the "notes" column.

The second half of the season unfolded with little drama. There was no team the equivalent of the 1951 Giants poised to make a charge.

Good thing, because in the second half of the season the Dodgers began to show their age as injuries large and small mounted. But unlike the Dodgers of a few years before, this club had some flexibility and depth. Robinson still bounced back and forth between third and the outfield, and Junior Gilliam occasionally ran down fly balls as well. Don Zimmer filled in all over the infield, veteran Frank Kellert supplied some right-handed power, and Don Newcombe, when he wasn't pitching, was the best left-handed pinch hitter in the league — and in 1955 arguably the best pitcher as well.

There was another pitcher on the Brooklyn roster who one day would earn the appellation "best" — Sandy Koufax. A product of the Brooklyn sandlots, Koufax had planned to attend the University of Cincinnati on a basketball scholarship before a $20,000 baseball contract, which included a

---

Don Newcombe led the National League in winning percentage (.800) with a superb 20–5 won-lost mark. The 6'6" right-hander also batted .359 with seven home runs.

$14,000 bonus, convinced him otherwise. To slow the prac-
tice of offering what organized baseball considered to be
obscene and inflationary bonuses, the baseball rules of the
time mandated that so-called bonus babies remain on the
major league roster for two years instead of gaining necessary
experience in the minors. In effect, the rule penalized precocious talent, and few bonus babies of the era ever made good
on their promise. After two years spent either stagnating or
overmatched in the majors, their confidence was shattered.

Koufax, only 19 years old, had started the season on the
disabled list with a convenient hairline fracture of the ankle.
When he was activated on June 8 to replace perennial borderline prospect Tommy Lasorda, he was very much the last
man on the roster and the last man on the pitching staff.

For the most part, he kept his mouth shut and gave the
veterans on the club a wide berth, doing little more than
pitching batting practice. He was ostracized by his age, his
status, and his Jewish background. Alston barely acknowledged his presence. Koufax later described his experience in
1955 as being "with the team, not of it."

Yet Koufax had the most precious commodity in all baseball, a *really fast* fastball. His gift was from the gods, for his
left arm could throw a baseball nearly 100 miles per hour, the
kind of pitch that makes a noise as it passes, that appears to
rise and hop at the last instant, that causes hitters to stop and
watch and ask out of the lineup. Other pitchers learn to survive with guile and trickery, but the pitcher with the phenomenal fastball needs to learn only how to control the gift,
to throw the ball where he wants to.

With a huge lead in the National League, Alston could
have—and probably should have—given Koufax regular
work, a few innings here and there to learn and gain confidence in low-pressure situations. And given the Dodgers'
problems at the gate, Koufax, a Brooklyn native who was born
in Borough Park and grew up in Bensonhurst, might well
have become a significant gate attraction.

Instead, and almost inexplicably, Koufax was all but
buried. In 1955 he was used only sporadically. He didn't make
his first appearance until June 24 in Milwaukee. He promptly

**The sparse crowds at Ebbets Field in their world championship
season in 1955 helped Walter O'Malley make the decision to leave
the borough for Los Angeles just two seasons later. For the season,
the Dodgers drew just over one million fans, only eighth-best in
the majors.**

loaded the bases but managed to escape the jam. After another appearance five days later against the Giants in which he again managed to wiggle out of a bases-loaded jam, Alston tabbed him to start a game against last-place Pittsburgh.

Koufax was all nerves and struggled with control, walking eight in just over four innings. The performance buried him and saddled him with an overstated reputation for wildness that the Dodgers would use for several years as an excuse both not to pitch him and not to believe that his occasional good outings were significant. After the start against Pittsburgh, it was seven weeks before Koufax was allowed to start another game, this time against Cincinnati. He struck out 14, the league high for 1955. A week later he threw another shutout against Pittsburgh, essentially duplicating what Karl Spooner had done a year earlier. Yet while Spooner's back-to-back shutouts seemed to target him for stardom, the organization treated Koufax as some kind of eccentric fluke — he would never appear in a postseason game for Brooklyn, and his contribution to his hometown team would, in the end, be negligible, the odd spectacular performance sandwiched between weeks of relative inactivity.

In mid-August Brooklyn fans began to look with confidence toward the World Series. Then O'Malley dropped a bombshell. He announced that in 1956 the Dodgers would play seven home games — nearly 10 percent of their schedule — in Jersey City.

Dodger fans were taken aback. Jersey City was Giants territory, the home of their triple-A team. "We'll have a new stadium shortly thereafter," added O'Malley. Ebbets Field, he explained, was too small, it didn't have enough room for parking, and attendance was dropping. Despite the fact that Jersey City's Roosevelt Stadium seated only 24,170 fans, there was also — significantly — parking for 7,000 cars. He hoped the games in Jersey City would prove profitable, but the arrangement was also a none-too-subtle reminder that like the Braves and the Browns and the A's, the Dodgers could play anywhere.

"Our fans require a modern stadium," he had concluded, "with greater comforts, shorter walks, no posts, absolute protection from inclement weather," etc., etc., etc. That was true, to a point, for the drop in attendance clearly revealed that there were significant problems with the Dodgers remaining in Ebbets Field, although "absolute protection from inclement weather" was not something fans clamored for or even thought about. But then O'Malley added a veiled threat: "We will consider other locations only if we are finally unsuccessful in our ambition to build in Brooklyn. But our stockholders are prepared to build in Brooklyn and not elsewhere." He would later add that the Dodgers were willing to build the park themselves — all they wanted from the city was land. Then, almost as an afterthought, O'Malley added the kicker: he was planning to sell Ebbets Field by 1958. The clock was ticking.

His statements were revealing. O'Malley had already determined the scope of what he wanted, and the timetable. That may have been the way he was accustomed to doing things in Brooklyn, but to get a new ballpark he would have to deal with New York, which operated through forces far larger and more powerful than O'Malley, including those who saw New York in its entirety and didn't recognize the sanctity of Brooklyn as anything but a part of New York. And no one had ever built a ballpark in New York — not even Ebbets Field — without submitting to a considerable amount of give-and-take, without ceding some control, and without considering the political realities.

But O'Malley wanted to jump past all that and set the agenda himself. That was his big mistake.

While the attempts to build a new ballpark in Brooklyn over the next few seasons have been explored in detail in two extremely fine books — Neil Sullivan's *The Dodgers Move West* and Michael Shapiro's *The Last Good Season* — the critical errors had already been made — everything that came afterward would be the result of O'Malley's missteps at the very beginning. He had matched Zeckendorf's offer for Rickey's shares in 1950, when the wiser path might have been to welcome him aboard as a partner. Zeckendorf, with his deep pockets and connections in the intersection between real estate development and politics, could have been an enormous ally. Now O'Malley compounded that error. He should have spent the interim five years building bridges to the powers-that-be, massaging egos, making friends, figuring out who his enemies were, and discovering what was and what was not possible. Instead, he proceeded in virtual isolation, oblivious to all but his own plans and desires, and then made his play.

But as he would soon discover, the future of the Dodgers in Brooklyn no longer rested in his hands — anyone who wanted civic government involved in the business of baseball had already agreed to give up territory in a turf war. And as with most development plans in New York, the power broker Robert Moses, the man who more than anyone else determined what was to be built where and when in New York,

1955

times in the past the Dodgers have chased the elusive championship only to meet with failure."

The Series opened in Yankee Stadium — not a good place for the Dodgers to play, for the cavernous park reduced their vaunted power from the right side. But at the same time, these Dodgers were configured for the Yankee pitching staff. New York's big winners in 1955, Whitey Ford and Tommy Byrne, were both left-handed, and National League managers had learned that you threw a left-hander against Brooklyn at your own peril — only one lefty starter had gone the distance against the Dodgers all year.

The best news the Dodgers received came from the Yankee doctors. Mickey Mantle, with his .300 batting average and 37 home runs, had ripped a hamstring in September and was day-to-day. That forced the Yankees to start the Series with Irv Noren in center and Elston Howard in left. The move should have been devastating for the Yankees, but if any club was designed to make up for the loss of a player like Mantle, it was the Yankees.

Newcombe and Ford started game one, and Alston loaded the Dodger lineup with right-handed bats, moving Gilliam into the outfield in place of Sandy Amoros, starting Don Zimmer at second base, and leaving Duke Snider — and Newcombe — as the only lefties in the lineup. In the second inning Furillo led off and went the other way. The hit curled toward the right-field corner, only 296 feet away, hit the top of the wall, and bounced into the stand for a home run. Jackie Robinson then sent a drive to Death Valley, Yankee Stadium's cavernous left-center field. The ball skipped between Noren and Howard and rolled to the wall. Robinson pulled up at third with a triple. Then Zimmer made Alston look like a genius and Stengel look like an idiot. The Yankee manager pulled the infield in, Zimmer lofted a soft drive just over Billy Martin at second, and the Dodgers led, 2–0.

But Ford settled down and got out of the inning. Joe Collins, who platooned at first with Moose Skowron, walked. Then Elston Howard drove a hanging curveball into the stands to tie the game.

Now Brooklyn came back. In the top of the third Snider turned on a Ford pitch and put it into the upper deck, giving the Dodgers a 3–2 lead.

But Newcombe wasn't right, something they had worried about in Brooklyn since July, when his record stood at 18–1; he'd gone on to win only two more games for the season. His shoulder and back were giving him trouble, and in recent days a virus had weakened him. It became clear that was the case when Whitey Ford led off the third with a single. The Yankees moved him around, and he scored to tie the game. And in the fourth Joe Collins was the genius maker, knocking Newcombe's second pitch, a low fastball, into the stands. In the sixth he did it again, this time with Berra on board, and suddenly the Yankees led 6–3. Billy Martin then followed with a triple.

That was enough for Alston. He pulled Newcombe and turned to Don Bessent, who had gone 8–1 in relief during the regular season.

New York went for the throat. Billy Martin tried to steal home.

He got a great jump on the startled Bessent and appeared to slide in under Campanella's tag. But umpire Bill Summers was out of position and called the volatile Yankee infielder out.

He bounced up in a rage and on his way swung an elbow at Campanella's face. Campy didn't retaliate, but the Dodger bench took notice. In the eighth they extracted a measure of revenge.

After Furillo singled, Gil McDougald botched a ground ball, putting Furillo on third and Robinson on second. Zimmer's fly ball scored Furillo and moved Robinson up.

Suddenly, Robinson turned back the clock. He began dancing off third, feinting toward home, dashing back, and then feinting again. But Ford wasn't pitching from the stretch. As he started his windup Robinson broke for home.

Berra stepped up and took the throw with his left foot on home, and then dropped to his knees, blocking the plate and forcing Robinson, making a hook slide, directly into the tag. Umpire Bill Summers made the wrong call again. He waved his arms and Robinson was safe. Now it was Berra's turn to act enraged.

In the terms of baseball's proverbial "book" of strategy, Robinson's dash made no sense. But Robinson wasn't trying to score as much as he was trying to light a fire under his team. As he explained later, "I suddenly decided to shake things up. . . . I really didn't care if I made it or not. I was just tired of waiting." So was the rest of Brooklyn.

The run made the score 6–5, but despite Robinson's dash, the Dodgers were done as Brooklyn native Bob Grim came on in relief in the ninth and shut them down. As Drebinger observed, "It may yet come to pass that the Dodgers will win their first world series. But they took one long stride in the wrong direction."

And after game two, it looked as if they were finished. Stengel eschewed convention and started Tommy Byrne, another left-hander. Alston stuck with the same lineup he'd used the day before and chose Billy Loes to start the game.

The Dodgers scored first. In the fourth Reese doubled, and then Snider drove a ball down the right-field line. As it bounced along the low wall, and Reese scored, Snider thought the ball was touched by a fan and began to pull up.

But it wasn't — or if it was, it wasn't seen by the umpires. Elston Howard, playing right field now in place of Hank Bauer — who had pulled a hamstring of his own in the first inning — fielded the carom and threw to second. Too late, Snider began running again, but he was put out, squandering the Dodger rally.

That would be the only break the Yankees needed. In the bottom of the inning, with two out and no one on, Loes suddenly lost it. Berra singled, Collins walked, and then Howard and Martin followed with base hits before Loes hit Eddie Robinson with a pitch.

It had all happened too fast for Alston to call for a relief pitcher, and Loes stayed in the game to face Byrne. He singled up the middle, and it was 4–1 New York. Byrne went the distance and became the first left-hander all year to pitch a complete game and beat the Dodgers.

"All Brooklyn needs to do," wrote Red Smith after the game, "is to win four times in the next five games. This task may be complicated by the fact that since man first crawled out of a cave and laid hold of a Louisville Slugger, no Dodger team has beaten a Yankee team four times in a whole year." Actually, things were even worse than that.

Newcombe was done and would be unable to pitch in the remainder of the Series. Mantle, although still hobbled, was getting closer to coming back. And now, as Drebinger noted, "crafty old Casey Stengel once again sits high and mighty. The Bomber manager tossed his two top left-handers . . . in the first two games and bagged both. Now he invades the more limited confines of Ebbets Field with his staff of right-handers available for the quick kill . . . the Dodgers won't have to be pushed back much farther to have their backs up against the walls." And when observers learned that Alston's pick to start the game was Johnny Podres, many felt they were all the way up against it. Pitching a left-hander against the Yankees at Ebbets Field was viewed as insanity. And Podres, like Newcombe, hadn't pitched particularly well in the second half. Tommy Holmes, now writing for the *Herald Tribune,* noted that "since June the Podres performances have ranged from mediocre to bad, and even on his mediocre days he was ready for the showers after five or six innings." He'd almost been left off the postseason roster and was saved only when he pitched effectively against the Pittsburgh Pirates late in the season.

Left fielder Sandy Amoros came to the rescue of Johnny Podres and the Dodgers in the sixth inning of game seven of the 1955 World Series with his running catch of a sinking line drive by Yogi Berra.

A TALE OF ONE CITY

Dave Anderson

I T'S THE TALE OF ONLY ONE CITY, BUT CHARLES Dickens would have cherished the Brooklyn where I grew up, the Brooklyn of the Dodgers.

I lived there in what I like to call the Pee Wee Reese era that spanned the shortstop's arrival as a baby-faced rookie in 1941 to his departure as the Dodgers' celebrated captain to Los Angeles after the 1957 season. I lived in the Bay Ridge section of Brooklyn, not far from where the Verrazzano Bridge is now. And in the sweltering summers of my early years there in the '40s, there were many more radios than television sets, many more open windows than air-conditioning units.

In those years, you never saw the Dodgers unless you went to Ebbets Field and bought a ticket. You read about them in the newspapers or listened to Red Barber's voice coming through the radio. More than any player, he was the Dodgers.

In Bay Ridge, Flatbush, Coney Island, or any other neighborhood, you could walk for blocks past the open windows of all those two-family homes or six-story apartments and never miss a pitch. "Oh, Doctor," Red Barber would be saying, "the Dodgers are in the catbird seat now." Or, "The bases are FOB"—full of Brooklyns. Or, "There's a high fly ball out toward the scoreboard and into Bedford Avenue for an Old Goldie." And you knew that, below the radio booth behind home plate, a carton of Old Gold cigarettes was bouncing down the screen to the batboy, who would hand it to the Dodger who had just hit a home run.

Not long after we moved from Troy, New York, to Brook-

lyn in 1938, my mother took me to my first game at Ebbets Field. "To see Babe Ruth," she said.

The Babe wasn't playing, of course. He had hit his 714th home run in 1935 with the Boston Braves, but Larry MacPhail, the Dodgers owner, had put him on display in 1938 as the Dodgers' first-base coach, an ornament for a bad team. He was fatter than he ever had been with the Yankees, but MacPhail, known as Loud Larry, knew the Babe would sell some tickets to people who just wanted to see him hit homers in batting practice. There wasn't much else to see. Those Dodgers of 1938 finished seventh in the eight-team National League. Only the Phillies were worse.

Baseball was really the national pastime then. Boxing was big, especially when Joe Louis defended the heavyweight title. So was thoroughbred racing; 1938 was Seabiscuit's year. College football was important, but pro football didn't mean much. College basketball had its fans, but pro basketball was in only a few small midwestern cities. Pro hockey was a seven-team lodge with two teams in New York. Only country club swells cared about golf and tennis. And when World War II canceled the 1940 and 1944 Olympics, Jesse Owens and 1936 in Berlin were fast fading from memory.

But slowly, the Dodgers improved. MacPhail's new manager was Leo Durocher, who had been the gassiest of the Gashouse Gang as the Cardinals' shortstop. MacPhail traded for first baseman Dolph Camilli, outfielder Joe Medwick, catcher Mickey Owen, and right-handers Whitlow Wyatt, Kirby Higbe, and Curt Davis. By 1941, with the arrival of Reese

and rookie outfielder Pete Reiser along with a trade for second baseman Billy Herman, the Dodgers were in a pennant race with the St. Louis Cardinals. Brooklyn would celebrate its first NL championship since 1920, but it also would suffer its first World Series torment by the Yankees.

In the fourth game, the Dodgers appeared to have squared the Series at 2–2 as Tommy Henrich swung and missed a third strike for what should have been the final out of a 4–3 victory.

But when right-hander Hugh Casey's pitch bounced past Owen, the alert Henrich beat Owen's throw to first base. Joe DiMaggio singled. Charlie Keller doubled for two runs. Bill Dickey walked. Joe Gordon doubled for two runs and a 7–4 lead. When the Dodgers went out quietly, I read later, somewhere in Brooklyn a man listening to the game with his little dog on his lap near an open fourth-floor window suddenly flipped the dog out the window. The next day the Yankees finished off the Series in five games.

On newsstands, the *Brooklyn Eagle* headline lamented, "Wait 'til Next Year." But next year was worse. The Dodgers were leading the league on July 10 in St. Louis when Reiser, chasing a fly ball, crashed into the concrete center-field wall, one of the first of many injuries that wrecked what should have been a Hall of Fame career. Although the Dodgers won 104 games, the Cardinals won 106. I must be honest here. Though growing up in Brooklyn, I was always more of a baseball fan than a Dodgers fan. The way the Cardinals played baseball appealed to me. I liked the way they flew around the bases with the red piping on their uniform sleeves. And back then you could go to Ebbets Field and clap for the Cardinals without worrying that you might be indicted for treason.

In 1942, when I was 13, heaven was going to a Sunday doubleheader with the Cardinals. You took the subway to the Prospect Park stop, then walked the few blocks to Ebbets Field with a big brown bag of bologna sandwiches and enough money for a few Cokes, trudged up the ramp to the center-field bleachers (for 55¢), and sat behind Hildy Chester, who stood in the front row clanging a cowbell. Halfway through the second game, when most of the ushers had gone home, you sneaked through the stands and slid into a box seat behind third base. Stan Musial, the Cardinals' young outfielder with the corkscrew batting stance, appealed to me

even more. In later years, he kept me in pocket money. Whenever the Cardinals came to Brooklyn for a four-game weekend series, I would bet my street-corner pals in Bay Ridge on how many hits Musial would get in the four games. The over-under was usually six, sometimes seven or eight. He almost always got enough hits for me to win. We were only betting quarters, but in those years you could go to the movies for a quarter.

Years later, when I told Stan Musial about how he had kept me in pocket money as a teenager, he smiled as if he had just doubled off the scoreboard in Ebbets Field. I wasn't alone in admiring him. During one of his many batting sprees at Ebbets Field, he was settling into the batter's box when a fan yelled, "Here's that man." Stan the Man had been christened.

During World War II, baseball wasn't the same. Most of the major league players were in the military. By 1946, they had been discharged, but when the Dodgers lost a pennant playoff with the Cardinals, it prompted another "Wait 'til Next Year" headline. And that next year was a historic year. Jackie Robinson arrived. I remember going to Ebbets Field just to see him that year, the first of the Dodgers' six pennants in his ten seasons. But little did I know that I would be covering the Dodgers and Jackie Robinson himself as a sportswriter for the *Brooklyn Eagle* a few years later.

I had wanted to be a sportswriter since I was 12, since I spread the sports sections on the floor of our Bay Ridge home and read them. I grew up reading the best sportswriters of that era: Red Smith, Jimmy Cannon, Frank Graham, W. C. Heinz, Arthur Daley. I had been a summer copy boy at the *New York Sun* while at Xavier High School in Manhattan and the sports editor of the Holy Cross student newspaper. Three months after my 1951 graduation I was hired as a clerk in the *Eagle* sports department for $40 a week. On October 3, 1951, the day of the decisive third game in the 1951 National League pennant playoff, I was in the *Eagle* composing room, checking the type on page 1 with the big eight-column headline "Dodgers Win." Moments later somebody shouted, "Bobby Thomson hit a homer. The Giants won." The printer yanked out the "Dodgers Win" headline and flung it into a bin.

In May 1953, the Dodgers beat writer, Harold C. Burr, broke his hip in a fall. I had covered Giants and Yankees home

1955

games occasionally, but suddenly the kid from Bay Ridge was covering the Brooklyn Dodgers day to day, the best beat in the business. I was traveling with the Dodgers in their chartered railroad cars to St. Louis and Chicago and, in 1954, going with my wife Maureen to Vero Beach for spring training. And I was watching and writing about Jackie Robinson, Pee Wee Reese, Gil Hodges, Roy Campanella, Duke Snider, Carl Furillo, Don Newcombe, Carl Erskine, and Preacher Roe as well as Walter O'Malley, Buzzie Bavasi, and the managers, Charlie Dressen in 1953 and Walt Alston in 1954. Never a dull day. Somebody was always doing something or saying something.

You never had to worry about what you were going to write. Just get to the ballpark early and pay attention, especially to Jackie Robinson. For all the current raves about Barry Bonds and for all of the splendor of Henry Aaron, Willie Mays, Mickey Mantle, Joe DiMaggio, and Ted Williams, the best baseball player I've ever seen was Jackie Robinson, because he could win a game so many different ways—with a single or a home run, with a spectacular catch or stealing a base. Stealing home if necessary; nobody steals home anymore. He also played wherever the Dodgers needed him without a murmur—first base, second base, third base, left field. And sometimes he would win a game by the sheer force of his competitive will that he imposed on his teammates.

Jackie Robinson couldn't win every game, of course. Nobody does. My favorite memory of him involves a photo taken in the moments after Thomson's home run in the most disheartening game the Dodgers ever lost. While the other Dodgers have turned toward the clubhouse in center field at the Polo Grounds, he is still standing near second base, his hands on his hips, staring at home plate to make sure Thomson steps on it. As it turned out, I would be the last baseball writer to cover the Brooklyn Dodgers for the *Brooklyn Eagle*. Put it on my tombstone. Six months before the Dodgers finally won the World Series for Brooklyn in 1955, the *Eagle* suddenly folded. I moved to the *New York Journal-American*, where I was an occasional pinch hitter for the regular baseball writers covering the Dodgers, Yankees, and Giants. I was in Yankee Stadium when the Dodgers won that 1955 Series on Johnny Podres's 2–0 shutout. And on September 24, 1957, with Walter O'Malley about to abscond with the franchise to Los Angeles, I was assigned to cover what everybody knew

would be the Dodgers' last game in Ebbets Field. Danny McDevitt, a little left-hander, blanked the Pittsburgh Pirates, 2–0, before 6,702 mourners as the organist Gladys Goodding played "Auld Lang Syne." In the press room two hours later, Bill Roeder of the *World-Telegram and Sun* and I were the last to finish writing. When we got to the night watchman's door near the marble rotunda, I stepped aside to let Bill walk out, then I walked out—the last writer to leave Ebbets Field after the last Dodger game.

Put that on my tombstone too.

Dave Anderson began his career in journalism with the *Brooklyn Eagle*. As a sports columnist for the *New York Times*, he is a past winner of the Red Smith Award for distinguished sportswriting and the author of more than 20 books.

But the Dodgers were going home, back to Ebbets Field, and that meant more to them than perhaps any other team in baseball — especially now. Stengel decided to throw Bob Turley, a 17-game winner and a fastball pitcher. After scuffling against the softer tosses of Ford and Byrne, the Dodgers, a fastball-hitting team, relished the thought.

It didn't take long for them to feel comfortable. In the bottom of the first, after a Reese walk, Campanella hit a home run to put the Dodgers ahead 2–0.

Podres gave it right back. Mantle was back in the lineup, and although he wouldn't remain healthy enough to play the remainder of the Series, the 23-year-old Podres, pitching on his birthday, made a mistake that Mantle hit out of the park. The blast seemed to unnerve him, and he struggled through the inning as the Yankees scored one more and tied the game when Campanella dropped a throw from Sandy Amoros after being bowled over at home by Moose Skowron.

But on this day the Dodgers wouldn't be denied. Robinson singled, Amoros was hit by a pitch, and Podres, trying to sacrifice, beat Turley's throw to first to load the bases.

Now Robinson turned back the clock again, feinting another dash to home, worrying Turley to distraction. He walked Gilliam to force Robinson home, and Stengel had to turn to his bullpen.

They fared no better, and with the Dodgers leading 6–3 in the seventh Robinson stole a run. He smacked a double to left and took a wide turn, making it look like he had decided, too late, to go to third and had now changed his mind. Yankee left fielder Elston Howard fell for the ploy and threw behind Robinson, thinking he might catch him returning to second.

It was an old Robinson trick, one he hadn't used in several seasons and now dusted off for the big game. The instant Howard threw, Robinson broke back toward third and slid in safely. The Dodgers went on to score twice, and Podres went the distance in the 8–3 win, finishing the game to a serenade of "Happy Birthday" played by Gladys Goodding on her organ. Drebinger wrote: "After two days of restless wandering the Dodgers yesterday came upon the trail that may lead them to their first world series title." The oddsmakers concurred. They dropped the odds on a Yankees championship from 19–5 all the way down to 8½–5 and made Brooklyn a 13–10 favorite in game four.

But that morning another warning shot in regard to the Dodgers' future was sounded. On October 1, Charles Kiley of the *Herald Tribune* broke a story that revealed that Walter

Brooklyn manager Walter Alston (right) embraces pitcher Johnny Podres following the left-hander's masterful 2–0 shutout victory over the Yankees to clinch the Dodgers' first world championship. Alston would capture three additional world titles as Dodger skipper following the team's move to Los Angeles.

O'Malley had commissioned R. Buckminster Fuller, a visiting professor of architecture at Princeton, to design a domed stadium with a plastic roof to house the Dodgers. According to Kiley, O'Malley had approached Fuller about the idea in April and Fuller and his graduate students had been at work on the project ever since. They had even created a model of an enormous, spherical geodesic dome (which Kiley referred to descriptively as made of "triangular grids") with a polyester resin skin reinforced with fiberglass. The structure would be 750 feet in diameter and nearly 30 stories tall.

Kiley's timeline is significant. Although others have dated O'Malley's interest in the domed park to November 1955, Kiley's story moves the timetable up some six months, long before O'Malley had made the announcement in regard to Jersey City. While the Dodgers were trying to win the pennant, O'Malley was already making substantive plans for a new park. According to Kiley, O'Malley and Fuller had met on a number of occasions throughout the summer, and O'Malley had even taken field trips with Fuller to inspect other domes he had built. "Mr. Fuller said he had Mr. O'Malley out to Huntington Station recently to inspect a fifty-five foot dome,"

NL STRIKEOUT LEADERS

Year	Player	SO	Year	Player	SO
			1936	Van Lingle Mungo	238
			1951	Don Newcombe	164
			1959	Don Drysdale	242
1921	Burleigh Grimes	136	1960	Don Drysdale	246
1922	Dazzy Vance	134	1961	Sandy Koufax	269
1923	Dazzy Vance	197	1962	Don Drysdale	232
1924	Dazzy Vance	262	1963	Sandy Koufax	306
1925	Dazzy Vance	221	1965	Sandy Koufax	382
1926	Dazzy Vance	140	1966	Sandy Koufax	317
1927	Dazzy Vance	184	1981	Fernando Valenzuela	180
1928	Dazzy Vance	200	1995	Hideo Nomo	236

wrote Kiley. "He said the Dodger president found the plastic dome so strong he could not throw rocks through it. There was no word on what Don Newcombe's fastball might do."

Any remote chance that remained for Walter O'Malley to get the cooperation he needed from local authorities to get a stadium built where and when he wanted it was now doomed. As Kiley's final quip indicates, the idea of a domed stadium, particularly one made of plastic and designed by Fuller, was, from the outset, an object of derision. Instead of making O'Malley look like a man ahead of his time, he came off as a man out of his mind. In 1955 the notion of a domed stadium was an untested pipe dream, and Fuller, while a darling of academic architecture and a true visionary, was far, far too "far out" to be taken seriously by the powers-that-be. Neither Robert Moses nor anyone else in authority would ever be willing to back O'Malley now. They already thought O'Malley was naive, presumptuous, and stubborn; now they thought

he was nuts. Even if O'Malley was using the notion of the domed stadium only to get attention and intended to then build a more traditional facility, he badly miscalculated. All the machinations he would go through over the next few years were an exercise in futility.

As Michael Shapiro goes on to describe the episode in *The Last Good Season,* in the end one of Fuller's students designed a smaller, scaled-down version of the dome. Over the next year O'Malley would take pride in publicly displaying the model, further cementing the perception that he was impractical and unrealistic.

Even the most dedicated old Dodger fan should shudder at the thought that such a facility might ever have been built. It would be 1965 before baseball got its first dome, Houston's Astrodome, and even with another decade of technological advances, the result would be an utter abomination. The facility was totally inappropriate to the game—the grass died after the roof had to be painted to reduce glare, and that led in turn to the development of Astroturf. Even the scaled-down version of Fuller's dome—had it been built at the time—might have made for an amazing building, but it unquestionably would have been a horrific excuse for a ballpark.

For now, that story was just a footnote to the Series. With Erskine scheduled to start opposite the Yankees' inconsistent Don Larsen, the Dodgers suddenly seemed to have the Yankees on the run.

They did. The Dodgers again pounded the Yankees, cracking three home runs and scoring three runs in both the fourth and fifth innings to chase Larsen. Erskine also struggled, but first Bessent and then Labine came on and held the Yankees at bay. Brooklyn emerged with an 8–5 win while Yankee owner Del Webb ended the game with an ice pack on his head after being struck with a foul ball.

His headache grew the next day. This time Bob Grim was Brooklyn's victim, or more precisely, Duke Snider's. The Dodger center fielder hit two home runs off Grim—his third and fourth of the Series—both with two strikes, both on change-ups, both driving Casey Stengel nuts. Meanwhile, Alston surprised everyone by starting rookie Roger Craig. He worked into the seventh and got the decision in the 5–3 Brooklyn win. All of a sudden the Dodgers were going back to Yankee Stadium needing only one more win to take the Series.

But it was different in the Bronx. In 1952 the Yankees had been in the same exact situation. Before game six the still-confident Yankees posted an announcement on the scoreboard that said, "Tomorrow, Brooklyn, 1 P.M.," a game they fully expected to play. Alston surprised everyone again by picking Karl Spooner to start the game. So far, a team starting a left-handed pitcher had won every game. Although Spooner wasn't the same pitcher as he'd been before he hurt his arm, he had found a way to get National League hitters out. Stengel turned back to Ford.

Unfortunately for the Dodgers, American League hitters were a different story, but then Spooner neither gave himself much of a chance nor received much help.

In the bottom of the first he walked Rizzuto, and as Martin struck out, Rizzuto tried to steal second. He got a lousy jump but made the base when Gilliam was late to the bag, causing Campanella to double-clutch before the throw. McDougald walked before Berra hit a hard grounder up the middle.

Gilliam took a few steps to his right, then planted for a back-handed grab and the start of a double play. But Berra's ball hugged the ground and Gilliam grabbed only air. The ball was ruled a hit. Bauer followed with a single, and then Skowron hit a three-run home run to give the Yankees a 5–0 lead. Spooner was done before he'd broken a sweat. Russ Meyer and Ed Roebuck shut New York down the rest of the way, but it was too late. Ford scattered four hits, the Yankees won 5–1, and the Series was tied.

After the game there was a measure of bitterness in the Dodger clubhouse as Spooner blamed Gilliam for his performance. "All I know," he moaned, "is that when a runner goes down to steal somebody had better cover second. Maybe I should have struck out everybody." But he didn't have the stuff to do that anymore.

Once again the Dodgers' season—in fact their legacy as a franchise—came down to one game, one game in which defeat would mean utter disaster, while victory would spell . . . what would it be? Joy? Everything, absolutely everything, came down—again—to one game, game seven.

It would not be easy. Although there was some speculation before the game that Newcombe would get the ball, he was finished. For the first time in the Series Alston turned to a starter for a second time and chose Johnny Podres to pitch opposite Tommy Byrne. That wasn't the only decision that Alston faced.

In game six Duke Snider had stepped on one of the infamous sprinkler heads in the Yankee Stadium outfield, the one that had ruined Mickey Mantle's knee. Snider had also wrenched his knee, and as the Dodgers had struggled to come back he had been pinch-hit for by Don Zimmer and pulled from the lineup. Alston was unsure whether he'd be able to play.

Ditto for Jackie Robinson. After game four his right Achilles tendon had started giving him trouble. After game six he told the press, "I can't tell right now whether I can play. It all depends on how the foot feels. It is up to Walt."

At the same time Don Zimmer was politicking to play. After game three, when Alston had sat him down against Bob Turley, he'd gone off. "I'm sick of sitting around, playing one week, sitting next," he snapped. "If I can't play here, I want to play somewhere else." Since then he hadn't played at all until pinch-hitting for Snider.

When Alston made out his lineup before the game, Snider was in center field and Zimmer was at second, which pushed Gilliam into left field and caused Sandy Amoros to take a seat. Don Hoak was at third, making his only start of the Series. Jackie Robinson was on the bench, presumably with the bad Achilles.

But there may have been a bit more to it than that. When he talked about the Series later, Alston never mentioned Robinson's heel as the reason he didn't play, instead saying simply that Robinson was "tired." And in postgame reports in New York newspapers, Robinson is nearly invisible. Odder still is the fact that later Robinson never spoke in any detail about the Series, not even in his own autobiography. Nor do any of Robinson's many biographers address the issue. The heart and soul of the Dodgers, and arguably the man most responsible for their record since he first stepped onto the field in 1947, neither started nor appeared in any capacity in the most important game in Dodger history.

Before the game Podres, from upstate New York, was blissfully unaffected by the pressure of pitching game seven. Bristling with the confidence of someone who didn't know any better, he had spent much of the previous 24 hours telling his teammates not to worry, that the game was in the bag.

It was Indian summer in New York, the rare autumn day when the sky was clear, the sun warm, and the wind negligible, more like a day in June. There was no great ceremony before the game, no inkling of the history about to be made. If anything, the crowd was a little subdued, and several thousand tickets went unsold. There were a fair number of Brooklyn fans in attendance, but this was clearly a Yankee crowd. Most Dodger rooters followed the pattern they had adopted in recent years and stayed home to watch on TV.

When the game started at 2:00 P.M., the diamond was bathed in sunshine. As the afternoon progressed the sun would start to drop behind the stands along first base, turning left into a notorious sun field and causing a shadow to creep across the diamond.

The Dodgers hit first. Gilliam led off with a chopper up the middle, but Phil Rizzuto streaked across the diamond and threw him out by a step. Byrne breezed through the rest of the first.

Podres was similarly effective, and the Yankees didn't manage a hit until two were out in the second. Moose Skowron drove a ball to right, causing most of Yankee Stadium to stand and start to yell, but it fell well short of the wall and skipped into the stands for a ground-rule double.

Podres didn't panic. He got the third out as he stuck to his plan, not just throwing but pitching with wisdom beyond his

years. The Yankees expected him to depend on his change-up, as he had in his earlier start, and some of them were laying on the pitch. But on this day Podres threw more fastballs than before, with just enough change-ups to keep the Yankees guessing.

Byrne too pitched smart. When he had first reached the majors, he'd been a power pitcher, totally dependent on his fastball. But that was gone now, and both Byrne and the Yankees had been surprised by his transformation from a raw thrower into a pitcher.

With two out in the third, the Yankees threatened again. Podres walked Rizzuto, and Billy Martin singled to right. Rizzuto, respecting Furillo's arm, stopped at second. Gil McDougald hit next.

He chopped a slow roller toward third whose path traced out the words "base hit." Don Hoak, playing back, was caught in between. As the ball trickled his way Rizzuto raced to third, knowing that he had to beat Hoak to the bag, for if the third baseman got to the ball, all he had to do was step on the base to end the inning.

Rizzuto, the ball, and Hoak all arrived in about the same place at the same time. Rizzuto slid just as Hoak bent to field the ball only a step or two behind the bag.

But in this Series, finally, the Dodgers got the break. The ball struck Rizzuto in midslide, just before he reached the safety of the base, and then caromed wide. Umpire George Ballinfant's call was clear — Rizzuto was out, and Podres was out of trouble.

Byrne struck out Duke Snider to start the fourth inning, but then Roy Campanella hit what might have been the hardest ball all day, sending a shot down the left-field line, then legging out a double as Elston Howard cautiously gathered in the ball. Furillo followed with a slow grounder to Rizzuto. He was out, but when Campanella saw that the ball was hit softly, he alertly went to third.

That brought up Hodges and left Byrne with a choice, one that Casey Stengel weighed in on with a visit to the mound. Byrne could walk Hodges, and his 27 home runs and 102 RBIs, and then pitch to Hoak, who was appearing in his first game of the Series and had hit only .240 for the season. Both were right-handed hitters.

The Yankee manager made a rare mistake. He made the decision to have Byrne pitch to Hodges. Although the pitch jammed him, the Brooklyn first baseman was so strong it hardly mattered. The ball shot just over Rizzuto's reach, over his head and into left field. Campanella scored, and now Brooklyn led 1–0.

Berra, batting cleanup for the Yankees, led off against Podres in the bottom of the inning. He hit a lazy fly ball to left-center. Snider and Gilliam converged on the ball, and at the last moment, as Snider slowed and Gilliam streaked into his line of sight, both men abruptly pulled up and shied away from the ball. Berra ran hard the whole way and made it to second with a cheap double.

Brooklyn fans grew nervous. This was the kind of play the Yankees always, always seemed to take advantage of.

But not this time. Bauer flew out to right, but Berra couldn't advance on Furillo. Skowron then grounded out to Zimmer, and Berra went to third, but when Bob Cerv popped up, the Dodgers were out of the inning.

And in the sixth they were on their way to paradise as Byrne, according to one writer, was quickly "beaten to a pulp by butterfly wings."

With the Dodgers still leading 1–0, Reese led off with a sharp single to center, bringing up Snider. Alston decided to play for one run and ordered Snider to bunt.

The play surprised New York. Both Skowron and Byrne started for the dribbler to the first-base side of the mound, then Skowron rapidly backed off and headed to first as Snider, bad leg and all, tore down the line.

Byrne fielded the ball cleanly and flipped to Skowron. Although he wasn't quite back to first yet, the throw still beat Snider. All Skowron had to do was slap on a tag.

He did, but with one hand, on Snider's shoulder. The ball popped free and Snider was safe.

Now Alston decided to try again. Roy Campanella would later be named the NL MVP for 1955, and now he proved his worth. He bunted. Campy was thrown out, but both Reese and Snider moved up.

The butterflies were battering Byrne. Stengel ordered Furillo walked to load the bases, then turned to right-handed Bob Grim to face Hodges.

It didn't work. Hodges drove a fly ball deep to right-center field. Cerv caught it on the track, but Reese jogged home and put the Dodgers ahead by two.

Grim wasn't ready. He threw a wild pitch, and Snider moved to third. Then he walked Hoak to set up a force at second. Alston countered by pinch-hitting George Shuba for Zimmer, but he grounded out to end the inning.

That move caused a series of changes, like ripples on a

All of Brooklyn rejoiced over the Dodgers' first World Series triumph and their conquest of the Yankees. One newspaper ran a banner headline that simply said, "We Win," and another referred to the team's long-time underdog image with block letters that read: "Who's a Bum."

pond, that Dodger fans have forever been grateful for. With Zimmer out of the game, Gilliam moved to second. Shuba was no great outfielder, so now Alston played defense, inserting Sandy Amoros and his glove into left field.

One other factor came into play. At the start of the inning the shadows from the grandstand and the light standards on the roof crossed into the path that went from the pitcher's mound to the plate. The ball became a bit harder to see as it flickered in and out of the sun.

Billy Martin led off the inning for New York with a walk, and Dodger fans shifted nervously on davenports all over Brooklyn and beyond. McDougald then pulled a surprise of his own. He bunted, and beat it out for a hit. That brought up Yogi Berra with no outs.

The Dodger outfield swung around toward right field. Berra, a left-handed hitter, liked to pull the ball, and Podres was tiring. In left field Sandy Amoros gave Berra the line and moved all the way over to left-center field, behind Reese, closing the gap to center.

With his first pitch, Campanella had Podres back Berra off the plate with a ball inside. This was not Ralph Branca facing Bobby Thomson four years before. The hitter wasn't going to get a pitch he could pull. Campanella and Podres weren't thinking on the fly. They had a plan and knew that a home run — Berra had hit 27 in 1955 — would put the Yankees up 3–2. On his second pitch Podres went away, throwing a pitch that Berra couldn't pull and one that, if he tried, would turn into a ground ball and perhaps a double play.

But Berra was a smart hitter. The ball was up, where he could drive it. The pitch was also hard to see in the flickering light, particularly against the background of the fans in the center-field bleachers. He swung and hit the pitch solid, but was late.

It sliced into the sunshine and started toward the left-field corner, swerving, as all such balls do, toward the line. The next few seconds were the longest in Dodger history as Sandy Amoros, the ball, and the left-field corner all converged.

McDougald broke with the sound of the bat on the ball. With the play in front of him, he knew that Amoros was in left-center and that if the ball dropped in he might be able to score. But on second Billy Martin had a better view of the hit, and he wasn't so sure. He took only a few tentative steps toward third and focused his attention on Amoros, waiting to see if the ball dropped.

Amoros just ran. The Cuban outfielder was a fine player and probably the fastest man on the team. He knew the situation.

He ran until he couldn't run anymore, until the ball began to drop, until he was only a step or two in front of the foul line, maybe 10, perhaps 15 feet from the foul pole, where the number "301" was painted on the concrete.

Knowing he was out of room, he started to brake and stuck out his glove on his right hand, palm up. Then, catching decades of frustration, he snagged Berra's drive, stopped inches short of the stands, then turned and made a perfect throw to Reese, who had floated out toward him to take the relay. The Dodger captain caught the ball, wheeled, and fired to Hodges on first base, where McDougald, forced to retrace his steps, slid back a fraction after the throw.

Double play. Rally over. The Dodgers still led, 2–0.

Or was it? There were only two outs, Martin was still on second, and Bauer, who could hit home runs too, was stepping in.

Podres stayed away from him too. Bauer grounded out to Reese, and the inning was over.

Dodger fans started counting the outs. Nine more meant the world championship.

They came quickly in the seventh. Two ground balls to Reese delivered two outs before Elston Howard singled.

Grim was due to hit, but he never came out into the on-deck circle. Mickey Mantle did.

His hamstring hadn't healed, and in the first inning of game three, when he'd started the game in center field, he'd reinjured the leg. Despite hitting a home run later, he had to move over to right field. He limped through game four, obviously subpar, and hadn't played since. Still, he was Mickey Mantle coming to bat in a game when one pitch and one swing could tie the score. And both Podres and home plate were well within the shadows now.

Batting from the right side, Mantle got his pitch but *just* missed, cutting under the ball by a fraction. He hit a towering fly that Reese caught behind third base. Six outs to go.

After the Dodgers went out without scoring again, New York mounted one last charge. Rizzuto singled hard to left, and Amoros raced over, blocking the ball in what one paper described as a "scrambling one knee stop," keeping the ball in front and Rizzuto on first. Then Billy Martin sliced a liner to right field. Furillo came in and caught the ball at his knees. McDougald followed with a slashing ground ball to Hoak.

Caught in between again, Hoak backed up on the ball, waiting for a big hop. He got it, but it wasn't true and the ball went off his shoulder into left field.

It was excruciating, being a Dodger fan. Why couldn't the Yankees just go down quietly, quickly? Why did the door always have to be left ajar?

In the dugout, Alston didn't move. Berra was coming up again, and the only lefty in the bullpen was Spooner. He wasn't warming up. The only guy throwing was Labine.

Podres and Campanella stuck to the plan. They jammed Berra with a pitch he could pull but couldn't drive. He flew out to shallow right field. Four outs to go.

Hank Bauer took a ball in, fouled one back, and then took another ball to go ahead in the count 2–1. A home run meant the ballgame.

Podres had struck out only three hitters the entire game, and two of those were on the pitcher, Tommy Byrne. But the cocky kid still had something left and threw a fastball at Bauer's shoulders.

He swung through it, grunting. Three outs to go.

All over Brooklyn fans fingered lucky amulets, said the rosary, grabbed a last beer, pulled on another cigarette, gave the baby another bottle to stay quiet, paced, rubbed their faces, fiddled with the antenna, sat back down, and tried to breathe.

The Dodgers went down quickly again in the ninth, as if not wanting to break the spell themselves, as if they couldn't wait to get Podres back on the mound, the coolest customer on the team.

The other Dodgers liked him and saw themselves in the ballsy "so what?" attitude of this young guy, still single, just having fun, a kid who'd grown up a Dodger fan in the Adirondacks, wanting to play for the Dodgers and now living the dream that every Dodger fan had dreamed for decades. Three outs to go.

Big Moose Skowron led off and hit a rocket, a ball that hit the ground and exploded on Podres. He stuck up his glove, and the ball stuck in the pocket, just like that, boom, ripping the webbing, and sticking there, wedged between the leather. Podres tugged at it while jogging to first, and then running, as if to make the play himself, until the ball came loose and he then flipped over to Hodges and there were two outs to go.

Bob Cerv took a big swing but hit a pop-up to Reese.

Now it was down to Elston Howard. Podres could hardly stand still. He was running on adrenaline. He drew a long deep breath.

Campanella noticed. The kid was throwing hard, harder than at any time in the game. If Howard got on, well, that was okay. The pitcher was due up next, and all the Yankees had on the bench were left-handed hitters—Noren, Eddie Robinson, Joe Collins. Podres could go after Howard. A home run wouldn't beat him.

Podres threw a fastball, and Howard fouled it off. Then the two went back and forth. A ball. A foul, a ball, and another foul, the count 2-and-2.

Howard was on to the fastball, but that's what Campy wanted, more fastballs.

Podres shook him off, shook off the sign from the league MVP, from the best catcher in baseball, from a guy who'd been catching for a living for almost 20 years.

Podres threw a change-up. Howard swung. The ball rolled to Pee Wee Reese.

Reese smiled. The Dodger captain had been waiting for this for a long time, a *long* time. He was the only Dodger left from 1941, when Reiser was still young and Hugh Casey struck out Henrich but lost game four when Owen lost the ball and everyone said, "Wait till next year." Reese remembered when all the players were white and the Dodgers were Bums, and he was the only guy left from 1942 when the Dodgers won 104 games but the Cardinals won 106 and everyone said, "Wait till next year," again. And he remembered Rickey being hired, and Durocher and 1946, when they had to wait till next year again after the Cardinals beat them in the playoff, and then 1947 and Jackie Robinson coming to the big leagues and his old friends in Kentucky giving him a hard time about it, then Robinson showing everyone, and showing Reese, that he was a man, a man who could play. But it was still "wait till next year," always next year, after almost every year. Always waiting.

He waited now, one last time, for the ball to bounce true and roll straight into his mitt. Then he turned and tossed it to Hodges, low, but Hodges stretched, reached out one hand like Amoros, and laid it on the ground. Hodges, who remembered too, reached out and grabbed it and didn't let go.

And next year was finally here, where it belonged, in Brooklyn.

LAST EXIT TO BROOKLYN

THE PARTY DIDN'T STOP FOR HOURS. AS SOON AS THE BALL SETTLED INTO Gil Hodges's glove, Johnny Podres leapt in the air, arms spread wide like a huge V for victory. Before his feet touched the ground again, thousands joined him, maybe millions, as every Brooklyn fan in the universe leapt in the air too. And the Dodgers started leaping and running, and Campy grabbed Podres, and Jackie Robinson, the tired man with the bad heel who didn't play in the biggest game the Brooklyn Dodgers ever played, was first out of the dugout and outraced every other Dodger on the bench to the big knot on the field where, as Red Smith noted, Podres was soon "lost from sight in a howling, leaping, pummeling pack that thumped him and thwacked him and tossed him around, hugged him and mauled him and heaved him."

And from there it spread, all the howling and thumping and hugging, downtown and across the bridge to Brooklyn, where it exploded. For once, Brooklyn rose higher than Manhattan, and in seconds there were people on the streets and cars honking and people dancing in their houses and swilling Schaefer beer just like the Dodgers in the Yankee Stadium clubhouse, pouring it over each other in delight.

Impromptu motorcades formed on the streets, and cars paraded down Fulton Avenue, dressed in shaving cream like

Jackie Robinson bids an unheralded, silent farewell to the Dodgers as he exits the Ebbets Field clubhouse on January 7, 1957. Robinson rejected a trade to the Giants and instead retired from baseball to work as vice president of human resources for the Chock Full o'Nuts restaurant chain. In less than a year the Dodgers themselves exited Brooklyn for Los Angeles.

newlyweds on the way to the honeymoon — "World Champs," "Bums No More," and "The Yanks Is Dead." Around Borough Hall businessmen tore up newspapers — Brooklyn ticker tape — and tossed it from office windows. Stores emptied, and their owners stood on the streets, closed early, and took it all in, though also watching out, a little afraid of what the crowds might do. But mostly people did nothing but smile and look for other faces smiling and watch the cars and listen to the horns as every cop with a Brooklyn beat was called on to keep the streets clear and make sure nothing bad happened. For now, next year had come and that was enough, and no one really knew what to do but breathe it in and feel something wonderful they had never felt before.

It changed toward nightfall as the liquor flowed and block parties broke out and joy was splashed with a little out-and-out frenzy and the bars filled and the business of Brooklyn shut down early. The Dodgers had a party that night at the Hotel Bossert, and thousands of fans gathered around outside, cheering the Dodgers as they entered the hotel, where they would dance throughout the night.

And it wasn't a dream. Best of all, it wasn't a dream. It was there, later that evening and the next day, in all the papers, "Brooks World Champs" in the *World-Telegram,* "Dodgers Win First World Championship" in the *Herald Tribune,* "Dodgers Capture 1st World Series" in the *Times,* and the best of all in the *Daily News:* "Who's a Bum!" and "This IS Next Year."

The writers had to struggle with words to describe it, for as Red Smith noted accurately, "One has to pause for a moment and consider before the utter implausibility of the thing can be appreciated." But not in Brooklyn. In the *Daily News,* Joe Trimble wrote: "They won't make October 4 a red-letter day in Brooklyn. They'll print it in letters of gold from now on because it's only the greatest date in the history of the batty borough." John Drebinger of the *Times* added simply, "Brooklyn's long cherished dream has come true," and Harold Rosenthal of the *Herald Tribune* couldn't help but observe: "The Brooklyn Dodgers won the World Series and if that reads a trifle peculiarly, it should. It's never been written before because it never happened before. But it happened yesterday."

The party was terrific, glorious, everything Brooklyn had asked for and waited for and hoped for and more, a party that would be replayed and talked about like the game that had just taken place, the shared stories of "Where were you?" and "Who were you with?" and "What did you do?" the chain of happiness wrapping its wide arms around every Brooklyn fan

everywhere, so much so that 50 years later the mere mention of the Dodger world championship would make old fans young again.

But the hangover that would soon follow proved to be more than sobering, for it would do two things — embolden O'Malley in his quest for a new ballpark, and make the Dodgers even more desirable to suitors. They weren't a team that was the clear second choice in the city of their birth, like the lowly Boston Braves compared to the Red Sox, the recently fallen Philadelphia Athletics compared to the more potent Phillies, or the historically pathetic St. Louis Browns compared to the proud Cardinals. The Dodgers were number one in Brooklyn, a place of three million people, and world champions, for now, second to no one, not even the Yankees.

And in only two short years those two facts would combine and conspire to take the Dodgers away, to sever the Dodgers from Brooklyn forever.

Only a few weeks after the World Series win, O'Malley decided to go on a public relations campaign to tout the plan for a domed stadium. There was far more interest in the Dodger team than in his plans for the franchise, and as O'Malley tried to explain the concept of Fuller's geodesic dome design, eyes glazed over, reporters stopped writing in their notebooks, and readers turned the page. His pipe dream cost O'Malley what little credibility he had, both with the press and with the political figures he was destined to deal with.

His argument in regard to the Milwaukee Braves also fell flat. O'Malley kept citing the Braves' financial success as a harbinger of their success on the field, warning that the Braves were on the cusp of outspending everyone for talent and intimating that the Dodger farm system couldn't compete. "I must make money," he said. How many kids could the Dodgers sign up, he asked, when the Braves scouts were saying, "Look, I'll get you four times as much"?

But reality did not match that perception — at least not yet. The Dodgers were reigning world champions — Brooklyn had finished 13½ games ahead of Milwaukee in 1955. Young Johnny Podres had just won two World Series games and seemed to be a star in waiting. The Dodgers' Montreal farm club had just won another International League title. Their double-A farm team from Mobile captured the Southern Association, and single-A Newport News won the Piedmont League. The only Milwaukee farm teams that had won anything were in C ball. The same bonus rule that forced the Dodgers to keep Koufax on the roster for two years was, in one sense, working. It was holding down the size of bonuses paid to amateur players. The competitive advantage of Milwaukee that O'Malley cited didn't reflect reality.

O'Malley's logic simply didn't resonate. He came off as a man who had neither a compelling vision of the future nor a sober assessment of the past, but as one who simply felt uncomfortable in the present. Although attendance at Ebbets Field was disappointing, fans weren't clamoring for a new park or citing it as a reason they weren't coming out to see the Dodgers, and no matter where a new ballpark was built, thousands of Brooklyn residents were destined to be displaced or inconvenienced and no one seemed concerned about that at all. If the Braves had been beating up on Brooklyn, or if the farm system had thoroughly collapsed, or if fans were recoiling in horror at Ebbets Field, the result might have been different. But at the time, even though Ebbets was sorely outdated, there just didn't seem to be a compelling *need* for a new ballpark apart from O'Malley's desire for one, and he was never ever able to convince anyone otherwise.

Meanwhile, the Dodgers had a world title to defend. Many thought 1955 would be the last hurrah for a team that had been together for nearly a decade. Despite the performance of their minor league teams, there wasn't a great deal of talent in the Dodger system — they were winning minor league championships with good minor league players, not major league prospects.

Yet the organization seemed stuck in a holding pattern, and the team did little to try to rebuild. In the off-season before 1956, the only significant trade sent Don Hoak to Chicago for Cub third baseman Ransom Jackson. While Jackson was a solid player, and Hoak something of a disappointment, the trade seemed to be made more to force Robinson out of the lineup than to respond to any need. And when Johnny Podres was drafted into the service, it appeared as if a long slide was ready to begin.

But the same resiliency that had enabled this team to finally succeed after so many failures was still in place. Although Robinson reported to spring training with his hair sporting more salt than pepper and a paunch above his belt, as if on a personal campaign to embarrass Dodger officials he played so well in the spring that he beat out Jackson and was in the lineup on Opening Day. Even Alston finally seemed resigned to Robinson's role on the club, saying, "If Robby sets his mind to beating out a man for a position, he'll beat anybody out." Although the two players would end up splitting playing time as Alston went with the hot hand, Robinson, despite diminishing skills, could still occasionally summon skills that had seemed long gone. So could Reese, Campanella, Hodges, and Furillo.

On Opening Day the club celebrated the raising of the first world championship banner in their history in a pregame ceremony never before seen in Brooklyn. It showed, because at the end, when the crowd rose for the singing of "The Star-Spangled Banner," there was no one assigned to raise the flag on the flagpole. After a delay, the Marine color guard took over, and then, as Tommy Holmes wrote, the Dodgers "tripped over their unprecedented eminence and fell flat on their manly faces," losing to Robin Roberts and the Phillies 8–6.

For the first month the club muddled along, looking old and nothing like the previous year's team, looking as if they were about to resume their perennial and now purely ceremonial search for next year. But in mid-May the Dodgers got some unexpected boosts from some unexpected places.

The press started writing the team's obituary, and in one report a scout from the Giants went right down the lineup

---

In the aftermath of the 1955 World Series, most Dodger fans felt like the fabled (and delirious) Brooklyn Bum, as depicted by cartoonist Willard Mullin.

and pronounced everybody over the hill. Then, on May 12, a sore-armed Carl Erskine bounced back to toss a no-hitter.

Two days later the Dodgers made a move.

Since starting in game two of the 1955 World Series, pitcher Billy Loes had done little to endear himself to the organization. He had never been the big winner they envisioned when he first came up, and by 1956 they considered him something of an odd duck. He once told Charlie Dressen that he never wanted to win 20 games because "then you'll expect me to do it every year." After an indifferent spring marred by a bout of tendinitis, on May 14 he was sold to Baltimore. One day later the Dodgers turned the money around and purchased the most hated man in Brooklyn, Sal Maglie, from the Cleveland Indians.

The previous summer, when the Giants finally admitted they were going nowhere, they'd dealt Maglie away. He was 38, and the Yankees were desperate to acquire him, but the Indians, who didn't need him, outbid New York just to keep him out of Yankee hands. Maglie hardly pitched in the last half of 1955, and by 1956 he was the last man on the staff, completely forgotten, when the Dodgers pried him away.

He could still pitch. Over the years he'd beaten the Dodgers 23 times, primarily in big games with a lot at stake. He just hadn't had much of an opportunity to throw since joining Cleveland.

Brooklyn fans could hardly bear it when they first saw Maglie in a Brooklyn uniform — it just didn't look right, it was like seeing Jackie Robinson in Yankee pinstripes. But the players were delighted to have him. Robinson, in fact, was the first man to greet him when he entered the clubhouse. Although Maglie had made him his particular target, Robinson never assigned a racial motivation to Maglie's bean balls — he knew the pitcher hated every hitter without prejudice. Robinson and the other Dodgers knew Maglie brought to the team a certain toughness that was lacking in their other pitchers.

After a few relief appearances to build up his arm strength, in June Maglie went right into the rotation, and in his first start he twirled a shutout against Milwaukee. Maglie's presence seemed to light a fire under Don Newcombe. The big pitcher was 9–5 at the end of June, but over the final three

On Opening Day 1956, Dodger captain Pee Wee Reese (left) and manager Walter Alston prepare to raise Brooklyn's first and only world championship banner over Ebbets Field.

months he would win 18 games as Maglie helped the cause with 13 wins.

All of a sudden the Dodgers were in the pennant race. The only problem was that everybody else was too. For much of June the Dodgers, Braves, Cardinals, Reds, and Pirates were tied together atop the National League in a huge knot. But the one-two punch of Newcombe and Maglie, backed by Clem Labine in relief, gave the Dodgers enough pitching to stay close to both the Braves and the Reds into September in what Red Smith called "the most ulcerous three-team race in living memory." Then Jackie Robinson, after being benched for a few weeks, got hot and suddenly moved back into the cleanup spot. He turned the clock back one last time, and the Dodgers clawed their way to the front. Over the final weeks Brooklyn and Milwaukee traded first place back and forth.

With three games left to play, Brooklyn still trailed the Braves by half a game. After a rainout against the Pirates on September 28, the Dodgers played a doubleheader on the 29th, a Saturday.

So far, Dodger fans had been lukewarm to the pennant race. On Thursday against Philadelphia, the club drew only 7,000. But for the Saturday afternoon doubleheader more than 36,000 packed their way into Ebbets Field.

Maglie was part of the reason. Four days before he had twirled a no-hitter against Philadelphia. This day he started and finished game one, a 6–3 win, and in game two Alston gave Clem Labine a rare start. He collected a complete-game win as well, and after the Braves lost in 12 innings to the Cardinals, the Dodgers entered the final day of the season leading by one game.

Newcombe, despite a heavy cold, started for Brooklyn. The game drew a big crowd — 31,000 — but there were still scattered empty seats. Nevertheless, as Tommy Holmes wrote, "beneath a Flatbush sky as dull and heavy as a Milwaukee rooter's heart," the Dodgers cracked five home runs and Newcombe held on to win the game 8–6. The Dodgers won the pennant too, and there was celebrating again throughout Brooklyn.

It put the Dodgers back into the World Series, but not all the news was good, at least not for Walter O'Malley. Over the past several seasons some observers had blamed Brooklyn's runaway pennant runs for the slide in attendance. But while the 1956 pennant race had been hotly contested all season long, attendance had risen only slightly, and most of that increase was due to the seven games played in Jersey City.

Still, that experiment had been less than successful. It wasn't as if Jersey City fans had been waiting to see major league baseball their whole lives — it was a short trip to both New York and Philadelphia. And because the Jersey City Giants were a Giant farm club, most Jersey City fans rooted for the Giants. The Dodgers were booed every time they played in Jersey City, and the players hated the inconvenience and felt that playing in Jersey City put them at a competitive disadvantage. Although they finished with a record of 6–1 at Roosevelt for the season, in a pennant race decided by the narrowest of margins, playing on unfamiliar and hostile ground could have cost them. And while attendance at Roosevelt was relatively good, and the parking revenue sent O'Malley to his abacus, it didn't cause Dodger fans to respond by going to Ebbets Field in larger numbers. In the end the experiment did nothing for O'Malley but cost him a measure of goodwill.

His response after Brooklyn's win on the final day was telling. Instead of touting the performance of his team, O'Malley told the press that "the time seems propitious to report that real progress is now being made to get a new stadium worthy of our team, our community, and our fans." It was a bald-faced lie. O'Malley hadn't budged from his insistence on the site at Flatbush and Atlantic Avenues, which still wasn't available, and any number of commissions and authorities were powerless to do anything about that.

The Dodgers had won their second straight pennant, but unlike 1955, in 1956 they had been pushed to the limit once again and began the series with an exhausted pitching staff. Newcombe in particular was out of steam. Despite winning 27 games, a performance that later in the fall would earn him both Cy Young and MVP honors, he had tired down the stretch. In his final two appearances he had been unimpressive.

The Yankees won the American League pennant in their usual fashion — easily — taking over first place in April and romping to a nine-game margin for the season, making them a 3–2 favorite entering the Series. Mantle had chased Ruth for much of the year before settling for 52 home runs.

In game one the Yankees eschewed conventional wisdom and despite Brooklyn's vaunted right-handed power chose to start left-hander Whitey Ford opposite Maglie. Ford had won 10 of his last 11.

After the Yankees hit in the top of the first, he appeared to be on his way to 11 of 12. Mantle cracked a long home run onto Bedford Avenue, where it reportedly "bounc[ed] off hoods of automobiles in the parking lot for half a minute."

CAN YEZ IM-AGINE! WUNST THERE WUZ A TIME WHEN I USEN'T NOT T'EVEN **LIKE** YEZ!

NO HITTERS! AT HISS AGE YET! ACH HIMMEL! 'IST INDECENT!

Former Giant pitcher Sal "The Barber" Maglie joined the Dodgers in 1956 in a trade with the Indians and proceeded to win 13 games for the defending world champions. In the 1956 World Series, Maglie won the opening game but lost 2–0 in game five as Don Larsen threw the first perfect game in World Series history.

But Ford had never beaten the Dodgers at Ebbets Field, and in 1955 the Yankees hadn't managed a win there either. After Ford held Brooklyn scoreless in the first, Robinson led off with a home run of his own, and the Dodgers started to tee off. Hodges hit a home run in the third, and Ford was knocked from the game, trailing 5–1. Sal Maglie again proved to be the master of the big game, and Brooklyn went on to win, 6–3.

After game two the Dodgers were ready to celebrate. The Yankees had jumped out to a 6–0 lead off Newcombe in the second, but then, as Tommy Holmes wrote, Brooklyn's "muscle hitters took complete charge." Duke Snider led a six-run rally off Don Larsen in the bottom of the inning with a home run, and the Dodgers went on to batter a host of Yankee pitchers to win 13–8.

Yet all was not well. After the game Newcombe got into it with a parking lot attendant who asked him, "Do you fold up?" Newcombe hit the attendant with his right hand before passersby pulled him off. Not only was he hurting, but the carping over his perceived inability to "win the big one"—he had yet to win a game in the World Series—had gotten under his skin. He even asked for permission to stay home for game three, but the Dodgers turned him down—Newcombe was occasionally used as a pinch hitter, and Alston thought he might need him.

And now the Dodgers were headed to Yankee Stadium. Brooklyn was a different team away from Ebbets Field, and the Yankees knew it. So did Whitey Ford.

In Brooklyn Ford stayed away from his off-speed pitches, owing to his fear that the Dodgers would pull the ball, and as a result they were able to sit on his not-so-fast fastball. But in Yankee Stadium he was able to use his full repertoire. The result made the phrase "would have been a home run in Ebbets Field" the most overused of the Series, for the Dodgers hit fly ball after fly ball that would have been out in Brooklyn but helped make Ford a Hall of Famer in New York. He cruised to a 5–3 win, and the Yankees were back in the Series.

In game four it was more of the same, only this time Tom Sturdivant did the trick for New York against Carl Erskine. The Yankees hit two home runs, the Dodgers none, and New York won 6–2.

The Dodgers were reeling. Newcombe was suddenly persona non grata on the Dodger staff. Alston announced that Maglie would start game five and Labine game six. Newcombe wasn't even in the conversation.

In game five Sal Maglie pitched perhaps the best game of his postseason career. He was perfect into the fourth inning, when Mantle pulled a chip shot home run into the right-field stands, and in the sixth the Yankees packaged two singles around a two-strike bunt by Larsen to score a second run. Apart from those two momentary lapses, Maglie was in complete control.

And completely outpitched. Yankee starter Don Larsen, after being knocked from the box in the second inning of game two, worked Yankee Stadium, good luck, an abbreviated wind-up, and a moving fastball to perfection. Twenty-seven Dodgers went to the plate and 27 sat down as Larsen, aptly described as "the imperfect man," twirled the first and only perfect game in World Series history, although there were three or four near-misses for base hits, and Maglie noted later that at Ebbets Field it would have been a different story. True enough, but Larsen still accomplished what no

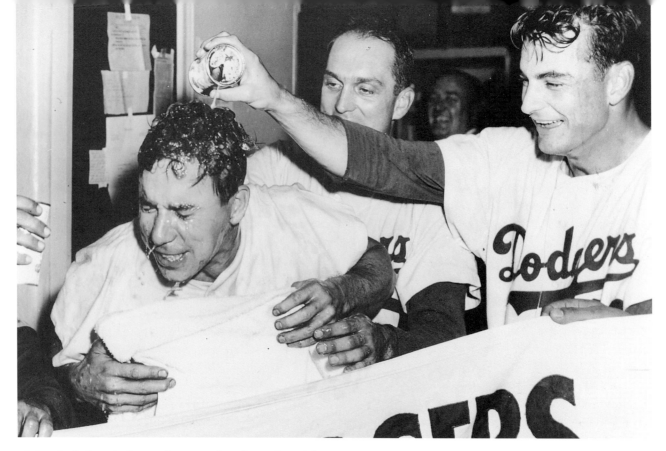

Pitcher Carl Erskine (center) watches as Don Bessant showers teammate Pee Wee Reese with beer as the Dodgers celebrate clinching the 1956 National League pennant on September 30.

pitcher had done before and no one has done since. The Dodgers were one game away from the end of the season, but they were going back to Ebbets Field.

Incredibly, game six was the best game of the Series, and probably the best pitched. Like Larsen, Yankee pitcher Bob Turley had abandoned a full wind-up late in the season, and like Larsen, he suddenly discovered he was possessed of an extra measure of command and energy. Over nine innings he shut Brooklyn down completely, giving up only three hits and striking out eleven in what he later called "my finest game of the season."

But Clem Labine was just as good, even better. Making only his fourth start of the season, he kept New York off-balance with a big overhand curve and responded with what he described as "the best game I've ever pitched." After nine innings the game was still scoreless.

Neither manager wanted to make a move. Labine held the Yankees in the top of the tenth, and Turley returned to the mound to face the Dodgers. With one out, he committed the pitcher's original sin and walked Gilliam. Reese followed with a sacrifice, putting the winning run on second base with two outs.

Duke Snider stepped in, and Stengel didn't hesitate. He ordered Turley to walk the left-hander, bringing up Jackie Robinson.

The move made total sense. Snider was in his prime, while Robinson was clearly near the end of his career. He not only looked old but felt old. Over the summer he'd begun to be bothered by the symptoms of what would later be diagnosed as diabetes.

But he was still Jackie Robinson. Down in the Dodger clubhouse, Ralph Branca, who was serving as Brooklyn's batting practice pitcher for the Series, was watching the game on television, surrounded by reporters who had anticipated the end of the game as soon as Gilliam reached second. As Robinson stepped in Branca intoned, "Come on, Jackie . . . come on, Jackie . . ."

Robinson fouled Turley's first pitch straight back. Then the pitcher went downstairs, trying to get Robinson to hit the ball on the ground.

Robinson reached down and hooked the ball to left. Enos Slaughter got a bad break and misjudged the drive. Instead of racing back, he ran directly toward the wall along the left-field line.

The liner didn't drop but rocketed over his outstretched glove. It hit the concrete wall then ricocheted toward the infield, ruining any remote chance he had to field the ball and make a throw to the plate. Gilliam scored. The Dodgers won 1–0, and the Series was tied.

Given what would soon take place, it would have made a nice story, a wonderful story, for the Dodgers to win the 1956 World Series at Ebbets Field, keyed by a Jackie Robinson base hit in what would prove to be his final season. But in the end the legacy of the Dodgers in Brooklyn, and of Robinson, would not be the stuff of fairy tales but hard, clear reality.

In game seven Alston reluctantly turned to Newcombe. Since his game two shellacking, he'd done nothing to give his teammates any confidence. He seemed to have succumbed to the fiction that he couldn't win the big one, not helped by the fact that his elbow had ached since pitching the season finale against Pittsburgh. He was, by turn, sullen and morose, testy and withdrawn. The Dodgers weren't optimistic.

The Yankees didn't wait around. Berra homered in the first and the third. By the fourth inning Newcombe was gone, about to go on a bender that would affect the rest of his career. And the Dodger bats, which so often had rattled the outfield fences at Ebbets Field and evoked screams of delight from the Flatbush faithful, were all but silent. Johnny Kucks scattered three hits, and the Dodgers fell, 9–0, a score that Tommy Holmes noted bitterly was "the formal statistical figure used to denote a forfeited game," after which he added that the most common reason for a forfeit is "the failure of a ballclub to put in an appearance." In this game the Dodgers did not show up. And although no one yet knew it, more than the World Series had just come to an end.

Jackie Robinson, appropriately, was the last man at bat that day for Brooklyn. He struck out, but when Berra dropped the ball, Robinson, for one final time, cut loose on the base paths.

Another player might have simply allowed himself to be tagged out, but not Robinson. He started running—hard as always—and forced Berra to make the throw to first for the final out.

The Dodgers had precious little time to mourn their loss. As soon as the Series ended, the club gathered for a postseason goodwill trip to Japan. Many players didn't want to go, and Robinson did not, but the others soon embarked on the long cross-country plane trip. They stopped in Los Angeles for a layover before continuing on, first to Honolulu and then to Japan.

Walter O'Malley made the trip too. But for him the stop in Los Angeles was far more significant than any goodwill generated in Japan.

Kenneth Hahn, a city councilman from Los Angeles, had traveled to the World Series hoping to entice an owner into moving his team to Los Angeles. For several years civic support for a major league team had been gaining momentum in L.A. Hahn had targeted Calvin Griffith, owner of the Washington Senators, who was desperate to get out of the nation's capital. Several months before he had tried to approach O'Malley but had been put off.

Things had changed. When O'Malley learned that Hahn was at the Series, he requested a meeting. This time he told Hahn straight up that the Dodgers would be interested in going to Los Angeles. It was becoming more or less common knowledge that the Giants were also contemplating a move west, would need a companion, and that Los Angeles was the more lucrative market.

O'Malley's sudden interest got Hahn's attention. The Senators would be nice, but the Dodgers were another animal altogether. L.A. wouldn't be getting just another failed franchise but perhaps the only other major league team, apart from the Yankees, that had a national following.

When the Dodgers stopped in Los Angeles on their way to Japan, O'Malley met with Hahn again and started discussing specifics. According to Hahn, it was then that O'Malley committed to Los Angeles, although he told Hahn he would continue to make public statements about staying in Brooklyn— he didn't want to ruin attendance in the 1957 season. Over the next few months it became even more certain that New York still wasn't going to give the Dodgers what O'Malley wanted and that Los Angeles was eager to accommodate him. He was even able to convince Los Angeles authorities that they wouldn't have to give the Dodgers as much as other teams. O'Malley didn't want the city to build a ballpark—he'd do that himself. All he wanted was land.

Of course, in the long run it would be far more profitable for the team to have its own stadium, since it wouldn't have to share revenue or pay rent, but for now it looked good to the pro baseball forces in city government. The antibaseball crowd had already been working overtime to convince the public that the city shouldn't be in the business of building a ballpark. Providing the team with land—and the ever-important infrastructure of roads—would prove to be a much easier sale.

Now the ball was rolling, and the Dodgers were beginning an inexorable shift toward Los Angeles. While the team was in Japan, on October 30, 1956, the tenth anniversary of the

OBIT ON THE DODGERS

Dick Young

New York Daily News, October 9, 1957

THIS IS CALLED AN OBIT, WHICH IS SHORT for obituary. An obit tells of a person who has died, how he lived, and of those who live after him. This is the obit on the Brooklyn Dodgers.

Preliminary diagnosis indicates that the cause of death was an acute case of greed, followed by severe political complications. Just a year ago, the Brooklyn ball club appeared extremely healthy. It had made almost a half million dollars for the fiscal period, more than any other big league club. Its president, Walter O'Malley, boasted that all debts had been cleared, and that the club was in the most solvent condition of its life, with real estate assets of about $5 million.

O'Malley contends that unhealthy environment, not greed, led to the demise of the Dodgers in Brooklyn. He points out that he became aware of this condition as long ago as 1947, when he began looking around for a new park to replace Ebbets Field, capacity 32,000.

At first, O'Malley believed the old plant could be remodeled, or at least torn down and replaced at the same site. But, after consultation with such a prominent architect as Norman Bel Geddes, and the perusal of numerous blueprints and plans, O'Malley ruled out such a possibility as unfeasible.

So O'Malley looked around for a new lot where he could build his bright, new, salubrious dwelling for his Dodgers; a dream house, complete with plastic dome so that games could be played in spite of foul weather, a plant that could be put to year-round use, for off-season sports and various attractions.

O'Malley suggested to the City of New York that the site of the new Brooklyn Civic Center, right outside the Dodger office windows in Boro Hall, would be ideal for the inclusion of a 50,000 seat stadium—a War Memorial stadium, he proposed.

That was all very patriotic, the City Planning Commission said, but not a stadium; not there. Sorry.

So, O'Malley looked farther, and hit upon the area at Flatbush and Atlantic Avenues—virtually the heart of downtown Brooklyn, where all transit systems intersect, and where the tired Long Island Rail Road limps in at its leisure. O'Malley learned that a vast portion of the neighborhood, which included the congested Ft. Greene market, had been declared a "blighted area" by city planners who had earmarked it for rehabilitation.

Here began one of the most forceful political manipulations in the history of our politically manipulated little town. With O'Malley as the guiding spirit, plans for establishment of a Sports Authority were born. It would be the work of such an Authority to issue bonds and build a stadium with private capital—utilizing the city's condemnation powers to obtain the land.

With O'Malley pushing the issue through his lifelong political contacts, the bill was drafted in Albany, passed overwhelmingly by the City Council, squeezed through the State Legislature by one vote, and ultimately signed into law by Governor Harriman.

At the moment, April 21, 1956, the prospects for a new stadium, and a continuance of Brooklyn baseball, were at their highest. Thereafter, everything went downhill. City officials, who had supported the bill originally, in the belief Albany would defeat it, went to work with their subtle sabotage.

Appropriations for surveys by the Sports Center Authority were cut to the bone, and O'Malley shook his head knowingly. He was getting the works.

O'Malley, meanwhile, had been engaging in some strange movements of his own. He had leased Roosevelt Stadium, Jersey City, for three years with the announced intention of playing seven or eight games a season there. Later, he sold Ebbets Field for $3,000,000 on a lease-back deal with Marv Kratter. The lease made it possible for O'Malley to remain in Brooklyn, in a pinch, for five years. He had no intention of doing so—it was just insurance against things blowing up at both political ends.

Why was Ebbets Field sold?

Politicians claimed it was an O'Malley squeeze on them. O'Malley claimed it was a manifestation of his good intentions; that he was a manifestation of his good intentions; that he was converting the club's assets into cash so that he might buy Sports Authority bonds and help make the new stadium a reality.

Then O'Malley moved in a manner that indicated he didn't believe himself. At the start of '57 he visited Los Angeles. Two months later, he announced the purchase of Wrigley Field. Shortly thereafter, Los Angeles officials, headed by Mayor Poulson and County Supervisor Ken Hahn, visited O'Malley at Vero Beach, Fla.

It was there, on March 7, that serious consideration of a move to Los Angeles crystallized in the O'Malley mind. He made grandiose stipulations to the L.A. authorities—and was amazed to hear them say: "We will do it."

From then on, Los Angeles officials bore down hard on the project, while New York's officials quibbled, mouthed sweet nothings, and tried to place the blame elsewhere. With each passing week, it became increasingly apparent the Dodgers were headed west—and, in an election year, the politicians wanted no part of the hot potato.

Bob Moses, park commissioner, made one strong stab for New York. He offered the Dodgers park department land at Flushing Meadow—with a string or two. It wasn't a bad offer—but not as good as L.A.'s.

By now, O'Malley's every move was aimed at the coast. He brought Frisco Mayor George Christopher to dovetail the Giant move to the coast with his own. He, and Stoneham, received permission from the NL owners to transfer franchises.

That was May 28—and since then, O'Malley has toyed with New York authorities, seeming to derive immense satisfaction from seeing them sweat unnecessarily. He was repaying them.

Right to the end, O'Malley wouldn't give a flat, "Yes, I'm moving"—as Stoneham had done. O'Malley was using New York as his saver—using it to drive a harder bargain with L.A.'s negotiator Harold McClellan, and using it in the event the L.A. city council were to reject the proposition at the last minute.

But L.A., with its mayor whipping the votes into line the way a mayor is expected to, passed the bill—and O'Malley graciously accepted the 300 acres of downtown Los Angeles, whereupon he will graciously build a ball park covering 12 acres.

And the Brooklyn Dodgers dies—the healthiest corpse in sports history. Surviving are millions of fans, and their memories.

The memories of a rich and rollicking history—dating back to Ned Hanlon, the first manager, and skipping delightfully through such characters as Uncle Wilbert Robinson, Casey Stengel, Burleigh Grimes, Leo Durocher, Burt Shotton, Charlie Dressen, and now Walt Alston. The noisy ones, the demonstrative ones, the shrewd and cagey ones, and the confused ones. They came and they went, but always the incredible happenings remained, the retold screwy stories, the laughs, the snafued games, the laughs, the disappointments, the fights, and the laughs.

And the players: the great ones—Nap Rucker, Zack Wheat, Dazzy Vance, Babe Herman, Dolph Camilli, Whit Wyatt, Dixie Walker; the almost great ones but never quite—like Van Lingle Mungo and Pete Reiser; the modern men who made up the Dodgers' golden era—Duke Snider, Preacher Roe, Hugh Casey—and the man who made history, Jackie Robinson, and the boy who pitched Brooklyn to its only world championship in 1955, Johnny Podres.

And the brass: the conflicts of the brothers McKeever, and the trials of Charley Ebbets; the genuine sentimentality of Dearie Mulvey and the pride of her husband, Jim Mulvey; the explosive achievement of Larry MacPhail, the unpopular but undeniable success of Branch Rickey—and now, Walter O'Malley, who leaves Brooklyn a rich man and a despised man.

Dick Young first gained fame as a reporter covering the Dodgers for the *New York Daily News*. After the Dodgers moved to Los Angeles, he became a columnist, and his work was featured regularly in the *Sporting News*. He was elected to the writers' wing of the Baseball Hall of Fame in 1978 and ended his career with the *New York Post*.

signing of Jackie Robinson, O'Malley sealed their fate: he sold Ebbets Field.

The buyer was Marvin Kratter — within a decade he would become familiar to many sports fans when he purchased the Boston Celtics. For now, however, Kratter wasn't interested in buying a team. Like William Zeckendorf, who developed commercial properties, the Boston-based Kratter was an equally high-powered developer of apartment complexes. It just happened that he wanted to build 6,000-plus apartments where Ebbets Field now stood, which was precisely what Robert Moses had wanted built there all along.

Moses had made it clear that the only place he would be willing to have a ballpark built for the Dodgers was not in Brooklyn at all but in Queens, at Flushing Meadows. There wasn't really anything wrong with the site except for the fact that it wasn't in Brooklyn. They weren't the Queens Dodgers, and never had been, even though that borough included many expatriate Brooklynites and Dodger fans and provided easier access to those who had moved out to Long Island.

The site also had an interesting history in regard to the Dodgers. Once upon a time Moses had wanted to offer it up as a home for the United Nations. That would not have been the best use for such a huge piece of undeveloped property, but it was the only option then available, for Moses didn't control a site in Manhattan large enough to meet the UN's needs. Then William Zeckendorf had swooped in and provided a wonderful solution, a Manhattan property that the Rockefeller family gladly purchased and then donated to the international organization. That had left Flushing Meadows available for other Moses projects, of which a ballpark was now one of many multiple uses under consideration. One can't help but wonder how Moses would have reacted if Zeckendorf had been able to buy into the Dodgers. Moses owed him a huge favor. Flushing Meadows certainly would have been available, but so might have been the site at Flatbush and Atlantic, perhaps in exchange for the housing space Moses wanted at Ebbets Field.

That was going to happen now, but not the way Moses had envisioned it. Instead of trading Ebbets Field for a ballpark site, O'Malley's sale to Kratter gave him cash to build a park on free land in Los Angeles, unrestricted by the plans of anyone else.

For all the sturm und drang that would take place over the next 12 months with the state legislature, the Board of Estimates, the impotent Brooklyn Sports Authority, and other

Ace right-hander Don Newcombe receives both the MVP and Cy Young Awards for the 1956 season in a 1957 Opening Day ceremony at Ebbets Field. Presenting the awards to Newcombe are writer Dan Daniel (left) and National League president Warren Giles.

governmental entities looking to stick a finger in the pie while at the same time washing their hands of responsibility if the Dodgers left, the deal was essentially done. While Kratter had agreed to give O'Malley a three-year lease, ostensibly to give New York time to meet O'Malley's demands for a domed stadium, that was all public relations B.S. Over the next few months O'Malley would pay lip service to New York's efforts to convince him to stay, using New York to extract more and more from Los Angeles.

Over the winter, in relatively rapid fashion, O'Malley and Los Angeles officials decided on a site for the ballpark—Chavez Ravine—and O'Malley acquired the Cubs' minor league franchise in Los Angeles, which simultaneously gave him territorial rights over the Los Angeles area. Everything was in line. All Los Angeles had to do was find a way to convey the land to O'Malley, and he was gone.

That would prove difficult, but not undoable, for O'Malley and Los Angeles officials had selected a parcel of the land that was already controlled by local government—183 acres had been designated for use for public housing, which local government then massaged to include "public use," a much broader definition. The remainder, some 300 acres, was in the private hands of those whom Los Angeles mayor Norris Poulson had described as "squatters and a handful of small homeowners whose goats, cows, and chickens roamed about." In other words, most residents of Chavez Ravine were Mexican immigrants with little political clout who could be steamrolled and made to disappear.

But in the winter of 1956 and 1957, that was still background noise. Oh, the press, particularly Dick Young in the *Daily News,* was beginning to beat O'Malley to death by typewriter about his overtures to Los Angeles, but to many Dodger fans, despite increasing evidence to the contrary, the notion that the Dodgers would ever leave Brooklyn seemed about as likely as the Brooklyn Bridge sinking into the sea. They saw the stories every day, and they even read some of them, but in their hearts they didn't believe it.

In a sense, many Dodger fans had left Brooklyn already, even if they hadn't moved yet. To them, Ebbets Field had already passed into the realm of nostalgia. They didn't go there anymore themselves—at least not very often. But in the rose-colored glasses of the mind's eye, Brooklyn was still the same place it had been when they were coming of age in the years surrounding the war, a colorful neighborhood of character and characters. Reality no longer matched that vision—

Jackie Robinson poses with wife Rachel and son Jackie Jr. at their Stamford, Conn., home following his short-lived trade to the New York Giants. At the time Robinson had already made a deal to retire from baseball and work as an executive for the Chock Full o'Nuts restaurant chain. He notified the Dodgers and Giants of his decision shortly after the trade.

Hubert Selby Jr.'s violent, hard-edged portrait of Brooklyn gone to seed, *Last Exit to Brooklyn,* would soon be the more accurate portrayal—but a more nostalgic viewpoint was kept under glass now, preserved in memory, untouchable. The irony would be missed by most, but the authors of most of the sticky nostalgia about Brooklyn that would flourish in another decade or two would all be written by people who, like Walter O'Malley, had also left Brooklyn. It was still a great place, but even more so from the vantage point of Staten Island, Westchester, or Long Island.

Their words would put the Brooklyn of their childhood in a kind of literary scrapbook, one that glossed over its rough edges and exalted its most mundane aspects into pure romance. They would create a place, and mourn for it, that had only existed the way childhood itself exists, as a transitory moment.

And they would blame not the passing of time for its demise but Walter O'Malley. He would become the villain—and rightfully so—but not for the reasons most chose to assign to him. He became a symbol for the alienation that many former and soon-to-be-former residents felt toward the

Famed clown and Dodger fan Emmett Kelly sits with catcher Roy Campanella in the Dodger dugout prior to the final game at Ebbets Field. The Dodgers' final game in Brooklyn was also Campanella's final game: the Hall of Fame catcher's career ended when injuries from an auto accident in January 1958 left him paralyzed.

forces that were changing their home forever and "forcing" them, like the Dodgers, to leave it. O'Malley abandoned Brooklyn, to be sure, but he had a face and a name and was an easy target. The truth was that a lot of people abandoned Brooklyn at about the same time—the fathers of kids just coming of age, young professionals, as well as city and state government, factories, and businesses. They were all Walter O'Malleys.

In one sense, O'Malley was a victim of that exodus as well—he was swept up in the same tidal forces that sent Brooklyn families to Long Island and shut down the *Brooklyn Eagle*. In recent years O'Malley's role in the Dodger move has been recast as one of reluctance, the story retold as a move forced upon him by larger forces—Robert Moses and other intransigent government authorities. To a degree, that is true. But from the first day he took over the team and turned his attention to getting a new ballpark built in Brooklyn, O'Malley himself made the wrong moves, at the wrong time, over and over again. From stiff-arming William Zeckendorf to signing on with Buckminster Fuller, every move O'Malley made reflected his egocentric myopia and his attendant lack of political skill and vision. In fact, he was damn lucky that Los Angeles bailed him out and that some other team didn't beat the

Dodgers to Los Angeles. For if that had happened, the alternatives for the Dodgers, in retrospect, aren't very appealing.

There is no evidence whatsoever that if O'Malley and the Dodgers had remained in Brooklyn the team would have ended up with a ballpark, domed or otherwise, that would still be standing today, or that the Dodgers would have been able to remain in Brooklyn as a Brooklyn team. At best, they might have ended up with a utilitarian structure like what had been constructed in Milwaukee. That ballpark—a place people drove to as long as the team was winning but didn't feel compelled to visit when it was not—would be abandoned by the Braves in little more than a decade. At worst, the Dodgers might have gotten a dome 30 years before technology and architecture knew how to build one successfully. And given the economic decline of New York in the late 1950s and early 1960s, even a new ballpark might not have been enough to save them, and the Dodgers certainly would not have been enough to "save" Brooklyn from the changes that were taking place everywhere. It would have been impossible to renovate Ebbets Field. The park was in rough shape by age 30, and by 1957 Lee MacPhail's repairs were starting to fail as well. The absolute worst-case scenario would have been for the Dodgers to stay in Brooklyn, at Ebbets Field. Had that happened, instead of being moved while still in their relative prime, the Dodgers would have died on the vine. There'd have been no nostalgia value in that.

The Dodgers and Brooklyn were successful together because each flowered at the same time. By 1957, however, summer was coming to an end for both.

Just two months after the World Series, an unthinkable trade demonstrated the degree to which that was true. As if determined to start breaking the bonds that bound the Dodgers to Brooklyn and the fans to the Dodgers in advance of their departure, on December 13 the Dodgers announced the trade of Jackie Robinson to the New York Giants for Dick Littlefield and $30,000.

In fact, Robinson had already made the decision to retire. He had signed on to become an executive with Chock Full o'Nuts and had even signed a contract with *Look* magazine to break the story in a ghostwritten article, a contract that required his silence on the matter until the story appeared. The trade blind-sided him, just as the story later blind-sided the Dodgers and the Giants.

Brooklyn howled, and in their anger over the loss of Robinson, many fans were prepared to bid the team good riddance.

Then Robinson's story appeared, and now fans believed he'd simply strung everyone along to line his own pockets. That seemed like another smack in the face. Everything, apparently, was for sale—the Dodgers, loyalty, the past. And even though Robinson admitted in the article that now "my legs are gone and I know it," the Giants had genuine interest in him. Owner Horace Stoneham was essentially prepared to offer him a blank check to play one more year—pinch-hitting, perhaps platooning with Red Schoendienst at second base, and mentoring Willie Mays and the next generation of Giants stars on the horizon.

Robinson was tempted—he knew he could still play—but if he backed out of his retirement now, it would look like he was motivated solely by money. He stayed retired, and the Dodgers and Giants rescinded the trade.

It was hard to believe how much had changed since Robinson arrived in the major leagues. There were now more than 50 African Americans in the majors, and another 100 in the minors. Every team but the Red Sox, Tigers, and Phillies was integrated. There was no going back.

But at the same time the Negro Leagues were dead—only a few all-black barnstorming teams remained of that legacy. Baseball, beginning with the Braves' move, had started a long slow movement toward suburbanization, abandoning the inner city and, significantly, doing nothing to make black fans feel welcome at big league ballparks. While Robinson would enter private business and take on a somewhat awkward public and political role in the civil rights movement outside the game, in baseball he was never awkward. Until his death, he would continue to push for equality in the game, taking his battle from the field to the front office.

His larger role as a symbol and figure of true courage sometimes makes it easy to forget just what a remarkable player he was. Almost by himself he brought speed back into major league baseball. From 1947 through 1953, he was clearly one of the best players in the game, if not the very best, a player whom Yogi Berra accurately described after his death as someone who "could beat you in a lot of ways." He wasn't a power hitter, yet he often batted cleanup on the Dodgers, and even after his legs were gone he remained the greatest baserunner of his time. Moreover, in his ten years with the Dodgers, they won six pennants, competed for another four, and won their

Members of the "Keep the Dodgers in Brooklyn Committee" make their views known in one of the last games ever played at Ebbets Field.

Dodger fans weep following the final game at Ebbets Field on September 24, 1957. Only 6,702 fans attended and watched the defending National League champions beat the Pirates, 2–0, as organist Gladys Goodding played "Auld Lang Syne" and "Say It Ain't So."

There was no yearlong celebration of what was about to pass, no long good-bye, just a slow, accumulating chill. Dodger fans stood on the porch and watched their ballclub slowly back up the truck. Some complained, wrote letters, signed petitions, or formed committees, but most just watched in silence, angry, and slowly drifted away. It had always been Brooklyn against the world, hadn't it? Well, guess what? The world won. Didn't it always?

Blame was tossed back and forth in the newspapers, and most of it landed, rightly, at O'Malley's feet, but he acted oblivious. He was already looking ahead.

Dodger fans couldn't do that. Ebbets Field looked the same and sounded the same and smelled the same in 1957. Gladys Goodding still played the organ between innings and after the game, and kids still gathered for autographs, and the ushers still took tickets, but already in 1957 it was beginning to seem inauthentic. The fans and the team were both caught playing out the string, and not even the return of Johnny Podres or the emergence of a 20-year-old kid pitcher named Don Drysdale, on his way to winning 17 games, was cause for much excitement. Hell, no one would get to see him grow anyway. And where was he from? *California.* Even that other kid, the one from Brooklyn, Koufax, was finally past the date he had to be kept on the roster, and all of a sudden it looked like he belonged. Early in the year he struck out 14 while beating the Cubs, and in June he was leading the league in strikeouts. He was starting to look good, and now Alston just stopped using him. Didn't it matter where he was from anymore? It didn't.

On September 1, the Dodgers threw in the towel on the season. Although Sal Maglie had pitched well when he could, that wasn't very often. Brooklyn just let him go, waived out the league. The Yankees picked him up for the stretch run, while the Dodgers, for the first time since World War II, played September baseball when the games meant nothing and October would be just another page on the calendar.

That's when the final, official, and irrevocable steps would be taken to send the Dodgers out of Brooklyn. Back on May 29 the National League had given its approval for both the Giants and the Dodgers to relocate to San Francisco and Los Angeles if they chose to do so. The Giants already had. On October 7, the L.A. city council, to no one's surprise, formally voted 10–4 in favor of conveying the 300-acre Chavez Ravine site to the Dodgers, as well as committing nearly $5 million in city and county funds for improvements. In exchange, the

only world championship in Brooklyn. Although he led the league in few individual honors and set no lasting records, he is unquestionably baseball's all-time leader in guts and courage.

To the Dodgers the loss of Robinson was like losing a leg. Without him, the team suddenly seemed to be exactly what they were—old and slow.

In 1957 they were never in the pennant race as the Braves finally fulfilled their promise. And as the season unfolded and it became clear that the Giants too were leaving New York, headed to San Francisco, there was little question that the Dodgers were destined to follow them.

Dodgers agreed to give up L.A.'s old Wrigley Field, home of the Angels, which they had acquired in the territorial swap with the Cubs. Brooklyn's formal announcement that they were moving would come the next day, October 8, with the release of a simple statement: "The stockholders and directors of the Brooklyn Baseball Club have today met and unanimously agreed that necessary steps be taken to draft the Los Angeles territory."

That would be simply the parting shot to a body already cold and dead. For by the time of Brooklyn's final home game at Ebbets Field, the move was a foregone conclusion.

The final game wasn't a party but a wake, and a poorly attended one at that — only 6,702 fans turned out. The crowd lifted Dodger attendance for the year to 1,028,258. Subtracting attendance at the handful of games in Jersey City left fewer than a million fans who had turned out at Ebbets Field, the club's lowest mark since 1944.

By the final game most Brooklyn fans, at least those that still cared to, had already said their good-byes to Ebbets Field, if they bothered at all. Now nobody wanted to put another nickel in Walter O'Malley's pocket.

No one brought up the names of Jim Creighton or Zack Wheat or Dazzy Vance or Bill McGunnigle or Wil Robinson or any of the hundreds and hundreds of names that made up the legacy of Brooklyn baseball. The future didn't exist, and neither did the past.

It was a quiet game, just another meaningless September contest between also-rans. Benny Daniels of the Pirates, in his first big league start, pitched opposite Brooklyn's Denny McDevitt. There were only a few dignitaries in attendance — Brooklyn borough president John Cashmore and Emmett Kelly, the sad-faced circus clown. Conspicuous in his absence was Walter O'Malley. Furillo and Snider didn't play. Gil Hodges started at third base, Campy was behind the plate, Jim Gilliam was at second, and Sandy Amoros was in left. Captain Pee Wee Reese started the game on the bench but came in late to play third after Hodges shifted back to first.

The Dodgers took an early 2–0 lead — Gil Hodges knocked in Gino Cimoli in the third inning for the final run. And in the bottom of the eighth, with the Dodgers still leading 2–0, Hodges became the last Dodger to bat. He struck out, and Gladys Goodding played "Say It Ain't So" on the organ.

McDevitt went the distance, getting Dee Fondy of the Pirates to ground out to Hodges for the final out of the game. After the final out, Tex Rickards, the PA announcer, warned fans not to go out on the field. "But use any exit that leads you to the street." Those words could have served as Brooklyn's epitaph.

As a few fans went down to the field anyway and tore up chunks of sod, a recording of the old Dodger theme song, "Follow the Dodgers," played for a moment on the PA before Gladys Goodding broke in on her own composition and finished with an oddly tuneful rendition of "Auld Lang Syne." Only a few dozen fans lingered for long in the stands behind the Dodger dugout. There were some tears, but mostly just silence.

Brooklyn and the Dodgers had come together at a special time, in a special place, with a special team. Now it was made even more special because it all just stopped, frozen in time, before any of those elements could deteriorate. They grew up, grew older together, and then it all just stopped. Pee Wee and Hodges, Oisk and Jackie, all not quite old enough to be considered old, Ebbets Field not yet quite falling down, old Brooklyn still just holding together.

Perhaps, in the end, that was the way it was meant to be, because for Dodger fans — Brooklyn Dodger fans — those days were never, ever going to be matched again anyway. America would never again be like it was those first years after the war, and neither would Brooklyn. For a split-second in time the pronouncement that "Brooklyn *is* America" had sounded neither boosterish nor boastful. The feeling that swept over everyone when Brooklyn won the 1955 World Series would never be repeated either. In a way, that was what made them special and makes them special still today. The Dodgers left Brooklyn, but they also left behind memories that, because of their departure, remain there still, pure and strong, a snapshot of the heart that has never dissipated or faded away.

The Dodgers then went on the road for the final three games of the season, wearing caps bearing the Brooklyn "B" for the last time. On their final day, September 29, they lost to the Phillies, 2–1.

Sandy Koufax pitched.

And L.A. was ga-ga.

1958–1961

GLADIATORS AT THE
COLISEUM

THE BUM WAS OFFICIALLY DEAD.

In Los Angeles he lost weight, got a shave, put on a toupee, went to the beach, and got a whole new wardrobe. He was another new Californian, a man with no past who before he had even unloaded the truck in the new apartment was invited to the cocktail party out by the pool, greeted by smiles of perfect white teeth, pulled to the dance floor to learn the cha-cha, and introduced to hordes of new best friends with names one never would have heard in Brooklyn. The team that in Brooklyn was steeped in tradition and the burden of history was free to reinvent itself. It would, and it did: by every tangible measure—attendance, profits, pennants, world championships—the L.A. Dodgers would outstrip the success of their predecessors in only a few seasons.

The trade-off, if there was one, may have been in terms of passion, but there was no way to measure that except in the cottage industry of nostalgia. In time that would grow to envelop the old Brooklyn Dodgers like so much ivy, obscuring the architectures

Dodger right-hander Don Drysdale was perfectly suited to the franchise's move to Los Angeles. The tall, imposing California native soon became a favorite of Hollywood long before his former high school baseball teammate Robert Redford made his mark as a leading man.

beneath the image, which over time would turn ever softer and more winsome.

Brooklyn's loss was L.A.'s gain. For most old Brooklyn fans, the Dodgers simply ceased to exist—few fans of the Brooklyn club would shift their allegiance to Los Angeles. L.A. looked at Dodger history, put it on the shelf like an old book, and moved on.

O'Malley's first challenge was to find a place to play, for even though he now had the land he so desired, the process of building a ballpark would take years and prove somewhat more problematic than he had imagined. By December 1957 opponents of the agreement that deeded Chavez Ravine over to the Dodgers had collected enough signatures that the entire question would have to be decided in a referendum of Los Angeles voters scheduled for June 3, 1958. If the referendum did not pass, the Dodgers would be left in a situation not dissimilar to the one they had faced in Brooklyn—playing in an antiquated facility. O'Malley, for all his assumed acumen in getting Los Angeles to give him everything he wanted, was really no more politically adept in L.A. than he had been in Brooklyn. He still didn't see the larger picture outside his own desires, and he failed to see the ramifications of what seemed to him to be reasonable requests. His early missteps gave his opponents a genuine chance.

Initially, the Dodgers expected to play their first season or two in Los Angeles in old Wrigley Field, the long-time home of the Pacific Coast League Los Angeles Angels. The park had been acquired by the city after the Dodgers swapped their rights to Fort Worth with Cub magnate Philip Wrigley, whose ballpark in Chicago also shared the name of his family.

But there was one enormous problem with L.A.'s Wrigley Field—it made Ebbets Field look big. At best—best—some 25,000 fans could be crammed into the simple, double-decked facility, although the official capacity of 22,000 was much more realistic. And like Ebbets Field, the park included virtually no parking or other lucrative amenities. It would be hard for the club to draw much more than 1.5 million fans there, and that was not quite what O'Malley had in mind.

The dimensions of the field itself proved another obstacle. While it was 412 feet to dead center field, it was only 345 feet to the power alleys—shorter than Ebbets Field and short enough to have turned players like Angel star Steve Bilko into local legends. While Dodger batters would certainly benefit from the park, the pitching staff would be shell-shocked. Even baseball commissioner Ford Frick considered Wrigley

Field inadequate for major league play. When the expansion Los Angeles Angels were forced to play there in 1961, the field would give up a record 248 home runs in only 81 games.

The club's other options were football stadiums—the Rose Bowl and the L.A. Coliseum, the eventual home of the team. Originally built for the 1932 Olympics, the Coliseum had since been used for just about everything but baseball—boxing, rodeos, religious rallies, track meets, car racing, and even, incredibly, ski jumping. But never baseball.

At length, and after a flirtation with the Rose Bowl, a compromise was reached that placed the Dodgers somewhat awkwardly in the west end of the Coliseum. That would create a notorious sun field in right and force many fans to stare toward the sun during the game. But it was even harder to fit the field inside. The diamond couldn't be aimed straight downfield, for that would leave each foul line under 200 feet. So the field was turned perpendicular, with the third-base line roughly parallel to the goal line. That left only 251 feet to the stands in left, a problem the club tried to fix by blocking the field off with a 40-foot screen 140 feet long into left-center, where the power alley was still only 320 feet. A chain-link fence would be installed in center and right, which was inexplicably deep—425 feet straightaway and 440 feet to right-center.

The stands themselves were no more accommodating, for they were simple bleacher benches with no backs. But there was room for thousands of cars. Despite the field's shortcomings, the Coliseum would be home.

Most fans didn't care about the field. The Dodgers were big league, and that meant L.A. was big league. Three dollars got you the best seat in the house, and there were a lot of them. They bought tickets in handfuls, not only for individual games but for the whole season. There were 17,500 box seats available for only $250 for the season and another 16,000 reserved seats for $180. The result was that by late January, when Brooklyn was still an icebox, the Dodgers had already sold nearly $2 million worth of tickets. In Brooklyn advance sales had never topped $800,000.

But the weather in New York still delivered a devastating blow. On January 27, 1958, Roy Campanella skidded on some ice after closing his Harlem liquor store, crashed his car, and was paralyzed for life (see prologue).

Campanella's tragic injury was symbolic of the changes about to take place on the Dodger roster as the team made the transition from the group Roger Kahn later dubbed "the Boys

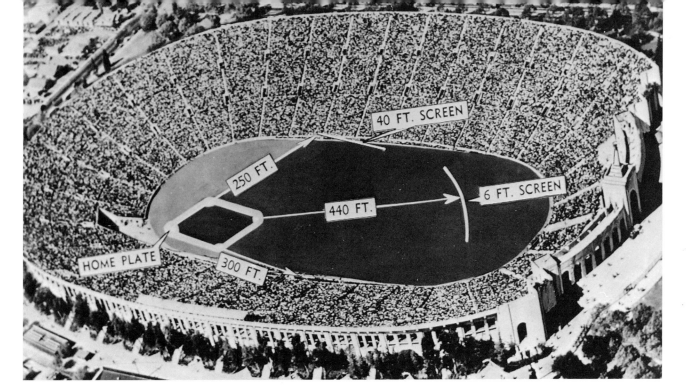

The Dodgers moved from one of baseball's coziest ballparks in Ebbets Field to the largest and quirkiest park of them all, the Los Angeles Coliseum. The makeshift park included two of the shortest foul lines in history as well as a towering 40-foot-high chain-link fence in left field.

of Summer" to a ballclub playing in an endless summer under the relentless sun. There was little romance in that.

The older Dodgers would be unable to make the transition. Although before the season Gil Hodges would offer that "the Coliseum should be a big help to right-handed batters," like himself, the results would say otherwise. No Dodger hitter would ever hit more than 14 home runs there in one single season. The Coliseum would rob both Hodges and Snider of their power — many of Hodges's long hits would smack into the screen for singles, and he later noted that because "the background is bad in the daylight," it was hard for anyone to hit there — and Snider's drives to right field would become some of the longest outs on record. Reese, at age 39 in 1958, was just about finished. The team would, at long last, have to turn to their farm system, but they would find no minor league talent there for playing in a ballpark made for speed, defense, and pitching. They were still stocked with players whose skills were more appropriate for Ebbets Field.

Before spring training the Dodgers found themselves part of a new Dodger public relations push. For years the Dodger front office had done the same old things the same old ways. But in L.A., with the help of a cooperative local press, they courted a giddy new constituency with a fervor they had never shown in Brooklyn. One can only wonder how much the drop in attendance in Brooklyn might have been countered had they tried similar campaigns there. In Los Angeles the club held endless clinics and tryouts in local parks, players were paraded before their new fans countless times in the off-sea-

son, cutting ribbons at store openings and endorsing everything, and the local press worked overtime running background stories on the history of the club. The *Los Angeles Times* ran a regular "Meet the Dodgers" feature on individual players and their families that let everyone know that this or that Dodger wife had joined the local ladies' club and was thrilled with her new home. Walter O'Malley in particular was lionized, as instantly popular in L.A. as he had been vilified in Brooklyn. He fed the press fictions that they presented as fact, diminishing Branch Rickey's historic role in the team history while exalting his own. One such puff piece in the *L.A. Times* even claimed that "O'Malley (and not Rickey) almost became the man to sign the first Negro for major league baseball." It made the specious claim that the Dodger owner had, at some point before Rickey signed Robinson, scouted and planned to sign a Cuban infielder only to have the Cuban military thwart his plans by drafting the young man.

In the Dodgers' first few seasons, coverage of the team would be overwhelmingly positive, almost an adjunct to the team's own public relations staff. Most ads in the sports section had a Dodger tie-in. The "Sunny Ranch" housing development in Fullerton "welcomes Dodgers." The local Sears store touted the "Silvertone" radio featuring a "magic disk" tuning device to "follow the Dodgers." ABC vending announced that it was "ready to feed the fans" at the Coliseum. Even song-meister Lawrence Welk, in ads for his twice-weekly show at the Aragon Ballroom, saw fit to send greetings to the club. The L.A. Chamber of Commerce almost required merchants to feature baseball in their storefronts.

Just before the start of the regular season the *Los Angeles Times,* in its Sunday magazine *This Week,* even went so far as to guarantee a Dodger pennant. Over the course of several weeks the "Royal Precision LGP-30 Datatron" computer was fed 12,000 baseball statistics for the last four seasons. Then, in 30 seconds, it concluded that the Dodgers would win the National League pennant with a record of 92–62. But in the same story baseball experts Joe DiMaggio, Dizzy Dean, and Bob Feller used different calculations to conclude that the Dodgers, at best, would finish second to Milwaukee, a con-clusion echoed by both Las Vegas oddsmakers and *Times* beat writer Frank Finch. He noted that after a spring in Florida fol-lowed by barnstorming through the Southwest on their way to L.A., "we'd like nothing better than to predict a pennant for our new horsehide heroes but as the club is now constituted it is too 'iffy' to merit a number one rating." He added that with Opening Day right around the corner, only Hodges, Gino Cimoli in left, and Carl Furillo in right were certain to start the season. Duke Snider was bothered by a bad left knee, and Alston had yet to make up his mind on who would play where in the infield from among Reese, Don Zimmer, Jim Gilliam, Charlie Neal, and rookie Dick Gray. And the pitching staff, apart from local hero Don Drysdale, was full of question marks.

But the Dodgers were not the only new team in California. The Dodgers opened the season on the road in San Francisco facing the Giants in their home opener at old Seals Stadium.

The first major league game played on the West Coast did not go well for the Dodgers. Don Drysdale, who drew the Opening Day start, suffered from wildness, and the Dodgers were futile against Giants starter Ruben Gomez's screwball. The Giants won, 8–0, although the Dodgers extracted a meas-ure of revenge the next day by thumping San Francisco 13–1

On April 18, 1958, a crowd of 78,672 at the Los Angeles Coliseum established a major league single-game attendance record but fell short of filling the 92,000-seat stadium. In their home opener, the Los Angeles Dodgers defeated the San Francisco Giants by a score of 6–5.

Dodger right fielder Wally Moon had the perfect right-handed swing for the left-field screen at the Los Angeles Coliseum. In his first season with the Dodgers in 1959, Moon hit 19 home runs. In this photograph he is crossing the plate after hitting a home run over the 40-foot screen in a 1961 game against the Reds.

combination of city civic leaders, businessmen, and Dodger officials, turned Opening Day into a daylong event.

After a welcome breakfast, the Dodgers gathered at 10:30 in the morning in uniform at city hall, where Mayor Norris Poulson officially welcomed them to town. Then O'Malley presented the mayor with his prize — home plate from Ebbets Field. It was inscribed "Los Angeles: We're Happy with the Move to Our New Home Base — the Dodgers," and signed by each member of the team.

The Dodgers thought they had seen it all back in Brooklyn, but this welcome wasn't like anything they had ever participated in before. Noted stripper Jennie Lee, known as "the Bazoom Girl," shimmied through the crowd, as the *Times* reported, "passing out advertising dodgers about her new strip set. She wore brief shorts and a tight jersey was lettered with the name of her team, the Barecats." After being given a California flag to fly over the Coliseum, the Dodgers and everybody who was anybody climbed into convertibles for an open-air motorcade to the ballpark. The press, more accustomed to reporting on movie premieres, covered the Dodgers like starlets. Every member of the team, it was noted, wore "white rubber shower sandals."

The parade threaded its way through downtown, where the players and their entourage were showered with confetti and occasionally slowed by crowds pressing for autographs and other memorabilia. At Eighth and Broadway, reported the *Times,* "a bevy of beauties in brief costumes pitched dozens of toy baseballs at the players," while on Seventh Street "a furrier threw out volleyballs covered with white fur made to resemble huge baseballs." Also in the parade was "a pretty girl dressed like a Dodger . . . in a golden chariot pulled by an ugly Giant." Then it was on to the freeways and to the Coliseum, where the players pulled into the lot at 11:30 and clip-clopped their way inside, but not before being surrounded by "gaily costumed senoritas from Oliviera Street . . . yanking off their caps and cracking their heads" with confetti-filled eggshells. If there was any remaining doubt, they were not in Brooklyn anymore.

The stadium was filling rapidly as many of the 78,672 fans arrived early to beat the traffic. The crowd included a who's who of the Hollywood elite, from Brooklyn native Danny Kaye to Jimmy Stewart, Burt Lancaster, Jack Lemmon, Nat King Cole, Danny Thomas, Gene Autry, Groucho Marx, and Ray Bolger, who mugged for the cameras under an Army surplus helmet labeled "L.A. Dodger Bean Ball Protector."

behind Johnny Podres. In the final game of the set the Giants beat Newcombe, who hurt his shoulder in the game, 7–4. That performance was the beginning of the end for Newcombe's career as a Dodger. He was drinking heavily and indifferent to the effects. Arguably the best pitcher in Brooklyn Dodger history, he failed to last the season and would never win a game for the Los Angeles edition of the Dodgers.

The Dodgers' 1–2 start didn't dampen enthusiasm in Los Angeles, where the only game anybody really cared about was the home opener on April 18. The Giants would return the favor by appearing in the Dodger home opener — each club was eager to jump-start what they both hoped would be a West Coast revival of the Dodger-Giant rivalry.

If there was anything L.A. knew how to do, it was how to hold a premiere party, and the city pulled out all the stops. The "Welcome Dodgers Committee," a group made up of a

Pregame ceremonies gave every politician in the crowd a chance to bask in the sun and the reflected glory of bringing big league baseball to Los Angeles. Mayor Poulson and his rival from San Francisco held a pitching duel. A choral group from the City Bureau of Music gave a concert. Assorted lesser dignitaries were installed in a special "coaches box" where they were supposed to provide Alston with strategic tips. And an 11-year-old boy won a newspaper contest for the honor of standing in for Roy Campanella when the players were introduced before the game. The ringmaster was another Hollywood symbol, actor and comedian Joe E. Brown.

And, oh yes, there was a game, although that seemed almost secondary. The Dodgers won, beating the Giants 6–5 behind Erskine and Dick Gray's home run, the first by an L.A. Dodger in Los Angeles. But the score seemed to matter about as much as the movie showing at a premiere—the fact that the movie was good was just icing on the cake.

It didn't matter to most Angelenos when the Dodgers took an almost immediate nosedive into the second division. They were on their honeymoon in 1958, at least with those fans who wanted baseball in Los Angeles. But that was a problem. Not everyone did—or at least, not everyone wanted the city to give O'Malley Chavez Ravine. As the referendum approached it became unclear whether or not it would pass. While polls over the winter indicated that some 70 percent of L.A. residents had once approved the deal, it was now a tossup. Old-time PCL fans and baseball purists were mortified by the conditions at the Coliseum and felt that O'Malley had pulled a bait-and-switch when he'd turned down Wrigley Field. He wouldn't broadcast the games on TV, and the growing number of retirees in the area felt shut out—listening to Vin Scully was fine, but in other cities fans could at least watch a game once in a while. A variety of opposition groups, from local morticians who wanted the site for a cemetery to social agencies worried about displaced residents to tightfisted taxpayers who thought the Dodgers were getting something for nothing all banded together to oppose the plan.

It didn't help that by the beginning of June the Dodgers were in last place. The Coliseum was proving to be a terrible place for hitters—there was too much glare during the day, and at night the lights were the worst in the major leagues. And the club's veteran pitchers—Erskine, Labine, McDevitt, Newcombe, and Craig—all had trouble getting untracked. A pitcher almost had to pitch backward at the Coliseum—hits were outs there and outs were hits. The only certain way to get a batter out was to keep him from hitting the ball at all. By midseason Alston had more or less thrown in the towel and settled on a rotation of Podres, Drysdale, Koufax, and rookie Stan Williams. Podres, at age 25, was the grizzled veteran by some three years.

As the June 3 date for the referendum approached, O'Malley and supporters of the measure grew increasingly nervous. Opponents spread the rumor that if the issue failed, O'Malley would pull out of town—perhaps even go back to Brooklyn. Ebbets Field, after all, was still there, the site of things like rodeos and car races. But win or lose, O'Malley was committed to Los Angeles. Although the Coliseum was the worst possible place to play baseball, at least for now fans were flocking to the facility and he was making money. The players hated it, but the bottom line ruled.

But not in everything—not quite. In regard to Roy Campanella, O'Malley stood tall. After some initial optimism in regard to his recovery, it soon became clear that Campanella would never walk again. He would remain paralyzed for life, in need of constant care. In the days before a strong players' union, when ballplayers had few rights and little protection, in a legal sense O'Malley and the Dodgers owed Campanella virtually nothing.

Yet O'Malley never stopped sending Roy Campanella a paycheck, and he never forgot him. He made certain that Campanella remained a part of the organization, employed by the club in some capacity, for the rest of his life. If one deems O'Malley a criminal for leaving Brooklyn, so be it, but his response to Campanella's tragedy reveals a level of sensitivity and compassion that also must not be ignored. As an organization, the Dodgers would stand up for the player who could not stand up for himself.

On the precipice of the referendum vote, known as "Proposition B" on the ballot, the Dodgers pulled out all the stops. Although O'Malley was enamored with the profit potential of a pay cable system known as Skiatron, problems both technological and political made the issue of pay TV an albatross. He backed off his opposition to televising Dodger games and in late April announced that the Dodgers had agreed to televise games against the Giants played in San Francisco on free TV.

Still, just a few days before the vote, with the outcome very much in question, desperate supporters of the measure sponsored a five-hour "Dodgerthon" on KTTV. The broadcast included a host of Hollywood stars such as Debbie Reynolds, George Burns, William Frawley, Danny Thomas, and Jack

NL ON-BASE PERCENTAGE LEADERS

1914	Casey Stengel	.404
1946	Eddie Stanky	.436
1952	Jackie Robinson	.440
1956	Duke Snider	.402
1961	Wally Moon	.438
1977	Reggie Smith	.432
1985	Pedro Guerrero	.425

it was nevertheless an important step, for it showed California's politically sensitive elected judiciary where the votes were.

The Dodger ballclub, unfortunately, continued their desultory play. By midyear they were clearly rebuilding. Don Newcombe was traded away, Reese mostly sat on the bench, and Snider and Furillo fought injuries. Koufax, Stan Williams, and Drysdale occasionally turned in impressive pitching performances, but the older Dodgers looked out of place at the Coliseum, waging a losing battle against its dimensions that made their skills disappear prematurely. The Dodgers finished seventh as Duke Snider slumped to 15 home runs and Hodges cracked only 22. Not since 1944 had the Dodgers suffered through such a dismal season.

In Brooklyn the club would have been excoriated for such a poor finish after so many years at the top. In L.A., hardly anyone noticed. Despite the problems at the Coliseum, where some seats were as much as 700 feet from home plate, the Dodgers drew nearly 2 million fans. Still, critics warned that once the shine was off, the Dodgers would need to win if they expected such crowds in the future.

They weren't quite as bad as they looked — or rather, seventh place wasn't as far from first as it looked. The National League was in transition, and baseball, which since the war had been in an age of offense, was starting to make a transition into an era when pitching and defense ruled, in part because many of the older, smaller parks such as Ebbets Field were beginning to be replaced by larger facilities. Over the next decade no team would be better positioned than the Dodgers to take advantage of that change.

In 1959 the club recognized that the Coliseum provided a unique opportunity. As awkward as it was for the Dodgers to play there, at least they became accustomed to its eccentricities. It was hard to hit home runs there, so the Dodgers stopped trying to. Opponents would out-homer them at the Coliseum, but the Dodgers would score more runs. Visiting teams never adjusted, and it soon became clear to the Dodgers that certain types of players were made for the park — namely, strikeout pitchers who kept the ball in the middle of the field and left-handed hitters who could take the outside pitch the other way. The Coliseum was not unlike Fenway Park — players who fit the park or made adjustments thrived there, while those who could not did not.

On December 4 the Dodgers made a deal that would pay a big dividend in 1959. Outfielder Gino Cimoli had tried to

Benny, all showing their support, and personal, ever more desperate appeals from O'Malley and Mayor Poulson. O'Malley made the claim that in Milwaukee the Braves were worth some $35 million to the local economy, while Poulson extolled the virtues of major league baseball as an effective tool to counter juvenile crime — both claims laughable on their face. The extravaganza ended with a welcome-home reception for the Dodgers as they returned from a road trip. An estimated 1.8 million viewers watched the telethon, and some 7,500 mobbed the airport.

Every vote mattered, and the result remained in doubt for several days while the ballots were counted. Finally, on June 6, it became clear that by the narrowest of margins, the Dodgers had won. Of more than 670,000 voters, the deal between the city and O'Malley was approved by just under 25,000 votes — barely a 5 percent margin.

While the vote would not end the opposition to O'Malley's plans, for opponents would continue to fight it in the courts,

hit the ball through the left-field screen, with little success, and when Alston had turned to other players, Cimoli had complained publicly. So the Dodgers swapped him for Cardinal outfielder Wally Moon. Moon was a good player coming off an off year and was suddenly the odd man out in the St. Louis outfield. But his defensive shortcomings would be hidden in left field at the Coliseum and his inside-out batting stroke from the left side was tailor-made for the park.

For the first time since 1940, Pee Wee Reese was not on the Dodger roster. He finally gave in to the inexorable erosion of his skills and retired. The only player on the team whose career had bridged the era of the Daffiness Boys to Los Angeles, who had been a teammate of both Fat Freddie Fitzsimmons and Don Drysdale, was gone. Only Zack Wheat had played more games in a Dodger uniform, but no Dodger had ever really meant more to the organization. For while the Dodger organization spun from MacPhail to Rickey to O'Malley and rode the emotional roller coaster of pennant races, playoffs, and integration, the one constant had always been Reese, their anchor and center, the bridge between various factions, black and white, northern and southern, regular and scrub. He made sure that in spite of anything else that

was going on, the players remained focused on baseball. After every game he remained in the clubhouse for hours, talking baseball and teaching, bringing the club together.

Some thought the L.A. Dodgers could not hope to win without his influence. They wanted Reese to take over as manager in 1959 — Alston's seventh-place finish left him vulnerable. Had Reese wanted the job, he probably could have had it. He didn't, although he agreed to stay on as a coach for the 1959 season. But he felt awkward in the role. Too many teammates were still on the roster.

In the early months of 1959 there was nothing, absolutely nothing, indicating that 1959 would be a special season. The old Dodgers were old, but the newer Dodgers — Moon, catcher John Roseboro, second baseman Charlie Neal — still suffered in comparison. The only person who predicted a Dodger

---

In his first full season with the Dodgers, right-hander Larry Sherry compiled a won-lost record of 7–2. In the 1959 World Series, Sherry was the big hero as he won and saved two games against the White Sox. In the sixth and decisive game, Sherry relieved starter Johnny Podres and picked up the win to secure the Dodgers' second world championship.

BLACK AND BLUE

Richard A. Johnson

THEIR RIVALRY SPANS THREE CENTURIES IN two states — first in one city, now in two. Like the most contentious blood feuds in professional sports — namely, the soccer wars fought between neighboring foes in flare-lit fury in cities like Madrid, Glasgow, Manchester, and Istanbul — the games between the Dodgers and Giants in Brooklyn, New York, Los Angeles, and San Francisco possess nothing short of operatic drama in even the worst of times. In the best of times their games exist in a dimension that binds players and fans across a time warp of shared memories.

Unlike the curious media-fueled "rivalry" of unequal partners that exists at Yankee Stadium and Fenway Park, the profanities traded between the Dodgers and Giants are almost always exchanged on the field and not in the stands. No curses here. Unless, of course, you still burn candles for Ebbets Field and the Polo Grounds and reserve your choicest expletives for the accursed houses of O'Malley and Stoneham.

Like their American League counterparts, the scope and magnitude of their battles grew from an enmity that existed before either franchise played a game. Shortly after the New York version of baseball won out as the nation's ballgame of choice over the "Massachusetts game," the best teams of the pre– and post–Civil War era played in Brooklyn and New York. Seventy years before Giant manager Bill Terry inquired if "the Dodgers were still in the league," the competition between the first and fourth largest cities in America as expressed in games between the Eckfords and the Atlantic

Club of Brooklyn was the topic du jour in saloons and salons alike. In the volatile atmosphere of the fastest-growing metropolis the world had yet seen, these teams were just more "gangs of New York."

It all started in Harlem on Friday, October 18, 1889, when the National League champion New York Giants hosted the American Association champion Brooklyn Bridegrooms at the Polo Grounds in the first postseason championship contest ever called the "world series." After the first four games in the eleven-game series ended in murky October twilight, Brooklyn held a commanding three-game lead. At this point both teams held banquets to both proclaim their superiority and sell more tickets. In the end the Giants swept the last five games of the series, and the Bridegrooms soon joined their rivals in the National League.

The rivalry born during the administration of Benjamin Harrison eventually became, and remains, baseball's best. From 1900 through the 2003 season the teams have played to nearly a draw, with the Giants holding a slender advantage of 1,040 wins versus 1,014 losses, which equals a difference of slightly less than one-quarter game per season.

Since 1890 the Dodgers have won 21 National League pennants and 6 World Series, and the Giants have weighed in with 18 National League pennants and 5 world championships. In the predivisional world of season-long pennant races, both teams finished second to each other on four occasions, including two memorable three-game championship playoffs won by the Giants in 1951 and 1962. Only purists

and San Franciscans remember the Dodgers' successive pennants in '65 and '66 won by margins of two games and one and a half games, respectively, over the Giants of Mays, McCovey, and Marichal.

On the East Coast the Giants were afforded the status of baseball royalty as the result of John McGraw's succession of championship teams populated with future Hall of Famers named Mathewson, Youngs, Ott, and Hubbell, among others. Across the East River, for nearly half a century, the Dodgers were America's quintessential lovable losers, led by characters like Dazzy Vance, Uncle Wilbert Robinson, and Babe Herman. Unlike the Giants, they won pennants only once or twice per generation.

The dynamic of the rivalry turned dramatically with the arrival of Jackie Robinson in 1947 and the subsequent relocation of the Dodgers to Los Angeles a decade later. Since the last Giant world championship in 1954, the Dodgers built one of the great ballparks and captured ten National League titles and all six of the franchise's world championships to date. In that same period the Giants built and abandoned Candlestick Park, then built and embraced Pac-Bell Park while playing and losing three World Series.

I am a Giant fan and have been ever since the early sixties, when my brother allowed me to "inherit" his Giant scrapbooks when he left for boarding school. Pasted on the cover of one of them was a color magazine photo of a smiling Willie Mays and the lines "Memories Are Made of This"—indeed. Another densely packed book was covered with a grainy black-and-white photo showing a Giant player hitting a catcher on the head with a bat. Only later did I ask my brother about the disturbing image and was told, "Oh, that was when Juan Marichal beat John Roseboro with his bat . . . the Giants hate the Dodgers . . . didn't you know that?"

Such was my introduction to the rivalry. In time I too created a Giant scrapbook, both literally and figuratively, and over the past four decades have savored the memories contained within. Many of these memories exist solely in the realm of imagination as inspired by radio broadcasts and box scores.

The most vivid of these experiences occurred in Milan, Italy, on October 3, 1993. After learning that my train connection to Paris was canceled owing to a strike, I retreated to a dimly lit hotel room near the Statione Centralle. There I fumbled with my Walkman and, much to my initial delight and ultimate dismay, found a static-rich Armed Forces Radio broadcast of the Dodger-Giant showdown on the final day of the season to decide the National League Western Division title.

The Giants had already won 103 games and after 161 games found themselves in a tie with the Braves. Only the Dodgers, who'd won just 80 games, stood between the Giants and a division title or a possible one-game playoff with Atlanta.

The familiar voice of Giant broadcaster Hank Greenwald described the scene: a sunny afternoon at Dodger Stadium on the 42nd anniversary of Bobby Thomson's "shot heard round the world," with Thomson in attendance seated next to Giant owner Peter Magowan. It was also the 31st anniversary of the Giants' best game ever at Chavez Ravine—namely, their other historic playoff-clinching victory over the Dodgers in Los Angeles.

It all seemed too perfect, and it was until the game started. Any fear that Giant rookie manager Dusty Baker might have perfectly imitated the inexplicably poor judgment displayed by his predecessor, Roger Craig, in big games was confirmed when a 21-year-old rookie named Salomon Torres surrendered five hits and five walks in three and one-third innings as part of the 12–1 rout suffered by the Giants.

Later that evening, in a short but necessary international telephone call to my brother in San Francisco, I listened to him complain that "Tommy Lasorda was practically waving pompons the entire game; you'd have been sick, just sick." I didn't feel the need to tell him I already knew all too well what had happened. As I hung up the pay phone and walked across the rain-coated cobblestones, I quickly remembered that the last Giant world championship had happened the year before I was born. Black and blue once again; I'd wait till next year.

Richard A. Johnson is curator of the Sports Museum, co-author of *Red Sox Century*, and photo editor of *Yankees Century* and this volume.

pennant was Dutch mind-reader Peter Hurkos, who'd taken over for Datatron as *This Week*'s resident prognosticator.

The highlight of the season appeared to take place on May 7. On that date the Dodgers held a benefit for Roy Campanella, an exhibition against the New York Yankees, who agreed to travel to L.A. at their own expense.

Over 93,000 fans packed the Coliseum. Another 20,000 or 30,000 milled around outside the park. Police had to stop general admission sales on three separate occasions to push fans back from the ticket booths to keep them from getting crushed.

Before the game started, Campanella was wheeled to a microphone near home plate to tremendous applause, welcomed, at last, to Los Angeles by nearly 100,000 people, most of whom had never seen him play an inning in person.

His "recovery" had been grueling. On several occasions pneumonia nearly took his life. He had limited use of his arms and hands, but that was all. Phantom pain tortured him. But earlier in the spring he'd attended spring training at Vero Beach, tutoring John Roseboro as best he could. And for the last month he had been in Los Angeles, attending every home game. It had taken nearly a year and a half, but he was back with the Dodgers, following them from Brooklyn to Los Angeles.

"I thank each and every one of you from the bottom of my heart," he said before a hushed crowd. "This is something I'll never forget as long as I live. . . . It's a wonderful tribute. I thank God I'm here and able to see it."

In between the fifth and sixth innings came the most poignant moment of the evening. The lights were turned off, and 93,000 fans lit matches and cigarette lighters in a silent tribute, bathing the field in a soft, golden, almost celestial glow.

Reality quickly returned. The Yankees won the game, which raised some $60,000 for Campanella, but two days later much of the goodwill was wasted when the front page of the *L.A. Times* showed pictures of sheriff's deputies carrying away displaced residents of Chavez Ravine against their will. A month earlier the California Supreme Court had ruled in favor of the land transfer, but some residents, despite the fact that land had been taken by eminent domain months earlier, were still balking at leaving their homes.

The Dodgers didn't need the bad press. Local TV stations splashed wailing residents on the news every night, and newspapers printed pictures of sheriff's deputies carrying crying women away from their homes. It mattered not that most

The Dodgers display their 1959 world championship banner at city hall in Los Angeles prior to the start of the 1960 season.

were squatters with no legal right to remain there anyway and that some were actually far better off financially than it appeared. The most notable family of protesters, the Arechigas, were soon revealed to be the owners of 11 other properties in L.A. That revelation quashed public sympathy for all the affected families and scotched further investigations into the matter by the city council.

The Dodgers wisely stayed silent. They let the politicians do the talking—Mayor Poulson called the whole event a "rigged demonstration."

Yet the incident raised a larger issue in regard to the Dodgers, one that they would struggle with in the future. It had been just over a decade since the Dodgers had led the way in the integration of baseball. Yet now there was little difference between the Dodgers and other major league baseball organizations in regard to minority issues. In the long run the Dodgers had not been much more aggressive in acquiring black and Latino players than a half-dozen other teams. And thus far, like virtually every other club, their front office remained lily-white. The incident over the displacement of the residents of Chavez Ravine served as a reminder that the signing of Jackie Robinson would not give the club a lifetime pass in regard to the issue. In fact, it would be decades before the club effectively reached out to L.A.'s enormous Latino population in any meaningful fashion.

By the time the controversy blew over in early June, the Dodgers were in fifth place. Although they trailed the Braves by only five games, the club was barely playing .500 baseball and giving little indication that the trend was about to end. Then, on June 5, the Dodgers brought up rookie shortstop Maury Wills.

Wills was a banjo-playing, banjo-hitting minor league veteran with five kids. In his ninth season in pro baseball, he still wasn't considered much of a prospect. The previous winter he had been sold conditionally to the Detroit Tigers, only to be returned. But he had just started switch-hitting and in 1959 he finally started to feel comfortable. At triple-A Spokane he thrived, hitting .313 while stealing 28 bases after adopting a philosophy in which he had promised himself that every time he reached first base he would "be daring." Besides, shortstop Don Zimmer was hitting only .212.

Wills began platooning at short with Zimmer, and soon the Dodgers went on a small run, winning seven in a row in late June to lift them more than ten games above .500 for the first time all year at 43–33. Wills didn't have a huge impact on

the club immediately. Entering September, he would barely hit above .200 and steal only seven bases for the year—but 1959 was the kind of season in which no team in either league was truly outstanding, where the smallest changes, like the addition of Wills, could have an enormous impact. In 1959 the Dodgers made a lot of those little changes.

Wally Moon, whose occasional blasts over the screen at the Coliseum were termed "Moon Shots" by the press, was a surprisingly effective hitter, particularly at the Coliseum. Young Larry Sherry emerged as one of the most effective relief pitchers in the league. He had shown little but speed without control since signing in 1953, but after learning to throw a slider while pitching in Venezuela the previous winter, he had suddenly become unhittable. And Roger Craig, after spending the first half of the year at Spokane, returned in late June and said, "I know I can help if they just let me pitch." He did—and finished the year with the best ERA on the staff.

The combination of Wills, Moon, Sherry, and Craig, plus the advantage the club enjoyed at the Coliseum, was just enough to put the Dodgers into the pennant race. After the seven-game winning streak in late June, the club hung in there for the next two months, playing .500 baseball. While the Giants tried to pull away and the Braves hung close, the Dodgers stuck close to both, although no one anywhere outside of L.A. considered the Dodgers a likely pennant winner. They were like the third wheel on a date, a team that general manager Buzzie Bavasi would later describe—accurately— as "the worst club ever to win a World Series."

In September the Giants slumped, allowing the opportunistic Dodgers to pull close. On September 19 they trailed the Giants by two games. Over the next two days, in the final three games ever played at San Francisco's Seals Stadium, Wills spurred the Dodgers to three wins, figuring in almost every scoring rally and knocking out seven hits in thirteen at bats—he hit .429 over the balance of the season. The sweep sent the Dodgers into first place and the Giants into a swoon that effectively ended their chances for a pennant.

That left Milwaukee, and over the next week the two teams mirrored one another, ending the season in a tie with so-so records of 86–68. The Dodgers won the coin flip and chose to play the final two games of the playoff at the Coliseum.

The first game was played in Milwaukee, where, despite the importance of the game, only 18,000 fans turned out to watch the Braves in what many believed would be a quick dismissal of the Dodgers. After pumping the stands full of fans since their arrival in 1954, Braves attendance was starting to erode. When McDevitt was knocked out in the second inning, the wisdom of the stay-at-home crowd seemed misplaced.

But Larry Sherry, a graduate of Fairfax High in Los Angeles, was in the midst of one of the greatest stretches of clutch pitching by any Dodger pitcher in history. Since September 11 he had given up only one run. He came on in relief and shut the Braves down the rest of the way as John Roseboro's home run proved to be the difference in the 3–2 win. The two teams then went to Los Angeles to decide the pennant.

Once again, in game two a Dodger victory seemed unlikely. Drysdale pitched against veteran Lew Burdette and was knocked out early. Entering the ninth inning, the Braves led 5–2 and Burdette was cruising.

The late afternoon start had left the Coliseum only half-full, still a big crowd but far short of capacity. By the ninth inning many were headed out to beat the traffic going home, an L.A. tradition that started at the Coliseum, where some fans came late and others left early purely because of the traffic. But they were also responsible for another L.A. tradition — the bugle-led "charge!" cheer, brought to baseball by Dodger rooters who were accustomed to using the cheer at USC football games. In the ninth inning, however, few fans were left to respond to the clarion call.

Then the Dodgers struck with a suddenness that left the Braves flat-footed. Moon, Snider, and Hodges all rapped singles to load the bases, bringing up Norm Larker. Don MacMahon and Warren Spahn rushed to warm up, but they didn't have enough time.

Burdette left a pitch over the plate, and Larker lifted a lazy fly ball to left field. In any other park played in by players older than Little League age, it would have been an easy out. But in the Coliseum it was off the wall. Moon and Snider read the hit perfectly and scored easily while Hodges made it all the way to third.

Now another one of the old Dodgers, Carl Furillo, took over. After Roseboro went out against MacMahon, Spahn came on to face Furillo. He needed a strikeout but gave Furillo a pitch to drive. He lofted a long sacrifice fly that scored Hodges and tied the game. From there, a brace of Dodger pitchers — Koufax, Labine, and Stan Williams — held the Braves scoreless. And in the 12th Furillo won the game when Felix Mantilla made a bad throw after making a great stop on a ground ball and Gil Hodges scored from second base. The Dodgers won, 6–5, and won the pennant, becoming the first team to do so after finishing in seventh place the year before.

The victory had been stunning in its ease and simplicity. Back in Brooklyn, pennants had been hard-fought affairs that lasted all season long and seemed always to require that the Dodgers overcome enormous odds in order to win — if they won a hundred games, so did some other team. The playoffs had been excruciating affairs that usually turned out badly. But in Los Angeles it was completely the opposite. The breaks all went the Dodgers' way, and a team that included no players in the starting lineup who could have played for the old Dodgers (save for the old Dodgers themselves) had somehow won the pennant.

Even the ballclub was surprised. They hadn't even issued World Series tickets. Now they had to print nearly 300,000.

Their good fortune continued in the World Series. The Yankees had a rare off year, and the Chicago White Sox stole past Cleveland to win the pennant. The "Go-Go" White Sox were not unlike the Dodgers, a quick, defense-oriented team deep in pitching. Their usual starting lineup included players whom few fans outside of Chicago would even remember as big leaguers — guys like Bubba Phillips, Jim McAnany, and Al Smith. In short, they were no better than the Dodgers, and the Dodgers were playing their best baseball of the year — they won 15 of their last 19 in the regular season. In such a strange season the Dodgers were fully capable of beating them.

And they did. After Craig was rocked in the opening game in Chicago, an 11–0 White Sox win as big Ted Kluszewski cracked two home runs, L.A.'s pitching took over, mainly in the form of reliever Larry Sherry.

In the third inning of game two, he came on in relief of Johnny Podres and gave up one run the rest of the way as Charlie Neal cracked two home runs in a 4–3 win. In game three, before 92,294 fans at the Coliseum — an all-time Series record — Furillo knocked in two runs with a pinch-hit single in the seventh. Drysdale pitched into the eighth, Sherry came on in relief, and the Dodgers won again, 3–1. In game four Sherry was the hero again. After the Dodgers erupted for four third-inning runs, Roger Craig tired in the seventh and the White Sox tied the score. But Sherry shut the White Sox down the rest of the way, and Gil Hodges floated a home run over the screen in right to give the Dodgers a 5–4 win. They were one game away from a most improbable world championship.

Alston wanted to pitch Sherry in game five — he'd been untouchable so far — but after pitching in three straight

Dodger wins, he needed some rest, and Alston could afford to gamble. Sandy Koufax got the call. No one quite knew what to expect from him, not even Koufax.

Frustrated by how his career was going, Koufax had almost quit the game entirely before deciding to give it another year or two. Koufax was getting better—much better—but Alston still put little faith in him. In June he had struck out 16 Phillies in a game that Frank Finch of the *Los Angeles Times* accurately called "one of the most remarkable strike-out performances in modern baseball history," ending only one strikeout short of Dizzy Dean's NL record. But then, inexplicably, over the next month he had barely pitched. In August Alston had stuck him in the rotation again, and on the last day of the month, in a must-win game, he had struck out 18 Giants—including 3 in the ninth on only ten pitches—to tie the major league mark. He even singled and scored what proved to be the winning run in the top of the inning. In his previous start he had struck out 13 in beating the Phillies, and in his next start, a 3–0 loss to the Cubs on September 6, he struck out 10 in ten innings, setting a major league mark with 41 strikeouts over three games.

But when he failed to win his next two starts—despite pitching relatively well—Alston forgot about him *again*. Over the last two weeks of the season Koufax had pitched only one and two-thirds innings, and in the Series he'd been absent apart from a mop-up appearance in game one.

Koufax, for a variety of reasons, just didn't sit well with Alston. He was Jewish, for one, and quieter and more remote than most ballplayers, something that for years Alston mistook as a lack of desire. He liked fiery, feisty ballplayers, "holler" guys, and Koufax's temperament put him off. In traditional baseball parlance, Koufax was considered a player with a "million dollar arm and a ten-cent head," too smart for his own good.

When pressed, Alston usually cited Koufax's lack of control as the reason he failed to stay in the rotation. It was true that, while he was often dominant, Koufax was also plagued by occasional bouts of wildness. Yet Alston never seemed to realize that lack of work was much of the reason Koufax struggled so much with his control. On the rare occasions when he pitched regularly, it wasn't much of a problem. In 51 innings over eight starts from mid-August to mid-September, he'd struck out 68 and walked only 26. But once he was relegated to the bullpen over the last two weeks, he had walked eight in less than two innings. Alston's attitude toward

In November 1960, Dodger owner Walter O'Malley shares his vision of Dodger Stadium with fellow major league owners, including Yankee co-owner and developer extraordinaire Del Webb.

Koufax was all or nothing. It was the dumbest of dumb luck that his abandonment of Koufax down the stretch hadn't cost his club a pennant.

In game five, before the third consecutive crowd of more than 90,000 at the Coliseum, Koufax gave Alston his all, turning in what was arguably the best Dodger pitching performance of the Series. Koufax was surprisingly economical, retiring the first seven hitters on 13 pitches. In the fourth, following singles by Nellie Fox and Jim Landis, the White Sox scored their only run on a double play. Before being pulled for a pinch hitter in the seventh, Koufax walked only one, struck out six, and gave up only five hits.

In any other game he would have won, but the Dodgers simply couldn't get the big hit against Bob Shaw and the White Sox relief staff. The White Sox won, 1–0, to send the Series back to Chicago.

For once, it wasn't close. The Dodgers jumped on Early

Wynn to take an 8–0 lead. And when Johnny Podres faltered in the fourth, Alston turned again to Larry Sherry. He shut the White Sox down the rest of the way. Somehow, the Dodgers were world champions.

What had taken generations to accomplish in Brooklyn had taken only two seasons in Los Angeles. It almost didn't seem fair, and plenty of naysayers tried to diminish the Dodger accomplishment by blaming conditions at the Coliseum for the White Sox demise. One Chicago columnist wrote that playing baseball in the Coliseum was "more than a joke. It was a travesty." He railed against the unfair advantage the Dodgers gained from "the matted grass and cement hard infield skin . . . no longer will our heroes have to look blindly into the glaring California sun and try to pick out a tiny sphere in a kaleidoscope of 92,000 sports shirts and blouses."

True enough, but that was mostly sour grapes — the White Sox had actually out-hit the Dodgers in the Coliseum, and the Dodgers had taken two of three in Chicago during the Series. While there is no question that the Dodgers, with a .590 winning percentage at home, had benefited from playing in the Coliseum during the regular season, they won the pennant on merit. Beginning with the sweep of San Francisco in mid-September, they'd won seven of nine on the road down the stretch. The Coliseum hadn't helped them then.

O'Malley was ecstatic. The Dodgers returned to L.A. on October 9 — his birthday — and were met by 5,000 fans. More than 2 million had made their way into the Coliseum during the regular season, and another 270,000 during the World Series. Including the All-Star Games and the Campanella benefit, more than 2.5 million fans had seen the Dodgers play at the Coliseum in 1959. No team in baseball had ever drawn so many fans anywhere. In the only ways that mattered to O'Malley, the move to Los Angeles had been an incredible success. In a new ballpark there was no telling what would happen.

In the wake of the victory, the U.S. Supreme Court confirmed rulings by their California counterparts that upheld the validity of the city's contract with O'Malley. At long last the final hurdle in the construction of the ballpark at Chavez Ravine was gone. Although O'Malley still saw fit to complain that the two-year delay had upped the cost of his ballpark by $2.5 million, the surprise world championship made that affordable. Already crews were at work moving earth in the ravine, even leveling an entire hill. To accommodate the park and surrounding construction, contractors would eventually move more than 8 million cubic yards of earth.

In the design of Dodger Stadium, O'Malley would get it right. Since he didn't have to worry about inclement weather in California, he had abandoned his plans for a domed stadium. Architect Emil Prager, faced with no other affordable option, wisely chose to work with the terrain instead of against it. To place a ballpark, parking lots, and access roads amid the gullies and hills of Chavez Ravine, he created a unique tiered design that created 21 separate, terraced parking lots that fed fans into the ballpark on six different levels. As much as Ebbets Field had been a ballpark of the past, Dodger Stadium would be one of the future. It was the only park built after Yankee Stadium in 1923 and before Royals Stadium in 1973 that would prove to be an architectural, financial, and artistic success. Even compared to many of the more contemporary retro parks, such as those in Detroit and Texas, Dodger Stadium remains a superior facility.

In many ways Dodger Stadium would be the anti–Ebbets Field — symmetrical, spacious, comfortable, and enormous. And in its own way, it was as reflective of Los Angeles as Ebbets Field had been of Brooklyn — a centrally located urban park would have been as out of place in L.A. as a park in the desolate expanses of Flushing Meadows would have been for Brooklyn. Yet the two radically different parks would share one significant trait. Dodger Stadium would be different enough from other parks that it would be possible for the Dodgers to build a team to fit the park. The Coliseum, for all its many faults, had already proven there were advantages to that.

O'Malley hoped that his new ballpark would be ready for the 1961 season, but a series of delays, many caused by landslides after heavy rains that moved hundreds of thousands of yards of earth to the wrong places at the wrong time, would push its opening day back to 1962. Meanwhile, the team stayed in the Coliseum.

For much of the next two seasons the franchise was on hold as work continued on Chavez Ravine, but no one really cared. The goodwill from the surprise world championship spilled over, and more than four million fans would travel to the Coliseum in the next two seasons to watch the Dodgers.

The team continued to slough off its Brooklyn roots. In 1959 Gil Hodges, Duke Snider, and Carl Furillo all took on secondary roles with the team. Furillo was released only a few days after the start of the regular season. He claimed he was injured and was protected by his contract. When the Dodgers disagreed, Furillo sued and eventually won his salary for

1960 — a significant event in the history of player-owner relations, but a bitter end to Furillo's career.

Although Maury Wills established himself as one of the most exciting players in the game — stealing 50 bases and hitting .295 — and gargantuan rookie Frank Howard, who stood 6'7" and weighed 255 pounds, hit 23 home runs, the 1960 Dodgers had a hard time scoring runs. They finished with a record of 82–72, just a few games off their record in 1959, but good enough for only fourth place behind surprising Pittsburgh. For all intents and purposes, they were never in the pennant race.

By 1961 the only players left from Brooklyn were Snider, Gilliam, Neal, Drysdale, Koufax, and Podres. Newcomers like Howard, Wills, and a trio of young outfielders, Ron Fairly and Willie and Tommy Davis, were becoming the club's key players.

The new Dodgers weren't quite ready in 1961. They were close, but like Dodger Stadium, their construction wasn't quite complete. After floundering for much of the first half, they surged into first place after winning an incredible 19 of 22, then experienced a landslide of their own, losing 11 in a row before bobbing back upright and making another late charge.

Koufax in particular had finally shown signs of becoming a big winner. Although in the Koufax myth his transformation was no more than a matter of finally learning to throw strikes, the truth was a bit more complicated. Beginning in 1960, when Alston finally put him in the starting rotation and left him alone, Koufax made a number of small adjustments that resulted in improved control, if not in results. He'd finished 8–13 in 1960.

In the spring of 1961, his improvement continued. He took advantage of the groundbreaking work being done by club statistician Allan Roth.

Roth had been on the Dodger staff since the days of Branch Rickey, accumulating all manner of arcane baseball statistics, breaking down performances at home and on the road, batting averages and earned run averages, against left-handers and right-handers, keeping track of pitch counts, etc. While keeping such stats is commonplace today, at the time no one besides Roth was performing such tasks for a major league team. Even on the Dodgers, most of his work

went virtually ignored — Roth was, after all, a Rickey hire. He compiled the usual baseball stats for visiting writers and for use in team publications, but most of his work was essentially ignored. The Dodger front office looked at his data and found it interesting, but rarely used it in their decision-making.

In the spring of 1961 Roth shared some of his findings with Koufax. His numbers had identified some troublesome areas for the pitcher — in particular, pitching to left-handed hitters and throwing strikes on the first pitch. When Roth showed him the numbers, Koufax instantly saw their logic and made the necessary adjustments.

The change he made to the angle of his curveball instantly made him much tougher for lefties to hit. And once Koufax saw the difference in a hitter's batting average when he threw a first-pitch strike and when he didn't, the old saw that the most important pitch in baseball is the first one was driven home dramatically. That insight, coupled with his own mental maturity, suddenly made him one of the best pitchers in baseball. He won 18 games in 1961, led the league in strikeouts, and more important, finally won over Alston for good. At long last the manager stopped jerking him in and out of the starting rotation after a loss.

At the end of the season, after 314 games over the course of four seasons, the Dodgers bade the Coliseum farewell. As Jim Murray of the *Times* noted, "The coast-to-coast sighs of relief were enough to post storm warnings." Yet for the Dodgers, their four years at the Coliseum had been a rousing success. They'd shed Brooklyn like an old coat and made money, for more than 8 million fans had passed through the turnstiles and consumed 12 million hot dogs, 16 million bottles of soda pop, and untold gallons of beer. (Even though sale of the beverage was banned at the Coliseum, fans had proven adept at smuggling it inside.)

But more important, the Coliseum had given the Dodgers an enormous competitive advantage — the club was 173–140 there — and taught them that it was not only possible but perhaps even preferable to win with a team built around pitching. In Brooklyn they might never have figured that out. The results were irrefutable — a pennant and a world championship.

After all, champagne was much better than beer.

NO RUNS, NO HITS, FEW ERRORS

AN OLD BALLPARK IS AN ARCHITECTURAL MEMOIR. A SOUND, A SMELL, AND a glance almost anywhere can cause a flood of memories. That's the way it had been, once upon a time, at Ebbets Field, where even when the park was empty the center-field bleachers echoed with the sound of Hildy Chester and her cowbell and the ghost of Jackie Robinson danced down the third-base line.

Dodger Stadium had none of that—yet. But in 1962 the Dodgers would begin to fill their new park with memories of their own and create a new history for the team. Their legacy would be different from that of the team that had called Brooklyn home, but in its own way it would fit the place just as the old Dodgers had fit Brooklyn. The Dodgers' first four years in Los Angeles had been wonderful, but playing in the Coliseum with a team still dominated by members of the old Brooklyn Dodgers somehow felt a little false. Now, with a home of their own, the Dodgers were prepared to become a full working part of Los Angeles. If L.A., in

Dodger Stadium was a baseball-only oasis in a "desert" of parking spaces. One of the main differences between Brooklyn and Los Angeles was that there were no trolleys to dodge in freeway country. For better or worse, Dodger Stadium served as the model for most of the baseball and multisport stadiums built in the 1960s and early 1970s.

the words of one observer, was "thirty-two neighborhoods in search of a city," the Dodgers, far more than Hollywood, Disneyland, or any other local attraction, embraced the identity of Los Angeles itself.

As Dodger Stadium had slowly risen in Chavez Ravine, so too had a new Dodger organization. The windfall of money that had landed in the team coffers since the move to Los Angeles had been poured back into the team, paying for both Dodger Stadium ($18 million) and the farm system, which, after years of decay, was now, at nine clubs, the biggest in baseball. General manager Buzzie Bavasi and Fresco Thompson, who was in charge of player development, were disciples of Branch Rickey, and it showed. Before the season, Thompson claimed, "We have spent over $3 million in bonuses to youngsters since coming to Los Angeles." Only four players on the forty-man roster hadn't been schooled in the Dodger farm system, and L.A. Dodger dollars had already delivered promising young players like USC bonus baby Ron Fairly and Willie Davis to supplement the last wave of players signed while the team was in Brooklyn, like Brooklyn native Tommy Davis.

With the opening of Dodger Stadium, the Dodger kitty was destined to grow even larger. Apart from an annual $350,000 payment to the city, O'Malley would keep almost every dollar the new facility made. The expansion Los Angeles Angels, who had played at Wrigley Field in 1961, would be the Dodgers' tenant beginning in 1962 until their own park in Anaheim was completed for the 1966 season. What little impact they had on the Dodger gate was more than offset by their rent—either $200,000 or 7.5 percent of net receipts, whichever was larger. The Dodgers also received half their concession receipts and all parking revenue, and they forced the Angels to pay half the maintenance costs for the park.

There was no lack of optimism before the 1962 season. When the oddsmakers in Las Vegas installed the Dodgers as 2–1 favorites to win the pennant, the players unashamedly agreed, and most echoed Maury Wills's comment that "the Dodgers should make a runaway of the race. We're that much better as a team."

They were. Everyone was a year older and presumably a year better. The old Dodgers had been replaced by a new team, one built around speed, pitching, and defense. Almost everyone could run, and with Koufax, Drysdale, Podres, and Stan Williams, backed by Sherry and reliever Ron Perranoski, the Dodgers had the best pitching in the league. They were so

confident that in the off-season they shipped Charlie Neal to the Mets for outfielder Lee Walls and $100,000. Earlier, the club had lost both pitcher Roger Craig and Gil Hodges to the Mets in the expansion draft, and several other spare parts to the new Houston Colt 45's. The moves didn't hurt the team at all, but cleared the way for a new wave.

Oh yes, the Mets. The new club aimed to fill the baseball void in New York left by the Dodgers and Giants. There was a new stadium in the works in Flushing Meadows, right where Robert Moses wanted it. It was even designed by Emil Prager, who had done similar work on Dodger Stadium. But Prager's New York park, Shea Stadium, would be a multi-use facility built by committee. The end result would be ugly and utilitarian, nothing like Dodger Stadium at all, a contrast that would not be lost on O'Malley. In the meantime, the Mets would play at the Polo Grounds. Ebbets Field was no more. It had been torn down in 1960, replaced by apartments.

Many Mets fans would be old Brooklyn Dodger fans, or their children, something the new club recognized. In addition to Neal, Craig, and Hodges, the Mets roster at one time also included ex-Dodgers Don Zimmer, Clem Labine, Billy Loes, and Joe Pignatano. Since the Dodgers had moved to Los Angeles, Brooklyn fans had left baseball behind. They couldn't bring themselves to root for the Yankees and wouldn't let themselves continue to root for the Dodgers of Los Angeles. For a few years the New York papers had given both the California editions of the old New York clubs extra attention, but they had stopped when they discovered that the allegiance of their old fans did not extend beyond New York's boroughs. Still, having the National League Mets in New York meant that in 1962 the Dodgers, in a sense, would be going back home for a visit.

On Opening Day, April 10, Dodger Stadium was unveiled in all its splendor. And it was something. Jim Murray almost ran out of similes when he called it the "Taj Mahal, Parthenon, and Westminster Abbey of baseball." And that wasn't the half of it.

Dodger Stadium represented a new paradigm, an exponential leap in ballpark design. With the faux nooks and crannies and brick faces of other contemporary ballparks stripped away, one can see that their model is Dodger Stadium. It was the first park designed with the comfort of the fan in mind—there were no poles, no uncomfortable or terribly distant seats, no steep concourses, no enormous lines at the concession stands, no cramped and confusing layouts. Fully 70 percent of the seats were within the infield, and it was built only for baseball, with no accommodations made for other sports.

Yet at the same time, in a sense, Dodger Stadium also helped inspire the horrific "cookie cutter" multipurpose stadiums of the 1970s, such as Cincinnati's Riverfront Stadium. Those parks would combine the worst aspects of Houston's Astrodome — minus the dome — with innovations that were first on display in Dodger Stadium, such as the multi-decked, cantilevered stands, color-coded seats, and massive electronic scoreboards. But in "stadiums" that were also made for football and lacked architectural elegance, paid no attention to detail, and were not organically adapted to the surrounding landscape, these features were empty gestures. Like Frankenstein, these awkward and monstrous amalgamations would not long survive. After 40 years Dodger Stadium, however, still seems almost brand-new and as a privately owned facil-

STADIUM OF THE STARS

Of the major league ballparks built after Yankee Stadium opened in 1923 and before Dodger Stadium was opened in 1962, none remain. Cleveland's Municipal Stadium, Milwaukee's County Stadium, Baltimore's Memorial Stadium, and Candlestick Park in San Francisco — all have been torn down. Dodger Stadium is now the fourth-oldest major league park, younger than only Fenway Park, Wrigley Field, and the House That Ruth Built. Incredibly, it has outlasted nearly a dozen ballparks and stadiums built after 1962 that have already been demolished — in Cincinnati, Pittsburgh, Philadelphia, Seattle, Houston, and Arlington, Texas, ballparks have been built, used up, and torn down. If there is one thing Walter O'Malley got right, it was Dodger Stadium.

When Dodger Stadium first opened, even though it was a cutting-edge facility full of new features, it did not appear as such. It still looked, and felt, like a ballpark, albeit a very clean one, and one as appropriate to its setting in Chavez Ravine and to its city as Fenway Park is to the Fens and the city of Boston. All the new features of Dodger Stadium served not the facility but the game, rather than the other way around. Most of the parks built after Dodger Stadium that have not survived shared the same flaw — the features served the building first. Monstrosities such as Riverfront Stadium in Cincinnati and the Astrodome were obsolete the day

they opened, for they had been built as if the game of baseball — their primary tenant — was an afterthought and the needs of baseball fans weren't worthy of consideration.

Dodger Stadium has survived because it is a baseball-only, integrated facility in which everything is focused on the field and fan comfort is paramount. When it first opened, the stadium was surrounded by 38 parking areas with a capacity of 16,000 cars, all color-coded to seat location so that fans could move from the parking area to their seats without climbing stairs or negotiating ramps. Tickets were also color-coded, as one observer noted, "to correspond with the hues of the section," with field level in yellow, the loge level in orange, the Stadium Club and dugout boxes in red, yellow, and blue, the third tier in green, and the top tier in blue.

Fully 70 percent of the seats were on the infield, and all seats offered an unobstructed view of the entire field and featured the then-revolutionary seat widths of between 19 and 22 inches, far more spacious than the then-standard 18 inches. Traffic, the great fear of southern California, proved not to be so bad as had been feared, and the game's largest scoreboard, at 75 by 34 feet, kept fans informed.

But perhaps the greatest innovation of the park was its recognition that while all fans deserve comfortable seats and unobstructed views, they are not all cre-

ated equal. The concept of the luxury box, the economic engine of specialty seating that drives ballpark construction today, can first be seen in the original Dodger Stadium.

Dodger Stadium allowed fans to pay for increasing levels of service. The park featured the exclusive Stadium Club and posh Diamond Room, which catered to the needs of stars and big shots in a city that made stars out of unknowns and big shots big. The innovative dugout boxes, on the same level and offering the same view as the dugout, were created for a select 234 patrons, the crème de la crème, and offered other fans a chance to see the stars on parade, go to work the next day, and say, "I saw Sinatra at the game last night."

In that way Dodger Stadium, and hence the Dodgers, responded to the aspirations of Los Angeles, a city of stars accustomed to special treatment, and, even more important, to the aspirations of those who aspired to be treated as stars even if they weren't. The result was that from the beginning, going to Dodger Stadium was perceived as an experience just a little bit more special, a little more exclusive, than simply going to watch a ballgame. As many as 56,000 fans, ushered back and forth by hundreds of nattily attired attendants, were made to feel not only welcome but even pampered.

In Dodger Stadium the fan has always been the real star.

Dodger Stadium opened in 1962 as baseball's version of the Hanging Gardens of Babylon. The park was deemed one of the most spectacular in sport. Yet for all its parking spaces and other amenities, it initially lacked public drinking fountains.

ity still sends virtually all its revenue directly into the Dodgers' coffers.

Only a few glitches marred Opening Day; most of the 52,564 fans in attendance wisely arrived early, and the predicted traffic jams weren't as bad as expected. The elevators operating between various levels weren't adequately marked, thousands of moths mysteriously hovered over the stands, the foul poles were mistakenly placed in foul territory, and there were no water fountains for patrons. The cynical viewed that as a plot by O'Malley to force fans to buy beverages—including beer, which the club was now allowed to sell.

The players were impressed. Hitters like Ron Fairly and Willie Davis, both of whom had thrived on the road but struggled at the Coliseum, were thrilled with the hitting background and the equity of the park's dimensions. There would be no so-called Chinese home runs at Dodger Stadium. And pitchers loved it, for in the spacious park it was 330 feet down the line but 385 feet to the power alley and 395 to center field.

Opening Day didn't go as planned: the Dodgers and Johnny Podres lost to the Cincinnati Reds, 6–3. But in the second game Sandy Koufax announced that his performance in 1961 had been no fluke as he shut down the Reds 6–2 behind Jim Gilliam's home run, the first by a Dodger in the new park.

The Dodgers were off and running—literally. After leading the NL in stolen bases in 1960 with 50 and with 35 in 1961, in 1962 Wills ran like no one had run in 50 years. He said he felt that there was "no such thing as an unimportant stolen base," and in 1962 he set out to prove it. Nearly every time the Dodger leadoff hitter had the opportunity to run, he did, whether the Dodgers were ahead or behind, no matter what baseball's fictitious "book" said, for Wills felt that the stolen base caused a cumulative disruption, changing the way pitchers pitched, catchers caught, and infielders fielded. Jim Gilliam was the perfect man to hit behind him: a patient player, he was adept at taking pitches and gave Wills the opportunity to run, then moved him along so the Dodgers' big hitters—Willie and Tommy Davis and Frank Howard—could knock him home. Tommy Davis in particular seemed to have a knack for knocking in Wills. Both Davises seemed ticketed for superstardom—Tommy Davis looked every bit the equal of Willie Mays, and Willie Davis's potential seemed unlimited.

By the end of May, Wills had already stolen 27 bases in 49 games. Every time he got on base Dodger fans chanted, "Go, go, go," driving the opposition nuts. Wills was the toast of L.A. Leo Durocher had taken over as third-base coach in 1961, and he gave the Dodgers entrée into Hollywood. Players like Wills became celebrities equal in status to the likes of Frank Sinatra, with all the same perks.

But pitching was where the Dodgers separated themselves from the pack, and Koufax separated himself from the pack of Dodger pitchers. On April 24 against Chicago, he tied the major league strikeout mark again with 18 strikeouts against the Cubs, and his performance seemed to inspire Don Drysdale to new heights. The tough right-hander, known for brushing back hitters at any time, was at his intimidating best. Together, he and Koufax were the best two pitchers in baseball.

On Memorial Day the first-place Dodgers came back to New York to play the Mets for the first time, and while they were not quite greeted as conquering heroes, they were not blamed for what their old fans saw as O'Malley's crime. Koufax, the last Dodger to pitch for Brooklyn, became the first to pitch in New York again, winning 13–6 despite giving up thirteen hits, the most of his career.

He made up for it a month later against the Mets at Dodger Stadium. He struck out the side on nine pitches in the first inning and then got better. Although he walked five and struck out "only" thirteen, no Met touched him for a base hit. Koufax pitched a no-hitter, something Dodgers beat writers were learning was a possibility almost every time he pitched.

Koufax was untouchable — his high-riding fastball and backbreaking curve, both thrown with impeccable control, were a devastating combination. And also one that would take a horrific toll.

Koufax threw *a lot* of pitches, most of them as hard as he could. Since batters didn't hit the ball very often, it often took Koufax 15 or 20 pitches to get through an inning, and his game totals were regularly well above 100. As the earlier game against the Mets demonstrated, Alston rarely pulled him from the game — even with a big lead, even with a great bullpen. Although the Dodgers were playing great and were in first place, they couldn't quite shake the Giants, and Alston was riding the team hard, particularly Koufax and Drysdale. In comparison, the other starters — Podres, Stan Williams, and a couple of kids, Joe Moeller and Pete Richert — were struggling. They got the bullpen.

In Koufax's next start he went the distance in a 16–1 win over the Phillies. But all was not well.

Since April the index finger of his left hand had been numb. Koufax ignored it — he was pitching well. As Koufax later recalled, "It had a white, dead look about it . . . as if it had been made in wax." He'd periodically show it to Alston and the team medical staff, and they would nod their heads and do nothing. But over his next two starts the numbness — and the "white, dead look" — began to expand to his entire hand.

Yet Koufax kept pitching until finally, in a game against Cincinnati on June 17, the finger split wide open. Finally, the club sent Koufax to a specialist. He had a blood clot. The fin-

ger was close to developing gangrene and dangerously close to the point where it might have been amputated.

Fortunately, through the use of blood-thinning medication and other drugs, the finger was saved, but Koufax was essentially done for the year. Had the Dodgers responded to his complaints earlier, the condition might well have been taken care of before it progressed to the point where it had nearly cost him his career. Despite their experience with Pete Reiser, Karl Spooner, and a host of other players over the years, the institutional attitude of the club in regard to injuries, even injuries to a player like Koufax, was unchanged. Although most teams at the time exhibited similar callousness toward player health, few were as cavalier as the Dodgers, and under Alston they weren't becoming more compassionate. Managing each season on only a one-year contract, he played for now. Koufax, in the end, would be another victim.

The Dodgers responded to Koufax's loss by surging. They won 17 of their next 21, expanding their lead over the Giants to five and a half games.

Credit Wills and Tommy Davis. Wills kept stealing, Davis kept knocking him home, and fans continued to pour into Dodger Stadium. Crowds averaged nearly 40,000 a game.

On September 16, after the Dodgers engineered a triple steal to beat the Cubs 6–4, they led the Giants by four games with only thirteen left to play. As the *Times* noted: "The Dodgers' magic number is ten . . . to give you a faint idea of how perilous the Giants' position is, should Los Angeles win only seven of its remaining thirteen, the Giants would have to win eleven of thirteen just to tie." Fans and players alike considered the World Series a sure thing. Most were more concerned about whether or not Wills would set a new record for stolen bases.

Ty Cobb had set the modern mark of 96 in 1915. On September 20, with the Dodger lead still four games with eight to play, just as it looked as if Wills would not only catch but pass Cobb, baseball commissioner Ford Frick chose to inject himself into the story. One year earlier he had elected to protect Babe Ruth's hallowed single-season home run record by adding the asterisk to Roger Maris's mark: because the length of the season had been expanded, he had played in more games than the Bambino. Now Frick did the same to Wills to protect Cobb. Frick said that Cobb's mark was "based on a 154-game schedule" and that to gain the record Wills had to steal a like number in the same number of games. But through 154 games in 1915, Cobb had stolen only 94 bases. Because of two tie games, the Tigers had played 156 games that season, and Cobb had stolen two additional bases. According to Frick's convoluted logic, however, 156 games in a 154-game season for Cobb equaled 154 games played for Wills.

Wills, with 94 steals in 153 games, was understandably bitter and disheartened. "I may as well forget trying to break Ty Cobb's record," he said. "I wish I'd known earlier . . . I could have taken some more chances in Milwaukee [earlier] and maybe could have gotten five or six stolen bases." Frick's ruling in regard to Maris had been bad enough, but at least he had made the point well in advance of Maris's record-breaking blast and his decision had been based on some kind of logic. In regard to Wills, by contrast, Frick was changing the rules at the last minute, grasping at any kind of straw to diminish Wills's achievement and preserve the name of Cobb atop the leaderboard. Not only was the ruling absurd, but its timing smacked of racism.

The next day, against St. Louis, Sandy Koufax returned to the mound for the Dodgers. He was eager to see if he could pitch before the start of the World Series. More significantly, Alston was getting impatient and already beginning to panic, even though he had no reason to apart from his own insecurity. He hadn't really wanted Durocher on his staff, and the presence of the Dodgers' ex-manager, who often ignored Alston's signs for his own, didn't make him feel secure. "Starting Koufax is not an experiment," said Alston, "it is a

necessity" — to keep a leg up on Durocher. Podres's back was giving him trouble, he added, and "we need all the pitching we can get for the stretch run."

But Koufax was bombed, and the Cardinals won 11–2. Wills stole base number 95 in game 154, ahead of Cobb's pace, but according to what Frank Finch of the *L.A. Times* gently referred to as Frick's "peculiar thinking," he was somehow not eligible for the record. Podres, his back miraculously better, pitched the next day, and the Dodgers won their 100th game of the year, reducing their magic number to four as Wills was kept in check.

Drysdale fell the next day to St. Louis, 12–2. And Wills forced Frick's hand by stealing two bases, giving him 97 in 156 games, one better than Cobb. Now the commissioner grudgingly admitted, "It's a record, whether we say it's a record in 162 games or not, there's no question it's a new record." But the Giants won that day too, and the lead was down to three games.

Over the next two days, September 25 and 26, the Dodgers split with Houston, losing 3–2 in ten innings in a game

---

Shortstop Maury Wills was quite the man about town in 1962, when he broke the major league single-season stolen base record. Wills was also a talented musician and made frequent appearances onstage, such as this photo opportunity with actress Polly Bergen at New York's Plaza Hotel.

started by Drysdale, and drubbing the Colt 45's, 13–1, as Will stole base number 100. But the Giants also won twice. Still, the Dodger lead was two with four to play. A collapse of historic proportion was about to begin.

Despite his poor performance four days earlier, Alston chose Koufax to start against Houston. For four innings he was the pitcher he'd been during the first half, but after he gave up two runs in the fifth, Alston pulled him. The Dodgers lost 8–6, when Ron Perranoski, in his NL record 66th appearance for a left-handed pitcher, gave up a grand slam. Fortunately, the Giants lost as well. With three games left, L.A.'s lead was still two games. But for the first time a playoff began to be seen as a real possibility. A coin flip determined that the first such game would be played in San Francisco, the next two at Dodger Stadium.

While the Giants were rained out against Houston, the Dodgers played another nail-biter versus the Cardinals. Larry Jackson beat Pete Richert and the Dodgers 3–2 as Ron Perranoski, whom Frank Finch was now bluntly describing as "overworked," lost again, this time in the tenth inning.

Now the Giants stumbled, splitting a doubleheader with Houston as former Dodger Norm Larker's home run beat them in the second game. But the Dodgers couldn't take advantage. Although they clinched a tie for the pennant, Drysdale lost his third straight bid to win his 26th game when monolithic outfielder Frank Howard, whom Jim Murray aptly described as "so big he wasn't born, he was founded," dropped Dal Maxvill's fly ball. That miscue led to two unearned runs, the only two the Cardinals needed in their 2–0 win. Once again, a pennant race between the Dodgers and Giants would come down to the final day, and once again the Dodgers were headed in the wrong direction. Finch noted that if the Dodgers blew it, their collapse would go down as "one of the most calamitous in baseball history, comparable to 1951," when the Dodgers blew a thirteen-game lead. They'd lost nine of twelve, and six of seven, all to the second-division Cardinals and Colt 45's. Podres, Drysdale, or Koufax had started every game except one because Alston had lost faith in Stan Williams and Joe Moeller.

Podres pitched magnificently on the final day of the regular season, giving up only one hit. Unfortunately, it was a home run to Gene Oliver that beat him 1–0 as veteran Curt Simmons was even better and the Dodgers, in a teamwide slump, were shut out again by St. Louis. Meanwhile, in San Francisco, Willie Mays's eighth-inning home run was the

NL WINS LEADERS

1901	Bill Donovan	25
1921	Burleigh Grimes	22
1924	Dazzy Vance	28
1925	Dazzy Vance	22
1941	Kirby Higbe Whitlow Wyatt	22 22
1956	Don Newcombe	27
1962	Don Drysdale	25
1963	Sandy Koufax	25
1965	Sandy Koufax	26
1966	Sandy Koufax	27
1974	Andy Messersmith	20

difference as the Giants pulled into a tie with a 2–1 win over Houston. There would be a playoff.

"WANTED," wrote Jim Murray, "ONE NEARLY NEW 1962 NATIONAL LEAGUE PENNANT, SLIGHTLY SOILED WITH TEAR STAIN IN CENTER. LAST SEEN BLOWING TOWARD SAN FRANCISCO. . . . WARNING: IF YOU RETURN PENNANT TO DODGERS DIRECT, BE SURE TO TAPE IT TO THEIR HANDS."

Alston was in a dilemma. Neither Podres nor Drysdale was

MONUMENT TO WALTER

Jim Murray

Los Angeles Times, April 10, 1962

I
F YOU HAD 37 OR 38 MILLION DOLLARS IN LIQuid cash and a line of credit that allowed you to borrow $10 million more, what would you do with it?

High on the list of things I would not do with it is build a baseball park. It is also, as it happens, high on the list of things most people would not do with it.

Which explains why more than one businessman in the City of Angels goes down to the hill overlooking Chavez Ravine in the hills athwart the city these days and stares incredulously at the scene before him.

There, by heaven and Walter O'Malley, just as he said it would, stands a baseball park. Not just any baseball park, but the Taj Mahal, Parthenon, and Westminster Abbey of baseball. It is a work of art even if you think the hit-and-run is an auto accident, a pitcher something to pour lemonade out of, and a slider an unexpected trip on a banana peel.

Like all works of art, it grew out of great travail, was conceived in controversy and executed under harassment. Like a Rembrandt, it is a one-purpose artifact. Its acoustics will not play host to the lyric soarings of great music, only the muted profanities of frustrated athletes and the off-key scratches of "The Star-Spangled Banner." No Greek tragedies will adorn the infield, just the minor ones of a shortstop who forgot to bend down, a batter who misjudged the plane of a thrown ball, and, perhaps, the pitcher who went to the well too often—and got full of good wine.

The ballet performed there will be the kind truck drivers understand and the Ballet Russe does not. The entrechats will be intended to elude hemorrhaging from spike wounds, not to outdo Nijinsky. The tour jetes will be meant to bring a run, not applause.

It is a strange monument to the career, life, and times of Walter F. O'Malley, a man who came into baseball like the explorer stumbled on the New World—i.e., looking for something else.

Walter F. O'Malley, it so happens, was a specialist in distress real estate—which baseball sure was—when he came into the game. It was like a man discovering girls after a lifetime on a desert island—an encounter neither one of them could quite break off. O'Malley stayed in the counting room only until he saw that assets and liabilities labeled "shortstops," "outfielders," "infielders," "catchers," and "pitchers" were the most fascinating and unpredictable in the whole world of business. No French bonds—or French women—could match them for hair-raising peaks and slumps.

He fed his addiction by acquiring more and more shares of this ravishing heart-breaker from former addicts who had taken the cure. His partner, Branch Rickey, perceiving the bright flush in the O'Malley cheeks and the feverish light in the eyes, dangled his portion of the prize at an outlandish million-dollar price tag. Rickey, too, was sentimental about baseball, but not about money. He knew O'Malley had to have it. Soon O'Malley—along with a partner, Jim Mulvoy, caught up in the same grasp of adoration for this strumpet baseball—had his prize.

BASEBALL INTRIGUE HOOKED HIM

It was a heady world of headline, haggling, hope, and hurt. Also intrigue. And if there was one thing O'Malley loved better than baseball, it was intrigue. Between the devious and the direct, he vastly preferred the devious — and baseball was the perfect spot for it.

He set about to conspire for a new ballpark in Brooklyn. He met his match in politicians. They, too, liked the devious. And were even more skilled at it. O'Malley hocked, not his soul, but two of his ballparks, which were the next dearest thing, to pony up $5 million. All the state, city, and county (O'Malley spared the federal government) had to do was tear down a railroad or two, a meat market, and a few hundred or thousand slum dwellers and he would move in with his park.

They said, "Let's haggle some more," and when they had looked up, O'Malley was gone. A western mayor, Norris Poulson, was offering what appeared to be the last remaining chunk of downtown Los Angeles for O'Malley's purposes. As Norris kept talking, it even appeared the city was prepared to tear City Hall down if the glare got in the hitter's eyes.

O'Malley fell to the glad cries. They died in his throat when he got to the Pacific and there, arrayed before him with hard eyes, seemed the entrenched wealth and established order of Los Angeles. "Give him 300 acres of downtown L.A. real estate for a chunk of land on Avalon Blvd. And a promise to use the land for only baseball — a game!" they shouted in disbelief. "What do you take us for? Why, he'll put up a tarpaper ballpark in one corner of the Ravine and department stores and lanai apartments on the rest of it — just like any other self-respecting businessman would do. He's not nuts about baseball. He's nuts about land."

VOTED CHANCE BY PEOPLE

O'Malley, bewildered, pointed out he was throwing something else onto the scales — a major league baseball franchise. There were only 16 in the world at that time and anything there's only 16 of has to be assayed in the millions whether it is a coelacanth or a formula for making gold out of coal.

The businessmen were skeptical. The Communists were purple. The people in between, the electorate, voted to give him a chance.

Walter O'Malley got his land. He poured his $18 million into a ballpark — not on the edge but smack in the middle of the Ravine. There isn't a department store or a high-rise apartment in sight. It is, by George or by Walter, a shrine to baseball. After all, if baseball perishes, so will Walter O'Malley, who will thereupon have the biggest rock garden in all civilization and the bills to prove it. Over ten million tons of concrete, enough to build a causeway across Santa Monica Bay (except you can't play baseball on a causeway) have been poured. Enough money has gone down to finance a revolution.

But baseball won't perish. O'Malley will, in time, as will all of us. The businessmen will go off scratching their heads and talking to themselves and the ones who said, "There never will be a baseball game played in Chavez Ravine," will be able to hear the umpire cry, "Play ball" — if they listen real carefully this afternoon in the hills where the goats used to single out the better tin cans.

Jim Murray was one of the giants of sports journalism, and his work for the *Los Angeles Times* earned him a Pulitzer Prize for commentary in 1990. Before joining the *Times*, he helped launch *Sports Illustrated*. His work has been collected in several volumes, including *The Quotable Jim Murray* and *The Best of Jim Murray*.

available to pitch. Now Alston turned to Koufax, the same pitcher he'd spent years passing over.

Koufax had nothing. Mays cracked a first-inning home run for two runs, and after Koufax gave up another to Jim Davenport, he was done. The Dodgers were shut out for the third day in a row as Billy Pierce shut them down on three hits.

The Dodgers came back to L.A. a beaten team, and for the first time since their arrival on the West Coast their fans seemed to agree. Only 25,000 turned out for what many expected to be the last game of the year.

For six and a half innings, they were right, as the Giants took a 5–0 lead off Drysdale. But after San Francisco starter Jack Sanford walked the leadoff hitter in the sixth, Giants manager Al Dark pulled him. The Dodgers exploded for seven runs as three straight pinch hitters came through, capped by Lee Walls's base-clearing double. Although the Giants came back to tie, Wills scored the winning run on a sacrifice fly in the ninth.

The next day, before 45,000 suddenly optimistic fans, the playoff came down to the last inning in a game in which the Dodgers made four errors, fell behind 2–0, and then came back to take a 4–2 lead into the ninth. With Ed Roebuck on the mound in relief of Podres, the end wouldn't be as dramatic as Bobby Thomson's walk-off home run. But for the Dodgers it proved just as painful.

Matty Alou led off with a single. Then Harvey Kuenn bounced a double-play ball to Wills. But second baseman Larry Burright, whom Alston had inserted into the game for his defense, was slow to the bag, and instead of a double play the Dodgers got only one out.

Roebuck unraveled and walked the next two. On the Dodger bench, the players were screaming for Alston to put in Don Drysdale, who had told Alston he could throw an inning. So too, reportedly, was Leo Durocher. But Alston was stubborn and left Roebuck in. Willie Mays then followed with a smash off Roebuck's hand, and the Dodger lead was only 4–3.

Now Alston turned back to his bullpen. But instead of Drysdale, whom he had already penciled in to start the Series, he called on Stan Williams. In the last two weeks Williams had hardly pitched and had struggled with control all year, walking nearly five players a game. Nothing he had done over the last half of 1962 marked him as the man the Dodgers wanted on the mound now. Orlando Cepeda greeted him with a sacrifice fly to tie the game. Then, after Williams

intentionally walked Ed Bailey to load the bases, and to the dismay of every Dodger fan everywhere, even the few left in Brooklyn, he walked Jim Davenport. The Giants now led 5–4, and after Burright bobbled Jose Pagan's ground ball, they led 6–4. The Dodgers went out quietly in the bottom of the inning, and 45,000 fans had a painful memory to place within the borders of Dodger Stadium.

But it didn't stay quiet. The players banned the press from the clubhouse and cut loose. Some started drinking and laying into Alston for all the mistakes he'd made down the stretch, and in particular for not using Drysdale in the finale. Tommy Davis screamed over and over, "You stole my money! You stole my money!" Alston stayed in his office as players tried to call him out, calling him a "gutless son of a bitch" before he left and offered congratulations to the Giants.

When the players finally emerged, they said little that was printable. According to the *Times*, "Drysdale broke through the door swearing to himself." Wally Moon bitterly asked, "How the hell would you feel if you all just lost $12,000?"— each player's expected Series share. Durocher later excoriated Alston's decision in his autobiography. Sid Ziff summed it all up in the *Times*: "The daffy Dodgers butchered it up with four errors, kicked away three runs, came back like gangbusters, loused up the set with some screwball strategy, still had it won until the ninth inning of a 165-game playoff season, and then blew the pennant. It was a lot like Brooklyn."

Well, the end result was the same, but the reaction was different. In Brooklyn the same club had been rolled out to try again, but in L.A. there was speculation that there'd be plenty of changes, starting at the top. Word was that O'Malley wanted to dump Alston in favor of Durocher, or perhaps coach Pete Reiser. But Buzzie Bavasi balked at the notion. He liked Alston and didn't blame him for the Dodger loss, concluding instead that the loss of Koufax had been key. Bavasi, like everyone else connected with the team, would remain oblivious to the role they had already played, and would continue to play, in Koufax's long-term health. Bavasi told O'Malley that if he fired Alston, he'd quit too. O'Malley didn't want to go looking for a GM — Bavasi was well liked in L.A. and kept the heat off the club owner. Besides, the Dodgers had set a record by drawing more than 2.7 million fans to Dodger Stadium. They had some goodwill to spare, and Durocher was a loose cannon. So Alston stayed.

But others did not. Like bad memories, over the next eight months the Dodgers jettisoned almost every player involved in the season-ending debacle. Stan Williams was dealt to the Yankees for Moose Skowron. Burright was sent in a package to the Mets. Duke Snider, who'd been open in his criticism of Alston, was sold and joined Burright in New York. And Ed Roebuck was dealt to the Senators. It was all very tidy.

The Dodgers were still formidable. Wills had finished with a record 104 stolen bases. Tommy Davis led the league with a .346 average and 153 RBIs. Drysdale had won 25 games.

The best news came in the spring, when Koufax showed up for camp healthy, something that instantly added another 10 or 12 wins to a club for which too many players —Wills, the Davises, Frank Howard, Perranoski, Drysdale — appeared to enjoy career years that were unlikely to be duplicated. Koufax could help make up for the expected drop-off. They were picked to win the pennant by almost half of the BBWAA's 255 members.

The Dodgers got off slow in 1963 —when they hit, the pitchers failed, and vice versa. The Cardinals got off quick and swept the Dodgers at the end of the month, putting them under .500.

The turnaround would eventually come, and for the press it took place on May 6, after the club dropped a doubleheader in Pittsburgh. Tired and angry, the Dodgers started griping about the condition of the bus driving them back from the airport.

Alston had had it. All spring the players had treated him like dirt, making it clear they'd lost a measure of respect. Alston barked at the bus driver to pull over and then challenged the whole team, telling them that anyone who wanted to could take a shot at him, just "get off and come outside." Then the manager climbed down and waited.

No one moved. Legend has it that the Dodgers surged after that — and they did — but a 12-day home stand that soon followed may have been just as important. Nevertheless, in June they struggled again.

The real move came in July and had less to do with Alston than it did with the schedule. Alston was on the hot seat, and L.A. was bubbling with rumors that Durocher was about to take over when the Dodgers dumped the Cardinals in three straight at the beginning of the month. Then, after the All-Star break, the Dodgers hit a stretch of 40 games in which 27 of them were against the league's bottom feeders, including the pathetic Mets and, almost as awful, the Colt 45's.

And then there was Koufax. He had only five subpar starts all year, and three of those came in the first two months of the

Brooklyn native Tommy Davis was the Dodger regular left fielder at age 21 in 1960. In 1962 he enjoyed one of the greatest individual seasons in baseball history when he led the National League with 230 hits, 153 RBIs, and a .346 batting average. The following season Davis repeated as National League batting champion with a .326 average.

season, when he battled some shoulder pain and started 8–3. From then on he was 17–2, and he started July by hurling three shutouts in a row.

Along the way he also picked up his second no-hitter, shutting down the Giants on May 11. Of his eventual four no-hitters, this was the only one in which he was not truly dominant. He struck out only four, his lowest total for a complete game all season.

On July 20, after the Dodgers beat Milwaukee for their 17th win in their last 20 games, their lead over the Giants, who had pulled ahead of suddenly slumping St. Louis, was seven and a half games. By September the Dodgers still led by six games, although the Cardinals had overtaken the Giants.

Then it happened again. All of a sudden it was a lot like 1951, only this time it was the Cardinals who got hotter than hot. With Stan Musial poised to play the final month of his stellar career, beginning on August 30 the Cardinals won 19 of 20. But the Dodgers didn't collapse—they won 13 of 19 over the same span. Still, the Dodgers came into St. Louis on September 16 with a record of 91–59, only one game better than the Cardinals' 91–61 mark. With the Dodgers' tortured late season history, everyone was half afraid to watch.

The knives were already out, looking for scapegoats. A lot of players were unhappy with Alston. He wouldn't settle on a lineup, and the players thought he was platoon-crazy. Murray quipped, "They're so unsure of their positions, a pitcher feels like a patient who climbed on the operating table and heard the doctor turn to his nurse and say, 'Now let's see, which side is it on?'" Fairly and Bill Skowron split first base, Gilliam and rookie Nate Oliver traded off at second base, and Moon and Howard shared an outfield spot. Dick Tracewski, who couldn't hit a lick, somehow started nearly half the games at short as Wills was put into a conga line at third base, where he was one of four players to play at least 30 games. The Dodger offense had dropped off the table as the club scored 200 fewer runs than in 1962. Their defense was somewhat better, but not enough to make up the difference.

Pitching bailed them out. It always did, making it hard for either Alston's players or the press ever to get a handle on him as a manager. Dodger pitching was so good that it justified almost everything he did. Yet over time a young Dodger club that had little trouble scoring runs would be transformed under his watch, and with his emphasis on "little ball," into a club that struggled offensively. At the time many blamed the dimensions of Dodger Stadium, but the club's performance in 1962 belies that notion.

In St. Louis pitching saved them again. In the first game of the series Johnny Podres scattered three hits, including a

---

In the third and final game of the 1962 National League playoff, Dodger shortstop Maury Wills steals his record-breaking 104th base in his 165th game. Despite his heroics, the Giants won 6–5 and claimed their first West Coast pennant.

No Runs, No Hits, Few Errors

On May 11, 1963, Sandy Koufax points to the scoreboard, which documents his second career no-hitter against the Giants, a game in which Koufax recorded only four strikeouts — his lowest total in a complete game for the entire season.

a close game with a home run in the ninth, Ron Perranoski pitched six innings of shutout relief, and in the thirteenth the Cardinals threw the game away. St. Louis was finished, and the Dodgers were so happy to have avoided another collapse that after the game Don Drysdale said of Nen, "That home run is going to cost us a lot of money. I'm going to propose a full share for the kid when we vote on the World Series split."

And that's precisely where the Dodgers were headed. The Cardinals faded, and the Dodgers finished 99–63, six games ahead, setting up another October confrontation with the New York Yankees.

Before the Series, New York was dismissive of the Dodgers. The mighty Yankees had hit nearly twice as many home runs as the increasingly anemic Dodgers, and both Whitey Ford and Jim Bouton had won 20 games. They knew Koufax was good, but the Yankees considered themselves a fastball-hitting team. They'd faced Koufax in spring training before and didn't think he was all that special. The consensus around baseball was that New York just had too much all the way around for the Dodgers to compete. Oh, Koufax — he of the 25 wins, 11 shutouts, one no-hitter, 306 strikeouts, and 1.88 ERA, the best in baseball — might win a game, but that was it.

But Koufax knew the Yankees too. He told a reporter, "I have faced every one of them four or five times during spring training"; while he admitted that "they're basically a fastball-hitting team and have power," he considered both the Giants and Cardinals their equal, and he was 6–1 against those clubs. Moreover, against the top ten hitters for average in the NL in 1963, a group that cumulatively hit .316 for the year and included eventual Hall of Famers Willie Mays, Hank Aaron, Roberto Clemente, and Orlando Cepeda, in 140 at bats Koufax had held them to a .235 batting average and had given up only four home runs. The Yankees didn't scare him, and this wasn't spring training.

The Series opened in New York on October 2. After Whitey Ford retired the Dodgers in order in the top of the first, Koufax took the mound. New York's confidence lasted all of five minutes.

Tony Kubek struck out to start the game, bringing up Bobby Richardson. In 630 regular season at bats, the second baseman had fanned only 22 times, and the Dodger scouting report said he feasted on high fastballs. That was Koufax's best pitch, but he wasn't about to change.

Three high fastballs later, Richardson had struck out for the 23rd time. Then Koufax blew away Tom Tresh. The Yan-

Musial home run, and the Dodgers scored two in the ninth to win 3–1. Koufax pitched the next night. It was automatic. He didn't give up a hit until the seventh, when Musial touched him for a hit, and he set a major league record for left-handers by twirling his 11th shutout of the season. As the Dodgers won 4–0, Koufax needed only 87 pitches: 57 fastballs — 47 for strikes — and 30 curves, 20 for strikes. A 2–1 ratio between strikes and balls is considered very, very good. Koufax's 4–1 ratio simply wasn't fair.

The Dodgers buried the Cardinals in the third game of the series. Rookie Dick Nen, just up from the minor leagues, tied

kees knew they were in trouble, and the Dodgers knew they weren't.

With one out in the second, Frank Howard hit a ball 455 feet over Mickey Mantle's head in center for a double. Ex-Yankee Moose Skowron scored him with a single, and after Dick Tracewski followed with a hit, John Roseboro homered to the upper deck to put the Dodgers ahead 4–0.

"The standard joke on the Dodgers," Dick Young would write in the *Post*, "is this: They get a run in the first or second inning and say to the pitcher, 'There's your run, now hold it.'" For Koufax that day, a four-run lead might as well have been forty, and when the Dodgers added a run in the third it might as well have been fifty.

The Yankees couldn't touch him. Through four innings he had nine strikeouts. New York didn't get a hit until the fifth, when they knocked three singles with two outs, but Koufax ended the threat by fanning pinch hitter Hector Lopez. In the eighth Koufax started to tire and was nicked for two runs when Tresh hooked a ball into the left-field stands, but he was never in trouble. He struck out Harry Bright to end the game and set a new Series strikeout mark with fifteen.

The Yankees were thoroughly beaten. Richardson had struck out three times. Although Tom Tresh boasted that "now that we've had a chance to look at him we'll get to him easier next time," Tony Kubek asked rhetorically, "Do they [National League hitters] hit him any better in September after seeing him all season?" The answer was no, and the Yankees knew it. Mantle said, "His fastball must sink or hop or something." And Yogi Berra wondered, "How come he lost five games this year?" It didn't make them feel any better when Koufax said after the game, "I felt a little weak." The Yankees felt considerably weaker.

Before the Series, much had been made of American League umpires' refusal to call balks on AL pitchers when they failed to pause when pitching from the stretch, and in a pre-Series meeting Alston was miffed when Ford Frick told him that was how it would be in the Series as well. Many observers expected this to halt L.A.'s running game.

Quite the contrary. The players took it as a challenge. In game two Maury Wills led off with a single against Yankee lefty Al Downing, whom Yankee manager Ralph Houk decided to pitch because he thought his pickoff move would keep the Dodgers from trying anything. When Downing tried to pick him off, Wills broke for second and beat the high throw from Joe Pepitone. Gilliam then singled, and Willie

Davis doubled. The Dodgers led 2–0, and the Yankees were back on their heels.

Back in 1955 Johnny Podres had boasted, "I can beat New York any day of the week." Well, it was a Thursday. The Dodgers won 4–1 as Podres pitched into the ninth and Perranoski finished the game.

Two thousand fans greeted the Dodgers at LAX when they returned home for game three. When Koufax walked off the plane, the *Times* reported, "men roared, women shrieked and teen-age girls all but swooned."

Don Drysdale took the mound for the Dodgers in game three, determined to match his counterparts. The Dodgers struck first when Yankee pitcher Jim Bouton walked Gilliam. He went to second on a wild pitch and scored when Tommy Davis hit a scorching ground ball off Bobby Richardson's glove.

Drysdale now had his run. All year long he'd pitched well, but the Dodgers hadn't scored, the only reason he'd been 19–17 instead of a 25- or 30-game winner. This time he made it stand up. He scattered three hits, the Dodgers won 1–0, and New York was down three games to none with Koufax available for game four. "Well," said Ralph Houk without any optimism, "we've got 27 more outs."

So did Koufax, and before the Yankees left their hotel the next day they packed their bags as if they knew what was coming and knew they weren't going to hit it. The Dodgers got Koufax his run off Ford in the sixth when Howard crushed a mammoth home run. But Mantle finally caught one off Koufax in the seventh to tie the score at 1–1, and for the first time in the Series the Yankees weren't behind.

They enjoyed the feeling for all of ten minutes. In the bottom of the inning Gilliam grounded to Clete Boyer at third, and first baseman Joe Pepitone lost his throw in the crowd. Gilliam went to third and scored on Willie Davis's fly ball. A second run was plenty for Koufax, who struck out "only" eight. He won 2–1, and the Dodgers captured their second world championship since moving to Los Angeles. "This," said Alston, thinking of the playoff the year before, "makes up for everything." When someone asked Sandy Koufax what his goals were in the future, he said simply that he hoped to finish his career with "the most victories" in NL history. And although so far he had won only 93 games and was still some 281 victories behind Christy Mathewson's NL record of 374, that mark did not seem out of reach and no one even blinked when he said it. Koufax was only 28, starting 40 or more games a year, and pitching as though winning 25 games was as easy as falling out of bed—had the Dodgers scored eight more runs at the right time in 1963 he'd have won 33. Hell, if he stayed healthy, he could break Mathewson's mark before he turned 40.

The Dodgers seemed similarly invincible. They'd just won one world championship and barely missed out on a chance to win another. Podres was their only pitcher over 30, and Jim Gilliam, about to turn 35, was the only regular who seemed to be slowing down. Koufax and Drysdale were coming into their prime, and four of the seven Dodger farm clubs had just finished either first or second. After off years, Tommy and Willie Davis both seemed poised to rebound. Fans still filled Dodger Stadium. The Dodgers didn't make any trades because they didn't think they needed to. Rolling out the balls, putting one in Sandy Koufax's left hand and another in Don Drysdale's right hand, seemed to cover just about everything.

The act of pitching is a constant process of breaking down and healing, not only from one game to the next but from one season to the next. During the season minute muscle tears are formed in a pitcher's arm. These never completely heal until the off-season and create small areas of scar tissue known as adhesions. When a pitcher starts throwing again in the spring, the adhesions break loose, causing passing pain with which most pitchers become familiar.

Koufax usually had to work through some arm pain each spring as his adhesions broke loose. But in the spring of 1964 the pain lingered, and his elbow, which always swelled slightly, became more swollen than usual and then remained puffy. Koufax took note of the phenomenon, but thought nothing of it. All pitchers pitch with some pain, and Koufax assumed that it was normal.

His arm still ached on Opening Day, although he beat St. Louis with a shutout. But in his third start a week later, against the Cardinals, he felt something pop in his forearm and had to leave the game.

That should have raised a very big red flag in the organization, and to a point, it did. After all, without Koufax the Dodgers weren't going anywhere. Dr. Robert Kerlan, the Dodger physician, examined him and diagnosed the injury as a small muscle tear, while also noting that Koufax's elbow was tender. Kerlan knew how to treat that. Over the course of the next week or so he gave Koufax three cortisone shots in his left forearm and elbow.

Cortisol, a natural hormone produced in the body by the adrenal gland in response to stress, allows the body to con-

tinue to function despite injury. In 1949 a synthetic version, the steroid cortisone, was created, and doctors discovered that it was something of a miracle cure. When injected directly into the site of an injury, such as the sore elbow or shoulder of a pitcher, cortisone breaks down scar tissue and tricks the body into suppressing antibodies and other responses that lead to swelling and cause pain. The effects of an injury, although not the cause, miraculously disappear. For a pitcher, a sore arm suddenly isn't sore anymore.

At the time no one knew much about cortisone beyond the fact that it was about the best anti-inflammatory available. Long-term effects were never even considered, and until very recently the drug was widely and repeatedly used in professional sports, often at dosages far above those recommended. In the last decade or so, however, researchers have learned that cortisone, particularly when used repeatedly and in high doses, causes severe long-term side effects. By masking pain, it often makes the underlying injury even worse. But that's not the worst of it. Cortisone can soften cartilage, weaken tendon fibers, cause high blood pressure, and leave fatty deposits in blood vessels that reduce blood flow to joints, leading to osteoporosis and bone loss. No one knew that in 1964.

They do now. Today doctors are much more judicious with their use of the drug. Dosages are much smaller, and many recommend no more than three injections *per year,* and only then if other therapies—including extended rest—have failed. But in the mid-1960s cortisone shots were given out like aspirin, and the result among pro athletes was carnage. Injured players took cortisone shot after cortisone shot, felt better, then got hurt even worse. Those who were able to continue playing racked up long-term side effects. Many former football players have had to undergo knee and hip replacements owing to excessive cortisone use—chronic joint problems such as bone loss have been the result not so much of old football injuries as of repeated use of cortisone. Baseball players are no different. In October 2003 a class-action suit filed against Major League Baseball by three former players included battery and negligence allegations specifically in regard to multiple cortisone shots given by team doctors without informing the players of the danger.

In effect, Koufax took a year's supply of cortisone in a week. And it worked. Boy, did it ever work. After missing twelve days, he pitched again—no brief test to see how he felt but a full ten innings against the Cubs, throwing at least 150 pitches while striking out 13. And on June 4, against

Philadelphia, he pitched another no-hitter, narrowly missing a perfect game when he walked Richie Allen, bringing his record to 6–4. Over the next ten weeks he went 13–1 and pitched six shutouts and twelve complete games.

But it didn't matter. The Dodgers weren't going anywhere. Johnny Podres was out for the year with a bad arm, and the club never found a third or fourth starter. They weren't hitting at all—Drysdale would finish the year with an ERA of 2.19 and still lose 18 games. The club couldn't move above .500, and by August it was clear that they were out of the race and destined to finish the season in sixth place, 80–82.

It was also clear that Koufax was hurting. He banged his elbow running the bases, and after his next few starts, every time he threw it swelled grotesquely. But Koufax never complained, and the ballclub never really monitored his condition. His league-leading ERA and strikeouts gave them all the feedback they were interested in.

On August 16 he shut out the Cardinals in the first game of a doubleheader and struck out 13, a season high. The press jumped on the fact that the 13-strikeout performance had come in a game in which Koufax had featured a new pitch, a forkball. "People are making too much out of it," he said after the game. "It's nothing special." But the Cardinals disagreed.

Koufax was now more than a fastball-curveball pitcher: in addition to those pitches and the forkball, he occasionally threw sidearm to left-handers and mixed in the occasional slider. All were thrown with impeccable control.

"My only goal is winning 20," he said, adding, "I feel fine." Dodger beat writer John Hall, noting that Koufax "didn't look too worn" after the contest, observed that "when he's on the mound Dodger Stadium still looks like the home of the world champions." Not only did the Dodgers usually win when he pitched, but Koufax was the biggest draw in the game—the Dodgers regularly drew near-capacity crowds with Koufax on the mound. Before the second game of the doubleheader, Vin Scully asked the question of the day when he approached game-two starter Larry Miller and asked, "How do you follow a performance like that?" As John Hall commented presciently, "You don't."

And neither did Koufax. When he woke the next day, his arm was swollen from the wrist to the shoulder—Koufax later described it as "a waterlogged log"—a condition way, way out of normal even for a baseball pitcher. He went back to see Kerlan and was diagnosed with traumatic arthritis, a chronic, incurable condition probably caused by wear and trauma but,

Sandy Koufax jumps for joy as he defeats the New York Yankees by a score of 2–1 in the fourth and final game of the 1963 World Series at Dodger Stadium. In the Series Koufax pitched two complete-game victories to supplement the 25 games he'd won during the regular season.

in retrospect, almost certainly exacerbated by cortisone shot after cortisone shot to mask pain and overuse. One can't help but wonder what Koufax might have done in his career if either he or the Dodgers had simply stepped back at some point, recognized what was happening, and taken another approach.

The joint was drained of fluid, he was given another cortisone shot, and, as Koufax later said, "they gave me some pills." The swelling went down. Two weeks later he tried to pitch in the bullpen. The arm swelled again. More shots, more pills. And two weeks later he tried again. More swelling, more shots, more pills. Finally, the Dodgers shut him down for the season.

He would never be the same, and he would never get better.

It is unfair to assign much blame to the Dodger organization for their treatment of Koufax through the 1964 season. Although most teams were drifting toward the five-man pitching rotation, the Dodgers were not among them — the four-man rotation was still considered sound strategy. Their starting pitchers threw every fourth day or they weren't starting pitchers, and no one worried very much about the consequences. If a pitcher couldn't throw every fourth day, the thinking was that there was something wrong with him, not with the method. Neither ballclubs nor pitchers put much

stock yet in things like pitch counts, and medical insight into the mechanics of pitching was virtually nonexistent.

Koufax was no dummy, but in regard to his left arm he was as ignorant as every other pitcher in baseball. Concepts like "rehab" and "prehab" were foreign concepts. When the season ended, a pitcher stopped pitching and in the off-season used his arm as much as an insurance salesman. Staying in condition meant not getting fat and doing a lot of walking. Once the season started, he ran a little.

Pitchers were as disposable as racehorses. When they broke down, they were sent to pasture and another horse was pulled from the stable. That's the way baseball was and always had been. The history of the game is littered with men who enjoyed short bouts of spectacular success but then broke down, their arms unable to take the strain. In 1903 New York Yankee pitcher Jack Chesbro won a record 41 games and threw 454 innings, but afterward was never the same. In 1912

To the victors go the spoils, and among the spoils for the '63 Dodgers was a plethora of show business appearances, including this stint on *The Bob Hope Show*. Joining Hope (seated, left) are (standing, left to right) Don Drysdale and Sandy Koufax, with Tommy Davis seated next to Hope.

Boston's Smoky Joe Wood went 34–5 but was never effective again. And the Dodgers had similar examples in their own history, such as Karl Spooner. Such breakdowns were considered unfortunate instances of individual weakness—a Darwinian inevitability that baseball was powerless to affect.

But after 1964 the Dodgers knew Koufax was pitching in a diminished, even dangerous, physical condition. So did Koufax. And they did nothing. Incredibly, instead of using extra caution or lessening his workload, instead of turning to a five-man rotation, instead of determining whether there was something Koufax was doing wrong that could be corrected, instead of asking questions about his condition, Koufax and the Dodgers took the opposite approach. Once they concluded that his time as a major league pitcher was running out, they didn't even try another approach in an attempt to extend his career. They didn't try to make his task just a little bit easier by adding offense and turning 2–1 squeakers in which every pitch meant the ballgame into 5–2 yawners. Instead, they squeezed as hard as possible to extract every possible pitch from his left arm. After being diagnosed with arthritis, Koufax would find his workload increased dramatically—he rested less, not more—and ever more dangerous treatments would be prescribed to get him through to his next start. A year before Koufax had talked about winning nearly another 300 games in his career, and no one had laughed. Now every game could be his last. And he pitched that way.

Yet even after Koufax and the Dodgers were aware that his career was hanging by a thread, he was not removed from games even when the Dodgers had a big lead. When he was obviously struggling, he was not removed from the game. When the game entered extra innings, he continued to pitch. When there was an opportunity to give him extra rest, he didn't get it. On the rare occasion when he didn't pitch a full nine innings, he was occasionally called on to pitch in relief between starts. Over the next two years he would throw not only more innings than any other Dodger pitcher but more than any man in major league baseball.

It would be a bit more understandable if the Dodgers had lacked effective relief pitching and had no other options. But they did have good relief pitching, and they did have other options. Even without Koufax, the Dodgers would have had the best pitching in the National League and the deepest relief staff in the majors. Yet instead of using other pitchers to give Koufax a rest, they used Koufax to rest the others—when he pitched, the relievers generally got the day off.

Yet Koufax never complained, never resisted. He knew the score and accepted it, trading longevity for momentary brilliance.

In a way it was courageous. In a way it was stupid.

Over the next two seasons the best pitcher in baseball would burn like a comet and then be gone.

Forty years later there is only the afterglow.

OF BEAN BALLS, BAND-AIDS, AND ELBOWS

IT WAS ALL OR NOTHING.

In the off-season before 1965 the Dodgers made one big transaction. Uncertain whether Podres, who had off-season surgery for bone chips, would return, and obviously concerned about Koufax, the Dodgers dealt Frank Howard, Dick Nen, and spot starters Phil Ortega and Pete Richert to the Washington Senators for shortstop John Kennedy, $100,000, and, most important, Claude Osteen, a 24-year-old pitcher who had somehow won 15 games in 1964 for the lowly Washington Senators.

The message was clear. The L.A. Dodgers would win with pitching or they would not win at all. Howard, despite hitting only .226 in 1964, was the only power threat the sub-.500 Dodgers had, hitting 24 of their 79 home runs. Yet they dealt him away for more pitching. If Podres returned, and if Koufax returned, and if Drysdale stayed healthy, the addition of Osteen would make for a pitching rotation second to none and give the offensively challenged team a chance. But if any of those things

At the height of his powers, Sandy Koufax was one of the most dominating pitchers in baseball history. He is shown here after his fourth career no-hitter, a perfect game against the Chicago Cubs at Dodger Stadium on September 9, 1965. Opposing pitcher Bob Hendley allowed just one hit but lost by a score of 1–0.

didn't happen, the Dodgers were finished. Then Osteen, instead of being the pitcher who put the team over the top, would become the pitcher the club would build around in the future.

By April it looked like time to rebuild. Koufax appeared to be on his way from all to nothing.

In spring training Koufax resumed his role as staff ace without blinking. One might expect that the Dodgers would have had him take it easy and build slowly toward the start of the season. Fat chance. He pitched more, not less, than any other Dodger pitcher that spring. He was the first Los Angeles pitcher to hurl a complete game in the spring—in fact, he did so twice, and led the club with 36 innings pitched and 27 strikeouts.

He paid for that mistake. After his second complete game of the exhibition season, against the White Sox on March 30, he awoke the next morning and his arm was not only swollen but also black and blue. He left Vero Beach and returned to Los Angeles, his career at a crossroads, to see Dr. Kerlan again.

Kerlan was not optimistic. On April 2 he told the *Times*, "He will remain here three or four days at least. It is too early to tell what the results of treatments will be."

Dodger officials were quick to distance themselves from the injury. Alston cited Koufax's ten strikeouts against Chicago and said, "I can't believe he'll be out any length of time," but then added, "He wanted to go [pitch] even longer than we allowed him a couple times." Bavasi claimed that "after he went the distance against the Tigers in Lakeland last Friday [a week before], he told me his arm never felt better." But Bavasi also said, "I'm resetting the club right now with the idea Sandy won't be with us," and admitted that concern over Koufax was the reason the Dodgers had made the Osteen trade.

The elbow, most certainly, wasn't getting better, and it wasn't going to. The hemorrhaging indicated that in addition to arthritis there was probably some ligament and muscle damage that had led to internal bleeding. All Kerlan could do was repeat the same pattern of treatment they had tried in 1964—draining the joint of fluid and giving Koufax a witch's brew of drugs and injections, this time adding to the mix painkillers and the anti-inflammatory Butazolidin, a horse drug. Kerlan was taking it himself for his own rheumatoid arthritis, using himself as a guinea pig. But "bute," as the drug was commonly called, wasn't approved for human use and was even controversial in equine circles—in 1968 Ken-

tucky Derby winner Dancer's Image would be stripped of his victory after testing positive for the drug. It killed bone marrow, and the user's blood count had to be monitored as if he were a cancer patient.

Kerlan wasn't entirely comfortable with that, but Koufax himself was insistent: he wanted to pitch, and the treatment worked—the pain and swelling went away. They discussed cutting back on his workload, turning him into what had once been called a "Sunday pitcher"—starting once a week, as Preacher Roe once had to do to preserve the dwindling number of pitches in his arm—but Koufax didn't want to hear it. Neither did the Dodgers.

They reached a compromise. Koufax decided to abandon his forkball, slider, and sidearm delivery, and he wouldn't throw at all between starts—he'd always thrown every day except the day immediately before he was scheduled to pitch. In addition to the various drugs he was taking, he also agreed to ice his arm after throwing. One day before the Dodgers opened the season against the Mets, he took the mound against the Senators in an exhibition game in Washington.

He pitched three innings, threw 52 pitches, struck out five, and gave up only one hit. His fastball and hard overhand curve were plenty to get out hitters. What sore arm?

That became the joke around the league. Drysdale got the Dodgers off to a winning start with a 6–1 win over the Mets on Opening Day, and Koufax made his first appearance in the Dodgers' fourth game, against Philadelphia. He went the distance and won, 6–2. All four pitchers the Dodgers needed to win were in place, all still backed by bullpen stalwarts Ron Perranoski and Bob Miller.

But the Dodgers still couldn't hit, and on May 1 what little offense they had appeared to have taken a hit. Tommy Davis, who'd been battling a groin injury since spring training, broke his ankle. While he had never fulfilled the Hall of Fame promise he showed in 1962, he was still one of the few dangerous hitters on the team. With light hitting second-year man Wes Parker at first base and rookie Jim Lefebvre, a former Dodger batboy, at second, the Dodger offense now came down to Willie Davis, Ron Fairly, and Maury Wills. That simply didn't match up with the Giants, who featured Mays, Willie McCovey, and Jim Ray Hart, or the Braves with Aaron, Eddie Mathews, and Felipe Alou, or the Reds with Frank Robinson, Deron Johnson, and Vada Pinson. In fact, in 1965 no Dodger would hit over .300 or have a slugging average over .400 except for pitcher Don Drysdale—he led the team in both categories, hitting .300 and slugging .508 in the 44 games he pitched plus his 14 appearances as a pinch hitter. Jim Murray would later aptly describe the Dodgers of 1965 as a team "trying to make a pennant out of a base on balls, a ball of string, a Band-Aid and a letter from their pastor." Another writer described their offense as consisting of "a withering base on balls to left field and two slashing errors to right."

There wasn't any help in the Dodger farm system, at least not any help that could hit major league pitching. L.A.'s triple-A team in Spokane was dreadful—they'd been forced to fill out the roster with veterans who had failed in previous major league trials, like 30-year-old Lou Johnson. Nevertheless, he got the call after Davis was hurt.

Johnson was a decent player, but not great at anything— an outfielder with a little power who could run a little, didn't walk much, and struck out a lot. He was no worse than dozens of other fourth or fifth outfielders, but this was a time when African American players generally weren't retained on major league rosters unless they held a starting position. In a 12-year professional career, Johnson had already played for 18 different teams and failed to stick in brief trials with major league Milwaukee, the Cubs, and the Angels. Thrown into a deal in 1964 when the Dodgers unloaded Larry Sherry, Johnson enjoyed his best season for Spokane, leading the PCL in

hits and batting .328. But he hadn't even been invited to spring training in 1965. After Davis was hurt, Bavasi tried to make a deal but had little to spare. Johnson became the Dodgers' left fielder by default.

On many other NL clubs he would have been on the bench, but on the Dodgers he was an unlikely star. He got off to a great start. In their anemic lineup, Johnson stood out, scratching and clawing for everything, and in his first two weeks in the lineup he was Mr. Everything. He gave the team a spark with timely hitting and more power than anyone else. Fans loved him, and so did the press for his convoluted way of speaking—"onliest" was a favorite word, and for much of the season he was the onliest Dodger doing any consistent hitting. Even after he was beaned and suffered a hairline fracture of his thumb, he kept playing. On a team of introverts and stolid professionals, Johnson wore his heart on his sleeve. He was major league baseball's original "Sweet Lou."

The Dodgers' pennant race against the Giants got ugly on August 22, 1965, when San Francisco pitcher Juan Marichal hit Dodger catcher John Roseboro on the head with his bat after Marichal claimed that the Dodger catcher was throwing balls close to his head when returning them to pitcher Sandy Koufax. Koufax is trying vainly to break up the fight.

Sandy Koufax loses his cap while pitching a perfect game against the Cubs at Dodger Stadium on September 9, 1965.

Koufax and Drysdale were everything people expected and more. And Osteen was as good as advertised, the perfect complementary part. Although by mid-July his record was a so-so 7–10, he was pitching better than that. In his ten losses the Dodgers had scored only fifteen runs. Over the second half he'd knuckle down and win eight of his last twelve decisions.

The Dodgers would need every one. Entering September, Los Angeles was in first place, but five other teams were within four and a half games of the top and still dreamed of winning the pennant. Never in major league history had there been such a close race, and the press was already speculating about the delicious possibilities of three-way or four-way playoffs.

One game in early September epitomized the strange nature of the Dodgers' season, one in which victory and glory sat so close to loss that games were won and lost on an almost cellular level.

On September 9 the Dodgers played host to the Cubs. After leading the league for most of the season, the Dodgers had dropped two in a row. The Giants had pulled ahead and now led both L.A. and Cincinnati by a half-game. The Braves and Pirates both trailed by only four.

The Dodgers, as they had done so often before, turned to Koufax. Although they had an opportunity to give him an extra day of rest, for they had played only twice since his last start, Koufax took the mound opposite Chicago pitcher Bob Hendley. Falling further behind the Giants was simply not acceptable, for reasons that had nothing to do with the pennant race.

On August 19 the two clubs had met at Candlestick Park in the first game of a key four-game series. The Dodgers had taken two of the first three and on August 22 looked to put the Giants away. The first three games had been contentious, full of fire. So was much of the rest of the West Coast. Simmering civil rights tensions had exploded. There had been riots in the Watts neighborhood of Los Angeles, and violence had spilled over into San Diego and San Francisco. The rivalry between the Dodgers and Giants, which had almost faded in the finals days in New York City, had been thoroughly revived. And now everyone was on edge.

It was a dream matchup, Koufax versus San Francisco ace Juan Marichal. In the estimation of most, Marichal, a native of the Dominican Republic, was the second-best pitcher in baseball.

Maury Wills had scored the first run of the game in usual Dodger fashion — after reaching first base, he stole second to put himself in scoring position and then scored.

By early May concerns over Koufax's arm began to fade under a tide of strong performances. The Dodgers swept past the Cincinnati Reds and into first place. Almost every game was a 3–2, 2–1, or 2–0 affair, but all the wins counted. Maury Wills, after being bothered by his legs in 1964, resumed his assault on the record books, stealing bases and runs at will, setting the tone for a team that kept constant pressure on the defense by always taking the extra base.

No, no, no. In the first game of the series Wills had ticked the Giants off when he'd faked a bunt and purposely pulled the bat back into Giants catcher Tom Haller's face mask, essentially drawing a catcher's interference call and getting on first. Now Marichal and the Giants had just about had enough of Wills.

When Wills came up again, Marichal sent baseball's universal message of tit for tat—a pitch under his chin that sent Wills sprawling. And just to make certain the Dodgers knew that it was no accident, he then flipped Ron Fairly.

Roseboro and the other Dodgers called on Koufax to retaliate and drill Marichal, but he refused. That just wasn't his style, and besides, the Dodgers were ahead, 2–1. Why risk that?

Roseboro took matters into his own hands. When Marichal came to bat, after a Koufax pitch he threw the ball back off Marichal's ear.

The pitcher started yelling, and Roseboro yelled back, none of it very repeatable. Then Marichal reacted. He raised his bat above his head and swung it down toward Roseboro's head three times, striking him hard at least twice.

A laboratory example of mob behavior ensued, mayhem worthy of anything going on in Watts as spark turned to flame. Roseboro was bleeding from the head. Umpire Shag Crawford tried to hold back Marichal. Giants coach Charlie Fox tried to wedge himself in between the two men. Koufax ran in and threw up his left hand as San Francisco's Tito Fuentes, also on deck, raised his bat. Soon there were a dozen players around home, then two dozen, then 60 players and coaches gathered around the plate. Willie Mays grabbed Roseboro, saw blood, and got him out of there. Cops poured onto the field.

It was 14 minutes before order was restored. Marichal and Roseboro left the game. Minutes later a rattled Koufax walked the next two hitters and gave up a three-run homer to Willie Mays, the only time Mays ever recalled beating Koufax with a long ball. The Giants won, 4–3. NL president Warren Giles fined Marichal $1,750 and suspended him for eight games plus the Giants' final two games of the season in L.A. Roseboro received a concussion, a two-inch gash in the head, and a handful of stitches, and he filed a lawsuit that would not be settled for nine years. The Dodgers thought Marichal got off easy.

A month later the two clubs were still in the same spot, half a game apart. In the end the fight had been a wash. Instead of collapsing, the Giants had responded by winning 14 in a row. And the Dodgers, who were scrapping for every win anyway, continued to do so. As did Koufax.

MAJOR LEAGUE CY YOUNG AWARD

1956	Don Newcombe	27–7
1962	Don Drysdale	25–9
1963	Sandy Koufax	25–5
1965	Sandy Koufax	26–8
1966	Sandy Koufax	27–9

Since his last win on August 14 against Pittsburgh, running his record to 21–4, Koufax—for Koufax—had been struggling. Including the game against the Giants, he hadn't won in five starts—and that included starts against both the Mets and Houston, who were both still lousy. In those five games Koufax had lost three times and left without a decision twice, all while giving up an un-Koufax-esque 14 runs. Fourteen runs in five starts made other pitchers All-Stars, but it was not up to Koufax's usual standard, and he was giving up too many runs for the Dodgers to win behind. After striking out 10 or more 17 times in his first 27 starts, he'd done so only once in his last five and had needed nearly 11 innings then. The press whispered that the incident against the Giants may have scared him or that his delicate arm was starting to fail.

So far the arm had been held together with everything he and Kerlan could throw at it. Koufax now took cortisone and Butazolidin to keep the inflammation down, "Atomic Balm," an aptly named heat-producing ointment slathered on before each game to stimulate blood flow, codeine the day of the start and sometimes midgame to control the pain, and an ice bath immediately afterward to slow the inevitable swelling so that the entire process could start again.

It is a measure of Koufax's control that he was able to pitch effectively on codeine, for the numbing effect of the drug could have wreaked havoc with the precision his fastball

THOSE WERE THE DAYS

Jane Leavy

O NCE UPON A TIME IN NEW YORK, THE parameters of turf were determined by dry cleaners. Eugene Raskin, a Columbia University architecture professor better remembered for writing the 1968 hit song "Those Were the Days," always said you could tell you were in a new neighborhood when you saw another dry cleaner.

Neighborhoods were organized into blocks. And blocks were subdivided into 250-foot lengths by manhole covers against which whole generations of boys measured their prowess.

Sandy Koufax, a onetime Columbia student who abandoned the study of architecture long before Gene Raskin arrived on campus, was a two-and-a-half-sewer man. Not with a fungo bat, like Willie Mays, the stickball wizard of upper Manhattan, whose Spaldeen clouts transcended four sewers and rational belief. Koufax couldn't hit a cow in the ass with a bag of rice at five feet. That was the word in his Brooklyn neighborhood.

Two and a half sewers — that's how far they said Koufax could heave a football. Jerry Goldstein, his sometime receiver in two-on-two touch football games, ran into a parked car 600 and some feet from the line of scrimmage trying to catch one of those apocryphal two-sewer throws. He can offer a chipped tooth as proof. Who's going to say different a half-century later? After all, Duke Snider once threw a ball out of the Los Angeles Coliseum, didn't he?

Koufax was a basketball star, captain of the Lafayette varsity, at a high school better known for its gridiron exploits.

"We played football games at Ebbets Field," captain Richard "Rug" Kauffman said. "We were in the home team locker room. I remember the stalls and the name of the players written in chalk."

Koufax had hands so big he could palm a basketball — or Freddy Horowitz's head in touch football, which is one way to bring down a receiver. Harry Ostro, Lafayette's football coach, drooled over him. Herb Stern was a 6'2", 175-pound defensive end on the all-city championship team whose roster included a future NFL all-pro, Sam DeLuca, and neighborhood legend Nick De Cicco. "One afternoon after practice Ostro told us that Sandy was going to be trying out the next day at quarterback. He said he would like to get Sandy on the team but wanted to be sure that he was serious about it and not just trying to get his third letter. So he told us not to pussyfoot around and to be really tough on him. We did our best and sacked him a few times."

Koufax never returned, intimidated, Stern assumed, by his less-than-genteel welcome from the Lafayette line — or perhaps by the coach's admonition that football wouldn't leave much time for cheerleaders. It wasn't until 50 years later that Stern learned the truth: Koufax's mother wouldn't let him play tackle football. "Jewish boys don't play football," his teammate Burl "Big Job" Abramowitz remembered Koufax's family saying. "They own the team." Herb Stern was relieved. His mother wouldn't let him play either. Those were the days when mothers were mothers, not soccer moms, and no meant no; when the captain of the football team, a future economist

nicknamed Rug for "rugged," topped the scales at 164 pounds; when bonus babies enrolled in college architecture classes — just in case.

Today vertical leap is measured straight out of the womb. Star athletes choose their sport before they can walk — or have it chosen for them by adults wielding biomechanical models and fat calipers. Kids play not to find out what they might become but to become what they are expected to be. Their muscles may be better stretched, their fibers (fast twitch and slow) better understood, but the elasticity of childhood is gone. There's no play in play, no room for Bill Cosby's improvisational play-calling: "You go ten steps and cut left behind the black Chevy. You run down to my house and wait in the living room." No room for George Burns's improvised field of play: "A manhole cover was home plate, a fire hydrant was first base, second base was a lamppost, and Mr. Gitletz who used to bring a kitchen chair down to watch us play was third base. One time I slid into Mr. Gitletz. He caught the ball and tagged me out."

And there is no room for the improvisation of self. In Koufax's day, you got to invent yourself as you went along. He wasn't groomed to become the greatest left-handed pitcher in the history of major league baseball. His dream was to play for the New York Knicks. He played sandlot ball in "Pop" Secol's Ice Cream League because it was more fun than homework. His father didn't even know he played baseball until he happened by the field one day. And he wasn't a pitcher. Plenty of guys claim they hit against Koufax back in high school. "Must have been a helluva throw since he played first base," Big Job said.

Much has been gained in the industrialization of sport, but something's been lost too. Premeditation has preempted serendipity. Who knows: if Koufax had started throwing curves in earnest at age 8, would his left elbow have lasted until he was 30? Would his interest have waned and a challenge been found elsewhere?

If his future was uncharted, his physique and character were already formed.

Raymond Conrad lived in the apartment next door. It was tough being a newcomer to Bensonhurst — not to mention being a short, Scandinavian 13-year-old in a neighborhood of rough-and-tumble Italians and Jews. "To me he was massive in size," Conrad said. "The young boys always gathered around this gentle giant, and he encouraged them to joust with him and try to punch him in the stomach. Sandy was virtually made of steel. I threw a very hard jab at him and was reduced to tears as my fist simply bounced off his body."

When he wasn't playing some kind of ball, Koufax was hanging out on the corner or at Seidman's Radio and Music Shop at 8509 Bay Parkway. "My grandfather sold and repaired record players, radios, and stereos," Seidman's grandson, Alan Goldstein, recalled. "The store also sold records and had what was billed as the most extensive collection of oldies. Mr. Koufax frequented my grandfather's shop and used to buy records, mostly classical, and work on radios and stereos at the workbench in the rear of the store. I believe that my grandfather helped teach Mr. Koufax how to repair and build radios and stereos. To allow Mr. Koufax to listen to records on the road, my grandfather built a record player into a suitcase. My grandfather said that Mr. Koufax was very shy, and when people came into the store, Mr. Koufax often would hide in the bathroom."

Years later an agent trying to do him a good turn was stunned when Koufax turned down an offer of $5,000. All he had to do was present a check at a banquet. "No," Koufax said. "They want a talker. I'm not a talker." In the fall of 1953 Koufax went off to the University of Cincinnati, not to play basketball on an athletic scholarship (he made the freshman team as a walk-on); nor was it on his agenda to become a big-league star. He begged for a tryout when he learned the baseball team was spending spring break in New Orleans and Florida, which sounded a whole lot better than Bensonhurst in April.

He arrived in Cincinnati with a nickname — "the Animal" — and determination that proved determinative. There were two Jewish fraternities on campus. One day the New York house took on the Cincinnati house in a game of three-on-three tackle football. His friend and teammate Ed Rothenberg played opposite him. "No shoulder pads — we hiked and ran and passed," Rothenberg said.

The game went on and on, the points and the bruises mounting. Finally only the two of them remained. "Everybody else faded away, bruised and beat up," Rothenberg said. "I know we had 100 points each. Can you imagine picking up

the ball and trying to run against Koufax? He was kind of gentle bringing me down. He wasn't about to quit. Finally, I just gave up and he won."

Sophomore year Koufax returned to Cincinnati with a $20,000 Dodger offer and a dilemma. "He wanted to know what I thought, because, y'know, Jews don't do that," Rothenberg remembered. "I said, 'Sandy, if these guys think you're that good that they're offering you that kind of money, take it. You can always go back to college.' That was the last time I talked to him. Then he was just gone."

The day he signed with the home team, Marv Raab saw him standing outside Dubrow's Cafeteria in Brooklyn, a lanky kid in a Lafayette sweatshirt, telling the world: "I just signed with the Dodgers!" He seemed as surprised as everyone else.

Later, much later, when he had become "good enough to pray against" — as Joe Torre, another Brooklyn kid, put it — Koufax gave Pop Secol an autographed ball. It said: "From all of us who you gave a chance to play."

Pop inscribed the words on a gold dog tag and adorned it with diamonds, one for each of Koufax's four major league no-hitters. He wore it around his neck until the day he died. His son, Steve, didn't dare take it from the old man until it was time to lay Pop in the ground.

Jane Leavy was a sportswriter and features writer for the *Washington Post*. She is the author of the novel *Squeeze Play* and the best-selling *Sandy Koufax: A Lefty's Legacy*.

required. Thrown at nearly 100 miles per hour, it was, after all, a potentially lethal weapon. But Koufax was no head-hunter—he'd proven that against the Giants. Koufax feared the consequences if one of his pitches got away, and he would hit only five men all year. Perhaps he hadn't wanted to go after Marichal because of how it might look if he beaned someone and hurt him and then it came out he was pitching on codeine. He didn't need to pitch inside very often anyway. The knowledge among hitters that he could, when he wanted to, was plenty to keep them off the plate. Still, throwing a baseball on codeine is something that perhaps no other pitcher in the game could have gotten away with. One slip and the results could have been devastating for everyone involved.

Maybe Koufax had grown tired of the whispers, or maybe leaving a few games early since August 14 had given his arm a measure of much needed rest, or perhaps in the wake of the Roseboro-Marichal debacle he had lost a certain measure of aggressiveness. After the game against the Giants, Koufax told San Diego reporter Gene Collier that he planned to retire after the 1966 season, a decision that may not have been coincidental with the events of August 19.

But against the Cubs he was sharp from the start. Perfect even.

Both Koufax and Hendley entered the fifth inning with a no-hitter. Koufax had given up only two hard-hit balls—a foul line drive by Glenn Beckert in the first and a hard drive to center field by Byron Browne in the second. Meanwhile, Hendley was pitching the game of his life, a game that against any other team in any other year would have been enough. But not against a team with Koufax pitching against him.

In the fifth Lou Johnson scored on a "withering walk" and a "slashing error." The walk was one of only 24 he would get all year. Ron Fairly sacrificed him to second, and Johnson stole third. When catcher Chris Krug's throw sailed into left field, he scored, and the Dodgers led 1–0.

That's all Koufax needed. He struck out 14. He didn't let a man reach base, and the Dodgers won 1–0. And as Vin Scully informed L.A. listeners after the last pitch, "On the scoreboard in right field it is 9:46 P.M. in the City of Angels, Los Angeles, California, and a crowd of 29,139 just sitting in to see the only pitcher in baseball history to hurl four no-hit, no-run games. He has done it four straight years, and now he capped it: on his fourth no-hitter, he made it a perfect game. And Sandy Koufax, whose name will always remind you of

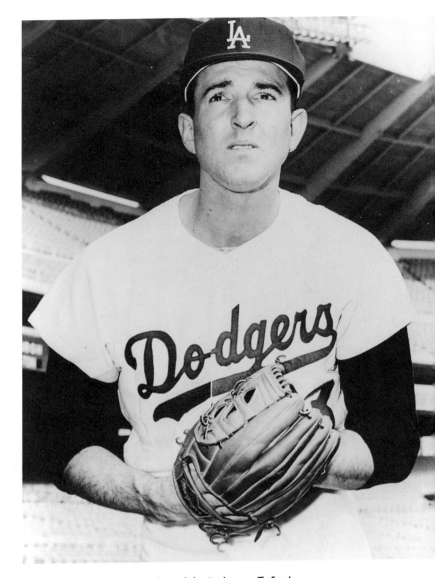

Left-hander Claude Osteen bolstered the Dodger staff after he arrived from the Senators in a deal that sent slugger Frank Howard to Washington. Osteen finished the 1965 season with a solid 15–15 record and went on to win the third game of the World Series with a 4–0 shutout of the Twins.

strikeouts, did it with a flourish. He struck out the last six consecutive batters."

Frank Finch called him "a Michelangelo among pitchers." Even Koufax seemed surprised by the performance. When a reporter asked if he'd thrown a pitch he'd wanted back all night, he said, "No, I don't think so," before adding that on the pitch to Browne, "I didn't want it back when I let it go but I wanted it back after he hit it." When Drysdale learned of the

NL COMPLETE GAME LEADERS

1910	Nap Rucker	27
1921	Burleigh Grimes	30
1923	Burleigh Grimes	33
1924	Burleigh Grimes Dazzy Vance	30 30
1927	Dazzy Vance	25
1965	Sandy Koufax	27
1966	Sandy Koufax	27
1975	Andy Messersmith	19
1981	Fernando Valenzuela	11
1986	Fernando Valenzuela	20
1987	Fernando Valenzuela	12
1988	Orel Hershiser	15
1989	Tim Belcher	10
1990	Ramon Martinez	12

perfect game, fully aware of how hard it was to pitch and win on this team, he asked of Koufax, "Did he win?"

But on that same day Marichal returned for San Francisco. He threw a shutout, and the Dodgers still trailed by a half-game. As late as September 20, they trailed by four games.

Then, as if keyed by Koufax's performance, the Dodgers got hot, or at least their pitching staff and Lou Johnson did. That was enough.

This was Sandy Koufax's and the Dodgers' year, not Marichal's and the Giants'. On September 26—the 154th game of the season—Koufax broke Bob Feller's single-season strikeout mark of 348, setting down Mike Shannon on his way to 12 strikeouts for the day and a 2–0 shutout of St. Louis. The win was L.A.'s eighth in a row.

Drysdale followed with a 1–0 win when Wills led off the game with a bunt hit, went to second on a pickoff play, and then advanced to third when the throw went wide. Gilliam singled, and that was it—another Dodger win.

The Dodgers couldn't lose and pulled into a tie with the Giants on September 27. On September 28 Lou Johnson's 12th-inning home run pulled them into first place, and the next day Koufax ran the win streak to 12 with another shutout, beating Cincinnati 5–0, to put the Dodgers ahead by two with only four games left.

Then Drysdale threw a shutout to make it 13 in a row—7 by shutout. And even though Osteen broke the streak with a loss on October 1, the Giants lost too.

Alston went for the throat. He brought Koufax back to pitch the next-to-last game of the season on two days' rest, and Koufax put an exclamation point on the season with a 3–1 win over the Braves. The headline in the *Times* said it all:

IT'S ALL OVER!
The Dodger Way: 2
Hits + Sandy = Flag

The game ended appropriately, with a fly ball to Lou Johnson. After being excellent over much of the season, he finished the year with 10 hits in his last 18 at bats and was every bit as responsible for the pennant as Koufax or Drysdale.

The Dodgers had three days before the start of the World Series against the surprising Minnesota Twins. They were bristling with confidence. Bavasi made the mistake of saying, "We can win it in four straight." The Twins were all right, he thought, but "three or four teams in our league would have won the pennant over there."

In fact, the Twins were much better than Bavasi thought. They had won 102 games despite playing nearly half the year without Harmon Killebrew, probably the most feared home run hitter in the American League. They had a little of everything — power, speed, defense, and pitching.

But over the final days of the season one big caution flag had been raised. The series was scheduled to begin on October 6, the Jewish holiday of Yom Kippur. Koufax didn't wear his religion on his sleeve, but he wouldn't pitch on Yom Kippur. The decision made him a hero to many Jews, but scared other Dodger fans to death.

At first it didn't seem like a big deal. Drysdale had been untouchable down the stretch, and he would open the Series. What was more important was that the decision seemed to preclude Koufax pitching three times in the Series. That was okay if the Dodgers fulfilled Bavasi's prophecy. But if they didn't, well, that would be tough for many to swallow.

After the pressure cooker of the pennant race, the Dodgers came out flat. Drysdale was routed in the second inning of game one when Zoilo Versalles, the AL MVP, cracked a three-run home run. Minnesota won going away, 8–2, leading Drysdale to quip to Alston, "I bet you wish I was Jewish too."

Koufax returned to the club the next day and got the ball, but on a cold and wet day in Minnesota, he didn't have it. Jim Kaat outpitched him, and the Twins won 5–1. Kaat hadn't even bothered to look at the scouting reports on the Dodger hitters. He credited Minnesota pitching coach Johnny Sain for getting him to "rely on your natural stuff and throw strikes." Against the L.A. lineup, even that seemed like overkill. "Shutout or nothing" baseball had worked down the stretch for the Dodgers, but this was the World Series.

Back in Los Angeles the Dodgers looked to Claude Osteen to stop the Twins, and he went back to the Dodgers' tried-and-true strategy. He knew the Twins from his time in the American League, and it showed. He shut them out, and the Dodger offense did more than enough against Camilo Pascual — Murray termed their ten hits "more than they got in July." He wasn't far off.

In game four they got another month's worth of hits against Mudcat Grant, even though six of the ten never left the infield. Of the four that did, however, two were home runs, one by Johnson and another by Wes Parker. Drysdale

pitched more carefully, and the Dodgers won 7–2. With Koufax ready again to face Kaat, the Series was square.

This time around it was different, although after the game Kaat offered that "the batters learned more than the pitchers from their first meeting," L.A. Times writer Al Wolf noted that Kaat was "half right and half wrong," for while Dodger hitters learned enough to hit Kaat, Minnesota hitters couldn't touch Koufax.

He shut them out and shut them down, 7–0, scattering four hits and striking out ten as the Dodgers parlayed fourteen hits into seven runs. Even Koufax got an RBI, something observers found far more remarkable than the fact that he pitched a shutout. So far, L.A.'s hitless wonders were stinging the ball, at least for them, out-hitting the Twins .302 to .212 and running wild on the bases.

But Claude Osteen couldn't close out the Series back in Minnesota. Bob Allison and Mudcat Grant both homered, and the Twins tied the Series.

All Dodger fans cared about now was Alston's pitching choice for game seven. Drysdale was in line for the start, but there was Koufax, with two days' rest and only one game to worry about.

Koufax wanted the ball, and his teammates wanted him to have it. Compared to everybody else, Drysdale was one of the best pitchers in baseball. Compared to Koufax . . . well, it just wasn't fair to compare him to Koufax.

Koufax's arm was sore, but that wasn't news. He told Alston he could pitch, and he got the ball. Drysdale would be the first pitcher out of the pen. If the Dodgers were going to lose, they'd do so with their best.

In game five Koufax had had a great curveball, but when he went out to the mound for game seven, it wasn't there. With two out in the first inning, he walked Tony Oliva and Harmon Killebrew. Drysdale got up and stayed up most of the game. Finally, the pitch bit, and Koufax struck out Earl Battey on a curve to end the inning.

Kaat was pitching on two days as well, but he hadn't lasted long in game five. Early on he was sharp while Koufax wasn't. Koufax didn't have many pitches left. In the third inning, after hanging a curve to Versalles, he bid farewell to Candy Cummings and turned to Jim Creighton. John Roseboro's job became extraordinarily simple — put down one finger and just catch the ball. For Koufax, it would be fastballs, nothing but fastballs, the rest of the way.

It was the oldest game in the world, call it what you want—good old country hardball or backyard baseball. It was Koufax's best against the Twins' best—hit-it-if-you-can baseball.

They couldn't. The Twins learned what hundreds of National League hitters already knew—you couldn't. Oh, once in a while a guy got lucky, or once in a while Koufax missed and somebody hit the ball hard or fought off a flare, and sometimes the hard ones were caught and the flares fell in, or vice versa, but unless both fell in, it was impossible. Koufax was pitching like it was the last game he would ever throw, making each pitch like it was his last, because, well, it might be.

Koufax gave up a single to Versalles in the third, a double to Frank Quilici in the fifth, a hard ball hit by Versalles that Jim Gilliam stopped at third, and a single to Killebrew in the ninth. Three hits.

In the second Sweet Lou Johnson reached out and caught a Jim Kaat pitch low and away and hit it where he shouldn't have been able to, down the line in left, high and deep and off the foul pole. Lou Johnson was having an entire season doing what he shouldn't have been able to. He stilled the crowd and clapped his hands while running around the bases. He *knew*. Koufax had his run. And when Fairly followed with a double and Parker singled, he had another. Two to nothing, Dodgers.

Bob Allison was the last Minnesota hitter, but that noun no longer applied to most batters facing Koufax, and with one out remaining and Koufax on the mound, the Dodgers had the safest two-run lead in the history of baseball. Koufax struck him out on five pitches, and the Dodgers were champions again.

They were almost too exhausted to celebrate much. John Roseboro was in awe of what Koufax had accomplished with one pitch. "It can't be done unless you are exceptional, and Sandy is the most exceptional pitcher in the game today," he said. Then Koufax and Roseboro told the story of the game.

If 1965 was the season Sandy Koufax became a legend, 1966 was the season he became human again, and it was also the season when the Dodgers pushed just a little too far and too hard, just about everywhere they could, from the front office to the playing field.

Two world championships in three seasons with the same core of players made the front office overconfident. Although the club screamed for more offense, in the off-season they made only a single move, sending Dick Tracewski to the Tigers for Phil Regan, a once-decent starting pitcher who

couldn't get anybody out in 1965. The Dodgers were hoping he could win a spot behind Osteen in the rotation. But by March the whole equation had changed.

In 1965 Drysdale had earned $80,000, Koufax $85,000. Not only had they carried the team on their collective back, but Koufax had risked becoming a cripple.

The two pitchers thought that counted for something. They also realized they had more leverage together than either did alone. And in Los Angeles, where each was a celebrity, they had options. Hollywood was calling, and although both were about as helpless in front of a camera as the hitters who faced them, they were nevertheless being offered roles for money that more than equaled their baseball salaries.

Walter O'Malley's financial success in L.A. had made him baseball's most powerful owner, and his paternalistic style and personality, while not unique, set the tone in regard to player-owner relationships. The one-year contract and the reserve clause, which left a player with no option but to sign the contract offered or not play at all, was entirely in favor of ownership. The Players' Association barely existed and was completely powerless. Each player was on his own.

That was just the way Walter O'Malley and his cronies liked it. To the other owners, O'Malley was the exemplar. They didn't necessarily like him, because Dodger success gave him disproportionate influence in league affairs, but it was hard to argue with the Dodgers' record, on the field and off.

Like most of his fellow owners, O'Malley erroneously believed that the unbalanced relationship between owner and player, which sent all the money straight into his own pocket, somehow made him a financial genius and a steward of this increasingly anachronistic arrangement. He would soon learn otherwise.

When he gave Buzzie Bavasi his budget for player salaries in 1966, it included only a minimal increase for Koufax, Drysdale, and other players. After all, went O'Malley's logic, they'd all made extra money winning the World Series the last two years. But the Dodger revenue stream was a river when it ran toward O'Malley—and only a trickle when it ran back out.

In the off-season, by chance, Koufax and Drysdale had dinner, started talking money, and realized that O'Malley and Bavasi had been playing one off the other, telling each player that the other was asking for less than he really had been, and holding salaries down for both.

That was it. Instant reality check. Despite all that each pitcher had done, the Dodgers had been cheating both of them *for years.* Loyalty was a one-way street that stopped at the wallet. So, in Koufax's words, he and Drysdale formed a "union of two."

Koufax in particular was feeling belligerent. Despite his decision to retire after the 1966 season, his contract request indicated that he was at least considering pitching longer. Clearly, however, he had made the decision to leave the game on his own terms, and the request was part of that. Koufax had more than earned his money in the past, and it is hard to believe that if he had signed a three-year contract he wouldn't have tried to pitch past 1966. But if he didn't get it, well, his decision was made for him. In a sense, the request was a litmus test to gauge the ballclub's faith in him and recognition of not only his unique value but also the extraordinary sacrifices he was willing to make to take the mound every day.

Koufax's lawyer, J. William Hayes, would handle the negotiations for the two. They did their homework and figured out how much each meant to the Dodgers at the gate. They concluded that games started by Koufax drew, on average, an extra 10,000 fans, while Drysdale drew an extra 3,000. Each pitched more than 40 times per season. Including the revenue from concessions and parking, the two pitchers were easily responsible for adding upward of $1 million a year to the Dodger coffers, and probably much more than that. They weren't greedy—each wanted only a three-year deal worth $500,000, a combined $1 million for the services of both pitchers, $166,000 each per year, far less than their value.

That request stood tradition on its head. Not only did it break baseball's unwritten $100,000 a year salary barrier, but each player wanted a multi*year* contract and had hired an attorney to serve as an *agent* and negotiator.

Koufax and Drysdale may as well have asked that the money be shared with a Soviet farm collective. Even though O'Malley could well afford it, even though the players were right, and even though they were still undervaluing their worth, they never had a realistic chance to win.

Neither the press nor the public had yet been educated about the long-standing inherent inequities of the player-owner relationship, and the reserve clause, which bound a player to a team for life, was still in effect no matter what. The fact that the holdout was doomed to fail is less significant, however, than the lasting impression it made on other players. In only a few years, after a long period of dormancy that began with the collapse of the Players' League, baseball players would begin to assert their rights. The Koufax-Drysdale

Dodger center fielder Willie Davis leaps high to rob Oriole first baseman Boog Powell of a home run in the fourth inning of the fourth game of the 1966 World Series at Memorial Stadium. Despite Davis's catch, the Dodgers lost the game 1–0 as the Orioles swept the defending world champions.

holdout is an important benchmark in the history of baseball labor relations.

When spring training began on February 26, Koufax and Drysdale stayed home. The Dodgers yawned. O'Malley knew that eventually they'd either cave in or sit out. And from the beginning the Dodgers categorically rejected the notion of negotiating with both players in some kind of package deal — that was a precedent they would not accept under any circumstances.

Wills was also a holdout. Once he saw what Koufax and Drysdale wanted, he reassessed his own value. He'd played for $60,000 in 1965. Now he wanted $100,000.

For the first two weeks of camp the Dodgers and their holdouts indulged in a public relations war. Once again, Drysdale and Koufax didn't have a chance. They were in L.A. — all the writers were in Vero Beach getting the party line from the Dodgers and the players in camp, most of whom were too insecure to say publicly what they felt privately. Stories featuring quotes like Willie Davis's "They treat me good here" abounded, as did statements from fans mocking Koufax and Drysdale as some kind of modern-day Bolsheviks, criticizing both for asking for such outrageous salaries for "two hours' worth of work every four days."

And every day there were more stories in support of O'Malley, pithy quotes from Bavasi such as, "They tell me they are independently wealthy — I wish them the best of luck," and intimations of morale problems among the Dodgers in camp. Then, in mid-March, Bavasi played hardball with Wills. He told Wills that O'Malley would have him blackballed. That was no idle threat — the shortstop knew that as a black man he didn't have the same leverage as the two white pitchers. Wills caved in and signed for a reported $75,000.

Yet Koufax and Drysdale stayed out and tried to make their threat of sitting out the season seem real. Koufax accepted a $110,000 advance for an autobiography to be written with Ed Linn. Drysdale was reportedly mulling an offer to pitch in Japan and was ready to sign a contract as an actor with Screen Gems. Both were reportedly ready to start working on April 4

Just prior to the end of their celebrated holdout in 1966, Sandy Koufax and Don Drysdale sit alongside actor David Janssen on the set of the film *Warning Shot*. Although the Dodgers rejected the duo's bid for multiyear contracts, they paid Koufax $125,000 and Drysdale $110,000 for the 1966 season.

in a movie with David Janssen, aptly titled *Warning Shot*. In late March they even appeared on the set. Paramount made sure there were cameras, and on March 29 *Times* readers saw each player flanking Janssen in his own personalized director's chair.

The next day the two signed with the Dodgers. In the end both sides wanted — and needed — the other. The club had

---

Right-hander Don Drysdale and lefty Sandy Koufax were one of the best pitching duos in major league history. Between them, they won 374 regular season games and seven World Series games for the Dodgers. Together they helped lead the Dodgers to six National League pennants and four world championships in their 12-year partnership.

been 6–12 in spring training and looked awful. Tommy Davis had shown up to camp still limping. The Angels were moving into their new park and taking their windfall with them. And in the end both Koufax and Drysdale wanted to pitch. It was who they were and what they did. In Hollywood you were good only because someone else said so. In baseball the scoreboard said it all.

The two sides had reached a compromise of sorts. The Dodgers rejected every aspect of the pitchers' request apart from a raise, and the players acquiesced. Each got more money — $125,000 for Koufax and $110,000 for Drysdale — and O'Malley and Bavasi were able to save face by rejecting both the package deal for their two stars and the notion of a multiyear pact. Drysdale was reportedly satisfied, but privately Koufax was not. He now knew exactly where he stood with the team. The club didn't know it, but by signing him to a one-year contract, they made it certain he would play only one more season.

If there was a silver lining for the team, it was the fact that during the holdout there were another 60 innings to spread around among the other Dodger pitchers in camp. Phil Regan, who made the team as a reliever, was impressive, as was rookie Don Sutton. Only 21 years old, Sutton came to camp with the nickname "Sutton Death." In only one year of pro ball, split between single and double-A, he had gone 23–6.

Koufax and Drysdale took a surprisingly short time to get ready. Both had stayed in shape during the holdout, and in back-to-back starts just before the start of the season at Dodger Stadium, both looked to be in midseason form — Koufax pitched six no-hit innings against the Indians, and the next day Drysdale also shut out the Indians for six innings.

Another pennant race ensued. And once again the Dodgers had to win with Band-Aids and balls of string — they would be shut out 17 times in 1966. Only Jim Lefebvre and Lou Johnson were significantly better than they were in 1965 — they would hit 24 and 17 home runs, respectively, giving the club more power than they had had in years. But Tommy Davis was now damaged goods, his speed gone, Wills was starting to wear down, and Jim Gilliam, after more than a decade of service as a valuable table-setter, was just about done. He, Koufax, and Podres were the Dodgers' only remaining links to the glory days in Brooklyn — Drysdale had played at Ebbets Field but missed out on 1955. Gilliam had simply done his job quietly and efficiently, playing second, third, or the outfield as needed, allowing Alston to mix and match with other players. But it was harder for Gilliam to be that flexible now.

And Podres was finished as well. In May, although the team needed offense, he was sold to the Tigers for cash. The emergence of Sutton, who, if not for the holdout of Koufax and Drysdale, would probably have been ticketed to Spokane, made Podres redundant.

It was pitching, pitching, pitching. Sutton came through, and for the first time in years the club had a fourth starter who could be trusted to take the ball every fourth day. Apart from the big four of Koufax, Drysdale, Osteen, and Sutton, only one other pitcher — Joe Moeller — would earn a start in 1966, and he would take the ball only eight times.

And the bullpen was never better. Miller and Perranoski continued their fine work, and Phil Regan emerged as the best in the league.

The Dodgers got off slow, trailing the Giants by seven in mid-May. They surged into contention in mid-June, but then faltered. Drysdale was struggling to win, and although Koufax was nearly as good as he had been in 1965 and Phil Regan swooped in to win so many games late that he earned the nickname "the Vulture," the Dodgers couldn't seem to put together the kind of streak that had swept them to the pennant in 1965.

By late August they looked done and trailed both the Giants and first-place Pittsburgh. They then won five in a row, sweeping past the Giants, only to watch as the Pirates also won five straight. The Dodgers had gained nothing but a place in the standings.

On September 5, they looked finished. Despite beating the Giants 4–1, Sutton pulled a muscle in his forearm. In the last week Osteen had been bothered by a groin pull, Drysdale had hurt a knee, and in his last start Koufax had had to leave because of exhaustion. On the 6th, Osteen couldn't take his turn. Drysdale stepped in and was pounded as the Giants pulled into a tie for second place. Early that day Koufax's book had come out, and as one writer noted at a book signing earlier that day, "Koufax was in a mood quite unlike the one in which Buzzie Bavasi found him last spring. He was ready to sign anything." At a downtown bookstore he reportedly autographed over 3,000 copies of his book. The next day Koufax pitched only seven innings against the Giants, leaving the game trailing 2–1. The Dodgers tied it up, but in the twelfth

Willie Mays scored when he kicked the ball out of John Roseboro's glove on a play at home.

The Dodgers were turning testy. In the middle of the game Wills and Davis had scuffled over a missed sign, and after the game, when Roseboro was asked if Mays had in fact kicked the ball out, he snapped, "How the hell do you think it got out of there?"

Then, just as suddenly, the Dodgers turned it around. True to form, pitching did it. The club went into Houston's Astrodome, and Osteen started things off with a shutout against the Astros, winning 7–0. The next day Drysdale and Regan turned the trick, combining to win 1–0. Then, in a doubleheader, Koufax shut them out 4–0 and Moeller, Miller, and Regan combined to win 1–0 in the second game. Four games, four shutouts, and the Dodgers were in first place for the first time since August 7, when they had led by a percentage point for one day.

They ran their streak to eight in a row, padding their lead, and into the last week looked as if they'd cruise to the pennant. Then they relaxed and stumbled, and on October 1 the Giants took a doubleheader from the Pirates for their sixth straight win. Going into the final day of the season, the outcome remained up in the air.

The Dodgers were in Philadelphia, forced to play a doubleheader to make up for an earlier rainout. All they needed was one win or a San Francisco loss to Pittsburgh. But if they were swept and the Giants won, then San Francisco would play a makeup game with Cincinnati. If the Giants won that, the Dodgers and Giants would be in another playoff.

Koufax had pitched and won only two days before, beating St. Louis 2–1 and striking out 13 for his 26th win. Alston hoped to save him for a potential World Series start and went with Drysdale in the first game.

It wasn't Drysdale's year, and somehow, despite pitching remarkably well for most of every season and for much of his career, when he pitched a game he had to win, when there was no tomorrow for him, he couldn't win. Maybe it was chance, or maybe it was because of Koufax, who always pitched the game after that and who always gave the Dodgers another tomorrow. Drysdale was shelled in the first inning, giving up two runs, and then was pulled in the second. Ron Perranoski passed the ball to Bob Miller in the fifth. Ron Fairly cracked a three-run homer in the sixth to give the Dodgers a lead and put them only 12 outs from the pennant.

But in the eighth the Dodger defense fell apart when Bob Miller threw a ball into center field and Jim Lefebvre's throw to the plate with the bases loaded went wide of Roseboro. The Phillies won, 4–3, and now game two meant something.

There was no question about it. Koufax would pitch on two days' rest. Like Superman, he'd even raced to the bullpen in the eighth inning of the first game, hoping to staunch the rally before that game was lost. Now he would have to go nine.

In Koufax's mind, everything was clear. The Dodgers needed to win. He was pitching for perhaps the last time with everything on the line exactly a year after he had come into almost the precise same situation at the end of the 1965 season.

And it unfolded in much the same way. In the first inning Koufax couldn't find his curveball and got in immediate trouble. But he fanned the Phillies' cleanup hitter, Richie Allen, with one out and two on and got out of the inning.

That taught him something. He threw away the curve and for the next eight innings just threw fastballs.

It wasn't easy and it hurt. Between innings he popped pills, rubbed on more Atomic Balm, and had people in the clubhouse tug on him to work out a crick in his back.

His fastball—and his arm, his pills, and shot upon shot upon shot of God knows what—got him into the ninth. The Dodgers led, 6–0.

Koufax needed three more outs. But Allen reached on an error by Lefebvre, then Harvey Kuenn and Tony Taylor singled to make the score 6–1. Bill White doubled, and it was 6–3, one on, no outs, no more margin for error.

Alston went to the mound. If one more man got on, Koufax was coming out.

The arm was gone now, and so was the fastball. All he had left was heart.

It was big enough to strike out Bob Uecker and to get Bobby Wine to ground out, scoring another run, bringing up leadoff hitter Jackie Brandt.

It was as if Koufax made a pact with the Devil: "Just give me three more pitches, just three more, then do what you want."

He got his wish, three fastballs equal to any he had ever thrown. Brandt struck out—Koufax's tenth—and the Dodgers had won another pennant.

This time they celebrated big, and through the champagne Koufax—27–6 for the season, with a league-leading 313 strikeouts—blubbered, "Thank God it's over," talking

about the game, talking about the season, talking about his career.

But it wasn't over, not yet. The Baltimore Orioles, fueled by former Reds star Frank Robinson's Triple Crown season and a pitching staff made up of hard-throwing baby faces who didn't know they were too young to win the pennant or the World Series, had won the American League.

While the Baltimore hitters knew that Dodger pitching could shut them down, Baltimore's pitchers didn't even think about that. They were brash, confident. They knew the Dodgers couldn't hit.

And that's what happened. Los Angeles had its best shot in game one. At least they scored in that one.

The Orioles made Dodger Stadium look small as Brooks and Frank Robinson both hit early home runs and Drysdale never made it to the third inning. The Dodgers came back to tie the score off Baltimore's Dave McNally, but then Moe Drabowsky came on in relief. He was a good pitcher, but not good enough to start for the Orioles. The Dodgers made him look like Koufax, and one had to wonder just how many strikeouts Koufax might have gotten in a game if he had ever had the opportunity to pitch against his own team. Drabowsky blew the Dodgers away, striking out eleven over the final six and two-thirds innings and giving up only one hit. Baltimore won, 5–2, and Baltimore's young pitchers took notice. Afterward, Jim Palmer bluntly told the press, after watching Drabowsky, that "you can beat the Dodgers with a fastball."

The 20-year-old Palmer started game two not bothered by the fact that he was pitching opposite Koufax, whom he had worshiped as a kid and seen pitch at both Dodger Stadium and the Coliseum. Palmer had grown up in Beverly Hills and was unfazed by being in the World Series. He'd seen stars all the time; Leo Durocher's son had been on his Little League team. Facing Koufax, he said, "would be a challenge." But Palmer already knew the Dodgers couldn't hit him.

In what would prove to be the last game Sandy Koufax ever pitched, neither he nor his teammates were up for it. Koufax, making his third start in eight days, was gassed, and the last line of defense, the Dodgers' fielding, let him down. Willie Davis made three errors in center field, losing balls in the sun. His teammates made three more. In six innings Koufax threw as many pitches as he usually did in nine. He gave up four runs, only one earned, and struck out only two.

It wasn't the way he wanted it to end. It wasn't the way any of them wanted it to end. But Koufax and the Dodgers had gotten absolutely everything they could from one another. Winning another pennant had taken everything. Koufax would walk away from the game with four no-hitters, four straight Cy Young Awards — the last four Cy Youngs given only to the best pitcher in *both* leagues — six years as nobody, then six years as one of the best pitchers the game had ever seen, and the last two as perhaps the best there ever was. For his career, he won 165 games and lost 87, but in his final four seasons he was 97–27.

And now, in the World Series, he had nothing left, and neither did the Dodgers — they had run out of ways to win without scoring. It was an easy 6–0 win for Jim Palmer as one Hall of Famer passed the torch to another. Then Wally Bunker shut them out in game three, beating Osteen and Regan 1–0. McNally did the trick in game four, beating Drysdale by the same score.

For years the Dodgers had been squeezing out wins like grains of sand through the narrow neck of an hourglass. And now, finally, it had all run out.

CALIFORNIA DREAMING

SIX MONTHS AFTER PLAYING IN THE WORLD SERIES, DODGER GM BUZZIE Bavasi made an admission that only a few months before would have been unthinkable.

"We always want to win the pennant, and we always expect to, but we don't think the public expects us to win this year. . . . So we think we're free to experiment." In the six months after the World Series the Dodgers had changed more dramatically than they had since before the days of Branch Rickey.

Since coming to Los Angeles in 1958, the Dodgers had enjoyed one long sweet ride. In less than a decade they had achieved more success than they had ever dreamed of in Brooklyn—at the gate, on the field, and everywhere else it mattered. For anyone except those who lived in Brooklyn, or maybe Long Island, the mention of the Dodgers evoked visions of palm trees and Dodger Stadium, fastballs and starlets, stolen bases and champagne.

If any team in baseball had adopted the swagger that until recently had belonged only to the Yankees, it was the L.A. Dodgers. Yet almost as soon as the 1966 World Series ended, despite possessing a pitching staff that still appeared capable of giving them a chance to win, the Dodgers were prepared to toss it away, to play "wait till next year" before next year had even started.

Walter O'Malley confers with Walter Alston in 1974. By this time O'Malley was the most powerful owner in baseball. He played a huge role in selecting Bowie Kuhn as baseball commissioner and helped Kuhn talk his fellow owners out of a proposed spring training lockout in 1976.

That approach would be an enormous mistake that would take nearly another decade to overcome fully. During that decade the team that had so long been ahead of the curve spent much of its time, if not behind the curve, behind other teams.

Of course, the wheels had started to fall off shortly after the end of the 1966 season. In the days following the loss to Baltimore, it was clear that there had to be some changes — scoring only two runs in the World Series was embarrassing.

Even Alston admitted, "It's pretty obvious we need a solid swinger," but he should have been thinking plural, not singular. And he dismissed the notion of getting a bona-fide slugger, saying, "I don't care so much for a long-ball hitter because our park isn't built that way." In a story headlined "Are Dodgers Due to Collapse Like Yanks?" the *Times* openly wondered if the loss to Baltimore was akin to the Yankees' loss to the Cardinals two years before, a herald of bad times ahead. And this was before anyone even knew Koufax wasn't returning.

A few days after the debacle against Baltimore, the team was scheduled to leave for Japan to represent American baseball in the annual goodwill tour. Koufax and Drysdale begged off, citing fatigue. Maury Wills also wanted out. Playing a 162-game season took a toll on Wills every bit as much as it did on the two pitchers. By October his legs were a mess, a mass of abrasions and bruises.

But Wills wasn't Koufax or Drysdale. The Dodgers bluntly told him he had to go, and Wills went — grudgingly. After only a few days, however, he left without club permission and went to Hawaii.

O'Malley took it personally. Ballplayers were changing. As the 1960s took hold, players were beginning to think for themselves. After being a holdout in 1966, Wills's defection was the last straw, a sign of egregious disloyalty. O'Malley wired Buzzie Bavasi — who didn't make the trip either but went on a cruise — and told him to get rid of Wills ASAP.

While Bavasi set out to do just that, Koufax was mulling over how to announce his retirement. He wanted to do it right after the Series, for there was already some speculation that he might call it quits — his recently published book was full of hints. Writers were pestering him with questions about his plans, and he tried to be diplomatic, telling them only, "I won't be able to say I'll return until I see how my elbow feels next spring," but he felt as if he were lying.

On November 16, while the Dodgers were in Japan and Wills was playing his banjo in a bar in Hawaii, Koufax told

Bavasi he was done. Bavasi begged him to hold off on any announcement for at least a week, until O'Malley returned from Japan — or even better, until after baseball's winter meetings. Bavasi knew he needed another pitcher, and if Koufax announced his retirement before then, he'd be dealing from a position of weakness. He hoped there was another Osteen out there.

But now Koufax had the hammer. And he remembered how he'd been treated the previous spring during the holdout.

He didn't wait for O'Malley or anyone else. He held a press conference on November 18 at the Beverly Wilshire Hotel and announced his decision. He was understated, as usual: "I don't have much to say, just a short statement. A few minutes ago I sent Buzzie Bavasi a letter asking him to put me on the voluntarily retired list." Then he took questions and told reporters that he was retiring, quite simply, because of his arm. The pain and fear of permanent damage to his arm was only part of it; the treatments he took were just as much of a concern. "I had to take a shot every ballgame," he admitted. "I don't know if cortisone is good for you." He added that he had been taking so many drugs that while pitching he felt "high half the time."

In Japan his teammates were stunned. Most echoed Ron Fairly, who said simply, "There's no way to replace him." The press concurred. Wrote Charles Maher in the *Times*, "This may appear to put the Dodgers in terrible trouble. But it is actually a little worse than that."

No kidding. Bavasi was already bemoaning the future. Although he said, "For fourteen years they've been telling me to get rid of my older players, and in that time we've won only eight pennants," he knew that now it was different. Koufax was completely irreplaceable.

It was common knowledge that the Dodgers were mad at Wills, but it wasn't yet public knowledge that he'd be traded. Now that Koufax was gone, did that move still make any sense?

No, but that didn't matter — that wasn't the point. Getting rid of Wills for skipping out on a series of exhibition games made little sense as it was. Getting rid of him after the Koufax retirement made no sense whatsoever. But he'd embarrassed O'Malley.

There wasn't a huge market for Wills. At 34, he was old for an infielder, and his skills weren't much in demand, for few other clubs had the need to scratch and claw for runs like the Dodgers. They didn't need a player to steal bases, and the consensus was that Wills was starting to slow down. The shortstop position was still viewed as essentially a defensive position, and Wills was no longer a very good fielder. He'd always been erratic, and while his shortcomings had been masked by playing half a season on the rock-hard infield of Dodger Stadium, that wasn't the case elsewhere.

The Dodgers also had to get a shortstop back in the deal. Bavasi opened shop but received few offers. "The line," he moaned, "is not forming to the right."

At the winter meetings he did what he could. For some reason the New York Mets thought Tommy Davis would regain his earlier form. The Dodgers, thinking he was babying his leg, had run out of patience waiting for him to be a star. Bavasi packaged him with infielder Derrell Griffith in exchange for second baseman Ron Hunt and outfielder Jim Hickman, a sometime slugger coming off a broken wrist. Hunt was actually pretty good but had trouble controlling his temper. During the 1966 season he'd written his ticket out of New York when in a fit of rage he'd thrown a bat into his own dugout. The Dodgers now planned to move Lefebvre to third, a perennial trouble spot. If they kept Wills, the Dodger infield was looking pretty good.

But that wasn't going to happen. Wills and the Dodgers started arguing in public. The shortstop said that his knees were bad and that if he didn't play with the Dodgers, he might not play at all. In response, the Dodgers announced that they were cutting his salary by the full legal amount, 25 percent. The end result made him even less valuable in trade.

Yet on December 1 Bavasi agreed to a trade with the Pirates. All he could get for Wills was Bob Bailey and Gene Michael. Michael was a triple-A shortstop who couldn't hit, while Bailey, a native of Long Beach, was a California high school legend turned bonus baby who had stagnated on the Pirate bench and never fulfilled his promise.

Wills couldn't believe it. He considered himself as much a part of the club's success as Koufax, and in a way he was. On a team that had a hard time scoring and played in a place like Dodger Stadium, he had been invaluable. And now he was being traded for a couple of spare parts because he flew to Hawaii? "I feel I've been as loyal and dedicated as any ballplayer that ever wore a Dodger uniform," he said.

And that was it. The L.A. Dodgers, the team that had used pitching, speed, and defense to win three world championships, were finished, just like that. The farm system, apart from pitching prospects, was barren. The Dodgers had been blind to their weaknesses, convinced that they could always

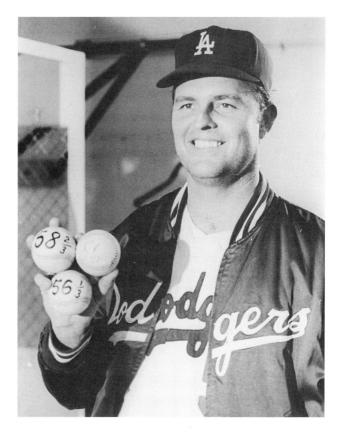

1968 was known as the "Year of the Pitcher," and nobody symbolized it better than Dodger right-hander Don Drysdale. He is shown holding the baseballs inscribed with the record-setting number of consecutive scoreless innings (58$\frac{2}{3}$) he reached on June 8, 1968, while breaking the previous record of 56 set by Hall of Famer Walter Johnson.

win with pitching, that hitting didn't matter. They stocked up on arms and let the offense take care of itself. But when they traded Wills, they lost any chance they had to remain respectable.

Bavasi was finished making deals. The Dodgers didn't even try to add a veteran starter to replace Koufax. Bob Miller started on Opening Day and lost to the Reds, 6–1. It wasn't long before the press began referring to the pitcher as "Bomb" Miller. Rookie Bill Singer soon took over for him in the rotation.

The Dodgers still had pitching, but even according to their low standards they couldn't hit, scoring nearly 100 runs less than in 1966, averaging barely three runs a game. In Don Drysdale's 16 losses, the Dodgers scored a total of 15 runs. Gene Michael hit .202 and couldn't field either. Bailey hit .227. Lou Johnson broke his leg.

1967

Wills hit .302 for Pittsburgh. Only the Astros and Mets kept the Dodgers out of last place. They finished 73–89. More significantly, attendance at Dodger Stadium dropped by a million fans, down to only 1.6 million, less than the pennant-winning Cardinals and Red Sox. It was the first time since moving from Brooklyn that the Dodgers hadn't led the majors in that category.

Some experiment. And it didn't look like 1968 would bring any improvement. It was obvious that the Dodgers missed Wills and needed offense, so in the off-season Bavasi made a trade he thought would take care of that, sending Roseboro, Ron Perranoski, and Bob Miller to the Twins for Zoilo Versalles and Mudcat Grant.

It would have been an interesting trade two years earlier. Now it was simply a swap of fading veterans.

It soon became clear why Bavasi had never made many trades — he didn't know how. He dealt for names, not talent. Lou Johnson was sent to the Cubs for Paul Popovich, an infielder with no pop whatsoever. Bavasi bought former slugger Rocky Colavito from the White Sox and sent Hunt to the Giants for catcher Tom Haller.

All those moves did was shuffle the deck — badly. Versalles was terrible and hit .196, and Colavito was almost as bad. Haller helped, but Popovich was dismal.

Just before the start of the 1968 season, the Dodgers made another monumental mistake. Civil rights leader Martin Luther King was assassinated on April 4, and America erupted. While the rest of baseball suspended operations, the Dodgers went ahead and played an exhibition game at Dodger Stadium against Cleveland. And when the rest of baseball pushed back Opening Day until after King's funeral on April 9, the Dodgers planned to play, even though their opponents, the Philadelphia Phillies, announced they would rather forfeit than participate. Hollywood even postponed the Academy Awards. But the Dodgers, the team that signed Jackie Robinson, insisted on playing their game.

Everything Bavasi said about the situation made him sound insensitive, and the organization appeared totally out of touch. "I talked to Willie Davis and [coach] Jim Gilliam," said Bavasi of the team's two high-profile African Americans.

On November 18, 1966, Sandy Koufax announced his retirement from baseball at a press conference held in Beverly Hills. The left-hander said he'd asked the Dodgers to place him on the voluntary retired list because his arthritic elbow compelled him to take "too many shots and too many pills."

NL MOST VALUABLE PLAYER AWARD

1913	Jake Daubert	1B (Chalmers Award)
1924	Dazzy Vance	P (NL Award)
1941	Dolph Camilli	1B
1949	Jackie Robinson	2B
1951	Roy Campanella	C
1953	Roy Campanella	C
1955	Roy Campanella	C
1956	Don Newcombe	P
1962	Maury Wills	SS
1963	Sandy Koufax	P
1974	Steve Garvey	1B
1988	Kirk Gibson	1B

"I told them the game would be played but they would not have to participate. It is similar to the time when Sandy Koufax did not play because of religious holidays." It was not.

He said the Dodgers planned to play "to give people some sort of amusement when they need it most. It may help keep people off the streets and to forget their anger." Besides, he reasoned, the Dodgers were playing a night game — King's funeral was in the morning.

The Dodgers were excoriated over the decision. On April 8 O'Malley and Bavasi met and finally backed down, but the damage to the team's reputation was done. Bavasi didn't help matters by saying afterward, "There's no sense bumping our heads against a stone wall," as if the decision had somehow been correct and everybody else was wrong. They simply didn't understand that choosing not to play was a matter of respect.

The Dodgers were trying to give the 1968 season a theme. They called it "Operation Bounceback." And when they finally opened on April 10, that's just what they did, bouncing back to where they'd ended 1967. Chris Short and the Phillies shut them out 2–0.

Dodger observers were finally starting to get impatient. Columnist Charles Maher in the *Times* referred to the club's home schedule as "eighty-one slumber parties" and offered that from the fan's perspective the season slogan should really be "We're tired of sitting on a stiff board when we are bored stiff." Lack of offense was a problem throughout baseball in the 1960s, but the Dodgers raised it to an art form. Even club vice president Fresco Thompson went on record as a supporter of the "wild card" hitter, a notion similar to the designated hitter. No team needed that more than the Dodgers. Unless they won by shutout, it was hard for them to win at all.

And no Dodger pitcher knew that better than Don Drysdale. Now that Koufax was gone, the pitcher they called "Big D" was supposed to fill Koufax's shoes. But as Dan Hafner of the *Times* commented after Drysdale's eighth start of the season on May 14, "The Dodgers can get a run for almost any pitcher [but] the pitcher had better be prepared to hurl a shutout . . . if he expects to win." After seven starts, Drysdale's only victory was a 1–0 whitewashing of the Mets, and L.A. had scored only a single run in each of their last four games. Hafner had no idea just how prophetic his words would be.

This time the Dodgers got one for Drysdale, and he followed Hafner's advice, shutting down the Cubs on two hits to win 1–0. After the game a clearly exhausted Drysdale was asked if he thought he could pitch 20 shutouts.

"Oh my heavens, no," he said. "I couldn't stand something like this every time out. I'm too old for that."

But he wasn't. In his next three starts Drysdale threw shutouts. The major league record was five shutouts in a row, set back in 1904 by Chicago White Sox pitcher Doc White.

When Drysdale took the mound at Dodger Stadium against the Giants on May 31 for a chance to tie White's mark, there was more excitement in the stands than at any time since

Dodger executive Peter O'Malley (right) attends the 1970 National League meetings and meets with Mets chairman Donald Grant (left) and Giants president Horace Stoneham (center).

1966. And more people. More than 46,000 fans packed the park for a chance to witness history.

The Dodgers gave him a lead in the second when, miraculously, Colavito doubled and Bailey followed with a single — for the Dodgers that was nearly the equivalent of batting around. They added single runs in the third and eighth, and Drysdale took the mound needing only three outs to make history.

Drysdale hadn't been in much trouble all night. Only one Giants hitter, the pitcher Mike McCormick, had made it as far as second base.

Still, Drysdale hadn't been particularly sharp. He'd thrown a ton of pitches, and although he hadn't walked anybody, he'd gone to a three-ball count on a dozen hitters. His fastball was tailing, and his sinker was dropping out of the strike zone, movement that led most hitters to believe that Drysdale was doctoring the ball.

In the ninth the Giants were determined to break his streak. There was still considerable bad blood between the two teams, and San Francisco, in first place, enjoyed looking down at the seventh-place Dodgers. Willie McCovey worked a walk — the first of the night — then Jim Ray Hart singled and McCovey stopped at second. Dave Marshall followed with a walk, and with no outs the bases were loaded.

Alston was in a quandary. As much as he wanted Drysdale to get the record, he also wanted to win the game. In the sev-

enth inning he made a few changes to put his best defensive team on the field. Now, with San Francisco catcher Dick Dietz up, Alston had to decide whether to play the infield in to cut off the run at the plate, or back for the double play, conceding the run. He kept the infield back, making Drysdale's task a little bit harder.

Dietz worked the count to 2–2. Then Drysdale came inside with a fastball. The pitch hit Dietz, a right-handed hitter, on the left elbow. The hitter dropped his bat and started to first base as McCovey started toward home.

Home plate umpire Harry Wendelstedt immediately called him back and called the pitch ball three. Dietz got in his face and started to argue, and San Francisco manager Herman Franks raced from the dugout.

Dietz, ruled Wendelstedt, had made no effort to avoid the pitch. In such an instance, the umpire did not have to recognize that the pitch hit him.

That's what the rule said, but such a judgment call was one of the rarest in baseball. Franks tried to argue, but Wendelstedt was unmoved. "It was the worst call I've ever seen," raged Franks later.

But now Drysdale, with the crowd threatening to explode,

Dodger manager Walter Alston was never allowed to risk failure as he lived his professional life on the basis of 23 consecutive one-year contracts. He won seven National League pennants and four of the six world championships won by the Dodgers in the 20th century.

still had to work out of the bases-loaded jam. With the count 3–2, Dietz flew out to short left field. McCovey had to stay put.

Alston kept the infield at double-play depth, but with pinch hitter Ty Cline at bat, he moved everyone in a single step. Cline smashed a pitch to the right side.

It went directly to first baseman Wes Parker, acknowledged by most as the best-fielding first baseman in the game. He dug the ball out of the dirt and fired home for the force-out. Now Drysdale was one out away from the record.

In his previous start, against Houston, Drysdale had wiggled out of a similar jam, giving up two hits, a walk, and a hit batsman in the ninth, only to be saved by a spectacular double play. But this was escape artistry of another order.

Jack Hiatt was the last hitter. Drysdale, who had already thrown more than 150 pitches, jammed him and Hiatt popped the ball up to Wes Parker. Drysdale had the record, and his teammates mobbed him as if he had just won the World Series.

But the Giants were still livid. Franks called Wendelstedt a "gutless son of a bitch" after the game and said, "Put Wendelstedt's name on the trophy first." Franks went on to claim that the pitch in question was a "Vaseline ball." Dietz denied being hit on purpose, saying the pitch froze him and all he had done was "flinch before it hit me."

The Dodgers backed their ace. Alston admitted that he had never before seen such a call in his long career, "but then it's the first time I ever saw anyone get deliberately hit by the ball." Dodger catcher Jeff Torborg concurred and said, "As soon as the ball hit Dietz, I yelled, 'Hey!' and Wendelstedt was already making his call." Drysdale, for the record, called the pitch a slider, and the victory "the biggest thrill of my life."

The shutout put a few more records within reach. He had not given up an earned run in his last 49 innings, and only two in 67 innings for the season. He needed only two more scoreless innings to match Carl Hubbell's NL record of 46⅓. Another shutout would give him that record all by himself and put Walter Johnson's major league record of 56 consecutive scoreless innings within reach.

In his next start against Pittsburgh on June 4, Drysdale was near-perfect again. He broke Hubbell's mark with a second-inning strikeout of Bill Mazeroski and cruised from there, shutting out the Pirates on three hits to win 5–0 and run his scoreless streak to 54.

Excitement over Drysdale's record assault obscured two events that would ultimately prove more important to Dodger history. At the end of May Buzzie Bavasi announced that he would resign as Dodger general manager and become part-owner of the expansion franchise in San Diego that was scheduled to begin play in 1969.

That was the first sign that changes were about to take place atop the Dodger organization. Walter O'Malley was getting old and maneuvering to put his son, Peter, at the head of the organization. Peter O'Malley had already served the organization for a number of years in the minor leagues and was ready to assume a greater role. Bavasi, who had never been cut into ownership by O'Malley, saw the San Diego opportunity as his big chance to cash in.

Next to O'Malley, Bavasi was as responsible for the shape of the organization as any man since Branch Rickey. But after Rickey's club grew old, Bavasi had been slow to react as Dodger offense took a dive, and he didn't have a plan after the retirement of Koufax. His trades since then had been disasters. The farm system, although under the control of player development director Al Campanis and Fresco Thompson, had not provided a first-rate position player in years. Most Dodger prospects seemed to follow a familiar pattern: early success, like that enjoyed by Tommy Davis and Jim Lefebvre, followed by a long slow decline. Dodger minor leaguers, many of whom had been considered absolute blue chippers when first signed, seemed to peak early, and time and time again the club rushed players to the majors a year before they were ready.

The system did a good job of identifying talent but was not adept at predicting future performance. Like the Yankees a few years earlier, the Dodgers signed prospects who looked like ballplayers instead of players who were the real thing. Although the Dodgers were the first team to put into place the now-standard numeric grading system that rates skills on a scale from 20 to 80, they also looked for what they called "the good face"—a ballplayer who looked the way they expected a ballplayer to look. The result was a good-looking team, but not a whole lot of talent.

Fresco Thompson took over for Bavasi, although many thought he was just a stopgap hire to prevent him from jumping to Montreal. In the 1968 free agent draft held a few weeks later, the Dodgers hit the jackpot. Either Bavasi had been the problem or it was just time for the Dodgers to get lucky. After all, if Drysdale could hit a batter with the bases loaded and still pitch a shutout, anything was possible. Among the players the Dodgers selected were unknown kids named Bobby Valentine, Steve Garvey, Bill Buckner, Ron Cey, Tom Paciorek, Joe Ferguson, and Doyle Alexander. Lee Lacy would be selected the following February. Few teams have ever had a more productive draft: none of these players would stay unknown for long, for these "good faces" also had some skills.

For now, the face everyone was interested in was still Don Drysdale's. On June 8 he took the mound against the Phillies in pursuit of a record seventh shutout in a row.

With Drysdale the big story in baseball, an overflow crowd filled Dodger Stadium. For the first time his nerves betrayed him. He had other things on his mind. In 1968 it was hard to play baseball without taking into account the madness that seemed to be breaking out all over the country. A supporter of Robert F. Kennedy, Drysdale had been shaken by his assassination on June 5. Seven of his first eight pitches missed the plate, and with one out he walked John Briggs. But Versalles then made a great stop, and Drysdale settled down.

On September 2, 1969, center fielder Willie Davis broke the Dodger consecutive game hitting streak held by Zack Wheat. Upon his retirement, Davis held the Los Angeles Dodger records in many departments, including hits (2,091), runs (1,004), at bats (7,495), total bases (3,094), and extra-base hits (585).

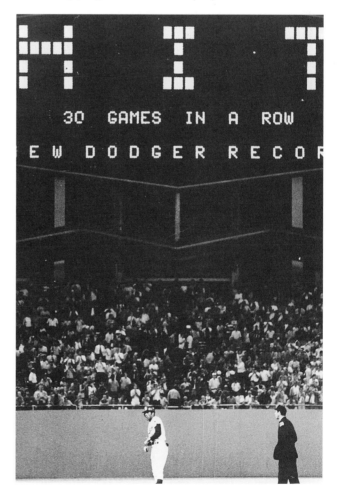

He passed Johnson in the third and induced Roberto Pena to ground out to Ken Boyer. Then he set his sights on the shutout.

But now that Drysdale had the record, Phillies' manager Gene Mauch wanted to win the game. He went out and spoke with umpire Augie Donatelli, and as Drysdale walked off the field, Donatelli stopped him, examined his wrist, and then had him take off his cap. The umpire ran his fingers through Drysdale's hair and found what he later referred to as "greasy kid stuff." Donatelli suspected Drysdale was doctoring the ball, using Vaseline rubbed in his hair, which he then transferred to his fingers between pitches. That enabled him to throw a pitch like a spitball, one that would squirt out of his fingers with little spin and drop sharply. When Drysdale took the mound to start the fourth, Donatelli, to emphasize the point, told him not to touch his head with his hand. If he did, he'd be thrown from the game.

The admonition bothered Drysdale. In the fifth Tony Taylor and Clay Dalrymple singled. With Taylor on third, pinch hitter Howie Bedell, just up from the minors, hit a fly ball to left. Taylor tagged and scored, giving Bedell the second and last RBI of his career. After 58⅔ innings, Drysdale had finally given up a run.

Now that he had, he couldn't stop. The Phillies added another in the sixth and one more in the seventh before Alston took Drysdale out. The Dodgers, however, hung on to win, 5–3. It was their sixth victory in a row and lifted them into second place behind St. Louis.

That was as close to first place as they would come. Drysdale, Vaseline or not, returned to mortal status. Over the remainder of the season he'd collect only one more shutout on his way to a 14–12 record, and the Dodgers soon slipped from their lofty perch, falling all the way to tenth place before a late surge lifted them into a tie for sixth, 76–86. They hit a collective .230 for the season and scored only 470 runs, the worst offense in the majors. Despite the big crowds that had come out to see Drysdale, attendance continued to tumble. Just over 1.3 million came to Dodger Stadium in 1968.

Change was coming. Desperate to create more offense across the board, major league baseball lowered the pitcher's mound and banned pitchers from licking their fingers. The National League added two teams in 1969, the San Diego Padres and the Montreal Expos, split into two divisions, and decided to play night games during the World Series. Jim Murray joked that in one fell swoop "baseball has eliminated

the second division, the home run, the spit ball, day games [and] the shirtsleeve World Series." Overnight there were suddenly two more teams even worse than the Dodgers. Now they had only five other teams in their division to overtake. It was almost as if the league had decided to make things easier on one of its flagship franchises.

There were also more changes in the Dodger organization. Walter O'Malley installed his son Peter as club vice president and began to loosen his grip on the franchise. In the off-season Fresco Thompson died of cancer, and Al Campanis became the new general manager.

He was no Bavasi. Campanis had actually played the game in the major leagues — albeit briefly — as a Dodger catcher in 1943. It was time, finally, for the Dodgers to rebuild, and Campanis was in a hurry, as eager to make trades as Bavasi had been loath to. That winter the Dodgers were more active than they'd been in years — Campanis even traded away his own son, Jim, a minor league catcher.

In the spring rookie Ted Sizemore took over at shortstop and Bill Sudakis at third. Willie Crawford, a local product and perennial contender for a starting job, took over one outfield spot. The other went to Andy Kosco, obtained in a trade with the Yankees. Rookie Bill Russell made the team as a backup. With L.A.'s pitching — and the presence of both San Diego and Montreal in the National League — the club had to improve.

They did — by midseason the Dodgers were in the midst of a fight for the division title in what the press called, not too inventively, "the wild, wild West."

But in early June Willie Davis broke his cheekbone. Everyone expected the Dodgers to fall off, but Campanis pulled a shocker — he made a significant midseason trade, something that hadn't been seen in Los Angeles, well, ever.

Incredibly, it had been more than a decade since the Dodgers picked up an impact player in midseason — 1956, when they had purchased Sal Maglie. Since then, Bavasi hadn't made a single important deal. Campanis did make a deal, and even better, it was for a player Dodger fans already knew and loved and, even better than that, needed desperately.

Since the spring shortstop had been a problem. Sizemore didn't have the range and had been moved over to second. Rookie Bill Grabarkewitz simply couldn't hit. And now, with Davis hurt, the Dodgers needed not only speed but also veteran leadership. They were, after all, in a pennant race of sorts.

Campanis had been pestering O'Malley to let him bring back Maury Wills. After two decent years in Pittsburgh, he had become available in the expansion draft and was picked up by Montreal, where his talents were wasted and he hated playing. He finally just stopped and said he was going to retire, only to come back after he learned that if he quit, the Expos couldn't trade him. He'd been awful in Montreal, but Campanis thought he'd come alive back in L.A. O'Malley, although still disdainful of Wills for his perceived "disloyalty," finally caved in. Campanis shipped Paul Popovich and Ron Fairly to the Expos for not only Wills but also Manny Mota, a bona-fide hitter who for much of the next decade would be the best pinch hitter in baseball.

Wills was thrilled and called it "the greatest thing that has ever happened to me." Now, somewhat incredibly and improbably, the Dodgers had a chance again. In the NL West, the divisional split worked perfectly as the Giants, Braves, Reds, and Dodgers all scrambled for first place.

There was just one problem—Drysdale. Until 1969 he had never missed a start. He had pitched despite broken ribs, shin splints, shingles, and God knows how many sore arms, propped up at times by taking the same assortment of medication on which Koufax had relied. Drysdale may not have enjoyed his counterpart's spectacular level of success, but he had been as dependable as the California sunshine and was the Dodger career leader in just about every pitching category worth mentioning.

In May he'd blown out his shoulder. He went on the disabled list, came back, went back on, came back off after the All-Star break, and had been terrible since then, yielding more than a run an inning. Like Koufax, Drysdale found that the pain wasn't the worst part. "I can't take any more medication," he said. "Sometimes I honestly felt I was becoming dopey. I was afraid the police would pick me up on a corner. I can't sleep. I roll over on this arm and the pain wakes me up. This morning I had to use my left arm to brush my teeth." In early August he retired.

Campanis didn't give up. He pried veteran Jim Bunning from the Pirates on August 15 for the stretch run as Willie Davis, healthy again, went on a tear and set a club record with a 31-game hitting streak. Although the Dodgers lacked punch, base hits weren't a problem. They just couldn't get into first place, however, and over the last two weeks the Braves pulled away as L.A. fell to fourth, eight games back at 85–77.

As the Dodgers watched the division title slip away, fans got a glimpse of the future. In the waning days of the season the Dodgers brought up a host of rookies to give them a taste

Mike Marshall, a student of kinesiology, believed a pitcher could pitch every day. In 1974 he not only set a record by appearing in 13 straight games but won the Cy Young Award on the basis of 15 wins and a league-leading 21 saves in 106 games.

of life in the major leagues, including Bobby Valentine, Steve Garvey, Bill Buckner, and Von Joshua. None were ready for the big leagues yet, but they were getting closer.

Peter O'Malley took over as club president in 1970, another sign of change, as Walter O'Malley took on the more ceremonial title of Chairman of the Board. In the spring there was optimism that glory days were about to resume.

One week into the season, those thoughts were gone. Cincinnati swept the club three in a row to open the season, and then the Dodgers dropped two to the woeful Padres.

Outfielder–first baseman Bill Buckner was part of a crop of young talent developed by the Dodgers at the end of the 1960s that included fellow first baseman Steve Garvey, Ron Cey, Bill Russell, and Dave Lopes. In eight years with the Dodgers, Buckner batted .289 before being shipped to the Cubs in a 1977 deal that sent outfielder Rick Monday to Los Angeles.

Alston reamed everybody out and called the club's performance "the worst exhibition of baseball in Dodger Stadium for a long, long time."

The season was effectively over. The Reds went wire to wire, and even though the Dodgers finally got on track, it was far too late. The "Big Red Machine" was starting to rev its engine, and the Dodgers didn't have enough horsepower. They finished second, 87–74, but 14½ long games behind the Reds. The difference between the two teams was obvious. While the Reds clubbed 191 home runs, the Dodgers hit only 87.

The Dodgers hadn't had a consistent power threat since Frank Howard. Since he'd been traded, only one Dodger, Jim Lefebvre, had hit more than 20 home runs in a season, in 1966, and he never came close again.

The talent bubbling up from the farm system was giving the team some flexibility. Campanis saw what was on the horizon and felt confident enough to start trading away the surplus and making room for the new recruits.

In October he dropped a bomb and dealt Ted Sizemore and highly touted catcher Bob Stinson to the St. Louis Cardinals for problematic slugger Dick Allen. With the farm system full of infielders and Joe Ferguson making his mark as the catcher of the future, the Dodgers weren't worried about finding replacements. And Allen was a slugger of the highest order. In fact, he was one of the most talented players in the major leagues — when he chose to play.

And that was the problem. Allen was also one of baseball's new breed, an individual who had no need or desire to go along to get along. After the press killed his career in Philadelphia, he was traded to the Cardinals in 1970. There he looked as if he had found a home and gotten off to a great start, earning All-Star honors at first base over Willie McCovey, Ernie Banks, and Orlando Cepeda — all eventual Hall of Famers. But in August he tore a hamstring, and instead of staying in St. Louis to heal, he went home to Philadelphia. Despite knocking in more than 100 runs in only 122 games, the Cardinals decided Allen wasn't worth the trouble.

Observers were surprised that the Dodgers went after him. He had everything but the "good face," and so he simply didn't fit their mold. Players in the organization were schooled in the "Dodger Way," and individualism in the increasingly conservative organization was frowned upon. The Dodgers, after all, were a lot closer to Orange County than Haight-Ashbury.

Other trades delivered veteran catcher Duke Sims and pitcher Al Downing. The influx of veterans allowed the Dodgers to take more chances, and they opened the year with three youngsters in the lineup — Steve Garvey at third, Bill Buckner in right, and Bill Russell, a former outfielder whom the Dodgers made not only an infielder but a switch hitter, at second base. Bobby Valentine was pressing for playing time if anyone faltered. Allen was installed in left field. In the spring one L.A. headline gushed, "Dodgers So Good It's Scary!"

But the kids were the ones who were scared. They weren't quite ready, and all had trouble hitting. Garvey kept throwing the ball into the first-base stands and broke his hand. Grabarkewitz and Sudakis were also injured. Alston couldn't seem to decide exactly who he wanted to play where — the only players with a set position were Willie Davis in center and Wes Parker at first base. That made the other veterans angry and the kids confused.

By the time Alston finally figured out who could play and who couldn't, the season looked to be over. The Giants jumped out to a huge lead, starting the season 37–14, and seemed likely to go wire to wire, just as the Reds had done the previous year. Meanwhile, the Dodgers struggled. At the end of May they trailed by ten and a half games. Although they pulled close several times, drawing to within three and a half games on both June 6 and August 11, each time, as Dodger pitcher Bill Singer put it succinctly, "we died." With 24 games left to go on September 5, they trailed the Giants by eight and a half games and needed a miracle.

They almost got one. The Dodgers had five games remaining with the Giants and won all five as San Francisco went into near-total collapse. L.A. pulled to within one game of the Giants with only four games left and looked to be closing.

But the Giants finally woke up, and with two days left in the season, the Dodgers suffered a devastating loss. Al Downing, with a new screwball, had emerged as the staff ace. He'd won 20 games, including six in a row, and in September had an ERA of 0.88. But the Astros drubbed him 11–0, while the Giants beat San Diego to clinch a tie for the division lead. On the final day of the season, although the Dodgers beat the Astros 2–1, the Giants won behind Marichal to capture the division.

Under Campanis and Peter O'Malley, the Dodgers didn't stand pat. Dick Allen, despite hitting .295 and leading the team with 23 home runs and 90 RBIs, hadn't fit in and had angered the club by speaking out before the last game of the season, telling Jim Murray he viewed his performance as "money well earned." When asked if he wanted to play another year with the Dodgers, he was noncommittal. "We [players] go where they tell us to go," he said. "If they want me, I'll stay, if they don't, I'll go."

That kind of talk didn't fit the increasingly important Dodger image. PR had become almost as important as RBIs. A show business, glad-handing atmosphere had taken hold within the organization. Players were supposed to be at the park at 5:00 P.M. for night games, but Allen, seeing no need to greet celebrities and sign autographs, often wouldn't arrive until much later.

Peter O'Malley didn't want Allen around anymore. After a couple of minor deals, on December 7 Campanis pried Frank Robinson away from the Orioles for a package of kids, none of them top-shelf. That made Dick Allen a spare part, and he was simultaneously shipped to the White Sox for pitcher Tommy John.

But it almost didn't matter what the Dodgers did in 1972. The Reds, after a year off-track, were back, and Frank Robinson, at age 36, was no longer the player who had won MVP Awards in each league. With the Dodgers holding a narrow lead going into June, Robinson, with 7 home runs and 27 RBIs, pulled a hamstring, and all of a sudden the Dodgers couldn't score runs again. Robinson never got back on track after that, and the Reds slowly pulled away. The Dodgers finished tied with the Astros for second place, ten and a half games back.

The Dodgers hadn't won anything since Koufax anchored the staff six long seasons before. Dodger Stadium had ceased to be a special place — that had been one of Dick Allen's complaints. The fans were too laid-back, arriving late and leaving early. "It was baseball as theater," he said later, complaining that the "polite" Dodger fans watched baseball like they were at the movies. And despite some improvement on the field in the past few seasons, the organization seemed stuck, unwilling to commit fully to a youth movement that was beginning to look overdue.

Part of the problem was Alston. Living contract to contract had become a way of life, and he wasn't willing to risk failure for a year or two. He tried to win as many games as possible every year, even after it became apparent that the Dodgers weren't going anywhere. All those Dodger kids had been shuffled in and out of the lineup so much that it was hard for them to get in a groove. A generation before, the Dodgers had ruined a host of minor leaguers by rushing them to the big leagues. Now the opposite was happening.

Down in the minor leagues, former Dodger pitcher Tommy Lasorda had been working wonders as a manager. In eight years in the organization his ballclubs had finished no lower than third. Campanis liked him. His draft picks had thrived under Lasorda. He was the polar opposite of Alston, whose "iron-hand" style didn't have the impact it had once had — younger players were different. Lasorda, on the other hand, was a pal, a pied piper, an enthusiastic advocate, as if by his own will and belief he could get his players to do what he had not been able to do as a player — reach the major leagues to stay. Many older players and long-time baseball men looked at Lasorda and rolled their eyes, but his players — at least those he played — seemed to buy it.

He had his eyes on the Dodger manager's job, and everyone knew it. Several years before, at a press conference when Walter O'Malley announced Lasorda's promotion to triple-A, Lasorda had said, "I want to continue working for the Dodgers even when I'm dead and gone." Amused, O'Malley asked him just how he proposed to do that. Said Lasorda, "Just put the Dodger schedule on my tombstone." Alston was also getting up in years — he couldn't manage forever. In 1973 the Dodgers brought Lasorda up as a coach, and the youth movement was put into full effect. Tellingly, his appointment was an organizational decision, not one made by Alston himself. In recent years the responsibility to select his own coaches had been taken away, a not-so-subtle message that the organization believed Alston's clock was beginning to wind down.

There was no turning back. Lasorda's appointment as third-base coach was a visible signal that the direction of the organization was about to change. Campanis, with the support of Peter O'Malley, was the key figure now. Personnel decisions were primarily his, not Alston's.

In the off-season Campanis broke the logjam. Frank Robinson was traded, sent to the Angels along with Bobby Valentine and Bill Singer for established starter Andy Messersmith. Maury Wills finally retired, as did Wes Parker.

By spring the Dodger roster had turned over. Its deep, experienced pitching staff was anchored by Osteen, Sutton, John, and Messersmith, backing up a team of unknown kids.

What would someday become the best-known infield in baseball was about to take shape, and the Dodgers were on

Steven Patrick Garvey was the son of the Dodgers' Vero Beach spring-training bus driver who made good with the home team. Following an outstanding collegiate career at Michigan State University, Garvey was drafted by Los Angeles and soon became a fixture at first base. In 14 years with the Dodgers, he batted .301 with 1,968 hits, 992 RBIs, and 211 home runs.

1976

the precipice of entering a new era. But not on Opening Day. Lee Lacy won the second-base job and started the season as the Dodgers' leadoff hitter. Bill Buckner played first. Veteran Ken McMullen was the third baseman. Bill Russell started the season at shortstop.

That configuration didn't hit, and the Dodgers got off to a slow start, despite a pitching staff that was strong from top to bottom. Alston started shuffling the lineup, looking for the right combination.

On June 13, finally, he found it. Suddenly everything snapped into place according to a kind of infallible logic. He moved Bill Buckner to the outfield. That opened up first base for Steve Garvey, whom the Dodgers had finally decided just couldn't cut it at third. Davey Lopes pushed Lacy off second base, and Ron Cey played third after Ken McMullen hurt his back. With Joe Ferguson supplying power behind the plate, all of a sudden the Dodgers had their best hitting team in years, and Willie Davis, Willie Crawford, and Lopes could all run. Defense was a concern at first, for of the four infielders only Cey was playing his natural position, but Russell, who'd been booed for his defense in 1972, suddenly settled down, Garvey was fine at first base, and Cey was a vast improvement at third, where in 1972 the Dodgers had made an incredible 52 errors.

That group would remain together for the next eight and a half years and prove to be as productive and sure as any core of players the Dodgers have ever had. For the next eight and a half years they made the task of the Dodger organization simple and clear-cut. All the front office had to do was supply complementary parts. It was not unlike the situation in Brooklyn from 1947 through 1955, when Robinson, Reese, Hodges, Campanella, and Snider had formed a similar core group. All this group lacked was experience — and a leader.

Although the Dodgers lost that day to Philadelphia, 16–3, in late June they won 14 of 16 to vault past the Giants and take over the lead in the National League West by an incredible 11½ games. The Dodgers appeared as if they would run away with the division title, and big crowds were again the norm at Dodger Stadium.

They weren't the only club coming together. The Cincinnati Reds rebounded from a slow start and in July began to take off. Still, in late August the Dodgers had the look of division champions.

But they hadn't been there before — the Reds had. Pennants are won and lost in September, and as soon as the cal-endar turned the Dodgers couldn't win as the kids stopped hitting. It didn't help that nagging injuries chipped away at the pitching staff.

On September 3 in Candlestick Park the Giants reminded the Dodgers that even though they were out of the race, they could still have a say in who won. The Dodgers led 8–1 entering the seventh inning, then collapsed. Bobby Bonds cracked a grand slam home run in the ninth, and the Dodgers fell, 11–8, leaving them in a tie with the Reds. "I never saw anything like it," moaned Alston. Then he made a huge error, telling the increasingly jittery club that maybe they needed to lose a few more before they could straighten themselves out.

That destroyed their confidence. The Reds took over first place for good the next day as the Dodgers went on to lose a total of nine in a row, and ten of twelve, including two to the Reds. The division title went to Cincinnati. L.A. finished 95–66, three and a half games back.

In the off-season Campanis got busy again, although with the infield settled, his task became much easier. Willie Davis, the club's senior statesman, had been named captain before the 1973 season, taking over from Wills. But he'd clashed with Alston, who wanted him to set the table for the Dodgers' younger hitters. Fresco Thompson had once complained that Davis never learned to use his speed. "You couldn't get Willie to bunt," Thompson maintained, "if the third baseman used a cane and was a certified alcoholic." Ever since he'd reached the majors, the Dodgers had expected him to become the next Willie Mays. He wasn't, but as the first Willie Davis he'd been pretty valuable. Now they decided that wasn't enough. On December 5 Campanis dealt him to the Montreal Expos for eccentric reliever Mike Marshall, and then he went after power, trading Osteen to Houston for slugging outfielder Jim Wynn and picking up onetime Mets star Tommy Agee.

Marshall was the key. The screwball-throwing right-hander was studying for his doctorate in the science of human movement at the University of Michigan and was convinced that he could pitch every day. So far it seemed as if he could — in 1973 he had pitched in 92 games for Montreal. In baseball circles his vocabulary alone made him a certified flake — Jim Murray aptly described him as a "prig," for the haughty pitcher considered most ballplayers far below his intellectual level. He called Dodger pitcher Jim Brewer's grasp of the screwball "infantile," but the Dodgers realized that despite his personality quirks, he was unlike any other pitcher in baseball.

The year 1974 was a cakewalk — for a while. Even when the

Dodgers lost, they won. They opened the season by sweeping the Padres, outscoring them 25–2, and then Al Downing allowed Hank Aaron's record-breaking 715th home run and the Dodgers lost, 7–4, as if in a sign of respect. As soon as history was out of the way, the club resumed its march through the NL West, opening up a ten-and-a-half-game lead over Cincinnati by July 10. Five Dodger players made the All-Star team, and Steve Garvey, who had emerged as both a power threat and the most popular player on the team, became the first write-in candidate ever elected to the All-Star Game.

In the second half the Reds started stalking L.A., and 1974 threatened to be a repeat of 1973. Yet this team was a year older and didn't collapse. In early September they stopped the Reds by taking two of three as Mike Marshall, on his way to a record 106 appearances, pitched in all three games. They finally clinched the division on October 1. For the first time in eight seasons they were going to play baseball after the first week of October.

The Dodgers faced the NL East champion Pittsburgh Pirates in the National League Championship Series and swept to victory in four games, completely outplaying the Pirates as Don Sutton won twice, Mike Marshall didn't give up a run in two relief appearances, and Steve Garvey, who would later be named NL MVP, cracked two home runs and knocked in five. All that stood between them and a world championship were the defending champion Oakland A's.

In terms of personality, the two teams seemed polar opposites. The A's were all swagger and bravado, fighting among themselves, hating owner Charlie Finley, grappling for headlines, and beating up on the rest of the league as if they were some kind of minor distraction that got in the way of their own internal turmoil. They were like a huge, extended dysfunctional family that used their own crises to create an us-against-the-world mentality. In contrast, the Dodgers were quiet and restrained, businesslike and professional. If the A's were baseball's equivalent of the Weather Men, the Dodgers were the Young Republicans. But the two clubs were not dissimilar in how they played the game on the field. Each was anchored by a strong set of starting pitchers. The A's triumvirate of Catfish Hunter, Vida Blue, and Ken Holtzman compared favorably to the Dodgers' Don Sutton, Andy Messersmith, and whoever else Alston chose to pitch. (Tommy John, after a great first half, had had elbow surgery.) And while the Dodgers had Mike Marshall, the A's had Rollie Fingers. He didn't pitch as often as Marshall but was just as effective.

WORLD SERIES MVP AWARD

1955	Johnny Podres	P
1959	Larry Sherry	P
1963	Sandy Koufax	P
1965	Sandy Koufax	P
1981	Ron Cey	3B
1981	Pedro Guerrero	1B
1981	Steve Yeager	C
1988	Orel Hershiser	P

Offensively the two clubs were near-mirror images, each with ample portions of power and speed. But the A's, with their experience, were heavily favored and exuded confidence. Before the Series, one unnamed Athletic player said of the Dodgers, "I'd like to know who they've beaten." Moreover, on the precipice of the Series, the A's seemed to be ready for battle. Before a Series workout at Dodger Stadium, Fingers and A's pitcher John Blue Moon Odom fought — Odom emerged on crutches, while Fingers had five stitches on the back of his head. For any other team such a fight might have been devastating. For the A's it was an announcement that they were primed for action.

The Dodgers, on the other hand, were not yet ready for prime time. After the two teams split the first two games at Dodger Stadium, Oakland winning game one 3–2 and the Dodgers winning game two 3–2, the Series moved north to Oakland.

In more ways than one, the A's won the Series in game three, or rather after it. After the A's dispatched the Dodgers with a workmanlike 3–2 win, Dodger outfielder Bill Buckner, whose eighth-inning home run had been the first Dodger score of the game, spoke out of turn.

"I definitely think we have the better ballclub," he said, despite being down two games to one. "The A's have only a couple of players that could play on our club. Reggie Jackson is outstanding. Sal Bando and Joe Rudi are good, and they have a good pitching staff. Other than that . . . if we played them 162 times we'd beat them 100."

As far as the A's were concerned, those were fighting words. They needed little motivation anyway, but Buckner's remarks fired them up. Before game four Oakland owner Charlie Finley had the comments pasted to a card and read them to his team. "What Buckner is saying," he said, "is that 22 of you aren't worth [expletive]." The A's then went out and won game four 5–2, and Buckner upped the ante afterward by making a disparaging comment about light-hitting Oakland center fielder Bill North.

Although the final score of game five was only 3–2, it wasn't that close. The A's and their fans were able to extract not only a world championship but a measure of revenge.

At the start of the seventh inning, with the score tied 2–2, a raucous A's crowd, which had been taunting Buckner all game, got ugly. The outfielder was hit in the head with a whiskey bottle. He got the umpire's attention and threatened to walk off the field.

The game was delayed for several minutes as Alston and several Dodgers, including pitcher Mike Marshall, on in relief of Don Sutton, discussed the situation with the umpires and Marshall consoled Buckner. When play finally resumed, it had been several minutes since Marshall had thrown a pitch. When he finally did, Joe Rudi sent the ball into the stands to give the A's a 3–2 lead.

The Dodgers had one more chance. In the eighth Buckner singled to center. A's center fielder Bill North misplayed the ball, and it squirted past him. Buckner, the tying run, raced to second. But instead of stopping, he kept going, ignoring third-base coach Tommy Lasorda's stop sign and trying for third. Reggie Jackson gunned him down.

That ended L.A.'s chances. Rollie Fingers set down the next six hitters, and the A's captured the world championship. The Dodgers took the loss hard. After the game Buckner said he'd make the same play again. North chortled that it was "stupid." When Mike Marshall was asked if it had been a mistake

not to stay warm during the delay, he responded, "If I don't answer your question, that means I'm not interested in it."

Before the Series there had been some speculation that if the Dodgers won, Alston, who would soon turn 63, would retire after 20 years as Dodger manager. Privately, there were many in the organization wishing he would do so, for he had the team in something of a fix. Although his contract only went year to year, in a sense that made it the most secure contract in the game. He was an institution, almost above reproach, and impossible to fire. Tommy Lasorda was in line for the job and getting impatient. Other teams were interested in Lasorda, but the only job he wanted was Alston's. While older players generally looked upon Alston favorably, the younger guys, most of whom had played for Lasorda in the minors, were starting to tune out the old manager. And while Lasorda wasn't overtly undermining Alston, his actions were having the same effect. Lasorda was all over the field in spring training and before regular season games, throwing batting practice, talking nonstop, playing the press and the crowd. Every day he made Alston look a little older in comparison.

In the end the Cincinnati Reds forced a change. For in 1975 and 1976, while the Dodgers were very, very good, the Reds were the best team in baseball. In both seasons Cincinnati pulled past the Dodgers in May and never looked back, winning the division by 20 games in 1975 and by 10 in 1976 and winning the world championship in back-to-back seasons as the Dodgers finished second. Nothing the Dodgers did — the trading of Mike Marshall, the acquisition of sluggers Dusty Baker and Reggie Smith, the addition of pitcher Burt Hooton, the emergence of pitchers Charlie Hough, Doug Rau, and Rick Rhoden, not even the miraculous comeback of Tommy John from the groundbreaking elbow ligament transplant surgery that now bears his name — was able to break Cincinnati's stranglehold on first place.

As the Dodgers grew accustomed to also-ran status, the squeaky-clean veneer that the fans and media had built around the team began to come unglued. Steve Garvey had become Mister Dodger, a status that, although earned by both his play and his fan-friendly behavior, appeared premeditated and disingenuous to some of his teammates. One guy's "Mister Dodger" was another man's "Mister Fraud."

Garvey had the ultimate "good face" and projected the precise image the organization loved — the clean-cut, hardworking family man. That was something that helped Garvey immensely both during contract talks and in off-the-field endorsement opportunities. Garvey's persona — he and his wife Cyndy appeared to be the perfect California couple — was making him rich, and that wasn't happening to the same degree for many of his similarly talented teammates. Both Ron Cey and Davey Lopes, for example, were every bit as important to the Dodger lineup. Cey was as good a hitter as Garvey and a much better defensive player, while Lopes was one of the first middle infielders to have both power and speed. Yet their contributions were overlooked as all the attention went to Garvey. L.A. was a city that loved a little scandal and inside dirt, and when Dodger watching — looking for cracks in the facade — became something of a cottage industry in 1975 and 1976, Alston seemed even more removed from the inner workings of his ballclub.

In the waning days of the 1976 season, as the Dodgers played out the string, there were rumors that Alston wouldn't receive one-year contract number 24. But neither he nor the Dodgers wanted to go through the indignity of a public ousting.

Alston, not altogether willingly, opted out when it became clear that his status was in doubt and no one on the Dodgers would tell him otherwise. There was no sense in waiting until the end of the season. On September 27 the Dodgers held an uncomfortable press conference and announced Alston's retirement. Both Walter and Peter O'Malley attended, but it was the son who did most of the talking, saying, "It was not until this afternoon that Walter told me he wanted to retire."

When asked if he had been prepared to offer Alston another contract, O'Malley parried the question by saying, "That question is hypothetical, since our discussion never got that far."

Alston looked tired and sounded bitter and resigned. "I'm not retiring because of criticism," he said and went on to list a few other reasons he wasn't retiring, including "the times," which made the contemporary ballplayer, in Alston's estimation, far less deferential and appreciative of being in the big leagues. What he didn't do was say *why* he was retiring, and he brushed off questions about his relationship to Campanis. He left with a record of 2,040 wins, 1,613 losses, and four world championships, one in Brooklyn and three in L.A. Since 1955 no team in baseball had won more.

Although coach Jim Gilliam, who had once been touted as Alston's likely successor, was blunt and said, "Do I want to manage? Yes, of course. The O'Malleys know where to find me," he also knew they wouldn't come looking. Forty-nine-year-old Tommy Lasorda was the only candidate.

The Dodgers made it official on September 29. "This is the greatest day of my life," said a beaming Lasorda. "To be selected as manager of an organization I love so deeply. To wake up and learn I had inherited a post being vacated by the greatest manager in baseball, is like being presented the Hope diamond." Baseball writers around the country would soon become accustomed to such hyperbole.

Alston didn't wait around but stepped aside and allowed Lasorda to take over immediately. In his first game Lasorda's Dodgers won the old-fashioned way, 1–0.

1977–1979

BLEEDING DODGER BLUE

FORMER CATCHER AND BASEBALL BROADCASTER JOE GARAGIOLA SUMMED it up. "You could," he said, "plant 2,000 rows of corn with the fertilizer Lasorda spreads around."

But if ever there was a team in need of Lasorda's brand of fertilizer, it was the Dodgers. Since Koufax retired, the team had lost its identity. The Brooklyn era was buried in the past—L.A.'s Dodgers had ignored the past for so long that it almost didn't exist anymore. Brooklyn's Dodgers, recently evoked in all their eloquence by Roger Kahn in his seminal portrait *The Boys of Summer,* made L.A.'s Dodgers appear colorless and unemotional. The Dodgers, in the worst way, were now simply an organization, a uniform that didn't seem to represent anything anymore, a team without an identifiable face or voice apart from the careful utterances of Steve Garvey. In his final years Alston had faded to gray, and although attendance had rebounded to more than two million fans annually, being a Dodger fan had ceased to be very exciting. Fans went to see the Dodgers like they went to the beach or the movies, almost automatically, without much thought or passion.

The Dodgers didn't need a manager in order to win; they had the talent. But they did need a salesman, someone to sell the

On April 15, 1977, a new era in Dodger history began as former Dodger pitcher and long-time Dodger minor league manager Tommy Lasorda took the helm of the big team. No less a celebrity than "the Chairman of the Board" himself, Frank Sinatra, came to San Francisco to celebrate his friend's managerial debut, a 7–1 triumph over the Giants.

Dodgers, to make their fans care, to make the media pay attention, to make their own players feel that being a part of the Dodgers was something special and unique.

Boy, did the Dodgers ever get a salesman.

As he constantly reminded everyone from the minute he took over, Lasorda was the Dodgers and the Dodgers were Lasorda. And Lasorda's Dodgers were not divided into the Dodgers of either Brooklyn or Los Angeles. He instinctively made "the Dodgers" a brand unto themselves. By embracing both the past and the present, he created something new. He liked to remind people that the Dodger name wasn't really used to describe anything else, that when "you say you're a Dodger, people know you're a major leaguer." And Lasorda presented himself as the ultimate Dodger. Jim Murray even dubbed him "Tommy Dodger," a not entirely complimentary nickname. Lasorda repeated his mantra, "Cut me and I bleed Dodger blue," so often that eventually some observers wanted to try just to see if it were true.

Lasorda had never been shy about evoking the Dodgers of Brooklyn. He often reminded everyone that he had played at Ebbets Field and was cut to make room for Sandy Koufax, laying out his genealogy as a "true" Dodger. Yet at the same time Lasorda was made for L.A. He thrived in the spotlight, loved being a celebrity, loved the way his shtick played and got him good press and into good restaurants and brought him close to people like Frank Sinatra and Don Rickles. Lasorda made Lasorda the story, and by extension the Dodgers. In the end he became as important a personality as there has ever been in the history of the franchise.

The Dodgers didn't need anything to win in 1977 except, perhaps, the belief that they could, both in the press and in the clubhouse. Baseball was entering the era of free agency, and while the Yankees signed Reggie Jackson and other stars went out to bid, the Dodgers stood still, wary of the new age even as they had resources equal to those of any team in the game. Before the 1977 season, they made only one deal of consequence, sending Bill Buckner to the Cubs for center fielder Rick Monday, who was coming off the best season of his career.

Underneath the one-liners, the glad-handing, and the mugging for the camera, Lasorda knew what he was doing. A lifetime in the minor leagues had given the former pitcher a clear grasp of baseball strategy, and surrounded by players he already knew from the minors, Lasorda was free to be himself, cheerleading his major league players just as he had done with them in the minor leagues. Had he become impatient

and taken a job as manager in another organization, it probably wouldn't have worked, but with the Dodgers it did. Having Lasorda in charge reminded some players of what it had been like a few years before, when they were young and hungry. His approach had worked then and helped them reach their goal of making the major leagues — and they didn't look at him any differently now. Veterans raised in other organizations, like Dusty Baker and Reggie Smith, had already become familiar with him as a coach and far preferred his gregarious style to that of Alston, who was from another generation.

Even better, Lasorda both took the heat and stood up for his players on the field. He didn't mind charging from the dugout to argue calls with umpires, and when the media needed someone to talk to, there was Tommy, always telling stories, cracking jokes, and sucking up all the oxygen.

The Dodgers rolled through the exhibition season with an NL-best 17–7 record knowing their only competition would be the Reds. But Cincinnati was not quite the powerhouse they had been in 1976, for the New York Yankees had signed away star pitcher Don Gullett as a free agent, leaving the Reds a little short.

Cincinnati traditionally opened the baseball season. They beat the Padres on Opening Day, and before the Dodgers had played a game they were a half-game behind. When Lasorda was asked about it, his answer was typical. Being a glass-half-full guy, he noted, "We're a half-game up on the Padres."

After four games both the Dodgers and Reds were 2–2. But the Reds lost their next game, and the Dodgers not only won their next one but went on to win 16 of their next 17. The division race was never close again.

The Dodgers, and virtually every player on the team, rolled, and with each win any lingering question about Lasorda faded away. He was the ultimate cheerleader. For his hitters, big hits and hard ground balls got the same reaction, while he praised pitchers for both strikeouts and balls caught up against the fence. Results were all that mattered, particularly when the Dodgers were winning, and particularly when it was one of Lasorda's favorites coming through.

And the Dodgers got results. The lineup was perhaps the most potent in club history, for despite playing in Dodger Stadium, Garvey, Cey, Reggie Smith, and Baker all cracked 30 or more home runs. They could create runs and win low-scoring games too, as Lopes stole 47 bases and the rotation of John, who won 20 games for the first time, Rhoden, Sutton, Rau, and Hooton was so good that only four games were started by other pitchers all year long. The Dodgers, quite simply, were a cliché — they had it all. They won the division with a record of 98–64, 10 games ahead of the Reds.

Unfortunately, the NL East champion Phillies also appeared to have it all. They won 101 games behind the power of Mike Schmidt and Greg Luzinski and the left arm of Steve Carlton, who, since the retirement of Koufax, was the best left-hander in baseball. He made the Phillies a particularly dangerous opponent, for with his devastating slider he was fully capable of shutting a team down completely.

The Dodgers were still narrow favorites. After Carlton, Philadelphia's starters didn't quite match up. The Dodgers celebrated their new age before game one at Dodger Stadium. Frank Sinatra — not Walter Alston — threw out the first pitch. Alston would have to wait until game two. A crowd of nearly 56,000 pushed Dodger attendance to more than 3 million for the season.

Dodger starter Tommy John threw ground balls, and his success depended on his fielders making the plays. In the opener Bill Russell, with 29 regular season errors, made two more that the *Times* aptly described as "plays a little leaguer should make," including missing second base while turning a double play. John was chased in the fifth, and even though Ron Cey broke an 0-for-31 slump with a grand slam to tie the game in the seventh, the Phillies scored twice in the ninth off reliever Elias Sosa and won the opener, 7–5.

The loss did not quiet Lasorda. In the clubhouse afterward he was his normal ebullient self and asked the reporters to make sure to return after game two to "taste the fruits of victory." They did, as Dusty Baker's grand slam off Jim Lonborg keyed a 7–1 win.

But the Phillies had been nearly unbeatable at home, and the next three games were to be played in Philadelphia. In game three, with the Phillies leading 5–3 with two outs and no one on in the ninth, the Dodgers looked done. Phillies' reliever Gene Garber had retired eight in a row.

Lasorda, to his credit, backed his never-say-die words with the same approach. He called on pinch hitter Vic Davalillo, who dragged a bunt past Garber for a hit. Lasorda turned next to pinch hitter Manny Mota. He drove a ball to deep left field, where oafish Greg Luzinski staggered under the ball before it fell in. The relay throw went awry, and Davalillo scored, putting Mota on third with the tying run.

Up came Lopes. He lined a screaming grounder to Mike Schmidt at third. The ball deflected off his glove directly to

Third baseman Ron Cey was known to all as "the Penguin" while playing for four Dodger pennant winners and five division runners-up in 12 years with the Dodgers. During that time he slugged 228 homers and was known as a clutch performer who batted .350 in the Dodgers' 1981 World Series win over the Yankees.

shortstop Larry Bowa, who made a quick throw to first. Ump Bruce Froeming called Lopes safe in a close play. Shaken, Garber then threw wild on a pickoff play, and Bill Russell's single up the middle scored Lopes with the go-ahead run. The Phillies went out in the bottom of the inning, and the Dodgers won, 6–5. The victory was as miraculous as any in club history.

Left-hander Tommy John will forever be remembered for the surgical procedure that carries his name and allowed him to continue his career following a year's layoff in 1975. He compiled an outstanding 87–42 won-lost record in six seasons with the Dodgers, including a 20-win season in 1977.

The Lasorda legend was secure. "Maybe," wrote Bill Shirley in the *Times,* "Dodger manager Tommy Lasorda is right. Maybe there *really is* a Big Dodger in the Sky." For while luck had played a huge role in the comeback, as it always does in such games, Lasorda had never stopped managing. He played

until the last out, and it had paid off. As Jim Murray wrote: "There is a cliché in baseball and it is as old as the game. It is 'a game is never over until the last out.' It is a lie." The next day Tommy John's sinker sank the Phillies and Carlton 4–1 to give the Dodgers a pennant.

Meanwhile, in Kansas City the New York Yankees were making the Oakland A's look like a sewing circle. Yankee owner George Steinbrenner did his best to buy a pennant, but then Steinbrenner, Reggie Jackson, and manager Billy Martin conspired to ruin those plans by indulging in a massive three-way battle of egos. After a tempestuous season, the result was both unlikely and predictable — the Yankees won the AL pennant, setting up the first meeting between the Yankees and Dodgers since 1963.

Lasorda was as thrilled as the ABC television executives over the matchup. He loved the attention. In his first season he had delivered the Dodgers to the biggest stage in a pairing of clubs from baseball's two biggest markets. Even better, in comparison to the Yankees, whom the press had dubbed "the Best Team Money Could Buy," the Dodgers seemed as pure as Little Leaguers. The opportunity to win a World Series was incentive enough, but for Lasorda the chance to beat the Yankees was a dream come true. "This is what we busted our ass for all year," he said, "the Big Apple. The two names synonymous with baseball." Besides, Lasorda was confident that his club could beat the Yankees; he didn't think they had a pitcher who could get his club out.

The Series opened in New York, and in the top of the first the Dodgers jumped out to a 2–0 lead off Don Gullett. But the Yankees responded with three straight hits off Don Sutton to make the score 2–1. That was it until the sixth.

Then, with one out, Garvey, described by writer Pat Jordan later as running "like a man trotting in a new silk shirt on a hot day," dropped a surprise bunt for a hit. With two out, Glenn Burke then singled to right-center.

Garvey was off with the pitch. Yankee center fielder Mickey Rivers, who, L.A. writer Charles Maher wrote, "couldn't out-throw Mickey Rooney," fielded the ball as Reggie Jackson shied away. Third-base coach Preston Gomez waved a reluctant-looking Garvey home. In a close play, he was called out. Willie Randolph then homered in the bottom of the inning to put the Yankees ahead. But the Dodgers tied it up in the ninth when Lee Lacy singled home Dusty Baker off Yankee reliever Sparky Lyle. Had Garvey scored, the Dodgers would have won the game. Now it entered extra innings.

Lyle didn't give up another hit. But in the 12th Lasorda had pinch-hit for pitcher Mike Garman. He went with Rick Rhoden in his first relief appearance all season to match up against the Yankees. Willie Randolph ruined the strategy, and Paul Blair singled him home to beat L.A. 4–3.

After the game, Garvey's mad dash was rehashed over and over, and he was criticized for everything from the way he slid to slowing up before third to not stopping on his own. Lasorda reportedly reamed him out for not thinking about scoring from the start—Dodger scouts had instructed everyone to take chances on the arms of Yankee outfielders.

Lasorda wasn't the only man with a low opinion of Yankee arms. New York manager Billy Martin felt the same way about his pitching staff. He had lost faith in almost everyone but Gullett, and he gambled in game two, passing over Ed Figueroa for Catfish Hunter, who'd been hurt and hadn't started a game in over a month.

Hunter wasn't the answer. In the first three innings he gave up home runs to Cey, Steve Yeager, and Smith. Hooton shut down the Yankees, and the Dodgers won 6–1 to tie the Series and send it back to L.A.

Everything seemed to be breaking the Dodgers' way. Martin's decision to bypass Figueroa pissed off Reggie Jackson, and Martin responded by telling Jackson, through the press, "to kiss my dago ass." Catcher Thurman Munson was so disgusted with everything that he was overheard muttering, "Only five more days of this, only five more days." The Dodgers were determined to make it only three days.

But like the A's of 1974, the more the Yankees fought, the better they played. In game three Mickey Rivers ran the Dodgers ragged, and apart from a three-run home run from Dusty Baker, Yankee starter Mike Torrez shut the Dodgers down as the Yankees beat John and the Dodgers 5–3. Although Dusty Baker said afterward, "We ain't losing, we're just behind," after game four that was a faint hope. Ron Guidry shut the Dodgers down on four hits, and the Yankees needed only one more win to take the Series. In his column Jim Murray compared the demeanor of the two teams and concluded that the Dodgers were a victim of their own "harmony, serenity and brotherly love."

Back in New York, the Dodgers stayed harmonious and made things interesting with a 10–4 win, but then came game six. Reggie Jackson's three home runs on three swings, off Burt Hooton, Elias Sosa, and Charlie Hough—and four if one counted his last at bat in game six—led the Yankees to

an 8–4 win and sent the Dodgers back to Los Angeles as losers. The difference between the two clubs in the Series, clearly, had been Jackson.

True to form, Lasorda was already looking ahead. As soon as the team returned to Los Angeles he was already trying to pump up his charges. "I wouldn't trade clubs, period," he said. Comparing the rosters of the Dodgers and the Yankees, "man for man I have to take the Dodgers." He announced he

Durable right-hander Don Sutton pitched for the Dodgers from the days of Koufax and Drysdale through Fernando mania and beyond. He retired as the all-time Dodger career pitching leader in wins (233), innings pitched (3,814), strikeouts (2,696), and games started (533), among other categories.

1977

wanted to return with the same club in 1978—man for man. "I already have a motto," he said. "We did it before and we can do it again."

He almost got his wish. In the off-season the Dodgers barely tinkered with the roster, only shoring up the bullpen by signing Pittsburgh reliever Terry Forster. The Yankees, on the other hand, after losing Mike Torrez to the Red Sox through free agency, signed two of baseball's premier relievers, Goose Gossage and Rawley Eastwick, and former Dodger Andy Messersmith. The Reds, like the Dodgers, more or less stood pat. The Dodgers knew that for the short term they had a lot more to worry about from the Reds than from the Yankees, for if they didn't beat Cincinnati, the Yankees wouldn't matter.

In 1978 it was almost as if the Reds and Dodgers looked at each other and decided to play a "do-over."

L.A. fans were ready from the outset, buying tickets in record numbers, looking forward to another Dodger waltz to the postseason. That winter Lasorda began to cash in on his success. After earning $20,000 annually as a Dodger coach, he was playing catch-up. Not only did he receive a hefty raise from his $50,000 salary in 1977, but he was suddenly presented with a wide variety of commercial opportunities; he made dozens of TV and promotional appearances, selling the Dodgers but also selling himself. A portion of the L.A. media, which had never fully bought his act to begin with, began to look at him with skepticism. They were particularly troubled by how easily Lasorda seemed to play both sides of the fence, having it both ways by acting one way in public and another in private. When no one was watching, he could be as brusque and cruel and profane as any man in baseball— many Dodger rookies soon discovered that Lasorda had little use for them until he needed them, and there was a reason why the names above the Dodger lockers were written in chalk. But in front of the camera Lasorda was always Tommy Dodger, and a good Catholic to boot. Some wondered what would happen when both sides were exposed and when what was good for Tommy and what was good for the Dodgers were in opposition.

Steve Yeager was a superb defensive catcher who shared duties with Mike Scioscia and Joe Ferguson much of the time during his 14 years in Los Angeles. Despite his .228 career batting average, Yeager batted .298 in four World Series for Los Angeles. He is shown here applying a tag to Felix Millan of the Mets, who was caught off base when teammate Rusty Staub laced a liner caught by Dodger first baseman Steve Garvey.

NL CHAMPIONSHIP SERIES MVP AWARD

1977	Dusty Baker	OF
1978	Steve Garvey	1B
1981	Burt Hooton	P
1988	Orel Hershiser	P

But if Lasorda was a phony, the fans didn't care. Los Angeles was suddenly wild about all things Dodgers. One local school district even renamed a school building Steve Garvey Junior High.

The Dodgers were just a little off at the start of 1978—not by much, but by just enough to make a difference—and the surprising Giants pushed their way into the race for the division title. By June there was real reason for concern in Dodgerland. Neither the Reds nor the Giants appeared likely to collapse.

But the Dodgers had something the other two clubs didn't—some real help on the horizon. Down in triple-A, rookie Bob Welch was blowing people away. He'd pitched well in the spring, and Campanis had admitted, "If I had any guts, I'd put Welch on the big club." He was only 21, but he could throw the ball almost 100 miles an hour.

The Dodgers needed a shot in the arm, and Welch was it. Although no one in the Dodger rotation was really struggling, Welch's fastball put him into the mix.

The Dodgers brought him up on June 18, and in his first 11 innings Welch struck out 13 and didn't give up a run. It appeared as if the next great Dodger ace, in the tradition of Koufax and Drysdale, was now in Dodger Stadium. Over the next six weeks he both pitched in relief and made a few starts.

The Dodgers were running out of time. On August 2 they went into San Francisco trailing the first-place Giants by two and a half. Two days later they trailed by four and a half. Then Welch got the ball. He was magnificent and beat San Francisco in baseball's "Game of the Week," 2–0. After he struck

out Jack Clark on three straight fastballs in the ninth, Tommy John joked that he'd done it as easily as his near-namesake, aging bandleader Lawrence Welk—"a-one, a-two, and a-three."

A week later in L.A. he beat the Giants and Vida Blue 12–2 to pull the Dodgers into first place, and a week after that he beat Philadelphia to put them there to stay.

But the do-overs weren't quite finished. As soon as the Dodgers pulled into first place, they took a page from the Yankees.

Under the facade of "bleeding Dodger blue" and worshiping the Great Dodger in the Sky, the Dodgers were also, like most teams, a club of simmering factions and cliques. And although Lasorda had become the dominant personality, on the players' side Steve Garvey still got all the attention. That didn't sit well with his teammates.

Garvey was a very good player, but as his teammates knew, he was also a player with limited skills. What he could do—rack up hits, show a flair for the big hit, play every day—he did well. He hadn't missed a game since September 3, 1975, and in 1979 he had even continued playing after an errant pickoff throw by Welch busted his mouth and he took 20 stitches. But at the same time he couldn't run or throw, and his play at first was average. For all his notoriety as a hitter, Garvey rarely walked and usually led in a category that few paid any attention to—in most seasons he made more outs than any man on the team. He would get his 200 hits and 100 RBIs and score nearly 100 runs, but it would take him a huge number of at bats to do so. In 1979, for example, Garvey made 444 outs—nearly three a game. Cey, Lopes, and Baker put up almost identical numbers while making far fewer outs. That didn't mean Garvey wasn't a good player—he was—but Garvey wasn't quite the superstar most fans thought he was.

But Garvey was glib, good on camera, and cooperative with the press. His wife, Cyndy, looked like a quintessential California blonde, although, like Garvey, she was from Michigan. She worked on camera for a local TV station, and together they were the ultimate California couple, so outwardly flawless they were dubbed "Ken and Barbie." A lot of his teammates felt that Garvey should have shown more humility, and in August pitcher Don Sutton unloaded, telling *Washington Post* writer Tom Boswell that "the best player on this team—and we all know it—is Reggie Smith," whom he called "a real person," while describing Garvey as "a facade." After the story appeared, Garvey and Don Sutton scuffled in the clubhouse at Shea Stadium. All of a sudden the Dodgers seemed a lot more like the New York Yankees.

That wasn't altogether bad, for after the clash the Dodgers began playing like the Yankees. They went into overdrive, winning 21 of 32 to put away the division title, although the Reds made a late run to make it close. Perhaps Jim Murray had been right. Perhaps the Dodger problem in 1977 had been too much "brotherly love." Maybe now they could beat New York.

First the Dodgers had to beat Philadelphia again. They did so quickly and without attendant drama. After blasting the Phillies 9–5 in the opener in Philadelphia and 4–0 behind a Tommy John shutout in game two, back in Los Angeles the Phillies' Steve Carlton proved he was still a formidable opponent with a 9–4 complete-game win in game three. If the Phillies could win game four, anything could happen.

It was the best game of the series. The Dodgers went ahead 1–0, fell behind 2–1 when Greg Luzinski homered, tied the game on a Cey home run, and then went ahead 3–2 when Garvey also smacked a solo shot. But in this home run derby the Phillies weren't finished. Bake McBride went deep off Rhoden in the seventh to tie the game, and it went into extra innings.

Philadelphia's colorful reliever Tug McGraw had the Dodgers flummoxed until, with two out in the tenth, he walked Ron Cey. That brought up Dusty Baker, hitting a cool .500 for the series.

He slapped a pitch into center field, a twisting, sinking knuckleball to Philadelphia center fielder Garry Maddox, widely acknowledged as one of the best center fielders in the game. But Maddox, incredibly, dropped the ball, and the Dodgers were still alive. Russell rapped McGraw's second pitch into center field for a hit and sent Garry Maddox into a long, embarrassed run in from center field as the Dodgers all poured out of their dugout and greeted Ron Cey at home.

This time the World Series opened in Los Angeles, and in game one a motivated Dodger team, still riding the wave of momentum from their win over the Phillies, jumped all over New York starter Ed Figueroa. After a scoreless first inning, Dusty Baker opened with a home run, and Davey Lopes followed later with a two-run shot to give the Dodgers a 3–0 lead. Two innings later Lopes cracked a three-run home run, and the Dodgers held a 7–0 lead before the Yankees could score off Tommy John. It didn't matter that they did, because the Dodgers won going away, 11–5.

Tommy Lasorda loved the spotlight and here cavorts with country singer Roy Clark on an episode of the television show *Hee Haw*. Broadcaster and former catcher Joe Garagiola once said of Lasorda, "You can plant 2,000 rows of corn with the fertilizer Lasorda spreads around."

But the Yankees still had Reggie Jackson. In the third inning of game two he doubled home two runs in the third inning, and the Yankees still led 2–1 entering the sixth.

By 1978 Yankee pitcher Catfish Hunter was no longer the pitcher who would later be elected to the Hall of Fame. And if he had a weakness, it was the home run. After Lopes and Smith singled, Ron Cey came up with two out.

More than any other player perhaps, Cey was most often overlooked in the Dodger lineup. He simply didn't look like a ballplayer — his legs were about two sizes too short for his torso, and his odd gait had earned him the nickname of "the

TRAVELS WITH TOMMY

Bill Plaschke

FIFTEEN YEARS OF MEMORIES CULLED AT THE sauce-stained elbow of the greatest of Dodgers can be summed up with one: the time I earned a scoop because of a slice. It was a couple of hours before a Sunday afternoon game in Chicago, and Tommy Lasorda was crammed into a tiny office underneath Wrigley Field, slices of cold pizza sitting in an open box on his desk, a crumb-filled empty box underneath, wadded-up napkins scattered to the side, a wrinkled lineup card in his lap. The Dodger manager looked up and was suddenly faced with something he considered more disturbing than a yawning ballplayer or an empty refrigerator. Lasorda looked up and found himself alone.

It is the great Dodger irony that the franchise's most exalted personality, the guy standing solo on the highest of pedestals, hated to be alone. Even in his managing prime, with the world watching, Lasorda needed an audience like he needed a power hitter, craved companionship like he craved a good pasta fagoli, couldn't drive the car without somebody riding shotgun. On this dank Sunday in Chicago, it was going to be me.

"Hey, Plaschke, get in here!" he shouted, and I knew what was coming — everyone around the organization knew about these moments, had lived them and consumed them and eventually belched them. So I hesitated for a second outside the office, mumbling something about needing to get upstairs and begin writing, when he shouted again. "Plaschke!" he said. "I got something for you!"

As the Dodger beat writer for the *Los Angeles Times*, I had to at least listen, so I sauntered inside and leaned against a doorway, the best place for those who weren't sure they had the time or appetite for a visit with a guy who always had plenty of both. Lasorda looked up at me with a smile, then pointed to one of the cracked leather chairs in front of his desk. "Sit down and have a piece of pizza," he said, which, in Lasorda speak, was a request to sit with him until he finished dressing and headed to the field.

I understood this. I empathized with this. I could not possibly do this. I had just eaten a giant Chicago breakfast that could not physically be topped with pepperoni. I refused. Lasorda wouldn't listen. I refused again. Lasorda grabbed a greasy slice and plopped it down on the desk in front of the chair and ordered me to sit.

I said, "Tommy, if I eat this piece, I will throw up."

He said, "Plaschke, if you eat this piece, I will give you a scoop."

I paused. Was I hearing him right? There were several personnel issues on the team that needed deciding. There were a couple of incidents that needed confirming. As with any Lasorda team, there was great news hidden in his giant shadow, and now some of that could be mine? For the price of one slice?

Lasorda said, "I'm not kidding. You eat this, I'll give you something to write."

I said, "Pass the napkins."

By the time I finished, while my stomach was bulging, so

was my next day's story. Lasorda talked so long, he was finally interrupted by the announcing of the starting lineups, at which point he hollered for a nearby coach to walk with him into the dugout, maintaining his perpetual company while leaving me with equal parts indigestion and inspiration.

So went the constant paradox of my travels with Tommy. Treacherous, yet tender. Filled with modern-day bluster, yet reeking of old-fashioned baseball. He was disliked by those players who felt his constant cheerleading was little more than a screech for attention, another way of avoiding being alone. But the same players never criticized him because he created such a fraternity atmosphere, it would have felt like criticizing family.

He was not as respected as Campy or as revered as Sandy or as admired as Bulldog. But I've stood on a field next to all of them and heard only an echo of the cheers, the embraces, the unconditional love that is showered on Lasorda.

How did this happen? How did a bowlegged, raw-knuckled, short-tempered little fat guy come to rule what was once the most glamorous kingdom in sports?

Searching for answers, I flew to Utah. In the little town of Ogden, old men still lean across Formica tables and talk about the time their minor league manager confronted a kid who complained of a sore ankle. "Stick it in the whirlpool," Lasorda told the kid, directing him to a toilet. Then there was the time, during one ornery road game, when he ordered a player off the field, into his street clothes, and into the stands, where the player spent nine innings threatening to punch out the hecklers. Or how about the time he pitched to his starters in an intrasquad game and threw at everyone's head? And, oh yeah, in his first year in the bush leagues, in Pocatello, Idaho, he called for 11 suicide squeeze plays in 66 games. "Tommy Lasorda?" remembered an elderly woman sitting behind an empty Ogden lunch counter, 30 years after his departure. "Wasn't he the loud one?"

Searching for answers, I met Lasorda in a restaurant in Las Vegas. It was late, we were the last customers there, the waiters and manager were standing behind our chairs, but none of them complained, they were too busy listening to Tommy talk about the miracle of 1988. "How did we do it?" Lasorda was saying, his voice rising. "Mike Marshall had a headache, that's how. In that World Series Marshall complained of a

headache the same time Bob Costas is on TV saying we had the worst lineup in World Series history, and I can't take it anymore. I start screaming, just screaming, about loving this team and this game and yourself. By the time I finished, I couldn't even talk." By the time Lasorda finished yelling this story, nobody else could talk, they were laughing so hard amid the flying crumbs and rattling knives, every person but one. "What's so funny?" asked Lasorda, silencing the room. "You think trying to win is funny?"

Searching for answers, I once flew to Sydney, Australia, where Lasorda was managing what appeared to be a horrible 2000 U.S. Olympic baseball team. "I never heard of half these guys," he had told me a couple of weeks earlier. "How am I going to pull this off?" So throughout the games I had written this view, that they had little chance, that even Lasorda couldn't handle this meal. But then they wound up winning the gold medal, defeating rival Cuba in the final game, and moments after tearfully listening to his anthem, Lasorda angrily came looking for me. "What do you say now, Plaschke!" he screamed during his press conference. "What are you going to write now? You didn't believe! Why didn't you believe?" I was stunned. I shouted back, "Tommy, wait a minute, *you* didn't believe." Lasorda broke into a big smile. "You should know me by now," he said. "No matter what I say, I always believe."

Searching for answers, I once traveled with Lasorda to a speaking engagement in Spokane, Washington. It wasn't until we arrived that I realized it was just a high school awards banquet. But Lasorda treated it like it was another World Series, shouting and gesturing and inspiring the kids such that afterward a dozen of them sprinted after his limousine, running several blocks to his hotel, where he stepped outside and signed autographs for them. Then he went to a sports bar run by one of the organizers, where a pitcher of beer was spilled into his lap, and he said nothing. Then he tried to convince a man wearing a Yankee cap that he had lost his mind. Then he finally went to bed after midnight, asking me to accompany him to his room, where I stood outside while he walked in, lay face down on the bed in his suit, and fell asleep. "Being out with the people like this . . . this is my linguine, this is my steak," he said.

Searching for answers, I realized I was looking in the right

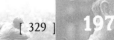

1979

places but the wrong era. Tommy Lasorda is beloved like antiques are beloved, respected like hard work is respected, embraced like devotion and admired like loyalty. During his 20 years as Dodger boss, the world changed, but Lasorda didn't. Players became free agents, but Lasorda wouldn't. Managers ripped their players, but Lasorda couldn't. Los Angelenos lost faith in that Big Dodger in the Sky, but Lasorda refused.

Baseball officials stopped learning the names of their players' families, but Lasorda never forgot. "How can I rip him when my kids still call him Uncle Tommy?" said reliever Jay Howell once.

Baseball protocol increasingly separated the rich players in plush clubhouses, but Lasorda wasn't buying. When he finally retired, he was the only manager who still set up the postgame buffet in front of his desk.

Lasorda still lives in a house with a den built by his former players. He still gives speeches at the service academies for free. He still wishes someone would ask him to pitch batting practice, where he says he would love to throw a curveball directly at a rookie's noggin.

And a slice wasn't the only thing that earned me a scoop. Another time it was steam. It was in Pittsburgh, and I had walked into Lasorda's office to ask an extra question just as he was stepping through the bathroom into the shower.

I said, "I'll come back later."

He said, "No, come in here now, what do you want?"

So I walked inside and stood at the sink as thick billows of white poured over the shower door, moisturizing my notebook even as it heated up my story.

About 10 minutes and 20 great quotes later, he climbed out, grabbed a towel, looked down at my soggy papers, and asked, "Do you need anything else? Could you understand what I was saying through all that steam?"

Speaking for all of Los Angeles, yeah, we certainly can.

Bill Plaschke covered the Dodgers for the *Los Angeles Times* for nearly a decade before becoming a columnist in 1996. His work has been recognized in the last two editions of *The Best American Sports Writing,* and he makes frequent appearances as a commentator on ESPN.

Penguin." But Cey could hit. He usually batted fifth in the Dodger lineup, after Garvey, giving him some protection.

He also had a good eye. He worked the count in his favor, 2–0, forcing Hunter to throw a strike. Cey turned on the ball and drove it deep into the bleachers for a three-run home run to put the Dodgers ahead 4–2.

The Yankees got a run back in the seventh when Jackson drove home Roy White with a ground ball, his third RBI of the day. Into the ninth the Dodgers still led, 4–3.

But Terry Forster, who had come into the game in relief of Hooton in the seventh, gave up a leadoff single to Bucky Dent. Roy White sacrificed him to second, and then Forster walked weak-hitting Paul Blair. That brought up Thurman Munson and Reggie Jackson, the last two men the Dodgers wanted to see at bat. To paraphrase Reggie Jackson, each was a hitter whose straw could stir the drink.

Out in the bullpen Bob Welch was warming up. A single would tie the game. A home run could conceivably send the Dodgers to a loss. For the last two months Welch had been almost untouchable, and he was well rested. He was also a stone-cold alcoholic. The Dodgers didn't know that yet, and for now it wasn't affecting his performance.

Lasorda waved him in. The Yankees knew what to expect—fastballs.

Munson got hold of one and hit it on a line to right, directly at Reggie Smith, for out number two. That brought up Reggie Jackson.

The next seven minutes were some of the most memorable in World Series history. The matchup between the fireballing rookie and the Yankee slugger who a year before had earned the nickname "Mr. October" was like a juvenile fiction novel being played out in real life, every kid's back yard dream under a microscope and broadcast live and close up coast to coast. The last inning of a World Series game, two out and the game on the line, the Hometown Hero versus the Bad Guy, the Rookie versus the Vet, Youth versus Experience, the Nobody versus the Star, the Immovable Object versus the Unstoppable Force. And the Ultimate Fastball Pitcher versus the Ultimate Fastball Hitter. It was the essence of baseball, distilled into a single matchup, with the result either joy or agony in Mudville. Dodger fans prayed for agony, for Casey to strike out.

Everyone knew Jackson played for just these moments—in fact, he had earned the name Mr. October against the Dodgers. But so far in his short career, Welch had shown

Bill Russell of Pittsburg, Kan., was a high school basketball star drafted from a school that was too small to field a baseball team. Despite this handicap, he went on to hold the Dodger shortstop job for 18 seasons.

nerves of steel, winning big game after big game. He was well rested and Jackson was hot. The matchup had everything.

Welch threw a fastball on the first pitch, over the plate but down. It surprised Jackson, and he was a hair late, swinging through the pitch. Strike one.

The crowd in Dodger Stadium was on its feet, as loud and raucous as it had ever been. Jackson stood there like the legendary Casey, gritting his teeth and trying to grind his bat into sawdust as Welch, looking younger with each passing second, looked in toward him.

Welch reared back and threw one up and in. Jackson spun away and went down, then jumped up. Ball one, but the crowd roared its approval.

On the exchange went. Fastball and a foul, fastball and a foul, fastball and a foul, Welch throwing harder and harder, Jackson trying to shatter the air with each swing.

After eight pitches, the count was 3-and-2. Now the runners would be running with the pitch, and now there was no question in anyone's mind that Welch was going to throw a fastball and that Jackson would swing. Either Welch would strike out Jackson and the Dodgers would win or Jackson would deliver and the Dodgers would lose.

On his ninth pitch, Welch cut loose another fastball, one that rode up and in. Jackson swung and missed—a mighty blow—then grimaced, grabbed his bat, and made a sound like an animal that had just missed his prey after a long time spent stalking.

The crowd roared with the thunder of the escaping herd. The Dodgers won 4–3 and now led the Series two games to none.

The Dodgers were ebullient after the game. Welch had made Lasorda look like a genius. Jackson called Welch's fastball "aviation fuel, pure octane," high praise from the game's dominant slugger. Reggie Smith said simply, "If it wasn't for Bob, we wouldn't be here." The Dodgers flew to New York absolutely certain they would return as champions.

They returned as Dodgers, knowing they would soon be waiting for next year. They had gotten a lesson in Yankee Stadium, where they were greeted by New York fans in all their dirty, gritty glory, taunted by insults, pelted by debris, and on the field completely intimidated as the Yankees reminded the Dodgers that Casey had struck out only in one game and the World Series was a best-of-seven affair.

Yankee third baseman Graig Nettles, almost by himself, won game three with his glove, saving five runs with spectacular stops as Guidry beat Sutton 5–1. Then in game four the Series really turned. Jackson was in the middle of it again.

The Dodgers led 3–1 in the sixth, with Munson on second, Jackson on first, and Lou Piniella at the plate facing Tommy John. Piniella hit a sinking liner to Bill Russell. He dropped the ball, then reacted, racing to touch second for the force-out and throw to first for a double play.

Reggie Jackson first got confused, and then got smart real fast. He broke for second, stopped when he thought Russell caught the ball, and then froze as he saw Russell touch sec-

ond and throw to first. But as the throw whizzed toward him, Jackson took a step, threw out his hip, deflected the ball wide, then turned his head and looked around as if saying, "Who, *me?*" Munson scored as the ball bounded away to make the score 3–2 and Lasorda and Russell and a host of Dodgers screamed bloody murder at umpire Frank Pulli.

Jackson should have been called out for the interference it clearly was, for a runner is not allowed to block a throw, but Pulli didn't see it that way. In fact, he hadn't seen it at all—Jackson's act had fooled him. The Dodger protest went nowhere except onto the World Series highlight film. Lasorda was wearing a wire, and every word ended up on tape, although not all of them could be used when the film was released.

The Yankees went on to tie the game in the eighth, and Lasorda turned to Welch again. In the tenth Welch walked Roy White and this time Mighty Casey—er, Jackson—singled, and Lou Piniella beat the Dodgers with a hit up the middle.

All of a sudden the Series was tied, and almost as suddenly the Yankees were ahead three games to two, because in game five they hit everybody and won going away, 12–2.

The Dodgers could not wait to get out of New York, not because they were going home, but just to escape. On their way out the door they bitched and moaned about the whole experience. "I don't like Yankee Stadium and I don't like the town," griped Rick Monday.

The Dodgers played game six with all the confidence of a New York tourist hurrying back to his hotel through Times Square late at night. The clock struck midnight on Welch, and the Yankees scored the last run of their 7–2 win when Jackson took him deep. Welch went from hero to zero.

The ballclub wore the loss like a stain. They had drawn 3.3 million fans, but the way the season ended made the whole year seem like a failure. This time Lasorda couldn't talk his club into beating the Yankees. "God doesn't deny," he said, "he just delays," but the Dodgers weren't quite buying it anymore.

In the off-season the Yankees rubbed the Dodgers' noses in it and signed ace Tommy John as a free agent. He had won 37 games over the past two seasons, but in response the Dodgers, who had been printing money for two seasons, didn't spend any of it apart from signing Andy Messersmith. They expected Welch to become a big winner and planned on promoting the promising rookie Rick Sutcliffe.

The Dodgers were about to pay a price for two years of almost unencumbered success. In Lasorda's first two years

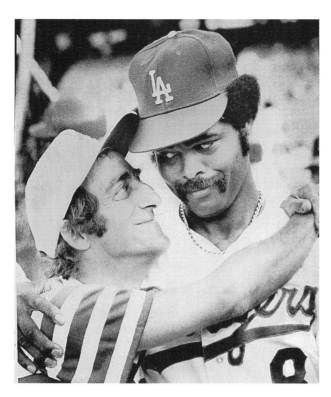

In six seasons with the Dodgers, Reggie Smith contributed to three National League pennant winners and one world championship while batting .297 with 97 home runs, including 32 in his first full season in 1977. Smith is shown with comedian Marty Feldman before the start of the annual Hollywood Stars exhibition game in 1978.

the club had gone almost injury-free, but in 1979 the disabled list took on the look of a hockey penalty box after a bench-clearing brawl.

Reggie Smith and Rick Monday were early casualties, and together they would combine for fewer than 40 RBIs. Pitcher Doug Rau got a sore arm, as did Terry Forster. Messersmith was cooked.

The only bright spot was the emergence of Sutcliffe, who won 17 games, a Dodger record for a rookie. But that was offset by a disappointing year for Jerry Reuss, who had been obtained in a trade for Rick Rhoden, and Bob Welch, who simultaneously fell off the table and the wagon.

Unbeknownst to the Dodgers, Welch had been an alcoholic when they signed him out of Western Michigan University, and his sudden success didn't help him stay sober. He spent a liquid winter and in spring training showed up out of shape, got a sore arm, and then deteriorated.

To their credit, the Dodgers were better than most clubs in handling such matters. Former pitcher Don Newcombe had been sober for years and worked for the club in community relations. Every spring he gave a talk on the dangers of alcoholism, but Welch was too young and immature to get the message. Besides, like most clubs, the Dodgers stocked beer in the clubhouse for after the game, and often Welch didn't even wait that long.

By the All-Star break the Dodgers were a pathetic 36–57 and starting to point fingers. Anonymous teammates accused Reggie Smith of "jaking" it, or quitting on them, and others spoke of some teammates as "cancers." Davey Lopes resigned as captain. Lasorda told them with unintentional, dead-on accuracy, "You're rusting on your laurels." He wasn't trying to be funny.

Although his job was safe, local media asked fans whether it should be. For the first time since Lasorda's arrival, the ball-club failed to respond to his approach. When he was on top, everything was sunshine, but when the Dodgers didn't win, his act quickly wore thin. And besides, in the last two years the rules had all changed. Free agency—the right of a player to go on the open market and sell himself to the highest bidder—changed everything. Neither the manager nor the club owner called the shots anymore. Players were no longer married to an organization until traded or discarded. Now, when a contract expired, they could choose to go. Rosters could change dramatically from year to year, making a manager's job even tougher than before.

It would no longer be possible for the Dodgers to depend on the strength of the organization to stay on top, watching while lesser clubs struggled to rebuild from below. Now, with enough cash, rebuilding could be done in a year or two. Helped by free agents, perennial also-rans like Houston and Montreal became instant contenders. The Dodgers could no longer afford to stand pat, watch players they developed leave as free agents, and restock from the farm system. They'd have to get in the game too.

On August 9 Walter O'Malley's death after a long bout with cancer caused mourning in Los Angeles and a last blast of bitter recrimination from old Brooklyn fans. L.A. Dodger fans loved him because he brought them the Dodgers and they won, albeit perhaps less than he probably could have. Brooklyn Dodger fans hated him because he took the Dodgers and Brooklyn lost it all. It was that simple, but some of the venom that still streamed his way was, to be fair, unfair. Over time

When right-hander Bob Welch arrived in Los Angeles in 1978, many pegged the tall flame-thrower as the new Don Drysdale. His matchup against Reggie Jackson in the World Series was unforgettable.

the Dodger move had taken on a symbolic significance larger than the loss of a baseball team — it symbolized the loss of an era and a time and place that didn't exist anymore. O'Malley was blamed because people grew up and moved away and buildings fell apart and time passed — all of which would have happened even if the Dodgers had never left Brooklyn.

The move of the ballclub to Los Angeles had been a resounding, staggering success, for both O'Malley and baseball. And even in the most basic terms, wins and losses, the Dodgers of Los Angeles far outstripped their forebears in Brooklyn. In Brooklyn a championship had often been only a distant dream, while in the 22 years since O'Malley had moved the club away from Brooklyn, championships had come with some regularity and were more or less expected. That made old Brooklyn fans even angrier — God hadn't penalized O'Malley for what he did, but rewarded him.

In many ways the Dodgers had become a model organization under his watch. They were forward-thinking, fan-friendly, and consistent, a team built from within that was loyal to its employees and incredibly lucrative. According to Buzzie Bavasi, in some seasons in L.A. in the 1960s the Dodgers earned a profit in excess of $6 million. Much of that stayed in O'Malley's pockets. He was, after all, a businessman.

But that was also his weakness — an inability to look beyond profit, beyond his own self-interest. As the Dodgers became more successful they also became, in a sense, narrower, their horizons more limited. Under O'Malley, in the wake of Jackie Robinson, the Dodgers became an organization that squandered its role as a leader in the integration of baseball and chose instead to pursue a pattern of disquieting paternalism, just like everyone else.

In a larger sense, it is perhaps most accurate to assess O'Malley's career apart from the prejudices of either L.A. or Brooklyn — indeed, apart from the Dodgers. For much of his time as Dodger owner — particularly after moving the team to L.A. — he was probably the most powerful and influential owner in the game, a status he earned by way of the Dodger bank account. Yet his legacy as one of baseball's movers and shakers in the 1960s and 1970s is, at best, a mixed one.

O'Malley wasn't so much a visionary as a fortunate opportunist. While he is often credited with making baseball a "coast-to-coast" game and ushering in a new era, those changes were inevitable. Neither was he a true leader among the club owners — he just had the most money and that made him one by default. As a leader, he was thoroughly average, a champion of the status quo and his own narrow self-interest. Under his watch, baseball scuffled, expanded too rapidly, built a bunch of terrible ballparks, and began to lose its pre-eminence as the national pastime. When free agency and labor relations between players and management were becoming ever more important issues, O'Malley never saw them coming. He helped engineer the appointment of Bowie Kuhn as baseball commissioner, and under Kuhn baseball made misstep after misstep, squabbling with itself, first toe-ing a hard line, then caving in, escalating salaries through ineptness, and creating the contentious and adversarial situation that today still threatens the game. But O'Malley made a lot of money. On that scorecard he was a success. In the end, however, his role on the larger stage may well prove to have been as muddled as his legacy as Dodger owner. Never-theless, O'Malley, along with Charlie Ebbets and Branch Rickey, remains one of the three central figures in the history of the franchise.

After none of it mattered anymore, the Dodgers did play better over the final two months of the 1979 season. In fact, in August and September they had the best record in baseball and finished a deceptive 79–83. While that record was some cause for optimism and may well have stopped the team from being torn apart, it still landed them in only third place, behind second-place Houston and eleven and a half games behind champion Cincinnati.

After coming so close to drinking champagne, in the end they had left the party with nothing but a season-long hang-over. And that was something that not even Tommy Lasorda could cure.

FERNANDO MANIA

IN THE OFF-SEASON BEFORE THE 1980 SEASON, PITCHERS DAVE GOLTZ AND Don Stanhouse were the two Dodgers everyone was talking about. They were the glitzy baubles acquired by the pure gold spun from the Dodger turnstiles, the supposed top-shelf return from three years of record-setting crowds in which the Dodgers averaged more than three million fans and had done everything but win. Goltz and Stanhouse, one a front-line starting pitcher and the other a slam-the-door reliever, were supposed to change that.

No one had ever heard of Fernando Valenzuela, whoever or whatever that was. He was a trinket picked up on the cheap while the Dodgers were headed somewhere else. He was just another guy, a curio of unknown value thrown in the pile at the bottom of the Dodger farm system. But in the end Goltz and Stanhouse were the forgotten acquisitions, overpriced chintz. Valenzuela became the priceless objet d'art, the masterpiece, the most significant Dodger since Sandy Koufax, and a story that couldn't have been made up because nobody would have believed it. Fernando Valenzuela—not Lasorda, not Garvey and Lopes and Russell and Cey, and most certainly *not* Goltz and Stanhouse—made the Dodgers champions again. And more than that, he gave the team something that recently had been in short supply—a

Dodger scout Mike Brito struck gold when he signed left-handed pitcher Fernando Valenzuela. In 1981 Fernando mania struck as Valenzuela captured both the Cy Young Award and the Rookie of the Year Award. His 13–7 record included a league-leading 11 complete games in the strike-shortened season.

heart and a soul in an era when baseball desperately needed both. When the business of baseball looked to be bigger than the game, Valenzuela made everyone stop and watch and remember why they cared at all.

The Dodgers were not fans of free agency. No baseball owner was really, but once it had become reality, some, like George Steinbrenner of the Yankees, jumped in with both feet. The Yankees' success in 1977 and 1978 led others into the fire. To compete, they had to play.

Yet apart from the cautious acquisition in 1977 of Terry Forster—who had one good year and then got hurt—the Dodgers had shied away from free agents. By 1979 their conservative approach was costing them. The Dodgers had lost to the Yankees because New York had added players to an already solid club, and the Dodgers had collapsed in 1979 because the others had gotten better while they hadn't. Not only did the Dodgers not have a "Mr. October," but in 1979 that month didn't even matter. After being lauded as the major league model of efficiency for so long, the Dodgers suddenly looked out of date. People both inside and outside the organization were starting to ask, "What's the point of making money if not to spend it to win?"

Since the days of Branch Rickey, Dodger success had been built from the farm system up, and since the team had moved to California the Dodgers had continually refueled that system with a steady influx of cash, outscouting and outspending other teams from the bottom up. This was what had enabled the Dodgers to remain at or near the top for so long and to contend annually for the National League pennant.

But thanks to free agency, that advantage was gone now, and 1979 had been a wake-up call. The amateur draft, Bavasi's do-nothing approach, and O'Malley's tightfisted monetary policy had combined to push the Dodgers to the back of the pack. Now they couldn't afford to wait on prospects when no one else was following that strategy. While the Dodgers would still resist diving full bore into the free agent market, before 1980 they decided to take a tepid dip in the waters.

In the off-season they were aggressive, for the Dodgers anyway. Bob Welch had entered rehab in the off-season, and while he was apparently succeeding in his quest for sobriety, no one knew what to expect from him in the future. The knowledge that the suddenly dangerous Astros, who had finished in second place in 1979, were certain to go after an impact player in the draft forced the Dodgers to react. They needed both a starting pitcher and some bullpen help.

The Angels' Nolan Ryan was the best fastball pitcher since Sandy Koufax. Although he lacked Koufax's control and sometimes struggled to win, he nevertheless had broken or matched two of Koufax's most significant records, setting a new single-season strikeout mark with 383 in 1973 and twirling four no-hitters. Everything about Ryan screamed that he belonged on the Dodger pitching staff, but he wanted a big contract and wanted to go home to his native Texas.

Although the Dodgers could spend with anyone, the franchise continued to find that notion repugnant—the O'Malley family business still served the family first. Even if Ryan had expressed an interest in Los Angeles, the Dodgers never would have spent the money. Had Walter O'Malley been alive, they might not have pursued anyone. But Peter O'Malley, who was calling the shots now, was eager to match his father by winning a world championship, and Lasorda, like Walter Alston, was on a year-to-year contract and impatient to win. Another sub-.500 record would probably send his act on the road. So in the reentry draft, which at the time determined which players a team could pursue, GM Al Campanis and the Dodgers decided to take a stab at Minnesota starting pitcher Dave Goltz, by default the second-best starter on the market, and the best reliever, Baltimore's Don Stanhouse. Goltz was an innings-eater who had won at least 14 games for five seasons in a row, with a high of 20 in 1977. Stanhouse had saved 21 games in 1979. He was known as both "Stan the Man Unusual" for his eccentric behavior and "Full-Pack," Baltimore manager Earl Weaver's nickname for him owing to the number of cigarettes Weaver claimed to smoke while Stanhouse performed another feat of brinkmanship in the late innings.

Neither Goltz nor Stanhouse was a truly upper-echelon player. Yet under free agency, and compared to the other players who were available, the skills of each appeared elevated. Unless the Dodgers were prepared to break the bank, there were few other choices. They had in fact selected two such players, Ryan and Reds second baseman Joe Morgan, but those were PR picks. L.A. never made a genuine offer to either man.

That was a mistake. When the Dodgers quickly signed Goltz and Stanhouse to contracts worth more than $5.5 million, according to the rules in effect at the time the club gave up its right to pursue Morgan. In a procedural move, he was made available to other clubs. The Astros, who, as expected, had signed Ryan, now nabbed Morgan too. The Dodgers had gotten what they wanted, but Houston had picked up two players on their way to the Hall of Fame — Goltz and Stanhouse would have to pay their way to Cooperstown. The Astros were becoming a lot like the Koufax-era Dodgers, a team built around pitching and speed. The starting rotation now included 21-game winner Joe Niekro, Ryan, and flame-throwing J. R. Richard, and the addition of Morgan made the team even faster.

As the 1980 season played out, it became clear that O'Malley, Campanis, and Lasorda had been completely outmaneuvered. Goltz struggled from the start, and Stanhouse had a bad arm. Rick Sutcliffe suffered through one of the worst sophomore slumps on record as he quickly lost his starting slot and his ERA ballooned to more than five runs a game. Fortunately, Welch, clean and sober, bounced back nicely, even making the All-Star team after a 9–3 start, but he slumped in the second half. Reuss, Hooton, and Sutton all pitched well, and hyperactive rookie left-hander Steve Howe took up the slack in the bullpen.

But the Dodger offense struggled. Only Garvey, Cey, and Dusty Baker performed to their usual standard as Rick Monday and Davey Lopes slowed, Reggie Smith underwent shoulder surgery, and catcher Steve Yeager couldn't hit. The Dodgers were able to plug some holes with rookies Rudy Law and Pedro Guerrero and veteran Jay Johnstone, but they didn't scare anybody. For most of the first half the Dodgers and Astros batted first place back and forth. Neither team was able to open up a big lead.

The key moment of the season — until the final week anyway — came just after the All-Star Game. Houston pitcher J. R. Richard, despite complaining of fatigue and a tired arm, had a great first half and even started the All-Star Game. Players reacted to his complaints of fatigue as they had after Koufax announced he had a bad arm — they laughed. Richard was throwing nearly 100 miles per hour and was harder to hit than Ryan.

Richard made only one more brief appearance after the All-Star Game before finally convincing Astros doctors that something was wrong. He was diagnosed with a circulatory ailment in his arm, and on July 30 he suffered a stroke. His season was over — and so was his career.

Richard's ailment helped the Dodgers, however, for it kept the Astros from running away with the division. The Dodgers finally caught them in early September, but after Bill Russell broke his finger, the Astros pulled ahead.

By October 1, four days before the end of the season, the Dodgers seemed finished. The Astros beat the Braves, while the Dodgers suffered what *Times* writer Mike Littwin called a "come-from-ahead loss" to the Giants, losing 3–2 to fall three games back with three left to play. Although those three games would be against Houston at Dodger Stadium and a *Times* headline had the temerity to ask, "Do You Believe in Miracles?" few did. To win the division, the Dodgers would need not only to sweep Houston but to then beat them in a one-game playoff, a near-impossible task. Yet over the next four days the expectation of a miracle would become palpa-

Dusty Baker was one of the more underrated players in recent Dodger history. In eight seasons with the Dodgers, Baker batted .281 with 144 homers, including 30 in 1977. His batting average in 17 National League championship series games was .371. In 1977 Baker was named MVP of the series.

ble and result in four of the most excruciating days of baseball ever seen in Dodger Stadium.

Don Sutton started the first game of the series on October 2, taking the mound for what he knew might well be his last time in a Dodger uniform. His contract was up, and it was no secret that the Dodgers weren't eager to re-sign him, at least for the money he was looking for. He was also 35 years old and had clashed with both Garvey and Lasorda, which in Los Angeles was like speaking out against Hollywood and sunshine.

There was a playoff atmosphere at Dodger Stadium for the game. The park was full, and as the Dodgers took the field they received a standing ovation. Sutton then proceeded to give them more to cheer about.

In 23 of his 30 starts he'd given up two runs or less. He made it 24 for 31 against the Astros. But he still left for a pinch hitter in the eighth trailing 2–1.

The Dodgers came to bat in the ninth still trailing by that score against the Astros' Ken Forsch. With one out, Rick Monday singled. Dusty Baker followed with a ground ball to short, but Astro second baseman Rafael Landestoy booted the ball. After an out by Garvey, Cey singled to tie the score.

And in the tenth Joe Ferguson homered to keep the Dodgers alive.

But the big story was not Sutton, Cey, or Ferguson, but a funny-looking pitcher with a funny-sounding name. Nineteen-year-old Fernando Valenzuela was making the major league minimum salary, considerably less than the $5.5 million due Goltz and Stanhouse. In relief of Sutton, he pitched two shutout innings for the win.

The Dodger organization had a long tradition of rookie phenom pitchers that stretched back decades — from Karl Spooner and Drysdale and Sutton all the way up to Welch and Rick Sutcliffe — but Valenzuela broke the mold. The other pitchers were players whose success had long been predicted. But Valenzuela arrived at Dodger Stadium like some kind of Carlos Casteneda–inspired creation, a magical apparition who seemed touched by the gods.

His parents were subsistence farmers near the Mexican town of Etchhauquila in Sonora. He had grown up poor, the

Right-hander Don Sutton pitched for 23 seasons with five teams over part of three decades. Sutton retired during the 1988 season.

youngest of 11 children. He had been pitching since he was just a young boy in pickup games on dusty fields, and at age 16 he began to pitch professionally in Mexico, earning a few hundred dollars a month.

Dodger scouts Corito Verona and Mike Brito discovered Valenzuela in 1978, when the 17-year-old was pitching in the Mexican Central League. In that rough-and-tumble circuit he was one of the youngest players.

They went to scout a shortstop but found something else—a pitcher who was also one of the most unlikely looking players in the league. That was saying something, for although there are many talented players in the Mexican League, there are also dozens who are too old, too troubled, or too one-dimensional to play anywhere else.

That was Valenzuela. He looked like he should have been sitting in a serape beside a dirt road. Throwing a baseball for a living seemed as unlikely a career for him as downhill skiing. He didn't look like a ballplayer—more like a much older man down on his luck, a vagabond who had been stuffed into a uniform while sleeping off a bender. He was short and pudgy, most of his 200 pounds or so concentrated in his torso and gut. His windup was unconventional—something a kid comes up with playing Wiffle ball in the back yard. He lifted his leg high, spun around almost backward, stuck out his tongue, and looked to the heavens as if sending up a prayer. Had he shown up at a tryout camp, he'd have inspired a few laughs and then been sent away.

But when he let go of the ball, his prayers were always answered. Like Don Juan, it was as if he suddenly gained access to some mystical powers and tapped into generations of pitching wisdom and acumen no one else could see. He was poised, determined, inventive, and confident. His control and big curveball were reminiscent of Sal Maglie, and he pitched with precocious command, changing speeds like a 20-year veteran. He seemed able to hit the target effortlessly and to always throw the ball at a speed and to a place that the batter least expected. Although he had a good curve, his fastball was only in the upper eighties. Nevertheless, the combination of his delivery and his control kept hitters on their heels, and he was able to strike out the best fastball hitters in the league.

And he was left-handed, an asset always in short supply. Had he been right-handed, the Dodgers probably would have looked the other way, but when room is made in baseball for the unconventional, it is usually for a left-handed pitcher.

NL CY YOUNG AWARD

1974	Mike Marshall	15–12
1981	Fernando Valenzuela	13–7
1988	Orel Hershiser	23–8
2003	Eric Gagne	55 saves

Even then, the Dodgers were almost too late and almost missed out. For years Campanis had jokingly asked Brito, "When are you going to come up with another Koufax?" and Brito had always responded, "Just give me time, just give me time." Now he thought he had a better answer.

Campanis wasn't impressed. Despite Brito's glowing reports, Valenzuela was short, out of shape, and didn't even throw 90 miles an hour. Campanis refused to sign him.

But Brito was insistent. In 1979 he convinced Campanis to take a look at Valenzuela with his own eyes. Now Campanis understood. But by then the Yankees had spotted him too, and even though some in their organization balked at his appearance and questioned his true age—one scout said bluntly, "He looks like he's 40 years old"—the Yankees had money to burn and tried to buy him.

A year before, the Dodgers could have gotten him for nothing. Now they found themselves in a bidding war for a player who looked like he could barely afford shoes. In the end the Dodgers outbid New York, paying $120,000 for Valenzuela's contract and sending him to their single-A team in Lodi. In three games he went 1–2. Good, but not great.

The Dodgers considered Valenzuela an intriguing project but not necessarily a player on the fast track. The Mexican League wasn't the majors, after all. In the off-season the club sent him to the Arizona Instructional League. With only a so-so fastball, the club thought the left-hander needed another pitch and asked veteran Bobby Castillo to try to teach him to throw a screwball, perhaps the most difficult pitch to learn, for it requires that a pitcher turn his forearm outward as he releases the ball, a completely unnatural motion. Yet if Valenzuela could learn to command the screwball, the Dodgers thought he had a shot at becoming an effective major leaguer in a few years.

Castillo told Valenzuela how to hold the ball and how to rotate his forearm to get the pitch to break in the opposite direction of a curveball. Valenzuela listened intently and just like that started throwing the pitch, not only for strikes but at two different speeds, all from the same identical motion. He had an inherent feel for the game that takes most pitchers years to learn and entirely eludes many others. In 1980 the club sent Valenzuela to double-A San Antonio, and he rapidly learned how to use the pitch in his repertoire. By the second half of the season nobody was hitting him. In a little more than a year he had become the best prospect in the entire organization.

There was some debate in the organization between those who thought he belonged in Los Angeles immediately and those who favored a more conservative approach. When Sutton was troubled by a toe injury in midseason, Valenzuela was almost called up, but in the end the Dodgers waited to call him up until September, when rosters expand from 25 to 40 players. Had they brought him up earlier, the team might well have collected another world championship.

Once he joined the team, he was a revelation. A skeptical Lasorda was told to use Valenzuela in any situation, and since it did not appear as if the Dodgers were going anywhere, Lasorda did just that. Down the stretch Valenzuela was both indomitable and inscrutable. Despite never before pitching in relief in pro baseball, in his first eight appearances he didn't give up a run, and he struck out nearly a man an inning.

And despite the fact that he didn't speak English — or maybe because of it — the press loved him. He was like no one else in the simultaneously polished and uptight organization. Valenzuela didn't have a care in the world. Speaking through translators, he was glib, funny, completely himself. In the locker room he sat back, lassoed passing teammates, and laughed. But the other Dodgers knew he was good. Davey Lopes called him simply "the smartest [pitcher] I've ever seen." Entering the final week of the season, Valenzuela was also the best pitcher on the Dodger roster, and perhaps the most important, for Welch was out with a groin injury and Valenzuela was holding the staff together. By the season-end-

ing series with Houston, Lasorda let it be known that if the Dodgers managed to push the Astros into a playoff, he would probably start Valenzuela. But that was still a long way off.

It got closer on October 4. Jerry Reuss went up against Nolan Ryan with the season on the line. On a smoggy day, Reuss outpitched Ryan. Steve Garvey scored the Dodgers' first run, then hit a home run for their second, and the Dodgers won again, 2–1, setting up a showdown on the final day of the regular season.

On the last day both clubs shot the works. At any other time during the season Davey Lopes, bothered by a pinched nerve in his neck, and Ron Cey, with a hamstring pull, would have been on the bench. Yet they were playing. And Houston pitcher Vern Ruhle, who had stepped up after Richard's loss to pitch the best baseball of his career, had cut a finger on his throwing hand a few days before but despite several stitches still took the mound.

When Burt Hooton gave up three straight hits in the second and the Astros took a 2–0 lead, Lasorda pulled him in favor of Bobby Castillo. In the third Ruhle's stitches began to give way, and Houston manager Bill Virdon also pulled his starter.

In the sixth the Dodgers trailed 3–1, and Lasorda, managing like it was the final game of the season, pinch-hit for Castillo and turned to Valenzuela. The Dodgers scored one in the seventh but in the eighth still trailed 3–2.

Garvey reached on an error. Ron Cey, who could barely walk, got the sign to sacrifice, but failed twice. Then a pitch fouled painfully off his foot gave him two bad legs. Nevertheless, he worked the count to 3–2 off pitcher Frank Lacorte, then fouled off another three pitches.

The fourth put him into a trot, about the only way he could move now anyway. He drove the ball over the wall to put the Dodgers ahead 4–3, and when the Astros threatened in the ninth off Steve Howe, who had followed Valenzuela after he had been removed for a pinch hitter, Lasorda took a page from Walt Alston. He brought in Sutton, who got the final out. The Dodgers would play another day, and if they won, perhaps for a few weeks longer.

By now, normally laid-back Dodger fans could hardly contain themselves. Over the last three days the Dodgers had captured the imagination of everyone, and the entire city suddenly turned into something of a neighborhood. For the Monday playoff game against the Astros, L.A. almost came to a stop. Businesses piped in the game on radio to keep workers from calling in sick or sneaking out to a bar. There was so much excitement that the arraignment of a woman who had committed a copycat murder in support of one of the notorious "Hillside Stranglers" was postponed. The detectives, reported the *Times,* were released to "pursue investigations in the field"—as in the infield and outfield at Dodger Stadium. Only in L.A.

Los Angeles mayor Tom Bradley threw out the first pitch. Toni Tenille sang the national anthem and then blurted out, "It's been the thrill of a lifetime to be here the last three days." She wasn't the only celebrity in the crowd—because of an actors' strike, half of Hollywood was there.

Meanwhile, Lasorda was running out of options. Cey's ankle ballooned up overnight, and he couldn't walk. Houston had Joe Niekro available to pitch the finale. Lasorda had only the $3 million man, Dave Goltz. The two innings Fernando Valenzuela had thrown the previous day left him unavailable to start.

He should have started anyway, because first Goltz and then Sutcliffe were rocked. By the time Lasorda turned to Castillo, Valenzuela, and Howe, it was too late. The Astros won going away, 7–1, to take the division title.

The Dodgers felt as if they'd walked off a cliff, and the disappointment after the game for their normally sedate fans was so acute that there was even a minor riot outside Dodger Stadium. Lasorda, for once, was almost speechless and fell back on clichés. He called the loss "heartbreaking."

"Everything was perfect," said Rick Monday, "except the ending." And for many the game did seem like the end, but for something larger than just a season.

These Dodgers were getting old, and their time was running out. Sutton was ready to move on, and after more than seven years together, every member of the Dodger infield was on the wrong side of 30 and still had no World Series ring. Dusty Baker's contract was up, and there were even rumors that the Chicago White Sox had their eyes on Lasorda and that he was thinking of jumping ship too. Even though the new free agent crop included San Diego outfielder Dave Winfield, a genuine five-tool player, the Dodgers felt burned by Goltz and Stanhouse. They might make a trade—there were reports of talks with the Red Sox about a deal for outfielder Fred Lynn—but they weren't going to throw more money away on free agents.

At the free agent draft in November the Dodgers were almost invisible as they made only three picks, selecting outfielders Claudell Washington and Jerry Morales and utilityman

Rhode Island native Davey Lopes made his mark as a solid fielder and superb baserunner with occasional power. He led the National League in stolen bases in 1975 and 1976 with 77 and 63 steals, respectively. He finished his ten-year Dodger career with 418 steals.

Dave Roberts. All three eschewed the Dodgers' lukewarm, "sensible" offers for more lucrative contracts. Meanwhile, Don Sutton, after entertaining an offer from the Yankees, joined Houston. Great. And Winfield signed with the Yankees. Apart from a trade with Minnesota for light-hitting center fielder Ken Landreaux, the Dodgers would enter the 1981 season with what they had.

At an off-season dinner honoring the Dodger infield, Davey Lopes said, "We have given you many things, except for one

Although Fernando Valenzuela won 20 or more games only once in his 11 seasons with the Dodgers, he is unquestionably one of the great pitchers in franchise history.

As Opening Day approached, the signs weren't good. Reggie Smith was still rehabbing his shoulder, and rookie Pedro Guerrero was named starting right fielder. The pitching rotation was a mess—Welch had been battling elbow problems, Goltz had a virus, Reuss had strained a calf muscle, and Burt Hooton was suffering from an ingrown toenail. Purely by default, that left Valenzuela, now 20 years old and penciled in as the fifth starter, as the club's only starting pitcher healthy enough to pitch on Opening Day. He'd had a fine spring, but the Dodgers were hardly comfortable with their pitching situation. Things were so up in the air that one day before the start of the season rookie pitcher Dave Stewart was told he was being sent back to the minors. He reacted violently, slamming the door shut on Lasorda. He then sought out Al Campanis, reamed him out, and took a swing at a concrete wall. He went to his locker and started packing only to be told, uh, not so fast. The club had decided to release Don Stanhouse. Meanwhile, Valenzuela had pitched batting practice before being told he would be starting the next day.

By now the Dodgers had high hopes for Valenzuela—he'd been featured on the back cover of the team's media guide—but starting him on Opening Day, particularly against Astros ace Joe Niekro, wasn't part of the plan. Valenzuela, after all, had never before started a major league game. Then again, he hadn't given up a run to a major league hitter either. Still, all the Dodgers hoped for was that he could last six innings.

But in a little over two hours, on April 9, 1981, "Fernando mania" would be born.

Valenzuela didn't just beat the Astros—he dominated the division champs, giving up only five hits. The headline in the *Times* said it all: "Did They Tell Him Batting Practice Was Over?" Jim Murray wrote, "The magic number for the Dodgers is now down to 161 games." Davey Lopes said bluntly, "We don't know what's going on inside of him. All he does is smile. All we know is the bottom line. The kid hasn't given up a run." Because Valenzuela was isolated by his age, his background, and the language barrier, his veteran teammates didn't know what to think about him. All they knew, and all that really mattered, was that when he took the mound, he knew how to pitch.

Then he got better, and as he did, so did the Dodgers. By the time he started his next game, the Dodgers were 4–0, and although Valenzuela gave up an unearned run, he beat the Giants and Vida Blue—who back in 1971 had been baseball's reigning phenom—7–1. The Giants said they weren't

thing—a world championship. You shall have it in 1981." The Dodgers were feeling the pressure to win. Lopes was on the final year of his contract, and few expected the infield to remain intact.

Expectations for the Dodgers ranged from very good to very bad. *Times* writer Mark Heisler, in true L.A. fashion, found a metaphor for the team in the advertisements for the controversial movie about wife-swapping *Bob & Carol & Ted & Alice*. The ads read provocatively, "Consider the possibilities." The 1981 Dodgers would either have the time of their life or be the odd man out.

impressed. Then he shut out San Diego, 2–0, and Houston, again, 1–0. Then he beat San Francisco for a second time, 5–0. Now they were impressed—it was hard to argue with four shutouts in five starts. Against Valenzuela, the National League was essentially 0-for-April.

It couldn't last forever, but Valenzuela made it seem like it could. After he started the season by going 36 innings without giving up an earned run—running his career streak to an ungodly 54 innings—the Expos finally scored a run off him on May 3. But he won anyway, 6–1, then shut out the Mets and beat the Expos again.

Every time he pitched, Dodger Stadium was the way it had been at the end of the 1980 season—a raucous, wild party, with fans actually showing up on time and staying for the whole game, many of them for the first time. Sellouts were the norm.

There was a reason for that: despite more than 20 years in Los Angeles, the Dodgers had not signed a Mexican player of note until Valenzuela. Although Dodger games had been broadcast in Spanish from the very beginning, the Dodgers hadn't really gone out of their way to court Mexican American fans. Since moving to L.A., the club had always taken the Mexican American fans for granted and marketed the club to wealthy suburbanites. Long-time broadcaster Jaime Jarrin estimated that over the years, at best, fewer than 10 percent of the fans in Dodger Stadium had been of Mexican descent.

That changed overnight. When Valenzuela pitched, there were suddenly Mexican flags waving in the stands, Mexican fans everywhere—L.A.'s Mexican American community was bursting with pride and self-awareness. A whole new constituency discovered Dodger Stadium, and crowds were just as enormous when he pitched on the road. In Latin America the number of radio stations that carried Dodger games doubled from 20 to 40. In Mexico the number of stations that broadcast Dodger games went from 3 to 17. Ever since, Dodger crowds have retained a distinctly Mexican American and Latino makeup. Twenty-five years after he made his debut, the Dodgers are still making money off Fernando Valenzuela.

And all the while, Valenzuela seemed blissfully unaffected. Although he did know some English, from the start he was smart enough to use the perceived language barrier to his advantage and to keep the growing media throng at bay, for few of them spoke Spanish. He communicated through either Bobby Castillo or Jaime Jarrin. After his Opening Day start, he admitted that he felt more nervous before the two

NL ROOKIE OF THE YEAR AWARD

1947	Jackie Robinson	1B
1949	Don Newcombe	P
1952	Joe Black	P
1953	Jim Gilliam	2B
1960	Frank Howard	RF
1965	Jim Lefebvre	2B
1969	Ted Sizemore	2B
1979	Rick Sutcliffe	P
1980	Steve Howe	P
1981	Fernando Valenzuela	P
1982	Steve Sax	2B
1992	Eric Karros	1B
1993	Mike Piazza	C
1994	Raul Mondesi	RF
1995	Hideo Nomo	P
1996	Todd Hollandsworth	LF

dozen reporters than the 50,000 fans in the crowd, but that he "slept like an angel." He pitched like one too.

The Dodgers were unprepared for the sudden onslaught of attention the media accurately dubbed "Fernando mania." By May he was the big story in baseball — the only story really. Valenzuela was bigger than Vida Blue had been in 1971, or Mark "the Bird" Fidrych, another phenom, in 1976. Valenzuela was 8–0. His earned run average was 0.50. He was even hitting .350, inviting comparisons to Babe Ruth that did not seem so far-fetched. The Dodgers were in first place. The infield, Steve Garvey, and Tommy Lasorda were all way, way, way below the fold. Fans seemed to sense that Fernando wasn't hype but 100 percent real and genuine, that he was all about performance, not an image of marketing. The Dodgers hadn't seen that since Koufax. The team suddenly seemed to have soul.

Valenzuela made his first off-field public appearance on May 16 at a clinic at City Terrace Park, an event scheduled long before the start of the season, long before Fernando mania.

Usually such events drew only a few hundred kids. Over 3,000 came to see Valenzuela, most of them adults. Valenzuela, one of five Dodgers at the clinic, was mobbed like a rock star. At one point he had to hide in the ladies' room just to take a breather. The other Dodgers at the clinic might as well have been the park's cleanup crew.

Two days later, on May 19, after giving up only four runs in 72 innings, Valenzuela finally showed that he was human. Against the Phillies, he gave up not only a first-inning home run to Mike Schmidt but, to the absolute incredulity of Dodger fans, *three runs* — a genuine rally — in the fourth inning as he temporarily lost control. He lost, 4–0, despite giving up only three hits during the game.

Dodger manager Tommy Lasorda nicknamed dour pitcher Burt Hooton "Happy." In ten seasons with the Dodgers, Hooton used his famed knuckle-curve to great effect while compiling a won-lost record of 112–84, including 22 shutouts. In 1981 he went 2–0 in the National League championship series with a 0.00 ERA.

When he was rocked in his next two starts, some observers started nodding knowingly. He had been too good to be true. Hitters had figured him out. He was just a flash in the pan. Whatever pact he had made with whatever god he worshiped had been broken. Now Valenzuela would become just another pitcher. He wasn't Koufax—he was Karl Spooner.

Not quite.

On June 2, as Mike Littwin wrote in the *Times,* "the interruption in the legendary exploits of young Fernando Valenzuela has ended." He beat the Braves 5–2 and struck out 11, a career high. While it was true that he would never again approach the lofty standards of his first 100 innings in the major leagues, neither would anyone else. In the last 25 seasons, no one has even come close.

There was a dark cloud looming on the horizon, however. It had little to do with Valenzuela apart from the fact that his spectacular performance had caused many fans to ignore the rumbling in the background.

In the off-season the players' union had authorized a strike on May 29 over the issue of free agent compensation. The players didn't want the restrictions of the reentry draft. Although both sides went through a charade of negotiations and the strike was forestalled for almost two weeks, in the end no agreement was reached. The players refused to bend, and ownership, as usual, underestimated the players' resolve and overestimated their own unanimity. The season was put on hold on June 12. The Dodgers were in first place in the Western Division with a record of 36–21, half a game ahead of the Reds.

Although the 1972 season had been delayed by a walkout, baseball's first extended midseason strike was under way. For the Dodgers it would prove to be less harmful than it would in many other places. Not only were they in first place, but Fernando mania had, to a degree, inoculated the ballclub from the most damaging effects of the strike, both at the gate and in the public's perception of ballplayers as selfish and greedy. As far as the fans were concerned, Valenzuela was neither. He was the antidote to the strike before even one game had been missed.

The strike wasn't settled until the end of July. After 50 days, the regular season resumed on August 10, one day after the All-Star Game.

A few days later the Dodgers learned that they had already clinched a berth in the postseason. Baseball would operate under a "split season" format. Since they had led the NL West

on June 12, the Dodgers were already in, even if they lost every one of their remaining 53 games.

Good thing, because although the Dodgers didn't lose all 53, they lost often enough that had the season been played to a full 162 games, they might not have made the playoffs after all. The Dodgers were only a so-so 27–26 in the second half, and their cumulative record of 63–47 was four games off the Reds' 66–42 mark. Yet the Reds, despite having the best record in baseball, wouldn't make the postseason. They lost the first half to the Dodgers by a half-game and the second half by the same margin to the Astros. But the Dodgers weren't the only first-half champions to struggle after the break—no first-half champion was able to repeat.

Even Valenzuela slumped, although he merely went from absolutely spectacular down to only very, very good. After going 9–4 in the first half of the season, he was 4–3 after the extended break. To be fair, the team struggled to score runs for him, then struggled to score at all after Ron Cey was lost for the balance of the regular season with a broken forearm. As Fernando mania quieted to a steady roar and the Dodgers limped through the second half, other stories began to dominate.

The first was a shocker—sort of. On September 12, Steve and Cyndy Garvey separated and filed for divorce. The couple the press sometimes referred to as "Ken and Barbie" were done. There had in fact been rumors to that effect ever since a profile on the couple by writer Pat Jordan appeared in *Inside Sports* in 1980. The Garveys had been so angry over that piece that they'd sued the magazine.

As the playoffs approached, it became clear that harmony in the Dodger clubhouse was still more myth than reality. When Lasorda told Rick Sutcliffe he wouldn't be on the playoff roster, Sutcliffe threw a chair against the wall in Lasorda's office, swept his desk clean, and said, "Tommy Lasorda is a liar. He told me three and a half weeks ago that I would get an opportunity to pitch, and that didn't happen. . . . I will never play for Tommy Lasorda."

It was one of those times when, like Valenzuela, most Dodgers wished they didn't know much English, for the team hardly needed the distraction heading into the postseason. Then, for the second year in a row, an injury to a Houston pitcher turned out to be a key factor in the fortunes of the Dodgers.

On October 2 the Astros played the Dodgers needing only one more victory—or one Reds loss—to clinch the second-half title. In the third inning Don Sutton came to bat against Jerry Reuss.

Since Sutton had left the Dodgers, there had been a fair bit of sniping back and forth. Before he had made his first appearance in Dodger Stadium in a Houston uniform earlier in the year, the Dodgers claimed that he was scuffing the ball and promised to have him checked on the mound. They did. Although umpires found nothing, Sutton was knocked out after four innings, but not before he decked Steve Garvey, whom Sutton disliked. In two later appearances against the Dodgers in Houston, Sutton had pitched much better, losing to Valenzuela 1–0 and tossing a four-hitter while winning 7–1.

With a man on third base, Sutton faked a bunt. On Reuss's next pitch, Sutton squared around for an attempted squeeze play.

Reuss did what pitchers are supposed to do in such a situation — throw at the batter. The fact that Sutton was batting was gravy, and Reuss didn't miss. His pitch struck Sutton flush on the left knee, shattering his kneecap. The Astros lost the game but still won the second-half title the next day when Cincinnati fell, but Sutton's loss left them undermanned entering the postseason. He'd been their best pitcher in the second half, going 7–1 with an ERA of 1.46. Now they'd have to face the Dodgers in the first playoff round, the best-of-five so-called divisional series, without him.

The series opened in Houston's Astrodome on October 6, and each club went with its best — NL ERA champ Nolan Ryan starting for the Astros and Valenzuela for the Dodgers. To win the world championship, a team had to win more postseason games than any team in history at the time — three in each of the first two rounds and four more in the World Series, for a total of ten games. Usually the regular season was the marathon and the postseason the sprint, but in 1981 that was reversed. The Dodgers had played the hare in the first half, then coasted. In the playoffs they would have to plod their way through three grueling series.

In game one, the first game that had really mattered to the Dodgers since June, Houston's Nolan Ryan was magnificent, as good as he had ever been in any of his four no-hitters to date. He gave up only two hits, faced only 29 hitters, and threw only 104 pitches, which the press believed was the fewest he had ever thrown in a complete game in his career. Apart from Steve Garvey's seventh-inning home run, he completely shut the Dodgers down.

But for much of 1981 even a no-hitter couldn't beat Valenzuela. He matched Ryan until Lasorda, and the bullpen, let him down. With the game still scoreless and two out in the sixth, Terry Puhl singled. Afraid that he might steal, Lasorda ordered pitchouts on consecutive pitches to Phil Garner. But Puhl stayed put, and Garner then walked, moving Puhl into scoring position anyway. Tony Scott followed with a bloop hit and put the Astros ahead 1–0 until Garvey's home run tied the score an inning later.

In the eighth Lasorda pulled Valenzuela for a pinch hitter who was hitting 50 points lower, Jay Johnstone. Johnstone made an out, and now Lasorda had to turn to the bullpen. In the bottom of the ninth reliever Dave Stewart, whose season had been marred only by a propensity to give up ninth-inning home runs, did so for the fourth time in 1981 as Alan Ashby took him deep. The Astros ended the game in a big happy knot at home plate, winning 3–2.

The next day the Astros put the Dodgers on the precipice. Reuss and Niekro each pitched shutout ball until the game was turned over to the bullpen. In the 11th Stewart came on again and immediately gave up two straight hits. After Terry Forster got a pop-up, Tom Niedenfuer gave up a run-scoring single to Denny Walling. Houston won 1–0 and was one game away from reaching the NLCS.

But the series was returning to Los Angeles, where the Astros were a different team, losers of 11 of their last 13 games. Lasorda said, "I really believe we can win three straight," but it sounded like so much fertilizer.

He did, however, make a bold move before game three. Bob Welch was penciled in to start the game, but the work of Stewart and Niedenfuer had made Lasorda wary of his relief staff, or at least of Stewart and Niedenfuer. He decided to put Welch in the pen, start Hooton in game three, and if the Dodgers made it to games four and five, pitch Valenzuela and Reuss on three days' rest in the last two games.

It worked to perfection. Garvey got the Dodgers a three-run lead with a home run in the first, and Hooton held on. Welch came on in the ninth to stop the Astros and give the Dodgers a 6–1 win.

In game four Valenzuela was not pitching opposite Nolan Ryan. Houston manager Bill Virdon, perhaps looking ahead, chose not to bring back Ryan on short rest but to take his chances with Vern Ruhle, a move that also meant the Dodgers wouldn't face knuckleballer Joe Niekro again in the series. That caused no frowns in the Dodger clubhouse — in his last

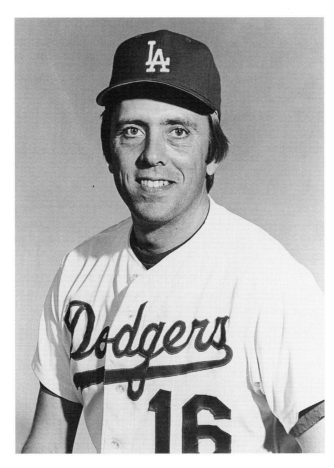

Outfielder Rick Monday arrived in Los Angeles in 1977 via a trade with the Cubs that sent Bill Buckner to Wrigley Field. In eight years with the Dodgers, Monday hit .254. He will forever be remembered for the day he prevented two protesters from burning an American flag in the Dodger Stadium outfield.

three starts against the Dodgers, Niekro had given up only three runs.

Even by the heady standards Valenzuela had already set in 1981, game four stood out. "Fernando's last stand went down as all of his other stands," wrote Mark Heisler in the *Times,* "a sellout, a masterpiece, some modesty on his part, some awe on everyone else's, a couple of *buenos,* a 'Hi-Ho, Silver,' and then he was gone, leaving the world to wonder just who the hell that was." All he did was carry a perfect game into the fifth and a shutout into the ninth, and then put everyone on the edge of their seat before sneaking off with a 2–1 win, beating Houston for the third time in 1981. "There was no way," said Lasorda, "I was going to take him out of the game in the ninth inning. . . . Sometimes when I look at him I think I'm

dreaming." Lasorda had learned his lesson in game one and rightly concluded it was better to take a chance on Valenzuela than to lose with anyone else, that Valenzuela was at his best when the Dodgers needed him most. As Lasorda once said, he knew better than anyone that Valenzuela was not only "good for the Dodgers . . . [but] very good for Tommy Lasorda."

The Astros were broken. In game five Reuss outpitched Ryan as the Dodgers scratched out three sixth-inning runs and won 4–0. They would play the Montreal Expos in the NLCS.

Montreal had come far since their desultory days as an expansion team. They'd narrowly missed out on a division title in 1980, come from behind to win the NL East in the second half of 1981, and beaten Steve Carlton twice to reach the NLCS. Moreover, they featured their own phenom, outfielder Tim Raines. In only 88 games he'd stolen a remarkable 71 bases.

The Dodgers received a spark before the start of the Series. Ron Cey, whom they had once thought would be lost for the season with a broken arm, pronounced himself fit and returned to the lineup, albeit with a plastic cast. In game one his two hits, Mike Scioscia's home run, and the performance of Burt Hooton were enough to dispatch the Expos 5–1, sending them to their 20th defeat in their last 20 games at Dodger Stadium.

Nothing would come easy in 1981. In game two, Valenzuela pitched well, but journeyman Ray Burris of Montreal shut down the Dodgers on five hits to win 3–0. When Steve Rogers set down the Dodgers 4–1 in game three, the Dodgers were again on the brink of elimination. But in game four, at last, the Dodger bats came alive, and they knotted the Series with a 7–1 win.

A rainout set up a game five showdown between Burris and Valenzuela. Montreal was an icebox for the contest — it was only 41 degrees when the game started, and snow flurries spun around Olympic Stadium.

The Expos got off quick. Raines led off with a double to the gap, and Rodney Scott followed with a bunt. Valenzuela pounced on the ball and tried to throw out Raines, but Raines beat the throw, and Andre Dawson knocked him home with a double play.

Then Valenzuela settled down. Unfortunately for L.A. fans, the Dodgers found Ray Burris just as much a mystery as in game two. But this was Valenzuela's year, not Ray Burris's.

In the fifth the Dodgers put runners on second and third, bringing up Valenzuela with one out. His was not a Ruthian response, but it was no less effective. With Burris trying for a strikeout, Valenzuela slapped the ball on the ground, just slow enough to score Rick Monday and tie the game.

That wasn't enough, but it kept Valenzuela in the game. Entering the ninth, the game was still tied 1–1.

An inning before, Expos manager Jim Fanning had pinch-hit for Burris. Now, after watching his bullpen implode in the later innings of game four, he turned to ace Steve Rogers, who was making his first relief appearance in three years.

He retired Garvey on a pop-up, and then Ron Cey drove a ball deep to left field but not deep enough. With two out, Rick Monday stepped in.

Since arriving by trade in 1977, Monday had been a disappointment—age and injuries had prevented him from being the player the Dodgers thought they would be getting. Dodger fans best remembered him not for anything he had done as a member of the Dodgers but for the time when, as a visiting Chicago Cub, he tackled a fan who tried to burn an American flag on the Dodger Stadium field. After hardly playing in the first half of the season as the Dodgers surged, Monday took over in right after Cey was hurt and Pedro Guerrero was moved to third. He'd been on the bench in the first two games, but then Lasorda, looking for left-handed power, had put him back in the lineup.

Monday worked Rogers to a 3–1 count. The pitcher would say later that he had planned to try to get Monday to waste the next pitch, to try to get him to chase it. If Monday didn't do that and walked instead, Rogers would take his chances with Guerrero, who was on deck.

But Rogers missed—badly. Monday lofted the ball over the right-field fence. Now the Dodgers led 2–1.

Valenzuela needed three more outs. But he had warmed up before the rainout the day before, and now he was starting to tire. After getting Rodney Scott and Andre Dawson out, he got ahead of both Gary Carter and Larry Parrish before walking both, putting the tying run at second and the winning run at first.

Lasorda had faith, but he wasn't stupid. He came out to the mound for the second time that inning. In Spanish the manager said to Valenzuela, "It's time for a fresh horse." Valenzuela laughed, and Bob Welch came in. He threw one pitch, Jerry White grounded to Lopes, and the Dodgers had won another pennant.

"You know the two faces of drama, comedy and tragedy?" asked Expos pitcher Steve Rogers afterward. "Monday got the smile, and I got the frown."

But Valenzuela was still the man of the year and the man of the moment, despite his last-inning hiccup. After the game a writer asked Rick Monday, "Is there anything left that would surprise you about him [Valenzuela]?"

Monday just laughed. "The only thing that would surprise me now," he said, "would be if he would finally tell us he was from Brooklyn."

Well, Brooklyn would get its chance to see him in the World Series, but it would have to be in the Bronx. The Yankees, after scuffling through the second half like the Dodgers, had beat Milwaukee and then swept Oakland to win the American League pennant. They'd been able to watch as the Expos exhausted the Dodgers, and they entered the World Series rested, their pitching rotation set. Their only significant injury was to Reggie Jackson, Mr. October, who had a bad calf muscle. But Jackson, who had hit only .237 for the year, wasn't the central figure in the Yankee lineup anymore, or the most highly paid. Dave Winfield was.

The Dodgers, on the other hand, were still beat up. Lopes was hurting now, and they would have to begin the Series in New York, where Yankees fans were still allowed to commit crimes and other misdemeanors frowned on in other parks, and where the Dodgers detested playing. The Yankees were 9–5 favorites.

In the first two games of the Series the Yankees made those odds look pessimistic. New York swept the first two games, never trailing for a second. Ron Guidry outpitched Reuss in the first game, and former Dodger Tommy John, 87–23 since the elbow surgery that had resurrected his career seven years before, shut out the Dodgers 3–0.

The Dodgers trailed in the Series two games to one, but it seemed like more. In the seventh inning of game two, pitcher Terry Forster and catcher Steve Yeager even got into a shouting match. After the game Lasorda closed the clubhouse.

The Dodgers, however, were returning to L.A. and Fernando mania. In a must-win game they had the pitcher on the mound most likely to win that game, and the Yankees were suddenly undermanned. Graig Nettles hurt his thumb and would have to sit the game out.

The Yankees had their own rookie on a roll, 22-year-old Dave Righetti, a hard-throwing left-hander. In two playoff starts he hadn't given up a run.

Righetti was the anti-Valenzuela, the Mexican pitcher's opposite in every way but results. Since high school he had been touted as the best prospect in baseball and was already considered en route to the Hall of Fame. And unlike Valenzuela, he looked the part. He was tall and long and lean with a fastball that approached 100 miles per hour and a slider that buckled hitters at the knees.

For the first time in the postseason, Valenzuela wasn't sharp. In the first inning he struggled, walking two before finally escaping. But in the bottom of the first the Dodgers gave him a break.

Lopes led off with a double. Playing for the lead at home, Lasorda had Russell bunt, and the Yankees botched the play, watching the ball stop dead as Righetti and the right side of the Yankee infield all made the wrong decisions. Then, on a

2–2 pitch and with two out, Cey blasted a home run to left-center, and the Dodgers led, 3–0. That was usually plenty for Valenzuela. But not today.

In the second the Yankees scored twice, once on a leadoff home run by Bob Watson and again after two hits. Then, as Dave Goltz warmed up, Valenzuela worked his way out of the jam, stranding two.

Lasorda let him bat for himself in the second, sending the message that he was in the game to stay. But in the third Rick

---

In game five of the 1981 World Series, Dodger third baseman Ron Cey was beaned by Yankee reliever Goose Gossage. He returned to the lineup to lead the Dodgers to victory in the decisive sixth game at Yankee Stadium. Cey shared the series MVP Award with teammates Steve Yeager and Pedro Guerrero.

Cerone cracked a two-run home run, and the Yankees threatened to score more before Valenzuela again escaped the inning and left two runners stranded. It was as if whatever shroud of invincibility that had hovered over him all season was gone and now he had to draw on other previously untapped resources to get the Yankees out. He pitched from behind. He shook off Yeager time after time. He tottered again and again and again. But he did not fall.

And Lasorda stuck with him. Stubbornly, perhaps even stupidly, in the middle of the game Lasorda decided that it was Valenzuela now and Valenzuela forever. He decided to risk everything — the season and perhaps his own managerial career — on that look to heaven Valenzuela gave each time he threw the ball.

Yankee manager Bob Lemon showed no such faith in Righetti. When Garvey led off the third with a single and Cey walked, Lemon pulled Righetti from the game in favor of reliever George Frazier, whom the *Los Angeles Times* accurately described as "a right-hander of no previous distinction." But in the regular season his ERA had been a minuscule 1.63.

Frazier got out of the inning and pitched into the fifth, holding the one-run lead as the Yankees tried to carry the margin into the later innings. Then the hard-throwing duo of Ron Davis and Goose Gossage would be almost automatic.

But in the fifth Garvey singled again and Cey walked. When Pedro Guerrero doubled Garvey home to tie the game, Lemon had Frazier issue an intentional walk and turned to Rudy May. Scioscia grounded into a double play, and the Dodgers had the lead.

By the ninth Fernando mania had returned — the Dodger Stadium crowd was on its feet, and Valenzuela, with 131 pitches already under his ample belt, was cloaked in invincibility again, somehow getting stronger with each pitch. He retired Jerry Mumphrey and Dave Winfield — 0-for-the-World-Series and called "Mr. May" by George Steinbrenner — then struck out Lou Piniella on pitch number 145 to end the game and change everything. "That was," said Lasorda, "one of the guttiest performances I've ever seen a young man do. He was like a poker player bluffing his way through a hand."

After the game Yankees owner George Steinbrenner was at his worst, which was good for the Dodgers. He called Valenzuela "beatable," Righetti "terrible," and the Dodger hits "chicken shit." The Yankees were still leading the Series, but their own owner had them behind and, even worse, had added to the pressure they felt to win. Now they started playing as if afraid to make mistakes, while the Dodgers had nothing to lose.

Steinbrenner wanted change, and he got it. For game four Reggie Jackson was suddenly back in the lineup, and Dave Winfield was playing out of position in center field as Jerry Mumphrey was benched.

At first it worked. Jackson knocked out Welch in the first with a single as the Yankees scored twice. Entering the bottom of the third, the Yankees led 4–0. But the Dodgers scratched out two in the fourth and another in the fifth before New York came back to score two more and go ahead 6–3. Now Lemon went for the kill and put Ron Davis in to pitch.

Pinch hitter Jay Johnstone ruined that strategy by hitting a two-run homer. Davey Lopes followed with a fly ball to Reggie Jackson in right field. Battling the sun, the Yankee outfielder staggered under the ball, which bounced off his chest for a two-base error. The *Times* would later note that although Jackson "beat the Dodgers once upon a time with his hip," he made up for it by helping them "win one with his chest." Lopes stole third and scored on Bill Russell's single, and the game was tied, 6–6.

New York was in a panic. In the seventh, as the Dodgers rallied, Lemon surprised everyone by turning to Tommy John in relief with no outs and the bases loaded. The Yankee sinkerballer gave up a sacrifice fly to Yeager and an infield hit to Lopes. The Dodgers now led 8–6, and although Steve Howe would stagger through the final two innings and Jackson would hit a home run, the Dodgers won 8–7 in a game Lasorda called "the most exciting game I've ever been involved in." It hadn't been pretty — Rick Monday conceded that it "wasn't your basic Picasso." Jim Murray noted, "The last time I saw a game like this the teams didn't have matching uniforms and there was a keg on third," but it counted anyway.

Better yet, it sent Steinbrenner off again. He called Ron Davis "lousy" and noted that "70 million people saw it," leading one reporter to ask rhetorically, "Has George ever fired a manager in mid-Series?"

If there was any player on the Yankee team immune to Steinbrenner, it was game five starter Ron Guidry. He threw the way they hoped Righetti would one day.

The Yankees gave Guidry a run in the second off Jerry Reuss when Jackson doubled, Lopes made an error, and Lou Piniella singled him home. For Lopes, the error was the first of three he would make that day, and six for the Series. Fortunately, it didn't cost the Dodgers the game.

Guidry and Reuss were both cruising, but in the seventh the Dodgers sent a dagger into New York's heart—actually two of them. After retiring 14 of the last 15 hitters and striking out 8, Guidry hung a slider and Pedro Guerrero hit it out to tie the game. One batter later, Steve Yeager followed with a home run, and it was 2–1.

It ended that way, although afterward all anyone could talk about was the eighth-inning Gossage fastball that almost made Ron Cey's wife a widow. Team doctor Frank Jobe was blunt: if not for Cey's batting helmet, the 94-mile-per-hour pitch, which hit him flush, probably would have killed him. As it was, it looked like it had done just that when he met with reporters afterward with his head wrapped like a mummy. Except for suffering a concussion, however, Cey was unhurt.

The same could not be said of George Steinbrenner. He showed up the next day in New York with his left hand in a bandage, a swollen lip, a lump on his head, a few small cuts on his right hand, and an enormous bruise on his gigantic ego. He claimed he'd been hurt while defending the Yankees' honor against two Dodger fans in the elevator of the Hyatt Wilshire Hotel in Los Angeles. Most observers found that notion laughable and Steinbrenner pathetic.

On October 27 former Dodger Pete Reiser died, and as if somehow honoring his passing, game six was rained out. The delay didn't help the Yankees, and it couldn't hurt the Dodgers. In fact, if the Dodgers didn't win game six, they now knew that in game seven a fully rested Fernando Valenzuela would be available. They liked those odds.

New York was reeling, and the Dodgers knew it. If the Dodgers needed another sign, or another small measure of motivation, all they had to do was look at the top four spots in the lineup card: Lopes, Russell, Garvey, and Cey, after eight and a half years together, in their last game. The longest-running and perhaps the most productive infield of all time, the four didn't necessarily like each other all the time, or even very often, but each knew that nevertheless they had accomplished something very, very special, and something that in baseball's free agent era wasn't likely to be seen again. All they needed now was the cherry, the final proof of their achievement—a World Series ring.

With the score tied at 1–1 in the fourth, New York manager Bob Lemon, knowing he had Steinbrenner looking over his shoulder, panicked. Although Tommy John was pitching well, with two out and two on he was pulled for pinch hitter Bobby Murcer. It didn't work. The Dodgers rapidly worked over New York's bullpen, scoring three in the fifth and four more in the sixth as Pedro Guerrero knocked in five all by himself to put the game away. In the sixth Lasorda took the ball from Burt Hooton and gave it to Steve Howe. And in the ninth Howe set the Yankees down to win the game, 9–2, make the Dodgers world champions, send their infield off on top of the world, and make Tommy Lasorda's job secure for a few more seasons.

It had been a long time coming, and game six would in fact prove to be the very last of the infield made up of Garvey, Lopes, Russell, and Cey, who had played the first half of game six before leaving, still dizzy from his beaning. He shared the Series MVP Award with Steve Yeager and Pedro Guerrero, but in truth that award could have gone to a half-dozen Dodgers: in their four wins no single player had dominated, and each had chipped in with a hit here, a play there.

Had there been an MVP of the entire championship season, of the franchise itself, it would have been, without question, Fernando Valenzuela. It had been his performance in the first half that got the Dodgers into the postseason in the first place; his performance in game five against Montreal that put the Dodgers into the Series; his performance in game three that stopped the Yankees in their tracks; his performance that allowed the organization to recover from the disastrous signings of Goltz and Stanhouse; his performance that caused the Dodgers to place their faith in kids like Howe and Guerrero; his performance that electrified a community and opened the door for the Dodgers to a whole new market; and his performance, almost by itself, that saved a baseball season.

What are you gonna do next, kid?

1982–1988

"I DON'T BELIEVE WHAT I JUST SAW"—OR HEARD

ON TOMMY LASORDA'S DESK WAS A NAMEPLATE WITH JUST TWO WORDS: "My Way." After the Dodgers beat the Yankees, the title of buddy Frank Sinatra's signature song could have served as the motto for the entire organization.

The World Series win over New York confirmed everything the Dodgers were and everything the franchise believed it was and represented. While George Steinbrenner was apologizing to Yankee fans for losing, the Dodgers gloated. "We're the champs," said Lasorda. "Can't nobody in this room take that away from us."

They were America's team—or at least they wanted everyone to believe they were. They even believed it themselves. In truth, the Dodgers were just as wealthy as the Yankees, if not more so, but Steinbrenner's Yankees made the Dodgers look as cuddly as a T-ball team. The Yankees were a bunch of mercenaries bought and paid for—the Dodgers were built from within. Baseball's highest-paid player, Dave Winfield, had one hit in the Series—one of the lowest-paid, Valenzuela, not only won a ring but was the biggest star in the game. Steinbrenner lambasted

As the 20th century drew to a close, Los Angeles fans were asked to name their sports moment of the century. The overwhelming selection was the dramatic ninth-inning game-winning home run by an ailing Kirk Gibson off Hall of Fame reliever Dennis Eckersley in the first game of the 1988 World Series at Dodger Stadium.

his players and publicly embarrassed them — the Dodgers were loyal, and Lasorda hugged them like they were his own kids. Steinbrenner thought tradition was something you could buy — the Dodgers grew their own.

The Series seemed to highlight important differences not only between the two teams but also between the two ruling paradigms of baseball in the free agent era. In the wake of the Dodgers' victory there was considerable gloating from those corners of the baseball world where free agency was still viewed as some kind of court decision that would be overturned.

Those perceptions played in Pasadena as well as in Peoria, even though in reality it wasn't quite so clear-cut. But the Dodgers were the champions, and that was all that mattered.

Well, that was all that mattered for about six minutes. Before the champagne had even been mopped up, the franchise was faced with a number of decisions that would call concepts like loyalty into question, and over the next few seasons the Dodgers, while not aping all of Steinbrenner's excesses, would not win another world championship until they became a bit more like the Yankees and less like the Bad News Bears. A little losing and more than a few failed prospects can do that to a team. Over the next few seasons, "My Way" also became a highway out of town for a generation of stars, and one that did not pass through a world championship clubhouse.

But for now the Dodgers were secure. Valenzuela's success gave the franchise confidence in their approach. Davey Lopes and baseball's best infield were history — it was time for new Dodger blood. Down in triple-A Albuquerque and double-A San Antonio, there was a generation of stars in waiting that the club was convinced would make everybody forget about not only Lopes but Cey, Russell, Garvey, and the others. The Dodgers thought that all they had to do was plug them in, one at a time. The organization was the star.

Al Campanis had never forgotten Branch Rickey's tenet that it is far better to get rid of a player a year too early than a year too late. Campanis would try to follow that same approach, and he would begin with Lopes and Reggie Smith. But he didn't learn the entire lesson. Rickey traded players when they still had value, when he could get something for them. But in February, Lopes was simply dumped on Oakland for a minor league second baseman, and the club made no effort to sign Reggie Smith, who eventually signed with San Francisco. Then, in the free agent market, the Dodgers

were quiet. Apparently the club felt their world championship run was more indicative of their strength than their so-so second-half performance.

In the spring, as expected, rookie Steve Sax took over for Lopes. Apart from that, the Dodgers opened the 1982 season little changed, although Pedro Guerrero, after spending several seasons trying to play third, appeared to settle in the outfield.

The Atlanta Braves quickly rendered those small changes moot. Braves owner Ted Turner fancied himself a kind of NL Steinbrenner. Before 1982, his purchases had lifted the club only to a .500 record. Now they jelled.

Under manager Joe Torre, the Braves opened the season with 13 straight wins as the Dodgers got off to a rough start. At the end of July the Dodgers were barely a .500 team and trailed the Braves by more than 10 games. Sax was a fine replacement, Guerrero matured into the best hitter on the team, and Valenzuela, while not quite the magician of 1981, was a workhorse. But Atlanta's quick start rocked the club. The front office figuratively threw in the towel and began to lay the groundwork for more changes and constantly reminded everyone that Garvey and Cey and Russell were just about done and the kids in the minors were going to be even better.

But a funny thing happened on the way to next year. The Braves completely and totally and utterly collapsed. They lost an incredible 20 of 21 games, and by August 10 the Dodgers, quite improbably, were in first place. The old guard was apparently making one last stand, their way.

Then, just as improbably, the Braves bounced back up and by the end of August were in first place again. Over the last month a division race of sorts ensued as in the final days the San Francisco Giants surged and inserted themselves into the mix. With the season entering its final three days, the result was still up in the air.

Atlanta still led by a game and controlled their own destiny. The Dodgers were a game behind, tied with the Giants. But the Braves were finishing with three games against San Diego. The Dodgers and Giants were playing each other one more time, with a title on the line.

The first two games decided nothing apart from the fact that the Giants were not going to win the NL West, for as the Braves took two from San Diego, the Dodgers knocked the Giants out of the race with two wins, setting up a showdown on the final day. If the Giants beat the Dodgers, L.A. was finished, no matter what Atlanta did.

Everything seemed to be tilting L.A.'s direction, for the Braves lost to San Diego and Fernando Valenzuela was able to start the game in search of his 20th win. If the Dodgers won, they'd play the Braves in a playoff. But Lasorda did not have quite the same faith in Valenzuela and his team that he had shown in 1981. With the game tied 2–2, he removed his pitcher for a pinch hitter. The Giants immediately rallied against Terry Forster, and Joe Morgan knocked the Dodgers out with a three-run home run.

That was all the excuse the Dodgers needed to hurry the youth movement along. Although Garvey and Cey had both performed near their accustomed standard, the Dodgers couldn't wait to replace them. On December 21, Garvey signed as a free agent with the San Diego Padres for $1.5 million a year. The Dodgers had first baseman Greg Brock waiting in the wings. Mr. Dodger was no more.

Few players have seen their reputation suffer the way Garvey's did after his departure from Los Angeles, for in time it became clear that his squeaky-clean image was just that. Garvey later admitted fathering children out of wedlock, and his postbaseball career has been dogged by a variety of legal issues. Those problems have combined to chip away at his reputation as a player, tarnishing the record of someone who at one time looked like he might be on his way to the Hall of Fame and who even aspired to a political career. For a time, however, Garvey fit the Dodgers perfectly, and they would eventually learn that he was not easy to replace.

The same could be said of Ron Cey, although he didn't leave as a free agent. He was traded for virtually nothing, dealt to the Cubs for two minor leaguers, pitcher Vance Lovelace, and an outfielder. Linda Lovelace would have been a better deal, for Cey, like Garvey, would continue to be a productive player for several more seasons.

It was a measure of both organizational arrogance and organizational greed that the Dodgers placed more faith in untested rookies than in proven major leaguers who had just won them a world championship. That pattern continued in the spring as Pedro Guerrero was moved back to third to make room in the outfield for another uber-prospect, Mike Marshall, and Greg Brock was handed the first-base job. Marshall had hit .388 in Albuquerque in 1982, and Brock had knocked in 138 runs. They were classic "good faces." But they couldn't *play*, at least not like Cey and Garvey, and it would take the Dodgers several years to admit that. Even Guerrero, who could play and was still young, was jerked around to

In 1982 second baseman Steve Sax replaced Davey Lopes and was named National League Rookie of the Year on the basis of his .282 batting average and 49 stolen bases.

accommodate the rookies. But he was just a Latino, and the Dodgers didn't know quite what to do with Latino stars who weren't named Valenzuela.

In many ways, the Dodgers were awful in 1983. Guerrero was a terrible third baseman. Brock couldn't hit. Neither could catcher Steve Yeager, while 35-year-old Bill Russell, the only surviving member of the once-cherished infield, was also struggling to keep his job.

But Steve Sax was something else again. The 1982 NL Rookie of the Year suddenly couldn't throw the ball to first base, a malady that led to one of the funniest lines in Dodger history. Pedro Guerrero, when asked by a sportswriter what he was thinking in a close game, was sweetly blunt. "I pray, 'Please don't let the batter hit the ball to me . . . and don't let him hit it to Saxy either.'"

Sax tried everything — extra practice, no practice, talking about the problem, not talking about the problem, even throwing blindfolded. So did Lasorda. In one memorable

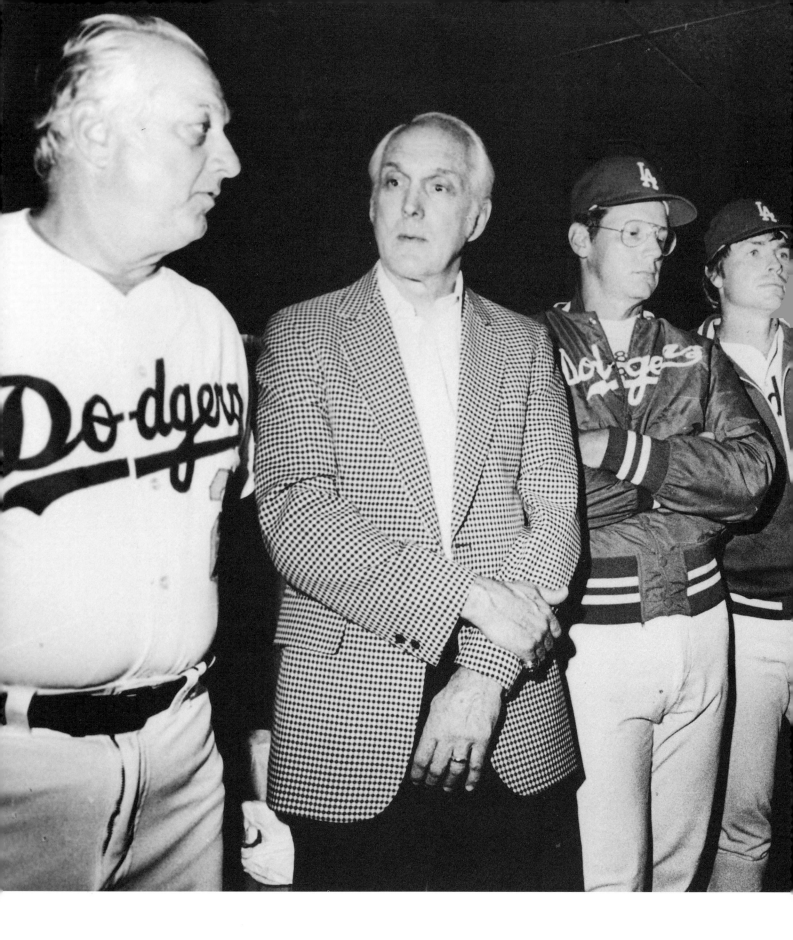

exchange he took Sax out onto the field and in classic Lasorda fashion pointed out to Sax that he could do things on a baseball field that only a few other people in the entire world could do. "But," added Lasorda, "how many *women* can throw the ball to first base? Every single one of them!" By early August Sax's error total was up to 25. Then, as mysteriously as the problem appeared, it miraculously evaporated.

And the word *miraculous* is appropriate for the 1983 Dodgers, for they were not really a very good club, and after relief pitcher Steve Howe left the club to enter a drug rehab program in midseason, they were considerably worse. But they still had enough pitching, not only enough to stay in the race but enough—in a season in which there was little difference between teams in the division, all of which finished within 17 games of each other—to win the NL West by three games. They won even despite the fact that Lasorda used more than 100 lineups during the season and the club barely played .500 baseball over the final three months.

They were then completely exposed in the NLCS against the Phillies, falling in four quick games. Playing horrible baseball and winning only when Valenzuela pitched, they made simple baserunning errors, threw to the wrong bases, and stumbled through as if they knew they didn't belong.

But the division title was another line on Tommy Lasorda's growing résumé. He was now something of a cottage industry: constantly busy in the off-season, he appeared regularly as the "Baseball Wizard" on the syndicated kids' show *The Baseball Bunch* and made other appearances. He was not only the most recognizable Dodger but, after seven years at the helm and four postseason appearances, the best-known baseball manager in the country.

George Steinbrenner even wanted him for the Yankees. Since falling to the Dodgers in the 1981 World Series, New York had lurched first one way and then another as Steinbrenner did everything he could to try to win—buying speed, buying pitching, buying power, firing managers, even bringing back Billy Martin again and again. Yet nothing had worked, and now he wanted Lasorda.

Lasorda didn't want to leave the Dodgers, but after seven years of one-year contracts, he wanted more money and more

In March 1983, former Dodger manager Walter Alston was elected to the Hall of Fame. Attending the press conference announcing the honor were (left to right) Tommy Lasorda, Carl Erskine, Burt Hooton, Bill Russell, Larry Sherry, and Ron Perranoski.

NL MANAGER OF THE YEAR AWARD

1977	Tommy Lasorda	Associated Press
1981	Tommy Lasorda	Associated Press
1983	Tommy Lasorda	BBWAA
1988	Tommy Lasorda	BBWAA

security. Multiyear deals were becoming the norm throughout the industry, and having a manager on a one-year contract when players both earned more and had multiyear deals themselves made it hard to enforce any kind of discipline. Lasorda received a three-year deal worth $1 million.

His timing was perfect. Had he asked for the contract after the 1984 season, he might have gotten a pink slip instead, although it wouldn't have been his fault. So far the Dodgers' youth movement was a bust: all they had was a bunch of guys who struggled to hit .250. In 1984 they added shortstop Dave Anderson, outfielder Candy Maldonado, and, after Greg Brock was sent back to the minors, first baseman Franklin Stubbs. The new Dodgers fit right in — all three struggled to hit.

To be fair, the 1984 Dodgers were hit with a rash of injuries and other disabilities, ranging from the predictable, such as utilityman Bob Bailor's dislocated shoulder, to the bizarre — Rick Honeycutt injured his shoulder when he tripped in the Dodger parking lot, and Tom Niedenfuer swallowed his tongue while passing a kidney stone. Others were sad. Steve Howe couldn't stay away from cocaine and was suspended for the season.

But the real story of the season was rookie pitcher Orel Hershiser. A 17th-round draft pick in 1979, Hershiser had made a slow but steady progression through the Dodger farm system, but without the flash that characterized so many of their young players. He made the club in 1984, pitching mostly in relief, and when Jerry Reuss went down with an injury, Hershiser was inserted into the rotation.

In his own way, Hershiser was as unlikely a prospect as Valenzuela had been. He looked like an accountant who spent his free time keeping stats for a rotisserie league rather than pitching in the major leagues himself. But when he put on a uniform and got on the mound, Hershiser underwent a transformation worthy of a comic book hero. He had control, a 93-mile-per-hour sinking fastball, a split-finger pitch, a good curve, uncommon concentration, and a distinct dislike of hitters. Lasorda gave him the unlikely but oddly appropriate nickname "Bulldog." Hershiser struggled at first, then was reamed out in what the unabashedly Christian pitcher later referred to as "the Sermon on the Mound" when both Lasorda and Perranoski told him, "Stop pitching like every hitter is Babe Ruth." He relaxed, got ahead of hitters, beat the Cubs 7–1 in his first start on June 29, and followed that performance with three straight shutouts, not giving up a run until the Braves' Dale Murphy knocked a home run on July 24.

There was no such thing as "Orel mania" surrounding his emergence, but in a season when prospect after prospect fell off the table, Hershiser, who finished with 11 wins, gave the Dodgers some cause for optimism. After all, Valenzuela was still only 23 — two years younger than Hershiser — Bob Welch was 27, and converted reliever Alejandro Pena was only 25. With relief pitcher Tom Niedenfuer and Ken Howell still in their early twenties, the Dodger pitching staff was full of promise. But the club needed hitting.

Yet the Dodgers stubbornly stuck to their guns and counted their money. They might as well have put a sign out in front of Dodger Stadium that read: NO FREE AGENTS NEED APPLY. While they didn't mind signing players they had developed — Pedro Guerrero and Valenzuela were both tied up in sizable multiyear contracts — or putting in some cash to juice up trades, as they had done with Texas to acquire Rick Honeycutt, they avoided free agents as if they were infected. And it cost them, or at least it cost Dodger fans, for after winning the Series in 1981, the organization seemed more or less content with just being a contender, a pretender to the crown.

One or two experienced, accomplished hitters at the right positions in the mid-1980s might have turned the club into a dynasty, and the youngsters who either struggled for too long or failed completely might have benefited from the protection in the lineup. But as long as three million fans streamed in and out of Dodger Stadium, who cared? Nearly 30 years after the Dodgers moved to Los Angeles, a fair number of their followers and many in the local media still had the welcome mat out. Bad deals and trades were rarely criticized. In the past few seasons, as the Dodgers shed the "lesser" lights of the farm system, they essentially dumped pitchers Sid Fernandez and John Franco for nothing. Together, they would go on to win nearly 200 games and save over 400. And the club seemed unable to separate reality from the rare air in Albuquerque that made every hitter in the system look like Rogers Hornsby.

Because they had pitching, however, they kept up the illusion that their approach was working. Just as Koufax and Drysdale had kept the cracks from showing in the mid-1960s, in 1985 so did the combined efforts of Hershiser, Valenzuela, and Welch.

The Dodgers started the season as if learning the game on the job, with terrible defense and a pathetic hitting attack that undermined the pitching staff. Finally, about three years too late, in June the Dodgers abandoned their wasted effort to turn Pedro Guerrero into a third baseman. Guerrero, with only 4 home runs and 16 RBIs over the first two months, became the best hitter in the league for the rest of the season. His offensive performance lifted everyone else — even Greg Brock, who at last began to perform like a bona-fide major leaguer. With Guerrero no longer at third, Dave Anderson was shifted to that position, a move that allowed Mariano Duncan into the lineup at shortstop.

It all came together in July, and the Dodgers got hot just as the Padres slumped. L.A. took over first place on July 13 and cruised through August and September, ending the year 95–67, 5½ games ahead of the Reds. Valenzuela finished 17–10. Welch was 14–4. And Orel Hershiser was a stellar 19–3, and 11–1 at Dodger Stadium, where his ERA was just

---

Dodger right-hander Orel Hershiser may have possessed the most deceiving looks of any pitcher of his era. Seemingly mild-mannered and gawky, the former hockey player was a rugged competitor on the mound. Tommy Lasorda called him "Bulldog," and in his second full season in 1985 he compiled a superb 19–3 won-lost record.

over a run a game. With home-field advantage against St. Louis in the playoffs, the Dodgers appeared to have a great shot to make the World Series.

The Cardinals were built around the speed of outfielders Vince Coleman and Willie McGee, the defense of shortstop wiz Ozzie Smith, the hitting of Jack Clark—their only power threat—and the pitching of John Tudor and Joaquin Andujar. Entering the Series, the Dodgers knew what they had to do to win—keep Coleman, with 110 stolen bases, off base and keep Clark from driving in runs. Lasorda, in fact, repeatedly told the pitchers not to let Clark beat them.

They listened. Playing a best-of-seven NLCS for the first time, in L.A. for games one and two Valenzuela and Hershiser stopped Coleman in his tracks, and Clark didn't have an RBI as the Dodgers won easily, 4–1 and 8–2. Although the Cardinals took game three when Welch was bombed early, before game four the Dodgers seemed to receive a break. In a freak accident before the game, a machine did what no catcher had been able to do all year. Vince Coleman was knocked out of the Series when an automatic tarp caught him napping and rolled over his leg.

Yet the Cardinals responded. In game four they belted Reuss and Honeycutt, exploding for nine second-inning runs to win big, 12–2. The Series was tied, but the Dodgers still had Valenzuela and Hershiser ready to go in games five and six.

And in game five Valenzuela was at his guttiest best. After giving up two first-inning runs, he didn't shut the Cardinals down, but he kept them from scoring again. The Dodgers scratched away and tied the game and seemed poised to go ahead in the seventh when they put two men on with no one out. Steve Sax, batting eighth, came up in a situation that screamed for a bunt—or something.

But Lasorda wavered and squandered both runners. After giving Sax the bunt sign on the first two pitches, both balls, he then took it off and gave Sax the take sign, hoping for a walk so he could keep Valenzuela in the game. Sax took another ball, then two strikes to run the count full. Now he got the hit sign, and Cardinal pitcher Todd Worrell struck Sax out. Lasorda then let Valenzuela hit. He grounded out, and Mariano Duncan popped up to end the threat. The score stayed tied.

That may have been the big play of the game. At the end of the eighth inning, Valenzuela, after throwing 132 pitches, told Ron Perranoski that he "had pitched too many pitches."

Lasorda brought in Tom Niedenfuer with the score still tied in the bottom of the ninth. Although Niedenfuer had pitched only once in the Series, after 106 innings in 64 appearances during the regular season he was feeling gassed too. Above his locker there was a cartoon of a relief pitcher with his arm dragging on the ground behind him. The caption read, "I know it's your 150th appearance, but we really need this one."

In the ninth he faced Ozzie Smith, the greatest fielding shortstop in the game and a good contact hitter, but not a power threat at all. He had only 13 career home runs, all from the right side, and he was batting lefty against the right-handed Niedenfuer.

But with the count 1–2, Smith and the law of averages beat Niedenfuer. The shortstop turned on a pitch and pulled it down the line, just fair, just over the right-field fence. The Cardinals won, 3–2.

The Dodgers were disconsolate after the game. Sax said he had had the take sign on 3-and-1. Lasorda said he didn't, and then he admitted to having made the ultimate manager's sin. Asked if he had been planning to pinch-hit for Valenzuela if Sax reached base, he said, "I wasn't sure what I was going to do." Valenzuela told reporters, "I don't think I can speak English today," and told them nothing in Spanish. The Cardinals were one win away from the world championship, and the Dodgers one loss away from losing four in a row.

Game six has been replayed as many times as any game since the Dodgers moved to Los Angeles, and in the minds of most, the result remains the same: Lasorda blew it, making the worst managerial decision in a championship series this side of Boston's Grady Little in 2003.

Back in Los Angeles after a day of travel, Hershiser didn't have his best stuff, but the Dodgers carried a 4–1 lead into the seventh. Then he tired, gave up two runs, and was replaced by Niedenfuer. Ozzie Smith resumed his power act with a triple, and the score was tied, but Niedenfuer got out of the inning by striking out Jack Clark.

Mike Marshall made Dodger fans delirious with an eighth-inning home run. The Dodgers were only three outs away from forcing a game seven.

Niedenfuer got pinch hitter Cesar Cedeno out to start the inning, then faced Willie McGee. He singled and, with Ozzie Smith at bat, stole second to put himself in scoring position, the tying run. Niedenfuer had little choice but to walk Smith and set up a potential double play.

Tommy Herr gave himself up and grounded to first base, putting Smith, the winning run, into scoring position at second and moving McGee to third.

Up stepped Jack Clark, the hitter Lasorda had told his pitchers time and time again not to let beat them. First base was open. Walking Clark would set up a force-out at every base. Andy Van Slyke, in a terrible slump, was on deck, and Lasorda had Jerry Reuss warming up in case he needed a lefty to match up against a left-handed hitter.

Lasorda didn't order the walk. He had Niedenfuer, on fumes, pitch to Clark. He didn't even tell him that he could pitch around Clark, that a walk would be okay, that Reuss would come in to face Van Slyke if Clark reached first.

As one writer noted later, "Hitters dream about situations like this." But they give managers nightmares.

Niedenfuer threw one pitch straight down the middle, "trying to get ahead," he said later, figuring Clark would take the first pitch. But Clark was a dead fastball hitter looking for one ball to hit. He got it and he didn't miss, sending the ball some 450 feet away to win the game 7–5 and end the Dodgers' season.

People thought of Branca and of Stan Williams. Some 20 years earlier the Dodgers had locked the locker-room door after Williams lost a pennant in a similar situation, and it had stayed locked for almost an hour. This time it stayed locked for only 17 minutes.

There was no screaming and no one was drunk — yet. And Lasorda met the press straight on, admitting, "This is the worst one of all; this one is tearing my heart out." He took the heat for not walking Clark, but he was also defensive. As writers peppered him with questions about the decision, he snapped, "Anybody can second-guess — I've got to have the first guess." Then the questions stopped, and he added, without prompting, "I thought about it, I thought about it, I thought about it, but [Niedenfuer] had struck him out the time before." But Niedenfuer had also given up a home run and a triple to Ozzie Smith.

The loss sent the Dodgers reeling. Injuries to Alejandro Pena and Pedro Guerrero early in the 1986 season made it clear that the Dodgers wouldn't repeat, and they didn't come close. Nobody but Steve Sax hit, and nobody but Valenzuela pitched, and nobody at all caught the ball. The Dodgers didn't make any deals and still wouldn't sign a decent free agent — they simply threw more kids out onto the field, stuffing them into the cracks like tar while the boat filled with

Dodger general manager Al Campanis embarrassed himself and the Dodger organization while being interviewed by Ted Koppel of ABC on the program *Nightline* in April 1987. When asked if he felt there was still that much prejudice in baseball, Campanis — Jackie Robinson's roommate on the Montreal Royals — commented, "No, I don't believe it's prejudice . . . I truly believe they [African Americans] may not have some of the necessities to be, let's say, a field manager or perhaps a general manager."

water. They listed to the end, finishing fifth, only a half-game ahead of last-place Atlanta. And in the off-season they again pursued a do-nothing policy, not making a genuine run at a free agent of merit, even though Tim Raines was available and no one else made a play for him. The Dodgers remained hard-liners when it came to free agency and were front and center when every baseball franchise illegally conspired to ignore free agents and prevent them from exercising rights they had earned through collective bargaining.

Even so, the 1987 season should have been a time for the franchise to celebrate, to take a look back and honor its past, even to reassess and refocus and reenergize. In recognition of the 40th anniversary of Jackie Robinson's first season in the major leagues, Major League Baseball had planned commemorative events all season long — retiring Robinson's number "42" in every ballpark, naming the Rookie of the Year Award after Robinson, and other similar measures. Although MLB was touchy when anyone intimated that baseball had in fact not been as conscientious or as sensitive about racial matters as it should have been and that such gestures were far less meaningful than they appeared, the desire to honor Robinson at least promised to inspire a dialogue over the issue of race and bigotry in baseball.

That it surely did.

In recent years the Dodgers had not been very concerned about race. After all, they had signed Robinson, and they had long been one of the few clubs to employ black faces; Gilliam, Newcombe, and Campanella had all been visible members of the organization at a time when other clubs didn't employ any African Americans in management at all. But over time the Dodgers had also grown complacent about the subject, as if signing Robinson had somehow given them a lifelong vaccine against the taint of racism.

In fact, by 1987 the Dodgers were little different from other organizations — which is to say, they had yet to move past tokenism in their hiring practices. Few blacks worked in positions of real authority. The ballclub made only the stan-

dard, cursory gestures at reaching out to the African American community, such as holding player clinics in parks and distributing free tickets. Even on the field there were few black faces. In the years before the amateur draft the Dodgers had been the team of choice for black prospects, but in recent years the game had lost its preeminence in the inner city, and even among the few young African Americans who played the game the Dodgers were now viewed as no different from other teams. Jackie Robinson was more a name in the history books than a living presence.

A number of former players, such as John Roseboro, had long detected within the Dodgers' organization a certain inherent paternalism and a patronizing attitude in regard to African Americans, for over the years there had been a certain amount of duplicity in the way the club treated white

Following the firing of Al Campanis, the Dodgers replaced him with former sportswriter and long-time Dodger PR and marketing executive Fred Claire. Here Claire talks to manager Tommy Lasorda. In the world championship season of 1988, Claire was named Baseball Executive of the Year by *The Sporting News*, with Lasorda earning National League Manager of the Year honors.

stars versus their black and Latino stars. Remember — Maury Wills hadn't been accorded the same star status as Drysdale and Koufax, and long-time stars like Willie Davis and Roseboro had been let go with little fanfare. In recent years the club had worked overtime to tout white prospects like Marshall and Sax and Brock, but the only real star in the lineup had been Pedro Guerrero, a black Dominican. Even Valenzuela had been shunted aside. Like every other organization in baseball, the Dodgers still had some work to do on racial equality. Signing Jackie Robinson didn't absolve them of that.

Yet since Robinson was so closely identified with the Dodgers, the organization was front and center for the anniversary tributes. Just a few hours after the Dodgers suffered an Opening Day loss to the Houston Astros, Al Campanis was scheduled to appear on the late-night ABC news program *Nightline* to speak with Ted Koppel about Robinson. He seemed the perfect choice. After all, Campanis had played with Robinson in Montreal and even been his roommate. The two men had been friends.

But Campanis was ill prepared for what was to come. He rarely appeared on camera and was far more accustomed to speaking with print reporters. And at almost midnight, sitting alone before a camera in the virtually empty Astrodome, he was at the end of a very long day.

Those were all excuses offered up later to explain away what he said to Koppel. When the three-way conversation between Koppel in a studio in Washington, author Roger Kahn in New York, and Campanis veered off from Robinson to focus on the larger issue of race in baseball, Campanis couldn't use the same old stories about Robinson that he had long told over and over and over. Oh, he knew how he felt, but no one had ever asked him those questions before.

Earlier in the segment, in a taped interview, Koppel had asked Rachel Robinson how her husband would assess baseball's record on race in 1987. She responded the same way her husband had at an interview in his last public appearance at the 1972 All-Star Game just a few days before his death. Robinson, rightly, had taken baseball to task for its failure to put African Americans into positions of authority either on the field or in the front office. Fifteen years later Rachel responded similarly to the same question, and Kahn echoed her statement, for since Robinson's death baseball had made little progress off the field. Apart from a few high-profile former stars, few African Americans had ever been employed in positions of real power in baseball. At the time only three

African Americans had served as major league managers (Maury Wills, Larry Doby, and Frank Robinson), and only one, Bill Lucas of Atlanta, had served as a GM. But no African Americans held such positions in 1987; nor were there any black Americans in similar roles in either triple-A or double-A baseball. Hank Aaron, the Braves' director of player personnel, was the highest-ranked black in the game. Yet 20 percent of the players were black.

Then Koppel spoke to Campanis, asking him, "Is there still that much prejudice in baseball?"

"No," Campanis responded, "I don't believe it's prejudice." He thought it was something else. "I truly believe," he went on, "they [African Americans] may not have some of the necessities to be, let's say, a field manager or perhaps a general manager."

Koppel could hardly believe what he had just heard, and the veteran newsman tried to throw Campanis a life preserver. "Do you really believe that?" he said.

Campanis could have gotten out of it if he'd simply known enough to speak the truth: baseball hadn't given many African Americans the chance to succeed or fail in positions of authority, and if they lacked a "necessity," that necessity was opportunity. But Campanis didn't believe that. He believed in the twisted logic of bigotry, in the spurious science that sought to justify racism with pseudo-scientific fact. He said the same things that a lot of bigots had been saying for years — that there were real physical and mental differences between blacks and whites. Campanis hadn't simply misspoken or accidentally blundered down some unfamiliar train of thought he hadn't been down before, for his logic wasn't original in the least. "Well, I don't say all of them," he blundered on, "but how many [black] quarterbacks do you have, how many pitchers do you have that are black?" Well, let's see — the Dodgers had Ken Howell. And former Dodger Dave Stewart was about to become a star with the Oakland A's — but Campanis had traded him.

Koppel was stunned. "That sounds like the same garbage we were hearing 40 years ago about players."

And then Campanis said what he *really* felt. Again, he made it clear that in his mind the absence of African Americans in baseball management had nothing to do with prejudice or opportunity — African Americans were really and truly *different*. "It's not garbage," he said, then asked rhetorically, as if providing proof of his thesis, "why are black people not good swimmers? Because they don't have the buoyancy."

Poof. A career of more than 50 years in baseball went down the drain in 10 seconds. And in the insular, deluded world of major league baseball, Campanis had been considered *enlightened,* one of the good guys, someone without a prejudiced bone in his body.

The excuses his defenders offered up were almost as pathetic as what Campanis himself said. He was not just having a "bad day," and he clearly hadn't "misspoken" or been "set up" or anything else. He had been neither inarticulate nor inattentive—Campanis had a college degree, spoke five languages, and was a leading executive in a multimillion-dollar corporation. His words were neither accidental nor unintentional. They aped the familiar, age-old, and oft-repeated logic of the racial supremacists who bucked up an indefensible belief system with spurious science. One doesn't say what Campanis did by accident. One expresses such ideas only after reading about them in the hate literature that espouses them and holding the same conversation time and time again either in the privacy of one's own thoughts or with other like-minded souls.

Campanis was guilty as charged. Being Jackie Robinson's roommate and signing dozens and dozens of African American ballplayers to contracts proved nothing except that Campanis had either changed or been extraordinarily duplicitous for years. And by the way, who *hadn't* Campanis scouted or signed or traded for? And why? Campanis had been a favored Dodger employee in a position of power *for years.* Suddenly an awful lot of things the Dodgers had done—or hadn't done—since 1947 made a whole lot of sense. They appeared capable of creating a dynasty to rival the Yankees but had always come up just a little short. Had they taken the next Koufax and made him a third baseman because he lacked certain "necessities"? Pennants and world championships, as the Dodgers knew better than any team in the game, are sometimes lost by the narrowest of margins. How many times had Campanis's latent bigotry—and by extension, institutionalized racism within the entire organization—left the Dodgers short? There is no answer to that question beyond a disquieting feeling that things might have been very different.

Campanis apologized, as did Peter O'Malley, but no apology could excuse Campanis's words. It was two long days before O'Malley fired him, and only then after black leaders were threatening a boycott of baseball and Campanis agreed to fall on his sword. O'Malley, incredibly, was prepared to keep him on even though Campanis was nearly ready to retire anyway. The firing hardly solved anything, for the attitude Campanis represented still enjoyed far more support in baseball than anyone was willing to admit, although at least now the problem was out in the open.

Campanis was replaced by Fred Claire, a former reporter for the *Long Beach Press Telegram* who had joined the club in 1969 in the publicity department and spent his tenure with the club in marketing and PR. There had long been speculation that Lasorda wanted to be both manager and GM, as Whitey Herzog had been in St. Louis, but the timing wasn't right for Lasorda. The 1985 playoff loss, coupled with the Dodgers' poor performance in 1986, had taken a bit of the shine off Lasorda's reputation, and the days of the manager-GM, given the complexity of player contracts, was just about over. Claire appeared to be the stopgap hire.

But he wasn't. He seized the job and spoke of his commitment to "sound business judgments." When the Dodgers followed up the Campanis incident by playing just as poorly as they had in 1986, Claire was given the authority to make some changes, and it soon became clear that "sound business judgments" meant something quite different to Fred Claire than to Campanis. Claire began by making some rare in-season deals, adding veterans like outfielder John Shelby. They didn't make much of a difference in 1987, but their acquisition seemed to signal that at long last the Dodgers were at least considering another approach, for Campanis's vaunted farm system was just about empty. In the future the Dodgers would reach outside the organization for answers. Meanwhile, they spent the season far out of the race and finished fourth, with a record identical to 1986.

They finally gave up on a generation of failed homegrown talent and, for a change, were busy in the off-season. Claire made a complicated three-way trade with the A's and Mets that delivered shortstop Alfredo Griffin and relief pitchers Jesse Orosco and Jay Howell while giving up Bob Welch, and he also signed Oakland outfielder Mike Davis, catcher Rick Dempsey, and 43-year-old Don Sutton on the cheap as free agents.

Yes, that's right—free agents. It was desperate measures for desperate men. And in a real shock, for the first time ever the Dodgers went after a top-shelf player.

Detroit Tiger outfielder Kirk Gibson, despite having a year remaining on his contract, was declared a free agent, for as a free agent in 1985 he had failed to receive an offer from any

GOLD GLOVE AWARD WINNERS

Year	Player	Pos	Year	Player	Pos
1957	Gil Hodges	1B	1972	Wes Parker	1B
				Willie Davis	OF
1958	Gil Hodges	1B	1973	Willie Davis	OF
1959	Gil Hodges	1B	1974	Steve Garvey	1B
	Charlie Neal	2B		Andy Messersmith	P
1960	Wally Moon	OF	1975	Steve Garvey	1B
				Andy Messersmith	P
1961	John Roseboro	C	1976	Steve Garvey	1B
	Maury Wills	SS	1977	Steve Garvey	1B
1962	Maury Wills	SS	1978	Davey Lopes	2B
1966	John Roseboro	C	1981	Dusty Baker	OF
1967	Wes Parker	1B	1986	Fernando Valenzuela	P
1968	Wes Parker	1B	1988	Orel Hershiser	P
1969	Wes Parker	1B	1995	Raul Mondesi	OF
1970	Wes Parker	1B	1997	Raul Mondesi	OF
1971	Wes Parker	1B	1998	Charles Johnson	C
	Willie Davis	OF			

team but the Detroit Tigers, the team for whom he already played. A federal arbiter ruled that baseball owners had indulged in collusion, a violation of baseball's Basic Agreement, which governed players' contracts.

Gibson, who had played tight end for Michigan State, brought a hard-nosed attitude to the baseball field. Although Detroit manager Sparky Anderson's comparison of Gibson to Mickey Mantle hadn't been quite accurate, Gibson was still a wonderful talent—fast and powerful, lacking only a strong arm to be a true five-tool player. Moreover, Gibson played *hard*. He didn't like to lose, and it showed. On the Dodgers that attitude had been sorely lacking. Lasorda still talked a good game, but his reputation as a master motivator had recently been more talk than real. The Dodgers signed Gibson to a three-year deal worth $4.5 million.

In the spring Gibson laid down the law. He'd won a world championship with Detroit in 1984 and had credibility. Hardly any Dodgers remained from the 1981 champions, and the whole team — apart from some pitchers — was made up of guys who had coasted their whole careers, accepting defeat, never playing hurt, just collecting paychecks, accepting mediocrity, and playing for individual goals. Gibson wasn't like that. Despite bad knees, he ran hard and didn't bitch. It helped that he was physically intimidating. He cracked a whip that Tommy Lasorda didn't even know existed.

L.A.'s attitude changed overnight. Orel Hershiser later cracked, "There were so many new faces I thought I'd been traded." Steve Sax opened the season by hitting a home run on the first pitch, the Dodgers won five in a row, and they were off.

Not everything went right, though, not even close. Don Sutton was done and the Dodgers cut him loose in midseason, and Valenzuela, after struggling, missed the second half with a bad shoulder. Mike Davis didn't hit a lick, third baseman Jeff Hamilton broke his ribs, and Alfredo Griffin broke a hand, missed almost two months, and hit .195. But it didn't matter. Gibson forced the issue all year, stealing bases and hitting for power. A deep and flexible bench, led by everyman Mickey Hatcher, dubbed themselves "the Stuntmen" and performed unexpected acts of brinkmanship and daring. The Dodgers moved into first place on May 24 and were never headed.

If Gibson gave the team backbone, the strong arms came from the pitching staff. Tim Leary, a perennial prospect for several clubs, learned a split-fingered fastball and won 17 games. Rookie Tim Belcher won 12. Howell, Alejandro Pena, and Orosco gave the Dodgers the best bullpen in baseball. And when the club needed help, Claire got it. In August, when it looked as if they were flagging, Claire traded Pedro Guerrero for St. Louis pitcher John Tudor, the league's ERA leader.

The Dodgers didn't lose more than three games in a row all season long, and with the approach of September, the

Kirk Gibson captured National League MVP honors in 1988 while helping lead the Dodgers to their sixth and last world championship of the 20th century.

1988

In 1988 Orel Hershiser earned the Cy Young Award after compiling a 23–8 record, which included 15 complete games and 8 shutouts. He capped his amazing season when he broke Don Drysdale's consecutive scoreless innings mark at 59. In the September stretch run, he went a perfect 5–0 with a 0.00 ERA.

time when pennants and championships are won and lost, the Dodgers began to entertain serious thoughts about playing in October. It was then that Orel Hershiser took a page from Dodger history, taking from both Don Drysdale and Sandy Koufax, with a little Sal Maglie and Johnny Podres thrown in for good measure. For the remainder of the season he may well have been the best pitcher ever to wear a Dodger uniform and gave the club a cloak of utter invincibility each and every time he went to the mound.

On August 30, against Montreal, he took a 4–0 lead into the fifth, then gave up two runs with one out before shutting them down the rest of the way for a 4–2 win, upping his record to 18–8. He was feeling good. Since being rocked by the Giants earlier in the month, he'd tweaked his wind-up and given up only three runs in his last three starts, all complete games.

He never gave up another.

His wins weren't meaningless victories either. In his next start on September 5 he beat Atlanta and stopped a three-game losing streak. In his next shutout, on September 10, he beat the second-place Reds and stopped a two-game losing streak, while his fourth shutout, on September 14 against the Braves, capped a five-game winning streak. He wasn't just winning—he was dominating and giving the bullpen some rest. Drysdale's record of 58⅔ scoreless innings was within reach.

Hershiser didn't buy it. "I don't see Don's record as one that will be broken," he said. He was no dummy. He had done the math, and although his streak was now more than 30 innings, it was still shorter than the one he'd enjoyed in his rookie season, and he was scheduled to make only three more starts before the playoffs. Unless he pitched in relief, he'd still be short. And besides, his wife was due to have a baby and he might even miss a start.

But Jamie Hershiser cooperatively went into labor between starts. Hershiser's daughter Jordan was born on September 16. He rejoined the team in Houston for his next start and shut out the Astros 1–0, his second consecutive 1–0 win.

The streak ended in the third inning of his next start against San Francisco—at least that's what Hershiser thought. With men on first and third, Ernest Riles hit a double-play ball, but Griffin's throw went wild and Jose Uribe scored.

But in a shades-of-Dick-Dietz moment, umpire Paul Runge ruled that Brett Butler had slid out of the baseline and gave the Dodgers the double play. Mickey Hatcher then cracked a three-run home run and Hershiser won, 3–0. His streak was now at 49 innings. As Jim Murray noted in the *Times*, "Five shutouts in a season is Cy Young stuff. Five shutouts in a row is Hall of Fame stuff."

With one more shutout, Hershiser could both tie Drysdale's shutout mark and come within a whisker of the consecutive scoreless innings mark. Everything was working out, for his final start, on September 28 in San Diego, would still leave Hershiser a full five days of rest before the start of the playoffs—he could go for the record without compromising team goals. The Dodgers clinched the division title on September 26, and now Hershiser's mark was the talk of the baseball world.

Hershiser was his usual efficient self against the Padres, getting ahead of the hitters and coaxing ground balls with his sinkers. Through six innings he had thrown only 65 pitches, given up only two hits, and not thrown as many as three balls to a single hitter. Of course, the Dodgers weren't having any more success against San Diego pitcher Andy Hawkins, but that somehow seemed appropriate. These were the Dodgers after all.

In the eighth, with two out, Roberto Alomar singled, and the crowd stirred. With the game scoreless, Alomar, a threat to steal anyway, was even more likely to try to get into scoring position.

Hershiser knew this. Few pitchers of his era have ever displayed more intelligence or awareness—he was one of the first to keep computer files on hitters. Alomar kept pushing his lead, and Hershiser kept throwing over. Finally, he caught Alomar out a little too far, leaning toward second, and this time his throw to first was not designed to keep Alomar close but to put him out. It did, and the streak was 57 innings, the tying shutout an inning away.

But the Dodgers could not score, and in the ninth Hershiser coaxed three ground balls from Padres hitters. Now he had pitched nine scoreless innings, and pushed his streak to 58, but since the Dodgers hadn't scored, he had neither the shutout nor the record. Both were still possible, but neither was certain.

Hershiser asked to leave the game. After only 98 pitches, he wanted the opportunity to break the record in Los Angeles, in a brief relief appearance. Lasorda refused.

Then Hershiser asked if he could just tie the mark, equal Drysdale, and, as he put it, "leave it there," but the manager

wouldn't hear it. After the Dodgers failed to score in the tenth, Hershiser took the mound again.

It wasn't easy. He struck out Marvell Wynne to start the inning, but his sinker, which dropped so much some thought he had scuffed the ball, escaped catcher Mike Scioscia and Wynne made first.

Benito Santiago sacrificed him to second, and now Hershiser was one out away from tying Drysdale, and one hit away from falling short. Randy Ready hit a ground ball. Out.

The record was tied. But Wynne moved to third. Garry Templeton stepped in and was walked intentionally, setting up a force play.

Now pinch hitter Keith Moreland came to bat. On Hershiser's fourth pitch he lofted a fly ball to short right field. Hershiser had the record.

He was mobbed by teammates, greeted by Drysdale, then hustled off—his work was done for the day. Drysdale still had the shutout record, but Hershiser held the scoreless innings mark of 59, one-third of an inning more than Drysdale. That somehow seemed appropriate, as did, in a way, the fact that the Dodgers lost, 2–1, in 16 innings. Drysdale quipped that it was "just like the 60's."

Entering the NLCS, the Dodgers were given little chance of defeating the mighty Mets, who had won 100 games and coasted to a 15-game lead in winning the NL East. Many considered them better than the team that won the 1986 world championship, for now, in addition to Dwight Gooden, their starting staff also included David Cone, 20–3 for the season. The Dodgers were considered overachievers, and it seemed inevitable that the Mets would again reach the World Series—they had more of everything. During the regular season, in fact, the Mets had defeated the Dodgers in 10 of 11 meetings.

But the Dodgers had Orel Hershiser. After imitating Drysdale to perfection, he now became Sandy Koufax. Not that he matched Koufax in terms of strikeouts, but over the next seven games Hershiser, like Koufax, took the ball and lifted his team on his back. Although he won only one game, the Dodgers would not have won the Series without him, or even come close.

Yet he "failed" in game one, when he carried a shutout into the ninth inning, running his unofficial streak to 67 innings (postseason appearances do not count in such records). Then in the ninth he gave up two hits and a run to start the inning, Jay Howell coughed up the lead, and the Dodgers lost, 3–2.

By getting to Hershiser, many observers thought that the Mets had broken the Dodgers and now they'd fall quickly.

But Mets pitcher David Cone, ghostwriting a column in a New York paper, unintentionally inspired the club with a series of insults, such as calling reliever Jay Howell "a high school teacher." The Dodgers clubbed Cone in game two and tied the Series.

Hershiser, pitching on three days' rest, was magnificent in game three, again carrying a lead into the late innings, leaving after seven with a 4–3 lead. Yet once again, the Dodger bullpen gave up the lead and the club lost, 8–4.

There would be no such collapse in game four. After Mike Scioscia cracked a two-run home run in the top of the ninth to tie the game, Gibson, hobbled by a hamstring pull, hit a solo shot in the top of the twelfth to put the Dodgers up 5–4. They were, Gibson admitted later, "on the edge of extinction."

And moving closer still, for Tim Leary and Jesse Orosco loaded the bases with two out. Then came Hershiser, making his third appearance in six days. He induced Kevin McReynolds to fly out, and the Series was tied two games to two. Gibson told reporters, "I don't know how we win and neither do you. But the fact is we do."

It came down to game seven, and now Hershiser, pitching for the third time in five days, and the fourth in nine, and starting on two days' rest, got the ball again. He was near-perfect, shutting out the Mets to send the Dodgers into the World Series against the Oakland Athletics.

The victory, however, left the American League champion Oakland A's cold. Earlier, slugger Jose Canseco had offered that the mighty A's, who had swept the Red Sox in ho-hum style in the ALCS, wanted to play the Mets so they could play "the best." The Dodgers somehow didn't count.

He was not alone in that estimation. The A's were supposed to be baseball's superteam. Ex-Dodger Dave Stewart won 21 games to lead a deep pitching staff that was backed by baseball's best reliever, Dennis Eckersley. And on offense Mark McGwire and Jose Canseco, the "Bash Brothers," paced baseball's most potent attack. Moreover, after beating Boston, they were rested and ready. It almost didn't seem fair, sending the Dodgers out to play the A's. It wasn't.

The Dodgers were spent. Hershiser needed rest, and Gibson had reinjured his hamstring in game five, then pulled ligaments in his other leg in game seven. At the start of the Series he could barely walk; he couldn't run.

He wouldn't have to.

Before game one Tommy Lasorda didn't think he'd play at all. When he was asked if Gibson, who was in the trainer's room having his legs taped up like a mummy, would be able to play, Lasorda was glum. "He can't do it," he said. "He just can't do it." Earlier in the day Gibson had received injections of both cortisone and Xylocaine, and he had been icing his legs ever since, with little effect. All Gibson could do was stand up — barely.

Before game one in Los Angeles, although Gibson was technically active, the Dodgers didn't even bother to include him in the pregame introductions. The only Gibson on the field was pop singer Debbie Gibson, who sang the national anthem. She had a better chance of playing than Kirk.

Tim Belcher started opposite Stewart, and for an instant it looked as if the Dodgers might somehow overcome the A's anyway as Mickey Hatcher struck for a two-run home run in the bottom of the first. But such optimism was short-lived. In the top of the second Jose Canseco belted a long grand slam off Belcher to put the A's ahead 4–2. With a lead, Dave Stewart's task was simplified. All he had to do was hold it into the ninth and give the ball to Dennis Eckersley. He was automatic.

Stewart did just that. The Dodgers scored one more in the sixth on three singles, but that was it. But at the same time, Tim Leary, Brian Holten, and Alejandro Pena managed to keep the A's quiet. Still, entering the bottom of the ninth, even a one-run lead against Eckersley seemed insurmountable.

It would have been different, of course, if Gibson had been available, the one player on the club with the ability to change the game with a single swing of the bat. But that apparently wasn't going to happen. Dodger broadcaster Vin Scully, announcing the game on TV for NBC with the authority of God, spoke up in the eighth inning and said, "The man who is the spearhead of the Dodger offense, throughout the year, who saved them in the League Championship Series, will not see any action tonight. He is not even in the dugout."

That was true. He was still in the clubhouse, still horizontal, still packed in ice, watching and listening on TV. But when Scully spoke, Gibson stood up, pulled on his uniform shirt, and looked over at the Dodger batboy. "I'll be there," he answered Scully. Then he grabbed a bat and ordered the batboy to follow him into the batting cage and place balls on a tee for him to hit. He would try.

Gibson was still in pain and still found it hard to walk, but a few swings told him he could hit. He told the batboy, "Go tell Tommy if someone gets on, I want to hit." He did.

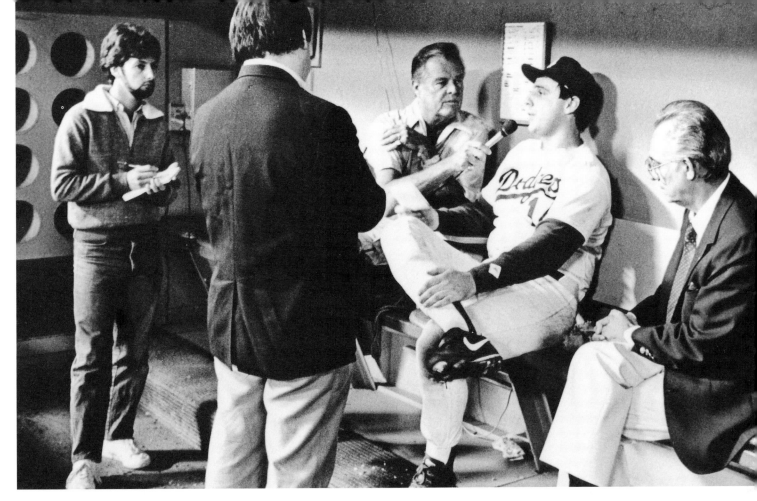

Former Dodger pitcher Don Drysdale interviews catcher Mike Scioscia at Dodger Stadium. In 13 seasons with Los Angeles, Scioscia batted .259 and was selected to play in the 1990 All-Star Game. Scioscia was a particular favorite of manager Tommy Lasorda and eventually went on to manage the Anaheim Angels to their first-ever world championship in 2002.

Lasorda bolted down the runway and met Gibson to make sure it was true. Again Gibson told him he could hit.

Yet as the game entered the bottom of the ninth it did not appear as if he would have the chance. If Hershiser had been the best pitcher in baseball in 1988, Eckersley was not far behind. He'd given up less than a baserunner an inning in the regular season and had allowed only three runners in six innings in the ALCS.

Scioscia and Jeff Hamilton went down quietly to start the inning. Then Lasorda called back Alfredo Griffin in favor of pinch hitter Mike Davis. Although the former A had been terrible all year, he did have the potential to hit a home run.

But Davis wasn't thinking that way. He recalled that the Dodgers had been admonished to step out against Eckersley, to make him impatient, to disrupt his rhythm. Davis did just that, stepping in and out of the box, calling time, checking his bat, and driving Eckersley nuts.

It worked. Eckersley, whose control was usually impeccable, walked Davis on a 3–1 pitch. But he wasn't worried. Lasorda had sent Dave Anderson on deck as a decoy. "If he [Eckersley] had seen Gibson, he would have pitched Davis differently," Lasorda explained later.

Gibson heard the crowd erupt and knew someone had reached base. He started limping up the runway. Lasorda called Anderson back into the dugout.

No one came out. Gibson hadn't reached the dugout yet. Plate umpire Doug Harvey finally came over to the dugout and yelled at Lasorda. "Tommy," he said, "you've got to have a hitter."

Gibson finally poked his head into the dugout, dragging his legs behind. "I've got a hitter," yelled Lasorda back.

Then Gibson ever so slowly, one uncertain step at a time, climbed the steps from the dugout and began a slow painful limp to home plate. Dodger Stadium erupted.

It was pure Hollywood, all schmaltz and hokum, a bad B-movie, the kind that didn't get made anymore and was only shown late at night on channels no one watched.

Kirk Gibson admires the flight of his historic ninth-inning game-winning home run in the opener of the 1988 World Series at Dodger Stadium.

Underneath Gibson's pants, the bandages on his legs stood out as he gingerly dug in. All 55,983 fans in Dodger Stadium were on their feet, roaring.

Eckersley wound up and threw a fastball. Gibson flailed at the pitch, swinging stiffly with his arms, fouling the pitch back and then almost falling over as his momentum threw him off balance and his legs couldn't support his weight. He stepped out of the batter's box and grimaced, then bent over and winced.

This was too much. Even B-movies didn't pile it on this thick. Eckersley threw another fastball, and again Gibson swung with his arms, fouling the ball off again and going behind in the count, down two strikes. Now Gibson would have to swing at anything close.

Knowing this, Eckersley threw his next pitch down and away. Gibson flicked at it again and just topped the ball foul down the first-base line. Once upon a time Gibson had been able to beat out toppers down the line like that. But on this day, even if the ball had been fair and even if the ball had been thrown around by the A's like a bunch of Little Leaguers, he knew he couldn't make it to first base. He was even worried that if he got a base hit to right field, he might be thrown out at first. After all, he had told Lasorda he could hit, but running was another matter altogether.

Eckersley threw again, another pitch off the plate, trying to get Gibson to chase it. The hitter watched it go by, and then breathed a sigh of relief as the umpire called it a ball. The count was one ball and two strikes. On the next pitch Davis broke for second.

The pitch missed the plate, and now Gibson didn't need to think home run but just base hit — just get the bat on the ball and limp all out to first — for Davis could score from second and tie the game. "It was important," Gibson said later. "Now I could shorten my swing."

Frustrated, Eckersley chose to go after Gibson now — he didn't want to walk another hitter, and instead of outside, he'd go inside. And instead of a fastball, he'd throw a slider.

Thirty-seven years earlier Dodger pitcher Ralph Branca, in a situation where one pitch could beat him, had made a similar decision, coming inside on a home run hitter in a situation where one pitch meant the ballgame. The result was perhaps the most famous home run in baseball history.

Now Eckersley made the same mistake: the ball sailed in, dropped down slightly, and Gibson dropped his bat head on the ball, barely striding, just shifting his weight, pulling, and then flicking the bat with his forearms and wrists.

Time slowed, and then stopped. When the ball came down, it started again: Gibson's drive to right field had dropped over the fence and beat the A's. Now he was running as fast as he could, which wasn't very fast at all. Dodger Stadium was awash in tears and cheers, and the credits were starting to roll as Jack Buck told the nation in his inimitable cadence, "I don't believe what I just saw!" Tommy Lasorda and the rest of the Dodgers gathered at home plate and waited for what seemed like forever as Gibson, pumping his fist and laughing, sort of ran and sort of walked around the bases before sort of jumping on home plate to give the Dodgers a 5–4 win and make Eckersley and Gibson as famous as Branca and Thomson.

The rest of the Series hardly seemed to matter — everyone now knew how this would end, and it followed the script. Hershiser shut out the A's in game two, 6–0, Oakland stole a 2–1 win in game three. Then the Dodgers beat the panicked A's in game four 4–3 and handed the ball in game five to Hershiser — he who had given up all of three runs in his last 92²/₃ innings, with seven shutouts in his last ten starts.

He gave up four hits and two runs, a virtual deluge. But the Dodgers scored four runs and won. Hershiser even hit 1.000 for the Series, going 3-for-3, which of course only tied him for the team lead. Because Kirk Gibson also ended the Series with a perfect batting average of 1.000 — after game one he never came to bat again.

He didn't have to. And he couldn't anyway. All he'd had left was one swing. That had been plenty. For the rest of time, or at least for a very, very long time, and at least for those Dodger fans who had never even heard of a Blackout cake, his home run marked the day the Dodgers franchise reached the top, the day the Dodgers of Los Angeles finally and definitively did something that equaled or maybe even topped anything that had ever, ever happened in Brooklyn.

In every way, at last, they'd won the way the Dodgers did.

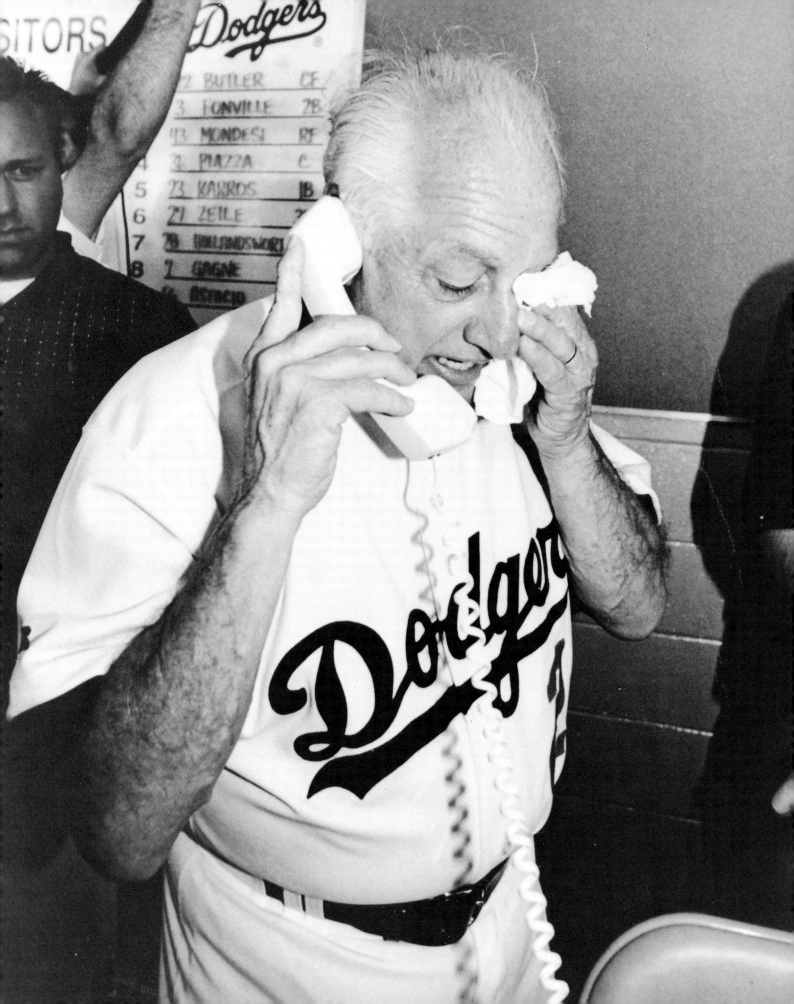

DODGER BLUES

IN MANY WAYS, JACK BUCK'S SIGNATURE CALL OF KIRK GIBSON'S HOME RUN still echoes over Chavez Ravine. But over time its meaning has changed, because since 1988 Dodger fans have hardly been able to believe what they have seen happen to their team. Over the last 15 years the Dodgers, the NL's signature franchise and in many ways its most successful and distinctive, have entirely lost their way. A rich tradition has essentially been squandered, frittered away in increments large and small. For most of those seasons, and especially recently, the Dodgers haven't mattered. Over this time period their story has rarely been written on the field, in the events of a game.

By the end of the 1988 season the Dodger name had come to mean as much as any in the game. Rich with tradition and history, the name "Dodgers" conjured up some of baseball's most enduring images—from Robinson dancing down the line to Koufax soaking his arm in ice to Tommy Lasorda dancing out of the dugout with his arms raised in triumph. Yet today those images almost seem anachronistic, as if they belong to another team from a long-gone era. The Dodgers have become a franchise without a face, a team of players but not personality winning a few games but losing ground. Instead of taking the

Former Dodger manager Tommy Lasorda wipes away tears of joy after learning that he has been elected to the Baseball Hall of Fame on March 5, 1997. He could just as well have been wiping away tears of frustration, as it had been nearly a decade since the last Dodger National League championship, the longest pennant drought since the days before MacPhail, Rickey, and O'Malley.

lead, they've followed, and along the way they've fallen further and further behind.

How did it happen?

In a sense, the 1988 world championship was a wonderful accident, a rare moment in time when just about everything worked out. It underscored Tommy Lasorda's ability as the best motivator in baseball and probably put him in the Hall of Fame.

Yet in the end it was a mirage that did not last. Great victories can do one of two things to a team. They can either set the tone for future success or endow a team with false confidence, causing the team to equate that victory with the methods that brought it to just such a moment. But if one were able to replay the 1988 World Series a hundred times, Kirk Gibson doesn't hit the ball out and the Dodgers probably don't win. The victory should have sent the Dodgers the message that they had a lot of work to do to repeat their triumph. But after the 1988 world championship, the Dodgers misread who they were and how they had gotten there. They thought the method had gotten them there, that Tommy Lasorda could take almost any team and make it a winner. In reality it was 25 gritty players who, in the blunt words of their heart and soul, Kirk Gibson, "busted our ass" and got extremely lucky. Yet the Dodgers acted as if the players didn't matter.

In the off-season Steve Sax became a free agent, and the Dodgers let him go. In return, they signed Yankee veteran Willie Randolph. He was still a fine player, but the Dodgers would miss Sax's spark. Gibson's success had convinced them to spend big again, and this time they picked up Baltimore first baseman Eddie Murray. On paper the Dodgers looked like a much-improved team: Valenzuela was back, Gibson and Murray sandwiched around Marshall looked formidable, and with Gibson and Hershiser they had plenty of star power, fire, and ice.

But the truth was that a whole lot of guys had peaked in 1988 and cumulatively achieved what they never would again. In 1989 Gibson's damaged hamstring would eventually require surgery, and Eddie Murray struggled to adjust both to the league and to Dodger Stadium. John Tudor was hurt and missed most of the year. Valenzuela was diminished. Only Belcher improved, throwing a league-best eight shutouts. On his way to 15 wins, he needed every single one—when he didn't throw a shutout, he was 7–12. The Dodgers couldn't score runs and were shut out 17 times themselves.

Hershiser went 15–15 and said, "I really feel like I pitched as well as I did last year." He was right, and he did, but this wasn't 1988. The Dodgers opened the year 3–7 and were never in the race. At the end of the season they were looking up from fourth place, 77–83.

The club had a decision to make in the off-season. Was there still a lesson in their victory in 1988, some key to success they had missed, or did they need to go an entirely different way? Their response was revealing.

The Dodgers continued to look at Gibson, age 33 and still fighting to get back into shape, as the catalyst, the key, and they chose to keep him as their central figure, the player they would build the team around. Looking in their minor league system and seeing some good arms just about ready but few bats, they chose to add offense, believing that if they could only surround Gibson with enough hitters, his will and their pitching would carry the team to victory again.

There was a flaw in their plan. For years, for better or worse, the Dodgers had followed an organizational road map. They had always been built from the bottom up. When their minor league clubs spit out pitchers, they built the team around pitching. When it provided more offense, they built the team around offense. Although that approach was not always successful, it gave a patient organization a certain balance, a certain consistency from year to year, and often a core group of players whom fans readily identified as Dodgers.

But Gibson, a mercenary free agent, had thrown that plan under the bus, and the 1988 championship convinced Fred Claire and Peter O'Malley that this new model was more effective. From that moment on the Dodger plan has fluctuated from year to year, and the organization has exhibited far less patience than before. As a result, their roster has been increasingly fluid and they have lurched back and forth wildly, first this way and then that, as players either exceeded or failed to reach expectations.

Before the 1990 season, they added Juan Samuel and free agent outfielder Hubie Brooks and looked forward to having Kal Daniels, a multitalented outfielder picked up from Cincinnati at the end of the 1989 season, for the full year. Surrounding Gibson and Murray, and supporting the Dodger pitching staff, that lineup seemed certain to deliver the Dodgers another division championship, and perhaps a world championship as well. Yet in only two years their lineup turned over almost completely and had virtually no homegrown products. They were an entirely different team.

After only a few starts, Orel Hershiser went down with a season-ending shoulder injury, resulting in surgery. Reliever

Jay Howell was already out with a knee injury, and before the season was over they would also lose Tim Belcher, Don Aase, and Jim Gott for significant periods of time. Although Ramon Martinez, in only his second major league season, blossomed into a 20-game winner, Valenzuela continued to slide, and the club never made up for the loss of Hershiser. Six different pitchers would start in his slot, and the club would use over 20 pitchers for the season, their most since moving to L.A. By late July they were 13½ games behind the Cincinnati Reds, who were on their way to a wire-to-wire division title. Murray and Daniels both came through big — Murray hit .330 after struggling in 1989 — but Gibson couldn't play regularly until the second half and even then didn't hit with power. Although the club closed with a rush and had the best record in baseball in the second half, they still finished five games behind Cincinnati and were never in the race.

The season was not without its moments, false indicators of impending greatness. On June 4, Ramon Martinez struck out 18 Atlanta Braves while fashioning a 6–0 shutout, the most for a Dodger pitcher since Sandy Koufax fanned the same number in 1962. Incredibly, Martinez could have — and perhaps should have — set an all-time record. He had two strikes on six other hitters, and late in the game Mickey Hatcher, hardly a Gold Glove candidate, made two spectacular plays on balls that on any other day probably would have been base hits and given Martinez even more chances to set a strikeout mark. But that's the kind of season it was for the Dodgers — even spectacular performances didn't mean much.

This was also true for the pitching job turned in by Fernando Valenzuela on June 29. Since his shoulder injury in 1988, Valenzuela had struggled. He lost a few key miles per hour on his fastball and could no longer sneak it past hitters as consistently as before. Yet on this day, after winning only once in six previous starts, he twirled a no-hitter, the first of his career. Then just as suddenly he struggled again.

Hershiser's recovery from shoulder surgery was long and uncertain. Entering the 1991 season, the Dodgers knew he wouldn't be ready until the second half, if then. And by now Gibson was a diminished player. His contract was up, and after the last two seasons the Dodgers didn't want to risk a contract on a player who had recently done so little.

Hall of Fame first baseman and Los Angeles native Eddie Murray played a little over three seasons with the Dodgers and enjoyed his best season in 1990 while batting .330 with 26 home runs and 95 RBIs.

NL RUNS LEADERS

Year	Player	Runs
1941	Pete Reiser	117
1943	Arky Vaughan	112
1945	Eddie Stanky	128
1949	Pee Wee Reese	132
1953	Duke Snider	132
1954	Duke Snider	120
1955	Duke Snider	126
1991	Brett Butler	112

The potential losses made the Dodgers nervous and impatient. There wasn't enough talent ready in the farm system to make a big contribution, and without Gibson and Hershiser they lacked a big star.

Valenzuela simply wasn't that guy anymore — Fernando mania was ancient history. And their other players, while talented, were without personality. Eddie Murray and Kal Daniels were both reticent, and Samuel and Martinez struggled to speak English.

The Dodgers decided they needed a superstar.

Darryl Strawberry was the biggest star on the market, arguably one of the most talented players in baseball. The L.A. native had been a star with the Mets since his rookie season and at age 28 was the youngest player ever to have hit 200 home runs. He was coming off a season in which he had just hit 37 home runs and knocked in over 100.

But those were only numbers. Strawberry was also one of the more troubled players in the major leagues. He had already been through alcohol rehab, there were rumors of drug use and domestic violence, and his battles with teammates and Mets manager Davey Johnson were well publicized. Over the past two seasons the Mets had decided his numbers weren't worth it. Things had come to a head over the last two weeks of the 1990 season, when Strawberry sat out seven games with mysterious back trouble while the Mets were fighting for a title. Team president Frank Cashen said, "We'll be a better franchise without him," and made no effort to retain his services.

The Dodgers had never had a player like Strawberry, not with his raw power and not with his egocentric approach, blunt tongue, and accumulated baggage. He was the opposite of absolutely everything the Dodgers had ever been.

But Claire and company were tired of waiting. It was as if after denying themselves the fruits of free agency for so long, now they couldn't stop. Claire had the notion that somehow, back home in his native L.A., Strawberry would avoid the trouble that had dogged him in New York. They signed Strawberry to a five-year, $20 million contract and over the next few weeks dropped another $16 million on center fielder Brett Butler, pitcher Bob Ojeda, Gary Carter, and others.

At first Strawberry said all the right things. He usually did—at first. "I don't want to be labeled as a bad guy, a person with an attitude. I'm a team player." Strawberry claimed that he had stopped drinking and was born again. The Dodgers certainly hoped so. His signing made Gibson an ex-Dodger, hero to zero.

That decision wasn't nearly as telling, or as shocking, as the one the Dodgers made at the end of spring training. Recently signed to a new contract, Fernando Valenzuela had looked great in the early spring. In mid-March the Dodgers traveled to Monterey, Mexico, to play an exhibition against Milwaukee, and Valenzuela gave up only one hit in five innings before a crowd of 29,000. Peter O'Malley said, "We all know of Fernando's popularity in this country, but to come down here and see it, hear it, feel it, it is one of the most extraordinary moments in my time with the Dodgers."

Two weeks later, after two subpar outings, he was cut. Still relatively young and with 141 wins over ten seasons, the Dodgers decided his $2.5 million were needed more than he was. These were not your father's Dodgers—or even yours anymore.

For the first half of the season Claire looked like a genius. The Dodgers were more potent than they had been in more than a decade. Although Strawberry got off to a slow start, the Dodgers jumped out and at the All-Star break had the best record in baseball, leading the NL West by five games over the Reds and by nine and a half games over the rapidly improving Atlanta Braves, who had finished at the bottom of the division a year before. The Dodgers were bristling with confidence. Strawberry crowed, "We aren't worried about the Braves. Why should we be worried about the Braves?" The Dodgers seemed impervious.

But there was already trouble. The Dodgers were terrible defensively, and Lasorda was distracted. His son Tommy died of AIDS in June, and in the second half of the season, as the Braves caught fire and the Dodger lead narrowed, the players started sniping at one another. Strawberry called Kal Daniels a "cancer," and Strawberry's teammates began to wonder if there were times he showed up at the ballpark impaired.

By September they were in a race with the upstart Braves, and after Lasorda charged that the rest of the division was taking it easy on Atlanta, the entire NL West lined up against the Dodgers as the already out-of-it Padres, Giants, Reds, and Astros openly rooted for the Braves.

Incredibly, with three games left in the season, the Braves caught the Dodgers as L.A. fell before the Padres in one of the worst performances in memory. Despite hitting only three balls out of the infield, the Padres scored six runs in the eighth to come from behind and win 9–4. "I have never seen anything like it," moaned Lasorda. "Ever."

That sent the Dodgers up against the Giants, a team up to the task and looking to play the spoiler on the last two days of the season. Giants fans greeted the Dodgers with Atlanta's "tomahawk chop," and the Giants lineup greeted Ramon Martinez, with only one win in his last five starts, with two first-inning runs. As Bill Plaschke noted in the *Times,* "The team that could not be intimidated seemed intimidated. The team that could not be outplayed in a big game was outplayed in a very big one." Atlanta beat Houston, and after four months in first place, alone, the Dodgers were now chasing the Braves on a very short track.

But they were already beaten. Atlanta had won 55 of their last 76 games. "The way the Braves are playing," said Lenny Harris, "it would be incredible if they lost," And it would be just as incredible if the Dodgers won.

They didn't. The Giants dumped them 4–0 on the final day

In 11 seasons with the Dodgers, Ramon Martinez compiled a record of 123–77, including 20 shutouts. His 1,312 innings pitched placed him sixth all-time among Dodger pitchers in Los Angeles.

of the season as the Braves took the division. No team since the 1962 Dodgers had ever lost so much ground so quickly. "It's like walking down the street and finding $1,000 in an envelope," said Lasorda. "Then when you get to your doorstop somebody taps you on the shoulder and says, 'Buddy, you got

In 1992 first baseman Eric Karros was named National League Rookie of the Year after hitting 20 home runs and driving in 88 runs. In 12 seasons with the Dodgers, he left as one of the top five all-time Los Angeles Dodgers in seven different offensive categories, including home runs, RBIs, hits, extra-base hits, doubles, at bats, and total bases.

my money.'" After the loss, when someone asked San Francisco first baseman Will Clark if he felt bad for the Dodgers, he let out a hearty, cartoon laugh.

The defeat would have a greater impact on the club than their victory in 1988. Since taking over, Fred Claire had played an ever more active role in the makeup of the club. Now, after the loss, he went beyond just providing players and began interfering more directly. In the off-season Eddie Murray, Alfredo Griffin, and Juan Samuel weren't re-signed, and Claire told Lasorda that two rookies, first baseman Eric Karros and shortstop Jose Offerman, were ready to play. That left a lot of holes, but Claire's big free agent acquisition was Strawberry's high school buddy, Eric Davis, an immensely talented player but one also prone to chronic injuries. Claire thought Davis's presence would help Strawberry, and Strawberry was thrilled. "Imagine what it is going to be like to play together at this level," he said. To help out the pitching staff, the Dodgers also picked up knuckleballer Tom Candiotti from Cleveland.

Karros and Offerman weren't ready, particularly Offerman. He could hit a bit and run, but his glove was atrocious, and he would eventually make a backbreaking 40-plus errors at shortstop. Because his failure threw off the rest of the infield, one of the most productive infields in all baseball in 1991 was one of the worst in 1992. And Dodger fans were left with Davis and Strawberry together only in their imaginations. Davis was hurt on and off all year, as was Strawberry, who eventually underwent back surgery and for all intents and purposes was lost for two seasons, tying up salary. Hershiser was back, but he wasn't the same, barely a .500 pitcher and sometimes not even that. Candiotti said accurately, "It wasn't this bad in Cleveland." The Dodgers fell fast, hard, and far, all the way to last place with a pathetic record of 63–99, 35 games out, their worst finish since 1905. In one season the Dodgers had thoroughly collapsed.

If they could have blown it all up they would have, but Strawberry's huge contract slowed Claire's pursuit of free agents. Nevertheless, he added second baseman Jody Reed and third baseman Tim Wallach to shore up the infield while cutting payroll by nearly $10 million. In 1992, for probably the first time since coming to Los Angeles, the club had lost money — by some reports that same $10 million. Attendance had tumbled to an un-Dodgerlike 2.4 million. For better or worse, in 1993 the Dodgers had little choice but to turn to something resembling a youth movement.

And for the first time in a long time, they actually had a few real players to offset pretenders like Offerman. The most notable was catcher Mike Piazza. The Dodgers hadn't had a player with his pedigree or potential since Steve Garvey. Piazza was born to be a Dodger.

Piazza's father Vince had been born only a few blocks away from Lasorda in Norristown, Pennsylvania. They were distant cousins and stayed in touch as Lasorda rose through the Dodger organization and Vincent Piazza became a millionaire running a string of used car dealerships. Vince Piazza and Lasorda dreamed that Mike, who served as the Dodgers' batboy whenever the club played in Philadelphia, would someday play for the Dodgers.

Vince Piazza did everything he could to make that come true, building a batting cage in the basement and even setting up a meeting between his son and the former slugger Ted Williams. Williams told Vince Piazza, "I guarantee you, this kid will hit the ball."

Williams was correct, and Mike Piazza, a first baseman, had a fine high school career. But pro scouts considered him a nonprospect. He couldn't run or throw, and while he could hit, on the professional level first basemen are guys who used to play somewhere else.

He went undrafted, and only his father's connections got Mike Piazza into the University of Miami, one of the top baseball programs in the country. But he couldn't cut it, quit, and went to junior college for a year.

To help Mike Piazza get an offer to attend another division 1 school, Lasorda arranged for him to be drafted by the Dodgers in 1988. He was selected in the 62nd round, the 1,389th player selected. His chances of making it to the big leagues were negligible—the Dodgers had no intention of signing him.

Two months later he still hadn't been offered a contract, but Lasorda pulled strings and got him a tryout. Piazza's bat shined, and the Dodgers decided that if he could learn to become a catcher, his bat would give him a shot at making the major leagues.

Given a chance, Piazza thrived, and he even volunteered to hone his skills at the Dodgers' training facility in the Dominican Republic. He made himself a passable catcher and hit well enough over the next two seasons to become a prospect. In the spring of 1993 he made the Dodgers, took over behind the plate, and started hitting.

The Dodgers still weren't very good—even an early season 11-game win streak left them nowhere—but Piazza was

Talented but troubled superstar Darryl Strawberry returned home to Los Angeles in 1991 and in three seasons with the Dodgers hit only 38 home runs while watching his batting average slide from .265 to .140. Strawberry is shown here with friend John Moseley.

for real. For the season he would hit 35 home runs and bat .318, remarkable numbers for a catcher, and incredible for a rookie. On a team without a likable star, Piazza earned a spot on the All-Star team with his bat, and his story made him stand out. The Dodgers had something to market again, a handsome, talented kid born to be a Dodger who made it through hard work. Lasorda became his PR man, for Piazza's Horatio Alger story reinforced Lasorda's reputation as a manager who could make something out of nothing. Piazza had the potential not only to make the Dodgers the Dodgers again but to make Lasorda Lasorda. He became their most important player since Fernando Valenzuela, a player to build a team around again and give the Dodgers back their identity.

But if Lasorda was right about Piazza, he was equally wrong about another prospect. Ramon Martinez, after winning 20 games, had never quite reached his potential while battling constant arm trouble. Little brother Pedro, a slender 5'11", put up great numbers in the Dodgers' farm system and at age 21 became the best setup man in baseball, striking out more than a hitter an inning in 107 innings of work over 65 appearances.

Pedro Martinez had it *all*—the great fastball, the command, the pitching savvy, and the work ethic. Like Piazza, he wanted to be great. Everything about him screamed the word *prospect*.

But Lasorda would ignore all that, ignore it as much as he had ignored everything about Mike Piazza that said *non-prospect*. Lasorda's old-school instincts told him that Martinez, who had been a starting pitcher in the minor leagues, was too small to be a starter in the majors and that perhaps, as he suspected of brother Ramon, Pedro was just too frail to succeed. It was a curious attitude to take, for Lasorda, the former pitcher, was only 5'9" himself.

If Mike Piazza represents one of Lasorda's greatest success stories, then Pedro Martinez is one of his greatest failures. The Dodgers had been looking for the next Koufax for 30 years. Now they had him and didn't know it.

Although the Dodgers were never in the race, the last game of the season offered them an opportunity at redemption. Entering the final day, the Giants had won 103 games and beat the Dodgers four in a row. But the Braves had also won 103. If Atlanta won and the Dodgers beat the Giants, San Francisco would miss a chance to play in the postseason. And for the Dodgers, 80–81, it was a chance to finish the season at .500, not a small accomplishment.

It was payback time, not just for 1991 but for 1982, 1962, and even 1951. The Dodgers raked the Giants, Piazza cracked two home runs, and pitcher Kevin Gross twirled a shutout as the Dodgers won 12–0. "They beat us in '91 and laughed at us," remembered infielder Lenny Harris. "Let them sit home during the Fall Classic and see how we felt."

The Dodgers' commitment to youth continued in the off-season. Although their recent draft picks had had a spotty record, their efforts in Latin America and in international scouting were beginning to pay off, and the farm system, which under Claire had collapsed as the Dodgers gave up high draft picks for free agents, had been rebuilt. Two outfielders, Raul Mondesi and Henry Rodriguez, were ticketed for jobs in 1994. The Dodgers felt as if they were getting close.

But they made one huge error that killed them. On November 19 they traded Pedro Martinez to Montreal for Delino DeShields, a second baseman.

DeShields was a nice player with speed, but serviceable second basemen are rarely in short supply, and much of DeShields's worth stemmed from his ability to make use of the artificial turf in Montreal, which made him appear better than he really was. He was a .287 hitter on turf, but only .254 on grass. The Expos would put Martinez in the starting rotation, and he would become a star, while in L.A. DeShields would slowly deteriorate and make the trade look worse year after year. Had Martinez stayed a Dodger—and been placed in the starting rotation—he may well have led a Dodger renaissance in the 1990s. Instead, he would serve as a constant reminder of what might have been.

They also expected Darryl Strawberry, his back apparently healthy, to return to form, but his star-crossed career in L.A. was just about over. He failed to show up for the Dodgers' final exhibition game, a traditional tune-up against the Angels. It had been a bad idea for him to return to L.A. and to old friends. He was on a two-day drug and alcohol binge. The Dodgers suspended him immediately.

Lasorda was not understanding. He had taken a harsh view of Steve Howe's drug use several years before, and he took the same attitude toward Strawberry. On Opening Day he was blunt. "First of all," he said, "it [drug use] is against the law. Number two, it is harmful to your body. Number three, it will lead you down a path of destruction." Then he added, "This is not a disease, like leukemia or cancer. This is a weakness."

Although there was little sympathy for Strawberry, Lasorda was, rightly, excoriated in the local press for the comment. The Dodgers, after all, were the team that had long employed Don Newcombe and had been way out in front in regard to alcoholism. Lasorda's comments seemed to be some unnecessary piling on. A month later Strawberry entered the Betty Ford Clinic, and on May 24 he was released. For $20 million Strawberry had hit 38 home runs as a Dodger.

The Dodgers, unlikely as it was, toyed with first place in 1994. It helped immensely that baseball's recent expansion had caused it to add a third division to each league and that the Braves, an emerging dynasty, weren't in the West anymore. Mondesi looked like a five-tool player, and Piazza thoroughly avoided a sophomore slump. Then, with the Dodgers 58–56, three and a half games ahead of the slumping Giants, baseball went on strike. The 1994 season was over.

Unlike most clubs, the Dodgers didn't sit on their hands as the strike stopped the season cold, canceled the World Series, and threatened to disrupt the start of the 1995 season as well. Their trouble with Strawberry and recent success with Dominican players such as Ramon Martinez and Mondesi convinced them that their dollars went further outside of the United States. O'Malley even liked referring to international baseball as his "hobby." In 1987 the club had opened an academy in the Dominican Republic, and in 1994 Korean pitcher Chan Ho Park had even had a brief trial with the Dodgers.

Only one Japanese player, Masanori Murakami, had ever played major league baseball, in the mid-1960s. Since then, professional baseball leagues in the two countries had chosen to respect each other's contracts. Although players from each nation were technically available to play in the other nation under certain conditions, since the 1960s only American players had played in Japan. Thus far, cultural differences, particularly the importance of loyalty in Japanese society, had discouraged Japanese players from going to the United States.

But that was about to change. Pitcher Hideo Nomo was a star in Japan. He wanted to be traded from the Kinetsu Buffaloes, but the club refused. Nomo then found a loophole in his contract, retired, and became a free agent. He was free to play in the major leagues, and after leading the Japanese Pacific League in wins, strikeouts, and walks in four years of the last five, he wanted to try.

Most clubs scoffed at the notion of a Japanese player succeeding in the major leagues. Not only were the Dodgers more open-minded, but they could afford to take a chance. They were intrigued by the notion of opening up the Japanese and Asian market to Dodgers baseball. In the emerging era of the Internet and cable TV, the Dodgers could reach into Asia almost as easily as they had done in Mexico during Fernando mania. In a sense, it was analogous to Walter O'Mal-

---

Catcher Mike Piazza was born to be a Dodger. Named National League Rookie of the Year in 1993, Piazza became one of the greatest hitting catchers in baseball history. Traded by Los Angeles to the Florida Marlins in a salary dump in 1998, Piazza left the Dodgers with a career batting average of .331, best in the Los Angeles era.

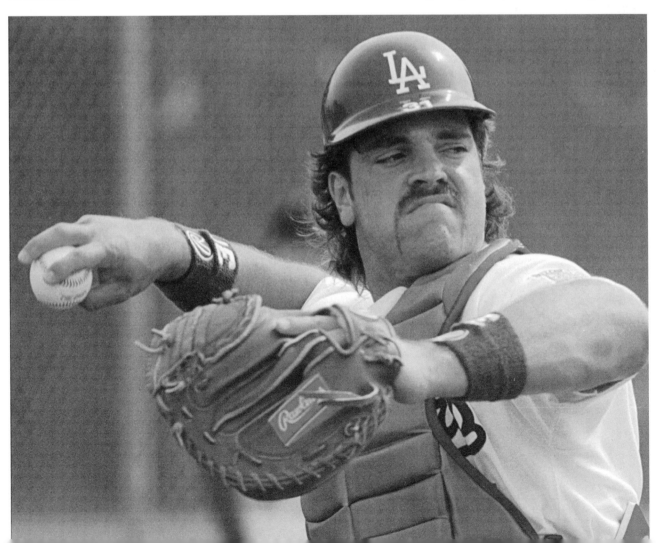

2004

1989

ley looking for answers to his problems in California. Son Peter saw solutions as well from a distant shore that offered the chance not only to make more money but to improve the ballclub.

Although no member of the Dodger organization had ever seen Nomo pitch — they'd seen a two-minute highlight film and knew his stats — on February 13, 1995, they gambled and signed him for $2 million. All they knew was that he had won in Japan, featured a wicked split-finger fastball, and pitched with a bizarre, contorted, halting wind-up that one writer described as "Haiku in motion." It earned him the nickname of "the Tornado."

One more situation factored into their thinking. In the wake of the strike — if it ever ended — fan interest would be low as they blamed players for the whole mess. Uninvolved in the strike, Nomo would be immune to that reaction. Moreover, there was a significant and as yet untapped Japanese American population in the L.A. metropolitan area. And while signing Nomo was certainly not as significant as signing Jackie Robinson, nevertheless, signing the first major Japanese player and opening up the Asian market would add to Peter O'Malley's legacy. Compared to his larger-than-life father, the son seemed weak and wishy-washy. He called for financial restraint, for instance, but had one of the biggest payrolls in baseball. Baseball union chief Marvin Miller summed up Peter O'Malley perfectly when he said, "His father was unusual. And he is not." Signing Nomo would make Peter O'Malley a kind of pioneer.

At length, and after baseball tried the charade of using "replacement players" during spring training, the strike was settled. On April 25 the 1995 season resumed, albeit after the loss of some 18 games.

In many ways the Dodgers came back after the strike a changed team. Hershiser, who never quite regained his form, left as a free agent and signed with Cleveland. The Dodgers had apparently abandoned their infatuation with free agents and were committed to building the club around Piazza, Mondesi, Karros, and other mostly homegrown talent, with more to come. Already they were touting minor league sluggers Todd Hollandsworth, Billy Ashley, and Karim Garcia as the next shade of Dodgers blue.

Pedro Martinez joined his brother Ramon on the Dodger staff in 1992. Manager Tommy Lasorda didn't think he had the stamina to succeed as a starting pitcher. His trade to the Expos prior to the 1994 season was one of the worst in franchise history.

Dodger president Peter O'Malley poses with pitchers Hideo Nomo (left) and Chan Ho Park (right) at a press conference on February 13, 1995, announcing the signing of Nomo to a Dodger contract. Park had signed with Los Angeles in 1994.

The Dodgers got off to a stumbling start, and Colorado, built by free agency, surged in front. Nomo debuted on May 2 against the Giants with five shutout innings, then struggled, but soon he found his groove and it became clear the Dodgers had gotten a bargain.

At first Nomo's emergence seemed to promise to give the Dodger organization a shot in the arm, a plan that they had long been lacking. "Internationalism" would be an apt description of the Dodger approach over the next few seasons as they increasingly looked to new markets like Japan, Korea, and Taiwan for players. At the time the club was thought to be ahead of the curve. Eventually, however, it would become clear that the policy was, at best, incomplete. Talent wasn't equal everywhere, and it would be increasingly difficult for the club to create from a collection of players a coherent team, particularly one that fans viewed, not as a collection of parts, but as all Dodgers.

Despite Nomo's success, by midseason the club was still stumbling along at .500, apparently underachieving. Now in his 19th season, Lasorda was facing some criticism. As he had grown older, he hadn't changed his approach. The younger Dodgers didn't go for his rah-rah style anymore, and in fact,

many seemed to shrink before that approach. Moreover, Lasorda seemed oblivious to the need to bring younger pitchers along slowly. In one stretch of games 21-year-old Ismael Valdes, a potential star, averaged nearly 130 pitches a game. Lasorda was feeling the pressure—one Dodger writer wrote that if Expos manager Felipe Alou were managing the Dodgers, "they'd win by ten, fifteen games."

But if Lasorda felt the pressure, his team didn't. They lacked a strong veteran presence, and their players were from everywhere—Mexico, Japan, Korea, the Dominican Republic, Puerto Rico, and Panama. They never came together as a team. Although Lasorda spoke Spanish, even he couldn't navigate the cultural differences between the various Latin players. The Dodgers left the impression that each player was out for himself, that winning and losing hardly mattered.

It didn't help when at the end of August Fred Claire recalled minor league third baseman Mike Busch. In the spring Busch had been a replacement player. When he joined the Dodgers, he was shunned.

But that made him a hero to fans. The club's staunch union supporters, such as outfielder Brett Butler, were booed mercilessly while Busch became a symbol. The already fractured club started to split apart. At length, they reached an uneasy peace.

Somewhat surprisingly, in the end the Dodgers outlasted the Rockies to win the West, but in the first round of the playoff the Cincinnati Reds bounced them out with dispatch: the Dodgers lost three straight, 7–2, 5–4, and 10–1. Three days later the Dodgers announced that Lasorda would return as manager in 1996. And Lasorda clearly wanted to keep the job—he had his eye on matching Alston's 23-year tenure.

In fact, the Dodgers were now in a position similar to where they'd been in Alston's final years. Even though the club made the playoffs, they were several dramatic steps behind the Atlanta Braves, and it was becoming increasingly clear that Lasorda might not be the man to lead the team into a new era. He'd always used the force of his personality to bring teams together, and that simply didn't work with the worldly new Dodgers. And just as Lasorda and Junior Gilliam had once been drumming their fingers waiting for Alston to retire, there was now a sizable and attractive line of candidates to replace Lasorda. Former Dodger reliever Phil Regan, recently fired as manager of the Orioles, was close to Claire and had long been rumored to be Lasorda's heir apparent. But now coach Reggie Smith, former catcher Mike Scioscia, and former shortstop Bill Russell all had their advocates. Peter O'Malley remained as comfortable with Lasorda, however, as his father had been with Alston.

The 1996 season played out in a rough repeat of 1995: after another close race, the Dodgers just made it into the playoffs again, although they did so on a sour note by losing three straight to San Diego to end the regular season and deliver the division title to the Padres and settling for a wild-card berth. In the playoffs they were quickly bounced out again, this time by eventual champion Atlanta. The Dodgers hadn't won a postseason game since 1988. But other matters dominated the season.

In May outfielder Brett Butler had a cancerous tumor removed from his tonsils, caused by his long-time use of smokeless tobacco. Then in late June Lasorda had a heart attack.

Although the attack wasn't life-threatening, Lasorda had to have an angioplasty. Coach Bill Russell took over as manager on an interim basis as Lasorda brashly predicted he would return by the All-Star break. But the longer Lasorda was out, the easier it became, both for the Dodgers and for Lasorda, to imagine the Dodgers without him in the dugout. Although O'Malley told him, "That uniform is waiting for you," at the same time the Dodgers didn't seem exactly enthusiastic over his return—his health was a concern.

And if they weren't enthusiastic, neither was Lasorda. He knew that managing a baseball team wasn't exactly stress-free, and after the past few seasons he had to know that eventually his time would come. His legacy was secure. For most of his years as Dodger manager, he had been, if not a great manager in his own right, certainly a great manager for the Dodgers. He had been what they needed when he was first hired, and that is what he had remained. Even when his act began to wear thin, the 1988 world championship had earned him several more seasons at the top. Should he have won more? Probably, but some of those losses arose from organizational failures as much as from Lasorda's shortcomings, and there were a few seasons, most notably coming back from two games down against the Yankees in 1981 and in 1988, when the Dodgers probably shouldn't have won at all. Personally and professionally, this was the perfect time for Lasorda to get out.

On July 29, he resigned. "As excitable as I am, I could not go down there and not be the way I've always been," he said, "and I have decided it was best for me and best for the organ-ization to step down." Bill Russell was named manager through the end of the season.

The Dodgers' collapse against San Diego and the three-and-out performance in the playoffs took a bit of the shine off Russell's 48–37 record after taking over for Lasorda, for whom the club had been only 41–35. In the off-season, however, the Dodgers left Russell in place and tried to address a glaring weakness elsewhere. Third base had been filled by committee in 1996. On December 9 they signed Baltimore third baseman Todd Zeile, a good, but not great, player. It was a rather typical Dodger free agent signing in the post-Strawberry era—the acquisition of a part rather than a player who was certain to have a major impact. Other than that acquisition, apart from finally giving up on Delino DeShields, whose performance had deteriorated annually, the Dodgers were strangely quiet. Big deals were for other teams now.

It became clear why on January 6, 1997. At age 58, Peter O'Malley announced he was putting the team up for sale. His children weren't really interested in running the franchise, and he cited "estate taxes" as the logic behind the sale.

But there was more to it than that. The Dodgers weren't on top anymore. The slow erosion of the club over the last decade and their failure to win a game in the postseason had taken a toll. While they were still competitive, and in fact, would be favored to win the West in 1997, they really weren't in the same league with Atlanta and the Yankees. Baseball commissioner Bud Selig was trying to enforce fiscal discipline and revenue sharing, essentially forcing big market clubs like the Dodgers to restrain their activities. O'Malley didn't want to practice such restraint, but unlike guys like George Steinbrenner, he also didn't want to run counter to the wishes of MLB.

His father had been a giant in the game, but Peter O'Malley was just one of 30 other owners, and not one whom Bud Selig turned to for advice. In recent years O'Malley had flirted with the notion of building a football stadium and bringing an NFL team back to L.A., but he had been thwarted. He simply lacked his father's aggressiveness and the brash confidence that comes after building something, which is how Walter O'Malley felt after winning the Dodgers' first world championship in Brooklyn and then winning in L.A. Peter O'Malley didn't have that—he didn't have any "Brooklyn" in him. The Dodgers had been delivered to him ready to wear. But by now the fabric was wearing thin. The Dodgers were a familiar old coat in Los Angeles now, but no more essential to L.A.'s wardrobe than the O'Malley name was anymore to the Dodger team.

As a business, under Peter O'Malley the Dodgers had been as successful as any in the game, and in 27 seasons the club had finished first or second 18 times. But in the divisional system that didn't mean as much as it once had, and the club had won only two world championships. Plenty of opportunities had been missed along the way.

Of course, putting the team up for sale wasn't quite the same as selling it. That would take a while, although O'Malley had already identified a buyer. Meanwhile, O'Malley clearly wanted to win on his way out the door. The 1997 season, however, would end up as just one more missed opportunity, in almost every possible way, and one more reminder of what the Dodgers had become.

It started with Piazza. He wanted a long-term deal — six years at $60 million, not an outrageous price at the time for such a prodigious talent. Although Piazza wasn't a commanding presence in the clubhouse, he was still the closest thing to Mr. Dodger the club had, and in the wake of Lasorda's retirement he was their only player with a national profile.

But now that O'Malley had decided to sell, he didn't want the team burdened with long-term contracts. Piazza signed for two years at $15 million and wasn't happy. He bitched and moaned during the spring and made it clear that he was a franchise player who was ready to move on.

In 1997, ten years after the Al Campanis incident, baseball celebrated Jackie Robinson again, this time on the 50th anniversary of his promotion to the major leagues. And now the Dodgers had one African American player on their roster, reserve outfielder Wayne Kirby. To be fair, the club also included many Latino players with African backgrounds, and for a wide variety of reasons, including MLB's abject indifference, there were fewer and fewer African American players in the majors every year. But for the Dodgers to have only one African American player was hardly the legacy Robinson had wanted to leave behind. Don Newcombe, still the club's director of community relations, was blunt. "If Jackie was alive today and saw what was going on," he said, "it would kill him." Newcombe went on to level some pointed criticism at the organization. "You don't see the Dodgers getting kids out of Watts," he observed, "but if they hear of a player in Japan, Korea, or Santo Domingo, they'll do it. . . . There's nothing you can do but go out and do your job and keep your mouth shut and hope it gets better." It didn't. By the end of the year

L.A. Times reporter Bob Nightengale, who wrote a two-part series on the Dodgers' problems with race that angered club officials, would file a suit in which he charged that the ballclub's ire over the series had led to his dismissal from the Times.

Meanwhile, the Dodgers went out and continued their dysfunctional underperformance. From the start the clubhouse was a mess, a fractured place of cliques and factions, often split along racial and cultural lines. Bill Russell was no Lasorda — one observer described Lasorda as someone who didn't spend five minutes a day not speaking, and Russell as someone who didn't talk for as much as five minutes a day.

What kind of year was it? Less than an hour after the team held a closed-door, players-only meeting to talk about "team unity," Ismael Valdes and Eric Karros nearly came to blows. Even the manager got into it, as Russell had harsh words with both Valdez and Pedro Astacio in the dugout after they were removed from games.

On an individual basis, the Dodgers seemed loaded. They had a deep pitching staff, speed, and power. Mike Piazza had the greatest offensive season by a catcher in the history of the game, hitting .362 with 40 home runs. Over six weeks in July and August the club showed their potential, going 39–17, and they even led the division until mid-September. Then they totally and completely collapsed and missed the playoffs altogether. As Eric Karros had commented, "You could spend every last dime on every world-class psychologist, and they couldn't figure this team out."

And the whole time, hanging over the club like a sword, was the impending sale. By the season's end it was common knowledge that the new owner would be Rupert Murdoch's News Corp. Murdoch was an Australian media mogul best known in the United States for his ownership of Fox and putting pinup girls on page 3 of his tabloids. Although Murdoch was loaded, no one was quite sure what Murdoch ownership would mean — Jim Murray wondered aloud, "He's Australian. What does he know about baseball?" In the go-go economic frenzy of the late 1990s, the word *synergy* was tossed around a lot — there was supposed to be some synergy between Murdoch's broadcasting empire and the Dodgers, although no one could ever say exactly what that synergy was or what it would mean. But Disney had recently purchased the Anaheim franchise in the National Hockey League — which they named the "Mighty Ducks," after a movie — and the American League Anaheim Angels. Perhaps that was why Murdoch was interested—he did eventually manage to thwart Disney's effort to build a cable channel around the Angels. The standard assumption was that Murdoch would try to out-Steinbrenner Steinbrenner and buy a pennant, for money had never been an object to anything Murdoch really wanted to do. Observers liked to cite his approach after he bought an Australian rugby team. He didn't just try to sign every player for the club—he tried to start his own league for them.

Yet at the same time, for such a high-profile player, Murdoch himself was oddly distant throughout the entire process. Unlike most baseball owners, who buy teams to become famous, Murdoch already was famous. As his interest in the Dodgers developed, he treated the deal like the inconsequential part of his portfolio it was, sending his underlings out to negotiate and make nice with MLB. He tended to get personally involved with projects only during a time of crisis, and only then when there was big money at stake. The Dodgers didn't qualify. They really weren't important enough.

On March 19, 1998, MLB finally approved Murdoch's purchase of the Dodgers for $311 million. It had taken nearly a year for all those dollars to assuage fears that Fox, which already owned baseball's national broadcasting rights and local rights for 22 of 30 teams through Fox Sports Net, wouldn't have too much influence on the game. Only the White Sox and Braves, owned by TBS honcho Ted Turner, voted against the deal.

And on that day, as would soon become apparent, the Dodgers as they had always been ceased to exist—or at least went into hiding. The sword proved to be double-edged. For a ton of money Fox bought a business, a product, and a franchise, but when it did, it cut the team off from its history and tradition. Fox left all that on the curb when it cleaned out the offices. And did it ever clean out the offices.

The Dodgers stumbled out of the gate 0–4 in 1998 and were effectively eliminated from postseason contention. While O'Malley stayed on as a consultant, Fox bean counters took over in the front office and took the attitude, "Gee, won't it be fun to run a baseball team?" For the next four years the theme of the Dodgers might as well have been a version of one of the network's reality shows—"When Fox Attacks" would have been an apt description for what took place at Dodger Stadium. Dodger fans got to witness the carnage over and over again.

Until May 17, Fred Claire thought he was still the general manager. Then Claire, O'Malley, Lasorda, and Russell all

Gary Sheffield was traded to the Dodgers in May 1998 as part of the deal that sent Mike Piazza to the Florida Marlins. Sheffield proved to be a solid performer in his brief stint as a Dodger, hitting .316 while averaging 36 home runs per season. On January 15, 2002, he was traded to the Braves for outfielder Brian Jordan and pitchers Odalis Perez and Andy Brown.

HAS ANYBODY SEEN THE DODGERS?

Howard Bryant

SINCE TIME IMMEMORIAL, OR AT LEAST SINCE the ball was held together with symmetric red stitching, the house of baseball has stood on four sinewy legs, each possessing its own considerable horsepower that far outmuscled any pretenders to the throne. If the great trumpeter Miles Davis said the entire history of jazz could be summed up in four words, "Louis Armstrong, Charlie Parker," so too can the history of baseball, but in five:

Yankees, Red Sox, Cardinals, Dodgers.

They are baseball royalty, the four monarchs that ruled the last century empirically, the tribute received being nothing less than sovereign title for generations — a lifetime pass of sorts. It used to be said that baseball survived on the illusion of importance, each nine innings a chapter in a daily, season-long book whose unknown outcome represents the suspense of summer. It is a narrative most often run through one or more of these dynastic main characters.

Some teams, like the New York–San Francisco Giants or the Philadelphia–Kansas City–Oakland Athletics, might try to barge in on this private gathering, but they would be nothing more than party crashers who would be asked to leave.

The Giants of John McGraw, Christy Mathewson, Willie Mays, Juan Marichal, and Barry Bonds might argue, eager to form a quintet. The Giants own a fine pedigree, replete with transcendent stars and championships (seven), but they cannot compete in the influence sphere of on-field dominance of the Yankees — who do not need their résumé reread — or the historic foresight of the Dodgers.

The Giants last won a World Series in 1954, when they were still in Harlem, in the Polo Grounds, plotting to flee both a changing neighborhood and a decaying ballpark. They too went to California, but it was the vision of Walter O'Malley, the Brooklyn Dodgers' owner — instead of their own baron, Horace Stoneham — that put them there. Had O'Malley had visions of moving to Havana, would Stoneham have brought his Giants to Puerto Rico instead of going to California?

The A's of Philadelphia boasted Mack, who built two machines, in the teens with Collins, Chief Bender, and Home Run Baker, then before the Depression with Foxx, Grove, and Waddell. The A's of Oakland fussed and feuded first with the mustachioed Fingers, Catfish, and Reggie, then were resuscitated a generation later with Eckersley, Jose, and McGwire. Of dynasty, there is no doubt. When the A's were great, they won in bunches, netting titles in '10, '11, and '13, then again in '29, '30, and a Series appearance in '31. In Oakland they won the trifecta from '72 to '74 and were the most fearsome team from '88 to '90, winning it all in '89.

But dynasties are made not only of muscle but of myth, and in between the winning was a whole lot of losing, evidenced by 15 — count 'em, 15 — 100-loss seasons in their history. Their old roommates the Phillies have 14, proof that the garbage wasn't the only thing that stunk in Philly.

For better or worse, none of the other franchises could power the game or boast more influence for nearly three-quarters of a century as the classic quartet.

The Cardinals, devoid of the promise of the West Coast and

the vast media reach of the East, are simply baseball's backbone. Their fans are not East Coast bitter ("What are we *paying* you for, you bum!") or West Coast cool ("Plenty of playoff tickets available, even on game day!"), but earnest and grateful. *Don't worry, that grounder won't eat you up next time, kid. We know you did your best.*

White loafers may be common at Busch Stadium, but the Cards did have star power. If the Giants claim the Say Hey Kid, then the Cardinals can parry with Stan the Man. The Dodgers had Koufax, but the Cards had Gibson. The Yankees had Murderers' Row, but the Cards had the Gashouse Gang.

They win too, without awe of the big dogs. The Yankees? No problem. Beat 'em in '42 and '64. The Red Sox? Beat them in '46 and '67. Nine World Series titles tie the Cards for second with the A's behind the Yankees' 26, and as recently as 1998, with Mark McGwire's breaking of Roger Maris's home run record, St. Louis returned to the epicenter of the baseball world.

The Cardinals, back in the dusty old days, were responsible for the growth and adoption of the farm system, which may not have made its founder, Branch Rickey, a hit with the journeyman looking for a shot at the Show or — back in the reserve clause days — the unfortunate talented first baseman playing behind Lou Gehrig. The Cardinals' impact on the game is unquestionable.

As has been duly noted ad infinitum, the Red Sox haven't won a World Series since 1918 and had in Tom Yawkey an owner for whom *progress* was a word as bad as *communism*. Nevertheless, the Red Sox are dominant, if not in the win column then certainly commercially, behind the scenes and on the bookshelves. The term "baseball book" would hardly exist as a genre without the volumes of chronicled, operatic futility produced by the New England literati.

Without the Red Sox, three of the last seven World Series champions would have had no reason to pop champagne, for the wild card exists only from the defeated mind of former Boston owner John Harrington, whose inability to beat the Yankees led to the advent of a concept — the second-place playoff team — never before realized in the century and a quarter of baseball theretofore. Every wild-card team that wins the World Series should kneel before Harrington and kiss the ring of the man who gave second place value.

The Yankees are, quite obviously, the Yankees. They carry the game when it is flush, and the game suffers when they are down. Some teams have beaten them, but they've beaten everybody more. There is only one sporting franchise in the United States that could argue that it owns an imperialistic cultural stamp similar to Coca-Cola or McDonald's, and it is the Yankees. Anyone believing this to be an overstatement is either in the hardest denial or is truly convinced all those kids in Tegucigalpa wear Yankees gear because they actually care about baseball. Where there is nothing else America, there is still the golden arches and the interlocked NY.

Schoolchildren learn the Pledge of Allegiance, memorizing it without knowing much of what it means or its origins, and are likely as unwitting about learning naked capitalism from the Yankees, but it is the Dodgers, not the U.S. Steel Yankees, who get taught in American history classes. Students might not know the origin of the name Brooklyn (it's Dutch!), but they know where the end of baseball apartheid took place. They know Jackie Robinson played for the Dodgers and was the first black player in the major leagues as surely as they know Washington crossed the Delaware.

The phrase "West Coast swing" was only a musical term before Walter O'Malley had his idea to make the Dodgers so big that they would have *two* histories, one in Brooklyn and one in Los Angeles. Was Walter O'Malley Lewis, or Clark, or both? As self-deprecating as Jewish humor is, Sandy Koufax resonated with the Dodgers to no less a degree as did the Brooklyn club with blacks and Robinson. In Jewish households, because of Koufax, the Dodgers *belonged*.

In the American League, on the East Coast, the West Coast Dodgers were always present, representing that shadowy, foreign National League, because they always won, which meant they were always on TV in a time when being on TV mattered (*everybody* is on TV today). They were the personality of that league in the 1950s, the '60s (along with the Cardinals), the '70s, and the '80s (along with the Cardinals — a theme is emerging here). They were the Anti-Yankees, clean-shaven Good Guys. They were identifiable by the little fat guy named Lasorda, who, like Los Angeles, fooled everybody.

When power is considered today, it is done so under the rubric of names like Steinbrenner and Selig, but baseball didn't move unless O'Malley offered an affirmative nod. He

was kingmaker and puppet master. Robinson provided the Dodgers the moral plane, O'Malley the biceps.

The Yankees won, but so did the Dodgers. From the time the Dodgers moved to L.A. in '58 until Kirk Gibson in 1988, the Yankees went to the World Series ten times, winning it five times. The Dodgers went nine times, and took the big trophy home—you guessed it—five times.

Maybe Faust was at game one of the 1988 World Series, because not long after Gibson's ball sailed away, out of the reach of the Eck and over the head of Canseco, so too did the Dodgers' soul. They have been gone since winning that last World Series, gone in the standings but more importantly in the imagination. They won, and then they left.

The Yankees are still here, in the mix, making headlines, winning titles. The Red Sox are still breaking hearts, and while the Cardinals haven't done much trophy-hoisting lately, thanks to McGwire, his restoration of Roger Maris, and his dignity during the summer of 1998, the organization can stand on the pantheon of giants.

Where, then, have the Dodgers gone? They weren't the black holes that you learn about in science class, exhausted giant stars, imploding with violence in one tempestuous, shattering moment. Somehow the Dodgers have gone underground, blended in, joined baseball's witness protection program. Worse, they went corporate, disappearing in a gray flannel suit.

As the millennium inches forward, the quartet is perilously close to becoming a trio, the lifelong pass not revoked as much as it's been surrendered. As baseball approaches the 2004 season, one question it never seemed necessary to ask has turned into baseball's greatest mystery:

"Has anybody seen the Dodgers?"

In football they wouldn't care. They wouldn't care that Rickey, Robinson, and Reese begat the Davises, Drysdale, and Koufax, which begat Garvey, Cey, and Fernando, which somehow begat Adrian Beltre, Chan Ho Park, and Billy Ashley. The football barons would light cigars to toast the puzzling reality that the Brooklyn Dodgers seem more alive than today's Dodgers, that Robinson dragging a bunt along first and battering the pitcher covering first is a more exciting story than anything the Dodgers did in the 1990s. Football would celebrate the death of the dynasty, that the Anaheim Angels and San Diego Padres, both created by the Dodgers and Buzzie

Bavasi, and the Giants, the little-brother foils, are all more successful than the Dodgers of today.

They would toast that in the 1990s the Dodgers didn't play for a championship at least once. The last arid decade of which this could be spoken was the 1930s, when for the first two years of the decade they weren't even the Dodgers. They were the Brooklyn Robins.

Of the four sports Americans care about, only the Yankees and hockey's Montreal Canadiens can say they've been as powerful as long. The Yankees have played for a title in every decade since the '20s, while *Les Habitants* have *won* at least one Stanley Cup in every decade since the teens. The Canadiens, though, find themselves nearly as rusty and withered as the Dodgers, fallen victim to a global and national economy that has shrunken the Canadian dollar as much as their muscular legacy. And the Canadian government, less concerned with hockey than governing, is not likely to offer a helping hand.

In baseball, which revels in money, cash was supposed to rule. The Dodgers were flush, and having boatloads of dough was supposed to guarantee an on-field colossus designed to stomp flat-busted opponents who had nothing but lint in their pockets (see New York Yankees, 1996–present, for reference). Not only did the Dodgers not win anything, but they would over the decade become the standard of what not to be.

The arrival of Fox, ousting an O'Malley dynasty tired of uncontrollable spending in baseball, may have provided the final, empirical evidence that Faust was sitting in those box seats that October night in 1988. The Dodgers, with all that Murdoch money, were going to be the West Coast Yankees, something they actually *were* during the 1960s and 1970s. During an era of corporate buzz terms like *synergy* and *convergence,* the Dodgers were going to flex their marketing muscle. Players would come to Los Angeles the way they were coming to the Lakers, not just to shoot hoop, but movies too. Fox possessed the power and reach to make it happen. Fox possessed everything, except soul.

The result, as the embers crackled over charred soil, was unmitigated disaster. The superstar for the millennium, Mike Piazza, was traded in a twister of accusations, hard feelings, and corporate hardball. The O'Malley family tradition, cultivated over a half-century, was dismantled, brick by brick, bringing tears and rage from the few holdovers who watched

the wrecking ball hit new targets daily. Lasorda left the dugout, replaced by company men named Hoffman and Tracy. Davey Johnson won, but found himself, as he always did, out of a job.

Murdoch money lined the pockets of Kevin Brown to a record $105 million, seven-year contract. Darren Dreifort received five years, $55 million, Shawn Green six years at $84 million. The Dodgers haven't played a postseason game since any of these contracts were signed.

The Dodger fade wasn't only about winning but about impression, about *presence*. The Yankees of the '80s didn't win, but Billy was there, and so was George, Mattingly, Winfield, and Howie Spira, reminding everyone that the shadow engulfing us wasn't a skyscraper but the ever-present specter of the Yankees. You knew they'd be back.

The Dodgers have eroded their own monument. The gallantry of Rickey, Robinson, and the "noble experiment" has given way to the last images of Al Campanis, a modern lineage of unhappy black stars — Darryl Strawberry, Eric Davis, Gary Sheffield—as well as a racially fractured clubhouse of blacks, whites, Koreans, Japanese, Dominicans, Puerto Ricans, and Cubans that underscores the complexities of diversity instead of its virtues.

West Coast baseball is still about cool, but San Francisco cool, Pac Bell Park cool, and for years ex-Dodger, Dusty Baker cool. Since 1988 the Giants have won four division titles, been to the World Series twice, and with Barry Bonds light the marquee. Nobody talks about the Dodgers, not like they used to.

So where are the Dodgers? And better yet, when are they coming back? Fox, not liking baseball on its balance sheet, finally began the process of selling out, like CBS did to Steinbrenner back in the day, and Disney did after winning the World Series down I-5. Murdoch money will soon be laundered clean again, and instead of taking the stairs, the Dodgers may yet ride the elevator back to the penthouse, where the Cardinals, Red Sox, and Yankees are playing cards, staring at the empty chair. Instead of asking the whereabouts of the Dodgers, maybe a better question should first be posed: do Faustian bargains have a statute of limitations?

Howard Bryant covered baseball for both the *San Jose Mercury News* and the *Bergen Record* before joining the *Boston Herald* as a senior writer. He is the author of *Shut Out: A Story of Race and Baseball in Boston*.

Right-handed pitcher Kevin Brown signed the largest free agent contract ever for a pitcher when he joined the Dodgers following the 1998 season. In five seasons in Los Angeles, Brown endured three stints on the disabled list yet compiled a record of 58–32.

found out that in the larger scheme of things they were way, way down on the chain of command. Chase Carey, a Murdoch lieutenant who served as chairman of Fox TV, engineered a trade with the Marlins. The Florida club, after winning the World Series, was dumping everyone. Carey traded Mike Piazza to Florida for slugger Gary Sheffield, catcher Charles Johnson, third baseman/outfielder Bobby Bonilla, and outfielder Jim Eisenreich.

Jaws dropped all around baseball as the Dodgers took on more than $20 million worth of contracts for 1998. But some hoped that, money aside, the trade made the Dodgers demonstrably better.

It didn't, for it didn't address the team issues that had been tearing the club apart, and it didn't deliver any pitching. Of

the four players the Dodgers acquired, only Sheffield would come close to earning his salary. The Dodgers were still a .500 team. But the Fox executives weren't done with their makeover.

When he first learned of the trade, Claire nearly resigned before being talked out of it. But now he got blamed for the club's desultory performance as the Fox pogrom axed everybody not with the program. Hideo Nomo was traded, and on June 21 Claire and Bill Russell were both fired. But Tommy Dodger got to stay—Lasorda popped up as the Dodgers' interim GM and named Glenn Hoffman, with a 27–41 record in triple-A, the new Dodger manager, then filled the coaching staff with his cronies. Fox even ditched the Dodgers' classic uniform, occasionally sending the team out onto the field in "Dodger blue" softball shirts. When one reporter asked Expos manager Felipe Alou how he thought Lasorda would fare as GM, Alou replied, "He didn't like Pedro Martinez and got rid of John Wetteland." On his way out the door, Bill Russell charged that Lasorda had undermined him from the start. "Everybody's numb," said Eric Karros.

Lasorda was busy, as if trying to make a fast impression, but activity was not the same as acumen. He traded the Dodgers' best prospect, Paul Konerko, to the Reds for closer Jeff Shaw, oblivious to the fact that Shaw had the right to demand a trade—a rookie mistake. He then dealt reliever Jim Bruske to the Padres, whom the Dodgers were fighting in the West, for a low-level prospect. "We're helping them out?" wondered one Dodger player.

The Lasorda era ended as abruptly as it began. With attendance dropping and the so-so Dodgers flirting with a .500 record, the club changed course again. After six months, Fox had finally concluded what everyone else in baseball knew—the farm system was empty and the whole organization needed to recharge. They hired Baltimore's assistant general manager Kevin Malone as GM. He was one of baseball's brash young guns, a former GM boy wonder in Montreal, where he had developed a reputation for being an astute evaluator of talent and for his ability to get a lot out of a little—which meant acquiring talent cheap. Malone was thrilled to be back in the big chair and told talk show host Jim Rome, "There's a new sheriff in town, and the Dodgers will be back." It was a bad way to start: his words would not pass unnoticed and would come back time and time again to haunt him.

The Dodgers finished third, 83–79, and no one gave a damn. Although, on the one hand, Fox wanted to take a long view, it now realized that dumping Piazza was a mistake and that the club needed a marquee player while they rebuilt. Fox sent Malone in pursuit of free agent Randy Johnson, the game's most dominant pitcher.

But Johnson didn't like the fast lane, and rather than come home to California, he chose to sign with Arizona. Like a pouting child denied a toy, the Dodgers then decided to make a run at power sinkerball pitcher Kevin Brown, a colorless loner who had recently jumped from club to club, helping both the Marlins and Padres to the World Series but warming few hearts and making few friends along the way. He was unquestionably a great pitcher, but he was as bland as his name, prickly to the press, and impossible to market.

Those were some of the reasons Brown wasn't exactly drawing contract offers like flies. Another was concern over his balky elbow. After missing out on Johnson, however, Malone wanted Brown badly. He bid against himself and finally signed Brown to the most lucrative contract in baseball history at the time, a seven-year deal worth $105 million. Most thought that by the end of the contract, at which time Brown would be 41, he would probably have a hard time changing lightbulbs with his right arm. Baseball laughed, and then laughed even more when Malone threw another $30 million around to land fading center fielder Devon White and keep pitcher Carlos Perez, then traded Charles Johnson and prospect Roger Cedeno for injury-prone catcher Todd Hundley. Malone wanted to hire Felipe Alou as manager, but the TV execs insisted he hire veteran manager Davey Johnson instead.

On paper, the Dodgers looked like a hit. They opened the 1999 season odds-on favorites to win everything. Johnson even said that with the talent the Dodgers had, "they could hire the village idiot and win."

But it was swings and misses all around, and maybe the village idiot could have done a better job. The Dodgers were horrible in 1999, at least for a team with one of the highest payrolls in baseball. Brown won 18 games, but Perez won only two. Sheffield hit 34 home runs—Todd Hundley hit .207. And the Mets, who had acquired Mike Piazza from Florida, won the pennant. The Dodgers finished third in the West, 77–85.

The answer was not more money, but it was the only answer the Dodgers had. On the plus side, in the off-season they dealt disgruntled Raul Mondesi to Toronto for talented outfielder Shawn Green, swapping huge contracts, and brought back Orel Hershiser. On the down side, they gave away Ismael Valdes and second baseman Eric Young to the

Cubs. Hershiser was 41, and Green, one of baseball's few Jewish players, was more publicity-shy than Koufax had been. Fox also started intimating that it might not be interested in sticking around for the long haul. It sold 10 percent of the team to former Warner Brothers executive Bob Daly, a Brooklyn native, made him chairman and CEO, and began to act like an absentee landlord.

As the Dodgers floundered, Malone took a beating. He was unprepared for the scrutiny that came with his job and put his foot in his mouth over and over again. One writer described his acquisitions as "has-beens, retreads, headcases and flameouts, all paid like future Hall of Famers." Worse, it made fans dizzy keeping track of who was coming

---

On November 8, 1999, the Dodgers shipped outfielder Raul Mondesi and pitcher Pedro Borbon to Toronto for outfielder Shawn Green and infielder Jorge Nunez. In 2001 Green enjoyed a breakout season, shattering the Dodger single-season home run record with 49 and driving in 125 runs while batting .297.

NL SAVES LEADERS

1947	Hugh Casey	18
1954	Jim Hughes	24
1956	Clem Labine	19
1957	Clem Labine	17
1966	Phil Regan	21
1974	Mike Marshall	21
1996	Todd Worrell	44
2003	Eric Gagne	55

the club's performance like the new-age GM he was — he'd done his job, everyone else had failed. Davey Johnson was fired and replaced by taciturn Jim Tracy, Johnson's bench coach.

Malone was running out of time and seemed to know it. In the spring of 2001 he asked for and failed to get a vote of confidence, and then on April 14, as Malone watched the Dodgers play the Padres in San Diego, he got into an altercation of sorts with several fans. Depending on whose account one believes, Malone either acted with dignity and restraint in the face of a withering verbal attack by a fan or was unnecessarily confrontational and aggressive. The fan went to the press, and the story took on a life of its own. Four days later Malone was asked to resign. Daly first installed former pitching coach Dave Wallace as interim GM before hiring Dan Evans, who had served a long apprenticeship with the White Sox, to the post. Whatever.

The Dodgers of 2001 would be no better than the 2000 team, but they would be more fun. By default, Paul LoDuca, a career minor leaguer who had failed in several brief trials with the Dodgers, took over as catcher. LoDuca grew up in Arizona but had been born in Brooklyn, and his heritage made him a story. His father, said LoDuca, was one of those guys who, after the Dodgers moved to California, "vowed never to root for them again."

But the way the son hit in 2001 gave the father little choice, because Paul LoDuca cracked 25 home runs and drove in 90 runs. That paled next to the numbers put up by Green and Sheffield, who struck 49 and 36 home runs, respectively, but LoDuca was making only $230,000, about 1 percent of their combined take. That made him a working-class hero to fans, and for the first time in several seasons the Dodgers seemed a little like overachievers. Despite the loss of Kevin Brown to an elbow injury, they contended into September before finally falling to the Giants and Diamondbacks and being eliminated for postseason contention on September 29. But there was finally a little life in Dodgers Stadium again.

Being in contention was at least on the radar again as something important to the team, and to that end, after the season — in which they again finished with an 86–76 record — the Dodgers dealt dissatisfied Gary Sheffield to the Braves for Brian Jordan and pitcher Odalis Perez. Jordan was no Sheffield, but Perez was a prospect, and it was estimated that in 2001 the Dodgers had lost somewhere between $30 million and $50 million. Under Fox, the team had been an unmit-

and going, who was pouting, and who wanted to be traded. Bill Plaschke wrote: "Fox has taken the corner grocery store and turned it into Wal-Mart, with huge aisles, fluorescent lights, and players you've never seen before. You go to a game now, and it's almost like you need a map."

Depending on one's perspective, the most notable event of 2000 was either the $100 million refurbishment of Dodger Stadium or one day in May when the Dodgers played the Cubs at Wrigley Field. The Dodgers had won eight of their last ten and were finally, perhaps, catching fire and playing to their potential when, in the ninth inning of a close game, a drunken Cub fan grabbed catcher Chad Kreuter's hat, which caused more than a score of teammates to charge into the stands and brawl with the Wrigley faithful. A total of 16 Dodgers were suspended for a total of more than 80 games. The Dodgers won 86 games for the season and ended up missing the playoffs again. Malone distanced himself from

igated disaster on the field and off. Even though the Dodgers had the second-largest television market in the country and all the muscle Fox could muster, ratings were down too.

That performance finally began to make an impression on the media conglomerate. Beginning in 2001, there had been rumors that Murdoch was looking to sell out. He had succeeded in using the Dodgers to help build the Fox Sports West regional cable network, fighting off Disney, and now that Disney was looking to sell the Anaheim Angels, Fox had made its point and was also looking to get out of baseball. In Murdoch's calculation, the value of the club had been extracted and transferred to the broadcasting arm, making continued ownership of the team immaterial. And after September 11, 2001, the economic outlook wasn't bright anyway. The club went on the block.

In such a situation, winning becomes almost untenable and insignificant as other issues become far more important than what happens on the field. In 2002 and 2003 Fox treated the Dodgers with caution. It made no bold moves to help the club but simply maintained the status quo. Only the acquisition of free agent Japanese pitcher Kazuhisa Ishii provided any real evidence that the club was looking ahead at all, for other transactions, such as the addition of first baseman Fred McGriff and Jeromy Burnitz, would be for players either clearly on the downside or coming off injuries. They were the kind of deals that clubs make to keep a team from collapsing, not to win. And while Ishii, with his monster curveball, would prove valuable, he would not inspire the same response as Nomo or the other Japanese players now playing in the major leagues, like Ichiro Suzuki.

In both seasons the Dodgers would again serve as nominal contenders, compiling an 92–70 record in 2002 and 85–77 in 2003, pretenders in the race for a division title or even a wild-card berth. Reliever Eric Gagne would often be their only distinguished player.

Before 2002, Gagne had struggled in parts of three seasons with the Dodgers, accumulating a record of 11–14. He was perhaps best described by Davey Johnson, who damned him with faint praise in calling him "the best French-Canadian player I've ever had."

Gagne, who grew up just outside Montreal and didn't learn English until he signed a pro contract, is one of only a handful of French-Canadians to play in the majors. As a kid, he played hockey, where his hulking physique made him a goon, but Gagne loved baseball better, and his fastball got

Brooklyn native Paul LoDuca spent eight seasons in the Dodgers' minor league system before securing the catcher's job in Los Angeles. In 2001 LoDuca led the Dodgers with a .320 batting average. That same season he hit 25 home runs with only 30 strikeouts—the lowest total for any player hitting 25 or more homers since Yogi Berra struck out only 29 times in 1956.

him into college in the United States. Entering the 2002 season, Gagne was at a crossroads in his career. He was essentially a fastball pitcher without a great fastball, the kind of pitcher apparently destined to struggle and fight to stay in the majors.

Then, by default, he got a shot in the Dodger bullpen. Gagne's hockey mentality turned out to be far better suited to

Quebec native Eric Gagne exploded on the scene in 2002 when the reliever saved 52 games while compiling a 4–1 won-lost record with a 1.97 ERA. The following season the right-hander became the seventh Dodger to win the Cy Young Award when he saved 55 games with a 1.20 ERA.

four saves in 2002 and converting every save opportunity he was presented with on his way to 55 saves and a Cy Young Award in 2003. For those two seasons the most compelling sight in Dodger Stadium was Gagne taking the mound accompanied by the ear-numbing sound of Guns 'n' Roses. Swathed in goggles because his eyes are so scratched up from hockey fights that he can no longer wear contacts, Gagne is many things the Dodgers haven't often been recently — emotional, aggressive, colorful, and oddly exotic. Unfortunately, the club has yet to take full advantage of either his dominant presence or his personality.

After the 2003 season, Fox's long-anticipated sale of the team finally appeared ready to take place. But Murdoch wasn't prepared to sell out entirely. News Corp would retain the lucrative Fox Sports West regional cable network. The sale would include only the ballclub, Dodger Stadium, and other Dodger properties in Vero Beach, the Dominican Republic, and elsewhere. Even though the Dodgers had lost money virtually every season since Murdoch acquired the club, Murdoch's asking price of more than $400 million made the sale of the club at least a break-even proposition — and that didn't include the hundreds of millions in value retained Sports West.

But the split scared off a number of suitors who might otherwise have been interested. Without the broadcasting revenue, and with a bloated payroll of more than $100 million, potential buyers were probably looking at several seasons of cost-cutting while bleeding red ink before turning a profit.

At length, and at last, one buyer looked upon favorably by both Murdoch's News Corp and baseball commissioner Bud Selig emerged. On October 10, 2003, 49-year-old Boston-based real estate developer Frank McCourt, who had failed in previous bids to build a new park in Boston, buy the Red Sox, and buy the Anaheim Angels, had his bid of $430 million accepted. "We have the deepest respect for the history and traditions of the Dodgers," he said at the time. "Our immediate goals are returning the Dodgers to the World Series and making each fan's experience at Dodger Stadium the absolute best that it can be." If those words hold true, Dodger fans should rejoice.

But words need to be followed by action, and there was precious little of that as the complicated transaction moved forward with the haste of a glacier. From the start the proposed deal raised some eyebrows. Although McCourt's grandfather had once owned a small piece of the Boston Braves and

the role of closer than starter. Almost immediately his fastball miraculously gained five to six miles per hour, putting him comfortably in the mid-nineties, and that made his change-up instantly more effective.

Armed with those two pitches, over the 2002 and 2003 seasons Gagne became the best closer in baseball, blowing only

McCourt himself has often been seen at Fenway Park and is a true fan of the game, his background and the price he was willing to pay caused some to question his motives and wonder whether real estate—particularly the 276 acres in and around Dodger Stadium—was the real reason McCourt was interested in the Dodgers. At some point in the future, a new ballpark, particularly one at least partially financed with public money, could make the Chavez Ravine site worth a not inconsiderable fortune.

Over the next few months questions about the deal only increased, a situation not helped by the gag order Selig put on McCourt, which also prevented the garrulous developer from courting local reporters. It soon became clear that McCourt wouldn't be buying the team with his own money—at least not very much of it. His personal fortune simply wasn't sufficient. Much of his worth was tied up in a 27-acre piece of the South Boston waterfront worth in excess of $200 million, which he leased for parking while waiting for the right time and the right plan to develop it. To make a deal for the Dodgers work, he needed to use the property as collateral and add some outside investors. The sale wasn't going to be a simple proposition but a much more complicated deal that would take months to finalize.

And all the while the Dodgers continued to founder. The Yankees came calling for pitching and, in exchange for Jeff Weaver, took Kevin Brown and the remaining two years of his contract, freeing the team of its most burdensome player. But with the club stuck in the netherworld of a "pending sale," the Dodgers were hamstrung in the off-season. GM Dan Evans didn't even know if he'd be retained, nor was manager Jim Tracy or anybody else assured of a job. Free agents interested in playing for the Dodgers couldn't get a commitment from the team. Boston apparently had shortstop Nomar Garciaparra on the block, but the Dodgers were cautious and couldn't find a way to make the deal work. Free agent outfielder Vladimir Guerrero also was reportedly interested in joining the Dodgers, but although the club kept saying they were prepared to make an 11th-hour offer, midnight came with no such bid, and in early January Guerrero signed with the Anaheim Angels.

With the delay of McCourt's proposed purchase as he structured the deal to satisfy MLB, many Dodger observers began to wonder whether he would be so encumbered by the details and debt of the deal that wins and losses would have to take a backseat to revenue issues. In December rumors that News Corp would in fact lend McCourt much of the money to buy the team raised even more questions, for the continuing involvement of Murdoch with the team on any level caused observers to blanch.

Finally, on January 29, the deal was unanimously approved by Major League Baseball, with News Corp retaining a small interest in the team and loaning McCourt approximately one-third of the $430 million purchase price. For better or worse, Frank McCourt takes his place in the lineage that stretches from Charles Ebbets through Branch Rickey, the O'Malley family, and News Corp. In his first move, he fired general manager Dan Evans and hired Paul DePodesta, a protégé of Oakland general manager Billy Beane. With no player salary commitments beyond 2005, McCourt and DePodesta have a chance to completely remake the team.

But McCourt's task may be far more difficult than those of his predecessors. The waning number of Dodger fans who still care are just about out of patience and the protracted sale process has left them skeptical. Somehow, some way, McCourt will have to find a way to succeed on the field while making the franchise profitable again. For years both of those goals were a given. Now he may well have to start from scratch. All he has to guide him are the lessons of the past.

The history of the Dodgers and the history of the game of baseball have been inextricably entwined from the start. At the beginning they were indistinguishable. Only a few other teams—the Giants perhaps—can make a similar claim, but none can claim a history as glorious and essential to the history of baseball, and hence to the fabric of the nation, as the Dodgers. The history of the game has been played out in the story of the Dodger franchise.

The Dodgers have survived because they have adapted and changed—not always quickly, and not without struggle, but in the end as effectively as any team in baseball. Indeed, they have not just survived but often thrived as the game evolved from its humble beginnings into its present form. Painful as it might be for some to recall, their move from Brooklyn stands as an example of the Dodgers' unique resiliency and is nearly as significant as the role they played in the successful integration of baseball.

For the Dodgers, it is in fact their struggles that have made them one of the game's most essential franchises. Others, such as the Yankees and Cardinals, have been more successful, and some—the Red Sox, Giants, A's, and a few others—have stories that are just as appealing, but none can match the drama of the Dodgers. The line between success and failure, between winning and losing, has been nearly invisible at times, yet the resulting emotional impact has been undeniable and unforgettable.

And that perhaps is what makes the Dodgers special — the intensity of emotion that the Dodgers have so long and so often inspired. There are fans of Brooklyn still angry about the move to L.A., fans of the Dodgers in the 1960s who can recall each excruciating moment of the team's battles with the Giants, and fans who recall precisely who they were with when Kirk Gibson struck his historic home run. In the course of writing this account, I spoke with fans for whom the drama of watching Koufax take the mound with the season on the line remains as fresh as the day it happened. One fan — nearly blind and in his eighties — spoke of how wondrous it was to travel to Montreal to see Jackie Robinson and then to realize, as Robinson danced off third base, "Hey, look! He's going to steal home!" and as Robinson feinted and faked, sending a ripple of anticipation through the crowd, to see him *do it* with a sense of ease and daring that took one's breath away, an act that instantly and irrefutably exposed the futility and idiocy of baseball's abominable insistence on the color line with more clarity than moral logic ever could.

Fans of other teams tend to recall only their moments of triumph, or perhaps the moments of their greatest disappointments, but Dodger history somehow lives between those extremes — in the Ebbets Field bleachers, in the austere achievements of Sandy Koufax, and in the joyous ballet of Fernando Valenzuela's wind-up. The losses, to be sure, have been painful, and the triumphs transcendent and sweet, but unlike with other clubs, one gets the feeling that the real Dodger fan has been there for the long haul, be he or she of Brooklyn or Los Angeles. The day-to-day ebb and flow has been as important as the final destination as long as the fans have not been made to feel that the daily journey was pointless or circular. One thinks of the Dodgers and does not think so much of the end of the season as of the pennant race — the anticipation that slowly builds from April to October and knits each season to the past.

In 2002 Dodger Stadium celebrated its 40th anniversary and was the second-oldest ballpark in the National League. Despite recent renovations, the park's lack of contemporary luxury boxes and other significant income-generating features has led some to question the park's future.

Dodger Blues

Boston developers Frank and Jamie McCourt celebrate the announcement of major league baseball's approval of their bid to purchase the Dodgers. Frank McCourt's grandfather had been a minority owner in the Boston Braves during the 1940s and the McCourts had only recently been one of many prospective bidders for the Red Sox in 2001.

And no team, not even the Giants or the Braves or the A's, has ever been cut in half like the Dodgers. These clubs had been abandoned by their fans long before they left. Brooklyn fans never let go, and most have stubbornly insisted that their club, betrayed by the man who owned them, has nothing whatsoever to do with that other team, that club in Los Angeles. And L.A. Dodger fans have tended to glaze their eyes before the pronounced nostalgia of the Brooklyn era, believing that their team is somehow ahistorical.

Yet they are not two clubs, and they are not as dissimilar as their two homes or their two constituencies. Try as one might to deny it, there are threads that run between Brooklyn and Los Angeles, parallels and echoes. Brooklyn had 1955, but L.A. got 1988. Brooklyn had Robinson, but L.A. got Koufax. Brooklyn had Durocher — L.A. got Lasorda. One of the goals of this book has been to deliver the Brooklyn era to those who know the Dodgers from their years in Los Angeles as well as to inform those who think Dodger history stopped in Brooklyn that they may have missed a pretty good game. The Dodgers are more than either place.

That may yet be what carries them through. Until recently, the Dodgers have always stood *for* something, and their recent failures may stem from the fact that, as an organization, they have forgotten that and have been behaving like other teams instead of like the Dodgers. To succeed again, they would do well to look to the past, for their history — rich and luxuriant — provides more direction than most. The way back may already be apparent, if only the Dodgers look for it.

For most of their history, on the field and off, the Dodgers have been led by a series of strong and unforgettable personalities. Yet in recent years those personalities have been silenced, cut loose, allowed to walk away, or left to hang on with nothing to do and no desire to change that. Their players have become as interchangeable as baseball cards, and their organizational leaders mere corporate functionaries. Peter O'Malley's last decade was spent serving masters other than the Dodger fans — the preservation of his own fortune and the desires of the increasingly corporate and remote interests of MLB, which has tried to enforce upon all its franchises a dulling sameness, taking the NFL, with its random parity and numbing glitz, as a model.

The sale to Fox was an almost logical result. When the always so independent Dodgers were subsumed beneath a larger corporate umbrella, they had one more master to serve before their fans.

And yes, the fans — remember them? Under this benign neglect, Dodger fans have become mere numbers, unimportant apart from the amount of money that the club can efficiently extract from them on their way into the ballpark. The success of the team in Los Angeles has never really been dependent on the fans or on the club's ability to promote itself, but rather on the larger "market," the economic engine of the area that has always guaranteed financial success. Over time the trade-off has been a loss of passion. It is almost as if the club made a Faustian bargain, trading baseball's natural, seasonal, manic-depressive fervor for a more predictable form of success, a dispassionate accent on Dodger Stadium and the larger experience rather than on the Dodgers and how they are doing.

It happened before with this team. In the dark past were times when Brooklyn's Dodgers took their rich legacy for granted and the predictable result was a team that few cared about, a team that at times nearly became the laughingstock of the National League. But once the Dodgers reached prominence again in the 1940s, for most of the next 50 seasons they fought hard to retain their place. At that time the organization still seemed aware of its more humble origins, of how hard the climb had been and what it had taken to get there. Even after the team moved to Los Angeles, there were people in the organization, on the field and off, who had been with the club in Brooklyn and remembered what it was like to fight for everything, to represent something, not only to entertain their fans but to enthrall them. And even though the Dodgers would sometimes struggle, until recently they never allowed the club to lose its identity and become just another team.

That can happen again. The recent sale of the team could be a moment of real promise, a chance for the club to grasp the future by recapturing a sense of its past. What the Dodgers need is simple: they need another *somebody*, a Lasorda, a Robinson, a Rickey, not someone identical in manner to these giants—for each time anoints its own champion—but someone whose personality can drive the franchise and give it passion again. In the past this somebody has sometimes been a player, like Robinson or Koufax or comets like Valenzuela, Hershiser, or Gibson; a manager like Durocher or Lasorda; or even a member of the front office, like Branch Rickey. But for most of their history the Dodgers have had someone who, in Lasorda's words, has "bled Dodger blue"— someone who has set the tone, created an attitude, or put into practice a philosophy that resulted in a team that was often successful not only financially and on the field but where baseball matters most: in the heart and soul of the fans.

And if all those figures in Dodger history and the dozens more who have told the team's story in this book have something in common, it is that none were really given the task to be that person. A crisis arose and they seized the role. Well, the next crisis is already here, and the next great Dodger leader may already be at hand. He—or she—may simply need the opportunity to make the Dodgers matter again and take them into the next era.

Then it may again be possible to recall the words of Walt Whitman, that old sportswriter, without nostalgia and to see the truth in them:

> Let us leave our close rooms, and the dust and corruption of stagnant places, and taste some of the good things. . . . The game of ball is glorious.

Appendix A: All-time Dodger Teams

1883 TO WORLD WAR II

MANAGERS

Wilbert Robinson (1914–1931): 2 NL pennants (1916, 1920)
Robinson, who played for and was a managerial disciple of
Ned Hanlon, left a coaching position with John McGraw
and the Giants to lead the Dodgers for 18 seasons. His overall Dodger record was 1,375–1,341 (.506).

Leo Durocher (1939–1946, 1948): 1 NL pennant (1941)
In nine seasons with the Dodgers, Durocher finished below
third only twice while winning 740 games against 566
losses (.567).

EXECUTIVES

Charles Ebbets (president, 1898–1925)
The owner not only built his namesake ballpark in 1913 but
established the Dodgers as both a force in the National
League and a national institution.

Larry MacPhail (executive vice president, 1939–1942)
MacPhail oversaw a successful overhaul of the Dodgers that
included night baseball, the first radio game broadcasts in
New York history, and the hiring of manager Leo Durocher,
which led to a pennant in 1941 and a subsequent string of
first-division finishes.

INFIELD

1b **Candy LaChance** (1893–1898): .290, 29 HR, 379 RBI
The switch-hitting LaChance was surprisingly speedy for
his size, scoring 99 runs in 1895. LaChance batted over .300
for three of his six seasons in Brooklyn, topped by his .323
batting average in 1894.

1b **Jake Daubert** (1910–1918): .305, 1,387 H, 87 3B
A two-time NL batting champion, Daubert captured his
crowns in back-to-back seasons with batting averages of
.350 and .329 in 1913 and 1914.

1b **Dolph Camilli** (1938–1943): .270, 139 HR, .497 SLG
The popular first baseman helped lead the Dodgers to their
first pennant in 21 seasons in 1941. He was named NL
MVP after leading the league in homers with 34 and RBIs
with 120.

2b **Tom "Tido" Daly** (1890–1901): .294, 76 3B, 44 HR
The versatile Daly also served as a valuable utilityman, sub-
stituting at catcher, third, shortstop, and the outfield during
11 seasons with the Dodgers.

3b **George Pinkney** (1885–1889, American Association;
  1890–1891, National League): .281, 781 R, 429 BB
For most of his days in Brooklyn, Pinkney was among the
leaders in runs scored in both the American Association
and the National League. In 1890 he helped lead the newly
formed Brooklyn Nationals to a pennant in their first season by batting .309 and scoring 115 runs.

ss **Ivy Olson** (1915–1924): .261, 486 R, 51 3B
Olson was the starting shortstop for the Dodgers for two NL
championships, in 1916 and 1920. In 12 World Series
games for Brooklyn, Olson batted .293.

OUTFIELDERS

LF **Zack Wheat** (1909–1926): .317, 2,804 H, 464 2B, 171 3B
As Dodger left fielder for 18 seasons, Wheat established
franchise records for games played (2,322), at bats (8,859),
doubles, triples, and hits while helping lead the Dodgers to
pennants in 1916 and 1920.

OF **Floyd "Babe" Herman** (1926–1931, 1945): .339, .557 SLG
Babe Herman entertained fans as much with his superb hitting as his atrocious fielding. Despite achieving back-to-
back single-season batting averages of .381 and .393 in 1929
and 1930, he never won a National League batting crown.

OF **Frank "Lefty" O'Doul** (1931–1933): .340, .505 SLG
A former pitcher turned outfielder, O'Doul led the National
League in batting average twice in his 11-year career, with
his second title coming with Brooklyn in 1932 when he
hit .368.

OF **Thomas "Oyster" Burns** (1888–1889, American Association; 1890–1895, National League): .302, 147 2B, .449 SLG

After leading his team to a win in the 1889 championship series against the New York Giants, Burns led the National League in homers (13) and RBIs (128) following the shift of his team from the American Association to the NL.

OF/3B **Cookie Lavagetto** (1937–1941, 1946–1947): .275, 763 H

Apart from beating the Yankees while breaking up Bill Bevens's no-hitter in the ninth inning of game four of the 1947 World Series, Lavagetto was a consistent performer for the Dodgers in a stint interrupted by World War II.

OF **Mike Griffin** (1891–1898): .308, 882 R, 544 BB

In his first season in Brooklyn, Griffin led the National League in doubles with 36. In 1898 he was named player-manager of the Dodgers.

OF **Willie Keeler** (1893, 1899–1902): .358, 845 H

Keeler's .358 career batting average as a Dodger is the highest in franchise history. His years in Brooklyn were interrupted by a stint with the Baltimore Orioles, a team that included such fellow Hall of Famers as John McGraw, Joe McGinnity, and Hughie Jennings.

OF **Jimmy Sheckard** (1897–1898, 1900–1905): .298, 212 SB

At the start of the 21st century, Sheckard still was among the top ten on the Dodgers' all-time career lists in both triples and steals.

CATCHERS

C **Al Lopez** (1928, 1930–1935): .279, 665 H, 274 RBI

The Hall of Fame catcher joined the Dodgers barely out of his teens and soon made his mark while batting .309 in his first full major league season.

STARTING PITCHERS

RHP **Adonis Terry** (American Association, 1884–1890, 1890–1891): 127–139, 3.38 ERA

Terry led the Brooklyn pitching staff in their first NL season in 1890 with 26 victories, a career single-season high.

LHP **Rube Marquard** (1915–1920): 56–48, 2.58 ERA, 444 K

Marquard helped lead the Dodgers to two World Series in his six seasons in Brooklyn. His 2.58 ERA is the fourth-best career mark in franchise history.

LHP **Nap Rucker** (1907–1916): 134–134, 2.42 ERA, 38 SHO, 186 CG

George Napoleon Rucker was the second-best left-hander in Dodger history behind Sandy Koufax. He was a .500 pitcher for sub-.500 teams who consistently was among the league leaders in ERA and innings pitched.

RHP **Jeff Pfeffer** (1913–1921): 113–80, 2.31 ERA, 157 CG, 25 SHO

Pfeffer was an early version of Don Drysdale, in terms of both size (6'3") and temperament. The hard-throwing right-hander led the Dodgers to the 1916 pennant with 25 wins and a 1.92 ERA. His career ERA of 2.31 is tops on the all-time Dodger list.

RHP **Bill "Brickyard" Kennedy** (1892–1901): 174–150, 279 CG, 2,857 IP

The incredibly durable Kennedy both won and lost 20 or more games four times during his decade in Brooklyn. He is the all-time Dodger leader in complete games.

RHP **Burleigh Grimes** (1918–1926): 158–121, 3.47 ERA, 205 CG

The spitballing Grimes won 20 or more games four times for the Dodgers and was always among the top two in either games started or complete games in the National League. Grimes was also a superior batter with a .251 career average in Brooklyn.

RHP **Clarence "Dazzy" Vance** (1922–1932): 190–131, 3.17 ERA, 212 CG, 1,918 K

Just two years after his first full major league campaign, the 33-year-old Vance enjoyed perhaps the greatest season of any Dodger pitcher in the 20th century: in 1924 he led the league in wins (28–6), ERA (2.16), complete games (30), and strikeouts (262).

RELIEF PITCHERS

RHP **Hugh Casey** (1939–1942, 1946–1948): 70–41, 50 SV, .631 WL%

Casey was the classic early reliever alternating between spot starting and bullpen duty. Of his career total of 70 Dodger victories, 46 came as a reliever.

POSTWAR DODGER ALL-STAR TEAM

MANAGERS

Walter Alston (1954–1976): 2,040–1,613
Alston never signed more than a one-year contract for 23 consecutive seasons and led the Dodgers to seven pennants and three world championships. In his second season he led the 1955 Dodgers to their first and only world title in Brooklyn.

Tommy Lasorda (1977–1996): 1,559–1,439
The effusive former minor league pitcher captured six division titles, four NL pennants, and two world championships in his 20-year reign as Dodger manager. During that time he tutored nine Dodgers honored as NL Rookie of the Year.

EXECUTIVES

Walter O'Malley (president, 1950–1970)
The former foreclosure attorney is still the most hated man in Brooklyn, having moved the team to Los Angeles in 1958. However, his business acumen and vision produced both Dodger Stadium and a team that more than maintained its place among the top two or three teams in the National League. The Dodgers have captured all six of their World Series titles to date under the stewardship of the O'Malley family.

Branch Rickey (president, general manager, 1943–1950)
In addition to breaking baseball's color line by signing Jackie Robinson, Rickey created the most formidable farm system in baseball.

INFIELD

1B **Gil Hodges** (1943, 1947–1961): .274, 361 HR, 1,254 RBI
In 16 seasons with the Dodgers in Brooklyn and Los Angeles, Hodges played on two world champions and seven NL champions. His 361 homers are second in franchise history to Duke Snider's 389.

1B **Wes Parker** (1964–1972): .267, 194 2B, 1,110 H
The slick-fielding Parker captured six Gold Glove awards in his nine years with the Dodgers. In the pennant-winning seasons of 1965 and 1966, Parker was part of the first switch-hitting infield in major league history, along with second baseman Jim Lefebvre, shortstop Maury Wills, and third baseman Jim Gilliam.

1B **Steve Garvey** (1969–1982): .301, 211 HR, 1,968 H
Garvey was one of the great stories in franchise history: his dad drove the team bus in Vero Beach, sent his son to Michigan State, and then saw him become one of the greatest players in franchise history. Garvey batted .344 in four Dodger World Series.

1B **Eric Karros** (1991–2002): .268, 270 HR, 1,608 H
One of the most underrated players in franchise history, Karros is among the top five or six Los Angeles Dodgers career leaders in every major offensive category. Most notable were his 270 homers, which are third in franchise history behind Snider and Hodges.

2B **Jackie Robinson** (1947–1956): .311, 137 HR, 947 R
The greatest American athlete of the 20th century started his major league career at age 28 and became a Hall of Fame performer in his fourth-best sport. He also played at first, at third, and in the outfield.

2B **Davey Lopes** (1972–1981): .262, 99 HR, 418 SB
Lopes was part of the infield with the longest continuous service in the majors along with first baseman Steve Garvey, shortstop Bill Russell, and third baseman Ron Cey. Lopes's 418 career steals are second overall in franchise history.

3B **Billy Cox** (1948–1954): .259 (.302 World Series), 659 H
Following his move from short to third, and from Pittsburgh to Brooklyn, Billy Cox performed as nothing short of an acrobat at third base. Cox was considered one of the best glove men of all time at third, along with Brooks Robinson and Clete Boyer.

3B **Jim "Junior" Gilliam** (1953–1966): .265, 1,163 R, 1,889 H
Gilliam performed virtually the same role for the Dodgers that Gil McDougald did for the Yankees — namely, serve as a full-time player with both the aptitude and attitude to play anywhere when needed. Serving mostly at third, Gilliam played in seven World Series.

3B **Ron Cey** (1971–1982): .264, 228 HR, 842 RBI

Known to all as "the Penguin," Cey played for four pennant winners and five division runners-up in twelve seasons in Los Angeles. During the 1981 World Series he was beaned by Goose Gossage in game five and returned to the lineup from a hospital bed to lead the Dodgers to victory in the decisive sixth game at Yankee Stadium.

SS **Harold "Pee Wee" Reese** (1940–1942, 1946–1958): .269, 2,170 H, 1,338 R

Reese was not only the captain of the Dodger juggernaut of the 1950s but also the heart and soul of the franchise. His career spanned a period from the '41 pennant to the inaugural season at Los Angeles Coliseum.

SS **Maury Wills** (1959–1966, 1970–1972): .281, 490 SB, 876 R

As a 26-year-old rookie, Maury Wills soon took the place of Don Zimmer at short. In 1962 he more than doubled his previous single-season stolen base mark of 50 when he set a then major league record of 104 steals.

SS **Bill Russell** (1969–1986): .263, 1,926 H, 293 2B

Russell's high school in Pittsburg, Kansas, was so small that it didn't have a baseball team, and the Dodgers drafted him on the basis of his sandlot reputation. The former high school basketball standout ended up holding the Dodgers' shortstop position for 18 years — longer than anyone in team history.

OUTFIELDERS

OF **Pete Reiser** (1940–1942, 1946–1948): .306, 666 H, 400 R

In his prime, many thought Reiser was the equal of Willie Mays. In his first full major league season in 1941, Reiser led the league in batting at .343, runs (117), doubles (39), and triples (17). He played the outfield with a reckless abandon that shortened his career after he suffered too many concussions and broken bones after colliding with concrete walls.

CF **Edwin "Duke" Snider** (1947–1962): .300, 389 HR, 1,995 H

The Duke may not have possessed the charisma and fire of Reiser, but the Californian was the perfect Ebbets Field outfielder, combining a sweet home run swing with superb athleticism. Snider suffered during the 1950s only in comparison with his fellow New York–based center fielders by the name of Mays and Mantle.

RF **Carl Furillo** (1946–1960): .299, 1,910 H, 1,058 RBI

Known as the "Reading Rifle," in honor of both his hometown and his incredible throwing arm, Furillo was also a superb batter who led the National League in batting average in 1953 at .344. Following his career, Furillo worked as one of the hardhats who built New York's World Trade Center.

LF **Tommy Davis** (1959–1966): .304, 912 H, 86 HR

The Brooklyn native was a hitting prodigy who captured the first of consecutive NL batting championships in 1962 at age 23, when he batted .346 with 230 hits and 153 RBIs. The following year he hit .326 during the regular season and .400 in the Dodgers' four-game World Series sweep of the Yankees.

CF **Willie Davis** (1960–1973): .279, 2,091 H, 335 SB, 110 3B

Known as the "man of a thousand stances," for the first part of his career Davis was one of the fastest men in baseball history and a player who got better with age. Upon his retirement, Davis held the Los Angeles Dodger records in many departments, including hits (2,091), runs (1,004), at bats (7,495), total bases (3,094), and extra-base hits (585).

RF **Frank Howard** (1958–1964): .269, 123 HR, .495 SLG

The former Ohio State basketball star took several years to make it into the Dodger lineup but blossomed in 1962 when he batted .296, hit 31 home runs, and drove in 119 runs. His home run percentage of 5.8 is second in franchise history to Duke Snider's 5.9.

LF **Dusty Baker** (1976–1983): .281, 144 HR, 1,144 H

In his second year in Los Angeles, Baker hit a homer in his final at bat of the season to join teammates Ron Cey, Steve Garvey, and Reggie Smith as the first quartet of players on one team to hit 30 or more home runs in major league history. In four NL championship series, Baker batted .371.

RF **Shawn Green** (2000–): .283, 134 HR, 423 RBI

The Dodgers traded Raul Mondesi and Pedro Borbon for Green and infielder Jorge Nunez in November 1999. In 2001 Green set a Dodger single-season home run record with 49 homers while batting .297.

CATCHERS

C **Roy Campanella** (1948–1957): .276, 242 HR, 856 RBI
A three-time NL MVP, Roy Campanella not only was a slugger but fielded his position with catlike quickness. On many backup plays, he routinely beat baserunners to first. He helped lead the Dodgers to five pennants and their lone Brooklyn world championship.

C **John Roseboro** (1958–1967): .251, 92 HR, 1,009 H
Roseboro succeeded Roy Campanella after the Hall of Famer was paralyzed in an off-season auto accident in the winter of 1958. During 11 seasons, Roseboro handled one of the great pitching staffs in modern history and contributed to four pennant winners and two world champions.

C **Mike Piazza** (1992–1998): .331, 177 HR, 563 RBI
Upon his trade to the Florida Marlins in 1998, Mike Piazza was the Los Angeles Dodger career leader in batting average at .331 and in the midst of one of the greatest offensive careers ever by a catcher.

STARTING PITCHERS

LHP **Sandy Koufax** (1955–1966): 165–87, 2.65 ERA, 2,396 K
For five seasons, from 1962 to 1966, Sandy Koufax was one of the greatest pitchers ever as he won three Cy Young Awards, an MVP Award, and two World Series MVP Awards in that span. He also pitched four no-hitters, including a perfect game.

RHP **Don Drysdale** (1956–1969): 209–166, 2.95 ERA, 2,486 K
The ornery right-hander was half of the formidable duo of Koufax and Drysdale that helped the Dodgers dominate the first half of the 1960s. In 1962 he won the Cy Young Award for his 25–9 season and six years later broke Walter Johnson's major league record for consecutive scoreless innings with 58, a string that included a record six consecutive shutouts.

RHP **Orel Hershiser** (1983–1994, 2000): 135–107, 3.12 ERA, 24 SHO
Nicknamed "Bulldog," Hershiser capped an amazing 1988 season when he broke Don Drysdale's consecutive scoreless innings mark at 59. In September he went a perfect 5–0 with a 0.00 ERA.

LHP **Fernando Valenzuela** (1980–1990): 141–116, 1,759 K, 107 CG
In his first full major league season in 1981, Valenzuela was a sensation while crafting a 13–7 season with a pitching motion that invited comparisons with Luis Tiant. Not only was he a great pitcher, but Valenzuela was the first major Mexican American star in Dodger history.

RHP **Don Sutton** (1966–1980, 1988): 233–181, 3.09 ERA, 2,696 K
Sutton retired as the all-time Dodger career pitching leader in wins (233), innings pitched (3,814), strikeouts (2,696), and games started (533), among other categories.

LHP **Claude Osteen** (1965–1973): 147–126, 1,162 K, 34 SHO
Osteen was the silent partner of the superb pitching staff of the 1960s dominated by Koufax and Drysdale. During his Dodger career, Osteen twice won 20 or more games and had a superb 0.86 ERA in 21 World Series innings.

LHP **Johnny Podres** (1953–1965): 136–104, 3.66 ERA, 1,331 K
Podres emerged from a mediocre 9–10 regular season record in 1955 to instant immortality in the World Series when he captured the third and seventh games to lead the Dodgers to their first-ever world championship.

RHP **Don Newcombe** (1949–1951, 1954–1957): 123–66, 3.51 ERA, 22 SHO
Newcombe was not only one of the great power pitchers of his era but one of the best ballplayers. When he won 20 games in 1955, he also batted .359 with 9 doubles, 23 RBIs, and 7 home runs. He was even asked to pinch-hit and batted .381 in that role.

RELIEF PITCHERS

RHP **Eric Gagne** (1999–): 17–18, 107 SV, 490 K
In 2002 Gagne came out of nowhere to become one of the best closers in baseball, if not the best. His large frame, chunky eyewear, and lively fastball intimidated hitters and helped him to a 55-save season in 2003, which earned the Montreal native the Cy Young Award.

RHP **Mike Marshall** (1974–1976): 28–29, 42 SV
Marshall was the best closer of his era and a student of
kinesiology who believed a pitcher could pitch every day.
In 1974 he helped lead the Dodgers to the pennant when he
shattered relief pitching records by appearing in 106 games,
pitching 208 innings, finishing 83 games, and appearing
in 13 straight games.

LHP **Ron Perranoski** (1961–1967): 54–41, 2.56 ERA, 101 SV
Perranoski saved many games for the Dodger big three of
Koufax, Drysdale, and Osteen and led the National League
with 16 wins in relief in 1963.

RHP **Clem Labine** (1950–1957): 70–52, 3.63 ERA, 83 SV
Twice Labine led the National League in relief wins and
saves, but not in the same seasons. The versatile right-hander also started the occasional game, including the sixth
game of the 1956 World Series, in which he shut out Bob
Turley by a score of 1–0 in ten innings.

Appendix B: The Dodger Record

Bold denotes World Series or Chronicle-Telegraph Cup winner (1900). In 1890 the Dodgers faced the American Association champions.

Italic denotes pennant winner but defeated in World Series.

<u>Underline</u> denotes division champion but defeated in division or league championship series. (Owing to the strike, no postseason play took place in 1994.)

* denotes defeated in playoff.

Year	Team	League	W/L	PCT.	+/-	Manager
2003	Los Angeles Dodgers	NL	85–77	.525	-15½	Tracy
2002	Los Angeles Dodgers	NL	92–70	.568	-6	Tracy
2001	Los Angeles Dodgers	NL	86–76	.531	-6	Tracy
2000	Los Angeles Dodgers	NL	86–76	.531	-11	Johnson
1999	Los Angeles Dodgers	NL	77–85	.478	-22	Johnson
1998	Los Angeles Dodgers	NL	83–79	.512	-15	Russell/Hoffman
1997	Los Angeles Dodgers	NL	88–74	.543	-2	Russell
1996	Los Angeles Dodgers	NL	90–72	.556	-1	Lasorda/Russell
<u>1995</u>	<u>Los Angeles Dodgers</u>	<u>NL</u>	<u>78–66</u>	<u>.542</u>	<u>+1</u>	<u>Lasorda</u>
<u>1994</u>	<u>Los Angeles Dodgers</u>	<u>NL</u>	<u>58–56</u>	<u>.509</u>	<u>+3½</u>	<u>Lasorda</u>
1993	Los Angeles Dodgers	NL	81–81	.500	-23	Lasorda
1992	Los Angeles Dodgers	NL	63–99	.389	-35	Lasorda
1991	Los Angeles Dodgers	NL	93–69	.574	-1	Lasorda
1990	Los Angeles Dodgers	NL	86–76	.531	-5	Lasorda
1989	Los Angeles Dodgers	NL	77–83	.481	-14	Lasorda
1988	**Los Angeles Dodgers**	**NL**	**94–67**	**.584**	**+7**	**Lasorda**
1987	Los Angeles Dodgers	NL	73–89	.451	-17	Lasorda

Year	Team	League	W/L	PCT.	+/-	Manager
1986	Los Angeles Dodgers	NL	73–89	.451	-23	Lasorda
1985	Los Angeles Dodgers	NL	95–67	.586	+5½	Lasorda
1984	Los Angeles Dodgers	NL	79–83	.488	-13	Lasorda
1983	Los Angeles Dodgers	NL	91–71	.562	+3	Lasorda
1982	Los Angeles Dodgers	NL	88–74	.543	-1	Lasorda
1981	**Los Angeles Dodgers**	**NL**	**63–47**	**.573**	**-4**	**Lasorda**
1980	Los Angeles Dodgers	NL	92–71	.564	-1	Lasorda
1979	Los Angeles Dodgers	NL	79–83	.488	-11½	Lasorda
1978	Los Angeles Dodgers	NL	95–67	.586	+2½	Lasorda
1977	Los Angeles Dodgers	NL	98–64	.605	+10	Lasorda
1976	Los Angeles Dodgers	NL	92–70	.568	-10	Alston
1975	Los Angeles Dodgers	NL	88–74	.543	-20	Alston
1974	*Los Angeles Dodgers*	NL	*102–60*	*.630*	*+4*	*Alston*
1973	Los Angeles Dodgers	NL	95–66	.590	-3½	Alston
1972	Los Angeles Dodgers	NL	85–70	.548	-10½	Alston
1971	Los Angeles Dodgers	NL	89–73	.549	-1	Alston
1970	Los Angeles Dodgers	NL	87–74	.540	-14½	Alston
1969	Los Angeles Dodgers	NL	85–77	.525	-8	Alston
1968	Los Angeles Dodgers	NL	76–86	.469	-21	Alston
1967	Los Angeles Dodgers	NL	73–89	.451	-28½	Alston
1966	*Los Angeles Dodgers*	*NL*	*95–67*	*.586*	*+1½*	*Alston*

Year	Team	League	W/L	PCT.	+/-	Manager
1965	**Los Angeles Dodgers**	**NL**	**97–65**	**.599**	**+2**	**Alston**
1964	Los Angeles Dodgers	NL	80–82	.494	-13	Alston
1963	**Los Angeles Dodgers**	**NL**	**99–63**	**.611**	**+6**	**Alston**
1962	Los Angeles Dodgers	NL	102–63	.618	-1	Alston*
1961	Los Angeles Dodgers	NL	89–65	.578	-4	Alston
1960	Los Angeles Dodgers	NL	82–72	.532	-13	Alston
1959	**Los Angeles Dodgers**	**NL**	**88–68**	**.564**	**+2**	**Alston**
1958	Los Angeles Dodgers	NL	71–83	.461	-21	Alston
1957	Brooklyn Dodgers	NL	84–70	.545	-11	Alston
1956	Brooklyn Dodgers	NL	93–61	.604	+1	Alston
1955	**Brooklyn Dodgers**	**NL**	**98–55**	**.641**	**+13½**	**Alston**
1954	Brooklyn Dodgers	NL	92–62	.597	-5	Alston
1953	Brooklyn Dodgers	NL	105–49	.682	+13	Dressen
1952	Brooklyn Dodgers	NL	96–57	.627	+4½	Dressen
1951	Brooklyn Dodgers	NL	97–60	.618	-1	Dressen*
1950	Brooklyn Dodgers	NL	89–65	.578	-2	Shotton
1949	Brooklyn Dodgers	NL	97–57	.630	+1	Shotton
1948	Brooklyn Dodgers	NL	84–70	.545	-7½	Durocher/Shotton
1947	Brooklyn Dodgers	NL	94–60	.610	+5	Sukeforth/Shotton
1946	Brooklyn Dodgers	NL	96–60	.615	-2	Durocher*
1945	Brooklyn Dodgers	NL	87–67	.565	-11	Durocher

Year	Team	League	W/L	PCT.	+/-	Manager
1944	Brooklyn Dodgers	NL	63–91	.409	-42	Durocher
1943	Brooklyn Dodgers	NL	81–72	.529	-23½	Durocher
1942	Brooklyn Dodgers	NL	104–50	.675	-2	Durocher
1941	*Brooklyn Dodgers*	*NL*	*100–54*	*.649*	*+2½*	*Durocher*
1940	Brooklyn Dodgers	NL	88–65	.575	-12	Durocher
1939	Brooklyn Dodgers	NL	84–69	.549	-12½	Durocher
1938	Brooklyn Dodgers	NL	69–80	.463	-18½	Grimes
1937	Brooklyn Dodgers	NL	62–91	.405	-33½	Grimes
1936	Brooklyn Dodgers	NL	67–87	.435	-25	Stengel
1935	Brooklyn Dodgers	NL	70–83	.458	-29½	Stengel
1934	Brooklyn Dodgers	NL	71–81	.467	-23½	Stengel
1933	Brooklyn Dodgers	NL	65–88	.425	-26½	Carey
1932	Brooklyn Dodgers	NL	81–73	.526	-9	Carey
1931	Brooklyn Dodgers	NL	79–73	.520	-21	Robinson
1930	Brooklyn Dodgers	NL	86–68	.558	-6	Robinson
1929	Brooklyn Dodgers	NL	70–83	.458	-28½	Robinson
1928	Brooklyn Dodgers	NL	77–76	.503	-17½	Robinson
1927	Brooklyn Dodgers	NL	65–88	.425	-28½	Robinson
1926	Brooklyn Dodgers	NL	71–82	.464	-17½	Robinson
1925	Brooklyn Dodgers	NL	68–85	.444	-27	Robinson
1924	Brooklyn Dodgers	NL	92–62	.597	-1½	Robinson

Year	Team	League	W/L	PCT.	+/-	Manager
1923	Brooklyn Dodgers	NL	76–78	.494	-19½	Robinson
1922	Brooklyn Dodgers	NL	76–78	.494	-17	Robinson
1921	Brooklyn Dodgers	NL	77–75	.507	-16½	Robinson
1920	*Brooklyn Dodgers*	*NL*	*93–61*	*.604*	*+7*	*Robinson*
1919	Brooklyn Dodgers	NL	69–71	.493	-27	Robinson
1918	Brooklyn Dodgers	NL	57–69	.452	-25½	Robinson
1917	Brooklyn Dodgers	NL	70–81	.464	-26½	Robinson
1916	*Brooklyn Dodgers*	*NL*	*94–60*	*.610*	*+2½*	*Robinson*
1915	Brooklyn Dodgers	NL	80–72	.526	-10	Robinson
1914	Brooklyn Dodgers	NL	75–79	.487	-19½	Robinson
1913	Brooklyn Dodgers	NL	65–84	.436	-34½	Dahlen
1912	Brooklyn Dodgers	NL	58–95	.379	-46	Dahlen
1911	Brooklyn Dodgers	NL	64–86	.427	-33½	Dahlen
1910	Brooklyn Dodgers	NL	64–90	.416	-40	Dahlen
1909	Brooklyn Dodgers	NL	55–98	.359	-55½	Lumley
1908	Brooklyn Dodgers	NL	53–101	.344	-46	Donovan
1907	Brooklyn Dodgers	NL	65–83	.439	-40	Donovan
1906	Brooklyn Dodgers	NL	66–86	.434	-50	Donovan
1905	Brooklyn Dodgers	NL	48–104	.316	-56½	Hanlon
1904	Brooklyn Dodgers	NL	56–97	.366	-50	Hanlon
1903	Brooklyn Dodgers	NL	70–66	.515	-19	Hanlon

Year	Team	League	W/L	PCT.	+/-	Manager
1902	Brooklyn Dodgers	NL	75–63	.543	-27½	Hanlon
1901	Brooklyn Dodgers	NL	79–57	.581	-9½	Hanlon
1900	**Brooklyn Dodgers**	**NL**	**82–54**	**.603**	**+4½**	**Hanlon**
1899	*Brooklyn Dodgers*	*NL*	*101–47*	*.682*	*+8*	*Hanlon*
1898	Brooklyn Dodgers	NL	54–91	.372	-46	Barnie/Griffin/Ebbets
1897	Brooklyn Dodgers	NL	61–71	.462	-32	Barnie
1896	Brooklyn Dodgers	NL	58–73	.443	-33	Foutz
1895	Brooklyn Dodgers	NL	71–60	.542	-16½	Foutz
1894	Brooklyn Dodgers	NL	70–61	.534	-20½	Foutz
1893	Brooklyn Dodgers	NL	65–63	.508	-20½	Foutz
1892	Brooklyn Dodgers	NL	95–59	.617	-9	Ward
1891	Brooklyn Dodgers	NL	61–76	.445	-25½	Ward
1890	**Brooklyn Dodgers**	**NL**	**86–43**	**.667**	**+6½**	**McGunnigle**
1889	*Brooklyn Dodgers*	*AA*	*93–44*	*.679*	*+2*	*McGunnigle*
1888	Brooklyn Dodgers	AA	88–52	.629	-6½	McGunnigle
1887	Brooklyn Dodgers	AA	60–74	.448	-34½	
1886	Brooklyn Dodgers	AA	76–61	.555	-16	
1885	Brooklyn Dodgers	AA	53–59	.473	-26	
1884	Brooklyn Dodgers	AA	40–64	.385	-33½	

Illustration Credits

Index